Personal Finance

AN INTEGRATED PLANNING APPROACH

Eighth Edition

Ralph R. Frasca

University of Dayton

Prentice Hall

Boston San Francisco New York
London Toronto Sydney Tokyo Singapore Madrid
Mexico City Munich Paris Cape Town Hong Kong Montreal

Editor in Chief	*Donna Battista*
Assistant Editor	*Mary Kate Murray*
Managing Editor	*Jeff Holcomb*
Senior Media Producer	*Bethany Tidd*
Rights and Permissions Advisor	*Dana Weightman*
Senior Manufacturing Buyer	*Carol Melville*
Text Design, Project Management, Composition, and Illustrations	*Gillian Hall, The Aardvark Group*
Copyediting	*Kathleen Cantwell, C4 Technologies*
Proofreader	*Holly McLean-Aldis*
Indexer	*Jack Lewis*
Cover Design	*Linda Knowles*
Cover Photograph	*© Masterfile*

Many of the designations used by manufacturers and sellers to distinguish their products are claimed as trademarks. Where those designations appear in this book, and Addison-Wesley was aware of a trademark claim, the designations have been printed in initial caps or all caps.

Library of Congress Cataloging-in-Publication Data

Frasca, Ralph R.
  Personal finance : an integrated planning approach / Ralph R. Frasca. -- 8th ed.
    p. cm.
  Includes bibliographical references and index.
  ISBN 978-0-13-606303-2 (alk. paper)
  1. Finance, Personal. I. Frasca, Ralph R. II. Title.
  HG179.W545 2008
  332.024--dc22   2008038450

Prentice Hall
is an imprint of

ISBN-13: 978-0-13-606303-2
ISBN-10: 0-13-606303-9

1 2 3 4 5 6 7 8 9 10—EB—12 11 10 09 08

Brief Contents

Contents

Boxed Features

Preface

As the economy moves along in its usual cyclical fashion with periodic financial crises, financial planning continues to be important. Equally important is how instructors of Personal Finance courses prepare their students to meet the challenges of a constantly changing economy. The most critical tasks are twofold: first, to have students appreciate the importance of planning and have a basic understanding of planning techniques; and second, to develop students' abilities to think critically and to make effective decisions. A Personal Finance course obviously includes other features and topics, many descriptive in nature. They make the course more in touch with current events and also make it lively. The instructor, as the artist, blends these topics to create an appropriate course for his or her audience. This Eighth Edition gives instructors a complete set of materials to craft their courses most effectively.

Changes in the Eighth Edition

This Eighth Edition largely follows the successful format of the Seventh Edition. Instructors should encounter an easy transition to this edition because there are no major changes in the structure of the text. Of course, the economic and legal infrastructure that serves as the backdrop for personal financial planning is constantly changing and these changes are introduced throughout. All of the discussions and illustrations have been updated to reflect the most current information. This includes the introduction of timely topics and a reexamination of previous issues.

New Topics

1. The appendix to Chapter 1 that previously generally covered career planning is expanded and discusses the option of becoming a professional financial planner.
2. New themed boxes that cover current topics such as the subprime crisis, retirement allocation funds, and payday loans are included.
3. Chapter 4, Taxes, now includes special considerations for military personnel.
4. Electronic check conversion and substitute checks are explained in Chapter 5, Cash Management.
5. Option and 2/28 mortgages, which were an important factor in the subprime crisis, are covered in Chapter 8, Housing.
6. The emergence of the electronic communications network and the integration of the NYSE into Euronext are covered in Chapter 9, Financial Markets and Institutions.
7. A section on calculating the capital loss or gain on a stock has been added to Chapter 11, Stocks and Bonds.
8. A box on mandatory health insurance in Massachusetts has been added to Chapter 14, Health Care and Disability Insurance.

Significantly Revised Topics

1. The financial information for the Steeles, our illustrative family, has been updated throughout to reflect today's cost of living and current tax laws.

2. The impact of bankruptcy on stored value cards is discussed in Chapter 5, Cash Management.

3. The section on student loans in Chapter 6, Short-Term Credit Management, has been significantly expanded and revised to reflect the new fixed rates on student loans.

4. The costs of owning and operating an automobile are updated in Chapter 7, Consumer Durables.

5. The subprime mortgage crisis is examined in Chapter 8, Housing.

6. The discussion of Series EE bonds has been revised to reflect the change from variable rates to fixed rates in Chapter 11, Stocks and Bonds.

7. The stocks used as a benchmark for examining MeadWestvaco have been changed in Chapter 11, Stocks and Bonds.

8. The discussion of ETFs in Chapter 12, Mutual Funds and Other Pooling Arrangements, now includes HOLDRs.

9. The changes in health care spending accounts and Medicare are included in Chapter 14, Health Care and Disability Insurance.

10. The impact of the Pension Protection Act on vesting schedules is incorporated in Chapter 16, Retirement Planning.

11. The Internet exercises at the end of each chapter have been thoroughly updated.

Distinguishing Features of the Text

A Flexible Outline

Realizing that not all students have the same needs, the text is designed to be used in different settings, the most common being a sixteen-week semester where the instructor seeks reasonably full topical coverage in both breadth and depth. However, Personal Finance has a unique situation in that it is frequently offered as a survey course, or as a course in a Life Skills program. Here, full coverage may be difficult to achieve, or perhaps not warranted. In these situations, the following adjustments will lead to streamlined coverage yet provide strong training in personal finance skills:

- In Chapter 2, The Time Value of Money, concepts can be omitted without losing continuity.
- Chapter 11, Stocks and Bonds, can be shortened considerably by deleting all or parts of the following sections: Fundamental Analysis of Common Stocks, Return and Risk Characteristics of Bonds, and Preferred Stock. An overview of stocks and bonds is presented in Chapters 9, Financial Markets and Institutions, and in Chapter 10, Investment Basics.

Most of the chapters and many chapter sub-parts (such as Estate Planning in Chapter 15) are self-contained units, making their coverage an instructor's option.

Decision-Making Approach

The analysis employs a four-part approach to decision making that involves setting goals, listing alternatives, measuring performance, and evaluating achievement. Important in this process are the concepts of opportunity costs and marginal analysis. These topics are introduced and explained in Chapter 1 and are used extensively throughout the text.

An Emphasis on Risk and Return

At the core of financial decision making is the balancing of risk and return. This concept applies in particular to investments, but it's also useful in decisions that involve uncertainty; thus, there is an expanded discussion of risk management in the insurance section. In the investment section, we treat risk in such a way that students can use the concept when making investment decisions. Thus, readers gain a practical tool as well as an understanding of the basic principles.

Integration with the Internet

The Internet is thoroughly integrated throughout the Eighth Edition. In addition to the Internet exercises, we continue to feature Topic Links, which are identified in the margins throughout each chapter. When you see the Topic Links icon, go to the Frasca Website (**www.prenhall.com/frasca**) for a direct hyperlink to a topic source. The links direct the reader to additional resources that supplement the material in the text.

TOPIC LINKS

www.prenhall.com/frasca

Focus on the Time Value of Money

The growing importance of achieving long-term goals through investing has increased the need for students to grasp the time value of money. Our explanation and use of these techniques are simple and well within the grasp of most students.

An Illustrative Family

As part of the decision-making approach, we continue to highlight a typical American family, the Steeles. Their financial situation is far from perfect, and, like most of us, they make mistakes. The Steeles' financial situation has been updated and revised. They still manage to live a reasonably comfortable and financially secure life, but they are encountering growing financial pressures as they consider their future needs to educate their children and to provide retirement income for themselves. The Steele family appears in each chapter, where they encounter problems common to most families. As they deal with financial issues and make decisions, so does the reader.

A Goal Planning Exercise for a Single Mother

The Marie Wilson Goal Planning Exercise gives students an opportunity to participate in the important job of framing goals, planning to achieve them, and properly budgeting to afford them. The exercise spans Chapters 1, 2, and 3 with Excel worksheets available at www.prenhall.com/frasca. Marie Wilson, a single adult with a four-year old son, is trying to get ahead financially on a limited income.

Boxed Features

Each chapter contains featured items that have been selected specifically for this edition to add interest and to provide background. All boxes have been selected to fit into four themes: Financial Planning for Young Adults, Saving Money, Simplifying Financial Planning, and Personal Finance News. These themes focus student attention and include practical and useful information.

An Informal Writing Style

To help the reader comprehend the many complex aspects of personal finance, the analysis employs a writing style that brings the student into the discussion without simplifying the concepts. We have been careful to explain new or unfamiliar terms, to use examples where appropriate, and to speak engagingly to the student.

A Complete Complement of End-of-Chapter Learning Aids

Each chapter concludes with the following features:

- Key Terms A list of important chapter concepts, accompanied by the page number where each key term is introduced and defined. To help the reader locate them, key terms appear in boldface type within the chapter.
- A Follow-Up on the Steeles Thought provoking questions designed to stimulate students to think about solutions to specific financial planning problems.
- Problems and Review Questions A list of questions meant to provide the basis for a review of textual material and to stimulate thought and discussion on the chapter's content. The questions and problems have been updated to reflect changes in the financial environment.
- Cases in Personal Finance When completed, two case studies provide additional insight into the topics covered. These study aids are more challenging than the problems and review questions and require a firm grasp of the fundamentals and more computation. In this edition all cases have been revised to reflect changes in the financial environment.
- Working Out on the Web Exercises designed to show students how the Internet can be used as a financial planning tool. The exercises are linked to informational sources on the Internet.

Supplementary Materials

This text is accompanied by a complete list of supplementary teaching aids for both the instructor and the student. As with the Seventh Edition text, the Internet is a major component of this ancillary package.

For the Instructor

(All instuctor supplements can be downloaded from the Instructor Resource Center at **www.pearsonhighered.com/irc**.)

- Instructor's Manual The Instructor's Manual, written by the author, is designed to assist instructors in their preparation of teaching activities. Each chapter of the Instructor's Manual includes key concepts for the chapter, a brief explanation of major topics, a detailed outline for the chapter, further insights on how the Internet may be used to enhance the current topic and, of course, the answers to the end-of-chapter questions and sample solutions for the cases.
- Test Bank The Test Bank, written by the author, contains more than 1,400 questions that vary in rigor and type.
- TestGen The Test Bank is designed for use with TestGen test-generating software. This computerized package allows instructors to custom design, save, and generate classroom tests. The test program permits instructors to edit, add, or delete questions from the test banks; edit existing graphics and create new graphics; analyze test results; and organize a database of tests and student results. This new software allows for greater flexibility and ease of use. It provides many options for organizing and displaying tests, along with a search-and-sort feature.

- **PowerPoint Lecture Notes** This lecture presentation, prepared by David Murphy at Kentucky Community and Technical College System, includes about 30–40 slides per chapter. Each chapter presentation includes an introduction to the chapter, chapter objectives, and a detailed chapter outline.
- **Companion Website** (www.prenhall.com/frasca) This site provides an interactive learning environment for students and a link to the electronic Instructor Resources.

For the Student

- **Companion Website** (www.prenhall.com/frasca) This site includes an *online study guide*, which offers different types of self-assessment exercises with immediate feedback; *Web destination links*, which are hyperlinks to the "Workout on the Web" exercises from the textbook; and links to the "Topic Links" that are highlighted in the margins of the text. The Companion Website also includes "Your Financial Review" worksheets.
- **"Your Financial Review"** Available on the Companion Website, the Financial Planning Worksheets consist of more than 40 forms and cover a wide array of topics, ranging from setting goals to evaluating individual stocks. The forms can assist students in preparing their own financial plans, or instructors can use them in conjunction with specific assignments. The forms are in Excel spreadsheet format, which can be used to complete the calculations for many of the exercises contained in the text.

We usually learn by doing, and this text gives students plenty of opportunities to do and learn. The decision-making approach enlivens the classroom, simplifies the teaching process, and encourages independent analysis on the part of the student. *Personal Finance: An Integrated Planning Approach* presents personal finance in such a way that is easy to understand, easy to teach, and interesting to learn. I hope that you enjoy it.

Acknowledgments

This edition is the result of a collaborative effort of many people—teachers, students, and financial planners—who contributed numerous suggestions, criticisms, and helpful insights. To begin, we are grateful to Jerry Basford (University of Utah), Margaret Chung (Northern Virginia Community College), John Sinton (Finger Lakes Community College), Anna Boulware (St. Charles Community College), Margaret L. Burk (Muskingum College), Craig Bythewood (Florida Southern College), Stephen G. Chambers (Johnson County Community College), Caroline S. Fulmer (University of Alabama), Sam S. P. LaMartina (MidAmerica Nazarene University), Frances Lawrence (Louisiana State University), Kenneth L. Mark (Kansas City, Kansas Community College), Manouchehr Mokhatari (University of Maryland), Cynthia Overgard (University of Connecticut), Ted Pilger (Southern Illinois University), Edward Stendardi (St. John Fisher College), Dick Verrone (University of North Carolina at Wilmington), Bashar Zakaria (Sacramento City College and California State University, Sacramento), Jim Bryan (Manhattanville College), Anthony Avallone (National University), Robert Emmer (University of California at Berkeley), Chris Austin (Normandale Community College), Deborah Kailer (Allegheny Community College), Abbas Mamoozadeh (Slippery Rock University), Dan M. Khanna (Golden Gate University), and Kyle Mattson (Weber State University), who provided important contributions to this edition. We also wish to thank those who have been so helpful with previous editions: Rick Deus (Sacramento City College), David D.

O'Dell (McPherson College), Steven E. Huntley (Florida Community College), Daniel T. Winkler (University of North Carolina–Greensboro), Clarence C. Rose (Radford University), Cliff Olson (Southern College), Robert C. Waldron (Southern Illinois University–Carbondale), William S. Tozer (Washington State University), Richard Trieff (Des Moines Area Community College), Paul Allen (Sam Houston State University), Anne Bailey (Miami University), Emerson R. Bailey III (Casper College), James W. Baird (Community College of the Finger Lakes), A. Frederic Banda (The University of Akron), Robert J. Bond (Los Angeles Valley College), Benny D. Bowers (University of North Carolina at Charlotte), Patrick J. Cusatis (Pennsylvania State University), Mary Ellen Edmondson (University of Kentucky), Loren Geistfeld (Ohio State University), George L. Granger (East Tennessee State University), Vickie L. Hampton (University of Texas at Austin), Donald Johnson (College for Financial Planning), Walter H. Johnson (Cuyahoga Community College), Jerry L. Jorgenson (University of Utah), Robert F. Kegel, Jr. (Cypress College), Robert W. Kilpatrick (University of Connecticut), Anthony J. Lerro (Winthrop College), Joseph T. Marchese (Monroe Community College), William C. Marrs (Morton College), Jerry Mason (Texas Tech University), Randolph J. Mullis (University of Wisconsin), Emily Norman (Delta State University), Dennis D. Pappas (Columbus State Community College), Myron S. Pharo (Penn State University), J. Franklin Potts (Baylor University), Jean R. Robinson (Cornell University), Joe Samprone (Purdue University), Michael Solt (University of Santa Clara), Mary J. Stephenson (University of Maryland), Skip Swerdlow (University of Nevada–Las Vegas), and Rosemary Walker (Michigan State University).

Finally, the Prentice Hall finance team—Donna Battista, editor-in-chief, and Mary Kate Murray, assistant editor—should be recognized for their excellent work and, more important, for their enthusiasm for the project. Special thanks to Jeff Holcomb, our managing editor in charge of production, who deserves credit for the outstanding quality of the text. Also, special recognition goes to Gillian Hall for correcting my mistakes. Of course, any remaining errors are mine.

—*Ralph R. Frasca*

The Basic Framework

organizing and managing your financial resources

We usually think of financial success as making the most of what we have. We can achieve it through planning: setting goals, establishing priorities, and making effective decisions. Our goals are likely to be both financial and nonfinancial. Indeed, nonfinancial goals—those pertaining to love, family, and religion—are probably more important. But our success in achieving financial goals often enables us to enrich the nonfinancial aspects of our lives.

Part 1 deals with effective planning techniques, the key to financial success. We begin, in Chapter 1, by outlining the planning process and presenting several basic concepts that can help you effectively evaluate financial choices. Among other issues, we consider the uneven match between income and needs during the life cycle, which requires us to respond by shifting resources through time to accommodate present and future needs.

This time shifting of resources creates an important need to understand the time value of money, which is covered in detail in Chapter 2. Here we explain the processes of compounding and discounting, and how knowledge of each helps us make financial decisions.

Long-run financial success is usually accomplished by achieving short-run goals. Budgets and financial statements, the subjects of Chapter 3, help you do just that. Financial statements show you where you are now so that you can plan effectively for the future; they help determine your existing worth and show how you managed your income in the past. Budgeting, on the other hand, helps you manage your future income, thereby increasing your net worth.

Part 1 concludes with a discussion of taxes emphasizing the federal personal income tax. Chapter 4 familiarizes you with tax law as well as tax minimizing strategies.

1

Financial Planning
why it's important to you

Objectives

1. To understand why setting goals is an important first step in financial planning

2. To appreciate that trends in the financial environment—inflation, taxes, and economic cycles—affect financial success and enhance the need for planning

3. To see why life-cycle financial planning is important and to understand the nature of a planning approach

4. To understand what is meant by marginal analysis and opportunity costs and to know how these concepts are used in financial decision making

5. To appreciate that financial success builds on a strong foundation and follows a building-block approach through time

6. To meet the Steeles, a family we will follow throughout the text

Steele family

The Steeles—Arnold (37), Sharon (35), Nancy (9), and John (7)—are a typical middle-class American family. By most measures, the Steeles have achieved a certain level of success. Arnold is a chemist with a major paint manufacturer and is currently next in line for vice president of plant operations. Sharon is a CPA and works part time at a local accounting firm. As the demands on her time by Nancy and John have diminished, she has steadily expanded her work hours. Eventually, she hopes to return to full-time employment.

The Steeles have thought about the future mostly in terms of aspirations and dreams. Nancy has shown an aptitude on the piano and the family would like to continue her music lessons, which could be expensive. Arnold and Sharon hope that both kids go to college and they expect to help them financially when each starts. The family vacations often, usually camping in Smoky Mountain National Park. If their resources were adequate, they would like to buy a vacation condominium near Pigeon Forge, Tennessee, and they also have thought about a family vacation in

Hawaii. As empty-nesters, Arnold and Sharon have dreamed of traveling extensively in Europe and, of course, they hope to enjoy a long retirement with a living standard comparable to the one they now experience. Finally, if everything works out well, they would like to leave a substantial estate for Nancy and John.

Arnold grew up in the town in which they now live, but Sharon is from Pittsburgh. Both Arnold's and Sharon's parents are living and in reasonably good health, given their ages. Each family is self-sufficient but not by any means wealthy. Arnold has a brother, Dave (33), who is divorced from his wife. His income is not substantial and he currently is taking classes at a local university with the hope of eventually earning a bachelor's degree in business management. The divorce has been reasonably amicable and he and his wife have joint custody rights of their two children. Arnold and Sharon try to help Dave raise the kids, who often are visitors at the Steeles' home. Arnold also has a much younger sister, Jody (22), who will finish college in the spring with a degree in education. She plans to teach kindergarten in the local school district.

TOPIC LINKS

Follow the **Topic Links** in each chapter for your interactive Personal Finance exercise on the Web. Go to: **www.prenhall.com/frasca**.

As we start our journey into personal financial planning, we would like to introduce you to the Steele family. You will meet them often in the succeeding chapters as they help us illustrate the application of financial planning techniques. After you finish a chapter, we encourage you to read some follow-up questions on the vignette in the chapter-end materials. As you will learn throughout the text, the Steeles are not experiencing any unusual financial stress. However, they have done virtually no financial planning for the future—an omission that many families make and one that could prove costly in the long run.

Like the Steeles, many of us would prefer avoiding financial problems or turning them over to someone else. Managing financial resources is time-consuming, usually difficult, and sometimes unsuccessful. We have often asked the federal, state, and local governments for help; Social Security retirement and federally funded health care are examples. But there is growing evidence that governments are no better—and perhaps worse than we—at solving these problems. If you are a young adult ready to start pursuing the American Dream, you will face some challenges far more formidable than those that faced your parents. The dream is becoming ever more elusive.

Many people of your parents' generation never worried much about health care and retirement. If they had a job, their employers provided health insurance, and Social Security was waiting for them at retirement. Many of you are unlikely to have these assurances. If there is one dominant social theme in recent years it is *self-reliance*. Self-reliance, though, is not an inherited trait; rather, it is an acquired skill. This leads us to personal finance. Becoming self-reliant financially begins with knowledge, and your decision to take a personal finance course was a wise one; it may be one of the most important decisions of your life.

Why Study Personal Finance?

You probably decided to take a personal finance course because financial success is important to you and you realize that in most cases it doesn't come easily. But what is financial success, and how is it measured? To some, it means making a lot of money—the sooner, the better. If that is your goal, then we are afraid this text won't help you very much; nor, we might add, will any other. You might as well save your time and go to Las Vegas or Atlantic City and hope for the best. **Financial success**, often elusive to define, is usually thought of as *obtaining the maximum benefits from limited financial resources*. This means you can be a financial success (or failure) regardless of your income level. A widow with many children and an income below the poverty line may be quite successful in allocating her very limited resources to achieve the goals her family feels are important, whereas a millionaire might misallocate most resources and achieve nothing.

Financial success Obtaining maximum benefits from limited financial resources.

Your Goals in Life

If personal finance deals with achievement of goals, then you might ask: What goals does it try to achieve? Does it suggest, for example, that we all should save as much as we can? Do we measure success in terms of our weekly contributions to the bank account? Not necessarily. Obviously, what we plan to do during our lifetimes differs considerably. You may want to have a big family and enjoy entertainment activities with the kids while they are young and growing; you might also want to provide for their education. We, on the other hand, might be skinflints who love money for money's sake and have virtually no other interests in life. (We're really not.) As Figure 1.1 indicates, we can categorize goals as either nonfinancial or financial.

Nonfinancial Goals

We should realize that many of our aspirations in life are nonfinancial. We hold moral, family, social, religious, or political ideals that have little or no connection to finance. You can't put a price tag on these goals, and you shouldn't try. On the other hand, the extent to which we succeed in achieving our financial goals might determine how much time and energy are available to pursue the nonfinancial aspirations. Sociologists tell us, for example, that one of the primary reasons for divorce is financial stress in the family. Achieving financial goals doesn't assure a happy life, but the evidence suggests that it helps far more than it hinders.

Financial Goals

Financial goals form the basis for financial planning. Indeed, without financial goals, planning is impossible. Setting goals and incorporating them in annual budgeting are important topics discussed in depth in Chapters 2 and 3. However, it is useful to introduce the topics here.

Financial independence
Having sufficient income or resources to be self-reliant.

Very broadly, one might list the most important financial goal as **financial independence**, that is, to have enough income or resources to be self-reliant. However, a goal defined this broadly really doesn't help us plan for the future. What does self-reliant mean? You might understand it as having a job with little threat of a layoff, while someone else may see it as never going into debt. Actually, there are two more concrete goals to shape financial plans: a consumption goal—current and future—and a savings goal.

Current consumption Goods and services used in a current time period.

Current Consumption. **Current consumption** refers to goods and services that we use in a current period of time, such as this year. These goods and services measure our scale of living. A low consumption budget means we use fewer of them and (probably) have a lower level of satisfaction than someone with a high consumption budget. If Mary's consumption budget is twice that of John's, chances are very good she has more consumption satisfaction than he. But she might not have twice as much. Economists often point out the

Principle of diminishing marginal satisfaction A decreasing *rate* of satisfaction in relation to increasing income.

principle of diminishing marginal satisfaction, which means that current consumption satisfaction increases as current income increases but usually at a decreasing rate. We still want that second piece of pie, but it provides us less satisfaction than the first. This principle explains why we begin to look more favorably at future consumption after we have achieved reasonable levels of current consumption.

Figure 1.1
Life's Goals

Nonfinancial	Financial
· Moral	· Current consumption
· Family	· Future consumption
· Social	· Savings
· Religious	
· Political	

saving money 1.1

Earn Less, Save More, Be Happy

Does more money always bring more happiness and do we ever have enough money? The answer to these questions seems to be "no." Actually, regardless of our income level, most of us think we need 20 percent more wealth than what we currently have, according to Harvard University sociologists who asked people how much it would take to make them "perfectly happy."

Another researcher, Richard Easterlin from the University of Southern California, notes that this perception leads us to chase a moving target. The result? We never hit it, even though we spend valuable time and effort trying, and we wind up being perpetually unhappy even though our incomes are constantly rising. In spite of increasing wealth the percent of Americans who say they are very happy has remained constant at 30 percent. Apparently spending time with family and friends carries too high a price when that time can be spent earning more income. Easterlin's research, though, indicates that it is pre-cisely good health and quality time with loved ones that make us happy.

Ironically, financial planning, which many people view as the primary tool of the wealth chaser, can play a critical role in shaping family happiness. When used properly, and when family members share common values, it forces us to put a price tag on our activities. Is it Yellowstone next year or a pool in the backyard? Or, should all of us work a little less and spend a few evenings in the park? The very act of asking these questions and then incorporating our answers into a family budget might slow the chase for more income. At the very least, it should help us determine what truly makes us happy.

Finally, perhaps the simplest way to save money is to realize we may not need as much of it as we think. Again, by having a firm grip on our financial situation, by making realistic plans for the future, and by providing adequately for emergencies, we will have a clearer idea of when we have enough money and that it is unnecessary to pursue the 20 percent "more."

Future Consumption. **Future consumption** refers to goods and services to be used in future periods. By itself, future consumption is less desirable than current consumption. Would you rather enjoy a good meal today or 20 years from today? In fact, if your annual income were to remain constant throughout your life, you might very well choose to spend a higher proportion on consumption while you are young, rather than waiting until you are old. But our incomes are seldom the same from year to year. Usually, they are quite low when we start our careers, increase substantially as we move into our most productive years, and then decline as we enter retirement. If we were forced to consume all our income each year, a very uneven consumption pattern would result. Fortunately, there is no such requirement. We try to smooth current consumption over time in order to get the highest overall consumption satisfaction throughout our lifetimes. This means we borrow heavily when we are young and repay our debts in later years.

Savings. **Savings** is simply the portion of our income *not* spent on current consumption. We have just mentioned one important reason for saving—to enjoy future consumption, perhaps in retirement—but there are others. One of the more important of these is to leave an estate to our heirs. Another might be to increase our investment assets, thereby gaining greater financial independence.

Future consumption Goods and services to be used in future periods.

Savings The portion of current income *not* consumed.

Important Economic Trends

Achieving financial goals would be much simpler if we lived in a predictable economic environment. But we don't. There are, however, certain trends that are likely to continue in the future. Let's see what they are.

TOPIC LINKS

Find current economic data at Economic Statistics Briefing Room.

Continuing Inflation

As Figure 1.2 shows, since the high rate of inflation at the end of the 1970s prices have generally risen at less than 5 percent a year. The consensus of economists is that inflation will likely continue at rates between 2 and 4 percent. Although these numbers suggest a tame inflationary environment, over long periods of time they can seriously erode the value of your savings. Your investments must earn more than the inflation rate if you hope to grow your wealth in real terms. Unfortunately, many people have been content to leave too much of their money in low-yielding savings accounts that often only match, or fall short of, inflation rates. We hope you won't make that mistake.

TOPIC LINKS

Visit the St. Louis Fed's site.

Persistent Business Cycles

Figure 1.3 provides a measurement of our economy's performance since 1979. As you see, there were four recessions, each of which had a serious impact on many American families, in terms of layoffs, reduced incomes, and spending cutbacks. There is no reason to suspect the pattern of recessions will stop, so you should develop financial plans that allow for economic instability. Build enough wealth to survive a financial shock and hold it in investments that aren't devastated in value by the cycle.

   If you will soon be a college graduate, you are likely to find the job offers fewer in number and perhaps for less money during a recession than offers made to graduates during boom years. Unfortunately, college recruiting is one of the quickest and easiest ways for companies to cut expenses.

Figure 1.2
Annual Inflation Rates

Source: Shaded areas indicate recessions as determined by the NBER 2007, Federal Reserve Bank of St. Louis: research.stlouisfed.org

Figure 1.3
Annual Rate of Growth in Real Gross Domestic Product (GDP)

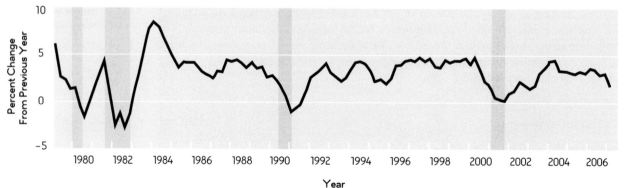

Source: Shaded areas indicate recessions as determined by the NBER 2007, Federal Reserve Bank of St. Louis: research.stlouisfed.org

Continued Instability in Financial Markets

The crash of the stock markets in 2000, the burst of the bubble in tech stocks and the current instability in the mortgage market should be a lesson that investment risk is still very much alive and a force to be considered in making plans for the future. The robust and consistent gains in stock prices prior to the crash created a type of investment euphoria where 20 to 30 percent gains each year were to be considered the norm. If you really wanted to get rich, you were urged to put your money in Internet stocks, which virtually doubled in price every three months. When it was all over, many of the Internet start-ups were bankrupt and even the blue-chip technology stocks, such as Intel, had lost 50 percent or more of their value. The popular NASDAQ index, loaded with big technology companies, declined to 1,620 from its record high of almost 5,000 one year earlier; and, as Figure 1.4 shows, returns on an index of 500 large companies have been very volatile over time. Note the significant negative returns in 2000, 2001, and 2002. But also notice that all of these losses were offset with gains in the next few years.

Now we are confronted with financial markets reacting to a meltdown in the subprime mortgage market and rising gasoline prices that are eroding discretionary income. Both of these problems were developing unforeseen while our attention was drawn to a resilient post 9/11 economy. Will financial markets overcome these setbacks or will they suffer from slower growth, unemployment, and rising prices? Every generation faces similar uncertainties. Wise investors assess how much risk they are willing to accept, and manage their investments accordingly. You should recognize the risk-return trade-off in financial markets. You can opt for safe investments like government bonds with modest returns or you could speculate in futures markets that have the potential for both significant gains and losses.

A High and Selectively Rewarding Tax System

Despite which party wins the presidency or holds a majority in Congress, we can usually count on two outcomes where taxes are concerned—rates will be high and the tax law will grow more complex. Indeed, it is already referred to as "the full employment act for accountants." From a financial planning perspective, it is appropriate to focus attention on attributes of the tax law that favor some courses of action over others. For example, the law encourages people to save and invest for their eventual retirement by allowing certain income tax deductions for contributions made to qualified retirement plans, such as IRAs (explained and discussed in later chapters). Put simply, not to take advantage of such

Figure 1.4
Stock Returns: Standard and Poor's 500 Index with Reinvested Dividends

Source: ©2007 Standard & Poors, a division of The McGraw-Hill Companies Inc.

SIMPLIFYING
financial planning 1.2

Financial Planning Software and the Internet

Managing your personal finances and keeping track of your expenses is not painless. However, financial planning software linked to the Internet can significantly reduce the pain. There are lots of free computer resources on the Internet, such as the spreadsheets and forms that can be downloaded from the publisher's Companion Website for this text. If you are serious about managing your finances, you need more comprehensive software, such as Microsoft Money or Quicken, which combines budgeting with investment tracking in one convenient program. Comprehensive planning software provides an instant snapshot of your net worth and an ongoing review of your expenditures. You can tag your expenditures with budget categories so that all expenditures with identical tags are aggregated and illustrated in a summary report that lets you determine whether your current expenditures are on track with your master budget. Tags can also be used to produce a summary of deductible expenses at tax time.

The two major commercial financial planning packages, Microsoft Money and Quicken, are both excellent personal management programs. They can be setup to provide a quick overview of all your accounts, from checking accounts to mutual funds. Better yet, the software can be linked through the Internet to automatically update your account balances. You can easily track your investment performance by downloading and updating the value of your investments with the most cur-

rent market prices. No doubt, the opportunity cost of time saved by electronically reconciling your checking account, instead of using a pen and hand calculator, may by itself exceed the purchase price.

There are Internet sites that provide free interactive comprehensive software for managing your personal finances. Two prominent ones are Wesabe.com and Greezeo.com. The interactive software on these sites can consolidate and update information from your bank accounts and brokerage firms. To do this, however, you may have to share your passwords with the site provider. The sites promise security, but there is not enough experience to judge just how safe those promises are. You might consider whether spending a few dollars on commercial software outweighs the trust you must place in these online Web sites to protect your financial information.

There are also lots of resources on the Internet for keeping up with the recent changes in the financial environment. Two top sites for financial information are the Wall Street Journal Online (**www.wsj.com**) and the Financial Times (FT.Com). The Wall Street Journal requires a paid subscription, but the Financial Times is free with registration. Other good sites that have a wealth of financial data are Bloomberg.com, Google Finance, Yahoo Finance, and Bankrate.Com. If you are looking for more informal advice by others who are also struggling to master their finances, check out the Personal Finance Blogs Aggregator (pfblogs.org). It contains links to entries to over 200 financial blogs that are updated every 30 minutes.

plans—and many people do not—is poor financial practice. Buying or selling your home or investment securities also has potential tax savings or pitfalls, which you should research before making decisions. Finally, it is important to follow the financial news to be aware of changes that could impact your financial plans.

Achieving Financial Goals Through Planning

TOPIC LINKS

Examine an overview of financial planning.

Planning is the key to personal financial success. Without it, your situation resembles that of an empty, rudderless ship floating on a lake. You can't tell where the ship has been or where it's going. Few people live this aimlessly, but many have very hazy and poorly defined ideas about what they hope to accomplish financially. Waking up one morning in your mid-forties and realizing you'd better do something about retirement is a poor approach. You may not have enough time to accumulate an adequate retirement nest egg, and you also lose all the income tax advantages that were available during the previous years, plus the earnings that earlier investments could have provided. One dollar saved and properly invested in your twenties could easily be the equivalent of $10 saved and invested during your forties. This view of planning as a lifelong process is called **life-cycle planning**.

Life-cycle planning A view of financial planning as a lifelong process.

Life-Cycle Planning

People go through different phases during their lives, as Figure 1.5 shows. Goals change in importance as we enter different phases, but the key to life-cycle planning is that *all* our lifelong goals are recognized and attended to at *each* phase in the cycle. The sooner a goal is stated and solidified, the better. Retirement, the children's educations, or a trip to Tahiti is more easily and effectively accomplished through preparation with advanced planning.

Major Financial Planning Areas

Certain areas require constant attention in all life-cycle phases. These areas are consumption and savings planning, debt planning, insurance planning, investment planning, retirement planning, and estate planning. Threaded throughout all of these areas is income tax planning. The government's share of your success is a fact of life that is probably already familiar to you. It certainly will become more familiar as this course progresses. The following sections discuss each type of planning.

Consumption and Savings Planning

Consumption and savings planning is an integral part of your strategy to achieve lifelong goals. As mentioned previously, you must decide each year how much of your income to allocate to current consumption and how much to save for the future. The topic of saving to acquire future goals is covered in Chapter 2. Also, two important activities related to consumption and savings planning are preparing periodic personal financial statements—an income statement and a balance sheet—and an annual budget. The latter is the instrument you use most often to make sure you are moving toward your goals. Financial statements and budgeting are covered in Chapter 3. Because taxes have a major impact on the household budget and affect many of our financial decisions this is covered next in Chapter 4.

Income Tax Planning

Almost no aspect of our financial lives is untouched by federal income taxes. The federal government will become a partner in all the income you earn. There are ways to minimize

Life-Cycle Phases	Financial Planning Areas
Young adult (18–25)	Consumption and savings
Family formation (26–35)	Debt
	Insurance
Family development (36–49)	Investment
Family maturity (50–60)	Retirement
	Estate
Retirement (60–?)	Income taxes

Figure 1.5
Life-Cycle Financial Planning

the tax bite, but it is up to you to find out what they are and how and when to use them. Two people with identical incomes and family situations could wind up with $100,000 difference in their assets after 30 years due to effective or ineffective tax planning. With this much at stake, it's worth your effort to become familiar with the income tax law. Chapter 4 will give you a good start.

Debt Planning

Very few people avoid debt throughout their lives—nor should they. Debt is the vehicle that allows us to even out our lifelong consumption. In addition, it is a shopping convenience, and it can help us hedge against inflation by permitting us to buy assets that match or beat the inflation rate. But debt must be managed carefully. We must avoid excessive debt and make sure we tap the lowest-cost sources of credit. Why borrow at 18 percent if you have access to funds costing 8 percent or less? Unfortunately, many Americans do. Debt management is discussed in Chapters 6 and 7.

Investment Planning

While saving part of your income each year, you must decide how to invest it. Choices here seem almost limitless, ranging from simply letting your bank account grow to speculating in raw land or commodity futures contracts. Successful investment often spells the difference between achieving your lifelong goals (and maybe even exceeding them) and failing to do so. An important first investment goal is to provide sufficient liquidity; this topic is discussed in Chapter 5. You can then turn your attention to riskier investments that offer potentially higher returns, as discussed in Chapters 9, 10, 11, and 12.

Insurance Planning

Life's uncertainties create continuous insurance needs. As a young adult with few obligations and no dependents, your primary asset is your ability to work and earn income. Therefore, you must protect yourself against the loss of that ability; that is, you need disability insurance. As you go through later phases of the life cycle, other insurance needs increase in importance. The needs of your dependents in the event of your death create a demand for life insurance, and as you accumulate assets—a house, cars, household furnishings, and others—you need more property and personal liability insurance. And, most important, you need medical insurance to protect against health or accident problems. The "average" illness can lead to hospital and doctor bills large enough to wipe out your entire savings, and then some. Insurance planning is explained in Chapters 13, 14, and 15.

Retirement Planning

Retirement planning consists primarily of estimating future consumption and other needs and then determining how you will meet those needs when you are no longer working. Most of us rely on Social Security and employer-sponsored retirement plans for retirement income, but we also realize that supplemental sources may be necessary to maintain a suitable lifestyle in retirement. We must invest during our working years to accumulate a retirement nest egg. The federal government has recognized these supplemental retirement efforts and has enacted favorable tax legislation to help achieve them. Retirement planning is the subject of Chapter 16.

Estate Planning

If you live forever, you can avoid the problem of estate planning: how to minimize taxes while giving away your wealth. Since the odds in favor of earthly immortality are not encouraging, your next best strategy is to make sure you have your financial house in order when you make the grand exit. Essential to this plan are a proper will and a sound tax strategy, which might mean distributing part of your wealth in the form of gifts while you are still alive. Estate planning is examined along with the life insurance in Chapter 15.

Career Planning

Choosing a career is clearly an important decision, not only financially but also in terms of mental and emotional health. To many people, their careers define them as persons and represent sources of both enjoyment and frustration. Moreover, career planning is not a one-time effort during senior year in college but, rather, it goes on throughout the whole life cycle, as people change careers or temporarily leave and then return to the labor market. Although career planning is a topic generally outside the area of personal finance, we examine careers in financial planning in Appendix 1.1.

A Planning Approach

As shown in Figure 1.6, planning involves four steps. First, you must state your broad goals in specific and concrete terms. For example, if buying a home is an important goal, eventually you must decide when you will buy it, how much to pay for it, the size of your down payment, and how to finance it. The second step is to create an action plan, which sets out in detail how you will achieve your goal. To achieve the goal of buying a home, you must save a portion of your income each year and invest the funds temporarily. After you have set a specific date to buy a home, you can decide which temporary investments are best suited to help achieve the goal. If the purchase date is relatively far in the future

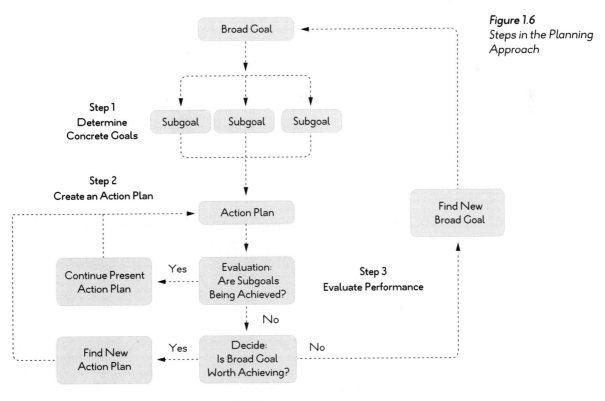

Figure 1.6
Steps in the Planning Approach

(say, five years or longer), you might choose investments that are somewhat riskier (with potentially higher yields) than you would choose if you intended to buy next year. The third step in the planning process involves evaluating your performance toward the goal. This step would be unnecessary if we lived in an unchanging world—but we do not. The type of home you want might increase in price, or financing costs might go up, or other changes could frustrate your effort to buy the home. The fourth and final planning stage forces you to decide if the goal is still worth achieving or if you should abandon it and search for another broad goal. If you decide the home is still worth the effort, for example, you must then revise your action plan by increasing the annual savings or perhaps by choosing other temporary investments that offer higher returns. (The latter approach could be very risky, though.)

Using the four steps shown in Figure 1.6 does not guarantee success, but you will certainly achieve goals far more easily if you use this method rather than a haphazard approach. Effective planning puts you at the rudder of the ship on the ocean, and it gives you the navigational aids you need to reach your destination.

Making Financial Decisions

Making a decision is a complex process. To decide is to choose among alternatives. You probably have encountered many situations in which making a choice was difficult; indeed, your biggest problem may have been simply identifying what choices were available. Then you had to find some basis for evaluating the expected outcomes of each alternative. With all that done, you picked the best alternative. Consider how difficult choosing a major in college can be; unfortunately, we face equally difficult financial decisions most of our lives. We can make better decisions if we follow guidance provided by basic economic theory, and we'll probably attain a more secure future if we follow a conservative approach when we plan.

Some Helpful Economic Insights

Economists have pioneered in the field of decision making. Two concepts—marginal analysis and opportunity costs—are useful to anyone who must make important decisions. Each is explained in the following sections.

Marginal Analysis

Marginal analysis Evaluating *changes* in important variables in relation to controllable decisions.

Marginal analysis means looking at *changes* in important variables that are related to changes in decision inputs you can control. For example, suppose you are ready to graduate and you are investing in a wardrobe you will need for your first job. You know that two good business suits are a must, but a third might be a luxury. To decide whether to buy the third suit requires that you compare the benefits it provides against its cost. If you think the added benefits are worth it, buy the third suit; if not, then don't buy it. But definitely do not consider benefits that the first and second suits provide, because they are totally irrelevant to the decision.

Marginal analysis should always be employed whenever a decision involves comparing different approaches to a problem. For example, suppose you are comparing two car insurance policies that differ with respect to coverage and cost. The two plans have the same basic coverage, but one includes protection against certain perils whereas the other does not. The former also has a higher yearly premium. In deciding between the two, you don't have to look at the total coverage and total premium of each; all you have to do is to compare the extra (marginal) coverage with the extra (marginal) premium. Then decide if the more comprehensive policy is worth the extra cost.

Opportunity Costs

Opportunity costs are benefits that you give up when you choose one alternative over another. If you decide to work during the Christmas holidays, you might give up a skiing trip to Colorado. The opportunity cost of the job is the fun you lose by not choosing the skiing trip, and the opportunity cost of the trip is the income you won't earn by turning down the job. Sometimes opportunity costs are obvious; at other times they are identified only by thoughtful consideration. For example, what is your opportunity cost of taking a course in personal finance, assuming you need the hours for graduation? It is not the tuition cost of the course; rather, it is the information and learning offered by another course that you can't take because you are taking this one.

> **Opportunity costs** Benefits given up when one alternative is chosen over another.

These examples might seem trivial, but opportunity costs arise in big decisions as well as small. Examples: What are the opportunity costs of choosing one career over another? What are the opportunity costs of your undergraduate education? What are the opportunity costs of renting versus buying a home or leasing versus buying a car? Carefully consider your responses to these questions. Some of the costs are clearly economic and probably easy to measure; others involve personal preferences and can be measured only by expressing personal value judgments. To get on the right track when using this technique, ask the following question: What do I give up if I choose one alternative over another? The answer will give you the opportunity cost for the alternative under consideration.

FINANCIAL PLANNING *for*
young adults 1.3

Five Simple Steps to Start Your Financial Life

Financial planning is not easy, particularly when it must be tailored to a specific family. But its complexities should not deter you from taking important steps as your financial life begins in earnest after graduation. The following steps are generalizations that may need to be changed as your situation evolves. But they should start you off on the right foot.

1. **Save 10 percent of your pretax income.** Try to have the amounts deducted automatically from your paycheck and invested directly so that you aren't tempted to slacken for a tempting expenditure.

2. **Use tax-deferred investment plans.** After you save 10 percent, try to invest as much as possible in tax-deferred plans, such as IRAs or 401(k)s. If your employer matches (fully or partially) your contributions to a 401(k), invest as much as you can even if the amount exceeds 10 percent; if you can't afford it, consider borrowing from your parents or another low-cost source. When an employer matches your contribution, you double your rate of return immediately—and that's hard to pass up.

3. **Take manageable risks with your investments.** Don't be afraid to invest in common stocks through a good mutual fund. To keep things simple until you can evaluate mutual funds, use index funds such as those offered by the Vanguard Group of Valley Forge, Pennsylvania. The percentage to invest in stocks is 100 minus your age; if you are 24, put 76 percent in stocks and 24 percent in high-quality corporate bonds (again, using mutual funds).

4. **Don't borrow on your credit cards.** You are likely to pay between 10 and 21 percent borrowing on credit cards in today's market, and these rates are simply too high, given current inflation and interest rates in general. You can't afford an item if you must borrow to buy—it's that simple.

5. **Buy term life insurance.** Don't buy *any* life insurance if you have no dependents who might be impoverished by your untimely death. But if you have dependents, you need life insurance—and probably far more than you think ($500,000 is not too much). Term insurance is far cheaper than cash value insurance, and with it you can probably afford $500,000 protection. That much cash value insurance is far too expensive for beginners. After you learn more about life insurance, you may want to switch.

The Building Blocks of Success

An important part of financial planning is setting priorities. All through life you will encounter both opportunities and risks, and you need to put them in perspective. Suppose you are a young person with family obligations and very little savings. A friend, who has recently become a securities salesperson, calls and tells you how you can double your money in a speculative investment. There is a strong temptation to take the offer, even though you know if it fails you will have to give up or delay other important goals. But if it succeeds, you can do so much more! Most financial advisors will tell you to forget risky propositions such as this until you have satisfied the goals you have already decided are the most important.

Setting priorities and sticking to the long-run plan suggests a **building-block approach to financial planning**, as illustrated in Figure 1.7. You begin with the lowest blocks, which means first you build a strong foundation of support. You proceed to the first

Building-block approach to financial planning Sequential investing, starting with a low-risk foundation and then moving to riskier investments.

Financial planner A professional who helps clients create, maintain, and execute a financial plan, designed to achieve their financial goals.

 finance news 1.4

What's a Professional Financial Planner—and Do You Need One?

The growing complexities of financial planning over the past 20 years have created a demand for a new professional—the **financial planner**. This person has a broad understanding of tax laws, insurance, investments, and finance. He or she is not necessarily an expert in any one area but is sufficiently knowledgeable in all to recognize problems and to suggest specialized professional help if it is needed. The planner's main function is to create a financial plan to help clients achieve their goals. This profession is not yet as organized and regulated as other professions, such as medicine, law, or accounting, and anyone can adopt the title of professional planner. But there is a growing trend toward regulation and, as the following table shows, there are a number of self-regulatory organizations that are active in establishing standards and a professional code of ethics.

Do you need a professional planner? Of course, the answer to that question depends on the complexity of your financial situation and how much of your own time you are willing to devote to the job. Assuming you have an average financial situation and you carefully complete this text (and the course, if you are using the text as part of a course), you should be able to develop your own financial plans. However, the professional planner may be able to add insights to a problem or use software to develop and evaluate your financial plans. These services could be worth their costs, which usually start at about $300 for a simple evaluation and could go to several thousand dollars for someone with a complex financial situation.

Some companies provide financial planning services to their employees as a fringe benefit. If you use this service, make sure the contact person is truly a financial planner and not a commissioned salesperson who may promote his or her products, whether they are appropriate for you or not.

Organization	Certification/Membership
Certified Financial Planner Board of Standards	Certified Financial Planner (CFP)
American College of Bryn Mawr, PA	Chartered Financial Consultant (ChFC)
Financial Planning Association	Individuals and companies engaged in financial planning
Registered Financial Planning Institute	Registered Financial Planner (RFP)
National Association of Personal Financial Advisors	Association of Fee-Only Planners
American Institute of Certified Public Accountants	Certified Public Accountant—Accredited Personal Financial
AICPA Personal Financial Planning Division for CPAs who specialized in financial planning,	Personal Financial Planning (PFP) Section and the Personal Financial Specialist (PFS) Credential

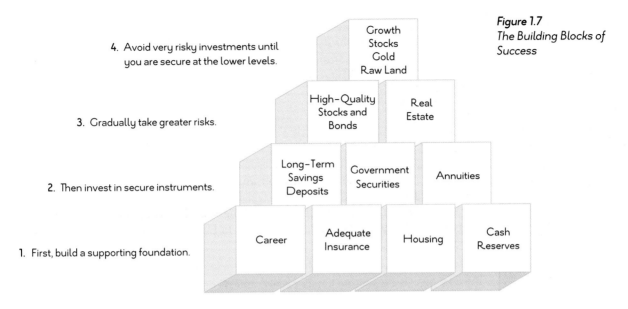

Figure 1.7
The Building Blocks of Success

4. Avoid very risky investments until you are secure at the lower levels.

Growth Stocks Gold Raw Land

3. Gradually take greater risks.

High-Quality Stocks and Bonds | Real Estate

2. Then invest in secure instruments.

Long-Term Savings Deposits | Government Securities | Annuities

1. First, build a supporting foundation.

Career | Adequate Insurance | Housing | Cash Reserves

investment level *after* the lowest blocks are secure. Likewise, you go on to riskier investments only after you have a suitable level of safe ones, deferring the very riskiest until last. Remember that if you fail at a higher level, the goals supported by success at the lower levels will not be achieved. You might have decided, for example, to invest in government bonds that will guarantee enough future return to put your kids through the state university. If you abandon this plan and put the money instead in speculative growth stocks, you might eventually have enough to put them through Harvard—or you might have to tell them there is very little money available to support their educations anywhere. You must make the choice, but at least you should understand the risks involved and the potential consequences of your choice.

key terms

building-block approach to financial planning (p. 14)
current consumption (p. 4)
financial independence (p. 4)
financial planner (p. 14)
financial success (p. 3)
future consumption (p. 5)

life-cycle planning (p. 9)
marginal analysis (p. 12)
opportunity costs (p. 13)
principle of diminishing marginal satisfaction (p. 4)
savings (p. 5)

follow-up on the Steele family

Reread the chapter-opening vignette.

1. In your view, have the Steeles *really* planned for the future? Discuss your answer.
2. Realizing the information is limited, indicate which of the family's goals or dreams are short range and which are long range.
3. If you were meeting with the Steeles, what advice could you offer them with respect to setting and achieving goals?
4. Again realizing that information is limited, discuss possible future events that could impact the Steeles financially.

problems and review questions

1. Give a definition of financial success, and discuss how it can be measured.

2. Discuss the choice of financial and nonfinancial goals and the part each may play in personal financial planning.

3. Explain what *financial independence* means to you. Might it have a different meaning to someone else? Explain.

4. Compare future consumption to current consumption. Is one necessarily better than the other? Discuss.

5. Some people argue that consumer debt should be abolished. Explain from a consumption-through-time perspective why this argument makes little economic sense.

6. Give a simple definition of savings. Explain reasons why people save.

7. What is the history of inflation over the past 25 years? If you were making financial plans for the next 25 years, what inflation rate do you feel is most relevant to those plans? Explain your answer.

8. What has been the history of the overall economy over the past 25 years? Explain if you think recessions no longer plague our economic growth.

9. Some people believe that the stock market is a safe place to put their money. Do you agree, particularly if the money might be needed on short notice?

10. Suppose that you are planning for your retirement in 30 years. What rate of return on stock investments is reasonable to use in making such plans?

11. Is our current income tax law neutral in terms of financial planning; that is, can you make such plans without considering tax impacts? Discuss.

12. What are the phases of the life cycle, and how are they related to financial planning?

13. Explain the steps involved in financial planning, and list the eight major planning areas.

14. Explain marginal analysis and opportunity cost, and then indicate why they are important concepts in financial decision making.

15. How would you measure the cost of spending a night at home watching television?

16. Martin has been asked by Jan to deliver a package on his way home for Christmas break. The trip would take him a total of 200 miles out of his way. Jan has offered to pay $40 for the service.
   a. What marginal costs of operating his car do you think Martin should consider in deciding to accept or reject Jan's offer?
   b. Identify an opportunity cost to Martin himself that might sway his decision.

17. What is a building-block approach to financial planning?

18. Bryan has saved $3,000. His friend Chris advises him to put it in a savings account because Bryan has very little cash reserves. Bryan wants to speculate in the stock market by trading biotech stocks. What's your view on this matter? Discuss.

case 1.1

The Haggertys' Financial Planning

Jan and Mickey Haggerty graduated from college several years ago. Each majored in biology, and they were fortunate to receive good job offers at graduation; their combined income last year was over $120,000. The Haggertys enjoy a high level of current consumption, but they also have saved about $20,000, which they invested in a bank savings account. They would like to buy a house eventually, but they are not certain when. Jan thinks they should have a definite plan for buying a house. This plan would indicate the date of purchase, the down payment, the expected purchase price, and other important details. Jan is so enthusiastic over the purchase that she thinks they should take their money out of savings and invest it in growth stocks. She has heard that they ought to get 20 percent on these stocks, which certainly beats the 3 percent they are getting at the bank.

Mickey thinks Jan worries too much about buying a house. In addition, there is much uncertainty in the housing market due to the recent crisis in subprime mortgages. He questions the necessity of a financial plan, believing instead that they should just continue saving in the future as they have in the past. Besides, he heard at work that a recession could be coming, and, if it does, he thinks it might be a good idea to delay buying stocks until their prices come way down. He heard you make money in the stock market by buying low and selling high. Jan would like to buy the house within five years; Mickey thinks setting a date is not wise. If the stocks work out well, they can get it sooner; if not, they have to wait. Besides, a friend of Mickey's told him he should worry more about all the income taxes he and Jan are paying, since they already are in a 28 percent tax bracket.

Questions

1. Without knowing more about the Haggertys, would you say they might benefit from financial planning? Cite specific examples.

2. What do you think of Jan's idea of investing in growth stocks? What additional information about the Haggertys would you like to have before you give a final answer to this question?

3. What is your opinion of Mickey's idea to delay buying common stocks until their prices fall? Do you think his source of information at work is a reliable forecaster? Do you think it's a good idea in general to base the success of your financial plans on accurately forecasting future economic events? Explain.

---

case 1.2

Lou Pirella and Vicki Wright: Two College Students

Lou Pirella and Vicki Wright are taking a course in computer science. They have been good friends for some time, and each will graduate at the end of the current term. Lou is going directly into the workforce, and Vicki plans to earn an M.B.A. degree at a university near her hometown. She is trying to convince Lou to join her, but he feels four years of college is enough—at least for a while.

Lou and Vicki have been talking quite a bit about their plans after graduation. Vicki is relying on her M.B.A. to earn a good income in the future. She also plans to invest, but only in very secure investments. Lou plans to take a more aggressive approach to investing, and he told Vicki he will probably earn considerably more than she each year. Lou has opened an account at a stock brokerage firm and plans to begin investing as soon as he can.

Neither Lou nor Vicki currently has life insurance or very much money in checking and savings accounts. Moreover, neither has given much thought to future housing needs. Both have fairly sizable outstanding student loan amounts and Lou has a credit card balance of $5,300 on which he makes monthly payments. He knows he pays interest on unpaid balances, but he isn't sure of the interest rate.

Questions

1. How should Vicki look at the opportunity costs of her M.B.A. degree? Explain.

2. Suppose that when Vicki registers at the university, she learns that she can pay a flat tuition of $3,000 a semester and take up to 15 credit hours (but no more). Or she can elect simply to pay $250 per credit hour and take as many hours as she wants each semester. Assuming it takes 60 hours to graduate, and also assuming she could handle

20 hours a semester without threatening her grades, what is the marginal cost of the second option—that is, paying $250 per credit hour? What might be the opportunity costs of the first option? Explain.

3. What advice can you give Lou with respect to financial planning? Touch on specific topics in your answer.

marie wilson goal-planning exercise

Setting Goals

Marie Wilson is a very good friend of yours. Married at 19, she is currently 28 years old, divorced for the past two years, and has a four-year-old son, Jake. She has a reasonably good relationship with Jake's father, who contributes to the child's support. Marie is employed full time as a paralegal in a large law office. Her salary this year is $36,000. While Marie enjoys her job, she would like to achieve a more rewarding position in the future, perhaps one day becoming an attorney.

Marie has recently earned a two-year paralegal degree from a local community college. She has tentative plans to start a four-year program with a major in either economics or political science. If she pursues this goal, Marie would take evening classes at the local university. She hopes that she could earn a degree in four years, if she can find the time and financial resources to support her efforts.

Marie lives close to town and commutes to work by bus. However, she owns a 1997 sedan that she uses on weekends and shopping trips. The car does not get very good gas mileage and seems to be in frequent need of repairs. The local university is located outside the city and not conveniently accessed by public transportation. Marie believes that she will need a new car within the next three years.

Marie likes her neighborhood, particularly its school system; however, she is cramped in her current apartment. Larger apartments are available, but Marie would prefer not to move until she can afford to buy a condominium. There are a number of condos available in the area; unfortunately, she cannot afford them at the present time.

Marie tries to be active in the community and is a choir member at a local church. The church runs a two-week summer touring program to various cities, but Marie has been unable to go because of the cost. She very much would like to join the group next year. She also enjoys doing things with Jake, particularly outdoor activities. Jake shows strong athletic skills, and Marie would like to enroll him in a golf clinic when he is eight or nine. Of course, a clinic is expensive and she would probably need to buy a set of clubs.

Marie has given no thought to eventual retirement, hoping that Social Security funds will be adequate when her retirement arrives. She feels that retirement is so far in the future that it is unwise to worry about it now. Marie has a strong relationship with her parents and her sister, but they are in no position to help her financially. Marie has considerable debt (credit card and school loans) and virtually no savings. On occasion, she is depressed by what she believes will be a bleak financial future, and she has often discussed this topic with you. You would like to help Marie, and you are excited by the opportunity to apply much of what you will learn in your Personal Finance course.

You will gain additional data about Marie as you go through Chapters 2 and 3. We will provide hints and suggestions at various points, but it will be your job to help Marie start a solid financial plan by framing financial goals, determining the required savings to achieve them, and incorporating a savings amount into her annual budget. Using Form 1.1, your first task is to prepare a list of financial goals.

Form 1.1

Identifying Financial Goals

Current Date: Month _____ Day _____ Year _____

	Date to Achieve	Number of Years in the Future

A. Short-range goals (to be achieved within two years)

_____

_____

_____   _____   _____

B. Intermediate-range goals (to be achieved in two to ten years)

_____

_____

_____   _____   _____

C. Long-range goals (to be achieved in periods over ten years)

_____

_____

_____   _____   _____

Discussion of goals

_____

_____

_____   _____   _____

Exercises to Strengthen Your Use of the Internet

working out on the Web

(Internet links for the following exercises can be found at **www.prenhall.com/frasca**)

Exercise 1.1 Getting Financial Planning Information

The American Association of Retired Persons (AARP) (**www.aarp.org/money/ financial_planning**) is concerned about family finances for all families, not only for those who are retired. Visit its Web site to learn more about financial planning.

Q. Click "How Good Are Your Money Management Skills?" How do you rate your own money management skills?

Exercise 1.2 Visit the White House for Financial News

The Economic Statistics Briefing Room at the White House (**www.whitehouse.gov/fsbr/ esbr.html**) gathers a wide array of financial and economic news used by the president and his advisors when making important political decisions.

Q. Click "Income" and find the most current value for household income. Then click the graphic and determine if household income is rising or falling.

Exercise 1.3 Following the Economy

Keep up with current economic events by using the Bureau of Labor Statistics (BLS) data (stats.bls.gov) and choosing the series that interests you. The link to the "Consumer Price Index" will provide information on the prices paid for consumer goods by urban consumers.

Q. What was the rate of inflation over the previous year?

Exercise 1.4 Finding Financial Planners

You may want the assistance of a professional financial planner. The National Association of Personal Financial Advisors (NAPFA) (**www.napfa.org**) provides information on locating and assessing financial planners. Under "Consumer Information" you can find helpful information on professional financial advisors.

Q. What is a fee-only financial planner? What questions should you ask the planner in your initial interview?

APPENDIX 1.1 # A Closer Look at Career Planning and Professional Financial Planners

Career planning is a complicated process in which you must consider your preferences, aptitudes, and current resources. Your school placement counselor and your state Bureau of Employment are good starting points for formalizing career plans. If you decide to use a private counselor, be sure to check references and review his or her credentials. The International Association of Counseling Services (**iacsinc.org**) and the National Board of Certified Counselors (**www.nbcc.org**) are the top accrediting services for career counselors.

Sources of Information

TOPIC LINKS

Occupational Outlook Handbook

The best source for a summary description of over 250 occupations is the *Occupational Outlook Handbook* published by the U.S. Department of Labor. This handy guide is available on the Internet and in print. For each occupation, you can discover the educational requirements, working conditions, and average earnings. The job outlook for each occupation is highlighted, along with sources of additional information.

The introduction to the *Occupational Outlook Handbook* contains a review of tomorrow's jobs. It shows occupations that are expected to experience the fastest growth over the next few years and those that will experience the greatest increase in demand. Market wages are set by supply and demand, and it is likely that occupations experiencing the greatest increase in demand will also reflect the largest increases in wages.

Other useful publications by the U.S. Bureau of Labor Statistics include the *Career Guide to Industries* and the *Occupational Outlook Quarterly*. The *Career Guide to Industries* reviews occupations from an industry perspective, indicating the kinds of occupations that can be found within a given industry. For in-depth articles on specific occupations or job-search strategies, you should examine previous issues of the *Occupational Outlook Quarterly*.

Potential Salaries

TOPIC LINKS

National Association of Colleges and Employers

Every few years the U.S. Census Bureau publishes an update to *What's It Worth: Field of Training and Economic Status*. Here you can find earnings by both undergraduate and advanced degrees. For the most recent information on salary offers for new graduates, go to Jobweb (**www.jobweb.com**) for a quarterly salary survey. Additional salary information on recent graduates can be found at the National Association of Colleges and Employers (**www.naceweb.org**). More comprehensive, but less recent, data are contained in the National Compensation Survey conducted by the U.S. Bureau of Labor Statistics.

Your potential salary is only one of many factors you should consider when choosing a career. The same caution applies when deciding among competing salary offers. Consideration should be given to relative working conditions, opportunities for advancement, job-related learning experiences, and most importantly, nonwage fringe benefits.

Fringe Benefits

In its survey of the employer cost of employee compensation the U.S. Department of Labor indicates that over 25 percent of total employee compensation consists of fringe benefits. Typically, the most valuable components of the fringe benefit package are health and pension benefits. In most cases, these and related benefits are either tax deferred or tax exempt. Tax-deferred benefits are those for which taxes become due only at some future date, the most common being employer and employee contributions to pension plans. The tax on such contributions typically does not become due until you retire and the funds are withdrawn.

Tax-exempt benefits are those that avoid taxes completely. One of the most important of these benefits is employer contributions to health and life insurance plans. Since a tax is never imposed, the dollar value of tax-exempt fringe benefits will understate the value it would cost employees if they were to purchase similar benefits with after-tax wages. For example, suppose you are in the 28 percent marginal tax bracket. This means that if you earn another dollar, you will have to pay the government 28 cents. You get to keep only 72 cents as after-tax income. Now suppose the prospective employer offers to provide $1,000 of medical insurance payments. In the 28 percent marginal tax bracket, you would have to earn $1,388.89 before taxes to provide these same benefits out of after-tax income. The before-tax cost may be calculated using the following formula:

TOPIC LINKS

Employee Benefits Survey at the BLS

$$\text{Before-tax cost} = \frac{\text{tax-free fringe benefits}}{\left(1 - \text{marginal tax rate}\right)}$$

$$\$1,388.89 = \frac{\$1,000}{\left(1 - 0.28\right)}$$

Regional Cost-of-Living Comparisons

If you are comparing salaries in two different regions of the country, you should consider differences in relative costs of living. It can cost more than twice as much to live in New York City and maintain the same living standard as living in a midsized Midwestern city such as Dayton, Ohio. The difference will depend on whether you rent or buy a home, how you commute to work, your tax bracket, and your particular lifestyle. There are a number of salary comparison calculators on the Internet that will help you compare the cost of living in different cities. For example, intercity cost of living calculators can be found at Homefair.com and BestPlaces.net.

TOPIC LINKS

Cost of Living at Datamaster

Careers in Professional Financial Planning

If you find personal finance interesting you might consider researching career opportunities in personal finance. Beyond an interest in finance, you must also have a sincere interest in helping others. Successful financial planners enjoy working with people and take pleasure in the success of others. Many professionals, such as lawyers, brokers, and accountants provide personal financial advice to clients. Their expertise in personal finance is one element in a wide range of services they offer. There are, however, some professionals who specialize in personal financial planning.

Personal financial planners assess the needs of their clients and help them construct financial plans that prepare them for life's major changes. They advise clients on most of the topics contained in this text, such as investment planning, insurance planning, retirement planning, and estate planning.

Job Description

Personal financial planners generally fall into two distinct categories including fee-based planners and commission-based planners. Fee-based planners charge a set fee that may be linked to the client's wealth or income. Commissioned planners receive a commission on the financial products the client purchases. The potential for a conflict of interest between the goals of the client and the financial planner are obviously less when the planner is paid on a fee-only basis. Unfortunately, many clients prefer not to pay an up-front fee for financial planning advice. Therefore, most financial planning services are provided by commissioned planners. An ethical commissioned financial planner with a good overview of available products can suggest financial products that benefit the customer while also providing an adequate return to the planner for his or her efforts.

A financial analyst is someone who specializes in analyzing and comparing various investment products. A financial analyst may specialize in researching investments. A financial planner may also be a financial analyst. However, a financial analyst is not necessarily a financial planner. Rather than specializing in a particular product, the financial planner must be more of a generalist. The planner must be able to piece together a plan that satisfies all of the client's financial needs. This requires knowledge of investments, tax laws, and insurance so that the financial planner may construct a plan that satisfies the client's short-term and long-term goals. A good advisor will follow the steps that are repeatedly reinforced in this text. He or she will help the client state and assess financial goals. The planner will then propose a comprehensive plan for achieving the stated goals and subsequently monitor the client's progress. The financial planner will typically meet with a client at least once a year to monitor progress and update the plan for life's major changes or changes in tax laws and the economy.

A financial planner may manage a team of legal and financial advisors each specializing in a particular area of personal finance. For example, while a financial planner may have knowledge of how a client's estate planning needs may be satisfied, the planner will need to work with a lawyer to oversee the writing of a will or the creation of trusts for transferring the client's wealth. Moreover, an estate plan may also transfer assets through life insurance that may require a knowledgeable expert in this area.

Educational and Professional Background

An educational background in business or law, which includes courses in finance and taxes, can provide good preparation for a career in financial planning. Other helpful courses are those covering real estate and insurance. Don't overlook courses in communications. A financial advisor must possess good communication skills.

You do not need professional certification to provide financial planning services, but advisors who sell financial investments may need a license. Many financial planners, however, obtain certification to enhance their business opportunities and professional reputation. (See Finance News 1.4 for a list of certifications and professional organizations.) The professional designations that financial advisors list after their names include CFP, Certified Financial Planner, and ChFC, Chartered Financial Consultant. The CFP is issued by the Certified Financial Board of Standards after the candidate has successfully completed a series of the exams covering all aspects of financial planning. The ChFC is bestowed by the American College in Bryn Mawr, Pennsylvania, after completing an eight-course program of study that is offered live and online. Both of these accreditations require practitioners to keep current by taking continuing education electives. Given the constantly changing financial environment, a good financial planner never stops learning new ways to help clients.

Employment Outlook and Earnings

The Bureau of Labor Statistic's *Occupational Outlook Handbook* reports that employment opportunities for financial advisors are likely to grow faster than the average for all occupations through 2014. This will be spurred on by the aging baby-boom generation needing advice on retirement and estate planning and by a rise in the general level of family wealth.

About 40 percent of financial advisors are self-employed. Accordingly, earnings are largely tied to the size of the client base, which means that there will be a wide earnings range for financial planners. The Bureau of Labor Statistics reports that mean annual earnings for personal financial advisors was $86,730 in 2006 with the middle 50 percent earning between $44,130 and $114,260.

For information on a career in financial planning, contact: The Financial Planning Association, 4100 E. Mississippi Ave., Suite 400, Denver, CO 80246-3053. Internet: http://www.fpanet.org

For information about the Certified Financial Planner (CFP) (R) certification, contact: Certified Financial Planner Board of Standards, Inc., 1670 Broadway, Suite 600, Denver, CO 80202-4809. Internet: http://www.cfp.net/become

For information about the Chartered Financial Consultant (ChFC) designation, contact: The American College, 270 South Bryn Mawr Ave., Bryn Mawr, PA 19010. Internet: http://www.theamericancollege.edu

2

The Time Value of Money
all dollars are not created equal

Objectives

1. To gain a general understanding that monies received or paid out at different times have different values and that these values can change dramatically depending on interest rate levels and when they are received or paid

2. To understand the process of compounding and to be able to compute a future value of a single payment or annuity

3. To understand the process of discounting and to be able to compute the present value of a single payment or annuity

4. To be able to find approximate values for unknown interest rates or unknown holding periods when the values for other financial variables are known

5. To recognize the importance of planning in the effort to achieve future goals

6. To be able to compute a required annual savings amount to meet future goals

7. To be able to construct a savings plan designed to show how savings will grow over time and be used to meet future goals

Steele family

Sharon Steele participated in a lunch discussion about the pending retirement of one of the CPA firm's partners. The talk was lively and there was spirited give-and-take on the topic of the amount of money needed to provide a comfortable retirement for a typical couple. Amazingly, the estimates varied from $200,000 to well over $2,000,000. Of course, although people were making different assumptions, Sharon had no doubt that coming up with a reasonable amount was not a back-of-the-envelope calculation. More importantly, as Sharon listened, it dawned on her that she and Arnold had a poor grasp of how much they might count on from Social Security and from Arnold's retirement plan. Would the combination be enough?

She later discussed her concern with Arnold and, as they pursued the issue further, it became clear that not only were they unsure about retirement funds, but also they had virtually no idea how much would be needed to finance other desired activities. A particularly troublesome part of the planning involved estimating values through time. Sure, they could determine how much one year at State U might cost for Nancy and John if they started school today; but what would be the cost when they actually enrolled in eight and ten years, respectively? Then, after these amounts are calculated, how much must they invest each year to reach their goal? Arnold and Sharon aren't going to kid themselves; they must allow a considerable amount of time to become familiar with time-value-of-money techniques.

TOPIC LINKS

Follow the **Topic Links** in each chapter for your interactive Personal Finance exercise on the Web. Go to: **www.prenhall.com/frasca**.

Perhaps one of the most difficult parts of financial planning is estimating future funds requirements. The Steeles aren't alone in their inability to measure a retirement need or the amount needed for future college costs. Many families experience similar difficulties. The trouble lies in two areas: First, since expenses occur in the future, sometimes the very distant future, the impact of rising prices over time makes it difficult to determine actually how much the expenses will be. Second, knowing how much to invest periodically to meet the expenses is equally difficult since actual earning rates on the investments may not be known.

This chapter presents a basic treatment of time-value-of-money techniques—approaches designed to measure the value of money over time. There are two fundamental activities—compounding and discounting. Each is explained and the chapter concludes by applying these techniques to the Steeles' goal-planning situation.

Compounding (Finding Future Values)

Compounding refers to the process of accumulating value over time. Two cases are considered: first, the accumulation of value from a single payment (*payment* is a more general term than *investment*); second, the accumulation of value from a periodic series of equal payments, called an **annuity**.

Compounding The process of accumulating value over time from a single payment.

Annuity A periodic series of equal payments.

Future Value of a Single Payment

A sum of money received or paid in the future is called a **future value**. For example, you might be considering an investment that costs $1,000 today and returns the same amount to you at the end of three years. Is it a good investment? Of course not! Why be content just to get your money back when other investments pay interest? If someone wishes to use our money, we insist on a return—one at least as good as those available on equal-risk, alternative investments. Suppose the borrower offered to give your $1,000 back at the end of three years along with $200 in interest. Is that acceptable, if you think you could earn 10 percent annual interest somewhere else? To answer the question we must calculate the future value (*FV*) of $1,000 invested elsewhere. This calculation follows:

$$FV \text{ at end of year } 1 = \$1,000 + 0.10(\$1,000) = \$1,100$$
$$FV \text{ at end of year } 2 = \$1,100 + 0.10(\$1,100) = \$1,210$$
$$FV \text{ at end of year } 3 = \$1,210 + 0.10(\$1,210) = \$1,331$$

An alternative quick calculation is

$$FV - (\$1,000)(1.0 + i)(1.0 + i)(1.0 + i)$$

where i = your required investment rate each period. Then

$$FV = (\$1,000)(1.1)(1.1)(1.1) = (\$1,000)(1.331) = \$1,331$$

In the preceding example, your $1,000 grows to $1,331 if you can invest it (and all the subsequent interest earned) at 10 percent. Comparing $1,331 with the $1,200 offered by the other investment tells us the other investment should be rejected.

The $331 of interest as calculated is called **compound interest**. It includes "interest on interest," which means that interest earned in earlier periods is assumed to be reinvested to earn interest in future periods. **Simple interest** assumes that interest earned in each period is withdrawn and not reinvested. The following formula is used to calculate simple interest:

$$\text{Simple interest} = (\text{principal}) \times (\text{rate}) \times (\text{time})$$

Future value A sum of money received or paid in the future.

TOPIC LINKS

Use a future value calculator.

Compound interest A future value that includes interest on interest.

Simple interest An assumption that interest earned in a period is withdrawn in that period.

Using the preceding data, simple interest would be $300 as calculated here:

$$\$300 = (\$1,000) \times (0.10) \times (3)$$

You can use either method to calculate interest, depending on which one is more appropriate to what you actually will do with earned interest. However, in most financial planning illustrations the compound method is used.

The Importance of Additional Yield

The future values of different investments are crucial to many financial decisions. For example, suppose you are considering investments *A* and *B*. *A* offers an 8 percent yield and has virtually no risk on either a short- or long-term basis. *B* offers a 10 percent yield and is about as risky as *A* on a long-term basis but somewhat riskier in the short term. (You might pay a penalty for early withdrawal, for example.) Since you plan to hold each investment for a long period of time, *B*'s added risk is not of major concern to you. On the other hand, you aren't sure that a mere two percentage points is enough marginal yield to pick *B* over *A*. By looking only at the difference of two percentage points, you may fail to see the substantial difference in future values between the two. Figure 2.1 shows this difference in dramatic detail. (The amounts were calculated using the compound interest techniques explained earlier.) At the end of three years, you will have only $71 ($1,331 minus $1,260) more with investment *B*, but at the end of 40 years you will have an extra $23,533—more than twice as much!

The Importance of Additional Time

Figure 2.1 also dramatizes the importance of investing early to achieve certain goals, such as retirement. Suppose you are 25 and plan to retire at age 65. You are considering investing now for retirement but wonder how much difference it would make if you waited 10 years to start. Assuming the 10 percent investment rate, the answer is $27,810 ($45,259 minus $17,449). You accumulate considerably more in the last 10 years than do you in the first 30!

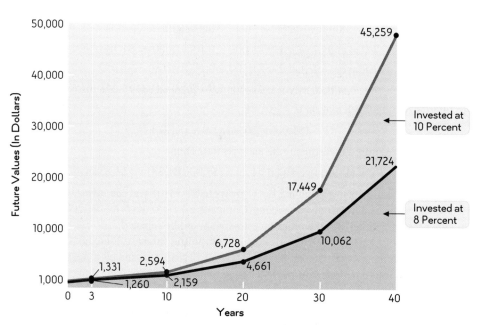

Figure 2.1
Future Value of $1,000
Invested at 8 and 10 Percent

Time-Value-of-Money Tables

Future value calculations are easy to make with a calculator or spreadsheet software, following the procedures just explained. As an alternative, many people use a *future-value-of-$1 table*. A portion of such a table is shown in Table 2.1. (More detailed tables appear in the Appendix at the end of the text.) A future-value table shows the future value of $1 invested for a specified number of periods and at a specified investment rate each period. To use the table, simply multiply the future value of $1 by the number of dollars you invest. If you invest $100, multiply $100 times 1.3310; if $200, multiply $200 times 1.3310, and so forth. You can see from Table 2.1 how the values in Figure 2.1 were determined.

The Rule of 72

A popular technique for examining the relationship between a future value and its associated interest rate is the **rule of 72**. It's quite simple to use. For example, suppose you would like to double the amount of funds you have placed in an investment. The length of time needed to accomplish this goal depends on the rate of interest you earn. If you suppose you can earn 6 percent, how long will it take to reach your goal? The answer is found by dividing the interest rate into the number 72; so, 72/6 = 12, or 12 years. A general formula follows:

$$\text{Doubling time } (DT) = 72/\text{interest rate}$$

An answer is always an approximation, but it is usually close enough for most problems. If you refer to Table A.1 in the Appendix at the end of the text, you will see that the future value factor for 6 years and 12 percent is actually 1.9738. A $1,000 investment grows to only $1,973.80, rather than the $2,000 needed to double the original amount.

The rule of 72 A simple technique to determine how long it takes to double an investment's value.

Time-Value of Money Calculations on the Internet

At a modest cost you can purchase a financial calculator that will instantly calculate most of the financial values explained in this chapter. If you lack a handy calculator or a spreadsheet program such as Excel, there are a number of very good Web sites to make time-value calculations. You enter the necessary data, click a button, and the calculation is done instantly. Most of these calculators are structured for a particular application, such as saving for retirement or paying off a mortgage loan. As such, they have limited use in general time-value-of-money situations that are presented here. However, once you have a basic understanding of the concepts, you probably will be interested only in specific applications as they arise. Then the dedicated-function calculators will be most useful to you. Some informative Web sites can be easily accessed at **www.prenhall.com/frasca** through the margin link.

TOPIC LINKS

Internet Time Value Calculators

		Interest Rate	
Number of periods (n)	6%	8%	10%
1	1.0600	1.0800	1.1000
3	1.1910	1.2597	1.3310
10	1.7908	2.1589	2.5937
20	3.2071	4.6610	6.7275
30	5.7435	10.0620	17.4490
40	10.2850	21.7240	45.2590

Table 2.1
Portion of a Future Value-of-$1 Table

(See Appendix, Table A.1 for an expanded table.)

Future Value of an Annuity

TOPIC LINKS

Use a future-value-of-an-annuity calculator.

Recall that an annuity is a series of equal payments. Many financial products, such as investments and insurance policies, involve making annual payments. So, suppose an investment requires a payment of $1,000 a year for the next three years, with payments made at the *end* of each year. How much will this investment accumulate at the end of the three years, assuming an annual investment rate of 10 percent?

Let's break down the investment into three separate single payments—one occurring one year from now (two accumulation years), one occurring two years from now (one accumulation year), and one occurring three years from now (no accumulation time). The accumulations are as follows:

First payment: $1,000 \times 1.1 \times 1.1 = $1,210
Second payment: $1,000 \times 1.1 \quad\quad = 1,100
Third payment: $1,000 \times 1.0 \quad\quad = \underline{1,000}
Total \quad\quad\quad\quad\quad\quad\quad\quad $3,310

The answer is $3,310. It could have been found much more quickly by referring to a future-value-of-$1 annuity table, an example of which appears in Table 2.2. As you see, the future value of a $1 annuity invested at 10 percent for three years is 3.310. Multiply this figure by the annuity amount—$1,000—and you have your answer. You have found the future value of an ordinary annuity (*FVOA*).

Ordinary annuity An annuity with end-of-period payments.

Annuity due An annuity with beginning-of-period payments.

If payments take place at the end of the period, the annuity is called an **ordinary annuity**; if they take place at the beginning of a period, it is called an **annuity due**. An annuity due simply involves one more compounding period than an ordinary annuity, thereby increasing the total accumulation. Let's return to the preceding example and calculate the accumulation:

First payment: $1,000 \times 1.1 \times 1.1 \times 1.1 = $1,331
Second payment: $1,000 \times 1.1 \times 1.1 \quad\quad = 1,210
Third payment: $1,000 \times 1.1 \quad\quad\quad\quad = \underline{1,100}
Total \quad\quad\quad\quad\quad\quad\quad\quad\quad\quad $3,641

The sum—$3,641—is called the future value of an annuity due (*FVAD*). Of course, there is a much easier way to find this value. Simply find the accumulation with an ordinary annuity and multiply it by 1.0 plus the interest rate (*i*, expressed as a decimal); that is,

$$FVAD = (1.0 + i) \times FVOA = (1.0 + 0.10) \times FVOA$$
$$FVAD = (1.10) \times \$3,310 = \$3,641$$

Since converting an *FVOA* to an *FVAD* is so easy, we present only an *FVOA* table in the Appendix at the end of the text.

Table 2.2
Portion of a Future-Value-of-$1 Annuity Table

(See Appendix, Table A.2 for an expanded table.)

Number of periods (n)	Interest Rate		
	6%	8%	10%
1	1.0000	1.0000	1.0000
3	3.1836	3.2464	3.3100
10	13.1800	14.4860	15.9370
20	36.7850	45.7620	57.2750
30	79.0580	113.2800	164.4900
40	154.7600	259.0500	442.5900

saving money 2.1

Time Value of Money— Big Bore or Big Help?

Financial products are becoming much more difficult to read and virtually impossible to understand unless you have a background in time-value-of-money techniques. Consider an example offered by Humberto Cruz, who writes a timely and very useful syndicated column on personal finance. A reader asked Mr. Cruz to evaluate an annuity package that included a long-term care insurance policy. Combination products are generally the most difficult to evaluate because the offering company seldom tells you how much you pay for each of the component parts. You have to determine that on your own.

In discussing one of the most popular of such policies, Mr. Cruz noted that the annuity component costing $58,900 (lump-sum immediate payment) provided a 55-year-old woman with a future payment of $258,874 at age 85. The con-

tract presumably offered an 8 percent return. Does it really? Without a basic training in time value of money, would you question the figures? Well, Mr. Cruz did, and he discovered that you only need to invest $25,229 to grow to $258,874, if indeed you earn an 8 percent return (check his calculation with a calculator or future-value-of-$1 table). So, where does the other $33,671 go? It's used to buy the long-term care insurance—a fact, as Mr. Cruz points out, that is not mentioned anywhere in the policy.

It's beside the point whether or not the insurance part of this product is a good or bad deal. In fact, you can't even begin to evaluate the insurance unless you know what it cost. And you won't know that figure unless you dig it out, as Mr. Cruz did. Unfortunately, we won't always have someone to help us evaluate "tricky" products—which highlights the importance of understanding personal financial tools. Maybe those time-value-of-money calculations aren't so boring after all.

Discounting (Finding Present Values)

In compounding we are finding future values, given present values; in contrast, **discounting** is the process of reducing future values to present values. Again, two cases are considered: first, finding the present value of a single sum that will be received or paid in the future; and second, finding the present value of an annuity to be received or paid in the future.

Discounting The process of reducing future values to present values.

Present Value of a Single Payment

Discounting is simply the reverse process of compounding. So, revising the preceding example, suppose an investment that requires an immediate $1,000 payment will pay $1,331 three years from now. Is it a good investment? The answer depends on the interest rate (now called a discount rate) we think should apply to the investment. Let's find the present value (PV) of the $1,331 future value ($FV$), discounting at 10 percent (i).

TOPIC LINKS

Use a present value calculator.

Using a Present Value Table

The easiest approach is to use a present-value-of-$1 table, an example of which appears in Table 2.3. As shown, the present value of $1 received three years in the future and discounted at 10 percent is $0.7513 (about 75 cents). Multiplying 0.7513 times the future value of $1,331 gives us the present value of the investment—$1,000.

The answer should reinforce the foregoing statement that discounting is simply the reverse process of compounding. We showed earlier that $1,000 *compounds* to $1,331 when invested at a 10 percent annual rate for three years. Clearly, then, $1,331 *discounts* to $1,000 when it is received three years from now and 10 percent is the annual discount rate.

Is the investment a good one, then? Actually, it's at the margin between good and bad—a situation we often describe as a "fairly priced" asset. To determine whether this is

	Interest Rate		
Number of periods (n)	6%	8%	10%
1	0.9434	0.9259	0.9091
3	0.8396	0.7938	0.7513
10	0.5584	0.4632	0.3855
20	0.3118	0.2145	0.1486
30	0.1741	0.0994	0.0573
40	0.0972	0.0460	0.0221

Table 2.3
Portion of a Present-Value-of-$1 Table

(See Appendix, Table A.3 for an expanded table.)

a good investment use the rate you could earn of similar investments with similar risk. For example, if you use an 8 percent discount rate, you get a present value of $1,056.55 (0.7938 × $1,331). Now, we could say the investment is a good one because the present value exceeds the $1,000 required to buy it. In contrast, if you discount at 12 percent, the investment turns bad because the present value is now only $947.41 (0.7118 × $1,331).

Present Value Graph

Figure 2.1 illustrates how $1,000 *grows* in value over time. Figure 2.2 shows how $1,000 *depreciates* in value over time. Two discount rates—10 percent and 4 percent—are used in the illustrations. As you see, the depreciation rate is much faster with the 10 percent rate. For example, the $1,000 received 10 years from now is worth only $386 today if the 10 percent rate is used; with the 4 percent rate, the present value is $676. No one should be indifferent as to when he or she receives money. The rule is always the sooner, the better. Moreover, no one should take lightly the interest rate used in the discounting process, since higher rates always lead to more rapid erosion of value. See *Saving Money 2.1* for a real-world example involving a discounting situation.

Present Value of an Annuity

Finally, we can find the present values of ordinary annuities and annuities due. Again, the easiest method is to use the present-value-of-$1 annuity table (see Table 2.4). As an exam-

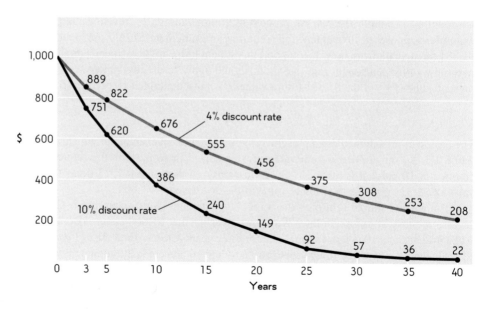

Figure 2.2
Present Value of $1,000 Received in the Future and Discounted at 10 Percent and at 4 Percent

	Interest Rate		
Number of periods (n)	6%	8%	10%
1	0.9434	0.9259	0.9091
3	2.6730	2.5571	2.4869
10	7.3601	6.7101	6.1446
20	11.4699	9.8181	8.5136
30	13.7648	11.2578	9.4268
40	15.0463	11.9246	9.7791

Table 2.4
Portion of a Present–Value-of–$1 Annuity Table

(See Appendix, Table A.4 for an expanded table.)

ple, suppose you are evaluating an investment that pays you $5,000 a year (end of year) for the next three years. What is the present value of the investment (ordinary annuity), assuming an annual discount rate of 6 percent? From Table 2.4 we find the discount factor for three years and 6 percent; it is 2.6730. So, the present value of an ordinary annuity (*PVOA*) = 2.6730 × $5,000 = $13,365.

Table 2.4 shows discount factors for ordinary annuities. If the investment required beginning-of-year payments, its present value (*PVAD*) would be $14,166.90. As before,

$$PVAD = (1.0 + i) \times PVOA = (1.0 + 0.06) \times PVOA$$
$$PVAD = (1.06) \times \$13,365 = \$14,166.90$$

Is this a good investment? The answer depends on its cost. Suppose the cost is $13,700 and payments are received at the end of three years. Then it is a bad investment because the present value of what you receive is only $13,365; in effect, you lose $335 ($13,365 – $13,700) if you buy it. But if payments begin immediately (annuity due), it's a good investment and you make $466.90 ($14,166.90 – $13,700.00). Receiving the payments one year earlier makes the difference.

More Applications of Future and Present Values

We can express the relationship between a present value (*PV*) and a future value (*FV*) as follows:

$$FV = [FV \text{ of } \$1 \text{ factor: } n, i] \times PV$$

The expression in the brackets refers to a value from a future-value-of-$1 table, where *n* represents the number of years and *i* represents the interest rate. There are four variables in the expression. Knowing any three allows us to solve for an unknown fourth. Several illustrations are explained next.

Finding an Unknown Interest Rate

Suppose we have the following problem. What interest rate must be earned to achieve a $6,000 goal in five years, assuming $4,000 is invested today? Rather than solving for a future value, we now must solve for an interest rate. Let's plug values into the preceding formula, knowing that *FV* = $6,000, *PV* = $4,000, and *n* = 5.

$$\$6,000 = [FV \text{ factor}] \times \$4,000$$
$$[FV \text{ Factor}] = \$6,000/\$4,000 = 1.5$$

Now, refer to Table A.1 in the Appendix at the end of the text. Go to the five-year row and go across the row until you find the closest value to 1.5. You should see that this value is 1.4683, which is found in the 8 percent column. So, the answer is approximately 8 percent.

Since 1.4683 is a bit smaller than 1.5000, the actual rate is a bit more than 8 percent. (We can get a more accurate answer by using interpolation techniques, which are covered in Appendix 2.1.)

Finding an Unknown Number of Years

Let's try another problem. You hope to earn 20 percent on a somewhat risky investment. You will put $3,000 into the investment and will "cash out" when the investment value reaches $10,000. How long will that take? Again, we go back to the basic formula and insert values.

$$\$10,000 = [FV \text{ factor}] \times \$3,000$$
$$[FV \text{ factor}] = \$10,000/\$3,000 = 3.3333$$

Returning to Table A.1, go to the 20 percent column and go down until you find the number closest to 3.3333. It is seven years, which has an FV factor value of 3.5832. Since 3.5832 is a bit larger than 3.3333, the actual number of years is a bit less than seven. (An interpolated answer is shown in Appendix 2.1.)

Approximation Methods with Annuities

The preceding examples relate to a single payment. However, we can also use approximation methods when annuities are involved. Again, two basic equations apply:

$$FV = [FV \text{ of } \$1 \text{ annuity: } n, i] \times \text{annuity payment}$$
$$PV = [PV \text{ of } \$1 \text{ annuity: } n, i] \times \text{annuity payment}$$

An Example Using a Future Value

We will illustrate with an example. You are committed to saving and investing $2,500 annually over the next 10 years. If you hope to accumulate $50,000 at the end of the period, what interest rate must you earn? Since the problem deals with compounding, refer to Table A.2 in the Appendix at the end of the text.

$$\$50,000 = [FV \text{ factor}] \times \$2,500$$
$$[FV \text{ factor}] = \$50,000/\$2,500 = 20.000$$

Go to the 10-year row and move across until you reach the number closest to 20.000; it is 20.303, which is associated with 15 percent. Since 20.303 is a bit more than 20.000, the actual rate is a bit less than 15 percent.

An Example Using a Present Value

You are thinking of buying a lottery ticket that will provide you with either a lump-sum payment of $2,000,000 right after you win or an annual payment of $160,000 for the next 20 years. You must make a choice at the time you purchase the ticket. What is the implied rate of interest embedded in the lottery payoffs? Since the $2,000,000 is a present value, use Table A.4 in the Appendix at the end of the text.

$$\$2,000,000 = [PV \text{ factor}] \times \$160,000$$
$$[PV \text{ factor}] = \$2,000,000/\$160,000 = 12.500$$

Go to the 20-year row and go across until you reach the number closest to 12.5000; it is 12.4622, which is associated with a 5 percent interest rate. (An interpolated answer is shown in Appendix 2.1.)

Knowing that the embedded rate is about 5 percent should help you decide how to take the money after you win. If you think that you could invest over the 20 years at rates higher

FINANCIAL PLANNING *for* young adults 2.2

Focus on the Asset, Not on the Daily Savings

Most of us establish daily consumption routines that on the surface seem trivially inexpensive. Coffee is $2, lunch costs at least $5, and maybe a snack or two from the vending machine. Add smoking to the mix and you can spend easily $10 to $20 every day. What's it worth to you to save some of this outlay, maybe by giving up smoking or by brown-bagging it for lunch? Aside from considerable health benefits gained, assuming you invest the savings, you can create an asset that is much larger than you might think. If you haven't been successful in the past breaking these "inexpensive" habits, you might have more luck if you focus on the asset you're giving up, rather than the small daily savings.

As an example, suppose you can save $15 a week. The table shows potential future values using weekly compounding and assuming different investment rates and periods of time that the asset is held. As you can see, the results are impressive. So, don't look at the $15 a week you can save; rather, plan on how you'll spend $307,533 when you are in your early sixties. (If you think $15 is too low—or too high—you can adjust the table amounts by multiplying them times your number over 15. For example, if you think $20 is a better estimate, multiply by 20/15, or 1.333.)

Changing a lifestyle is not easy. Moreover, the physical act of depositing money in an investment account involves some time and effort. The candy bar gives us immediate satisfaction; the investment only gives us numbers on paper. We must decide their relative importance, but at least this little exercise shows the long-run impact of what we are giving up as we munch on our Tootsie Rolls.

Years held	Investment Rates		
	3%	6%	9%
10	$9,093	$10,680	$12,633
20	21,367	30,131	43,682
40	60,293	130,103	307,533

than 5 percent indicates that you want the lump-sum payment. If you can't earn more than 5 percent elsewhere, take the extended payout.

Goal Planning for the Steeles

Time-value-of-money techniques are useful tools for determining the required amount of funds to achieve future goals, some taking place 20 to 30 years in the future. The application of these tools in the Steeles' case is illustrated in the following sections.

In the plan, the Steeles' last goal is 28 years away, when Arnold begins retirement. You might question the realism of trying to determine goals and preferences so far in the future. Who knows if either Arnold or Sharon will live for 28 more years? So why go to all the bother? But what is the alternative? You can't ignore the future, unless you are not particularly concerned about what happens to you or people you care about in the future. The odds are very high that Arnold and Sharon will live well past the estimated retirement date. The odds are also good that both Nancy and John will go to college. So, the Steeles can either plan for these very important events, or they can "wing it" and hope the money is there when the time comes.

Making Goals Concrete

The first phase in the planning process involves identifying particular goals, setting the future years when the goals are to be achieved, and establishing an initial dollar amount for each goal. You should understand that a goal is something far more concrete than a dream.

While there is nothing wrong with the latter—indeed, most goals probably begin as dreams or wishes—a goal implies a commitment toward its achievement. Moreover, you should only set goals for activities that are very important. If these can be achieved through a savings plan, then you can add other less important goals over time.

What and When?

Table 2.5 illustrates the first phase in columns 1 and 2. The Steeles have specified the following four major goals:

1. Providing four years of college education to Nancy and John, starting 8 years from the present and ending in 13 years.
2. Adding a greenhouse to the home 18 years in the future.
3. Taking a European vacation 20 years in the future.
4. Accumulating a retirement nest egg 28 years in the future.

Although these are the most important goals, the list could be expanded if the Steeles determine that these goals can be achieved without undue stress on their yearly budget, which is a topic we explore in Chapter 3.

How Much if Undertaken Today?

The amount of funds needed to achieve a goal is established initially by determining the cost of the activity if it were undertaken today. These amounts appear in column 3 of Table 2.5. So, if Nancy started college in the current year, the associated costs would be $12,000 for the year. It takes $48,000 for Nancy's four years, and a similar amount for John's education. If each can finish in four years, the annual outlays cover a six-year period, begin-

Table 2.5
Determining Required Savings Amounts

(1) Goals	(2) Years Until Goal Is Achieved	(3) Amount Required	(4) Inflation Rate	(5) Future Value-of $1 Factor	(6) Inflation Adjusted Amount $(3) \times (5)$	(7) Future Value-of-$1 Annuity Factor (8% rate)	(8) Required Annual Savings $(6)/(7)$
1. Nancy starts college:							
year 1	8	$ 12,000	6%	1.5938	$ 19,126	10.636	$1,798
year 2	9	12,000	6%	1.6895	20,274	12.487	1,624
2. John joins Nancy at college:							
year 3	10	24,000	6%	1.7908	42,979	14.486	2,967
year 4	11	24,000	6%	1.8983	45,559	16.645	2,737
3. John finishes college:							
year 5	12	12,000	6%	2.0122	24,146	18.977	1,272
year 6	13	12,000	6%	2.1329	25,595	21.495	1,191
4. Add greenhouse to home	18	40,000	3%	1.7024	68,096	37.450	1,818
5. Take European vacation	20	10,000	3%	1.8061	18,061	45.762	395
6. Accumulate retirement							
nest egg	28	100,000	3%	2.2879	228,790	95.338	2,400
Totals		$246,000			$492,626		$16,202

ning in eight years. There are two years when both kids are at the university. Also, as you can see, the greenhouse would cost $40,000 to install today and the European vacation would cost $10,000. Finally, Arnold and Sharon would like to have $100,000 in today's purchasing power to use in a variety of ways at retirement. They might spend all of it before their deaths, or they might save it as a legacy for Nancy and John.

Adjusting for Inflation

Unfortunately, since these goals take place at very distant future points in time, inflation will most likely increase their costs above the amounts specified in column 3. Therefore, the costs must be adjusted to reflect inflation. The assumed inflation rates are shown in column 4. Arnold and Sharon expect that the overall rate of inflation over the planning period will be 3 percent. However, college costs have been increasing in recent years at about twice the overall inflation rate, and there is no indication that this rate will diminish. Therefore, college costs are presumed to increase at a 6 percent rate.

Determining an inflated amount is accomplished by using the *compounding process,* discussed earlier in this chapter. An inflation rate (or, more generally, a growth rate) works the same as an interest rate. If inflation is 6 percent, then an item costing $100 today will cost $106 a year from today. You should see that this is the same as saying that $100 invested today at 6 percent interest will be worth $106 a year from today. Recognizing this similarity, we can then calculate the inflated amounts by using the future-value-of-$1 tables.

For example, Nancy's first year in college is eight years in the future and the $12,000 cost will grow 6 percent per year. From Table A.1 in the Appendix at the end of the text, we find the future-value-of-$1 factor for eight years and 6 percent is 1.5938. Therefore, the inflation-adjusted amount is $19,126 (1.5938 × $12,000). Similar calculations are made for the remaining items in Table 2.5. You might note the severe impact of inflation over time, which just about doubles the cost of future goals for the Steeles ($492,626 versus $246,000). The lesson is simple: Ignore inflation at your own peril!

Determining a Savings Schedule

By far the most difficult part of the planning process is determining how much must be saved each year to achieve the goals. Usually, planners go through a series of attempts (trial and error) until a workable saving schedule is reached. Column 8 of Table 2.5 shows a step in a first trial, one the Steeles are *not* likely to accept.

Required Annual Savings

A required annual savings amount is determined by using the compounding process again, only this time we use the future-value-of-$1 annuity. Assuming that the Steeles will earn 8 percent on their savings, we can illustrate one of the calculations. For example, the Steeles have 18 years to save for the greenhouse; so we find from Table A.2 in the Appendix the future-value-of-$1 annuity factor for 18 years and 8 percent is 37.450. Divide this figure into the inflation-adjusted cost of $68,096 and arrive at the required annual savings of $1,818.

Summing the amounts for all the activities gives a total required annual savings of $16,202. However, this is *not* an amount that must be saved each year over the next 28 years. Indeed, as each goal is achieved, the need to save for it is eliminated. The process is illustrated in Table 2.6.

Table 2.6
The Steeles' Savings Plan:
First Trial

Year	Deposit	Interest Earned (8% Rate)	Withdrawals	Ending Balance
1	$16,202	$ —	$0	$16,202
2	16,202	1,296	0	33,700
3	16,202	2,696	0	52,598
4	16,202	4,208	0	73,008
5	16,202	5,841	0	95,051
6	16,202	7,604	0	118,857
7	16,202	9,509	0	144,567
8	16,202	11,565	19,126	153,209
9	14,404	12,257	20,274	159,595
10	12,780	12,768	42,979	142,164
11	9,813	11,373	45,559	117,791
12	7,076	9,423	24,146	110,144
13	5,804	8,812	25,595	99,165
14	4,613	7,933	0	111,711
15	4,613	8,937	0	125,261
16	4,613	10,021	0	139,895
17	4,613	11,192	0	155,699
18	4,613	12,456	68,096	104,672
19	2,795	8,374	0	115,841
20	2,795	9,267	18,061	109,843
21	2,400	8,787	0	121,030
22	2,400	9,682	0	133,112
23	2,400	10,649	0	146,161
24	2,400	11,693	0	160,254
25	2,400	12,820	0	175,475
26	2,400	14,038	0	191,912
27	2,400	15,353	0	209,665
28	2,400	16,773	228,790	49

A First Trial

As you see in column 2 of the table, an annual savings amount of $16,202 lasts for only eight years, after which Nancy's first year in college is over. Thus, the $1,798 of annual savings to meet the first year's cost of $19,126 is no longer needed. In year 9, then, the required deposit to the savings account falls to $14,404 ($16,202 − $1,798). As all the goals are eventually reached, the savings account is depleted at the end of 28 years. (The $49 remaining in the account is trivial and due to rounding.)

Note that we are assuming end-of-year deposits (ordinary annuities—not annuities due). Thus, the interest of $1,296 earned in year 2 is based on year 1's deposit of $16,202. Also note that the ending balance of $33,700 consists of the $16,202 deposit made in years 1 and 2 and the interest earned in year 2 ($16,202 + $16,202 + $1,296 = $33,700).

The Steeles are not likely to follow this savings plan since it requires the most savings in the early years, when their incomes are probably lower than what they will be in future years. Generally, our incomes rise as we advance in our careers or become more skilled at trades. Even though the plan is rejected, its creation is still worth the exercise because it serves as a test for accuracy in the construction of Table 2.5. If our ending balance were not close to zero, we would know we made a mistake.

A Second Trial

Sharon decided to create a spreadsheet in an effort to find a workable savings plan. In a second trial, she and Arnold decided to set the initial annual savings amount at $8,000 and then increase it by $1,000 every four years. They felt that these amounts would likely be around 10 percent of their pretax incomes. This is not an unduly high savings goal but, as we shall learn in Chapter 3, it is one that far exceeds their present savings effort.

Table 2.7 shows the results of the second trial, and the picture is not good. As you see, a negative balance of $8,081 appears by year 12. Of course, a negative figure could not exist in the real world. It actually implies that the Steeles would have to borrow an amount to make up any deficiency. The savings account is then replaced by a loan account, and interest earned becomes interest owed. This situation is not acceptable to the Steeles.

Table 2.7
The Steeles' Savings Plan: Second Trial

Year	Deposit	Interest Earned (8% Rate)	Withdrawals	Ending Balance
1	$ 8,000	$ —	$ 0	$ 8,000
2	8,000	640	0	16,640
3	8,000	1,331	0	25,971
4	8,000	2,078	0	36,049
5	9,000	2,884	0	47,933
6	9,000	3,835	0	60,767
7	9,000	4,861	0	74,629
8	9,000	5,970	19,126	70,473
9	10,000	5,638	20,274	65,837
10	10,000	5,267	42,979	38,125
11	10,000	3,050	45,559	5,616
12	10,000	449	24,146	-8,081
13	11,000	(646)	25,595	-23,322
14	11,000	(1,866)	0	-14,188
15	11,000	(1,135)	0	-4,323
16	11,000	(346)	0	6,331
17	12,000	506	0	18,838
18	12,000	1,507	68,096	-35,751
19	12,000	(2,860)	0	-26,612
20	12,000	(2,129)	18,061	-34,801
21	13,000	(2,784)	0	-24,586
22	13,000	(1,967)	0	-13,552
23	13,000	(1,084)	0	-1,637
24	13,000	(131)	0	11,232
25	14,000	899	0	26,131
26	14,000	2,090	0	42,222
27	14,000	3,378	0	59,599
28	14,000	4,768	228,790	-150,423

A Third Trial

Arnold and Sharon did not believe they could increase their savings above the 10 percent of income target. This decision implies that they must cut back on one or several of their goals. Fortunately, the Steeles have accumulated some investments (we'll learn more about these in Chapter 3) that are worth approximately $30,000. The Steeles were thinking of using these funds for a Hawaiian vacation and/or a down payment on a vacation condo in the Smoky Mountains. However, it now appears that one or both of these dreams must be abandoned. Thus, Sharon assumes that $18,000 of the $30,000 is transferred to the savings account related to their goal-planning activity.

Table 2.8 shows a third trial at a savings plan, which will serve as the final version. Sharon assumes the $18,000 deposit is made immediately and so earns interest for a full year. At the beginning of year 1, then, there is $18,000 in the account, which earns interest of $1,440 during year 1. The Steeles are satisfied with this third trial since there are no neg-

Year	**Deposit**	**Interest Earned (8% Rate)**	**Withdrawals**	**Ending Balance**
1	$ 26,000*	$ 1,440	$ 0	$ 27,440
2	8,000	2,195	0	37,635
3	8,000	3,011	0	48,646
4	8,000	3,892	0	60,538
5	9,000	4,843	0	74,381
6	9,000	5,950	0	89,331
7	9,000	7,146	0	105,478
8	9,000	8,438	19,126	103,790
9	10,000	8,303	20,274	101,819
10	10,000	8,146	42,979	76,986
11	10,000	6,159	45,559	47,585
12	10,000	3,807	24,146	37,246
13	11,000	2,980	25,595	25,631
14	11,000	2,050	0	38,681
15	11,000	3,095	0	52,776
16	11,000	4,222	0	67,998
17	12,000	5,400	0	85,438
18	12,000	6,835	68,096	36,177
19	12,000	2,894	0	51,071
20	12,000	4,086	18,061	49,096
21	13,000	3,928	0	66,023
22	13,000	5,282	0	84,305
23	13,000	6,744	0	104,050
24	13,000	8,324	0	125,374
25	14,000	10,030	0	149,404
26	14,000	11,952	0	175,356
27	14,000	14,028	0	203,384
28	14,000	16,271	228,790	4,865

Table 2.8
The Steeles' Savings Plan: Final Version

*Consists of beginning-of-year deposit of $18,000 and end-of-year deposit of $8,000.

ative years and only a small surplus of $4,865 at the end year 28. Given this final version of their savings plan, they will budget in the upcoming year to save and invest at least $8,000.

A Final Note on Goal Planning

It is important to recognize that the usefulness of goal planning depends to a large extent on the validity of the assumptions embedded in the plans. In the Steeles' case, the two major assumptions are the inflation rates (3 percent and 6 percent) and the earning rate (8 percent). How realistic is it that any of these rates will not change over the plan's life? It is in fact totally unrealistic. Inflation may increase or abate, and earning rates are very likely to change over the period. Does this make planning a fruitless endeavor? No, it means simply that planning is not some activity undertaken once and then left unchanged. Rather, it is an ongoing process as we discussed in Chapter 1.

The Need to Monitor Progress

Sharon and Arnold must constantly monitor progress toward achieving their goals, and they must respond immediately to changes in the financial environment. Rising inflation

 finance news 2.3

Retirement: A Distant Goal or a Distant Dream?

Some 80 million Americans, those born between 1946 and 1962, are in deep trouble. A generation not accustomed to the word *no* where spending is concerned are getting ever closer to retirement with very little savings. And it's starting to dawn on them that $2,000 a month from Social Security is petty cash to a family used to spending $5,000 a month to keep happy.

Put simply, too many families are not saving enough for retirement. A recent study by the Employee Benefit Research Institute shows the average balance in a 401(k) plan for workers investing continuously from 1999 to 2006 was $121,202. Given the significant gains in the stock market this was almost double account values in 2002. Unfortunately, the study also shows that only 54 percent of workers between ages 25 and 34 work for employers who offer such plans. More unfortunately, other studies indicate that perhaps less than 50 percent of such workers participate in the plans when offered the opportunity. While $121,202 is a respectable number, the median value that separates the top 50% from the bottom 50% is only about half as much. Moreover, this represents only one in four workers. What do the other three in four have? Apparently, not much. The Federal Reserve Consumer Finance Survey showed that the median amount invested in retirement assets by all U.S. families was a mere $35,200 in 2004 (the most recent survey year).

Unfortunately, many families pursue retirement planning as though they live in Oz. Some plan to *never* retire; now, that's a realistic approach, particularly if you have a job that is physically or emotionally demanding and not much fun. Others are counting on Mom and Dad to leave them a bundle. True, trillions of dollars of savings are held by the over-55 generation, but most of that belongs to a handful of very wealthy families. The average baby-boomer family will probably get around $25,000—just enough to buy a new car. And, no kidding, some families actually believe that a winning ticket in the state lottery will bail them out in the end.

Avoiding such a situation requires a thoughtful savings-investment plan. As the following table shows, the sooner you start, the easier is the task. A $250,000 nest egg is not an excessive amount for two spouses who are likely to live 15 to 20 years beyond age 65. The 4 percent column is the most realistic when inflation is taken into consideration, but no tax-savings retirement plans (such as IRAs or 401(k)s) are used; if such plans are available, you could achieve the 6 or 8 percent columns. You would have to be very lucky to earn an inflation-adjusted 10 percent rate of return.

Required Monthly Savings to Accumulate $250,000 by Age 65

Age you begin to invest	Interest Rate Earned on Investments			
	4%	6%	8%	10%
25	$ 211	$ 125	$ 71	$ 39
35	359	248	167	110
45	680	539	422	327
55	1,692	1,518	1,358	1,210

rates or falling investment rates will increase the need to save more each year; if the situations reverse, the need to save each year lessens. Sharon's spreadsheet is an extremely useful tool in terms of simplifying the planning activity. It only takes a few seconds to enter different numbers and observe the changes in required annual savings.

How Should the Steeles Invest?

We shall defer a complete discussion of this question to various chapters later in the text. At this point we can make some general observations. First, the rate earned on savings must be an after-tax rate; that is, the Steeles must net 8 percent. If it were a pretax rate, then the amount remaining after taxes would be inadequate to fund the goals. Earning an after-tax rate of 8 percent is not all that easy unless you use certain tax shelters, such as IRAs, tax-deferred annuities, or State Higher Education plans.

Second, the Steeles might want to set up specific savings/investment accounts for each goal. This would be a requirement for the tax-sheltered plans mentioned earlier, but it might be a good idea even if there were no legal requirement. For example, the Steeles can probably afford to take greater investment risks with funds specified for the very long-run goals. The long investment horizon—a period in which the funds are not needed and can remain invested—allows the Steeles to, say, put all the funds in growth stocks in which they might achieve a return greater than 8 percent. On the other hand, the investment vehicles selected to fund Nancy's and John's education will probably be more conservative and will probably earn less than 8 percent. Finally, if different earning rates are planned, Sharon will need to revise her spreadsheet, which now assumes only one rate.

key terms

annuity (p. 25)
annuity due (p. 28)
compound interest (p. 25)
compounding (p. 25)
discounting (p. 29)

future value (p. 25)
ordinary annuity (p.28)
rule of 72 (p. 27)
simple interest (p. 25)

follow-up on the Steele family

Much of this chapter has dealt with the Steeles' goal-planning activities. You may need to refer to some of the chapter material to answer the following questions.

1. Table 2.5 assumes inflation rates of 6 percent and 3 percent. Granting that these are perhaps the best estimates, nevertheless, rework columns 6 and 8 assuming college costs increase 8 percent annually and that all other costs increase at a 5 percent annual rate. How much must the total required annual savings be, assuming the investment rate remains at 8 percent? (Use Your Financial Review Spreadsheet 2.2 at the author's Web site.)

2. Continuing with Table 2.5, don't change the inflation rates. Now let's consider the possibility that the Steeles can do better than 8 percent on some of their investments. Specifically, assume they continue to earn 8 percent on investments held for the kids' education but they can earn 10 percent on investments for the greenhouse and the European vacation, and they can earn 12 percent on their retirement investments. Now determine the required annual savings. (Use Your Financial Review Spreadsheet 2.2 at the author's Web site.)

3. The Steeles abandon the first savings plan (shown in Table 2.6) because it places too great a strain on their incomes over the next 8 to 13 years. However, by going to the

savings plan shown in Table 2.8, aren't they introducing greater risk into the process, in the sense that one never knows what can happen in the future, and saving greater amounts earlier in their lives provides a cushion in later years if something goes wrong? Discuss this point, addressing both sides of the issue.

problems and **review** questions

1. What is compounding?

2. What is compound interest? How does it differ from simple interest?

3. Suppose you invest $5,000 for five years at an interest rate of 8 percent. How much simple interest would you earn over the five years? How much compound interest would you earn? What is the explanation for the difference between these two amounts?

4. What is a future value?

5. Suppose you can earn 10 percent on an investment rather than 8 percent. After 20 years, the future value will be 25 percent greater. True or false? Explain.

6. Future values always grow larger the longer an investment is held. But do they grow proportionately larger? For example, if you hold an investment for 40 years, do you earn twice as much as you would if you hold it for 20 years? Discuss.

7. You want to double your money in six years. Approximately what rate of interest must you earn?

8. If inflation in the future runs at a 3 percent annual rate, how long will it take for prices to double?

9. What is an annuity? What is meant by the future value of an annuity?

10. How does an ordinary annuity differ from an annuity due? Which one provides the larger value in a compounding situation?

11. Explain the difference between compounding and discounting.

12. Find the following future values, using Table 2.1 or Table 2.2:
    a. $500 invested today at a 6 percent rate and held for 20 years
    b. $800 invested at the end of each of the next 10 years to earn 10 percent
    c. $300 invested at the beginning of each of the next 40 years to earn 8 percent

13. Find the following present values, using Table 2.3 or Table 2.4:
    a. $6,000 received 30 years from now, discounted at 10 percent
    b. $4,000 to be received at the end of each of the next 10 years, discounted at 6 percent
    c. $2,000 to be received at the end of each of the next three years, discounted at 8 percent

14. Suppose an investment has been offered to you that requires an initial outlay of $10,000. Ten years from now the investment will pay you $20,000. If you think an investment of this type should offer a return of 8 percent, should you make the investment? Explain, showing your analysis.

15. You can buy an annuity contract that will pay you $1,000 a year (end of year) for the next 10 years. The contract costs $6,000 today. If you think you should earn 6 percent on such investments, should you buy the contract? Explain, showing your analysis.

16. You have $15,000 to invest today. You hope to buy a new car that costs $25,000 in four years. What approximate rate of interest must you earn to achieve your goal?

17. You can invest $40,000 today toward your eventual retirement that will earn 14 percent interest over the period. You want to have $500,000 at the retirement date. How many years away from retirement are you?

18. You can invest $3,000 annually at the end of each of the next 12 years. You hope to have $60,000 in the investment account by then. What rate of interest must you earn to meet this goal?

19. Your grandmother died recently. She named you as a beneficiary on an insurance contract that will pay you $60,000 immediately. However, the contract gives you the alternative of taking $20,000 a year (end of year) for the next five years. You think that you will earn 6 percent on your investments over this period of time. Given this information, what is the better choice—immediate cash or the extended payout? Explain.

20. Distinguish between a goal and a dream.

21. The first phase of goal planning involves three steps. List them.

22. How is inflation handled in the goal-planning process? Explain.

23. Explain, as best you can, what is meant by a required annual savings amount.

24. What is a savings schedule?

25. Explain why it is necessary to monitor a savings plan over time.

case 2.1

Judy Shipley Plans for the Future

Judy Shipley graduated recently from Columbia University with an M.B.A. degree. Judy had five years of experience with a stockbrokerage firm before she entered Columbia, and this experience plus a very salable degree have landed Judy a fantastic position as an assistant portfolio manager with a mutual fund company. Her starting salary will be $110,000. Judy is unmarried and not contemplating marriage in the immediate future. She currently has no debts and no significant assets. Judy will move to Philadelphia shortly, with all moving expenses paid by her new employer.

Judy has assembled a list of goals that she would like to achieve over the next 10 years. The list does not include a retirement goal because her employer has a 401(k) plan in which she will participate. Judy hopes that her high income will support an ambitious goal plan because she wants to avoid any short-term debt. Judy anticipates an inflation rate of 4 percent on all the activities except the down payment on the town house. She has learned that housing prices in the neighborhood she favors have been increasing at an 8 percent rate. She will use that figure. Because Judy intends to make rather conservative investments, an investment rate of 6 percent seems reasonable to use.

Intended Activity	Future Date	Amount
1. Trip to Asia	2 years	$ 20,000
2. Purchase a new Lexus for cash	4 years	60,000
3. Make a down payment on a town house	6 years	80,000
4. Furnish the town house	8 years	100,000

Questions

1. Using Table 2.5 as a guide, prepare a similar schedule and calculate a required annual savings amount for each activity. How much must Judy save and invest each year (assume end-of-year payments) to achieve all of her goals? (Use Your Financial Review Form 2.2 at the author's Web site.)

2. Using your analysis from Question 1, prepare a savings schedule similar to the one shown in Table 2.6. (Use Your Financial Review Form 2.3 at author's Web site.)

3. Do you think that Judy will be able to meet her savings requirements, assuming taxes and 401(k) contributions will take about 40 percent of her income? Discuss your response.

Herman and Grace Rohrbach are in their mid-thirties. They are reasonably well off financially insofar as Grace's mother has established a trust fund to educate their two children, Barbara and Frances. The Rohrbachs lead rather simple lives and have no desires for lavish spending. However, they do face one major financial challenge: how to have sufficient resources in their retirement years. Herman owns his own camera shop and Grace has no employment income, although she often works in Herman's store.

The Rohrbachs have accumulated around $50,000 in savings, which is invested in a bond mutual fund, currently earning 5 percent after taxes. They have no other savings programs, either personal or through the business. If Herman retired today, his only income would be Social Security, which he estimates to be $18,000 annually. He would sell the business immediately prior to retirement. He has no idea what it will be worth then, but he believes he could get $100,000 for it today. To live a comfortable retirement, the Rohrbachs think they need an annual income comparable to their current one, which is $60,000 after income taxes. The Rohrbachs clearly need help to determine if they need to increase their annual savings to meet their retirement goal. Finally, the Rohrbachs will live off Social Security and interest from accumulated savings available at retirement. They will not touch any principal in their savings accounts, preferring instead to leave that money to their children. Retirement is planned in 30 years.

Questions

1. Social Security is indexed to inflation. If the inflation rate is 3 percent over the next 30 years, how much Social Security income will the Rohrbachs receive? How much will their income (currently $60,000) be at that time, assuming it grows at the 3 percent rate? How much, then, will be the shortfall—the difference between the two?

2. How much will be in the bond fund at retirement, assuming that it continues to earn 5 percent?

3. Herman has a very good location for his camera shop and can renew the lease indefinitely into the future. Suppose that its value increases by 10 percent annually over the next 30 years. How much will it then be worth?

4. Combine your answers to Questions 2 and 3. The total represents an amount available to the Rohrbachs at the beginning of retirement. Now assume that they sell the camera shop and put the proceeds into the bond fund, and the fund continues to earn 5 percent during their retirement years. Are these annual earnings sufficiently high to meet the income shortfall determined in Question 1? Your answer should be "no." Determine how much they must invest each year to accumulate a sufficient amount, which can also be deposited into a bond fund. Assume they earn 12 percent on these annual (end-of-year) investments.

case 2.2

The Rohrbachs Plan for Retirement

marie wilson goal-planning exercise

Preparing a Savings Schedule

Marie appreciates the help you have given her in formulating her financial goals. By putting the goals within specific time frames, she has a sharper focus on the savings effort she must make to achieve her goals. Her current problem is one of estimating an amount to save each year. At first, this task seemed relatively easy, but its complexity began to grow when certain financial factors were considered. These factors are the expected inflation rate on the costs of goals and the rate of return she might earn on periodic savings.

Some of the goals you and Marie have discussed must be achieved out of current income or with borrowed funds; these include pursuing a college degree, buying a new car, and paying off college loans. Marie will focus on these goals later when she attempts to prepare a budget. Also, although Marie thought retirement planning was out of the question, you have convinced her that she should consider it, even though her retirement date is probably 40 years away.

Marie has four goals that she will consider in her current savings plan: (1) sending Jake to a golf clinic five years from now at a cost of $4,000; (2) making a $14,000 down payment on a condo 10 years from now; (3) saving $32,000 for Jake's four years of college costs ($8,000 a year) beginning 14 years from now; and (4) accumulating $50,000 in a fund to be used when retirement begins in 40 years.

Form 2.1
A Simple Savings Schedule

Goals in Action	Year	Amount Required	Planned Savings	Account Balance
	1	$	$2,500	$2,500
	2		2,500	5,000
	3			
	4			
Golf Clinic	5	4,000		
	6			
	7			
	8			
	9			
	10			
	11			
	12			
	13			
	14			
	15			
	16			
	17			
	18			
	19			
	20			
	21			
	22			
	23			
	24			
	25			
	26			
	27			
	28			
	29			
	30			
	31			
	32			
	33			
	34			
	35			
	36			
	37			
	38			
	39			
	40			
Totals				

Assist Marie in preparing saving schedules for the planned goals. First, complete a simple schedule (Form 2.1) that ignores inflation and interest earnings. (This schedule will show a required annual savings amount of $2,500 ($100,000/40). Also, negative account balances will appear in years 16 and 17. This means Marie must borrow to meet her goals. For simplicity, assume that she will do this, but ignore any interest on the loans.

Second, complete a schedule (Form 2.2) that shows a required annual savings amount when inflation and interest are considered. Assume an overall inflation rate of 3 percent and an investment-earning rate of 6 percent. The total required annual savings should be $5,386.

Since Marie expects that her income will increase over time, she will not start her savings amount at $5,386 per year. Instead, she will begin her savings plan at $2,000 for each of the first five years and then increase the annual amount by $500 in each of the following five-year intervals. Use Form 2.3 to determine if this is a workable plan.

(1) Goals	(2) Years Until Goal Is Achieved	(3) Amount Required	(4) Inflation Rate	(5) Future Value of $1 Factor	(6) Inflation Adjusted Amount	(7) Future Value of $1 Annuity Factor	(8) Required Annual Savings
1. Golf clinic							
2. Condo down payment							
3a. College Year 1							
3b. College Year 2							
3c. College Year 3							
3d. College Year 4							
4. Funds in retirement account							
Totals							

Form 2.2
Determining an Annual
Savings Amount

Form 2.3
Determining a Savings Plan

Year	Deposit	Interest Earned	Withdrawals	Ending Balance
1				
2				
3				
4				
5				
6				
7				
8				
9				
10				
11				
12				
13				
14				
15				
16				
17				
18				
19				
20				
21				
22				
23				
24				
25				
26				
27				
28				
29				
30				
31				
32				
33				
34				
35				
36				
37				
38				
39				
40				

working out on the Web

Exercises to Strengthen Your Use of the Internet

(Internet links for the following exercises can be found at **www.prenhall.com/frasca**.)

Exercise 2.1 Using a Financial Calculator

There are many great online calculators, and most are designed to deal with a particular type of financial calculation. Locate a savings calculator on the Web. Go to Google.com and search for "savings calculator."

Q. Determine how long it will take to achieve a savings goal. Assume a target savings of $10,000, $200 monthly savings, an interest rate of 6 percent, and a tax rate of zero. Your answer should be approximately 3 years and 9 months (3.75 years).

Exercise 2.2 Saving for College

You may be advising someone about saving for college. These calculations can be somewhat extended and difficult, but FinAid (www.finaid.org/calculators/) offers considerable help on its great Web site.

Q. Click "Savings Plan Designer (Flat Contribution)" and notice the financial variables involved. Let's make some assumptions: Current savings are $2,000, interest rate is 8 percent, 10 years to enrollment, 100 percent of projected college costs, one year costs are $20,000, increasing at 6 percent. Find that monthly savings must be $826.68 to finance the future college costs.

Exercise 2.3 Finding the Future Value of a Single Payment and Annuity

Several of the calculators can be used for time value problems in general. For example, go to Centura Financial Calculators (www.rbccentura.com/tools/). Go to "Savings Calculators" and then "How much, at what rate, when?" to answer the first question and "How much faster will my money grow?" to answer the second.

Q. You hope to receive $5,000 in graduation gifts, which you will invest for your retirement in 30 years. If you can earn 12 percent each year, how much will you have in the retirement fund at the end of 30 years?

Q. You want to buy a $20,000 car in three years. If you can invest $6,300 a year and earn 8 percent each year, will you have enough funds at the end of three years?

Exercise 2.4 Finding the Present Value of a Single Payment

Money received in the future has less value than money available today. MoneyChimp (www.moneychimp.com/calculator/) has a present value calculator that finds the discounted present value of a future payment.

Q. Assume you expect to receive $6,000 seven years from now. If the discount rate is 10 percent, what is the present value?

APPENDIX 2.1   Interpolation Techniques

While handheld calculators and computers are frequently used to make time-value-of-money calculations, when we begin studying time value of money, it is helpful to use tables. Unfortunately, tables often provide answers that are not as accurate as we might like. Interpolation techniques add considerable accuracy to our calculations. Some examples from Chapter 2 are illustrated.

Finding an Unknown Interest Rate

> *FV* at 5 years, 8% = 1.4693
> *FV* at 5 years, 9% = 1.5386
> Difference   = 0.0696 (call this the *total difference*)

Then find:

> *FV* at 5 years, 8% = 1.4693
> *FV* at 5 years, ?% = 1.5000
> Difference   = 0.0307 (call this the *partial difference*)

Now solve:

Rate = lower rate + (partial difference/total difference) × rate increment

Rate = 8% + (0.0307/0.0693) × 1%

    = 8% + (0.443) × 1% = 8% + 0.443%

    = 8.443%

A financial calculator shows the actual rate is 8.447 percent; so, the approximation is very close.

Finding an Unknown Number of Years

20%, 7 years   = 3.5832

20%, 6 years   = 2.9860

Total difference   = 0.5972

20%, 6 years   = 2.9860

20%, ? years   = 3.3333

Partial difference = 0.3473

Number of years = 6 + (0.3473/0.5972) × 1.0 year

                  = 6 + 0.5815

                  = 6.5815 years

A financial calculator gives an answer of 6.6036 years. Again, the approximation method provides a fairly close answer.

An Example Using Present Value

20 years, 4%   = 13.5903

20 years, 5%   = 12.4622

Total difference   = 1.1281

20 years, 4%   = 13.5903

20 years, ?%   = 12.5000

Partial difference = 1.0903

Rate   = 4% + (1.0903/1.1281) × 1%

             = 4% + 0.9665%

             = 4.9665%

Financial Statements and Budgets

*where are you now and
where are you going?*

Objectives

1. To understand the importance of the balance sheet as a tool for measuring personal wealth
2. To prepare a balance sheet by identifying and valuing assets and liabilities
3. To prepare an income statement and to recognize its role in measuring financial performance
4. To evaluate financial performance by using appropriate financial ratios
5. To prepare an annual budget by constructing a master budget worksheet and a monthly income and expense plan
6. To monitor monthly activities by creating a system for recording actual income and expenses and then comparing them with budgeted amounts
7. To evaluate and control expenses during the year through a monthly review process

Steele family

Arnold and Sharon Steele have become increasingly concerned about their financial situation. A recent exercise in setting future goals has revealed a need to save about $8,000 a year. They never have been able to save that much and are concerned about their ability to achieve important future goals unless they modify their spending habits. It is clear to the Steeles that they need a budget to help them plan and control income and expenses in the upcoming year. Although they have prepared budgets in the past, they usually discarded them as the year progressed and seldom followed up to see if their actual expenses in certain categories bore any resemblance to what they had planned to spend. That practice would have to change.

It also dawned on the Steeles that they really did not have a firm grasp of their current financial status. They seemed reasonably well off, but then they never had the need to deal with a serious financial shock, such as a disability, the loss of a job, or a sick parent who needs considerable care. In truth, neither Arnold nor Sharon could answer the simple question: "What are you worth financially?" Even more embarrassing was the fact that neither could determine the amount of savings, if any, that they had accumulated in the year just ended. Before working on a budget, they felt it was important to determine their current financial strengths and weaknesses.

The Steeles' failures at budgeting and their lack of personal financial information are not characteristics unique to them. Indeed, many, if not most, families probably share the Steeles' experiences. Successful financial planning begins with a clear assessment of where you are and where you hope to be in the future.

TOPIC LINKS

Follow the **Topic Links** in each chapter for your interactive Personal Finance exercise on the Web. Go to: **www.prenhall.com/frasca**.

In Chapter 1 you learned that financial planning is a four-stage process: First, financial goals are set; second, action plans are devised for achieving those goals; third, a system is developed to measure the degree to which success is achieved; and fourth, on the basis of an evaluation of achievement, goals and action plans are reexamined to determine whether they should be dropped, modified, or left unchanged. In this chapter, our attention is directed toward the third task—measuring achievement. We are helped in this effort by accountants who have devised three particularly useful statements that measure success: the balance sheet, the income statement, and the cash budget. Each is structured to answer a specific question about financial performance. The balance sheet determines your financial position *at a particular point in time,* usually at the end of the year. The income statement shows your income, expenses, and contribution to savings *over a past period of time,* usually the preceding year. The cash budget details estimates of your income, expenses, and contribution to savings *in the upcoming period,* usually the next year. Each of the three statements plays an important role in helping you achieve your financial goals.

The Balance Sheet

Personal balance sheet
A statement designed to measure your wealth.

Assets Items of value you own.

Liabilities Your bills and other obligations.

Net worth Your wealth (assets minus liabilities).

What are you worth? It's a good practice to ask yourself this question periodically. A loan officer at a bank most certainly will ask it if you apply for a loan. She will also ask you to prepare a **personal balance sheet** to aid her in determining whether you should get the loan. The balance sheet is designed to determine someone's wealth. It has three components: **assets**, items that are owned and are measured by their fair market values; **liabilities**, bills and other obligations owed creditors that must be paid in the future; and **net worth**, the difference between assets and liabilities. (*Net worth* is actually the accounting term for wealth.) A simple balance sheet for Mike Mason, a second-year college student, appears in Figure 3.1. Mike has only a few assets, the most important being his television, stereo, iPod, and DVD player, and he has only two liabilities—$40 he owes Ed Bates and the balance due on his Visa card. Since the total value of Mike's assets is $2,178, and his liabilities are only $277, he has a net worth of $1,901 ($2,178 – $277) on December 31, 2008.

The word *balance* in balance sheet suggests a particular relationship among its three components. As Figure 3.1 shows, the balance is between assets on the one hand and the sum of liabilities and net worth on the other. Arithmetically, it is shown by the following equation:

$$\text{Assets} = \text{liabilities} + \text{net worth}$$

Figure 3.1
A Balance Sheet for Mike Mason Prepared as of December 31, 2008

Assets		Liabilities and Net Worth	
Cash on hand	$ 56.00	Loan from Ed Bates	$ 40.00
Balance in checking account	338.00	End-of-month balance	
Clothing inventory	450.00	on Visa card	237.00
Textbooks, school supplies, and similar items	234.00	Total liabilities	$ 277.00
		Net worth	$1,901.00
TV, Stereo, iPod and DVD	1,100.00		
Total assets	$2,178.00	Total liabilities and net worth	$2,178.00

The equality always holds, because net worth can be either positive or negative. It is positive when the market values of assets are greater than the total value of all liabilities; it is negative when the reverse is true.

Listing liabilities ahead of net worth on the right-hand side of the balance sheet is done for a purpose, too: It reflects the legal claims creditors have on assets. Specifically, it means that in most cases (except bankruptcy), their claims to your assets rank before your own claims. This relationship can be seen with an example. Suppose you purchase a new car for $20,000, putting down $2,000 and financing $18,000 with a local bank. If we ignored all other balance sheet items, immediately after the purchase your balance sheet would appear as follows:

$$\$20,000(\text{assets}) = \$18,000(\text{liabilities}) + \$2,000(\text{net worth})$$

After the first year of ownership, you may have paid off $2,000 of the loan, but if the car depreciated by $3,000, the new balance sheet would be

$$\$17,000(\text{assets}) = \$16,000(\text{liabilities}) + \$1,000(\text{net worth})$$

If the car had to be sold at this point to raise cash, the bank's $16,000 loan balance would be satisfied first. After that is taken care of, then you can take what is left—in the preceding example, $1,000. You should also be able to see how negative net worth arises. If the car depreciated by $5,000 in the first year while the loan payoff remained at $2,000, net worth would now be a negative $1,000. Before we look more closely at assets, liabilities, and net worth, remember that financial planning aims to maximize net worth; it does not attempt to maximize assets. As you can see, regardless of how much your assets are worth, if your liabilities are greater, you have negative net worth. Technically and legally, you're insolvent.

Assets

Assets are things you own that have market value. They might have physical substance, such as jewelry or a house; or they may be pieces of paper, such as stocks and bonds, that give you rights to receive income or other benefits. Determining the total value of your assets takes two steps. First, you must identify and count all the items you own, and second, you need to determine each item's market value. This second step is often harder, even though some assets' values are easily determined: For example, a quick glance at the morning newspaper will tell you what a share of IBM stock is worth. But other assets, such as a diamond engagement ring purchased many years ago, have market values that can be only roughly approximated unless an expert is consulted.

Assets and liabilities are often grouped on the balance sheet to make evaluation easier. In this respect, there are three asset categories: assets to satisfy liquidity needs, assets that are a part of our lifestyles, and investment assets that can increase net worth or provide income for current use or for retirement. We now take a closer look at these three categories.

Liquid Assets

A **liquid asset** is cash or any other asset that can be converted to cash with a minimum amount of inconvenience and with no loss in market value. Examples of liquid assets are currency, checking accounts, savings accounts, money market deposits, and certificates of deposit. Managing liquid assets is a very important part of personal financial management, and the topic is discussed thoroughly in Chapter 5.

Figure 3.2 shows a comprehensive balance sheet for Arnold and Sharon Steele. Arnold and Sharon have $27,440 in liquid assets, with most of it being held in their checking account, passbook savings account, and certificates of deposit.

Liquid asset Cash or any other asset easily convertible to cash with no loss in market value.

Figure 3.2
Balance Sheet for the
Steele Family (Part A)

Balance Sheet At	December 31, 2008		
For	Arnold & Sharon Steele		

Assets

Liquid Assets:

Coins and currency in hand		$	440
Checking account balances			5,400
Other deposits at financial institutions:			
Passbook Savings			10,600
42-month certificate of deposit			5,000
			—
Money market mutual funds			—
U.S. Series EE or HH bonds			6,000
Other liquid assets:			
none			—
none			—
Total liquid assets	(a)	$	27,440

Lifestyle Assets:

Residence			255,000
Vacation home			—
Furniture, household furnishings, and supplies			30,000
Automobiles and recreational vehicles:			
2007 Voyager van			17,000
2006 Honda sedan			11,000
2003 Coleman camper			4,100
Jewelry			4,000
Clothing			1,400
Sporting equipment			600
Hobbies and collections			400
Other lifestyle assets:			
2006 Toro riding mower			1,000
Total lifestyle assets	(b)	$	324,500

Investment Assets

Preferred stocks		$	—
Common stocks InChemCo shares			26,000
Corporate bonds			—
Government bonds			—
Mutual funds 2000 shares of Fidelity			6,800
Business interest			—
Cash value of life insurance			4,000
Cash value of annuities			—
Cash value of retirement fund			41,000
Individual retirement accounts:			
Arnold – none			—
Sharon – none			—
Total investment assets	(c)	$	77,800
Total Assets = (a) + (b) + (c) =	(d)	$	429,740

Figure 3.2
Balance Sheet for the
Steele Family (Part B)

Liabilities

Current Liabilities:

Unpaid bills Gas, Electric, and Telephone	$	460
Credit card balances due		1,720
Estimated taxes due		1,750

Installment loan balances due in one year:

Autos _____		8,046
Others: ___*none*___		—

Other current liabilities:

___*none*___		—
Total current liabilities	(e) $	11,976

Noncurrent liabilities:

Installment loan balances due after one year:

Autos _____		9,195
Others: ___*none*___		—
Mortgage loans		188,263
Loans on life insurance policies		2,000
Debit balances on margin accounts		—

Other noncurrent liabilities:

___*none*___		—
Total noncurrent liabilities	(f) $	199,458
Total Liabilities = (e) + (f) =	(g) $	211,434
Net Worth = (d) – (g) =	(h)	218,306
Total Liabilities and Net Worth = (g) + (h) =	(i) $	429,740

Lifestyle (Use) Assets

Things that help us achieve the quality of life we want are our **lifestyle assets** (also called use assets). Most families hold the greatest percentage of their total assets in them. This is particularly true if a house is purchased, since it is such a large investment. But many other similar assets are also "big ticket" items, such as household furniture and accessories, appliances, cars, and possibly hobbies like coin and stamp collections. Naturally, ownership of these assets varies considerably from one family to another, depending on family members' interests and activities.

Referring to Figure 3.2 Part A, you can see that of the Steeles' total lifestyle assets of $324,500, $255,000 is in their home. They determined this value by observing the selling prices of homes similar to theirs and then deducting 7 percent to allow for a realtor's commission.

Lifestyle assets Assets that influence our quality of life.

Investment Assets

Investment assets are purchased for the purpose of providing additional income or increasing your net worth over time. There are many different kinds of investment assets, as Figure 3.2 shows, and the Steeles have accumulated a reasonable amount of them. However, the Steeles realize that they must increase their investment assets substantially if they are to achieve their retirement goal and the goals they have for educating John and Nancy.

Investment assets Assets that provide income or increase our net worth.

Adding the total of investment assets to the total of lifestyle assets and liquid assets determines total assets. As you can see in Figure 3.2 Part B, for the Steeles this is $429,740.

Liabilities

At any point in time, most people have debt obligations. These obligations arise for a variety of reasons. You might use a bank credit card because of its convenience. If you don't want to use all your liquid assets to pay for one item, you might arrange an installment loan. Because you simply don't have enough resources, you obtain a mortgage loan to buy a house. Liabilities such as these are usually arranged on the balance sheet as current or noncurrent.

Current Liabilities

Current liability A debt that must be paid within one year.

A **current liability** is any debt that must be paid within one year. There are two sources of current liabilities. First are unpaid bills. These come from your use of credit cards, or from direct purchases, as in the case of gas, electric, and telephone bills. The Steeles have $2,180 ($460 + $1,720) of these items. The second source consists of portions of installment loans that are due within one year. The Steeles are paying off two car loans over four years. The current liability on the car loans is $8,046. We distinguish between current and noncurrent liabilities in order to better evaluate the Steeles' liquidity position, a topic we'll explain in more detail later in this chapter.

Noncurrent Liabilities

Noncurrent liabilities Debt obligations beyond one year.

Noncurrent liabilities are all debt obligations beyond one year, and they are also of two types. The first type represents the noncurrent portion of loans with specific repayment schedules. Examples are installment loans on cars, furniture, and major appliances, or credit card balances being paid off on an installment basis. To illustrate, one of the Steeles' car loans extends into 2009 with portions payable in 2010 and 2011, which explains their $9,195 noncurrent liability. Another important example is a mortgage loan on a house or other property. The second kind of noncurrent liability consists of loans that do not have repayment schedules. A loan on your life insurance policy, such as the $2,000 loan the Steeles have on Arnold's policy, is an example. While these loans do not require repayment, you do pay interest on them periodically. Adding current and noncurrent liabilities gives total liabilities; for the Steeles, this figure is $211,434 ($11,976 + $199,458).

Net Worth

As indicated previously, net worth is the difference between total assets and total liabilities. Even though this form of measurement has its problems, it is still the single best estimate of one's wealth. The Steeles' net worth on December 31, 2008 was $218,306. This figure was calculated in Figure 3.2 Part B by subtracting total liabilities (item *g*) from total assets (item *d*). Net worth plays a crucial role in estimating financial strength, so we need to understand how it can change from one period to the next. Net worth can be changed in two ways.

First, net worth increases whenever cash income exceeds cash expenses during a period. This situation is called a **positive contribution to savings;** conversely, if expenses exceed income, a negative contribution—call it **dissavings**—occurs, and it reduces net worth. Second, changes in net worth also occur when the market values of assets you own at the beginning of a period increase or decrease during the period. For example, if you own a home that increases in value, your net worth increases by an equal amount. (This assumes, of course, that you do not increase your mortgage or other loans.)

TOPIC LINKS

Determine your net worth.

Positive contribution to savings Increase in net worth.

Dissavings Reduction in net worth.

The Income Statement

The **income statement** (sometimes called the statement of cash flows) presents a detailed breakdown of cash income and expenses over a past period. It also provides a figure for the period's contribution to savings and, thus, it becomes an important companion statement to the balance sheet. The income statement provides the opportunity to review how well you have done financially in the past period and helps you budget your income and expense items for the upcoming period. The Steeles' income statement for 2008 is shown in Figure 3.3 and discussed in the following sections.

Income statement Detailed breakdown of cash income and expenses over a past period.

Income

Income usually consists of cash inflows. As Figure 3.3 shows, there are many potential sources of income. For many people, Arnold and Sharon included, by far the largest percentage of their total income consists of wages and salaries. Arnold has a full-time position with InChemCo, but Sharon works only during the tax season—roughly January through April—with a CPA firm. The data arrangement in Figure 3.3 shows gross wages rather than after-tax, or take-home wages. You probably will do your financial planning with the take-home figure, but it is also instructive to detail the actual amount of taxes you pay. This puts the total expense in perspective and underscores the need for effective tax planning. It is surprising how few people actually know how much they pay in total taxes—much less their effective tax rates—because they focus on take-home pay. You should look carefully at both.

Income Cash inflows, consisting primarily of salaries and wages.

The Steeles' total wages in 2008 were $95,700. Deducting from this the total payroll taxes of $14,050 leaves their combined take-home salary of $81,650. Arnold's and Sharon's salaries have increased rather nicely in the last several years, making it easier for them to achieve their financial goals.

The Steeles' $937 of interest income came from their passbook savings account, certificates of deposit, and U.S. Series EE bonds. They did not actually withdraw the interest earned on any of these deposits (there is limited access to the latter two) but instead allowed it to accumulate. The $1,090 of dividend income was earned on their common stocks and Fidelity Fund shares, and they did receive those dividends in cash. Adding the interest and dividends to their wages and salaries gives their total income of $97,727.

Expenses

Expenses are cash outflows that sustain our scale of living. They do not include all cash outlays, however. You would not, for example, consider the purchase of investment assets as expenses. Payments made on installment and mortgage loans are viewed as expenses even though formal accounting rules would probably require us to distinguish between payments of interest and payments of principal in measuring income. (We are required to do this for tax purposes, because interest may be an itemized deductible expense whereas principal payments are not. But our focus here is not on taxes.)

Expenses Cash outflows that sustain our scale of living.

The breakdown of expenses in Figure 3.3 is typical of most income statements you are likely to encounter in loan applications and elsewhere. The list of expenses is fairly comprehensive, although you might prefer to arrange them differently. We'll distinguish between inflexible and flexible expenses when budgeting is discussed later, but it is useful to introduce and explain these terms here.

Inflexible Expenses

Inflexible expenses (also called fixed expenses) are often defined as those over which you have very little control in the short run. Some expenses are perfectly inflexible, meaning

Inflexible expenses Expenses that are hard to control in the short run.

Figure 3.3
Income Statement for the
Steele Family (Part A)

Income Statement for the Period   Year Ended 12/31/2008

For _____ The Arnold and Sharon Steele Family _____

Income

Wages and Salaries:

Arnold - InChemCo		78,300
Sharon - Todd and Talbot CPAs		17,400
Total wages and salaries	(a)	95,700

Other Income:

Interest		$	937
Dividends			1,090
Capital gains or (losses)			—
Others			—
Total other income	(b)	$	2,027
Total Income = (a) + (b) =	(c)	$	97,727

Expenses

Housing:

Rent		$	—
Mortgage payments			15,967
Maintenance fees on condos and co-ops			—
Maintenance and home furnishings			8,500
Total housing expenses	(d)	$	21,467

Transportation:

Automobile loan payments		$	8,045
Gas, oil, other maintenance, and repairs			2,100
License, parking, and other auto			310
Other transportation			—
Total transportation expenses	(e)	$	10,455

Food and Other Consumption Items:

Food and household supplies		$	5,300
Meals taken out			2,210
Personal care—barbers and beauticians			820
Others			—
Total food and other consumption items	(f)	$	8,330

Utilities:

Telephone		$	1,540
Internet		$	660
Gas and electric			2,280
Water and sanitation			512
Garbage pickup			360
Cable TV			420
Others			—
Total utilities	(g)		5,772

Sunk costs Costs that cannot be avoided regardless of what happens in the future.

that the amount doesn't change. Such expenses arise typically from contractual arrangements requiring periodic payments. As you review the expense categories in Figure 3.3, you most likely will pinpoint the following as examples: the mortgage payments of $15,967, the car loan payments of $8,045, and maybe the life insurance premiums of $480. These expenses are often called **sunk costs** because the fixed amount must be paid regard-

Taxes:			
Payroll		$	14,050
Real estate and personal property			5,500
Others			—
Total taxes	(h)	$	19,550
Insurance:			
Health and medical withheld from wages		$	1,800
Life			480
Property and liability		$	870
Automobile			2,470
Disability			—
Others			—
Total insurance	(i)	$	5,620
Leisure and Entertainment:			
Theater and sporting events		$	570
Health club memberships			1,000
Newspapers, magazines, etc.			430
Vacations			5,380
Hobbies			280
Sporting equipment			230
Others— Holiday gifts			1,200
Total leisure and entertainment	(j)	$	9,090
Clothing:			
Clothing			2,630
Laundry and dry cleaning			490
Others			—
Total clothing	(k)	$	3,120
Others:			
Charitable contributions		$	2,080
Dues and subscriptions			200
Tuition, books, other education expenses			390
Babysitters			540
Family members' personal allowances			3,400
Unreimbursed medical–dental			1,500
			—
			—
			—
Total others	(l)	$	8,110

Total Expenses $= (d) + (e) + (f) + (g) + (h) + (i) + (j)$
$+ (k) + (l) =$ (m) 94,514

Contribution To Savings $= (c) – (m) =$ (n) $ 3,213

Figure 3.3
Income Statement for the Steele Family (Part B)

less of what happens in the future; the only way out of them is to drop, pay off, or renegotiate the underlying contracts. Other inflexible expenses are not fixed in amount from period to period, but they are nevertheless difficult to control. The Steeles' taxes of $19,550 are a good example of this type of expense; we know they must be paid each year, but the actual amounts might differ each year, or even in each month of the year.

Flexible Expenses

Flexible expenses Expenses that are generally controllable in the short run.

Flexible expenses (also called variable expenses) are those over which you have some control, at least in the short run. A good example is home maintenance. Of course, some of these expenses are more flexible than others. Home maintenance expenses, along with doctors' and dentists' bills, are very irregular and are the most troublesome to deal with in budgeting. Others, however, are far more predictable, such as purchases of food and household supplies. Some flexible expenses might be paid in such a way that they become inflexible expenses. For example, gas and electric usage can be billed in equal monthly payments regardless of seasonal variations. Also, some flexible expenses go up or down along with your income. For example, if you use your car on the job, and you work more hours during a period, your car expenses will increase as your income rises.

Figure 3.4 shows a breakdown of the Steeles' $94,514 of total expenses in 2008. As you can see, the larger percentage is in the inflexible category, indicating that quite a bit of their expenses were set and uncontrollable during the year.

Contribution to Savings

As explained earlier in this chapter, the excess of income over expenses is a positive contribution to savings (or savings, for short). It increases net worth and is a source of increases in assets or reductions in liabilities. In 2008 the Steeles made a positive contribution to savings of $3,213. This amount is 3.3 percent of their gross income, which is significantly below the Financial Planning Associations guidelines on saving for retirement of about 10 percent. However, the amount of their income exceeds the national average; so, they should be able to save considerably more—a goal they have set for the future.

Evaluating Past Financial Performance

Ultimately, your financial performance can be judged successful or unsuccessful only within the framework of your personal goals. If your plans call for buying a house or a new car, or saving $5,000, then you are successful if you achieve those goals. Apart from this

Figure 3.4
A Breakdown of the Steeles'
2008 Expenses

Inflexible Expenses		Flexible Expenses	
Mortgage payments	$15,967	Family members' allowances	$ 3,400
Automobile loan payments	8,045	Leisure and entertainment	9,090
Car licenses	310	Home maintenance and furnishings	8,500
All utilities	5,772	Gas, oil, and car repairs	2,100
All taxes	19,550	All food and other consumption items	8,330
All insurance	5,620	Clothing, laundry, and dry cleaning	3,120
Dues to professional societies	200	Gifts and charitable contributions	2,080
Tuition and books	390	Babysitters	540
		Medical–dental expenses	1,500
Totals	$55,854		$38,660
Total Expenses			

$94,514

Percentages
_____
Inflexible = $55,854/$95,514 = 59%
Flexible   = $38,660/$95,514 = 41%

personal evaluation, however, there also are objective yardsticks, called **financial ratios,** to measure present financial strength and its growth over time. Actually, to an outsider, such as a bank from which you are seeking a loan, your personal goals are not important. The bank must evaluate your request with an impersonal, objective attitude, asking whether you are a good credit risk. Periodically, you should use similar objective criteria to assess your situation. Three areas that are particularly important to evaluate are your financial performance as compared with the annual inflation rate, the liquidity of your assets, and your level of debt.

Financial ratios Yardsticks to measure financial strength and progress.

Matching or Beating the Inflation Rate

It is always sound financial management to compare the annual inflation rate with annual changes in both your income and net worth. In periods of high inflation, such as the early 1980s, it is doubly important because failure to match inflation will lead to an eroding scale of living and a diminished real net worth. However, even low rates of inflation can significantly lower the real return on your investments and decrease your real wage.

TOPIC LINKS

Find the current inflation rate.

Income and the Inflation Rate

Let's suppose that your **nominal income** (the amount you actually receive) increases by 6 percent during a year when prices in general increase by 10 percent. In real terms—that is, in terms of what your nominal income buys—your **real income** (the amount your nominal income is worth in purchasing power) declines by 4 percent. You are worse off this year because you have not kept up with the inflation rate. You may not feel much worse off, at least not immediately, because some items in your budget are fixed, as we explained earlier. So, you will continue to make the same payments on your auto or furniture loans, or on your home loan, as you did in the past, and you may continue to meet your savings goals. But eventually items being financed will need to be replaced, and you must then confront the reality of a deteriorated financial condition.

Nominal income Actual income received.

Real income Nominal income adjusted for inflation.

FINANCIAL PLANNING *for*
young adults 3.1

Pay Yourself First

Most financial planners agree that if saving money is truly important to you, then put savings in a proper focus—first, and not last—in the budget. In short, pay yourself first out of each paycheck. Seriously, when you get paid, take whatever percentage amount you have targeted and put it in a savings vehicle; then spend the rest.

This strategy works even better if you never get your hands on the money. So consider using a "forced-savings" approach. For example, many employers let you channel funds into U.S. savings bonds, mutual funds, or optional retirement plans. Or your bank may have automatic transfer plans that reposition cash from your checking account to a savings account. If you own mutual fund shares, choose the option to reinvest all dividends and capital gain distributions. Also, some companies have dividend-reinvestment plans; if you own shares in them,

take the option. If you are very poor at voluntary savings, consider buying whole life, rather than term insurance. This type of policy has a built-in savings feature.

Millions of Americans willingly choose to have more taxes withheld from their paycheck than the IRS requires and then count on their tax refund for extra spending or saving funds. Of course, this is the least effective way to do it, since you give up interest on money that could go into interest-earning assets. If you are currently allowing over withholding, check with your employer to see if an alternative savings arrangement is available.

Finally, some people argue that buying a home is the ultimate forced savings, since living in rented housing produces nothing more than canceled checks. Frankly, this argument stretches the point a bit. Buying versus renting is a complex issue, where the forced-savings feature might be considered, but should not dominate, when making a housing decision.

An important first test, then, is to compare your increase in nominal income with the inflation rate for the year. The simplest approach is first to calculate a percentage change in nominal income, as shown here:

$$\% \text{ change in nominal income} = \left(\frac{\text{this year's nominal income}}{\text{last year's nominal income}} \right) - 1.0$$

After you have this figure, compare it with the inflation rate (which is frequently reported in the newspaper and on television) to judge your relative performance. Using the Steeles as an example, and assuming that the 2008 inflation rate was 3 percent, we have

$$\% \text{ change in nominal income} = \frac{\$97,727}{\$92,324} - 1.0 = .07, \text{ or } 7.0\%$$

Thus, we know that the 7 percent increase in the Steeles' nominal income was more than twice the inflation rate.

Net Worth and the Inflation Rate

Inflation's impact is not limited to your income. If the market values of your assets do not increase at inflation's rate, your real net worth will decline. The same arithmetic procedures shown earlier can be used to calculate the change in real—as opposed to nominal—net worth. To prevent a decline in net worth, you must own assets that appreciate in value equal to the inflation rate. In the past, personal residences and common stocks have performed well in this respect.

Maintaining Adequate Liquidity

Adequate liquidity means having sufficient liquid assets to pay your bills on time. You may have a very high net worth, but if most of it is represented by assets with poor liquidity, such as your house, you still could be illiquid. To avoid becoming illiquid we often hold a portion of our total assets in cash or other liquid assets, such as savings accounts. Two ratios are frequently used to measure liquidity: the ratio of liquid assets to take-home pay and the ratio of liquid assets to current liabilities.

Liquid Assets to Take-Home Pay

Financial advisors often use the rule of thumb that you should hold liquid assets equal to three to six months of take-home pay to serve as a buffer. If you have good loss-of-income protection through your employer or union, then the low figure might be adequate. If your protection is poor, you should strive for the higher amount.

Liquid assets to take-home pay ratio A liquidity measurement.

Using data for the Steeles, we can calculate their **liquid assets to take-home pay ratio**. Recalling that their 2008 take-home pay was $81,650 and their liquid assets on December 31, 2008 were $27,440 (see Figure 3.2), we have

$$\text{Liquid assets to take-home pay ratio} = \frac{\text{liquid assets}}{\text{take-home pay}} = \frac{\$27,440}{\$81,650} = .34$$

The number can then be expressed as months of the year; for example, 0.34 means about 34 percent of 12 months, or about 4 months. (Notice that an answer of 0.5 indicates half the year, or six months.) Thus, the Steeles fall at the lower rule-of-thumb figure of three months, suggesting they should build their liquid reserves. Since Arnold does have rather good loss-of-income protection at InChemCo, the lower figure is the more appropriate one for them to use. (Note that take-home pay is an appropriate value to use if there are no other major sources of income, as in the Steeles' case. If there are other major sources, they should be included in the denominator, after allowing for related income taxes.)

Liquid Assets to Current Liabilities

The ratio of liquid assets to take-home pay does not consider the level of existing liabilities. Another family may show an identical ratio to the Steeles but be in far worse shape because their existing current liabilities are much greater. To augment the first ratio, then, it is helpful to calculate another ratio, called the **liquidity ratio**, which measures liquid assets against current liabilities. For the Steeles, it is

Liquidity ratio Liquid assets divided by current liabilities.

$$\text{Liquidity ratio} = \frac{\text{liquid assets}}{\text{current liabilities}} = \frac{\$27,440}{\$11,976} = 2.29$$

This number tells us the Steeles have $2.29 of liquid assets for every $1.00 of existing current liabilities. There is no hard-and-fast rule indicating what this ratio should be, but any number greater than 1.0 shows fairly good strength, assuming the ratio of liquid assets to take-home pay is also adequate. Of course, the larger the number, the better the liquidity. With a ratio of 2.29, the Steeles are in reasonably good shape.

Avoiding Excessive Amounts of Debt

Adequate liquidity protects you from temporary cash emergencies, and liquidity ratios are designed to warn you of liquidity problems. However, they do not reveal whether total debt is being used properly or is excessive. *Excessive* doesn't mean too much debt in absolute dollars but rather in relation to your underlying assets and income that support the debt. Two important ratios are often used to evaluate total debt: the ratio of total liabilities to total assets and the ratio of take-home pay to debt repayment obligations.

Total Liabilities to Total Assets

Technically, you are judged insolvent when your total liabilities exceed your total assets. Being insolvent doesn't automatically mean you are illiquid; you might still have sufficient cash to pay your bills for a while. What it does mean is that, unless the situation changes, you will ultimately not have enough assets to pay all your bills. Many people in this position eventually file bankruptcy as a means of settling with creditors or establishing an orderly plan for paying their bills over an extended period of time.

Bankruptcy (discussed more fully in Chapter 6) is not to be taken lightly or viewed as a convenience to avoid paying obligations. You should look for early signals of impending trouble. The **debt ratio,** which measures total liabilities against total assets, is one such signal. Using the Steeles' data from Figure 3.2 as an example, it is calculated as follows:

Debt ratio Total liabilities divided by total assets.

$$\text{Debt ratio} = \frac{\text{total liabilities}}{\text{total assets}} = \frac{\$211,434}{\$429,740} = .49$$

The Steeles have about $0.49 in total debts for each $1.00 of total assets. Looking at it in another way, the value of their assets could shrink up to 51 percent (1.00 − 0.49) before the Steeles would encounter insolvency problems. The smaller the ratio, the better from a safety point of view, but again, there is no iron-clad rule telling us what the ratio should be in every instance. The less volatile the market prices of your assets, the higher the ratio could be, all other things considered. In general, we like to see ratios below 0.5 to be on the relatively safe side. The Steeles are at the margin.

finance news 3.2

What's Happening to Savings?

Clearly, Americans are saving less and less of their incomes, to such an extent in recent years that savings have actually turned negative during some months. The last time we saw negative savings was back in the 1930s during the Great Depression. In contrast, the 1995 to 2000 period showed some of the strongest economic gains on record. Yet savings fell dramatically. See the accompanying graphic, which shows personal saving as a percentage of disposable personal income. What the graph does not show is that in the third quarter of 2005 the personal savings rate reached a low of negative 1 percent.

Disposable income is what we have left after paying personal taxes. Personal savings is equal to what is left after all personal consumption expenditures have been subtracted from disposable income. Accordingly, the personal savings rate doesn't include purchases of tangible property, such as homes, that some might consider savings. However this doesn't fully explain the dramatic decline in the personal savings rate over the last half century.

All sorts of explanations of the phenomenon have come forth. A current popular idea is the so-called "wealth effect"—

Americans have built considerable wealth in their homes and stock portfolios through rising market values, making savings less needed as a mechanism to build wealth. Indeed, many families continually refinance their homes, drawing out the built-up equity to finance even more spending. This is a successful strategy as long as home prices or stock prices are rising. However, when the housing market hits a slump, like it has recently, many families must confront the mistakes of their overspending.

No doubt, we have become a nation of spenders. Mom and Dad want $60,000 Saabs and Porsches, and the kids want $200 gym shoes. Many families earn the incomes to afford such luxuries if they don't worry about retirement. But, of course, that's when the fiddler gets paid. Saving 0 percent of our incomes, coupled with collapsing stock prices in our retirement accounts, is not exactly how one goes about building a retirement nest egg.

Of course, when retirement comes, we can simply refinance the house again, or sell it for a king's ransom. The house should last almost forever, shouldn't it? And housing prices never go down, do they? Frankly, if our retirement funds must come from a highly mortgaged house, we are in very bad shape, as the recent mortgage crisis has demonstrated.

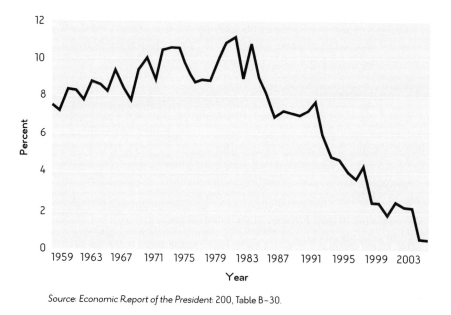

Source: Economic Report of the President: 200, Table B-30.

Debt Service Coverage

Your capacity to carry debt is reflected not only in the market value of assets you own but also by the relationship of your take-home pay to your total debt-servicing charges. By debt service, we mean monthly (or yearly) payments of both principal and interest on those loans requiring periodic repayment. The debt service coverage ratio measures take-home pay against total debt service charges. The Steeles have two auto loans and their home mortgage. In addition, they borrowed $2,000 on Arnold's life insurance policy. Although this loan does not require periodic repayments, they pay interest of $160 each year. The total annual payments are $24,172 ($15,967 + $8,045+ $160), and the following **debt service coverage ratio** can be calculated:

Debt service coverage ratio Take–home pay divided by debt service charges.

$$\text{Debt service coverage ratio} = \frac{\text{take-home pay}}{\text{debt service charges}} = \frac{\$81,650}{\$24,172} = 3.38$$

The Steeles take home $3.38 in pay for each $1.00 of required debt repayment and interest. Higher ratios, of course, indicate greater debt-carrying capacity than lower ones. A ratio of 1.0 means that all of your after-tax income is needed to repay existing debts, and a ratio less than 1.0 indicates that your income will not even cover your existing repayments. (Again, if other major sources of income exist, they should be included, on an after-tax basis, in the numerator.)

A single number is never enough to distinguish strength from weakness, but it is usually felt that a ratio of 3.0 or better signals adequate strength and reasonable flexibility in future budgeting. In such a situation, a large portion of your income will not be committed to repaying existing debt. The Steeles' ratio of 3.38 indicates strength in this area.

Review of the Steeles' Financial Situation

Now that you have learned about financial statements and have seen them applied to the Steeles' financial situation for 2008, what impression do you have? Are they a wealthy family? Are they "sailing right along" with few financial concerns? Actually, their situation is not quite as successful as it might first appear.

True, they have a net worth of over $218,000. But there are a number of areas of concern. First, their residence of $255,000 is more than one-half of their total assets. Housing prices do often increase over time at the inflation rate or greater, but real estate markets can become very soft in the short run. The recent subprime mortgage crisis has had a negative impact on housing prices. A decline of 10 or 20 percent over several years, while not likely, would decrease their net worth substantially.

Second, Arnold and Sharon have $28,000 invested in late-model cars, which depreciate in value rather rapidly. If they continue to turn over their cars after three or four years, they will perpetually carry a rather high amount of expensive installment debt. By lengthening the period between trade-ins they could shift their wealth into assets that appreciate rather than depreciate over time.

Third, and most important, the Steeles are enjoying a high-consumption budget that produces little savings in relation to their income. At their current pace, they will not accumulate sufficient funds to educate Nancy and John or to achieve other important future goals such as retirement income. Put simply, the Steeles must rethink their priorities, become smarter consumer-investors, or do both. We will follow them in this process as the remaining chapters unfold. But their most pressing immediate need is to learn the budgeting process.

Achieving Goals Through Budgeting

What is a **budget**? Put very simply, a budget is any plan—simple or complex—that expresses your financial goals and how you will allocate your limited resources to achieve them. A budget can be so simple that you keep it on the back of an envelope to monitor

Budget A plan indicating financial goals and how resources will be allocated to achieve them.

your monthly progress with checkmarks. Or it can be as complex as the one the federal government prepares each year, detailing how over $2 trillion will be spent. But size is no guarantee of success. Your envelope approach might work, and there are many critics who feel the federal budget never has. We'll discuss principles of effective budgeting in this chapter, but before doing so, we will set forth some simple rules for budgeting success. Our discussion will revolve around the following:

- Set realistic budget goals. The plural is important here. The budget is a device for achieving all your important goals; it is not a straitjacket to produce only savings.

- Stick to simple procedures. A $50 journal or an expensive computer is nice if you use it properly, but a waste of money if you don't. Trying to categorize every conceivable expense misses the whole point of budgeting and creates an unnecessary work burden that makes budgeting unpleasant.

- Use the budget to control and direct expenses. The main strength of a budget does not lie with its record-keeping function, although that is a necessary part. A budget allocation, say, for dining out, is a commitment you and your family make to an underlying activity. If you exceed the budget amount, ask yourself why. If the answer is because you want to, then you need to reexamine your goals to see if more funds should be allocated to this activity and less to others. If the answer reflects a temporary "overindulgence," then cut back next month to bring the activity back within budget. Knowing you have exceeded your budget and then deciding what to do about it is the essence of successful budgeting.

TOPIC LINKS

Compare your spending to that of others like you.

Goal setting A complex process that involves a hierarchy of wants—abstract at the top and tangible at the bottom.

Goal Setting

When you set goals, you are effectively managing your finances rather than merely letting them take place as you go about your routine activities. Actually, **goal setting** is a rather complex process, and it has been studied by professionals from many disciplines, including social psychology, economics, and behavioral management. Goals can be viewed in a type of hierarchy, with very general and abstract goals at the top and more specific and tangible ones at the bottom. Figure 3.5 illustrates such a hierarchy of financial goals. At the top is the general goal of attaining financial independence for each member of the family. But what does this mean? You might understand it to mean sufficient wealth to be self-reliant; another person might understand it as having a job free of possible firing or layoff. To be meaningful, the general goals must be expressed in specific terms. For example, in Figure 3.5 finan-

Figure 3.5
A Hierarchy of Personal Financial Goals

cial independence is structured into three distinct goals: to enjoy a current living scale that reflects a moderate to high level of consumption, to provide a college education for the children, and to achieve a scale of living in retirement that is on a par with the current living scale. As we move to the lowest level on the triangle, goals become even more specific and can be broken down to yearly savings and current consumption targets. Things to be acquired in the future—the children's education and retirement funds—must be saved for out of current income. Savings must be budgeted if these goals are to be achieved. The Steeles have decided to set a goal of saving about 10 percent for the coming year.

Preparing the Annual Budget

Armed with a clear understanding of the importance of expressing goals, you are in position to prepare the annual budget. This budget and the willingness to stick with it will determine success in achieving goals. There are two parts to budget preparation: the **master budget worksheet**, which details planned income, expenses, and contribution to savings in total for the budget year; and the **monthly income and expense plan**, which shows how each month's income, expenses, and contribution to savings will take place.

The Master Budget Worksheet

Each year budgeting begins by trying to forecast what your total income and expenses will be in the upcoming year. Some income and expense items are easy to forecast because they are known in advance (recall our previous discussion of fixed expenses): your mortgage payments on the house, for example. Others can vary widely and will be much more difficult to estimate: Dentist or doctor bills are good examples here, as is home maintenance. Despite the difficulties, estimates must be made and the budget finished.

Figure 3.6 illustrates a master budget worksheet the Steele family prepared for 2009. You probably recognize immediately that the budget has the same format as the income statement shown in Figure 3.3. The budget for a year should lead directly to the same kind of actual income and expense items after the year is over. In fact, budgeted and actual figures should be compared very closely at the end of a budget year, both for evaluating results for the year just ended and for preparing a budget for the year to come.

It almost goes without saying that budget figures should be determined as realistically as possible. Each line item should be reviewed and some reason found for making the estimate; that is, your figure should be defensible. A common mistake is to set a consumption item unrealistically low. If you think there is a good chance you will spend $40 a week on dining out and if that is what you want to do, then don't budget $20 a week for this activity. Doing so will only lead to frustration and eventual discarding of the budget.

The Monthly Income and Expense Plan

After the master budget worksheet has been prepared, the next budgeting step is to determine how income and expense items will occur during the year. Usually this is done on a monthly basis. Some expenses occur sporadically and in rather large amounts. It is important to plan for these expenses so that sufficient funds are available when these expenses must be paid. The monthly income and expense plan details income, expenses, and contribution to savings on a month-to-month basis. Arnold and Sharon Steele programmed their personal computer to show their monthly income and expense plan; it is shown in Figure 3.7.

Estimating the Monthly Activity

Some of the expense items were estimated in total by determining a budget monthly figure and then multiplying by 12. The monthly allocation, then, is this same monthly figure. For

Master budget worksheet Budget allocations detailing planned income, expenses, and contribution to savings.

Monthly income and expense plan A monthly breakdown of amounts listed on the master budget worksheet.

Figure 3.6
Master Budget Worksheet for the Steeles (Part A)

Master Budget Worksheet for the period   <u>Upcoming Year 2009</u>

For   <u>Arnold and Sharon Steele Family</u>

Income

Wages and Salaries:

<u>Arnold – expect 5% raise this year</u> $ 82,215

<u>Sharon – expect 10% raise and more hours</u>   19,140

Total wages and salaries   (a)   101,355

Other Income:

Interest   should be about 7% on average balance $ 984

Dividends   expect 10% increase   1,199

Capital gains or (losses)   —

Others   —

Total other income   (b) $ 2,183

Total Income = (a) + (b)   (c) $ 103,538

Expenses

Housing:

Rent $ —

Mortgage payments   fixed   15,967

Maintenance fees on condos and co-ops   —

Maintenance and home furnishings   cut back a bit   4,500

Total housing expenses   (d) $ 20,467

Transportation:

Automobile loan payments   fixed $ 8,045

Gas, oil, maintenance, and repairs   rise in price of gas   3,000

Licenses, parking, and other auto   should be $20 a month   360

Other transportation   —

Total transportation expenses   (e) $ 11,405

Food and Other Consumption Items:

Food and household supplies   about $550 a month $ 6,600

Meals taken out   let's budget $120 a month   1,440

Personal care–barbers and beauticians   about $60 a month   720

Others   —

Total food and other consumption items   (f) $ 8,760

Utilities:

Telephone   increase budget for cell phone $ 1,680

Internet   660

Gas and electric   last year was $190; go higher   2,470

Water and sanitation   last year was $128 per quarter; go higher   720

Garbage pickup   —

Cable TV   likely increase in basic cable   480

Others $ —

Total utilities   (g)   6,010

example, the Steeles' telephone bill was budgeted at $140 a month, so that figure is entered for each month. In Figure 3.7 note the expenses that do not occur uniformly. For example, all the property insurance bills come in January, February, and July; real estate taxes are paid in January and August, and vacation expenses are expected in July and August. Note further that Sharon's salary comes only in January through June and that dividends are

Taxes:			
Payroll	based on 2009 estimated taxes		$ 14,050
Real estate and personal property	last year's; didn't go up		5,500
Others			—
Total taxes		(h)	$ 19,550
Insurance:			
Health and medical withheld from wages	6% increase expected		$ 1,908
Life fixed			480
Property and liability	budget 5% over last year		914
Automobile budget 5% over last year			2,594
Disability InChemCo pays			—
Others			—
Total insurance		(i)	$ 5,896
Leisure and Entertainment:			
Theater and sporting events			$ 570
Health club memberships			1,000
Newspapers, magazines, etc. budget $30 a month			360
Vacations a camping vacation this year			4,000
Hobbies a digital camera and software			900
Sporting equipment kids soccer equipment			230
Others Holiday gifts			$ 1,200
Total leisure and entertainment		(j)	$ 8,260
Clothing:			
Clothing let's budget $250 a month, kids growing			3,000
Laundry and dry cleaning reduce to $30 a month			360
Others			—
Total clothing		(k)	$ 3,360
Others:			
Charitable contributions about $200 a month			$ 2,400
Dues and subscriptions last year's amount			200
Tuition, books, other education expenses expect big increase			480
Babysitters estimate $50 a month			600
Family members' personal allowances we agree on this			2,400
Unreimbursed medical–dental			
Medical Insurance copays based on last year's expenses			1,500
Nancy may need braces - one year's cost			1,000
Total others		(l)	$ 8,580
Total Expenses = (d) + (e) + (f) + (g) + (h) + (i) + (j) + (k) + (l) =		(m)	$ 92,288
Contribution to Savings = (c) – (m)		(n)	$ 11,250

Figure 3.6
Master Budget Worksheet for the Steeles (Part B)

TOPIC LINKS

See how other people spend their money.

received quarterly. In planning the monthly activity, you should try to determine as well as you can when the expected income or expense will occur.

Getting Through the Lean Months. Because of the irregularity of some income and expense items, it is possible that your expenses will exceed your income in a given month. Of

Figure 3.7
Monthly Income and Expense Plan for the Steele Family for 2009

Income	Jan	Feb	Mar	Apr	May	June	July	Aug	Sept	Oct	Nov	Dec	Total
Arnold's salary	6,851	6,851	6,851	6,851	6,851	6,851	6,851	6,851	6,851	6,851	6,851	6,851	82,215
Sharon's salary	3,190	3,190	3,190	3,190	3,190	3,190	—	—	—	—	—	—	19,140
Interest	82	82	82	82	82	82	82	82	82	82	82	82	984
Dividends	—	—	300	—	—	300	—	—	300	—	—	300	1,199
Total income	10,123	10,123	10,423	10,123	10,123	10,423	6,933	6,933	7,233	6,933	6,933	7,233	103,538
Expenses													
Mortgage payments	1,331	1,331	1,331	1,331	1,331	1,331	1,331	1,331	1,331	1,331	1,331	1,331	15,967
Maintenance and home furnishings	375	375	375	375	375	375	375	375	375	375	375	375	4,500
Automobile loan payments	670	670	670	670	670	670	670	670	670	670	670	670	8,045
Gas, oil, maintenance, and repairs	250	250	250	250	250	250	250	250	250	250	250	250	3,000
Licenses, parking	10	10	10	10	10	10	10	10	10	10	10	10	360
Food, household supplies	550	550	550	550	550	550	550	550	550	550	550	550	6,600
Meals taken out	120	120	120	120	120	120	120	120	120	120	120	120	1,440
Personal care	60	60	60	60	60	60	60	60	60	60	60	60	720
Telephone	140	140	140	140	140	140	140	140	140	140	140	140	1,680
Internet	55	55	55	55	55	55	55	55	55	55	55	55	660
Gas and electric	206	206	206	206	206	206	206	206	206	206	206	206	2,470
Water and sanitation	180	—	—	180	—	—	180	—	—	180	—	—	720
Cable TV	40	40	40	40	40	40	40	40	40	40	40	40	480
Payroll taxes	1,392	1,392	1,392	1,392	1,392	1,392	950	950	950	950	950	950	14,050
Real estate taxes	2,750	—	—	—	—	—	—	2,750	—	—	—	—	5,500
Health and medical insurance	159	159	159	159	159	159	159	159	159	159	159	159	1,908
Life insurance	—	—	—	—	—	—	—	480	—	—	—	—	480
Homeowners insurance	—	914	—	—	—	—	—	—	—	—	—	—	914
Automobile insurance	1,297	—	—	—	—	—	1,297	—	—	—	—	—	2,594
Theater and sporting events	48	48	48	48	48	48	48	48	48	48	48	48	570
Newspapers, magazines	30	30	30	30	30	30	30	30	30	30	30	30	360
Vacations	—	—	—	500	—	—	1,700	1,800	—	—	—	—	4,000
Hobbies and holiday gifts	—	—	300	—	300	—	—	100	—	—	700	700	2,100
Sporting equipment	—	—	80	150	—	—	—	—	—	—	—	—	230
Clothing	250	250	250	250	250	250	250	250	250	250	250	250	3,000
Laundry and dry cleaning	30	30	30	30	30	30	30	30	30	30	30	30	360
Charitable contributions	200	200	200	200	200	200	200	200	200	200	200	200	2,400
Dues and subscriptions	—	—	—	—	100	—	25	25	25	25	—	—	200
Tuition, books, etc.	—	—	—	—	—	—	—	480	—	—	—	—	480
Babysitters	50	50	50	50	50	50	50	50	50	50	50	50	600
Personal allowances	200	200	200	200	200	200	200	200	200	200	200	200	2,400
Unreimbursed medical expenses	208	208	208	208	208	208	208	208	208	208	208	208	2,500
Total Expenses	10,600	7,288	6,754	7,204	6,774	6,374	9,133	11,566	6,196	6,136	6,631	6,631	91,288
Contribution to Savings	-477	2,836	3,669	2,920	3,350	4,049	-2,200	-4,633	1,037	797	302	602	12,250

SIMPLIFYING financial planning 3.3

Budgeting with Envelopes and Play Money

At first glance, the bulletin board in Mark and Carla Spielman's kitchen looks pretty much like anyone else's—but there's a difference. Along with the reminders, recipes, and other assorted notes that usually adorn bulletin boards, theirs has nine letter-size envelopes, one for each of the most important ways the Spielmans spend money; there's also a red envelope for savings, red meaning: "Stop before entering." In each of the 10 envelopes Mark and Carla put a predetermined amount of play money at the beginning of each month, which represents their monthly allotment for the activity marked on the envelope; for example, the entertainment envelope starts with $200 each month.

These envelopes are the Spielmans' complete budgeting system. Every evening they go together to the bulletin board and withdraw money from the appropriate envelopes to represent the money they spent that day, whether by check or cash. At the end of the month all the envelopes should be empty, except those that include things such as vacations, where funds are being temporarily saved for later use. If all goes exactly as planned, on the last day of the month every envelope except savings should be empty. But what happens if the money runs out before the end of the month? Unless they come up with a good reason for transferring from one envelope to another (but never from the red one unless it's an absolute emergency), that

activity is over for the month. So if $200 is taken out of the entertainment envelope by mid-month, the Spielmans watch a lot of television or find other things to do for the rest of the month.

The envelope system of budgeting probably dates back to the time envelopes were invented. Of course, the system itself doesn't guarantee success, but supposedly the discipline you gain by touching and feeling the money as you slip it out of the envelope makes you more budget conscious than do other approaches, such as writing things down on a budget work-sheet, or, in today's environment, inputting data into your home computer. But what about play money? Will you have the same emotional reservations about spending it as you have about spending real money? Some financial planners think so, and if you haven't done well at budgeting in the past, it's worth a try. It has several big advantages over the real thing: It's not that important if you lose some, and hardly anyone wants to steal it. And, just as important, you can leave your actual cash in the bank to earn interest. Don't take this last advantage lightly. If you have an expense budget of $5,000 a month and pay expenses uniformly over a month, your average balance for the month—and for the year as a whole—is $2,500. If you had a bank account earning 4 percent interest, you would give up $100 a year by stuffing cash in those envelopes. So, use play money and sleep at night—and have a night on the town with the interest you earn.

---

course, you must have the funds available to meet the deficit, and you may have to borrow to do so. In looking at Figure 3.7 you see that the Steeles will have three deficit months. The other nine months show positive contributions to savings. By knowing they are likely to need extra funds in these three months, the Steeles can expect the need for effective cash management. For example, as they end the year they should ensure they have enough in their checking account to cover the expected deficit in January. It would not be wise to put the surplus in December into some type of account—say, a certificate of deposit—that is not readily available for withdrawals because they will need $477 in the next month. Unquestionably, the year's activity will not unfold exactly as the Steeles see it in Figure 3.7; there are sure to be some surprises along the way that will change things, but the Steeles are now in a far better position to cope with these changes than they would be without their monthly income and expense plan.

Monitoring and Controlling Activities

With the master budget worksheet and the monthly income and expense plan finished, the first phase of budgeting is completed. You now have a road map to guide your financial activities through the year. The second phase of budgeting begins as the year unfolds and events take place. This phase involves three separate tasks: First, you need a system to record your actual income and expenses. Second, you must periodically update your income and expense accounts to see if actual amounts received and spent are in line with amounts planned. (This is usually done on a monthly basis.) Third, you need to evaluate and control activities as the year progresses.

Recording Income and Expenses

Record keeping is perhaps the most unpleasant aspect of budgeting, but it's necessary. Our concern should be primarily with how to do it most efficiently, since most people resent doing extensive bookkeeping each evening or weekend. The following list of suggestions might help you simplify the work.

Don't Use Cash. Pay as many bills as you can with checks or by charges to your credit cards (assuming neither method induces you to spend more). These will give you a written record of expenses that can be recorded at the end of the month. Paying bills with cash means, in effect, that you must create your own record, either by saving invoices or by writing things on odd pieces of paper. These activities are time-consuming, and the records are easily lost. Whenever you do pay with cash, standardize the recording by creating your own little voucher, which can be a small piece of paper like the one shown in Figure 3.8. You can make many of these if you have access to a copy machine. Stick a few in your pocket each day and get in the habit of using them.

Code Income and Expense Accounts. Assign an account number to each line item (particularly those used frequently), and, as you pay a bill, code the check stub with the appropriate number. A good software checking program will prompt you to categorize each check. This practice will facilitate summing expenses by category each month. Also, code your income items as you make bank deposits in order to identify the income source. If you receive a check from someone and cash it instead of depositing it, you also will have to record the amount received and identify the source. It is almost always better to deposit checks and cash in your checking (or other) account so that they can be identified; if you need cash, write a check.

Use a Personal Computer. If you tagyour expenses and deposits by your major budget categories, most personal finance software will provide an instantaneous report for tracking your household budget. In addition, your personal computer has capabilities to store all the data and make it readily available for other purposes, such as comparing one month's expenses in a given category with similar monthly expenses of the previous year or exporting data to tax preparation software. You can link through the Internet to your bank and broker for downloading your checking statement and updating your investments.

Figure 3.8
A Simple Voucher to Record Cash Expenses

Date _____ 6/8/XX

Amount Paid _____ $12.50

To Whom _____ Burger King

For What _____ Eating Out

And much more can be done; for example, the budget can be connected directly to your year-end balance sheet and income statement, so that making entries on the computer keyboard is virtually all you ever have to do for the entire financial recording process. All data manipulation and storage—and even printed copies—are provided automatically by the software.

Updating Income and Expense Accounts

After all income and expense items have been accounted for, the next step is to update your monthly income and expense plan by recording actual amounts and then comparing them with the budget. This is usually done monthly, and it is done best with an income and expense plan update, such as the one shown in Figure 3.9. If the actual amount for a line item differs from the budgeted figure, it is called a **variance**. Variances can then be either favorable—meaning they assisted in the saving effort—or unfavorable—meaning they detracted from it. An **income variance** is favorable whenever actual exceeds budgeted; it is unfavorable when the reverse is true. An **expense variance** is favorable whenever actual is less than budgeted, and it is unfavorable in the opposite case. Unfavorable variances are indicated in Figure 3.9 by a minus sign in front of the amount. The **cumulative variance** figure results from adding the current month's variance to variances of previous months; thus, the cumulative variance for maintenance—the second expense item—in February is a favorable $364, which is the sum of the favorable $319 variance in February and the favorable variance of $45 in January. In March, maintenance showed an unfavorable variance of $205, and subtracting this from February's cumulative variance gives a new cumulative variance of $159 at the end of March.

> **Variance** Actual income or expense item that differs from the budgeted amount.
>
> **Income variance** Income item variance—favorable when actual exceeds budgeted; unfavorable in the reverse situation.
>
> **Expense variance** Expense item variance—favorable when actual is less than budgeted; unfavorable in the reverse situation.
>
> **Cumulative variance** Monthly accumulation of variances.

Figure 3.9 shows the Steeles' activity for the first three months of 2009. Although you see all three months at once, you should assume that each month's activities were recorded separately. The flow of data gives you a fairly good picture of how the Steeles' financial events took place during the quarter. Sharon began working more hours than she anticipated, which led to most of the favorable income variance in January, and this continued in February and March. By the end of the quarter, Sharon had earned $1,718 more than budgeted. The estimates for Arnold's salary and dividends were accurate, and the interest variance is trivial.

Evaluating and Controlling Activities

Being able to stay within budget means you are continuously adjusting your expenses during the year. Evaluating and controlling activities really make the budget work; an elaborate recording system does little good if you choose to ignore the information it provides. For example, the Steeles were $43 over their budget for new clothing in January. This tells them they have only $207 ($250 – $43) to spend in February. You must subtract the cumulative variance (add, if it's favorable) from the current monthly budget figure to determine how much of current funds is available for a given line item. In February, the Steeles were $127 under budget for new clothing, which offset the unfavorable $43 variance, leaving an $84 favorable variance for March. However, March's figure was $124 over budget, meaning the Steeles ended the first quarter with a cumulative unfavorable variance of $40 in this account. Unless their goal is changed here, they should try to reduce this variance to zero by the end of June.

Even though you are monitoring activities and calculating cumulative variances at the end of each month, a year-end review can be helpful. It serves mainly to assist in making budget estimates for the next year. It also provides an opportunity to prepare the current year's income statement, because the figure for each line item on this statement is simply the budget amount for the year plus its cumulative variance on December 31.

Figure 3.9
Monthly Budget Update for the Steeles for the First Quarter, 2009

	January				
Income	Budget	Actual	Variance	Cumulative Variance	Budget
Arnold's salary	6,851	6,851	—	—	6,851
Sharon's salary	3,190	3,220	30	30	3,190
Interest	82	84	2	2	82
Dividends	—	—	—	—	—
Total income	10,123	10,155	32	32	10,123
Expenses					
Mortgage payments	1,331	1,331	—	—	1,331
Maintenance and home furnishings	375	56	319	319	375
Automobile loan payments	670	670	—	—	670
Gas, oil, maintenance, and repairs	250	220	30	30	250
Licenses, parking	10	—	10	10	10
Food, household supplies	550	601	-51	-51	550
Meals taken out	120	160	-40	-40	120
Personal care	60	120	-60	-60	60
Telephone	140	125	15	15	140
Internet	55	55	—	—	55
Gass and electric	206	173	33	33	206
Water and sanitation	180	153	27	27	—
Cable TV	40	40	—	—	40
Payroll taxes	1,392	1,396	-4	-4	1,392
Real estate taxes	2,750	2,750	—	—	—
Health and medical insurance	159	159	—	—	159
Life insurance	—	—	—	—	—
Homeowner's insurance	—	—	—	—	914
Automobile insurance	1,297	1,297	—	—	—
Theater and sporting events	48	96	-49	-49	48
Newspapers, magazines	30	21	9	9	30
Vacations	—	—	—	—	—
Hobbies and holiday gifts	—	—	—	—	—
Sporting equipment	—	—	—	—	—
Clothing	250	293	-43	-43	250
Laundry and dry cleaning	30	23	7	7	30
Charitable contributions	200	200	—	—	200
Dues and subscriptions	—	—	—	—	—
Tuition, books, etc.	—	—	—	—	—
Babysitters	50	35	15	15	50
Personal allowances	200	200	—	—	200
Unreimbursed medical expenses	208	316	-108	-108	208
Total Expenses	10,600	10,490	110	110	7,288
Contributions to Savings	-477	-335	142	142	2,836

key terms

assets (p. 50)
budget (p. 63)
cumulative variance (p. 71
current liability (p. 54)
debt ratio (p. 61)
debt service coverage ratio (p. 63)
dissavings (p. 54)
expense variance (p. 71)

expenses (p. 55)
financial ratios (p. 59)
flexible expenses (p. 58)
goal setting (p. 64)
income (p. 55)
income statement (p. 55)
income variance (p. 71)
inflexible expenses (p. 55)

| February | | | March | | | |
Actual	Variance	Cumulative Variance	Budget	Actual	Variance	Cumulative Variance
6,851	—	—	6,851	6,851	—	—
3,940	750	780	3,190	4,128	938	1,718
75	-7	-5	82	70	-12	-17
—	—	—	300	300	—	—
10,866	743	775	10,423	11,349	926	1,701
1,524	-193	-193	1,331	1,331	—	-193
330	45	364	375	580	-205	159
670	—	—	670	670	—	1
388	-138	-108	250	287	-37	-145
—	10	20	10	—	10	30
534	16	-35	550	321	229	194
111	9	-31	120	144	-24	-55
80	-20	-80	60	65	-5	-85
98	42	57	140	89	51	108
55	—	—	55	55	—	—
221	-15	18	206	187	19	37
—	—	27	—	—	—	27
40	—	—	40	40	—	—
1,496	-104	-108	1,392	1,522	-130	-238
—	—	—	—	—	—	—
159	—	—	159	133	26	26
—	—	—	—	—	—	—
914	—	—	—	—	—	—
—	—	—	—	—	—	—
67	-20	-68	48	87	-40	-108
33	-3	6	30	28	2	8
—	—	—	—	—	—	—
—	—	—	300	137	163	163
—	—	—	80	89	-9	-9
123	127	84	250	374	-124	-40
31	-1	6	30	56	-26	-20
200	—	—	200	200	—	—
—	—	—	—	—	—	—
54	-4	11	50	67	-17	-6
200	—	—	200	200	—	—
155	53	-54	208	166	42	-12
7,483	-195	-85	6,754	6,828	-74	-159
3,383	548	690	3,669	4,522	852	1,542

follow-up on the
Steele family

This entire chapter has focused on the Steeles. If you have read it carefully, you should have a good understanding of their present financial situation and what they hope to accomplish in the upcoming year. Let's consider a few other points.

1. The Steeles saved $3,213 in 2008 and plan to more than triple this amount in 2009. Judging from your own experiences at saving money, do you feel the Steeles will accomplish their goal?

2. Reviewing their expense allocations in the master budget worksheet, in what area(s) do you think the Steeles are likely to go "over budget" during the year?

3. The review of the Steeles' situation on page 63 of the text seems rather harsh. Do you agree with it? Explain.

4. Your family background may be quite different from the Steeles. Without interjecting personal value judgments, how would you compare your family situation with the Steeles'?

problems and review questions

1. Explain the following elements of a balance sheet and give an example of each:
   a. liquid assets
   b. investment assets
   c. lifestyle assets
   d. current liabilities
   e. noncurrent liabilities

2. Explain how asset values are determined on the balance sheet and whether these valuations are made easily.

3. What is net worth? Does it have anything to do with wealth? Explain two factors that can change net worth from one period to the next.

4. Explain the difference between a current and a noncurrent liability. Give an example of each. Explain whether liability amounts are difficult or easy to determine.

5. Lisa Rich spent every cent she had and then borrowed $1,000 to purchase an elaborate wardrobe worth $2,000. Ignoring all of Lisa's other assets and liabilities, construct her balance sheet after the purchase. Suppose that a year later, Lisa's wardrobe—now completely out of style—is worth only $100. If Lisa has paid off $500 of her loan, what does her balance sheet look like now? Comment on her present financial position.

6. What is an income statement, and what are its components? In your answer, distinguish between flexible and inflexible expenses.

7. Would you classify the following expense items as flexible or inflexible? Which one(s) would you consider sunk costs?
   a. property taxes
   b. house mortgage payments
   c. clothing
   d. car licenses
   e. insurance
   f. family members' personal allowances

8. Explain how planned savings differs from savings as something left over.

9. The following items, arranged alphabetically, belong to either the income statement or the balance sheet. Put them in their correct place and then construct each statement. (You must also calculate net worth and contribution to savings.)

Car (2006 Ford)	$14,000	Jewelry	850
Car loan payments	1,200	Mortgage loan on residence	60,000
Cash value of life insurance	2,000	Mortgage payments	6,200
Coins and currency	300	Property and liability insurance	300
Credit card balances due	500	Real estate taxes	1,200
Federal income taxes withheld from wages	4,000	Residence	80,000
Food and household supplies	6,000	Telephone	240
Gas and electric expenses	2,200	Theater and sporting events	700
Gifts	400	Tuition	1,100
Hobbies and collections	650	U.S. Series EE bonds	1,600
Installment loan balances due in one year	1,200	Unpaid bills	700
Interest	700	Wages and salaries	26,000

10. You are given the following data for Kim Zerussen:

	2007	2008
Income during the year	$60,000	$64,000
End of year: Assets	50,000	60,000
Liabilities	40,000	49,000

Assuming that inflation was 10 percent during 2008, evaluate Kim's financial performance for the year.

11. Explain a financial ratio and then identify the following ratios, indicating what they are supposed to test. How would you evaluate each, given its specific numbers? After you complete that assignment, discuss whether you think the person to whom these ratios apply is a good credit risk.
    a. liquid assets to take-home pay = 0.08
    b. liquidity ratio = 0.75
    c. debt ratio = 1.20
    d. debt service coverage ratio = 1.10

12. Explain three simple rules that often lead to success in budgeting. Do you agree that the more complex a budget is, the more successful it will be? Explain.

13. Discuss the process of setting goals. List several general goals that you think will be important to you after graduation and then indicate which specific goals you will use in your annual budgets.

14. Describe the master budget worksheet, indicating some expenses you think are easy to forecast and some that are more difficult.

15. Explain how you would forecast the following expense items for an upcoming budget year:
    a. mortgage payments
    b. food and household items
    c. income and other payroll taxes
    d. family members' personal allowance

16. How does a monthly income and expense plan help in managing your cash and checking account?

17. Explain how a budget helps achieve effective cash management.

18. Briefly describe four procedures that might simplify bookkeeping activities connected with recording monthly income and expense amounts.

19. Explain the relationship among the budget, the income statement, and cumulative variances. Also discuss possible situations that might warrant making changes in a budget during the year.

20. Following are budget and actual figures for selected income and expense accounts for June and cumulative variances for each account through May. (Parentheses indicate an unfavorable variance.)

	Cumulative variance through May	June Budgeted	June Actual
Salaries	$(1,600)	$3,000	$3,400
Expenses:			
Rent	(100)	300	320
Transportation	85	200	215
Food	125	550	575
All others	(160)	850	780
Payroll taxes	400	900	1,000

Answer the following, assuming that the foregoing list of accounts is all that needs to be considered.

a. Calculate June's variances and the cumulative variances through June.

b. If the budgeter planned at the beginning of the year to save an equal amount each month and has not revised that plan, how much has he or she actually saved through June? (Show your work.)

case 3.1

Can Arnold and Sharon Afford a Vacation Condominium?

At the end of 2008 Arnold and Sharon Steele were considering buying a condominium in Gatlinburg, Tennessee. Gatlinburg is a resort town next to the Great Smoky Mountain National Park area, where the Steeles have often camped. The condo they particularly liked was priced at $97,000, and the seller offered to finance 90 percent of the purchase price with a 15-year mortgage loan requiring monthly payments of $737 during the first year. To make the $9,700 down payment and $2,200 of closing costs, the Steeles planned to sell their Coleman camper (which was worth $4,100 at that time) and their U.S. Series EE bonds (then worth $6,000). The balance of $1,800 would be borrowed from Sharon's parents, who would not expect regular repayments of the loan but would charge interest of $100 each year. Arnold and Sharon decided against the purchase for a number of reasons, one of which involved finances. They felt that the condo would have placed an excessive strain on their budget, given their alternative goal of adding to their investments and liquid assets.

Questions

1. Using the data given in this case and elsewhere in this chapter, calculate what the Steeles' contribution to savings would have been in 2008 if they bought the condo on January 1, 2008. (Assume mortgage interest payments would have been $5,736 for the year and that they benefit from the mortgage interest deduction. Also assume that the marginal tax rate is 28 percent and that all other expenses and taxes not related to the purchase remain the same.)

2. Prepare a new balance sheet at December 31, 2009 for the Steeles, again assuming that they made the purchase on January 1, 2008, and that payments of principal on the mortgage were $3,108 for the year. Assume that any reduction in savings was funded with current assets.

3. Using the four ratios given in this chapter to evaluate liquidity and total debt, make new calculations for the Steeles, assuming the condo purchase, and compare them with those calculated in the chapter. Assume that any reduction in savings was funded with current assets. Discuss the comparisons.

4. Do you agree with the Steeles that the purchase would have been a financial strain? Explain your answer.

case 3.2

The Terrels' Budget for 2009

Donna and Sherman Terrel are preparing a budget for 2009. Donna is a systems analyst with an airplane manufacturer, and Sherman is working on a master's degree in educational psychology. The Terrels do not have any children or other dependents. Donna estimates her salary will be about $59,000 in 2009; Sherman expects to work only during the summer months, doing painting and remodeling work for a building contractor. He anticipates an income from those activities of $2,400 a month in June, July, and August. Sherman does have a scholarship that pays his tuition and also provides $2,100 a year, payable in equal amounts in October and February. The Terrels don't expect to have any other income in 2009.

Donna and Sherman have listed their expected total expenses in 2009 as follows:

Rent	$10,760
Transport	7,800
Food	7,920
Utilities	3,880
Payroll taxes Donna	10,800
Payroll taxes Sherman	1,200
Life Insurance	600
Car Insurance	2,320
Vacation	4,152
Leisure other	5,728
Clothing	3,292
Others	5,840
Total	$64,292

The Terrels will begin 2009 with about $1,200 in liquid assets, and they prefer not to draw this balance below $600 at any time during the year.

Questions

1. Prepare a monthly income and expense plan for the Terrels in 2009.

2. On the basis of the plan you have just prepared, discuss the Terrels' expected financial situation in 2009. Explain if you foresee any difficulties.

3. During the quarter break in April Sherman's employer landed a major remodeling project and asked for Sherman's help. Sherman agreed, and he expects to earn $1,800 from the job before taxes but probably won't receive a check until early June. Discuss how this unexpected event might affect the Terrels' activities and their budget for the balance of 2008. It is not necessary to prepare a revised monthly income and expense plan, but do refer to specific accounts and amounts (make appropriate assumptions) in your discussion.

marie wilson goal–planning exercise

Preparing a Budget

You have helped Marie establish financial goals and prepare a plan for achieving them. A tentative plan requires that Marie save $2,000 annually over the next five years. Since Marie has saved very little until now, she is concerned that this amount may be excessive. She has asked your help in preparing a budget for the upcoming year.

Marie expects to earn $32,000 next year in salary and $6,000 in support payments from Jake's father. Other income is minimal and can be disregarded. Her monthly rent is $400 and she estimates a gas and electric bill of $150 a month. Payroll taxes have been

Form 3.1
Budget (Part A)

	Amounts	Percent
Income		
Salaries and wages: earner 1	$	
Salaries and wages: earner 2		
Total salaries and wages	$	
Other income		
Interest		
Dividends		
Capital gains		
Alimony/ support payments		
Others		
Total other income	$	
Total income	$	100%
Expenses		
Housing		
Rent or mortgage payments	$	
Maintenance		
Home furnishings		
Other housing –		
Total housing	$	
Transportation		
Auto loan payments	$	
Gas, oil, maintenance		
Licenses, parking fees		
Other transportation		
Total transportation	$	
Food and other consumption items		
Food and household supplies	$	
Meals eaten out		
Personal care—barbers, beauticians		
Total food and consumption	$	
Utilities		
Telephone	$	
Internet connection		
Gas and electric		
Cable		
Water		
Other utilities		
Total utilities	$	

about 10 percent of her gross salary and her employer withholds $200 a month for health insurance. Last year, she paid babysitters $4,800 and she paid $1,200 on her student loans. Her telephone bill is $20 a month and she pays another $18 a month for Internet service. While she hasn't kept good records, Marie estimates she spends about $400 a month on auto expenses (not counting auto and property insurance of $1,500 a year) and about $6,000 annually on food, both at home and dining out.

Marie realizes that the previous list is not inclusive, and she expects that you can help her identify possible outlays related to other areas. Explain to Marie why you believe these areas are important. However, do not consider any expenses related to Marie's intent to begin law school. Marie feels this goal is very important but first she must determine if it

Form 3.1
Budget (Part B)

	Amounts	Percent
Taxes		
Payroll	$_____	_____
Real estate	_____	_____
Other taxes	_____	_____
Total taxes	$_____	_____
Insurance		
Health and medical	$_____	_____
Life	_____	_____
Auto and property	_____	_____
Disability	_____	_____
Other insurance	_____	_____
Total insurance	$_____	_____
Leisure and entertainment		
Theater, sporting events	$_____	_____
Memberships	_____	_____
Newspapers, magazines	_____	_____
Hobbies	_____	_____
Other leisure and entertainment	_____	_____
Total leisure and entertainment	$_____	_____
Clothing		
New clothing	$_____	_____
Dry cleaning	_____	_____
Other clothing	_____	_____
Total clothing	$_____	_____
Other expenses		
Baby sitting and child care	$_____	_____
Educational outlays	_____	_____
Charitable gifts	_____	_____
Personal allowances	_____	_____
Unreimbursed medical and dental		
Student loans		
_____	_____	_____
_____	_____	_____
_____	_____	_____
Total other expenses	$_____	_____
Total Expenses	$_____	_____
Contribution to Savings	$_____	_____

can be accommodated within her budget. Use Form 3.1 to help her prepare an annual budget. Try to be as realistic as possible in setting expense items. After finishing the budget, prepare a report on Marie's financial situation. Discuss whether she will have adequate financial resources to pursue the goals identified in Chapter 1.

working out
on the Web

Internet Exercises to Strengthen Your Use of the Internet

(Internet links for the following exercises can be found at **www.prenhall.com/frasca.**)

Exercise 3.1 What Is Your Spending Personality?

Your spending personality assessment may be revealed by answering a questionnaire from MyVesta (**myvesta.org/tests/moneypersonality**).

Q. What are your buying habits? Explain if you may have shopping problems that can hinder your saving effort.

Exercise 3.2 Is Your Income Matching the Inflation Rate?

Find the most recent inflation rate by reviewing the Consumer Price Index at the Bureau of Labor Statistics (**www.bls.gov/cpi/**).

Q. How much must your income increase each year to match the most recent inflation rate, as measured by the "Consumer Price Index"? Check out the latest news release and the "Inflation Calculator."

Exercise 3.3 How Do Other People Spend Their Money?

In the BLS Consumer Expenditure Survey (**stats.bls.gov/cex**) you can find expenditures for the average American family. The Steeles spent 28 percent of their income on housing.

Q. What percentage does the average family spend on housing? Suppose your rent is 40 percent of your income. What problems can this create in your effort to balance your budget?

Exercise 3.4 Do You Have a Typical Budget?

You can find Money 101 under "Personal Finance" at CNNMoney.com (**money.cnn.com**). The site contains helpful information on controlling your expenses. Their Instant Budget Maker (**cgi.money.cnn.com/tools/instantbudget/instantbudget_101.jsp**) allows you to enter your personal data and then analyze your spending.

Q. Enter appropriate data for the Steeles and then compare their spending to that of other people shown in the example.

Taxes

the government's share of your rewards

Steele family

This is the weekend Arnold and Sharon have reserved for filing their taxes. As usual they have waited until the week of April 15. Tax-filing season typically puts the Steeles in an unpleasant mood. However, the task is less time consuming now that they are using computer software to complete their federal and state tax forms. Given the appropriate information, the software program automatically computes a number of entries such as their tax credits and tax liability. In addition, it also simultaneously completes federal and state forms, avoiding the need to repeat the process.

Last year the Steeles purchased a computer program to aid them in filing their taxes. This year they bought the annual update. The updated program for the current year eases some of the time burden by accessing the personal data from last year's tax forms and automatically entering them on this year's forms. It keeps track of the previously entered data to ensure the entry of repeat information in the current year. For example, if they claimed a home interest deduction in the previous year, the program automatically prompts them for information in the current year.

The Steeles feel well prepared to tackle this year's taxes. In addition to using computer support, they have also been keeping track of their tax-deductible expenses. Receipts for expenses that might be deductible, such as medical and child care, have been filed in special folders. They have also been noting tax-deductible items on check stub memos and credit card statements. They view their tax planning as a success, since it appears they will be receiving a significant refund this year. Nevertheless, they still feel they may be paying more in taxes than their neighbors and would like to improve their tax planning.

TOPIC LINKS

Follow the **Topic Links** in each chapter for your interactive Personal Finance exercise on the Web. Go to: **www.prenhall.com/frasca**.

Taxes are an important part of our everyday lives. We pay sales and excise taxes on many items that we purchase to consume. Our houses, cars, and other assets—tangible and intangible—are subject to property taxes. The income we earn is taxed, and when we die, our estate is taxed. Figure 4.1 indicates the size of the federal "tax bite" in relation to income; note that the table considers only so-called direct federal taxes levied on households. When all taxes are considered, the percentages are considerably higher. Indeed, the Tax Foundation estimates that the average family had to work about 120 days in 2007 to support government services. The largest single tax is the federal income tax, and Figure 4.1 gives a clear indication of the federal government's role in American society. Not only does its size make it important, but also it is structured such that most people can reduce their tax liability through effective tax planning. The percentage of your income you pay in taxes is directly related to the size of your income. Note that those filing returns with $200,000 or more in adjusted gross income paid almost 50 percent of all federal taxes.

TOPIC LINKS

Tax Foundation

Determining Your Federal Income Tax

Almost all individuals with moderate levels of income are required to file a federal income tax return. In 2007 most single individuals with more than $8,450 in gross income and married couples living together with more than $16,900 in gross income were required to file federal tax returns. There are different income thresholds for the self-employed, those age 65 or older, and dependents. In addition, those owing special taxes, such as Social Security and Medicare, must also file a return. Even when it is not required, you may want to file a return to receive a refund for an overpayment of withholding taxes or a tax credit.

The name on your tax return must match the name on your Social Security registration. Newlyweds and the recently divorced should notify the Social Security Administration of any name change. You can obtain a name change form at your local Social Security or the agency's Web site (**www.socialsecurity.gov**). If you have changed your address be sure to notify your employer so that you receive your W-2 Wage and Tax Statement on time.

Figure 4.1
Federal Taxes as a Percentage of Adjusted Gross Income

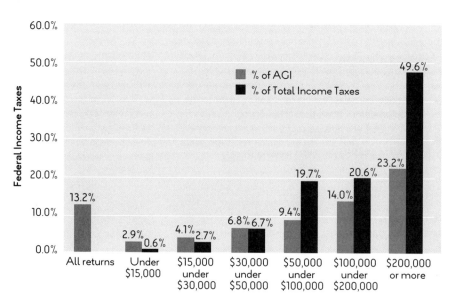

Source: Preliminary Individual Tax Return 2005, Internal Revenue Service.

The federal income tax follows the steps illustrated in Figure 4.2. The entire process is explained in greater detail in the following sections, and later we'll illustrate the topic by showing Arnold and Sharon Steele's income tax return. This discussion in this chapter is meant to familiarize you with the general process of filing your personal taxes. It is only an illustration. The main purpose is to provide a general appreciation for how the personal income tax is structured. It should not serve as a tax guide. Tax rules change regularly and can be extremely complicated even for professionals. Before you file your taxes, you should review the latest taxes guides, tax software, and IRS publications. If you find that you have special circumstances that might require more technical advice, consult a CPA or an attorney who specializes in tax preparation.

TOPIC LINKS

See IRS Pub. 17 "Your Federal Income Tax."

Gross Income Items

To begin, some items that you might look on as part of your **global income** (income from all sources) are not considered taxable income by the Internal Revenue Service (IRS). A partial list of included items is shown in Figure 4.3. Specifically excluded from global income are those items listed in Figure 4.4. Your **gross income** includes income from all sources except if it is specifically excluded by the tax code.

Global income Income from all sources.

Gross income Income from all sources less specifically excluded items.

1. **Determine Gross Income after Nontaxable Exclusions**

> Global Income

less

> Nontaxable Exclusions
> (see Figure 4.4)

equals

> Gross Income
> (see Figure 4.3)

2. **Reduce Gross Income by Adjustments to Gross Income**

> Gross Income

less

> Adjustments to Gross Income
> (see Figure 4.5)

equals

> Adjusted Gross Income

3. **Reduce Adjusted Gross Income by Personal Exemptions and Standard or Itemized Deductions to Calculate Taxable Income**

> Adjusted Gross Income

less

> Itemized or Standard Deduction
> (see Figure 4.6)

less

> Personal and Dependency Exemptions

equals

> Taxable Income

4. **Determine Tax Rates and Tax Liability**

> Taxes Based Upon Taxable Income and Family Status
> (see Tax Rates Figures 4.7–4.8)

less

> Tax Credits
> (see Figure 4.9)

plus

> Other Taxes

equals

> Tax Liability

5. **Calculate Refund or Amount Due at Filing**

> Tax Liability

less

> Tax Payments
> (Taxes Withheld and Estimated Tax Paid)

equals

> Refund or Amount Due

Figure 4.2
The Five Steps to Calculating Your Federal Income Taxes

Figure 4.3
A Partial List of Gross Income Items

Alimony
Awards, prizes, and lottery winnings
Back pay
Bargain purchase from employer
Bonuses
Breach of contract damages
Business income
Cash gift from employer
Clergy fees and contributions
Commissions
Compensation for services
Damages other than personal injury
Death benefits
Debts forgiven
Director's fees
Dividends
Embezzled funds
Employee awards
Employee benefits (excepting certain fringe benefits)
Employer-paid disability benefits
Estate and trust income
Farm income
Fees for services
Gains from illegal activities
Gains from sale of property
Gambling winnings

Group term life insurance, premium paid by employer (coverage over $50,000)
Hobby income
Interest income
Jury duty fees
Living quarters, meals (unless furnished for employer's convenience)
Mileage allowance
Military pay (unless combat pay)
Partnership income
Pensions
Professional fees
Punitive damages
Reimbursement for moving expenses
Rent
Retirement pay
Rewards
Royalties
Salaries
Severance pay
Social Security benefits (partial inclusion)
Strike and lockout benefits
Supplemental unemployment benefits
Tips and gratuities
Travel allowance
Unemployment compensation
Wages

Figure 4.4
A Partial List of Exclusions from Gross Income

Accelerated death benefits and long-term care benefits
Accident insurance proceeds
Annuities (to a limited extent)
Casualty insurance proceeds
Child support payments
Cost-of-living allowance (for military)
Damage for personal injury or sickness
Disability benefits you paid for
Disability pensions (to a limited extent)
Fellowship grants (to a limited extent)
Gifts
Health insurance proceeds not deducted as a medical expense
Inheritances
Life insurance paid on death
Long-term capital gain on personal residence

Meals and lodging (furnished for employer's convenience)
Military allowances
Municipal bond interest
Qualified employer contributions (to a limited extent) for
    — adoption expenses
    — educational expenses
    — long-term care service
    — moving expenses
    — pension benefits
    — health, life, and disability benefits
    — health and medical savings accounts
Relocation payments
Scholarship grants (to a limited extent)
Survivor benefits for public safety officers
Veterans' benefits
Welfare payments
Workers' compensation

Some of the excluded items are important in tax strategy. Note that municipal bond interest is an excluded item. All other factors being the same, it is to your advantage to own municipal bonds as opposed to those whose interest payments are fully taxable. Also, such items as group term life insurance and health insurance are often offered as fringe benefits by employers (or as part of a salary-reduction plan). If you had to purchase these items with after-tax income, they may cost you considerably more. For example, if you are in a 28 percent tax bracket, you must earn $1,389 to net $1,000. (You get this figure by dividing the $1,000 by 1.00 minus the tax bracket; that is, $1,389 = 1,000/[1.00 − 0.28]$.) Clearly, if your employer gives you a choice between the $1,000 in wages or a nontaxed $1,000 fringe benefit, choose the latter if you intend to buy the benefit anyway.

Adjustments to Income

Adjusted gross income is equal to gross income less certain adjustments permitted by the tax law. These are significant adjustments because they reduce your income before you itemize deductions. A partial list of adjustments is shown in Figure 4.5. The education-related adjustments are discussed in a later section of this chapter. A discussion of some of the other important adjustments follows.

Adjusted gross income Gross income plus or minus certain adjustments.

Health and Medical Savings Account Deduction

If you satisfy certain IRS requirements, you may be able to set up a special account for health care expenses. Funds in this account are an adjustment to your gross income and can be used to pay for qualified medical expenses. These are explained in IRS Publication 969, "Health Savings Accounts and Other Tax-Favored Health Plans" and IRS Publication 502, "Medical and Dental Expenses." These accounts are also discussed in Chapter 14, "Health Care and Disability Insurance."

Moving Expenses

You can deduct certain moving expenses if your new home is at least 50 miles from your previous home and these expenses are incurred within one year of the date on which you began a new job. These deductions are available to both individuals changing jobs and those entering the job market for the first time. Generally, you can deduct the cost of traveling to your new home and the cost of moving your furnishings. See IRS Publication 501, "Moving Expenses."

TOPIC LINKS

See IRS Pub. 501 "Exemptions, Standard Deduction, and Filing Information."

IRAs and Keogh Plans

IRAs and Keogh plans will be explained in greater detail in Chapter 16, but a few words about each are appropriate here. A Keogh plan can be established by anyone with self-

IRAs and Keogh plans Retirement plans that reduce gross income.

Figure 4.5
A Partial List of Adjustments to Income

Alimony paid
IRA deduction
Health and medical savings account deduction
Moving expenses
Penalty for early withdrawal of savings
Payments to self-employed SEP, SIMPLE, and qualified plans
Self-employed health insurance deduction
Self-employment tax (half)
Student loan interest deduction

employed income (i.e., income from a business). This plan is used by many small business operators and professionals, such as artists and writers. Allowable contributions to a Keogh are considerably greater than IRA contributions, so if you earn self-employed income, you should become familiar with the Keogh provisions.

The tax-deductible IRA (Individual Retirement Account) can be used by anyone (employed or self-employed) whose income does not exceed certain limitations. Its intent is to encourage individual retirement planning, and it accomplishes this by allowing deductions to qualified IRA investments. Most investments people make—such as deposits in banks and savings and loans, common and preferred stocks, bonds, certain partnership interests, and more—are qualified investments The contribution limits for 2008 are the lesser of $5,000 or your taxable compensation if you are below age 50 and $6,000 if you are older. After 2008 the limits will increase according to the rate of inflation.

It goes almost without saying that the IRA is one of the easiest and most generous tax concessions provided by Congress. Many tax advisors call it the best tax shelter for the middle-income family. Not only is the IRA a generous deduction but also it's virtually the only one you can take after the tax year is over, because you have until April 15 of the following year to make your investment. Unfortunately, if your income exceeds certain limits and you have an employer-sponsored retirement plan, the deductibility of an IRA is gradually eliminated. The current limits can be found in IRS Publication 590, "Individual Retirement Arrangements."

There is also an alternative to a traditional IRA called a Roth IRA. With a Roth IRA the initial contributions are not tax deductible. However, the fund's earnings and future distributions are tax free. The relative tax consequences of a traditional IRA and a Roth IRA will be examined when we discuss retirement savings in Chapter 16.

Alimony Payments

In general, **alimony payments** as the result of a court decree of divorce or separation are generally included as income by the person receiving them and deductible for the ex-spouse making them. Child support you pay is never deductible and child support you receive is not taxable. Divorce or separation often involves deep emotional feelings, and the last thing on the spouses' minds is how to structure the divorce to minimize future tax liabilities. This is unfortunate, because a cooperative approach can benefit both people. You need good tax advice in this area, and it's usually worth retaining an attorney or CPA to help with the settlement.

Adjusted Gross Income

Gross income less adjustments is adjusted gross income. This is an important figure because itemized deductions are phased out if your adjusted gross income exceeds annually determined limits. In addition, there are itemized deductions you may not take unless they exceed a specified percentage of your adjusted gross income.

Taxable Income

Taxable income consists of adjusted gross income less **personal and dependency exemptions** and deductions for specific personal expenses. This latter item consists of either taking a standardized amount or itemizing allowable deductions.

Personal and Dependency Exemptions

The law allows most taxpayers a personal exemption. We are each allowed a certain minimal income that is exempt from federal taxation. In 2007 the amount was $3,400. It is

---

TOPIC LINKS

See IRS Pub. 590 "Individual Retirement Arrangements."

Alimony payments Added to gross income of the receiver but a reduction of the payer's gross income.

Taxable income Adjusted gross income less personal and dependency exemptions and allowable personal expense deductions.

Personal and dependency exemptions Deductions from adjusted gross income based on the number of people in a household, their ages, and eyesight quality.

indexed to the price level; therefore, the exemption is adjusted upward each year to reflect the current cost of living. Each spouse on a joint return is entitled to the exemption, and it also applies to any of the taxpayer's dependents. Therefore, a married couple with two dependents could claim $13,600 in exemptions for tax year 2007.

It is important to note that someone claimed as a dependent on another's return, such as parents claiming a dependent child, cannot also take the personal exemption. A working college student, for example, might provide most of his or her own support, thereby earning the exemption amount but preventing the parents from taking it. If the parents are in a high tax bracket, this is poor tax strategy.

Personal and dependency exemption deductions are gradually eliminated when taxable income exceeds certain limits. In 2007 the threshold level of income was $234,600 for married couples filing a joint return and $156,400 for single filers.

The Standard Deduction

In addition to personal and dependency exemptions, the law also allows a **standard deduction** for personal expenses. The deductible amount depends upon taxpayer filing status as indicated later. Generally, the standard deduction in 2007 was $10,700 for married couples filing jointly and $5,350 for individuals. Standard deduction amounts also are inflation indexed. Age or impaired sight allows taxpayers *additional* standard deduction amounts beyond those just described. If you are claimed as a dependent on your parents' tax return, you still received a small standard deduction of about $850 in 2007.

Standard deduction
Deduction from adjusted gross income based on the taxpayer's filing status.

Itemized Deductions

If your **itemized deductions** are greater than your standard deduction, you may take these as an offset to adjusted gross income instead of the standard deduction. In general, the IRS

Itemized deductions
Deductions from adjusted gross income based on actual amounts spent by a taxpayer.

SIMPLIFYING
financial planning 4.1

How Do Your Deductions Compare?

Below are average amounts written off by taxpayers who claimed these deductions on 2005 returns filed in 2006. *Note:* This does not mean that taxpayers with $35,000 to $99,999 in adjusted gross income averaged $5,994 in medical deductions. Most such people did not qualify for medical write-offs. The figure instead is the average deduction among those who *could* deduct medical expenses.

Adjusted Gross Income	Itemized Deduction						
	Medical and dental expense	State and local income taxes	Real estate taxes	Home mortgage interest	Charitable cash contributions	Casualty and theft loss	Unreimbursed employee business expense
Under $35,000	6,791	1,245	2,297	7,422	1,687	16,715	4,703
$35,000 to under $100,000	5,994	3,116	2,713	8,651	2,254	16,639	4,407
$100,000 to under $200,000	10,106	6,959	4,355	11,989	3,578	18,097	4,922
Over $200,000	29,677	38,667	9,216	19,557	15,812	36,351	9,410

does not allow personal expenses as deductions except in those cases where the tax law clearly indicates the contrary. Most allowable itemized deductions reflect activities regarded as socially desirable (giving to charity, for example) or alleviating undue financial hardship (medical expenses). Probably, some are allowed because strong vested interests were influential in having them included in the tax law. Figure 4.6 indicates the more common deductions. While it is a good idea to keep good records to support all items on your tax return, it is particularly important in the case of itemized deductions. A lack of supporting evidence—canceled checks, invoices, or carefully written logs—will often lead to a disallowance of the claimed deduction.

There are limits on the amounts you can deduct for medical expenses, charitable contributions, casualty losses, and miscellaneous expenses. You can take only amounts greater than 7.5 percent of your adjusted gross income for medical expenses, which include hospital and doctor bills and drugs and medical supplies. Special rules apply if charitable contributions exceed 20 percent of adjusted gross income. The IRS now requires proof of all cash and noncash contributions. Also, for a charitable contribution to qualify, it must be made to an IRS-recognized charity; gifts made to individuals or political causes do not count as deductions.

As is the case with personal and dependency exemptions, taxpayers lose a portion of itemized deductions when their incomes exceed certain limits. The elimination of these tax preferences at high incomes is scheduled to be gradually phased out by 2010 unless Congress changes it.

Determining Your Tax Liability before Tax Credits

After calculating taxable income, many taxpayers can proceed directly to the tables excerpted in Figure 4.7 (if their taxable income is less than or equal to $100,000) or the tax schedule shown in Figure 4.8 (if their income is above $100,000) to calculate their income tax before tax credits. For example, a married couple with taxable income of $65,799 would have had a corresponding tax of $9,291 in 2007. If you have qualifying dividends or capital gains, you must use a special worksheet for computing your tax instead of the tax tables.

Federal marginal tax rates can be found in the third column of Figure 4.8. The federal marginal tax rate on taxable income ranges from 10 percent in the lowest tax bracket to 35

Figure 4.6
Frequently Claimed
Itemized Deductions

Medical expenses (including payments to medical insurance) in excess of 7.5% of adjusted gross income
State and local income taxes
Property taxes
Personal property taxes
Interest on home mortgage (possible limitations)
Charitable contributions (subject to limitations)
Casualty and theft losses (subject to limitations)
Miscellaneous expenses in excess of 2% of adjusted gross income:
    Union dues
    Professional dues and subscriptions
    Certain educational expenses
    Tax return preparation fee
    Investment counsel fees
    Unreimbursed business expenses

If line 43 (taxable income) is—		And you are—			
At least	But less than	Single	Married filing jointly *	Married filing separately	Head of a household
			Your tax is—		

65,000

At least	But less than	Single	Married filing jointly	Married filing separately	Head of a household
65,000	65,050	12,680	9,104	12,703	11,431
65,050	65,100	12,693	9,116	12,717	11,444
65,100	65,150	12,705	9,129	12,731	11,456
65,150	65,200	12,718	9,141	12,745	11,469
65,200	65,250	12,730	9,154	12,759	11,481
65,250	65,300	12,743	9,166	12,773	11,494
65,300	65,350	12,755	9,179	12,787	11,506
65,350	65,400	12,768	9,191	12,801	11,519
65,400	65,450	12,780	9,204	12,815	11,531
65,450	65,500	12,793	9,216	12,829	11,544
65,500	65,550	12,805	9,229	12,843	11,556
65,550	65,600	12,818	9,241	12,857	11,569
65,600	65,650	12,830	9,254	12,871	11,581
65,650	65,700	12,843	9,266	12,885	11,594
65,700	65,750	12,855	9,279	12,899	11,606
65,750	65,800	12,868	9,291	12,913	11,619
65,800	65,850	12,880	9,304	12,927	11,631
65,850	65,900	12,893	9,316	12,941	11,644
65,900	65,950	12,905	9,329	12,955	11,656
65,950	66,000	12,918	9,341	12,969	11,669

Figure 4.7
A Portion of the 2007 Tax Table

Schedule X — Single

If taxable income is over-	But not over--	The tax is:
$0	$7,825	10% of the amount over $0
$7,825	$31,850	$782.50 plus 15% of the amount over 7,825
$31,850	$77,100	$4,386.25 plus 25% of the amount over 31,850
$77,100	$160,850	$15,698.75 plus 28% of the amount over 77,100
$160,850	$349,700	$39,148.75 plus 33% of the amount over 160,850
$349,700	no limit	$101,469.25 plus 35% of the amount over 349,700

Figure 4.8
2007 Tax Rate Schedules for Single Filers and Married Couples Filing Jointly

Schedule Y-1 — Married Filing Jointly or Qualifying Widow(er)

If taxable income is over--	But not over--	The tax is:
$0	$15,650	10% of the amount over $0
$15,650	$63,700	$1,565.00 plus 15% of the amount over 15,650
$63,700	$128,500	$8,772.50 plus 25% of the amount over 63,700
$128,500	$195,850	$24,972.50 plus 28% of the amount over 128,500
$195,850	$349,700	$43,830.50 plus 33% of the amount over 195,850
$349,700	no limit	$94,601.00 plus 35% of the amount over 349,700

percent at the top bracket. Within the income bracket defined in the first two columns, the marginal tax rate is the percent of each addition dollar of income that you owe in federal taxes. As indicated in Figure 4.8, if you are single tax filer with taxable income of $40,000 you are in the 25 percent marginal tax bracket. You only get to keep 75 cents of each additional dollar. Your overall marginal tax rate, which includes payroll taxes (FICA) and state income taxes, will be higher. Moreover, the phase out of deductions at high incomes may further increase your effective marginal tax rate.

Tax Credits

Tax credit A dollar-for-dollar offset against the tax liability.

A **tax credit** is a direct reduction against your tax liability. It provides a dollar-for-dollar offset to your tax liability. Tax credits can be either "nonrefundable" or "refundable." The size of a nonrefundable tax credit is limited by the taxes you owe. If a refundable tax credit exceeds the taxes you owe, the excess is returned in a check from the government. Many low-income families with one adult over age 24 qualify for the Earned Income Tax Credit (EITC). Because it is a refundable tax credit, low-income earners who owe little or no tax on their income can receive a refund check. Most of the other popular tax credits, such as the child care credit and the educational expense credits are nonrefundable. A partial list of tax credits is presented in Figure 4.9.

Your tax liability for the year is determined by subtracting the total of your credits from the taxes you calculated using the tax table or one of the schedules. This tax liability is an important figure—one you should be very much aware of as you make financial decisions. An even more important figure to know is the marginal tax rate on your last income dollar.

Do You Get a Refund or Owe More Taxes?

The amount you receive or pay depends on how much tax has been withheld from your wages or, if you earned income not subject to withholding, how much you have paid in estimated taxes. (By the way, if you expect to earn such income, you are required to file an estimated tax. Failure to do so can lead to penalties and interest.) If withholding was greater than your tax liability, you are entitled to a refund; if the reverse is true, you must pay additional tax. Every employer is required to provide employees an annual report of their wages and all the taxes (and possibly other items) withheld from their wages. This report is called a **W-2 form**, and you should review yours each year to make sure it is correct. You need to attach copies to your federal and state income tax returns.

W-2 form A form prepared by an employer showing an employee's earnings and withholdings.

The IRS will charge penalties if you withhold substantially less than you should during the tax year. On the other hand, the IRS does not pay interest on excess withholding. Despite this fact, many taxpayers claim fewer exemptions than they need to on withhold-

Figure 4.9
Partial List of Tax Credits

Adoption credit
Child and dependent care expenses credit
Earned income credit
Education credit
Elderly or disabled credit
Foreign tax credit
Health coverage tax credit
Retirement savings contribution credit

ing forms filed with their employers (called a **W-4 form**). They do this because it is a form of forced savings or because they enjoy getting a big refund. Actually, this is very poor financial management. You can do better if you invest the money in a way that offers you a return. When you withhold more than you owe, you are lending the government your money at 0 percent interest.

Determining the Steeles' 2007 Income Tax

The Steeles used Form 1040 , the so-called long form shown in Figure 4.10, to complete their federal taxes. In 2007 Arnold and Sharon Steele had the following items to consider in preparing their income tax return. Arnold earned $76,200 at InChemCo and had $8,723 of federal income tax withheld from his salary. Sharon earned $20,400 at Todd and Talbot and had $1,233 of such taxes withheld. Accordingly, they had total wages on Line 7 of $96,600 and paid total federal withholding taxes of $9,956 on Line 64. They received $937 in interest on savings accounts and $1,090 in dividends on stocks they owned. On their 2006 state income tax return they received a $210 refund, which they must now declare on their 2007 federal income tax return. The Steeles did not sell any stock during the year and, therefore, did not have any capital gains or losses. Altogether, their total income for 2007 on Line 22 was $98,837.

The Steeles had no adjustments to gross income; therefore, their gross income for the year was also $98,837. Given their large mortgage interest payments, local and state taxes, and charitable contributions, the Steeles itemized their deductions and arrived at an allowable total of $19,438. The Steeles' adjusted gross income is reduced first by their net itemized deductions of $19,438, which was more than the standard deduction of $10,700. The subtotal of $79,399 (Line 41) is further reduced by the $13,600 of exemptions (four exemptions claimed times $3,400 per exemption) to arrive at their taxable income of $65,799 on Line 43. The Steeles are filing a joint return, and they are claiming four exemptions. They could have filed under option 3—married filing separate returns—but they found their tax liability would have been greater. This isn't always the case, so you should check your liability each way to determine the appropriate option.

At this point you might expect that the Steeles could go directly to the tax tables and find their Line 44 tax. If they did, the tax on taxable income of $65,799 would be $9,291. However, those with qualified dividends or capital gains must use special worksheets included in the Form 1040 instructions, because these items might be taxed at a lower rate than ordinary income. After completing the related worksheet, the Steeles compute a Line 44 tax of $9,193. Were it not for the tax software program the Steeles are using, they would now have to complete Form 6251 to determine whether they must pay the alternative minimum tax. The tax preparation software indicates they do not owe the alternative minimum tax.

Their next step is to see if they qualify for any of the tax credits. The Steeles had two potential credits in 2007. The first was a dependent care tax credit and the second was a child tax credit. The credit for dependent care and child care expenses is related to your total qualifying expenses and level of adjusted gross income. The maximum is $3,000 if you have one qualifying dependent and $6,000 if you have two or more. The Steeles paid $540 in child-care expenses for after school care while they were at work. Consequently, the dependent care credit was 20 percent of $540 in qualifying expenses, or $108. The Steeles were also eligible for a $1,000 child tax credit for each child. The child tax credit is phased out for upper-income couples and individuals. Given the Steeles' income for 2007, they were entitled to the entire child tax credit for each child.

Finally, since the Steeles had a combined total of $9,946 of federal taxes withheld from their wages, they overpaid their 2007 tax liability by $2,861. They could have applied this overpayment to a 2008 estimated tax but chose a refund instead.

TOPIC LINKS

Get IRS Forms and Publications.

Figure 4.10
1040 U.S. Individual Income Tax Return (Page 1)

Form 1040 Department of the Treasury—Internal Revenue Service
U.S. Individual Income Tax Return **2007**   IRS Use Only—Do not write or staple in this space.

For the year Jan. 1–Dec. 31, 2007, or other tax year beginning _____ , 2007, ending _____ , 20 ___   OMB No. 1545-0074

Label
(See instructions on page 12.)
Use the IRS label.
Otherwise, please print or type.

LABEL HERE		
Your first name and initial Arnold S.	Last name Steele	**Your social security number** 000 : 00 : 0000
If a joint return, spouse's first name and initial Sharon P.	Last name Steele	**Spouse's social security number** 000 : 00 : 0000
Home address (number and street). If you have a P.O. box, see page 12. 496 Mulberry Lane	Apt. no.	▲ You **must** enter your SSN(s) above. ▲
City, town or post office, state, and ZIP code. If you have a foreign address, see page 12. Middlebury, Missouri 64131		Checking a box below will not change your tax or refund.

Presidential Election Campaign ▶ Check here if you, or your spouse if filing jointly, want $3 to go to this fund (see page 12) ▶ ☐ **You** ☐ **Spouse**

Filing Status
Check only one box.

1 ☐ Single
2 ☑ Married filing jointly (even if only one had income)
3 ☐ Married filing separately. Enter spouse's SSN above and full name here. ▶
4 ☐ Head of household (with qualifying person). (See page 13.) If the qualifying person is a child but not your dependent, enter this child's name here. ▶
5 ☐ Qualifying widow(er) with dependent child (see page 14)

Exemptions

6a ☑ **Yourself.** If someone can claim you as a dependent, **do not** check box 6a . . . .
b ☑ **Spouse** . . . .

If more than four dependents, see page 15.

c **Dependents:**

(1) First name Last name	(2) Dependent's social security number	(3) Dependent's relationship to you	(4) ✓ if qualifying child for child tax credit (see page 15)
Nancy T. Steele	000 : 00 : 0000	Daughter	☑
John L. Steele	000 : 00 : 0000	Son	☑
			☐
			☐

Boxes checked on 6a and 6b **2**
No. of children on 6c who:
• lived with you **2**
• did not live with you due to divorce or separation (see page 16) ___
Dependents on 6c not entered above ___

d Total number of exemptions claimed . . . .   Add numbers on lines above ▶ **4**

Income

Attach Form(s) W-2 here. Also attach Forms W-2G and 1099-R if tax was withheld.

If you did not get a W-2, see page 19.

Enclose, but do not attach, any payment. Also, please use Form 1040-V.

7	Wages, salaries, tips, etc. Attach Form(s) W-2	**7**	96,600	00
8a	**Taxable** interest. Attach Schedule B if required	**8a**	937	00
b	Tax-exempt interest. **Do not** include on line 8a . . . ☐ **8b**		
9a	Ordinary dividends. Attach Schedule B if required	**9a**	1,090	00
b	Qualified dividends (see page 19) . . . ☐ **9b** 1,090 00		
10	Taxable refunds, credits, or offsets of state and local income taxes (see page 20) . .	**10**	210	00
11	Alimony received	**11**	
12	Business income or (loss). Attach Schedule C or C-EZ	**12**	
13	Capital gain or (loss). Attach Schedule D if required. If not required, check here ▶ ☐	**13**	
14	Other gains or (losses). Attach Form 4797	**14**	
15a	IRA distributions . . ☐ **15a**	b Taxable amount (see page 21) **15b**	
16a	Pensions and annuities ☐ **16a**	b Taxable amount (see page 22) **16b**	
17	Rental real estate, royalties, partnerships, S corporations, trusts, etc. Attach Schedule E	**17**	
18	Farm income or (loss). Attach Schedule F	**18**	
19	Unemployment compensation	**19**	
20a	Social security benefits ☐ **20a**	b Taxable amount (see page 24) **20b**	
21	Other income. List type and amount (see page 24) ---------------------	**21**	
22	Add the amounts in the far right column for lines 7 through 21. This is your **total income** ▶	**22**	98,837	00

Adjusted Gross Income

23	Educator expenses (see page 26) **23**		
24	Certain business expenses of reservists, performing artists, and fee-basis government officials. Attach Form 2106 or 2106-EZ **24**		
25	Health savings account deduction. Attach Form 8889 . . **25**		
26	Moving expenses. Attach Form 3903 . . . . . **26**		
27	One-half of self-employment tax. Attach Schedule SE . **27**		
28	Self-employed SEP, SIMPLE, and qualified plans . . **28**		
29	Self-employed health insurance deduction (see page 26) **29**		
30	Penalty on early withdrawal of savings **30**		
31a	Alimony paid b Recipient's SSN ▶ _____ : _____ **31a**		
32	IRA deduction (see page 27) **32**		
33	Student loan interest deduction (see page 30) . . . **33**		
34	Tuition and fees deduction. Attach Form 8917 . . . **34**		
35	Domestic production activities deduction. Attach Form 8903 **35**		
36	Add lines 23 through 31a and 32 through 35 . . . . ▶	**36**	
37	Subtract line 36 from line 22. This is your **adjusted gross income** . . . . . ▶	**37**	98,837	00

For Disclosure, Privacy Act, and Paperwork Reduction Act Notice, see page 83.   Cat. No. 11320B   Form **1040** (2007)

Figure 4.10
1040 U.S. Individual Income Tax Return (Page 2)

Form 1040 (2007)							Page **2**

Tax and Credits

38 Amount from line 37 (adjusted gross income) . . . . | **38** | 98,837 | 00

39a Check if: ☐ **You** were born before January 2, 1943, ☐ Blind. ☐ **Spouse** was born before January 2, 1943, ☐ Blind. Total boxes checked ▶ **39a** ☐

b If your spouse itemizes on a separate return or you were a dual-status alien, see page 31 and check here ▶ **39b** ☐

Standard Deduction for—

● People who checked any box on line 39a or 39b or who can be claimed as a dependent, see page 31.

● All others:

Single or Married filing separately, $5,350

Married filing jointly or Qualifying widow(er), $10,700

Head of household, $7,850

40 **Itemized deductions** (from Schedule A) **or** your **standard deduction** (see left margin) . . | **40** | 19,438 | 00

41 Subtract line 40 from line 38 . . . . | **41** | 79,399 | 00

42 If line 38 is $117,300 or less, multiply $3,400 by the total number of exemptions claimed on line 6d. If line 38 is over $117,300, see the worksheet on page 33 . . . . . . | **42** | 13,600 | 00

43 **Taxable income.** Subtract line 42 from line 41. If line 42 is more than line 41, enter -0- | **43** | 65,799 | 00

44 **Tax** (see page 33). Check if any tax is from: **a** ☐ Form(s) 8814 **b** ☐ Form 4972 **c** ☐ Form(s) 8889 | **44** | 9,193 | 00

45 **Alternative minimum tax** (see page 36). Attach Form 6251 . . . . | **45** | |

46 Add lines 44 and 45 . . . . ▶ | **46** | 9,193 | 00

47 Credit for child and dependent care expenses. Attach Form 2441 | **47** | | |

48 Credit for the elderly or the disabled. Attach Schedule R . | **48** | 108 | 00 |

49 Education credits. Attach Form 8863 . . . . . | **49** | | |

50 Residential energy credits. Attach Form 5695 . . . . | **50** | | |

51 Foreign tax credit. Attach Form 1116 if required . . . | **51** | | |

52 Child tax credit (see page 39). Attach Form 8901 if required | **52** | 2,000 | 00 |

53 Retirement savings contributions credit. Attach Form 8880 . | **53** | | |

54 Credits from: **a** ☐ Form 8396 **b** ☐ Form 8859 **c** ☐ Form 8839 | **54** | | |

55 Other credits: **a** ☐ Form 3800 **b** ☐ Form 8801 **c** ☐ Form | **55** | | |

56 Add lines 47 through 55. These are your **total credits** . . . . | **56** | |

57 Subtract line 56 from line 46. If line 56 is more than line 46, enter -0- . . . . . . ▶ | **57** | 2,108 | 00

Other Taxes

58 Self-employment tax. Attach Schedule SE . . . . | **58** | |

59 Unreported social security and Medicare tax from: **a** ☐ Form 4137 **b** ☐ Form 8919 . . | **59** | |

60 Additional tax on IRAs, other qualified retirement plans, etc. Attach Form 5329 if required . . | **60** | |

61 Advance earned income credit payments from Form(s) W-2, box 9 . . . . | **61** | |

62 Household employment taxes. Attach Schedule H . . . . | **62** | |

63 Add lines 57 through 62. This is your **total tax** . . . . ▶ | **63** | 7,085 | 00

Payments

If you have a qualifying child, attach Schedule EIC.

64 Federal income tax withheld from Forms W-2 and 1099 . . | **64** | 9,946 | 00 |

65 2007 estimated tax payments and amount applied from 2006 return | **65** | | |

66a **Earned income credit (EIC)** . . . . | **66a** | | |

b Nontaxable combat pay election ▶ | **66b** | | | |

67 Excess social security and tier 1 RRTA tax withheld (see page 59) | **67** | | |

68 Additional child tax credit. Attach Form 8812 . . . . | **68** | | |

69 Amount paid with request for extension to file (see page 59) | **69** | | |

70 Payments from: **a** ☐ Form 2439 **b** ☐ Form 4136 **c** ☐ Form 8885 . | **70** | | |

71 Refundable credit for prior year minimum tax from Form 8801, line 27 | **71** | | |

72 Add lines 64, 65, 66a, and 67 through 71. These are your **total payments** . . . . ▶ | **72** | 9,946 | 00

Refund

Direct deposit? See page 59 and fill in 74b, 74c, and 74d, or Form 8888.

73 If line 72 is more than line 63, subtract line 63 from line 72. This is the amount you **overpaid** | **73** | 2,861 | 00

74a Amount of line 73 you want **refunded to you.** If Form 8888 is attached, check here ▶ ☑ | **74a** | 2,861 | 00

b Routing number ▶ **c** Type: ☐ Checking ☐ Savings

d Account number

75 Amount of line 73 you want **applied to your 2008 estimated tax** ▶ | **75** | |

Amount You Owe

76 **Amount you owe.** Subtract line 72 from line 63. For details on how to pay, see page 60 ▶ | **76** | |

77 Estimated tax penalty (see page 61) . . . . | **77** | |

Third Party Designee

Do you want to allow another person to discuss this return with the IRS (see page 61)? ☐ **Yes. Complete the following.** ☐ **No**

Designee's name ▶   Phone no. ▶ (   )   Personal identification number (PIN) ▶

Sign Here

Joint return? See page 13.

Keep a copy for your records.

Under penalties of perjury, I declare that I have examined this return and accompanying schedules and statements, and to the best of my knowledge and belief, they are true, correct, and complete. Declaration of preparer (other than taxpayer) is based on all information of which preparer has any knowledge.

Your signature	Date	Your occupation	Daytime phone number
Arnold Steele	4/15/05	Engineer	(000) 000-0000
Spouse's signature. If a joint return, **both** must sign.	Date	Spouse's occupation	
Sharon Steele	4/15/05	Accountant	

Paid Preparer's Use Only

Preparer's signature ▶		Date	Check if self-employed ☐	Preparer's SSN or PTIN
Firm's name (or yours if self-employed), address, and ZIP code ▶			EIN	
			Phone no. ( )	

Form **1040** (2007)

Average tax rate Total tax liability divided by total income.

Marginal tax rate Additional tax liability divided by additional income.

It is time for Arnold and Sharon to reflect on their tax situation. Their tax liability is $7,085 out of their pretax total income of $98,837. Therefore, they paid 7.2 percent ($7,085/$98,837) of their total income in 2007 in federal income taxes. This is their **average tax rate**, but a far more useful figure is their **marginal tax rate**. This rate is more or less buried in the tax table. Arnold and Sharon found it by using the tax rate schedules in Figure 4.8 to calculate their tax. This schedule clearly highlights their marginal rate at a taxable income of $65,799, which is 25 percent.

The marginal rate is the rate being applied to the bracket in which their taxable income falls. If the Steeles' taxable income increased enough to put them into the next higher bracket, their marginal rate would jump to 28 percent. The marginal rates are the ones to consider in making financial decisions concerning future sources of income or deductions, because additional income will be taxed, or additional deductions will save taxes, at the marginal rate. For example, suppose Sharon has considered working additional hours at Todd and Talbot, and she could earn $1,000 more by doing so. Should she work the additional hours? If she does, the Steeles' taxable income will increase by $1,000. Assuming that everything else remains the same, they will pay $250 more in federal taxes and their after-tax income will increase by only $750. They must decide if the additional $750 is worth the extra time and effort on Sharon's part. Of course, this does not take into account payroll taxes or state and local income taxes that would further increase the effective marginal tax rate.

 # saving money 4.2

Do Your Own Tax Return

Why do so many Americans not prepare their own tax returns? A recent study by the U.S. Government Accountability Office found that over half of taxpayers paid someone to prepare their return. This was true for every income category, even those with less than $20,000 in income. In fact, one-third of those filling a 1040EZ and two-thirds of those in the low income group claiming an Earned Income Credit used a paid preparer. Completing the 1040EZ usually takes no more time and is no more challenging than completing a credit application. The 1040A is only a bit more involved, and even the so-called long form—the 1040—should be relatively simple for most taxpayers, considering that 60 percent of 1040 users do not itemize deductions. Is it fear of the IRS, unwillingness to undertake an unpleasant task, or simple year-to-year inertia? Some people feel that the signature of a professional preparer on the return lessens their chance of being audited, although there is no evidence to support this. Why you use an outsider is unimportant; what matters is that you will pay anywhere from $50 to $2,000 when you hire professional help.

If you have used outsiders in the past, the trick is to break the cycle by deciding to go it alone this year. It is extremely helpful to have a copy of your previous year's return when you begin. In most cases, doing this year's return is no more involved than following last year's return but using this year's numbers. (If your preparer did not give you a copy of last year's return, call and ask for one.) Along with "plugging in" the new numbers, you should read the information booklet mailed to you along with your return. This will alert you to any current-year changes. Moreover, if you use tax preparation software you will be prompted for the required information and you will not need to calculate each entry individually.

Actually, the IRS booklets are easy to read and reasonably clear in indicating the steps to take in preparing a return. They are keyed to the line items on the returns, which makes it easy to start at the beginning and work toward the end. If you have a question and cannot find a suitable answer in the booklet, you can call the IRS assistance line (800-829-1040).

Whether you go it alone or use an outsider, it is important to keep good records along with the documents provided by your employer and financial institutions. These latter items indicate your wages and interest or dividends earned during the year. They also will show any deductible mortgage interest. It's a good idea to put the documents in a large envelope or box as soon as you receive them; also, put your tax returns there when they arrive.

Finally, file your return early. You should have all your needed documents by January 31, so set mid-February as your target. Waiting until April accomplishes nothing and may create a feeling of desperation that you won't be able to finish the return on time by yourself.

Other Aspects of the Federal Income Tax

In addition to understanding how the federal income tax formula is used to determine your tax liability, it is important to be familiar with other aspects of the tax. In the following sections we will explain capital gains and losses and the role of the Internal Revenue Service (IRS). Finally, we will discuss the issue of seeking outside help in preparing your return.

Capital Gains and Losses

As your income and wealth increase, you can expect to have a growing number of transactions involving the sale or exchange of capital assets. Almost always, an exchange results in either a gain or a loss that may have to be reported when filing your annual return.

What Is a Capital Gain or Loss?

A **capital gain or loss** results whenever you sell a capital asset for more or less than what you paid for it (or your "adjusted basis" in the asset when special tax rules apply). The next logical question is: What are **capital assets**? For the most part, everything you own and use for personal purposes, pleasure, or investment is a capital asset. Examples are stocks, bonds, and other securities; your house, car, and household goods; or your hobbies, such as stamp and coin collections, and fishing gear.

Capital gain or loss Gain or loss resulting from the sale of a capital asset.

Capital assets Assets held for personal pleasure or investment.

Tax Treatment of Capital Gains and Losses

On certain assets the tax on capital gains is reduced below the tax on ordinary income. Whether the gain or loss qualifies for a lower tax rate depends on the holding period. Changes in the value of assets held for one year or less are termed *short-term* capital gains or losses. These are evaluated at ordinary income tax rates. The appreciation or depreciation in the market value of assets held for a longer period qualify as *long-term* capital gains or losses. The steps for calculating your net gain or loss are as follows:

1. Determine your net short-term gain or loss.
2. Determine your net long-term gain or loss.
3. Combine your net short- and long-term gain or loss to arrive at your overall net gain or loss.

If you have net short-term gains and net long-term gains, the long-term gain receives favorable tax treatment. The maximum tax rate on net long-term capital gains is either 5 percent if you are in the 15 percent marginal tax bracket or 15 percent if you are in a higher tax bracket. This does not apply to collectibles (items such as stamps, coins, and rare wine) or depreciated real estate, which have higher maximum rates. If you have a net gain in one category and a net loss in the other, but have an overall gain, the category in which there is a gain will determine the tax treatment. If you have an overall net loss, you can deduct up to $3,000 of losses in a single year. If losses exceed $3,000, the unused portion can be carried forward to future years and taken as a deduction. There are special tax loss regulations for deductions by individuals who actively manage a business. These are explained in the IRS Publication 925, "Passive Activity and At-Risk Rules."

Any gain on the sale of property held for personal use—your car, for example—must be reported and is taxed in full. Losses on the sale of such assets, however, cannot be deducted against other income. Of course, you seldom sell personal property at a gain, but it is possible.

> **TOPIC LINKS**
>
> See IRS Pub. 925 "Passive Activity and At-Risk Rules."

Selling Your Home

Your home is a personal property, so it is also subject to capital gain taxation. However, special provisions have been written into the law to soften the tax's impact. Under most circumstances you can exclude a $250,000 ($500,000 for married couples) gain on the sale of your main home. To qualify, you must have owned the home for at least the past two years and have used it as your main home for two years. In addition, you must not have excluded the gain from the sale of another home within the past two years. If you lived in the home for less than two years, you may qualify for a partial exclusion. You cannot deduct a loss from the sale of your main home.

It is obvious that a home is a tax-advantaged investment. This feature, coupled with the fact that home prices have generally increased over the years, has made home ownership a very solid investment. This aspect is explained more fully in Chapter 8.

TOPIC LINKS

See IRS Pub. 523 "Selling Your Home."

Alternative Minimum Tax

Alternative Minimum Tax (AMT) Alternative tax calculation to ensure upper income families pay a minimum tax.

The original purpose of the **alternative minimum tax (AMT)** was to ensure that the rich pay at least something. In effect, the AMT computation eliminates many deductions and credits and creates a tax liability for those who would otherwise pay less in taxes. It has a greater impact on individuals living in states with relatively high state and local taxes who itemize deductions.

Those above the statutory income limit must pay at least the AMT. Because the income limits have been stated in dollar terms that are not adjusted for inflation ($66,250 for a married couple and $44,350 for a single filer in 2007), an increasing number of individuals who are not rich now have to undertake an additional calculation of their federal taxes. The procedures for calculating the AMT are difficult and time consuming. This one calculation may make tax preparation software worth the cost. As an alternative you can use the AMT Assistant at the IRS Web site. It is an electronic version of the AMT worksheet provided with Form 1040.

Congress had been debating either eliminating the AMT or raising the income limits at which the AMT takes effect. It is presently unclear how Congress plans to deal with this widely unpopular tax.

The Role of the Internal Revenue Service

Internal Revenue Service (IRS) Federal agency assigned the task of administering the federal income tax.

The **Internal Revenue Service (IRS)**, a division of the Treasury Department, is the federal agency assigned the task of administering the federal income tax. Two of its most important functions are providing taxpayer assistance and auditing tax returns. In addition to understanding these functions, you should be aware of the filing deadline and extensions and the statute of limitations as it applies to the federal income tax.

Taxpayer Assistance

The IRS attempts to make filing your return as easy as possible. (Don't blame the IRS if the return itself is difficult to complete; blame Congress, because the tax law is its responsibility.) If you have filed a return in the past, you are automatically sent a tax form for the current year. If you have never filed a return or if you need to file one different from the previous year, you can find forms at practically every public library and many banks or savings and loans. Forms and instructions are also available from the IRS home page (**www.irs.gov**). In addition to Form 1040 (illustrated with the Steeles' example), there are two simpler forms—1040A and 1040EZ—that many taxpayers can use.

It is often helpful to read IRS publications to handle a tax item properly. The instruction booklet that accompanies your tax return contains a list of IRS publications and forms and shows where in your state to write to get them. We strongly recommend Publication 17, "Your Federal Income Tax," as a handy and reliable general reference on many tax matters. If you file Form 1040EZ or Form 1040A, the IRS will figure the tax for you, if you wish. You must provide all the relevant information, however. The IRS will also figure your tax on Form 1040 if you meet certain criteria.

IRS Audits

The strength of our tax system rests on the integrity of millions of taxpayers to file an honest and reasonably correct return. An important function—the IRS audit—is to ensure that such filing takes place. The IRS has three basic audit approaches: the field audit—where an IRS agent visits your premises to examine your return; the office audit—where you visit an IRS center; and the correspondence audit—where the IRS mails you a tax notice questioning some aspect of your return and asks you to examine the item again to determine its appropriateness.

An audit may involve questioning just one item on your return, or the whole return might be audited, which means you must have documentary support for each line item. Returns selected for audit are determined by a formula (known only to the IRS) and random procedures. Generally, as indicated in Figure 4.11 your chance of audit increases significantly with income and self-employment. The high rate at the lower incomes was a result of special audits of the Earned Income Tax Credit.

It is illegal to file a fraudulent return or not to file a return at all, and stiff penalties can be assessed in each case. A mistake or an alternative interpretation of the law may not lead to a penalty, but you will pay interest on any deficiency. The interest rate changes periodically, depending on market rates of interest. For assessments of additional taxes, the interest period begins on the due date of the return—not from the time the deficiency is found.

Filing Deadline and Extensions

Your tax return must be filed before April 16. If you can't meet that deadline, you can get an **automatic extension** of four months. However, before April 16 you must file Form 4868 asking for the extension. Remember, though, an automatic filing extension does not extend the time you have to pay your tax. You must estimate your tax for the year and pay any tax due along with Form 4868. There is a penalty for late payment unless you have reasonable cause for not paying your tax when due. You can request extensions beyond the automatic four-month extension, but you must meet certain criteria before the IRS will grant them.

TOPIC LINKS

See IRS Pub. 17, "Your Federal Income Tax."

TOPIC LINKS

See IRS Pub. 967, "The IRS Will Figure Your Tax."

Automatic extension An extension of time for filing an income tax return, given automatically by the IRS.

Figure 4.11
IRS Examination Coverage: Fiscal Year 2006

Individual Income Tax Returns	Percent Audited
All individual tax returns with income	1.0
Under $25,000	1.5
$25,000 under $50,000	0.6
$50,000 under $100,000	0.6
$100,000 or more	1.3
Self-Employed Schedule C Returns	
Under $25,000	3.8
$25,000 under $100,000	2.1
$100,000 or more	3.9

Source: 2006 IRS Annual Data Book.

TOPIC LINKS

Explore the IRS e-file options.

TOPIC LINKS

Get a list of companies and software accommodating electronic returns.

TOPIC LINKS

Go to online tax preparation sites.

TOPIC LINKS

Download federal fill-in forms.

Refund anticipation loan A loan provided by a tax preparation service based on a taxpayer's refund.

Statute of limitations A period of three years given the IRS to impose additional taxes on a filed return.

Electronic Filing

As an alternative to mailing your tax return, you can file it electronically through the IRS e-file program. In 2006 73 million tax returns were e-filed (20 million on home computers). You can have a tax professional e-file your return or you can file it yourself using tax preparation software. The IRS does not provide free software for e-filing. With e-file software you are more likely to file an accurate return and receive a quicker refund. Moreover, in most states you can simultaneously file federal and state tax returns. The two major software packages, TurboTax and TaxCut, allow you to file one electronic return without additional cost. There are also a number of sites on the Internet that let you prepare your tax forms and calculate many of the entries online. If your adjusted gross income falls below certain limits, $54,000 in 2007, you can use Free File at the IRS Web site (**www.irs.gov**) to file an electronic return without charge. Go to the IRS Web site (**www.irs.gov**) click "Free File," and then press the "Start Now" button and choose a tax preparation company from the list provided. You cannot access Free File by going directly to the company's Web site.

You can have your refund directly deposited in your bank account or you can pay the taxes you owe by debit or credit card. Taxes owed can be paid with an electronic funds withdrawal or, for a fee, with a credit card. If you can't wait for a refund, a number of preparers will give you a **refund anticipation loan** of $300 to $3,000. In this case, you receive a direct deposit following the acknowledgment by the IRS that you have filed a valid return. Naturally, you should determine if the fees associated with electronic filing and a refund anticipation loan are worth it. Unless you need the refund desperately, determine the equivalent annual interest on the latter item. For most individuals, this will be an unreasonably high rate. Consequently, it has not proven popular among middle- and upper-income tax filers.

The Statute of Limitations

The **statute of limitations**, as it generally applies to the federal income tax law, gives the IRS three years from the time a return is filed to impose additional tax liabilities. This fact suggests that tax records should be kept at least this long. But a special six-year limitation applies if you omit a gross income item that is greater than 25 percent of reported total gross income. Moreover, the statute of limitations does not apply if a return is never filed or if a fraudulent return is filed. If you discover a mistake, indicating that you owe more or less tax, you should file an Amended U.S. Individual Tax Return (Form 1040X).

Also, be forewarned that if you overpaid taxes in a given year, you must file a claim for a refund within three years from the date the return was filed or two years from the date the tax was paid, whichever is later. Failure to file within these periods usually leads to loss of the refund.

Getting Outside Help

Preparing returns has become a very big business, and you are probably familiar with H & R Block, the largest tax preparation service in the United States. Should you use an outside firm? The answer to that question depends on several factors. If you have a complex tax question that cannot be answered by referring to Publication 17 or a tax reference manual at the public library, and if the item is large enough to matter, then you need an expert's opinion. Second, you may not care to spend the time doing your return. There are two broad types of preparers: the tax service companies such as H & R Block and professionals such as CPAs and attorneys.

Tax Service Companies

Many tax service companies open their offices in January and close them in May. Others remain open all year in some of their locations. Fees for their services vary, but a Form

1040 with several supporting schedules will usually cost between $50 and $100. The short forms cost less, but there are additional charges for state and local income tax returns. While most of these companies do a good job in filing your return, a recent government study found that a surprisingly large number of commercial preparers made significant mistakes. You should know that most of their work consists of simply entering the data you give them in appropriate places on the return. While they claim their staff is instructed to ask the right questions to save you taxes, you shouldn't count on it.

After you finish this chapter, if you get Publication 17 and also keep reasonably alert to newspaper and magazine articles on how to reduce your taxes, you will have a good chance of doing a better job on your return than many of these preparers will. Actually, you're more likely to save taxes by planning throughout the year rather than finding clever loopholes at year's end.

CPAs and Attorneys

CPAs and attorneys with specialized training in federal income taxation are the tax experts. If you are fortunate to have a high income, or if you are involved in activities with many income tax implications (running a business, for example), you probably need a professional. As just mentioned, you may want his or her services to guide you throughout the year. You most likely want assistance not only in preparing the return but also in setting up trusts or gifts or advising you about the income tax implications of various investments, including self-employed retirement plans (if they are applicable). Fees for these services are very high: Count on $100 to $200 an hour or a minimum annual retainer of $1,000.

Financial Planners

Many financial planners do not specialize in income tax advice, although they may have contact with people who do. Also, a number of business firms are now engaging financial planners to advise their employees on financial planning. Their services are offered as a fringe benefit to employees. Ask if this service is available at your company and, of course, take advantage of it. The financial planner may not do tax returns, but he or she should be able to help with tax planning.

Tax Publications and Software

If you decide to prepare your own tax return, consider buying books that offer tax advice. The oldest, and still one of the best, is J. K. Lasser's *Your Income Tax*. However, there are several other excellent guides available at modest prices.

Using computer software to prepare your return can save you considerable time. A good program will lead you through the return by providing information on likely deductions and signaling probable omissions. TurboTax and TaxCut are the two major competitors in this market. When selecting software, be sure to check out the following features:

- The ability to complete both federal and state tax returns. (Most software packages charge an extra price for a state module.)
- The capability of importing data from your existing word processing or spreadsheet programs into the tax software. Some tax packages accept data directly from the popular budget management programs.
- Telephone support providing information on both software and tax questions.
- The cost of an annual upgrade.

The tax law has become increasingly complicated over the last decade. It is no surprise that more people than ever before are using tax preparation software to ease that burden. It represents a nice solution for middle-income individuals who have to fill out more than the 1040EZ, but who do not have a special tax situation that requires expert advice.

Special Considerations for Students

College isn't all about money, but you can't get a college education without overcoming a significant financial obstacle. To help you over the hurdle Congress has enacted several tax incentives that encourage expenditures on education. Detailed information on the related tax benefits can be found in IRS Pub. 970, "Tax Benefits for Education." What follows is a brief review of some important educational incentives.

TOPIC LINKS

See these IRS publications on educational expenses.

If you are under age 24 and a full-time student, you may be claimed as a dependent on your parents' return. This is typically advantageous because they are likely to be in a higher marginal tax bracket. Being listed as a dependent on your parents' tax form does not necessarily relieve you of the responsibility of filing a return. In general, you must file a federal income tax return if you had earned income of more than $5,350 (2007) or if you had unearned income of more than $850. However, you should file if you are due a refund on taxes withheld from your paycheck.

Scholarships, Grants, and Fellowships

Scholarships, grants, and fellowships may or may not be included in taxable income. If you are in a degree program and those awards cover purely educational expenses such as tuition, fees, books, supplies, and equipment, then they are most likely tax exempt. However, awards for noneducational living expenses such as room and board are taxable. One exception is an ROTC subsistence allowance paid to students participating in advanced training. Your school's bursar should be able to tell you if your scholarship is taxable.

Employment–Related Advantages

Work-related educational expenses that meet certain restrictive requirements are deductible. The education must be required by your employer or serve to maintain or improve your skills in your present work. It doesn't qualify if it is needed to meet minimum educational requirements for your present job or if its purpose is to prepare you for a new trade or business. This deduction reduces your taxable income only if you itemize and your total job-related deductions exceed 2 percent of your adjusted gross income.

Some employers pay for part-time schooling under a qualified educational assistance plan. Either a portion or all of these payments up to $5,250 may be tax exempt. Your employer can tell you if the plan qualifies. If you do receive tax-exempt payments, you cannot receive both a reimbursement and a tax deduction for the same expense. There is a special exception for educational institutions. A qualified tuition reduction for graduate or undergraduate studies is tax free. This is a reduction in tuition provided to an employee, or the wife and child of an employee, by the educational institution.

Tax Credits

The Hope Scholarship Credit and the Lifetime Learning Credit are available for qualified educational expenses. For each eligible student you may claim only one of the tax credits. The Hope is available for the first two years of postsecondary education. For additional years of schooling, you may be entitled to a Lifetime Learning Credit. Both credits are eliminated for higher-income households.

To qualify for the Hope Scholarship Credit you must be enrolled at least half time in one of the first two years of higher education. In addition, you must be enrolled in a program leading to a degree, certificate, or other recognized educational credential. If you are claiming a Hope Scholarship Credit for a particular student, none of that student's expenses for that year may be applied toward the Lifetime Learning Credit.

In the years in which you are not entitled to Hope Credit, you may still receive a Lifetime Learning Credit. The Lifetime Learning credit is available for all years of post-secondary education and for students who have taken one or more courses.

Tuition and Fees Deduction

If you do not use either of the tax credits listed previously, you may be eligible to deduct some of your or your dependent's educational expenses. Both of you cannot deduct these expenses. Subject to income limits, $2,000 to $4,000 of annual expenses are deductible in 2007 as an adjustment to gross income. This is an adjustment to gross income that can be claimed regardless of whether you itemize.

Coverdell Education Savings Account (ESA)

Subject to income restrictions on contributors, you can contribute up to $2,000 each year in a Coverdell Education Savings Account meant to fund the qualified educational expenses of a designated beneficiary. These funds can be used for qualified primary, secondary or college expenses. Deposits in a Coverdell Account are not tax deductible but they grow tax free until distributed. Withdrawals are taxable if they are used for nonqualified expenses.

Qualified Tuition Programs (QTP)

These are also called "529 plans." Several state-run QTP programs let you prepay college expenses or contribute to an account to pay for a future education. The contributions to a qualified state tuition program are not tax deductible, but there is no tax on distributions for qualified educational expenses. Unlike an Education Savings Account, there are no income restrictions on contributors and there is no limit on contributions as long as combined distributions from a QTP and ESA do not exceed the amount of potential educational expenses.

Early Distributions from IRAs

A tax penalty is generally levied on distributions from an IRA before age 59 1/2. However, funds withdrawn to pay for qualified educational expenses are exempt from the penalty. Withdrawals from a traditional IRA will be taxed at ordinary income rates in the year they are disbursed.

Student Loan Interest

Generally, personal interest you pay on a loan, other than mortgage interest, is not tax deductible. There is an exception for interest you pay on a qualified student loan used for qualified educational expenses by you or your dependent. The student loan interest deduction is taken as an adjustment to income. Therefore, you get the tax benefit even if you do not itemize your deductions. The amount you can deduct is limited and is phased out at higher incomes.

Education Savings Bonds

You can exclude from your gross income interest on qualified U.S. savings bonds, if you have qualified higher educational expenses during the redemption year. The savings bond must be a Series EE or I bond issued after 1989. The bond must be issued in your name and you must be at least 24 years old before the bond's issue date. This exemption is subject to limits on your income.

Special Considerations for the Military

Men and women serving in our armed forces are accorded special tax benefits. Military pay is divided into basic pay and allowances. Federal and state taxes must be paid on basic pay, bonuses, incentives, and special pays. However, allowances for such things as living, travel, and moving are excluded from federal gross income on a military W-2 Statement of Earnings. There is also an exclusion for combat pay for enlisted members and a limited exclusion for officers. Information on rules governing tax benefits provided to the military appears in IRS Publication 2 "Armed Forces Tax Guide." Many states provide similar tax benefits, but they vary by state. Pay officers should have details on which pay is taxable.

Special benefits are provided to those serving in a combat zone. The combat zone exclusion from federal income taxes applies to active duty pay, reenlistment bonuses, student loan repayments and other types of reimbursement. These exemptions extend beyond time in the combat zone for those hospitalized for injuries or illness sustained while in a combat zone. However, they do not extend to the income of other family members.

Reservists often experience a significant drop in income when called to active duty. Short-time needs may require the use of long-term savings. Accordingly, reservists on active duty for a sufficient period may be able to access tax advantaged retirement accounts. Ordinary income taxes may be still due on early withdrawals; however, the hefty 10 percent early withdrawal penalty is waived for qualified reservists on active duty.

Planning to Reduce Your Income Taxes

Effective tax planning is an ongoing process. Among other things, it requires selecting investments carefully, holding them for a sufficient length of time, and then selling them at the most opportune time for tax purposes. It also means that you must use provisions of the income tax law that are specifically designed to lower your tax liability. Tax planning attempts either to avoid taxes altogether or defer them to a later time. It works within the tax law, not outside of it as is the case with tax evasion. Following are some of the more common and useful tax-planning techniques.

Invest Where You Receive Tax-Advantaged Income

The tax law favors some forms of income over others. You can reduce your taxes by investing first in those favored investments, which are discussed here.

Buy Municipal Bonds

Municipal bonds Bonds paying interest that are exempt from federal income tax.

All interest on **municipal bonds** is tax exempt. These bonds are explained in more detail in Chapter 11, but you should see at this point that the after-tax yield on a municipal bond is the same as its pretax yield.

Buy a Home

We have already explained the income tax treatment of your personal residence. In effect, you can enjoy a $250,000 tax-free, long-term capital gain each time you replace your principal residence. It's hard to beat that anywhere. Also, most mortgage interest is deductible as an itemized expense.

Actively Invest in Real Estate

Despite the disadvantage of limited deductibility of business losses, actively managing your own business, such as real estate, offers certain tax advantages for most taxpayers.

The appeal of real estate rests in the fact that a large portion of many losses is represented by a noncash charge called depreciation. This means that even though the property shows a loss for tax purposes, you might still have a decent cash return.

Plan for Retirement

Many types of tax-advantaged retirement accounts, discussed in this and later chapters, defer taxes on contributions and earnings until they are withdrawn after age 59 1/2. If your marginal tax rate is lower in your retirement years than it is now, the difference will result in a net savings.

Take Capital Losses Quickly

If you have a capital loss, it is usually to your advantage to take it before a tax year ends. Even if you believe the security's price might rebound and eliminate the loss, you should consider selling the security you own and replacing it with a similar security. For example, suppose you buy Exxon common stock, and after your purchase, its price falls to half of what it was. You believe the international oil companies will do well in the future, but the year is about to end. Consider selling Exxon and buying Mobil, another international oil. You will then be able to deduct all the loss in Exxon (up to $3,000), and the tax savings will enable you to buy that many additional shares of Mobil. Why not just sell Exxon and buy it right back? You can't; that's called a *wash sale*. You must wait at least 30 days, which also may not be a bad idea if you think Exxon is a far better stock than Mobil over the long run. This strategy works well for stocks, but it works even better with bonds since their characteristics are more similar from one bond to another. The general rule of thumb is that you take your losses quickly and let your gains run.

Split Your Income

Dividing income among family members so that it is taxed at a collectively lower marginal rate is a favorite tax-reduction technique. If you are in a 28 percent tax bracket and your child is in a 15 percent tax bracket, then the family will save $0.13 on each dollar of income earned by the child rather than the parent. This approach is used often when people wish to establish educational funds for their children. It can also be used to create retirement income for aging parents, who may also have high medical expenses. The two most frequently used techniques for transferring income are making outright gifts and setting up trusts. They should be utilized with caution, only after seeking advice for a professional planner. Incorrectly applied, they can backfire and actually increase your tax liability.

Gifts

A husband and wife can give someone as much as $24,000 a year without reducing their gift or estate tax exemption; and since it is a gift, it is not considered income of the recipient. Regardless of the amount given, any future earnings on the invested funds become income of the recipient. Suppose you are interested in providing funds for your child's future support. It's a simple matter to set up a **custodial account** (at a bank or other financial institution) and make a gift each year, the amount depending on how much you wish to accumulate.

Custodial account An account set up by parents in their children's names.

For minors under 18 years of age, the first $850 of income from gifted assets (or any assets) is tax free by virtue of a modified standard deduction. The tax consequences for unearned income above that amount are complicated (see IRS Publication 929, "Tax Rules for Children and Dependents"). keep in mind that once you make gifts to your children, they become the children's property. In effect, you lose control of the money and cannot access it legally.

Trusts

A trust is a legal arrangement that allows assets to be managed by a trustee for the benefit of individuals called beneficiaries. Trusts are more expensive to establish than a gifting program, but they can be structured in many ways, making it wise to seek legal advice when establishing one. Trusts are often used to provide income for someone who is aged or infirm and in need of medical or other care. If properly structured, income earned by the fund may be taxed at a lower rate than the trust's creator.

Stagger Income and Expenses

If you can control the timing of expenses and income, you may be able to reduce your taxes. For example, you may have a very large doctor or hospital bill that can be paid in either 2008 or 2009. But you might find that even by paying the bill in 2008, you don't have enough other itemized expenses to exceed the standard deduction. If you pay the bill in 2008 anyway, you may lose the benefit of the deduction in 2009. By delaying payment you hold the expense until 2009, when you may be able to itemize.

Even if you itemize in both years, it could be advantageous to stagger as many itemized expenses as you can into one of the two years. Again, this difference results from the income tax's progressive rate structure: A large deduction in one year could put you in a lower tax bracket that year, whereas taking an approximately even amount each year might leave you in the same higher bracket both years. As the months of November and December get closer, you should review your tax situation and see if expenses can be staggered profitably. Of course, staggering income—if that's possible—should also be considered.

Defer Income to Later Years

Deferring income to be taxed in later years is different from avoiding taxes altogether. However, deferring can be as attractive as avoidance for several reasons. First, deferred income is free to accumulate, and it will grow to a substantially larger sum than income that is taxed each year. Second, your marginal tax rate on deferred income (usually during retirement) might be lower than your current marginal rate. Some commonly used income-deferring investments are IRAs and Keogh and 401(k) plans; tax-deferred annuities; and U.S. Treasury Series EE bonds. In addition to these formal plans, any investment that defers your return to the future offers tax advantages. For example, a growth stock typically pays little or no current dividends that would be taxable. Rather, you can enjoy your total return as a capital gain when you sell the stock in the future. Moreover, the tax rate on capital gains will be less than the rate on earned interest taxed as ordinary income. The "saved" taxes can be invested and earn a return during the entire investment period.

IRAs, Keoghs, and 401(k) Plans

We will discuss each of these in greater depth in Chapter 16. Certainly one of the major advantages of these plans is the deduction against current income of amounts invested.

With regular IRAs, you should be aware that you can always take your money out before retirement. Withdrawals, however, must be included in determining taxable income in the withdrawal year. (*Remember*: You excluded the IRA contribution in the year you made it.) If you do so before age 59 1/2, you must pay a 10 percent penalty unless the withdrawal was for an exempted reason.

Tax-Deferred Annuities

A **tax-deferred annuity** is an investment usually written by an insurance company. It also defers income to later years, but in contrast to IRAs, Keoghs, and 401(k)s, you cannot take a deduction on your current return for amounts invested, which makes them less attractive.

Tax-deferred annuity An investment, usually sold by insurance companies, that allows tax deferral on current interest earned.

U.S. Treasury Series EE Bonds

Series EE bonds give you the option of either reporting income as it accrues on the bond each year or reporting it when you cash the bond. The main advantage of this bond is its flexibility. You choose when to cash it and pay the tax, and choosing a year when your marginal tax rate is low can save taxes. These bonds are explained further in Chapter 11.

finance news 4.3

Congress Struggles with the Alternative Minimum Tax

The Alternative Minimum Tax (AMT) was instituted in 1969 to ensure that millionaires could not avoid paying their fair share of taxes by exploiting loopholes in the tax code. It was targeted to reach 155 households that paid little or no taxes. Sometime between then and now the definition of a millionaire seems to have changed. Today, those much less wealthy feel the impact of the AMT. This is because the AMT is not adjusted for inflation. Accordingly, as the cost of living increases more and more Americans are impacted by the AMT.

Rather than remedying this underlying problem, Congress has chosen to deal with it by periodically raising the effective minimums. The adjustment in the AMT by Congress in 2007 was so late in the year that the IRS warned taxpayers not to file their returns until February 11 because they had to reprogram their computers to handle the changes. Without this last minute reprieve, up to 20 million taxpayers might have been impacted. Given the increasing share of tax revenues collected by the AMT, Congress has been reluctant to eliminate or reduce the AMT.

Many taxpayers must now calculate their taxes the ordinary way and then also calculate their taxes under the AMT. Good tax software automatically checks to see if you are liable for the AMT. Just this one calculation, makes most tax software worth the cost. The AMT uses special rules for determining taxable income and allowable deductions. The two major deductions eliminated by the AMT are state income and local property taxes. Based on your AMT Taxable Income you calculate your Tentative Minimum Tax. You then compare this with your ordinary tax liability and pay whichever is greater. This tax was originally set at 10 percent. There is now a minimum tax burden of 26 or 28 percent, depending on your AMT Taxable Income.

The main purpose of the AMT was to close tax loopholes used by high-income individuals. Unfortunately, these are generally the same tax deductions that benefit most taxpayers. Therefore, the AMT tax is not easily avoided or reduced. You need to complete IRS Form 6251 to determine your Tentative Minimum Tax. An inspection of the line items on that form should provide some insight on tax planning opportunities.

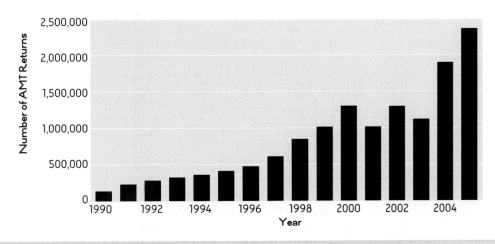

Other Important Taxes

Although the federal income tax is the most important tax to most of us, others should also be understood. For example, people in low- or middle-income brackets might pay more in Social Security taxes than in personal income taxes; if you are very wealthy, you may pay substantial estate and inheritance taxes when you die or gift taxes if you give your estate away before you die. The growing fiscal needs of state and local governments have brought forth an array of income, sales, and property taxes at these levels.

Social Security Taxes

Most of us are familiar with the Social Security system. We are counting on it as an important part of our retirement income or for survivor benefits to our families if something happens to us. But, as you probably also know, it has come under financial stress because benefits seem to be outpacing revenues. As a result, Social Security taxes have escalated rapidly and will continue to do so in the future.

The taxes withheld from your wages for Social Security are called **FICA taxes**; FICA denotes taxes collected under the Federal Insurance Contributions Act. FICA taxes consist of three components: health insurance (HI), old age and survivor's insurance (OASI), and disability insurance (DI). HI is paid for by a 1.45 percent tax on all wages. There is an annually adjustable limit on the taxable base for OASI and DI taxes. In 2008 wages up to $102,000 were taxed at 6.2 percent for these components. Accordingly, at below the adjustable limit, FICA taxes add up to 7.65 percent of your wages.

It is important to realize that you might overpay FICA taxes. This could happen if you change employers during the year or if you work for two or more employers. You can claim excess payments as a credit against your federal income tax liability at the time you prepare your return. By all means, check the W-2 forms your employer gives you in January to make sure you have not overpaid. However, both spouses must pay the full amount of the tax, so you cannot have an overpayment simply because the sum of the two exceeds the maximum.

Also, you should be aware that your employer must pay FICA tax equal to the amount withheld from your wage. This is an expensive payroll cost for employers. Self-employed individuals must pay both the employer's and employee's portions of the tax.

State and Local Taxes

The maze of state and local taxes in most states not only takes a fairly large amount from your bank account but also creates considerable confusion as to what is being taxed and for how much. Very few people thoroughly understand all these taxes; in fact, some of the taxes are buried in the prices of items that we buy. There is little that can be done about the situation except to make the best of it. Table 4.1 indicates how state and local tax burdens vary by income. Of course, governments that collect high taxes may also provide high levels of services. In this sense, then, high taxes aren't necessarily bad.

Income Taxes

All states except Alaska, Florida, Nevada, South Dakota, Texas, Washington, and Wyoming levy income taxes. These are usually withheld from your wages, but you must file an annual return, similar to the federal return, to calculate your tax liability and to determine any overpayment or underpayment. The tax bases and rates vary among the states, and they can be quite high. A New York City resident whose income is in the highest bracket will pay over 20 percent in combined state and city income tax.

TOPIC LINKS

Find state income tax rates.

	Income Level				
Type of tax	$25,000	$50,000	$75,000	$100,000	$150,000
Income	$390	$1,189	$2,523	$3,992	$7,028
Property	1,633	2,231	2,641	2,983	3,679
Sales	663	897	1,387	1,574	2,128
Car	211	295	518	641	775
Total	$2,792	$4,379	$6,614	$8,518	$12,479
% of income	11.2%	8.8%	8.8%	8.5%	8.3%

Table 4.1
Average State and Local Tax Burden for a Hypothetical Family of Three: Average for the Largest City in Each State, 2005

Source: Tax Rates and Tax Burdens in the District of Columbia: A Nationwide Comparison, 2005, Government of the District of Columbia.

Many local governments—mostly cities and villages—impose income taxes. While these are often called payroll taxes, they are imposed on all forms of income. These also require filing an annual return if you have taxable income not subject to withholding. It is not uncommon for someone (such as a sales representative) to file more than a dozen returns if he or she earned income in 12 different communities. To make matters more confusing, there is always the question of whether you pay tax to the city where the income was earned or the city in which you live, assuming they are different. In general, the tax follows the place of employment unless the city of residence imposes a higher tax rate; then you usually pay the difference between the two rates to the city of residence. Of course, you must file a tax return with that city.

Property Taxes

Property taxes are still the mainstay of local governments, particularly school districts. All states have taxes on real property (houses and buildings), and most also tax personal property (equipment, furniture, fixtures, and the like) of businesses; some also tax household personal property. Many impose taxes on intangible property, such as stocks and bonds. The property tax rate that you pay depends very much upon the community where the property is located. It varies from a high of about 1.86 percent of a home's value in Texas to a low of about 0.23 percent in Hawaii.

Sales Taxes

Forty-five states and the District of Columbia have sales taxes. Some tax all consumption items—services as well as commodities—and others omit services. Some tax necessities, such as food; others do not. The sales tax rates vary among states and even within states when local governments enact their own taxes to "piggyback" the state tax.

Death and Transfer Taxes

If you think you can avoid paying taxes by dying, you are wrong. Those who have been lucky enough to accumulate a sizable estate at death may have to share their financial success with the government. Some call this double taxation, since it was already taxed when it was earned. With proper estate planning, however, even wealthy individuals can significantly reduce their tax liabilities at death. Through the use of life transfers and special trusts they can ensure that their wealth is transferred intact to desired beneficiaries. The strategies for accomplishing this objective for high-income individuals are too complicated for us to discuss in this introductory text. You need the help of estate planning professionals if you find yourself in this category. Nevertheless, a basic understanding of estate and transfer taxes can benefit most individuals. With it, even moderate-income individuals may avoid tax liabilities and know when to seek professional financial help.

Federal Gift and Estate Tax

Federal estate tax A tax levied on a decedent's estate.

Federal gift tax Excise tax levied on the transfer of property; supplements the federal estate tax.

The **federal estate tax** is a tax that is levied on the value of a decedent's estate at the time of death. The **federal gift tax** is an excise tax charged on the transfer of property by a living donor. A gift tax is necessary to supplement an estate tax; otherwise, you would be able to transfer wealth during your lifetime and, therefore, avoid the estate tax. The federal gift allows "modest" nontaxable gifts each year of $12,000 (as of 2008) to as many individuals as you wish. Therefore, a husband and wife can together transfer $24,000 each year to each child while avoiding gift and estate taxes. For most families the "modest" gift provision allows a substantial transfer of their wealth each year.

The interaction of the federal estate and gift tax is fairly complicated. However, the tax is only applied to large gifts and estates because of a rather large tax credit on taxable transfers and specific exclusions. The most notable is the marital exclusion that permits an unlimited nontaxable transfer to a living or surviving spouse. Taxable gift transfer above the annual exclusion and taxable death transfers above allowable exclusions are subject to a unified tax and a unified credit. This means that the tax and the credit are applied to the combined value of the taxable gift and death transfers. Under the Tax Relief Act of 2001, the unified credit gradually increases over the next few years until the unified tax is entirely eliminated in 2010. However, the present law does retain a separate gift tax in 2010 in order to reduce the incentive for transferring income-generating property from high-rate taxpayers to low-rate taxpayers. Given the planned expansion in the unified credit, taxable transfers below the amounts listed in Table 4.2 will be exempt from gift and estate taxes. If Congress does nothing, which is unlikely, the estate tax will be reinstated in 2011.

State Death Taxes

Estate tax State tax imposed on the property of the deceased before transfer.

Inheritance tax State tax levied on the heirs to an estate.

A tax on the property transferred or received upon the death of the owner is known as a death tax. There are two types of death taxes: an estate tax and an inheritance tax. An **estate tax** is imposed on the property of the deceased before it is transferred; an **inheritance tax** is levied on the property when the beneficiary receives it. At the federal level, only an estate tax exists. However, state governments impose either estate or inheritance taxes, and sometimes both.

Table 4.2
Planned Changes in the
Estate Tax

Tax Year	Top Rate	Estate Exemption Amount
2008	45%	$2 million
2009	45%	$3.5 million
2010	repealed	
2011	55%	$1 million

Source: Joint Committee on Taxation.

Each state has its own inheritance or estate tax. The exact tax rate and the exemption accorded each beneficiary differ from state to state. About one-third of states have inheritance taxes. These are levied somewhat differently than estate taxes in that heirs are classified according to their relationship to the decedent. Inheritance tax statutes generally segregate beneficiaries into classes similar to the following:

- Class 1: Spouse
- Class 2: Parents, children, grandparents, lineal descendants
- Class 3: Brothers and sisters, aunts and uncles
- Class 4: Children of brothers and sisters, children of aunts and uncles
- Class 5: All others

The tax rates on classes of beneficiaries are structured so that the larger the estate and the more distant the relationship to the deceased, the higher is the tax rate. Inheritance taxes play an important role in estate planning by providing an incentive to leave property to closer relatives. Furthermore, because exemptions are low—in one state $5,000 for a spouse—and because rates can be high on large estates, approaching 30 percent, inheritance taxes also provide an incentive for lifetime gifts.

Transfers of Appreciated Property

Most of us are not wealthy enough to worry about the gift or estate tax. However, the method in which our property is distributed can still be important because it can affect the federal income taxes paid by beneficiaries. In some situations it may be preferable to let the property transfer at death rather than as a gift. This is because the property of the deceased receives a stepped-up cost basis for tax purposes at death. This means that the cost basis for valuing the taxable capital gain is set at the market value of the property at the time of death rather than what it cost when it was initially purchased by the deceased.

If you were lucky enough to buy stock in Microsoft when it was first issued, you probably own some shares that are worth a lot more than you previously paid for them. If you sold them today, you would have to pay a tax on that capital gain. Suppose instead those shares transferred to your children at your death, your children would receive a new cost basis in the stock valued at the time of your death. Consequently, the entire appreciation in the value of the stock that occurred while you were alive would escape taxation. Regrettably, new rules are planned to take effect when the federal estate tax is temporarily eliminated in 2010. With some modification, beneficiaries will have to pick up the cost basis of the deceased.

If you gift property to others while you are alive, the recipient of a gift must assume your cost basis when the property has appreciated in value. Therefore, if you gift your children that Microsoft stock, they will have to pay a capital gain tax on the entire appreciation in the value of the stock from the time you purchased it. The basic rule of thumb is that you let those goods that have appreciated in market value transfer at death rather than as gifts. In this way a new cost basis is established, and potential capital gains taxes are eliminated.

Alternatively, don't bequeath property that has depreciated in value. The beneficiary will not be able to receive the tax benefit from the capital loss. Don't give depreciated property away, either. The best strategy is to take the capital loss yourself. On gifts that have depreciated in value, the cost basis to the recipient is the lower of the cost to the donor or the fair market value at the time the gift was made. Thus, the recipient of a gift that has depreciated in value since its initial purchase would not be able to take the reduction in value before the property was transferred as a loss for tax purposes.

key terms

adjusted gross income (p. 85)
alimony payments (p. 86)
alternative minimum tax (AMT) (p. 96)
automatic extension (p. 97)
average tax rate (p. 94)
capital assets (p. 95)
capital gain or loss (p. 95)
custodial account (p. 103)
estate tax (p. 108)
federal estate tax (p. 108)
federal gift tax (p. 108)
FICA taxes (p. 106)
global income (p. 83)
gross income (p. 83)
inheritance tax (p. 108)

Internal Revenue Service (IRS) (p. 96)
IRAs and Keogh plans (p. 85)
itemized deductions (p. 87)
marginal tax rate (p. 94)
municipal bonds (p. 102)
personal and dependency exemptions
    (p. 86)
refund anticipation loan (p. 98)
standard deduction (p. 87)
statute of limitations (p. 98)
taxable income (p. 86)
tax credit (p. 90)
tax-deferred annuity (p. 105)
W-2 form (p. 90)
W-4 form (p. 91)

follow-up on the Steele family

Reread the chapter-opening vignette.

1. The Steeles postponed filing their federal return until the last possible date. Was this a wise strategy?

2. How do you find the Steeles' marginal tax rate?

3. What tax strategies can you offer the Steeles for reducing their future tax liabilities? Do you agree with the Steeles that this year's tax refund is an indicator of successful tax planning?

problems and review questions

1. Arrange the following items in their appropriate sequence according to the federal income tax formula:
   a. adjusted gross income
   b. adjustments to income
   c. itemized deductions
   d. tax credits
   e. gross income items
   f. nontaxable exclusions
   g. federal income taxes withheld
   h. exemptions

2. What is the personal exemption and how does it differ from the standard deduction?

3. How can an IRA affect your tax liability?

4. Chrissy, Jack, and Janet are friends. Jack and Janet have grown fond of each other and are thinking of marrying. Chrissy has told them, however, that if they do, their income taxes will increase. Jack and Janet don't see how that's possible. Assume each made $47,000 and took the standard deduction in 2007. Using the tax schedules in Figure 4.8 to approximate their taxes, determine whether Chrissy is right.

5. John and his wife Clara had $36,000 of adjusted gross income in 2007. They filed a joint return and took the standard deduction. Is it likely they had to pay any taxes? If so, how much?

6. Steve has a 28 percent marginal tax rate. What is it worth to him to have the following?
   a. an additional itemized deduction of $100
   b. an additional $100 invested in a tax-deductible IRA
   c. an additional tax credit of $100
7. Explain the tax treatment for capital gains and capital losses.
8. In 1995 Miguel purchased a home for $130,000. In 2000 he sold it for $170,000 and immediately purchased another one for $180,000, which he sold in 2007 for $235,000. How much taxable capital gain, if any, does Miguel have?
9. Identify, explain, or elaborate upon the following items:
   a. functions of the IRS
   b. automatic extension of time for filing
   c. statutes of limitations
   d. assistance in tax-return preparation
   e. income splitting
   f. staggering expenses
   g. avoiding taxes
   h. deferring taxes
10. Explain how expenses for a college education might reduce your tax liability.
11. Is all military pay taxable? Explain.
12. How are FICA taxes calculated? Is it possible to overpay them? If your answer is yes, what should you do?
13. What are estate, gift, and inheritance taxes?
14. Identify frequently levied state and local taxes.

case 4.1

Preparing Becky Sell's First Tax Return

Becky Sell graduated from a Midwestern college in 2007 and began work as a marketing manager trainee for a large consumer products company. Becky had never prepared her own tax return, but she was determined to do it for the first time. Becky got all pertinent information together in February 2007, and it appears as follows:

- Data on two W-2 forms (Becky worked part-time prior to graduation) showed wages of $44,000 and federal income tax withheld of $4,600. In addition, they showed she paid $1,600 in state and city income taxes and $3,366 in FICA taxes.
- Becky paid most of her bills with checks and kept all canceled receipts of purchases. Examination of these and her check stubs shows the following major classifications of expenses: rent = $5,000; charitable contributions = $500; interest on installment loans = $1,900; food and clothing = $8,000; dues to professional marketing society = $200; hospital and doctor's bills = $1,000; state sales tax = $600; contributions to a political candidate in her hometown = $110; contributions to a panhandler she often sees outside the office of the political candidate = $50.
- Becky received $12,000 in gifts at graduation, and with it she purchased shares of GM stock in April. Three months later she sold these shares for $8,500.

Becky wants to file a return that will minimize her 2007 tax liability. She has cash from the GM stock sale that could be used for an IRA investment, but she isn't sure of the maximum allowed.

Questions
1. If Becky itemized personal expenses, how much can she deduct? How much is her standard deduction? Should she itemize or take the standard deduction?

2. Using the schedules in Figure 4.8, and taking the standard deduction, determine Becky's 2007 tax liability. (Assume she will make a $2,000 tax deductible IRA investment.) How much will Becky owe or have refunded?

3. Determine Becky's marginal tax rate and explain to her what this rate means.

4. By how much did the IRA contribution reduce her current tax liability?

5. Becky worked for two employers; did she overpay her FICA taxes? Explain.

case 4.2

The Brittens' Investment Alternatives

Bernie and Pam Britten are a young married couple beginning careers and establishing a household. They will each make about $60,000 next year and will have accumulated about $40,000 to invest. They now rent an apartment but are considering purchasing a condominium for $100,000. If they do, a down payment of $10,000 will be required.

They have discussed their situation with Lew McCarthy, an investment advisor and personal friend, and he has recommended the following investments:

- The condominium—expected annual increase in market value = 5 percent
- Municipal bonds—expected annual yield = 5 percent
- High-yield corporate stocks—expected dividend yield = 8 percent
- Savings account in a commercial bank—expected annual yield = 3 percent
- High-growth common stocks—expected annual increase in market value = 10 percent; expected dividend yield = 0

Questions

1. Calculate the after-tax yields on the foregoing investments, assuming the Brittens have a 28 percent marginal tax rate.

2. How would you recommend the Brittens invest their $40,000? Explain your answer.

working out
on the Web

Exercises to Strengthen Your Use of the Internet
(Internet links for the following exercises can be found at **www.prenhall.com/frasca**.)

Exercise 4.1 Keeping Up with Changes in the Tax Code

Each year Congress makes at least minor changes in the tax code. Those people who are aware of the changes can often modify their personal financial plans so that the changes work in their favor. Money Central (articles.moneycentral.msn.com/taxes/home.aspx) and Yahoo! Finance (finance.yahoo.com/taxes) highlight recent changes in the law that affect individuals. In addition, the IRS tends to highlight recent changes in each of its publications, such as IRS Publication 553 (**www.irs.gov/publications/p553/**).

Q. How might recent changes in the tax law influence your current or future financial decisions?

Exercise 4.2 What's an Enrolled Agent (EA)?

If the IRS audits you, an enrolled agent can appear at the IRS in your place. How do you locate an enrolled agent? The answers to this and other questions concerning enrolled agents appear at the Web site for the National Association of Enrolled Agents (**www.naea.org**).

Q. How does one become an EA, and what are the entry requirements for this profession?

Exercise 4.3 Getting the Tax Information You Need

The IRS Web site provides access to all of its publications (**www.irs.gov/formspubs**). Publication 17 "Your Federal Income Tax." is a good starting point for individual filers. At the beginning of this booklet is a section that highlights the important changes for the most recent tax year.

Q. What are the most important changes for the latest tax year?

Exercise 4.4 Locating Information on State Taxes

The IRS provides tax forms, informational publications, and tax tips. Determine what type of information is available from your state government. In your hunt, you can use a general Internet search engine such as Google, or you can use one of the special pages with state government links. For example, try Federal Tax Administrators (**www.taxadmin.org/fta/link**) or the TaxSite.Com (**www.taxsites.com/state.html**).

Q. Can you electronically access information on your state taxes? If so, at what site can you access this information?

Exercise 4.5 Determining the Top State Marginal Tax Rate

Most states tax income in a manner consistent with the federal government's taxation of income. If your state has an income tax, what is its top marginal tax rate and at what level of taxable income does this rate become effective? Which state has the top marginal tax rate in the nation? This information is available from the Federation of Tax Administrators (**www.taxadmin.org/fta/rate**), an association of major state tax collection agencies.

Q. If your state has an income tax, what is the top marginal rate in your state, and at what level of taxable income does this rate become effective?

part 2

Liquidity Management

managing current assets and current liabilities

The management of any unit that has financial transactions—business, government, or family—recognizes the need to maintain adequate liquidity. Cash is received from employment or other sources, held for a while, and then used to pay bills or invested in savings accounts or other financial assets. Managing these cash flows should be undertaken in a way that embraces both a cash management strategy and a short-term credit management strategy. Together, these strategies aim to reduce the overall costs of liquidity, which can be explicit costs, such as interest expenses on amounts borrowed, or opportunity costs, such as interest-earning opportunities forgone because cash is deployed in other ways.

Chapter 5 focuses on cash management. It discusses some basic features of cash-type assets, such as savings accounts, certificates of deposit, and U.S. savings bonds. For readers who are unfamiliar with checking accounts, the chapter provides specific steps for managing one properly. The topic of how interest is determined on savings accounts is also discussed, and the chapter concludes with a discussion of cash management strategy.

Chapter 6 examines short-term credit, which can be viewed broadly as simply another source of cash to pay bills or make investments. But it can be an expensive source and not one to be taken lightly or overused. The chapter focuses on various sources of credit and how to manage credit effectively. It also highlights courses of action if credit is denied, or if borrowers' rights are abused by lenders or by credit card fraud. Finally, advice is offered for resolving personal debt problems.

Cash Management
funds for immediate needs

Objectives

1. To identify the important deposits for holding cash balances and the advantages and disadvantages of each
2. To determine how much liquidity is usually necessary, given your income and preferences for safety
3. To decide on the appropriate type of checking account and to learn how to make transactions with your account and reconcile it each month
4. To understand how compounding makes your deposits grow over time and why deposits with long maturities are riskier than those with short maturities
5. To devise a strategy for managing your total liquid asset portfolio

Steele family

Arnold and Sharon Steele are increasing their familiarity with financial planning. Recently, they have prepared and analyzed financial statements, which have uncovered some financial strengths and weaknesses. Their liquidity position seems strong. They have $27,440 in liquid assets that were accumulated more or less at random. They have a savings account that was opened right after their marriage, and it has been untouched since then. Recently, they put funds into certificates of deposit because of an advertisement they read in the newspaper, and they invested in savings bonds because of certain tax advantages they hoped to achieve with them. Finally, they had $5,400 in their checking account at year-end. This amount varies from month to month and, on average, is considerably more than they need to have on hand. However, occasionally they buy an antique and must have sufficient funds available to make the purchase.

The Steeles are trying to resolve two issues with respect to their liquid assets: First, is the current amount adequate, or should they hold more or fewer such assets? Sharon is concerned about the safety of their investments, particularly those earmarked for John and Nancy's education. Most liquid assets are very safe, an appealing feature to Sharon, who feels that a good portion of their future savings should be allocated to them. Arnold leans more toward minimizing their liquid asset holdings in favor of greater allocations to long-term investments, such as stocks, bonds, and mutual funds.

The second issue they must resolve is the selection of specific liquid assets. Should they continue to hold the current mix, or should they look for alternatives? How much additional yield can they reasonably expect to achieve by rearranging the liquid asset mix? And does the greater yield bring greater risks?

TOPIC LINKS

Follow the **Topic Links** in each chapter for your interactive Personal Finance exercise on the Web. Go to: **www.prenhall.com/frasca**.

Like the Steeles, many people do not seem overly concerned about managing liquidity. Perhaps they view liquid assets as a temporary reservoir that grows higher occasionally because they can't spend their incomes fast enough. Since these assets have a short "shelf life," why worry about achieving high relative returns? The money won't be there long enough to matter anyway.

This is a poor approach to liquidity management. What is needed is a **cash management strategy**, which is a plan determining how much cash to hold, in what form, and in which financial institutions. This chapter discusses the important aspects of cash management.

> **Cash management strategy** A plan determining how much cash to hold, in what form, and in which financial institutions.

Meeting Cash Needs

Few of us hold the same amount of cash. One person's income might be far greater than another's, and some people are financially more conservative than others. Despite such differences, people share some common characteristics that determine their cash needs. And to satisfy them, most of us keep some pocket money and hold the rest of our cash in checking or savings accounts.

Why Hold Cash?

There are three reasons why people hold cash: to undertake transactions, to have a cash reserve in case of an emergency, and to have a temporary store of value. We will examine each of them.

Undertake Transactions

Each day you make small transactions. You may buy lunch at the cafeteria or perhaps you stop at a vending machine to buy a candy bar or some other item. It takes cash—specifically, **pocket money** (coins and currency)—to do these things. How much pocket money do most people have on hand? Normally, they keep enough to get through a week or two; so, if you spend an average of $10 a day, you might cash a check each week for $70. Or if you have access to an automated teller machine (ATM), you can use your bank card to make withdrawals, and this method is usually more convenient than cashing a check. Actually, it is convenience, along with safety, that dictates how much pocket money to have on hand: The more convenient it is to get it, the less you need to hold. Since pocket money is easily lost or stolen, it is usually worthwhile to put up with some inconvenience to keep your balance low.

> **Pocket money** Coins and currency a person holds.

These inconveniences lead most people to open a **checking account** to pay larger monthly bills, such as rent or utilities. You wouldn't want the risk of losing currency in the mail or the inconvenience of visiting the creditor just to pay the bill in cash. Moreover, a canceled check serves as evidence of having paid the bill. The advantages of checking accounts so heavily outweigh their disadvantages that a much larger portion of our total liquid assets is held in them than in coins and currency. Checks account for more than 80 percent of the dollar value of all transactions.

> **Checking account** Funds held with a financial institution and available upon demand.

Emergency Reserves

In addition to needing cash for everyday transactions, most people want to hold a portion of their assets in liquid form in case of emergencies. An illness, the loss of a job, or any other unfortunate event can severely strain a family's budget, and without some liquid assets, a family could be forced to sell other assets, such as their house or automobile, to

Emergency reserves Liquid deposits held to meet unexpected cash needs.

meet daily living expenses. While most people agree that some cash should be held for **emergency reserves**, *how much* should be held isn't clear. Individual circumstances must dictate the amount. If you have disability income insurance or other protection that would maintain your income at close to its previous level while you are unemployed, you need a smaller emergency reserve than does someone whose income stops altogether. Also important is the amount of medical insurance carried: The more you have the less cash you need. Many financial planners recommend a reserve equivalent to three to six months' after-tax income; so if you take home $3,000 a month, a reserve of $9,000 to $18,000 is suggested. Remember, though, this is only a rule of thumb.

Since emergency reserves are not intended to be used for making transactions, they should be held in deposits that offer the highest potential return consistent with reasonable liquidity. Holding them in a checking account that pays no interest, for example, would be a mistake.

Store of Value

You may be saving to make a major purchase in the future: a house, an automobile, a computer, or a vacation. Until you have enough money, you need to save each pay period and then hold your savings in a form that will earn a return. You should be aware, though, that if you are holding funds for a fairly long period of time, the return on your deposits may not match the inflation rate on the item you are saving to buy. In this case, the deposit would not serve well as a store of value. It is important to balance earnings against liquidity in your savings effort; to achieve your target you may have to sacrifice some liquidity to capture a higher return.

In addition to saving for a major purchase, some people hold cash balances as temporary "parking places" for their money. They really plan to reinvest their funds in less liquid investments in the future but are waiting for the investment environment to improve. Whatever the motive for holding cash, it must be held in specific kinds of deposits, to which we now turn our attention.

Fundamental Deposits

Many people meet their cash needs by holding deposits in checking accounts and passbook savings accounts. These are the basic deposits, but other types are often used as well. Table 5.1 shows frequently used deposits and grades them in terms of availability, safety, liquidity, and yield. We will explain these deposits in this section and the next, but first, remember that what makes a deposit liquid is your ability to withdraw it easily, with no delays or other complications, and your ability to withdraw it with *no loss in principal*. This last feature rules out many kinds of investments for serving liquidity needs. Common stocks, for example, can be sold quickly and relatively inexpensively—but there is never a guarantee they can be sold without loss, so they fail the liquidity test. Some of the deposits examined later are much more liquid than others. Certificates of deposit are the least liquid because of interest penalties for early withdrawal.

Closely related to the issue of losing principal is the question of safety. Many depositors view safety as their most crucial concern because a large portion of their total investments may be in liquid accounts. Certainly a major advantage of holding deposits in most banks, savings and loans, and credit unions is the availability of federal insurance.

Indeed, the failures of major financial institutions in the past clearly indicate that you could make a tragic mistake by using a nonfederally insured institution. Be sure, then, to look for the following abbreviations when opening an account:

TOPIC LINKS

Current rates on savings assets.

- *FDIC* (Federal Deposit Insurance Corporation)—insures commercial banks

Table 5.1
A Scorecard for Liquid Deposits and Accounts

Deposit	Availability	Safety	Liquidity	Yield (average rate)[a]
Regular checking account	A+ (no or small minimum less than $100)	A+	A+	F (0.0%)
Interest–bearing checking account	A (small minimum about $400–$500 to open an account, much larger minimum to avoid fees)	A+	A+	D (.50%)
Savings account	A+ (no minimum)	A+	B+	D (.50%)
Money market deposit account	C (fairly large minimum)	A+	B+	B– (3.66%)
Money market mutual fund	B+ (minimum varies)	A to C (depending on securities held)	A+ to B (depending on check writing privileges)	B+ (4.98%)
Certificates of deposit (CDs)	A (minimum varies)	A+	C (early withdrawal penalties)	A (5.30%)[b]
Series EE bonds	A (small minimum)	A+	B	B– (3.40%)

[a]Approximate rates at August 1, 2007. Rates vary considerably within and among regions, making comparative shopping very important. Helpful information can be found at **www.bankrate.com/**.

[b]On 60–month CDs; longer maturities offer higher rates, shorter maturities less.

- *SAIF* (Savings Association Insurance Fund)—insures savings and loans and mutual savings banks
- *NCUA* (National Credit Union Administration)—insures credit unions

It's important to know also that insurance is provided up to $100,000 for the *depositor*, not for the deposit. So, if you are fortunate enough to have more than $100,000, you should open a second account with a different institution, or you could make additional deposits with the same institution in another person's name. There is a higher $250,000 limit on certain retirement accounts held at banks and credit unions. In addition, on joint accounts each co-owner's share is insured up to $100,000. This is separate from the coverage on individual accounts. A husband and wife have individual accounts and a joint account could be insured up to $400,000 at a single bank.

Checking and NOW Accounts

Checking and NOW accounts are used primarily to satisfy transaction needs. While there is a slight technical difference between a regular checking and a **NOW (negotiated order of withdrawal) account**, for all practical purposes they are identical. The major difference to you is that a NOW account pays interest on balances in the account, whereas a regular checking account does not. Most banks advertise their NOW accounts with names such as *Checking Plus* or *Checking Plus More*, to indicate that interest is earned on the account. The interest may be paid in several ways. Amounts below the minimum earn interest at a relatively low rate, and amounts above the limit earn higher rates. The higher rates are usually pegged to current money market rates, which means the interest you receive depends on the level of interest rates in general; as they go up, so does the amount earned. Of course, the reverse is also true.

NOW (negotiated order of withdrawal) account Interest-earning checking account, usually with a minimum balance requirement.

If you can meet the minimum balance requirement of a NOW account, it is usually the best choice. However, get complete information on all accounts the bank offers before making a choice. Then compare their benefits and costs.

Savings Accounts

Savings account Account with virtually no restrictions but with no check writing privileges.

Many Americans have had a **savings account** at one time or another. Savings accounts used to be known as passbook accounts because a record of your activity in the account was recorded in a passbook. Today these books are mostly replaced by the type of statements used for checking accounts. However, the rate of interest earned on savings accounts is still called the **passbook rate**. Because these accounts require no minimum balances, they are used frequently when only small deposits can be made. The passbook rate is generally the lowest rate of interest available, and it may be to your advantage to invest funds in alternative liquid accounts if you have enough cash to qualify for one. Comparison shopping may work to your advantage, even with savings accounts. For example, your credit union might offer a higher rate than your bank or savings and loan.

Passbook rate Interest rate on a savings account; usually the lowest savings rate offered by a financial institution.

Other Deposits

In addition to checking and savings accounts, investors have access to a variety of other deposits. These are explained briefly in the following sections.

Money Market Deposit Accounts

Money market deposit account (MMDA) Savings account with an interest rate that is tied to money market rates of interest.

Money market deposit accounts (MMDAs) offer current money market rates and easy access through check writing privileges, usually limited to three checks (or six transfers in total) a month. Federal depository insurance also enhances their appeal, as does access through ATMs. Unfortunately for small depositors, they have minimum deposit balances.

Money Market Mutual Funds

Money market mutual fund Pooling arrangement that invests in money market securities having very large denominations.

Money market mutual funds pool the resources of many investors to purchase short-term securities issued by the U.S. Treasury, large commercial banks, and financially strong corporations (more information about mutual funds is provided in Chapter 12). Since most of these investments are very safe, so too are the money market mutual funds that invest in them. Nevertheless, your deposit is not insured as it is in a money market account or other federally insured deposit. All money market mutual funds have a minimum balance requirement and a minimal withdrawal requirement, which is usually $1,000, although some are as low as $500.

Certificates of Deposit

Certificate of deposit (CD) Savings account with a set maturity and restricted access to funds until maturity.

Certificates of deposit (CDs) are somewhat different from money market deposit accounts or money market mutual funds. When you buy CDs, in effect you are freezing your money for the maturity of the deposit, which can vary from seven days to eight years, or even longer. For instance, a 60-month deposit of $1,000 might be purchased to yield 6 percent. At the end of 60 months you will get $1,338.23, which is the principal plus interest (assuming annual compounding). But suppose you need the money before the 60 months' end. You will then pay an interest penalty, the amount depending on when withdrawal takes place. A very early withdrawal can mean you get less back than your initial deposit. Naturally, this penalty discourages investors from using these deposits indiscriminately to obtain higher rates. The interest rate at the time of purchase is locked in for the entire term of the deposit. If interest rates fall during that period, you benefit by having your money invested at the higher rate. But if interest rates rise, the certificates will have been a poor choice.

U.S. Series EE Bonds

U.S. Series EE bonds are intermediate-term investments, particularly for small investors. There is a three-month penalty for cashing in EE bonds before they are five years old, which makes them ill-suited for short-term needs. Each May and November the U.S. Treasury sets a rate on new issues equal to 90 percent of the rate on five-year Treasury securities. The Treasury guarantees that at the end of 20 years they will double in value.

The interest you earn on Series EE bonds is free of state and local income taxes and can be deferred for federal income tax purposes until you redeem them. Moreover, federal income taxes may be avoided altogether if interest on the bond is used to pay for a child's college or vocational education. This exclusion phases out at upper incomes. More information is available at the IRS Web site. Clearly, this possible avoidance of taxes on Series EE bonds makes them very attractive.

Interest is earned on the Series EE bond by redeeming it for an amount greater than what was paid to purchase it. Another important consideration in purchasing Series EE bonds is their widespread availability. They can be bought or redeemed directly from the government or at most federally insured commercial or mutual savings banks or savings and loans.

U.S. Series EE bonds
Treasury-issued bonds with indexed interest rates, low denominations, and other attractive features.

U.S. Series I Bonds

You can lock in a fixed rate with Series EE bonds, but that fixed rate might be worth much less than you expect because of rising prices. I bonds provide inflation protection. They are inflation-indexed savings bonds, whose redemption values adjust semiannually to reflect the rate of inflation in the previous six months. I bonds grow at what is termed the "composite rate," which is determined by a fixed rate set at the time of issue and the inflation rate. The composite rate changes every six months. Here's how the composite rate for I bonds issued May 2007–Oct. 2007 was set:

Fixed rate = 1.30%
Semiannual inflation rate = 1.21%
Composite rate = [Fixed rate + (2 × Semiannual inflation rate) +
                  (Fixed rate × Semiannual inflation rate)]
Composite rate = [0.0130 + (2 × 0.0121) + (0.0130 × 0.0121)]
Composite rate = [0.0130 + 0.0242 + 0.0001573]
Composite rate = [0.0373573]
Composite rate = 0.0374
Composite rate = 3.74%

I Bonds have the same tax advantages as EE Bonds, such as being free of state and local taxes on interest, federal income tax deferral, and possible avoidance if the bonds are used to finance a child's higher education, and widespread availability at banks and other financial institutions. Also, as with Series EE Bonds, interest is not paid to you but rather accumulates in the bond's redemption value and there is an interest penalty if cashed in before five years.

So, should investors rush out and buy as many of the new bonds as they are allowed in any calendar year (a separate limit on Series EE and I bonds of $5,000 in Treasury Direct purchases and $5,000 in paper bonds purchases)? Maybe not. Suppose the fixed rate on I bonds was 2 percent versus 5 percent on noninflation adjusted bonds. Now you must forecast future inflation rates. If you think that inflation is likely to average more than 3 percent a year, take the indexed bond; in the reverse case, the nonindexed bonds are a better choice. As usual, making a personal financial decision is not easy.

U.S. Series HH Bonds

The Treasury no longer issues Series HH bonds. We mention them here since previously issued bonds are still outstanding. If you own some you should consult your local bank for advice on whether to hold or sell them. Their current interest rate of 1.5 percent makes them unattractive.

Treasury Direct

You can open an account at **www.treasurydirect.gov** that will allow you to purchase savings bonds and other government securities directly from the government. With a Treasury Direct account you can move funds electronically between your local bank account and treasury securities. The minimum account value is $1,000. Once you have an account, you can buy and sell government securities without brokerage or transactions fees that would be charged by a private investment service. You can participate in auctions for treasury bills with maturities of less than one year, treasury notes with maturities of two to ten years, and treasury bonds with longer term maturities. Through Treasury Direct you can redeem your government securities at maturity for no charge. Treasury Direct will even handle a sale of your investments before maturity for a small fee.

TOPIC LINKS

TreasuryDirect Savings
Bond Calculator

Using Your Checking Account

The convenience of paying bills by checks, rather than with cash, was noted earlier in this chapter. Maintaining a checking account properly, however, involves some work. Care must be taken in making deposits and writing checks, and it is important to keep an adequate balance in the account, both to avoid overdrafts and to stay above any minimum that applies to the account. In addition, each month the bank will provide a statement of activity in the account, which you should reconcile with your activity records to ensure that neither you nor the bank has made a mistake. The first order of business, though, is to select a bank. We use the term **bank** to refer to any financial institution that offers checking account services. These can be commercial banks, savings and loans, mutual savings banks, or credit unions.

Bank Any financial institution offering checking account services.

Selecting a Bank

A variety of factors usually determines your choice of a bank. Perhaps the most important of these is convenience, but also consider the range of services provided by the bank. Finally, you must evaluate what the bank charges to service the account and what it offers in interest on average balances. Shop around to find a checking account that fills your needs best.

Geographic Convenience

Depositors often cite geographic convenience as an important factor in choosing one bank over another. Although many transactions can be made indirectly through such means as preauthorized savings or bill payments, people nevertheless still conduct most of their banking business by direct contact with the bank. They visit it frequently to cash checks, make deposits, pay off loans, and so forth. It's not surprising, then, that geographic convenience and hours of operation still matter the most. But closely related to the geographic convenience of the main office and branches is the existence of automated teller machines at convenient locations and Internet access to your banking information. Finally, conve-

finance news 5.1

Electronic Check Conversion

You hand the clerk a check. The check is run through a machine that marks it void and the clerk hands it back to you. You wonder what just happened. Does the clerk know what he is doing? Has your check just been rejected? Can you leave the store without being arrested?

Don't be alarmed. Your written check has just been converted into an electronic deduction from your checking account. The merchant uses the information on your check to receive an electronic payment from your account. Your paper check is not processed as a check. Instead, the payment is debited from your account as an electronic fund transfer. You must receive notice of the conversion. There may be a posted notice in the store or you may be asked to sign a written agreement. The merchant should mark the check void and return it to you. When paying through the mail, the original check may be simply destroyed.

The number from the voided check will not be listed on your monthly bank statement. Instead, you will see an electronic transfer to the merchant. Your store receipt and your bank statement should contain enough information to serve as proof of payment. Your transaction is protected under the Electronic Funds Transfer Act. Have your bank investigate any electronic fund transfers you believe are unauthorized or incorrect. You have 60 days from the day your statement was mailed to notify your bank of a potential problem. After that, you could be out of luck.

A merchant does not have to accept your check. If you don't want your check to be used for electronic check conversion, the salesperson may be willing to accept some other form of payment such as a credit card or cash. For additional information see the "When Is Your Check Not a Check?" at the Federal Reserve Board Web site: **http://www.federalreserve.gov/pubs/checkconv/**.

nience and courtesy at the bank will probably influence your choice to open or keep an account there. Drive-in window facilities are obviously important to many of us, judging by the long lines of automobiles we often see at banks.

Bank Services

As Figure 5.1 shows, full-service banks and many other institutions now offer a wide array of services to their depositors. You might notice the items of convenience, such as the arrangements available for paying bills and transferring funds.

Service Charges and Earned Interest

Competition among banks has led to significant differences in service fees and interest paid on deposits. So comparative shopping is essential. There is little reason to pay any fee, no matter how small, for a service when you can get the same service free elsewhere. However, if a bank's charges are low for some services, they might be high for others. Decide which services are important and then do your shopping. A study by Bankrate.com found that the average monthly fee for a noninterest checking account is about $3 and an interest earning checking account is about $10.

Checking Account Procedures

Using a checking account is a relatively simple process if you are careful. Once an account is opened, you will make periodic deposits to increase your balance, and you will draw it down by writing checks. A record of these transactions is kept in a check register, which may be a journal but is more often simply stubs to the checks written. Regardless of what forms are used to keep records, it is a good idea to take a little extra time to record all pertinent data. Very often a check is written in haste at a crowded checkout line, for example, and the stub is left for your memory to fill in later. Unfortunately, memories fade with time, particularly with respect to the exact amount of the check, and after several such instances,

Figure 5.1
A Partial List of Services
Offered by a Large
Midwestern Bank

Savings/Investing
· Passbook accounts
· Money market deposit accounts
· Certificates of deposit—maturities of one week to 10 years
· Savings reserve, to protect against accidental overdrafts
· IRAs
· Mutual funds
· Annuity products
· Brokerage services

Loans
· Personal loans—autos, trucks, recreational vehicles, home improvements
· Business loans—lines of credit, term loans
· Mortgage loans—business and residential (conventional, FHA, VA)

Major Credit Cards
· American Express Gold Card/Executive Credit
· MasterCard/Visa

Other Services
· Internet banking
· Bill-paying services
· Automated teller machines
· Safe deposit boxes
· Trust services
· Business services—payroll, accounting, leasing, direct deposit
· Preauthorized savings—automatic transfers from checking to savings
· Direct deposit of retirement checks (Social Security, Civil Service,
  or Railroad Retirement)
· Direct deposit of payroll checks
· Wire transfers
· Bank by mail
· Money orders, cashier's checks, traveler's checks
· Utility payments

you'll have no idea how much is in the account. Along with filling out the stub completely as the check is written, it is also a good idea to earmark certain expenditures if they have particular importance. For example, many people use a check mark or other symbol to identify tax-deductible expenses. This identification helps when filing next year's tax return.

You may also keep a check register on your computer. Most checking software allows you to earmark expenses and will automatically tally you expenditures by categories. This is only helpful if you make a practice of entering whatever data you have in your paper register into your electronic register. Almost all banks provide online access to information on your accounts and many banking sites allow you to download data from your bank into a compatible software program that will automatically reconcile your check register with your bank statement.

Opening the Account

Opening a checking or savings account requires nothing more than filling out a simple signature card. If a joint account is opened, both (or all) signatures are required. It's important to use your legal name on any account. A married couple should consider a joint account rather than separate accounts for several reasons. First, the monthly service charges on two accounts are generally higher than for just one account. Second, and more important, if one of the spouses were to die, the funds in a joint account would pass immediately to the remaining spouse. This right of survivorship is associated with most bank accounts. However, in some states a joint account that does not specifically state **right of survivorship** will presume that **tenants in common** applies, in which case the survivor receives only his or her share of the account. Be sure to inquire about right of survivorship when you open an account.

Making Additional Deposits and Endorsing Checks

Making deposits to a checking account is a regular activity. These deposits consist of currency, coins, and checks written to you. Deposits are made with a deposit slip, such as the one shown in Figure 5.2. Note that the deposit is for $600, consisting of $100 in currency and a check for $500. The arrangement of numbers 01-4/435 is the bank transit number on the check deposited. This number is of no particular importance to you, but it is used in the Federal Reserve's check-clearing process, and it should be listed carefully to help this process. Also, use a separate line for each check deposited even if all the checks are from the same bank.

Checks can be endorsed (signed on the back) in three different ways, as shown in Figure 5.3. You use a **blank endorsement** when withdrawing cash from the account, but remember that once you sign a check it becomes a negotiable instrument and can be used as such by anyone. If you happen to lose the check, all the finder needs to do is sign it under your signature and cash it. As a safeguard, don't sign the check until you are at the

Right of survivorship An owner of an account has access to all funds upon the death of a co-owner.

Tenants in common An owner of an account has a legal claim only to his or her share of an account upon the death of a co-owner.

Blank endorsement Unrestricted endorsement of a check; anyone possessing the check can cash it.

Figure 5.2
A Deposit Slip

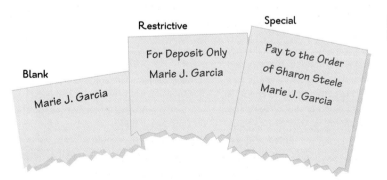

Figure 5.3
Ways to Endorse a Check

Restrictive endorsement Limits the use of a check to a single purpose, usually to make a deposit.

Special endorsement Using a check to pay a third party.

bank and ready to make the withdrawal. A **restrictive endorsement** limits the use of the check to a single purpose. "For deposit only" is written on a check when it is deposited by mail. If the check is lost in the mail and subsequently found, it cannot be cashed. A **special endorsement** is used when you use the check to pay someone else. All that you need do is indicate the payee and sign, as shown in Figure 5.3. It is usually not a good idea to pay bills in this manner, however, since you will not have a record of the payment unless you take the time to make one. Remember, the check will be returned to the person who issued it, not to you.

Writing Checks

Writing a check is a simple procedure, as illustrated in Figure 5.4. As mentioned earlier, the stub should be filled in at the same time the check is written, and, naturally, they should agree. Your account number is printed on the bottom of the check, as well as on the deposit slip. This number identifies the account and is needed whenever inquiries about the account are made. As a safeguard, the amount of the check is indicated numerically and in written form. Be particularly careful about the written amount because it is the legally binding figure. Also, your signature should appear exactly as you signed the signature card to open the account.

"Bouncing a Check"

The "float" is the amount of time between when you write a check and the amount is deducted from your account. It is unwise to write a check with insufficient funds in the hope of depositing the necessary funds in your account before the check clears. With the new electronic banking checks can clear rapidly.

Overdraft (bounced check) A check lacking sufficient funds to cover it.

If you happen to write a check without sufficient funds to cover it, you will have an **overdraft**, commonly referred to as a **bounced check**. It's an expensive oversight, since most banks charge about $30 for each such check. Moreover, it can lead to a poor credit rat-

saving money 5.2

Check Cashing—Your Bank Wants a Piece of the Action

What does Wells Fargo (a major U.S. bank) and Cash America International (a pawnshop operator) have in common? They have formed an alliance to bring check-cashing services through vending machines in grocery and convenience stores. This union is further evidence that major banks plan to tap into a very lucrative market, one they had disdained in the past as perhaps too "seamy" for blue-blooded bankers.

Well, the lure of huge profits is enough to make any banker rethink his or her bloodlines. But what's good for bankers and pawnshops is definitely very bad for the rest of us. Consider that the going charge to cash a check (most often a payroll check) is 2 to 3 percent of the check amount plus transaction fees. The Consumer Federation of America found that the average charge of 2.44 percent has increased significantly over the last few decades. Let's take the 2 percent figure, ignore the transac-

tion fee, and assume that you cash a $500 check each week. That's $10 a week or $520 a year. Of course, what you really have here is a perpetual short-term loan of $490 (the interest is paid in advance), and the annual rate of interest is about 106 percent a year! Even the Shylock in *Get Shorty* would go for this deal.

As banks probe more deeply into the market, they have learned that many customers are not poor; indeed, Fisca (a check-cashers trade group) reports that 60 percent of them have accounts at banks or credit unions. Why incur such an exorbitant expense for cash? Convenience. Apparently, we like to get our cash when it's convenient for us, not for bankers. We sometimes want it at night or on weekends.

Once in a while we all slip and find ourselves short on cash. Look at the outrageous fee, then, as the price of forgetfulness. It won't break our budget or put us in the poorhouse. But, if we use check cashers on a routine basis, we're certainly heading for trouble and might as well forget the budget.

Figure 5.4
A Sample Check

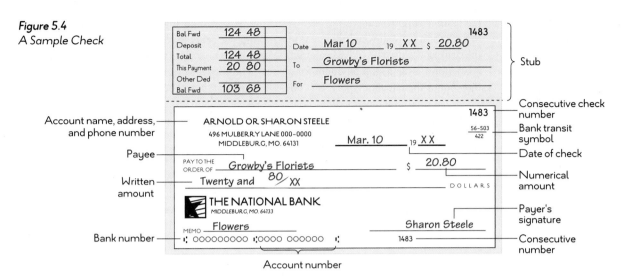

ing. Either of these factors should motivate you to balance your account accurately on a timely basis. After writing one or two overdrafts, some people go to the opposite extreme and keep an excessive balance to avoid the problem in the future. But this practice is costly if the account does not pay interest. Another precautionary step is to arrange a savings reserve that ties the checking account to a savings account and automatically transfers funds from the latter to the former whenever an overdraft takes place. Although this arrangement is better than "overloading" the checking account, it too has a drawback if interest earned on the savings account is only at the passbook rate. You might get a better rate than this in another account. A third alternative is to prearrange for a loan that will cover the overdraft. This is known as overdraft protection. You avoid the merchant's return check fee, but it is still the worst alternative. The bank will charge you a fee on each bounced check and interest on the cash advance at your credit card rate, which is usually at least 16 percent.

Availability of Funds

Current federal law requires all banks to comply with the following standards in making funds available after deposits have been made to the account: Cash, wire transfers, government checks, cashier's checks, and certified checks must be available on the next business day. Checks written on a local bank or other local financial institution must be available two business days after the deposit day, and checks written on a nonlocal financial institution must be available five business days after the deposit day. However, in some situations, a bank may hold the funds for longer periods. It is a good idea to check your bank's policy if you intend to write checks against a current deposit.

Stopping Payment on a Check

Sometimes it's necessary to stop payment on a check already issued. Perhaps you paid someone for merchandise and after inspection found it defective or incomplete. You simply go to the bank and fill out a form, called a **stop-payment order**, directing the bank not to pay the check. You are charged for this service, so it shouldn't be used casually. It's a better idea to delay payment by charging the purchase on your credit card. Then, if you are not satisfied with the service or merchandise you can protest the charge on the credit card.

You may not have to issue a stop-payment order for a lost or stolen check. Contrary to what you may have heard, such checks are the bank's responsibility and not yours; that is,

Stop-payment order
Directive to a bank not to pay a check.

the bank is supposed to verify your signature before honoring a check. However, you may incur liability if you were negligent in handling your checks. So, to avoid problems, inform the bank and close the old account while opening a new one (which may involve a charge). Also, don't issue a stop payment for a check you forgot to sign. Let it process and the bank may honor the check anyway. If it doesn't, write another check to the payee.

End-of-Month Activities

At the end of each month, the bank will send you a monthly statement showing all transactions the bank has recorded in your account. It is important to reconcile this statement each month, both to update and audit your records for accuracy and to make sure the bank hasn't made a mistake.

Bank Reconciliation

Bank reconciliation End-of-month analysis comparing the cash balance per bank statement with the cash balance per checkbook.

A **bank reconciliation** means that the end-of-month balance as shown on the bank statement is the same as the end-of-month balance shown in the check record. Figures 5.5, 5.6, and 5.7 illustrate the steps in the reconciliation process. Figure 5.5 shows the stubs from a

Figure 5.5
Sample Check Stubs

Figure 5.6
Sample Bank Statement

THE NATIONAL BANK

ARNOLD OR SHARON STEELE
496 MULBERRY LANE
MIDDLEBURG, MO 64131

YOUR BANKING NO.   211 4003

STATEMENT PERIOD	PAGE
FROM 2/04/XX TO 3/07/XX	1

CHECKING

TYPE	PREVIOUS BALANCE	DEPOSITS & CREDITS		CHECKS & DEBITS		NOW INTEREST	SERVICE CHARGE	CURRENT BALANCE
		NUMBER	AMOUNT	NUMBER	AMOUNT			
FREE&EASY 02	384.18		600.08	1	601.70		2.00	382.48

DAY	AMOUNT	CHECK NO. OR DESCRIPTION	DAY	AMOUNT	CHECK NO. OR DESCRIPTION	DAY	AMOUNT	CHECK NO. OR DESCRIPTION
07	2 00	SERVICE CHARGE						
05	52 60	1483						
08	16 80	1484						
18	35 30	1485						
24	600 00	DEPOSIT						
25	495 00	1487						

Figure 5.7
A Bank Reconciliation

To balance your checking account:

Step 1 Subtract from your checkbook balance all charges or other transfers that are shown in the checking section on the front of the statement such as Service Charges, Automatic Transfers, Reorder of Checks, or Others. Your Checking Plus Loan Payment is shown in the bottom right section on the front of your banking statement. Subtract only the payment amount from your checkbook balance. Add your NOW Account Interest to your checkbook balance.

Step 2 Compare checks shown on this statement to your checkbook records and list checks outstanding by dollar amount.

Step 3 Enter Current Balance shown on this statement. $ ___382.48___

Add Deposits made after Statement Period. $ ___—___

Total $ ___382.48___

Subtract total of checks outstanding. $ ___250.00___

Step 4 This Balance should agree with your checkbook. $ ___132.48___

Checks Outstanding		
Date or No.	1486	$ 220.00
	1488	30.00
Total	$	250.00

series of checks, numbers 1483 through 1488, written from the account. Note that the running balance is maintained and that the end-of-month balance is $134.48. Figure 5.6 shows the bank statement sent to the depositor at the end of the month. A glance at it reveals several bits of information. First, the bank has deducted a service charge of $2, which wasn't known and, therefore, was not recorded up to now. So the first task is to reduce the book balance from $134.48 to $132.48. Second, you can see that of the six checks written during the month, only four have cleared; checks 1486 and 1488 are still outstanding. That is why the bank's balance is so much greater than the book balance. Figure 5.7 is a reconciliation form that appears on the back of this particular bank statement. By following steps 1 through 4, you should be able to reconcile the statement. Note that after the outstanding checks are deducted from the bank's balance, the book balance (after the service charge has been deducted) of $132.48 is confirmed. This reconciliation is a fairly simple one, since there are only six checks to review, no deposits in transit, and no other activity to make things more difficult. However, before you start to reconcile your statement, it is a good idea to compare each cleared check with the data recorded on the stub, because errors seem to occur no matter how carefully we try to keep our books. Cross-checking before you start to reconcile can prevent a headache later on if the two balances fail to agree after a first reconciliation attempt.

Checking account software can also guide you through this process. You may be able to download you account data from your bank directly into your software program. Your program may automatically attempt to match the checks in your register with the withdrawals from your account. Once you have approved the matches and corrected any other missing entries the program has discovered, it should automatically reconcile your account.

Your Bank Statement and Substitute Checks

After reconciliation, the bank statement can be filed for later reference or you can download a copy of your statement for storage on your computer. You probably will not receive your original canceled checks. You account agreement should indicate whether you receive originals or substitute checks, or simply images of your canceled checks. Banks are not required to return original checks and may charge you a fee for copies.

Banks now save time and money by exchanging substitute checks electronically, rather than the originals. A law called "Check 21" governs the use of substitute checks. A substitute check is a digital picture of your original check that can be electronically transmitted. Not all copies of your original check are substitute checks. A photocopy or a copy you download from the Internet is not a substitute check. A substitute check is specially formatted for bank processing. Images of multiple checks you may receive with your bank statement are not substitute checks.

A substitute check is the legal equivalent of the original check and can be used as proof of payment just as you would use the original cancelled check. The bank may not make a payment from your account unless you authorize a withdrawal. If you receive a substitute check from your bank and believe there is an error, the law allows you to claim a refund known as an "expedited credit." If the bank believes your claim is valid you should receive your funds back within a relatively short time period. The bank must provide an explanation if your claim is rejected. For additional information on substitute checks visit the Federal Reserve's Web site at **www.federalreserve.gov/check21**.

Save the documents the bank returns to you or you download from the Internet. These items—not your check stubs or other documents that you generate—are necessary to support a claim that payment has been made. For example, the Internal Revenue Service requires these source documents, such as substitute checks, to support your personal income tax deductions.

Checks That Guarantee Payment

On occasion you may need a check that guarantees payment. Maybe you are buying something from a person who doesn't know you and is also not familiar with your bank. Conversely, there are instances when you want to be sure a check you are receiving will not bounce. There are three popular approaches to guaranteeing a check: have a personal check certified, buy a cashier's check, or buy traveler's checks.

Certified Check

A person can take a personal check to his or her bank and ask to have it certified, making it a **certified check**. This means that the bank will verify that sufficient funds are in the account to cover the check. After this verification, the bank deducts the amount of the check from the account, making the funds immediately available to the payee. A certification is then stamped on the check.

Certified check Bank verification that a payer has sufficient funds to cover a specific check.

Cashier's Check

People without checking accounts often use a **cashier's check** to pay bills. Such a check is also used when the amount involved is very large. It is written by a bank against itself and is accordingly much more acceptable than a personal check. There is a small service charge for a cashier's check unless you are a special customer to the bank, in which case the charge might be waived. Counterfeit cashier's checks, unfortunately, have become a convenient vehicle for Internet fraud. Typically, the victim receives a cashier's check for more than the item being sold on the Internet, with the request that the excess be wired back to the buyer. The counterfeit check fools the teller who credits the victim's account for the amount of the fraudulent check. When the bank discovers the check is counterfeit, it reclaims the funds from the victim's account. The victim loses both the merchandise and the excess amount wired to the fraudulent buyer.

Cashier's check A check issued by a bank against itself.

Traveler's Checks

A **traveler's check** is generally used when you are traveling, although they have become less important since credit cards are now readily accepted abroad. These checks can be purchased at any bank or other financial institution in denominations that usually range from $10 to $100. At the time you buy these checks, you sign each one in the presence of a bank officer; later, when you cash one, you sign again in the presence of the person cashing it. The payees can thus compare signatures to guard against forgery.

Traveler's check Check purchased from a bank, generally used when traveling away from home.

Traveler's checks are protected against loss or theft. You get a small journal to record the check serial numbers and other pertinent information. It's a good idea to keep this journal somewhere other than where you keep the checks, since theft or loss of the checks must be reported to the bank to stop payment. Otherwise you may not know what specific checks are actually missing. Traveler's checks are accepted practically everywhere throughout the world. They are a wise purchase (some banks will provide them free) whenever you travel.

Electronic Banking and Debit Cards

Growing computer and electronics technologies have created important changes in the way banking transactions can be made. As previously mentioned, it's now possible to do much of your banking business on the Internet. Table 5.2 indicates that percentage of households that have taken advantage of the various electronic technologies. A 2007 study by the Federal Reserve indicates that the number of electronic payments has risen dramatically

Table 5.2
Percentage of Households
Using Selected Banking
Technologies: 2004

Electronic	Percent
Direct deposit of any type	74
ATM card	65
Debit card	61
Preauthorized debts	50
Automated phone system	20
Computer banking	34
Nonelectronic	
In person	78
Mail	51
Phone (talk in person)	42

Source: 2007 U.S. Statistical Abstract, Table 1166.

over the last few years. Electronic payments now account for twice as many noncash transactions as checks.

Automated teller machines (ATMs) Machines that perform certain banking functions.

Most of us are already familiar with **automated teller machines (ATMs)**. With them you use a plastic ID card and a personal access code to conduct a number of bank activities such as withdrawing cash (in limited amounts only), transferring funds from one account to another, or paying routine monthly bills. You may be able to withdraw funds from your account through a networked machine owned by another bank. Be aware that banks normally charge a fee for the use of their machines by non-account holders.

Your ATM card may also function as a debit card or what has also been called a check card. There is no float with a debit card. Debit cards are typically accepted at most gas stations and retail stores. When you use a debit card, funds are taken directly from your account. Debit cards are convenient to use for small transactions. Unfortunately, if you use your card for a lot of minor purchases you will probably lose track of how much you have in your checking account unless you enter these expenditures in your check register. Overdraw your account and you are likely to get hit with an over-the-limit fee of $35 or more.

You should exercise care in using an ATM because it is a fertile area for consumer fraud and theft. For example, don't leave your access card in the machine or in other unprotected places, and don't use obvious code numbers such as your street address or phone number. Your potential losses from a stolen debit card are capped at $50 by the Electronic Funds Protection Act if you notify the bank in less than two days and $500 if you notify the bank between 2 and 60 days. After that you could lose everything in your account.

Keep all receipts. You may need them if you want to dispute an incorrect debit. It is almost always better for you to pay with a credit card. As discussed in Chapter 6, your consumer protections are much better if you use a credit card and there are lower loss limits. The maximum you can be liable for a lost or stolen credit card is only $50 and you can stop payment on unsatisfactory merchandise. With a debit card there is no opportunity to deny payment because the funds are immediately withdrawn from your account.

Electronic funds transfer systems (EFTS) Electronic payment of bills and other transfers of cash.

Electronic funds transfer systems (EFTS) extend beyond ATM services and debit cards. You may have an arrangement whereby your payroll check is wired directly to your bank; or, if you are a retiree, you may receive your Social Security check through an electronic transfer. You also may arrange for automatic monthly withdrawals from your account for utility payments and loans. Although electronic banking lacks a personal touch, it does add convenience.

SIMPLIFYING
financial planning 5.3

Banking by Computer: A Bank That Never Closes

You may have heard the term "banker's hours." It was a term used to ridicule someone who only works a few hours. Well, the Internet has eliminated banker's hours. If your computer is linked to the Internet, you have access to an Internet bank that never closes. All major banks offer online Web sites where you can check your account balance, download your check statement, transfer funds between accounts and pay bills. If you want, you can download your banking data to add-on software, such as Intuit's Quicken or Microsoft Money. With personal management software you can reconcile your checking account and manage your budget electronically.

One big advantage of computerized banking is the ease of paying bills. With a PC, you pay bills by writing checks on the screen and clicking a payment box. Data for payees that you pay frequently, such as the telephone company, are stored on your computer or the online bank site. This means the next time you write a check to a vendor you don't have to enter the payee's information again. Your electronic check can be sent in one of two ways. You may have a service that actually writes a check and mails it to the payee for a small fee. Or the payee may have an electronic hookup to your bank, in which case the funds are simply transferred from your account to the payee's.

You don't have to use online banking to benefit from electronic services. You can set up an agreement with your broker or mutual fund manager to wire deposits to your bank account and withdraw funds to pay for investments. Through electronic funds transfer you can have your tax refund and most likely your paycheck directly deposited in your bank account. The benefit of online banking is that you easily and immediately check on those transfers to ensure they are correct.

There are additional advantages beyond the easy access to your banking information and check account reconciliation. When your banking software is one part of a more general personal finance software program, check payments can be automatically allocated according to expenditure categories. This will help you monitor the household budget and track expenses for tax purposes. Learning how to use the software will cost you time and money in the short-run. However, over the long-run the time saved updating your accounts and managing your budget may more than outweigh the short-run costs.

Understanding How Your Account Earns Interest

What does a financial institution mean when it offers to pay you, say, 12 percent interest on your account? On the surface, this looks like a simple enough calculation: If you put $1,000 in the account, in one year you would have $1,120, which is the initial $1,000 plus $120 ($0.12 \times \$1,000$) of earned interest. Simple as it seems, complications can arise if your account is structured differently from the one just mentioned, and many are.

One source of confusion in the simple interest calculation is that it assumes that interest is paid only once—at the very end of the year. But you probably have seen accounts that advertise interest paid weekly, daily, or even continuously. Do you earn more with these accounts? If so, how much more? To answer these questions we need to understand basic interest calculations. Suppose you make periodic deposits and withdrawals to and from an account. Will interest be earned on the deposit balance at the beginning of the month, at the end of the month, on the average for the month, or just when? Clearly, these questions, too, must be asked before you open an account.

How Interest Is Calculated

The actual interest dollars (I) earned on a deposit depend on three factors: the amount you invest (P); a stated interest rate (i), expressed in decimal form; and the length of time (t)

the deposit is held, expressed as a fraction or multiple of a year. This relationship is shown as follows:

$$\$I = (\$P)(i)(t)$$

Thus, in the earlier example we have

$$\$120 = (\$1,000)(0.12)(1)$$

If the deposit were held for only six months, then the interest earned would be

$$\$60 = (\$1,000)(0.12)\left(\frac{6}{12}\right)$$

The future value (FV) of any deposit is simply the sum of principal invested and interest earned; that is,

$$\$FV = \$P + \$I$$

The $FV for the deposit held 12 months is $1,120 ($1,000 + $120), and it is $1,060 ($1,000 + $60) for the six-month deposit. Which of these two deposits would you rather have? If you thought that at the end of six months you could take the $1,060 and reinvest it at a 12 percent annual rate for another six months, you would clearly prefer the two six-month deposits to the one 12-month. Why? To find out, calculate the $FV of the six-month deposit at the end of the second six months. You must first calculate $I, which is

$$\$63.60 = (\$1,060)(0.12)\left(\frac{6}{12}\right)$$

Then, $FV is $1,123.60 ($1,060 + $63.60). What you have determined is the future value of a deposit with a 12 percent stated interest rate (also called the *nominal rate*) *compounded semiannually*. In comparison with the annual compounding, it provided $3.60 more over the one-year holding period. From this illustration, you probably also recognize that the more often compounding takes place, the greater is the future value of any given deposit for any given stated interest rate. Table 5.3 shows future values for a $1,000 deposit and an 8 percent stated rate for various compounding periods, assuming the deposit is held for 1, 2, 4, 8, or 16 years. As you see, more frequent compounding leads to greater future values. The table also shows a fairly common phenomenon in compounding. Small differences compounded over a long period of time eventually become a big difference. For example, daily compounding added only $3.28 more than annual compounding for one year, but over 16 years the difference grows to $170.19 ($3,596.13 − $3,425.94). *Continuous compounding* may not be familiar to you. It assumes that interest is calculated even more frequently than every second of every day. It sounds impressive but, as Table 5.3 shows, it adds little above daily or weekly compounding.

Table 5.3
Future Values of $1,000 Invested at an 8 Percent Stated Rate with Interest Calculated for Selected Compounding Frequencies

Frequency of Compounding	Number of Years Deposit Is Held				
	1	2	4	8	16
Annually	$1,080.00	$1,166.40	$1,360.49	$1,850.93	$3,425.94
Semiannually	1,081.60	1,169.86	1,368.57	1,872.98	3,508.06
Quarterly	1,082.43	‘1,171.66	1,372.79	1,884.54	3,551.49
Weekly	1,083.22	1,173.37	1,376.79	1,895.55	3,593.11
Daily	1,083.28	1,173.49	1,377.08	1,896.35	3,596.13
Continuously	1,083.30	1,173.51	1,377.13	1,896.48	3,596.62

Determining Interest on Your Account

All savings accounts are not alike in the way interest is determined on your balance. Differences arise with respect to the length of time balances in the account are judged to qualify for earning interest. In some cases, if a deposit is not held for an entire quarter, it earns no interest at all, even if it was withdrawn on the very last day of the quarter. Four different methods are in general use: (*a*) day of deposit to day of withdrawal (or daily interest), (*b*) minimum balance, (*c*) FIFO (first in, first out), and (*d*) LIFO (last in, first out). Table 5.4 illustrates these four methods. It is assumed that a deposit of $1,000 is made on the first day of the quarter; another $1,000 is made on the 30th day; and a $900 withdrawal takes place on the 60th day. The account has a stated interest rate of 6 percent.

Most banks use the daily interest method. However, some do not, making it important for you to ask how your bank determines interest.

Cash Management Strategy

At the beginning of this chapter we said that the object of cash management is to minimize cash balances while maintaining an adequate level of liquidity. By now you can see that the problem is made more complex by the many forms of liquid deposits. No one would argue

Table 5.4
Quarterly Interest Earned Under Four Determination Methods with a 6 Percent Stated Interest Rate

Activity in the Account		
Day	**Deposit (Withdrawal)**	**Balance**
1	$1,000	$1,000
30	1,000	2,000
60	(900)	1,100
90	Closing	1,100

Interest Calculations

1. Day of deposit to day of withdrawal:
   a. $\$1,000 \times 30/360 \times 0.06 = \$\ 5.00$
   b. $\$2,000 \times 30/360 \times 0.06 = \$10.00$
   c. $\$1,100 \times 30/360 \times 0.06 = \underline{\$\ 5.50}$

   Total $\$20.50$

2. Minimum balance:
   $\$1,000 \times 90/360 \times 0.06 = \underline{\$15.00}$

3. FIFO:
   a. $\$\ 100 \times 90/360 \times 0.06 = \$\ 1.50$
   b. $\$1,000 \times 60/360 \times 0.06 = \underline{\$10.00}$

   Total $\$\ 11.50$

4. LIFO:
   a. $\$1,000 \times 90/360 \times 0.06 = \$15.00$
   b. $\$\ 100 \times 60/360 \times 0.06 = \underline{\$\ 1.00}$

   Total $\$\ 16.00$

FINANCIAL PLANNING *for*
young adults 5.4

Stored Value Cards: Don't Pay for a Picture

A recent but rapidly growing phenomenon is the use of stored value cards. Technically, these are debit cards that consumers use in a variety of ways, such as making purchases at retail outlets or withdrawing cash at ATMs; some value cards may also be recharged. Well over 1,000 companies now offer such cards to their employees, and the number is growing rapidly. The cards are convenient, particularly for transient workers or young adults who may not have checking or savings accounts, and who may find it difficult or expensive to cash a payroll check. For students living away from home, parents can reload the cards by direct deposit. Parents may prefer a stored value card over a credit card because it imposes a strict limit on the child's spending.

Another form of stored value cards is the gift card, which various companies issue as a substitute for the old form of gift certificate. These cards can be insidiously expensive. For example, there may be a transaction fee or a shipping fee. Equally bad, after a year or two, unused balances on the cards (called "breakage") are frequently confiscated by the issuer through steep monthly service charges. Recently Kmart settled a law suit brought by the Federal Trade Commission for not prominently advertising that its gift cards expired after a period of nonuse. Is it really worth giving a $50 gift card if a good part of it gets gobbled up in fees?

As with cash itself, you need to be careful with any stored value card. Anyone who finds a lost card may use it. Also, these cards could induce extra spending because of their convenience. Even worse, your card may become worthless if the issuing company goes into bankruptcy. This happened when Sharper Image announced that it was suspending the acceptance of gift cards because of a Chapter 11 bankruptcy. The Tower Group estimates that consumers could lose more than $75 million from store and restaurant closings in 2008.

A gift card is an interest-free loan that may not be repaid if the store goes under. When you purchase a gift card you are extending the store a loan at a zero rate of interest. You can do a lot better than that and earn a risk-free return by simply leaving your money in a savings account. Just think what $25 billion in a savings account could earn in one month. The National Retail Federation reports that this is close to the total value of gift cards purchased during the holiday season.

---

against keeping currency and coin holdings to a minimum, but differences of opinion arise over how other cash should be held. If you want to manage your cash actively rather than putting it all into one account, then you should follow these steps:

1. Resolve to your own satisfaction which direction you think interest rates will move in the planning period.

2. Obtain current information about various deposit accounts, particularly current interest rates and possible account restrictions.

3. Allocate your liquid funds among the accounts to satisfy your preferences for yield, safety, and liquidity.

Remember: The more yield you want, the less safety and liquidity you must take. These three aspects are brought together in the action plan for the Steele family, but we should keep in mind the instability of interest rates.

Interest Rate Volatility

The advent of money market funds introduced many of us to the volatile behavior of interest rates. Up to that time, most saving deposits were in passbook accounts with their virtually constant rates. Rates on money market funds will closely parallel the rates on short-term government securities. Figure 5.8 shows what has happened over approximately the last 20 years to government obligations with a six-month maturity. Short-term rates have declined from a peak of over 9 percent in 1989. However, it has been a bumpy downward

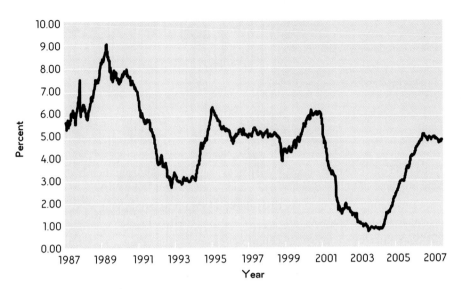

Figure 5.8
*6-Month Treasury Bill:
Secondary Market Rate*

Source: Federal Reserve
Economic Data,
http://research.stlouisfed.org/

ride, with local peaks above 6 percent in 1995 and 2000. Moreover, these peaks were not far from lows in 1993 of close to 3 percent and in 2004 of just less than 1 percent. Since this most recent low there has been an upward move with rates approaching 5 percent in 2007.

Such volatility in rates makes cash management very difficult. For example, when rates are low, there is a temptation to shift your money into higher-yielding accounts, such as two-year certificates of deposit, to "pick up" the higher yield. But doing that could be a mistake if rates then increase. It may be wise to always hedge your bets by not shifting too far in any direction.

TOPIC LINKS

Treasury bill rates over the past six years

key terms

automated teller machines (ATMs) (p. 132)
bank (p. 122)
bank reconciliation (p. 128)
blank endorsement (p. 125)
cash management strategy (p. 117)
cashier's check (p. 131)
certificate of deposit (CD) (p. 120)
certified check (p. 131)
checking account (p. 117)
electronic funds transfer systems (EFTS) (p. 132)
emergency reserves (p. 118)
money market deposit account (MMDA) (p. 120)

money market mutual fund (p. 120)
NOW (negotiated order of withdrawal) account (p. 119)
overdraft (bounced check) (p. 126)
passbook rate (p. 120)
pocket money (p. 117)
restrictive endorsement (p. 126)
right of survivorship (p. 125)
savings account (p. 120)
special endorsement (p. 126)
stop-payment order (p. 127)
tenants in common (p. 125)
traveler's check (p. 131)
U.S. Series EE bonds (p. 121)

follow-up on the Steele family

Reread the chapter-opening vignette.

A breakdown of the Steeles' $27,440 of liquid assets at December 31 appears on the next page.

The Steeles like to shop at flea markets and antique malls where purchases must often be made in cash. So, they typically keep about $2,000 or more in their checking account

Account	Amount
Coins and currency	$ 440
Regular checking	5,400
Savings account	10,600
60-month CDs	5,000
U.S. Series EE bonds	6,000
Total	$ 27,440

than would otherwise be necessary. Also, as you may recall from their budget in Chapter 3, there are three months—January, July, and August—that show negative cash flows.

1. Considering their income, does the total liquid asset amount of $27,440 seem adequate for the Steeles?

2. Is the Steeles' reason for keeping an excessive checking account balance sensible? Can you offer a better approach, assuming they will continue their shopping habits?

3. Assume that the deposit rates shown in Table 5.1 currently exist. How would you advise the Steeles to allocate the $27,440 among the various types of deposits? Show the specific amounts you suggest for each type of deposit. If you think the appropriate amount is zero, so indicate.

4. Hopefully, your plan created in your answer to Question 3 shows superior returns to the Steeles' existing arrangement. Show the enhanced yield, but also discuss whether or not your plan offers more or less safety and more or less liquidity.

problems and review questions

1. Explain the reasons for holding cash. How much pocket money (coins and currency) should most people hold? What advantages does a checking account have over pocket money?

2. List and briefly explain three fundamental deposits and five other popular types of deposits, ranking them according to availability, safety, and liquidity.

3. What is a *federally insured* deposit? Is deposit insurance important to you? Explain.

4. Explain all the advantages and disadvantages of U.S. Series EE and Series I bonds.

5. A local bank offers a "free" checking account if you maintain a minimum balance of $1,000. Is the account really free? Explain.

6. What institutions are "banks"? What makes an institution a bank, according to the text?

7. Discuss factors that should be considered in choosing a bank.

8. Identify or explain the following items:
   a. certificate of deposit
   b. bank
   c. right of survivorship
   d. bounced check
   e. stop-payment order
   f. certified check, cashier's check, traveler's check
   g. ATM
   h. EFTS

9. Explain three ways to endorse a check; explain which is the riskiest and why.

10. Explain what is meant by interest rate volatility and then discuss the risk of investing in CDs in periods of interest rate volatility.

11. Juan Mendez has just opened a savings account that pays interest at a 4 percent annual stated rate, compounded semiannually. If he puts $1,000 in the account, how much will he get back a year later? After he opened the account, Juan learned that another account was also available that quoted a rate of 4.25 percent, compounded annually; now he isn't sure whether he got the best deal. Did he?

12. Which method of determining interest is the most favorable to consumers?

case 5.1

Mark's First Checking Account

During his junior year in college, Mark Sutherland opened a checking account at the First National Bank of Westerly, Nebraska. His account does not have a minimum balance requirement, but he does pay a monthly service charge of $3. Mark has just received his first monthly bank statement and notices that the end-of-month balance on the statement is quite different from the end-of-month balance he shows in his check record. He has asked your help in explaining this difference and has provided you with the following bank statement and check record:

ACCOUNT: Mark J. Sutherland

ACCOUNT #:   43967   PERIOD: January 3, 2008 through January 31, 2008

Bank Statement of Activity This Month

Beginning Balance		Deposits and Other Credits to Your Account	Checks and Other Charges to Your Account	Ending Balance
	00.00	300.00	163.80	136.20
03	Deposit	300.00		
05	100	16.50		
07	101	20.00		
12	103	42.96		
14	104	16.87		
17	105	5.00		
17	106	11.43		
19	107	25.00		
24	108	14.04		
28	109	9.00		
31	Service Charge	3.00		

Mark's Check Record

Date	No.	Payee	For	Amount	Balance
1/3		Deposit		300.00	300.00
1/3	100	Harmon Foods	Food	16.50	283.50
1/4	101	Cash		20.00	263.50
1/5	102	VOID			
1/7	103	Mel's Sporting Goods	Gym shoes	42.96	220.54
1/10	104	Valley Cleaners	Dry cleaning	18.67	201.87
1/13	105	Sharon Mackey	Birthday present	5.00	196.87
1/14	106	University Bookstore	Supplies	11.43	190.44
1/14	107	Cash		25.00	175.44
1/19	108	Harmon Foods	Food	14.04	161.40
1/24	109	Mom	Repay loan	9.00	152.40
1/25	110	Poindexter's Cafe	Sharon's birthday party	20.00	132.40
1/26		Deposit		50.00	182.40
1/28	111	Exxon	Monthly statement	12.96	169.44

Questions

1. Reconcile Mark's account for him, and explain the difference between his balance of $169.44 and the bank's balance of $136.20.
2. How careful was Mark in keeping a record of his checking activities? Discuss.

case 5.2

Choosing Liquid Accounts for Marcia and Philip Helm

Marcia and Phil Helm have been married for several years. They have no children, and each has a professional career. Marcia is a trainee for a management position at a large department store, and Phil is an engineer at an electronics firm. Their careers have promising futures, but neither has exceptionally good income protection in the event of a layoff. The Helms have saved around $8,000, and $7,400 of it is in a 3.5 percent savings account at the credit union where Phil works. They have about $600 in a regular checking account (with Mid-City Bank) that doesn't have a service charge or monthly minimum requirement but also doesn't pay any interest. The Helms' combined take-home pay is about $5,000 a month, and Phil thinks they should take the $7,400 out of their savings and invest in the stock market to earn a better return. He points out that, excluding their life insurance policies, they have no other investments. Marcia thinks this plan might be too risky, but she does agree that the 3.5 percent yield is not very good. Recently, while at a party a friend suggested they take out certificates of deposit (CDs) with long maturities, since they were paying around 6 percent. The Helms liked her advice and stopped at Phil's credit union to get more information on the CDs. After talking with the office manager for a while, though, they became even more confused. He didn't favor CDs, although the union had them available. He pointed out that interest rates on the new money market accounts were around 4 percent and didn't require "freezing" your money for a year or more. He also indicated that the union could offer a super NOW account that would allow the Helms to close their current unproductive checking account with Mid-City. This account would give them unlimited check writing privileges with no service charges and would pay 3 percent interest; however, it would require a minimum balance of $2,500. If their balance went below the minimum in a month, interest would be only 2 percent.

The Helms left the credit union without taking any action. They have asked you for advice on managing their liquid deposits.

Questions

1. Do you feel the Helms' $8,000 liquid balance is adequate? Explain.
2. Explain the relative risks and potential advantages of CDs. Explain under what condition(s) you would recommend them for the Helms.
3. Do you agree with Phil that some of their funds should be invested in the stock market? Explain.
4. Prepare and defend a cash management plan that you think is most appropriate for the Helms.

working out on the Web

Exercises to Strengthen Your Use of the Internet
(Internet links for the following exercises can be found at **www.prenhall.com/frasca**.)

Exercise 5.1 How Can You Join a Credit Union?

If your employer does not have a credit union, you still may have an opportunity to join one. CUNA, the Credit Union National Association (**www.cuna.org**), provides information on joining a credit union at its consumer site (**www.creditunion.coop/how_to_join.html**).

Q. What are the seven ways to find a credit union?

Exercise 5.2 Where Can You Earn the Highest Returns on Your Cash Deposits?

Bankrate.Com (**www.bankrate.com**) helps you find financial institutions offering the highest yields on bank deposits, money market funds, and Treasury securities. Choose "CDs & Investments."

Q. Suppose you are helping your parents invest $80,000 over the next six months. Where can you get the highest return with a six-month CD in your state? Find the phone number of the offering institution, and then call to determine if the account has federal insurance.

Exercise 5.3 What Is the Trend in Short-Term Interest Rates?

Interest rates are often volatile over time. Economagic.com (**www.economagic.com/ fedbog.htm**) provides an array of interest rate data. This data can also be found at the Federal Reserve Board (**www.federalreserve.gov/releases**). You can use this site to examine the trend in financial data.

Q. What is the current trend in the one-year Treasury bill rate (constant maturity)?

Exercise 5.4 Can I Pay Bills over the Internet—and How Much Does It Cost?

You can use the Internet to pay bills. Many banks, such as Chase (**www.chase.com**) provide this service.

Q. Click "Site Map," and then scroll down to "On Services." What is the monthly fee for the Online Bill Payment feature? At this price, would you find this service useful?

Exercise 5.5 Finding Nominal and Effective Yields

The Mortgage Calculators Finance Center (mortgage-calculators.org) has several financial calculators. If you follow the link to the Calculators page and click the link for additional calculators you will find the "Nominal/effective rate" calculator.

Q. What is the effective yield on an account that compounds more frequently than once a year? Enter: $10,000 for future value, 1,000 for present value, 30 for years, and 1 for "Compound Periods Per Year." What are the nominal and effective rates? Now leave the other data the same, but change the compounding periods to 12 per year. What are the nominal and effective rates? Compare your answers. Repeat the process for 365 compounding periods per year. What inferences can you draw from your results?

6

Short-Term Credit Management

consumer credit

Objectives

1. To evaluate reasons for and against using credit and decide whether credit is appropriate for you
2. To be able to take the necessary steps to establish credit and develop a credit history
3. To identify what is meant by sales credit and how it is used
4. To understand how to use credit cards properly and to know your legal rights as a borrower against credit mistakes
5. To identify the important characteristics of installment loans
6. To compare the various sources of credit and to learn what to do if you experience credit problems

Steele family

"Just when you think everything is going fine, something comes along to upset your day," Sharon thought, as her car was towed away. A call from the mechanic brought more bad news. The transmission was shot and it would cost $4,000 to repair. The transmission was out of warranty; therefore, the Steeles would have to decide how to finance the payment. They thought the car was running fine and had not planned for this expense. They are not sure whether they should use their savings to pay for the repair or finance the expenditure. They have other major bills, such as property taxes coming due in the next few months. There is no way they could get by with just one car and a replacement would cost them

far more. The garage is promising them a lifetime guarantee on a new transmission.

Their credit card carries a substantial credit limit. They could charge the repairs to the credit card and pay it off over the next few months. However, the APR on the card is 18 percent, which seems high to the Steeles. The Steeles are also considering the sale of a few shares of stock, but this would trigger some capital gains taxes. Another option is to take out a temporary home equity loan. For a $50 application fee, Arnold's credit union will provide him with a $10,000 line of credit on his home equity. Amounts borrowed on this line of credit will carry an 8 percent APR.

TOPIC LINKS

Follow the **Topic Links** in each chapter for your interactive Personal Finance exercise on the Web. Go to: **www.prenhall.com/frasca**.

When you are faced with unexpected expenses, as the Steeles are, credit can be a useful tool for managing your expenses and your household budget. There are, however, unfortunate examples of those who have let credit work against them rather than for them. They find themselves in a vicious circle of increasing debt. With some care, credit can become a useful instrument in financial planning. Borrowing to purchase assets, such as a home, which are likely to increase in value, can be a wise investment strategy. On the other hand, borrowing to increase present consumption, or to purchase assets that will decrease in value, places a burden on our future ability to consume. Too much, and it can result in a vicious cycle, with an ever-increasing burden of obligations as we attempt to repay old debts with new loans.

All of us use credit in one form or another. When the paperboy or papergirl delivers your newspaper each day and stops by only at the end of the month to collect, he or she extends credit to you for the month's bill. The same is true for the local gas and electric company or any business that does not demand immediate payment for its product or service. Much of this credit—called **service credit**—we take for granted, probably because it is readily available and usually provided without cost. The forms of credit we are more aware of—sales credit and cash credit—are more difficult to obtain and often carry interest and other expenses; these forms of credit are the topics of this chapter.

Service credit Credit extended by the merchant from whom you have purchased the good or service.

Arranging and Using Credit

Before applying for credit, you should carefully consider why you want it and what possible disadvantages are connected with its use. It is important to avoid too much debt, as this often leads to serious financial problems, including the possibility of bankruptcy. If your cash outflows constantly exceed your cash inflows, you can't solve the problem by using credit. You should consider changing your lifestyle.

TOPIC LINKS

Credit Guide from the Federal Reserve Bank

Reasons for Using Credit

People sometimes think that the only reason for using credit is a lack of sufficient cash to pay for a purchase. Although this factor can be important, it may not be the only one. Furthermore, your lack of sufficient cash does not necessarily mean that the item's cost exceeds all the cash you have. You may have more than enough to pay for it, but in so doing you would reduce your cash reserves below what you consider a safe level. Furthermore, you would give up the financial return on those reserves. So you may choose not to use cash to maintain adequate liquidity and earnings. You might choose credit over cash for other reasons, too, and these are discussed next.

As a Shopping Convenience

Using credit instead of cash can make shopping much more convenient. You avoid the risks of loss or theft associated with carrying cash, and your end-of-month statement provides a clear and complete record of expenses to help with budgeting and income tax preparation. A credit card also simplifies shopping by phone or returning merchandise. A national credit card, such as Visa or MasterCard, allows you to enjoy many of these advantages throughout the entire United States, even throughout the world.

To Increase Total Consumption Benefits

Credit can be used to correct a temporary mismatch between income and expenses. Borrowing allows you to consume in a given year at a level greater than your current income would otherwise permit. This consumption in turn can lead to a higher scale of living and greater satisfaction from total consumption over time. This point is illustrated in Figure 6.1, in which we show a four-year period to keep things simple. Assume that you would like to have an even amount of consumption over the four years, as indicated by the line *AB*, and also assume your total consumption for the four years equals your total income; that is, assume zero savings over the four years. If your income is low at the beginning and then rises, as shown by the line *CD*, and if your consumption is tied to your income, it would also be low at the start and higher at the end. Borrowing allows you to even out consumption and achieve your goal. You borrow in years 1 and 2 and repay the loans in years 3 and 4. The illustration does not consider interest, which would reduce total consumption, since part of your income would be needed to pay it, but the added satisfaction you gain from an even level of consumption might far outweigh the satisfaction you lose by paying interest.

As an Inflation Hedge

When the rate of inflation increases, many people tend to use credit in an effort to soften its impact. We hear such expressions as "paying back your debt with cheap dollars" and "buy now and avoid higher future prices." All too often, these words have been true and symbolic of a high-consumption approach toward life. Credit makes this approach possible. Buying now to avoid higher future prices, however, is often not as simple as it appears, since a high inflation rate is almost always accompanied by a high rate of interest on money borrowed.

As a Source of Emergency Funds

Having easy and quick access to credit gives you funds that could be used in case of emergency if your available liquid assets were not adequate. Some people regard this feature as the single most important advantage of credit, since it allows them to hold a larger portion of their total investments in nonliquid assets, where yields have historically been higher. It would be a mistake, though, to rely upon credit too much or for too long a period of time. Borrowed funds must be repaid, meaning that eventually you must sell nonliquid assets and suffer potential losses if market prices are low when you sell them.

Figure 6.1
Consumption and Credit over Time

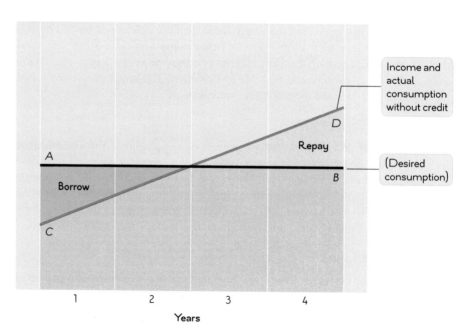

Disadvantages of Using Credit

After considering the reasons for using credit, you should also be aware of its disadvantages. The final decision to use credit—and how much to use—requires your careful consideration of both the advantages and the disadvantages. The easy availability of credit can entice us into a lifestyle we cannot afford and burden us with future obligations that can destroy relationships with family and friends.

A Temptation to Overspend

As previously mentioned, after you qualify for credit, you will probably be surprised at how willing lenders are to extend credit. Given these temptations, and without proper credit planning, you are in real danger of allowing the consumption component of your budget to get far out of hand. The only solution to this problem is to develop the discipline to stay within a planned budget, as we discussed in Chapter 3. Also, some people become so accustomed to using credit cards that they often forget purchases they made during a month. Consumption naturally becomes excessive, and the rude awakening arrives with the monthly statement. To guard against this form of overspending, some financial planners urge you to maintain a credit card expense journal, which is similar to the check stubs in a checking account (see *Simplifying Financial Planning 6.1*).

Credit Costs

There may be expenses directly connected with credit, such as an annual maintenance fee on your account. However, the biggest cost associated with credit is the interest you must pay. You wouldn't buy a product if you didn't know beforehand how much it would cost you. The interest you will owe is the cost of a loan. At a minimum, you should know what the annual percentage rate (APR) is on the loan, how interest will be calculated, and the total amount of interest that must be paid over the life of the loan. We'll cover those topics in detail later in this chapter.

Indirect costs can be important, too. If your loan involves a credit card, you must be concerned about its safety: If your credit card is lost or stolen, it can be used by someone else, with you paying the bill. The **Truth in Lending Act (TILA)** limits your loss to $50 per account, but this amount could be substantial if you lose five or six cards. You will also have the aggravation of notifying creditors and taking other steps to be protected under the law. Another indirect cost is the time it takes to review creditors' monthly statements for accuracy and then to write and mail your checks. Many people are not concerned with these indirect costs, but they may be important to you.

Truth in Lending Act (TILA) Sets rules regulating credit market. It also sets limits on your credit-related financial responsibilities.

TOPIC LINKS

A summary of consumer credit laws

Less Flexibility with Future Budgets

The more we spend in one period, deferring payment until a later one, the less flexible is our future budget. In effect, we increase the fixed-expense component of the future budget. By itself, this practice isn't necessarily bad; but it sometimes happens that items purchased with credit fail to satisfy us as we thought they might at the time we purchased them. Holiday gifts usually come to mind as examples here. In these cases, we are left with the bills to pay, along with the temptation to buy new items to satisfy current consumption demands. An overreliance on credit can strain your future budget.

How to Get Credit

Having decided you want credit, the next step is to apply for it. You can apply in person, by mail, or on the Internet. You probably will be asked to complete an application form that

SIMPLIFYING financial planning 6.1

A Credit Card Register

If you update the register each time you write a check, your check register should indicate just how much you have in your checking account. Unless you or the bank makes a mistake, you are not likely to be surprised by your monthly checking account statement. The same people, however, who keep excellent check registers are often surprised by the outstanding balance on their charge account, because they fail to keep similar information on their credit card use.

The first sign of credit card misuse is an expectedly large credit card balance. If you use "plastic money" often, you are likely to forget just how much you have charged. You might keep the receipts in your wallet with the good intention of periodically totaling your charges, but somehow that gets put off until the credit card statement arrives. But then it is too late: You have already overspent your budget.

You may have heard of food diets in which you are required to keep a running list of everything you eat. If each little snack is added to the list, you may eventually come to the realization that all those little snacks add up to one big eating spree. The same should hold true for a credit diet. If you maintain a running tally of your credit charges, you must inevitably confront your own excesses and reduce your overspending. You can do this by creating a credit register that you update just as you would a check register.

Use the accompanying illustration as a guide for creating your own out of an unused check register or in a computer spreadsheet program such as Excel. Quicken and Microsoft Money provide credit card registers as part of their financial planning software. Each time you charge a purchase, receive a credit for returned merchandise, or make a monthly payment, enter the transaction in the register and update the outstanding balance.

Some banks let you download the information on your credit statement directly into your software program. Moveover, you don't have to wait to the end of the month. Online statements will often post charges after a lag of only a few days. If you get in the habit of making entries with each use of the account and checking your online statement, you will eliminate the unexpected by knowing just how much you owe at any time.

Date	Description	Credit for Returns and Payments	Amount of Charge	Balance $74.20
1/2/xx	Marshalls—sweater		$56.19	130.39
1/6/xx	Sunoco—gas and milk		18.75	149.24
1/8/xx	Kmart—return of defective garden hose	$11.08		138.16
1/9/xx	Lotus Blossom—dinner with the Williams		48.96	187.12

asks for personal and financial information. It's important to know what a lender looks for in a credit applicant and what steps you can take to begin a credit record.

What the Lender Looks For

Put simply, the only concern of the lender is your ability to repay the loan along with any related expenses. To assess this ability, lenders often look at the three Cs of credit—*character, capital,* and *capacity.* Character has to do with how you have handled yourself in previous financial dealings. Do you have checking and savings accounts and use them regularly? Have you used credit properly by repaying your debts on a timely basis? These are some of the questions lenders frequently ask to judge creditworthiness. Capital refers to your financial strength, usually measured by net worth, a topic discussed in Chapter 3. Capacity means your ability to repay debt out of your future income. Here the lender looks not only at the amount of such income but also at future commitments that might restrict it.

Lenders may apply rules of thumb before granting a loan. For example, only consumers with monthly mortgage loan payments less than 25 percent of income and total loan payments less than 30 percent of income may be deemed creditworthy. Others may

TOPIC LINKS

Know your credit rights.

use a more specific evaluation technique to weigh important factors in the credit-granting decision and arrive at a numeric guide as to whether credit should be made available to you (see *Finance News 6.2* on credit scoring). The scoring system will be based on the lender's bad loan experience. Factors that are likely to weigh in your favor include home ownership, residential and job stability, education, and income.

Regardless of the system lenders use to evaluate your credit application, the **Equal Credit Opportunity Act (ECOA)** insists that fairness be applied. You cannot be discriminated against because of race, color, age, sex, marital status, or related other factors. This does not mean that someone is automatically given a loan because of one or several of these characteristics; what it does mean is that lenders may not base their loan decision on any of these characteristics. The ECOA also ensures that lenders do not use such factors in credit-scoring formulas that might discriminate against any protected group.

Equal Credit Opportunity Act (ECOA) Ensures that you cannot be denied credit because of your race, color, age, sex, or marital status.

Beginning a Credit Record

Being aware of the factors lenders look at to assess your creditworthiness helps you improve your score and your chances of receiving credit. here are some practical things you can do:

- Open both checking and savings accounts (if you don't already have them) and, of course, use them properly. This means no "bounced checks" and a history of regular deposits to the savings account.
- Open a retail charge account with a local store or major oil company. These accounts are often easier to obtain than other loans. Then use the card and make sure you are prompt in remitting the monthly balance due. Not all retail creditors report to credit bureaus. Make sure that yours does. In this way you will begin to build a credit history.
- If you have recently moved, write for a summary of any credit record kept by a credit bureau in your former town. It will be helpful in establishing credit in your new town.
- Have a telephone installed; this item often appears as a factor in credit-rating formulas. If you have a cell phone, make sure you pay your monthly bills promptly.
- Apply for a credit card and use it responsibly. However, don't over apply for credit and hold multiple cards. Too many credit applications can hurt your creditworthiness.

Special Concerns for Married Women

You may face special problems in getting credit if you are a woman, so you should take additional steps:

- Always use your own name when applying for credit. If you are Nancy Brown, who marries Edward Hall, you should use *Nancy Hall* or *Nancy Brown Hall* as your legal name, if you choose to use your husband's last name. You are not required to do so, however, and you can continue to use your maiden name. But definitely do not use a social title such as *Mrs. Edward Hall*. Not only could other women have this name, but also any credit information under it goes to your husband's credit file and does not benefit you individually.
- Make sure all credit information is reported under your name as well as your husband's. With a **joint credit account** both spouses are responsible for the debt. Obviously, if you are separated or divorced, you should immediately cancel all joint accounts. On an **individual credit account** only you are responsible for the debt, and the account will appear only on your credit report.
- If you are recently married, inform creditors accordingly and indicate that you wish to maintain your own credit record. For individuals who live in a community-property

Joint credit account Both spouses are responsible for the debt.

Individual credit account Only you are responsible for the debt.

state, a creditor may consider your spouse's credit history. Nevertheless, you should make certain that the local bureau has a separate file in your name.

The Role of the Credit Bureau

Once you begin using credit, you will establish a credit history. It contains a record of credit previously granted you and how responsible you were in handling that credit. Many lenders do not maintain their own credit-investigating facilities but instead use such services provided by major credit bureaus. In all likelihood, one or more of these bureaus will keep your credit history.

The United States has approximately 1,000 credit bureaus that function as clearing-houses for information about borrowers' credit histories. These bureaus are connected by computer, so if you wish to make a credit card purchase in California, the seller can check your credit history even if you have never used your card outside of New York. These local credit bureaus are either interconnected with or owned by the three major national credit bureaus are Equifax (**www.equifax.com**), Experian (**www.experian.com**), and TransUnion (**www.transunion.com**). The largest of these firms, Experian, maintains over 90 million credit files.

It is sometimes believed that the credit bureau decides whether you receive credit, but this is not true. A credit bureau only stores information about how you have handled credit in the past and any legal actions that might impair your financial strength in the future. lenders may buy a credit report from the credit bureau. They use this report in their decision to extend you credit, although it is not the only factor they consider, and a good credit record doesn't automatically guarantee that credit will be given. Your report may also be checked by a potential employer and periodically checked by your current employer.

The credit report includes the credit accounts that you have with banks, retailers, credit card issuers, and other lenders. Information on each account states your credit limit, the loan amount, the account balance, and your payment history. Public record information such as bankruptcies, tax liens, and monetary judgments are also included. Bankruptcy information may remain on your credit report for up to ten years, and other negative information may remain up to seven years. The report also indicates if anyone besides you is responsible for paying any of your accounts. Finally, it lists all credit inquiries over the last year, and all employment-related inquiries over the past two years.

If You Are Denied Credit

According to the Federal Reserve Bank of Chicago, the following are the most common reasons for being denied credit:

- Too little time in current job or at current residence
- Too much outstanding debt
- Unreasonable purpose for requesting credit
- Cosigner cannot take on additional debt liability
- Errors on applicant's credit record
- Strictness of creditor's standards

Under the **Fair Credit Reporting Act (FCRA)**, you are entitled to one free report each year from each of the three major credit bureaus. In addition, the credit bureau is required to notify you in writing the first time negative information is added to your file. You should take advantage of this free opportunity to view your credit history. You can request your free annual report from all three major bureaus at **AnnualCreditReport.com**.

If you are denied credit, insurance, or employment because of your credit report, the creditor must give you the name, address, and telephone number of the credit-reporting

TOPIC LINKS

Credit reporting agencies and a sample credit report

Fair Credit Reporting Act (FCRA) Establishes standards for credit reports and procedures for correcting an inaccurate report.

agency that supplied the report. Review your credit report and insist that any incorrect information be removed from the file. If the facts are correct, but you feel they do not fairly present your side of the story, you may submit your own statement to be included in the file. You can also insist that all those who have requested your file within the last six months be notified of any unsubstantiated or incorrect entry.

You can review your credit report even if you are just curious about it. The bureaus in your area can be found in the Yellow Pages under such headings as "Credit" or "Credit Reporting Agencies." They can also be found on the Internet.

A **secured credit card** can be helpful if you are trying to reestablish a good credit record. The card is secured by funds on deposit at the bank, assuring the bank repayment for your purchases. Consequently, banks that might not consider issuing you a typical credit card will have no problem granting you a secured credit card. This is particularly useful for those who are trying to overcome a poor credit history.

TOPIC LINKS

Obtain a credit report.

Secured credit card A credit card secured by funds held at the bank issuing the card.

Sales Credit

Sales credit arises from the sale of merchandise or services. Traditionally, most of this credit was offered by merchants, such as department stores, major oil companies, automobile dealerships, and furniture and appliance dealers, in an effort to expand their sales. While they are still important in supplying such credit, the major bank credit cards—Visa and MasterCard—are the primary sources. Sales credit is often symbolized by a credit card that is used to make service or merchandise transactions, although many of these cards can now be used for financial transactions as well, such as making a cash loan.

Sales credit Any credit arising from the sale of merchandise or services.

Kinds of Accounts

You can obtain sales credit in three different forms: (1) as a regular (or 30-day) account; (2) as a revolving account; and (3) as a retail installment account. The first two are called open-end credit accounts; they are discussed next. The third is referred to as a closed-end account, and it is discussed in an upcoming section. When you establish an **open-end account** you sign an agreement that covers all credit purchases and cash advances made in the account. This one agreement is binding as long as the account is open. In contrast, a **closed-end account** requires a separate retail installment contract for each purchase; consequently, these are usually for large amounts and longer periods of time.

Open–end account Establishes an ongoing line of credit covering future purchases.

Closed–end account Credit for a single purchase with a set repayment schedule.

Regular Charge Account

People who use a **regular charge account** are typically those who view credit as a shopping convenience. Your purchase transactions for a month are accumulated and sent to you at the end of the month. You agree with the terms of this account by paying the total amount billed within 10 to 30 days after the billing date, and generally you avoid interest charges by making timely payments. Fees and interest charges may be attached to late payments.

Regular charge account A credit account for which complete payment at the end of the billing cycle usually avoids all interest charges.

Revolving Account

A **revolving credit account** allows you to make purchases up to a credit limit that is usually determined by your credit record and net worth. If you then pay the full amount due at the end of the month, you are using the account as a regular charge account. You must at least make a partial payment. the minimum amount depends on how much credit you have

Revolving credit account An open–end credit account with rules for minimum monthly payments and interest charges.

finance news 6.2

Scores Revealed

For several years, you have been able to get a copy of your credit report. Until recently, however, credit reporting agencies were prohibited from making credit scores available to consumers. Your credit score is a single number that summarizes and grades your creditworthiness. The most commonly accepted summary grade is your FICO score. It is named after Fair, Isaac & Co., (**MyFico.com**) the originator of the scoring methodology.

For a small fee you now can obtain both your credit report and your FICO score from a credit reporting agency. Your credit score is a three-digit number from 300 to 900, which may determine whether you get that car loan or home mortgage. It may even influence whether you get that next job. If you are not denied credit, it may influence how much you will pay in loan origination fees and on interest rates. Potential borrowers with scores above 700 may get preferential treatment, whereas those with scores of less than 600 are likely to be placed in the high-risk category.

The credit agencies will not tell you how they determine the score. However, it is generally understood that your credit score will be based upon the following factors. Fair, Isaac reports that it weights each of these factors by the indicated percentage.

- A history of on-time payments (35 percent) and the length of your credit history (15 percent)
  The longer your credit history and the longer your track record of on-time payments, the higher your score

- Your amount owed (30 percent)
  The smaller your use of credit relative to your credit limit, the higher your score.

- New credit (10 percent)
  The fewer the number of inquiries, the higher your score.

- Types of credit in use (10 percent)
  The larger the variety of debt (auto loans, mortgages, credit cards) you have successfully managed, the higher your score.

You must have free access to your credit score when you apply for a home mortgage and if you are denied credit. Otherwise, you can obtain your credit score at any time for a small fee.

Improving Your Credit Score

Given weights placed on each of the factors included in your credit score, there are some obvious steps you can take to keep a good credit score or improve a bad one.

Annually review your credit report. Review your reports from all three major credit bureaus annually and when applying for a loan. Identify problems in your credit history and correct any mistakes in your reports.

Pay your bills on time. Make sure all your payments are up to date and plan for future payments. Paying your bills promptly and avoiding excessive debt is the basic recipe for good credit. If you have trouble making payments, contact creditors and make an appointment with a legitimate credit counselor.

Reduce your credit card balances. Large outstanding balances can lower your credit score. Generally hold balances to less than 24 percent of your credit limit.

Pay off debt rather than moving it around. Owing the same amount, but having few cards can lower your credit score. You need to reduce your outstanding balances.

Don't open a number of new accounts. This can increase the number of inquiries and lower your credit score. Don't open several new accounts all at once. Spread out new applications over time.

---

used and the interest charged on the account, but it can be as low as 2 percent of the outstanding balance. However, government agencies have recently been pressuring credit card issuers to increase the minimum payment and several credit card companies have responded to this pressure by raising the minimum to 4 percent of the outstanding balance. As the balance is reduced by payments, you may again make purchases up to the limit, so the account may never actually be paid off. Interest is charged each month on the unpaid balance.

The Survey of Consumer Finances found that about 55 percent of households almost always pay off their credit card balance each month. About one-quarter of households, however, almost never pay off the balance. Using a credit card to finance a long-term outstanding balance is a sign of credit mismanagement. There most likely are cheaper sources of credit.

Your monthly payments are presumed to cover interest first. If the payment exceeds the interest charge, the excess reduces the principal that you owe. The creditor must inform

Ranges of Creditworthiness

Range	Credit Worthiness
720–850	**Very Good to Excellent** • Best interest rates on loans. • Your mailbox will be overflowing with credit offers. • Average score is about 720.
650–720	**Good** • Likely to get credit, but not the best interest rate.
630–650	**Fair** • May get credit but your creditor will take a second look at your ability to handle the risk.
580–630	**Poor** • Missed payments or lack of credit record. • May get credit but only at higher rate.
350–580	**Bad** • Likely to be denied credit by all but a high cost lender. • Your mailbox will be overflowing with offers from credit repair services.

Distribution of Individuals by Credit Score History

Source: Federal Reserve Bulletin "Credit Report Accuracy and Access to Credit," Robert B. Avery, Paul S. Calem, and Glenn B. Canner, Federal Reserve Bulletin, Summer 2004.

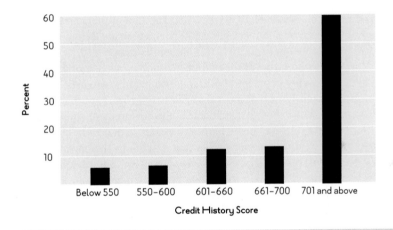

you each month as to the interest rate applicable that month, the applicable rate expressed as an annual percentage rate (APR), and the method used to determine the balance on which the monthly rate is applied. A revolving credit agreement will also include information about the following:

- the time available to pay your balance due without being charged interest
- the minimum amount you must pay each month, and the penalties if you don't pay it
- permission you give the creditor to investigate your credit history

You will receive a monthly statement for each credit account you have. An example of such a statement is shown in Figure 6.2, where the period covered is the month of July. This statement is patterned after one used by a major bank card but it is typical of most monthly statements. Note that the borrower made three purchases during the month and one payment; there were no credits for returned merchandise. The lender charged interest of $4.32 for the month, based on the monthly rate of 1.65 percent (which is an annual per-

Figure 6.2
A Monthly Statement for a Revolving Credit Account

Reference Number	Date	Description of Transaction		Amounts (Credits indicated by—)
89453987	7/05	Walmart 7549	Centerville, OH	$ 38.15
42874908	7/10	Payment		20.00–
69426933	7/12	Days Inns 033M	McDonough, GA	32.50
75538521	7/20	Mendelsons Retail	Dayton, OH	17.64

Finance Charge	Computed on an Average Daily Balance of	Monthly Periodic Rate	Annual Percentage Rate	Payment Due Date	Statement Closing Date
$ 4.32	$ 261.83	1.65%	19.80%	8/15/XX	7/31/XX

Previous Balance	Payments	Credit Transactions	Debit Transactions	Finance Charge	New Balance
$ 215.00	$ 20.00	$ -0-	$ 88.29	$ 4.32	$ 287.61

Credit Limit: $2,000
Available Credit: $1,712.39
Minimum Monthly Payment: $20.00

centage rate of 19.80 percent). The sum of this interest and purchases was $92.61 ($4.32 + $88.29). Subtracting the $20 payment made during the month gives the net change during the month of $72.61; this amount is then added to the $215 beginning-of-the-month balance to arrive at the end-of-the-month balance of $287.61. This amount or the minimum monthly payment of $20 must be paid by August 15. Also notice that the borrower has a credit limit (the most that can be borrowed) of $2,000, and there is $1,712.39 ($2,000 – $287.61) of credit available at the beginning of August. You may have outstanding charges up to this amount. Charges in excess of the credit limit may result in a penalty.

We mentioned earlier that it might be the borrower's intent to use a revolving account as a somewhat permanent form of credit. Before doing that, a person should consider other sources of credit that might be less expensive. In the preceding example, the APR was a rather high 19.80 percent. Generally, revolving credit is expensive credit if it is used on a permanent basis.

Determining Interest on a Revolving Account

Interest on a revolving charge account is determined by applying the monthly rate to the balance in the account. It seems simple enough, except that there are various ways of determining this balance. The three most commonly used methods are the previous balance method, the adjusted balance method, and the average daily balance method. The method used by the card issuer should be prominently displayed on the contract. Using data from Figure 6.2, each of these methods is illustrated in Table 6.1.

Previous balance method: The interest rate is applied to the outstanding balance at the end of the previous billing period.

Adjusted balance method The interest rate is applied to the previous balance less any payments or returns made during the current billing cycle.

The **previous balance method** is the simplest of the three. The rate is applied to the balance at the end of the previous month. As you see in Table 6.1, this means you multiply the rate, 1.65 percent, by the previous balance, $215, to arrive at the month's interest of $3.55. This method works to your advantage if you have considerable charges in the current month.

The **adjusted balance method** is more favorable than the previous balance method. The adjusted balance is equal to the previous balance less any payments or returns you made during the current billing cycle. Thus, in Table 6.1, the adjusted balance is simply

I. Previous Balance Method		

Interest is charged on the previous balance

$$1.65\% \times \$215.00 = \boxed{\$3.55}$$

II. Adjusted Balance Method		

Interest is charged on the previous balance less any current credits

$$1.65\% \times (\$215.00 - \$20.00) = \boxed{\$3.22}$$

III(a). Average Daily Balance Method (including current purchases)		

Interest is charged on the updated balance considering the day a charge or credit takes place

	(a)	(b)	(c)
Period	Number of Days	Balance	(a) × (b)
7/1–7/4	4	$215.00 + $0 = 215.00	$ 860.00
7/5–7/9	5	215.00 + 38.15 = 253.15	1,265.75
7/10–7/11	2	253.15 – 20.00 = 233.15	466.30
7/12–7/19	8	233.15 + 32.50 = 265.65	2,125.20
7/20–7/31	12	265.65 + 17.64 = 283.29	3,399.48
	31		$8,116.73

$$\text{Average daily balance} = \frac{\$8,116.73}{31} = \$261.83$$
$$1.65\% \times \$261.83 = \boxed{\$4.32}$$

III(b). Average Daily Balance Method (excluding current purchases)		

Interest is charged on the updated balance considering the day a current payment is made but ignoring current purchases or returns

	(a)	(b)	(c)
Period	Number of Days	Balance	(a) × (b)
7/1–7/9	10	$215	$2,150.00
7/10–7/31	21	$215.00 – $20.00 = 195	4,095.00
			$6,245.00

$$\text{Average daily balance} = \$6,245.00/31 = \$201.45$$
$$1.65\% \times \$201.45 = \boxed{\$3.32}$$

Table 6.1
Three Methods for Computing Interest on a Revolving Credit Account (Based on Data from Figure 6.2)

$215 less the credit payment of $20. Applying 1.65 percent to $195 determines a finance charge of $3.22. This is the most advantageous method for cardholders.

There are two variations to the **average daily balance method**; one includes purchases for the current billing cycle, the other does not. The *average daily balance method including current purchases* gives the most correct balance for applying interest. In this procedure, you weight a balance for the number of days it is outstanding. In the example, the beginning balance of $215 was applicable only for the four days, 7/1 through 7/4. Thereafter, other balances were appropriate for varying numbers of days. By weighting each balance for the number of outstanding days, you arrive at the total weighted balance of $8,116.73, which is then divided by 31 to arrive at the $261.83 average daily balance. This figure multiplied by 1.65 percent gives the interest amount of $4.32.

The other variation is the *average daily balance method excluding current purchases*. Again, an average daily balance is computed. However, in this variation of the average daily balance method, the finance charge is less because new purchases are not included in the daily balance. As indicated in Table 6.1, the finance charge is only $3.32 when new purchases are excluded.

Lenders traditionally provide a **grace period** of 25 days during which interest on the loan balance is forgiven. This usually applies only when you have fully paid off the previ-

Average daily balance method The interest rate is applied to the average outstanding balance over the billing cycle.

Grace period Period in which interest charges are forgiven on the condition that the outstanding balance is fully repaid.

ous month's balance. The grace period normally lasts between the statement closing date and the payment due date. Recently, some lenders have eliminated the grace period; others have offered their customers a choice between credit accounts with or without grace periods. Finance charges on the account with the grace period are based on a higher annual percentage rate, making it less desirable for someone who does not regularly pay off the entire amount due.

Two-cycle average daily balance method Collects interest over two billing periods when an unpaid balance is begun.

Some major card issuers are now applying a **two-cycle average daily balance method**. This eliminates any grace period applied in a previous month when you fail to completely pay off the balance in the present month. Thus, the creditor can in effect go back two months to collect interest on unpaid balances. If you pay your balance in full each month or you carry a balance from month to month, your interest payments are the same as under the one-cycle average balance method. Those hit the hardest with increased interest charges are consumers who pay off their balances in alternating months.

For each revolving account you have, you should determine how the monthly balance is calculated and verify the monthly statement to make sure it is correct. Of course, you aren't likely to go through all the calculations for the average daily balance method, and it may not be necessary that you do. A quick glance between this month and last month should indicate if the number is approximately correct. A last piece of fairly obvious advice is to use those accounts that determine the monthly balance to your best advantage.

Credit Cards

"Plastic money" is indeed an appropriate name for what we use to purchase many goods and services. About one-half of all families hold at least one retail store card. Most retail store cards are charge cards issued in conjunction with a regular charge account. An even larger percentage of all households have at least one bank credit card. The major names of issuers include Visa, MasterCard, and Discover.

Credit Card Issuers

Bank credit cards Credit cards that are issued by banks, such as MasterCard and Visa.

The **bank credit cards**—MasterCard and Visa—are by far the largest suppliers of consumer installment credit. When you use one of these cards, you are actually borrowing from a bank, perhaps a local one, or you may have a card issued by one of the major banks, such as Chase. We illustrated and discussed a typical credit card account earlier, which showed how the card is used to make purchases. But bank cards can also be used to make financial transactions. For example, you may be able to get cash advances from money machines with your card, and in some places you can use it to buy securities, such as stocks or bonds.

TOPIC LINKS

Locate credit card companies.

Specialty Cards

Affinity card Returns a small percentage of sales to the sponsoring organization.

A bank card that carries the name of a sponsoring organization is known in the industry as an **affinity card**. The card's sponsor receives a small percentage of card sales. Part of this may be returned to cardholders in the form of frequent flyer miles, discounts on purchases, or cash rebates. Some sponsors, such as environmental groups and alumni organizations, use the revenues from affinity cards to support socially desirable causes. Visa estimates that 22 percent of their cardholders have these cards.

Travel and entertainment (T&E) cards Credit cards issued by finance companies catering to businesspeople and travelers.

Traditionally, **travel and entertainment (T&E) cards**, such as American Express and Diners Club have catered to travelers—usually businesspeople—who frequently buy goods and services away from their hometowns. The cards are used to pay for hotel and motel accommodations, to buy airline tickets, and to pay restaurant bills. However, the T&E cards are expanding their services. The usual annual fee of $50 or more for a T&E card is much higher than that of a bank credit card, and it is questionable whether it is worth it, since bank credit cards are so universally acceptable. The annual fee for the American Express Black Centurion card is about $2,500.

We mentioned earlier that many retail establishments issue their own credit cards, known as **private-label cards**. These stores generally prefer that you use their card rather than a bank card (many will not accept bank cards), since consumer credit is often a profitable part of their business.

Private-label cards: Credit cards issued by a retail establishment.

Selecting a Credit Card

Many people who are good credit risks find their mailboxes overflowing with solicitations from credit card companies. Their major problem is not in getting credit but rather in selecting the best credit from among the numerous offers. In order to make comparison shopping easier and also to eliminate potentially misleading sales practices, Congress empowered the Federal Reserve Board to set down rules governing the information that credit card companies must furnish potential consumers. The rules enacted under this law require detailed and uniform disclosure of rates and other cost information in applications and solicitations to open credit and charge card accounts. The most important information should be prominently displayed in a box similar to that shown in Figure 6.3.

The Federal Reserve Board periodically collects and publishes information on credit card plans offered by major financial institutions. The Bankrate Monitor (**www.Bankrate.com**) also provides a survey of recent rates. The cost of credit can vary significantly among issuers and over time in response to changing conditions in credit mar-

Figure 6.3
Sample Disclosure Box for Credit Card Offer

Annual percentage rate (APR) for purchases	2.9% until 11/1/08 after that, 14.9%
Other APRs	Cash-advance APR: 15.9% Balance- Transfer APR: 15.9% Penalty rate: 23.9% See explanation below.*
Variable-rate information	Your APR for purchase transactions may vary. The rate is determined monthly by adding 5.9% to the Prime Rate. **
Grace period for repayment of balances for purchases	25 days on average
Method of computing the balance for purchases	Average daily balance (excluding new purchases)
Annual fees	None
Minimum finance charge	$.50

Transaction fee for cash advances: 3% of the amount advanced
Balance-transfer fee:3% of the amount transferred
Late-payment fee: $25
Over-the-credit-limit fee: $25

*Explanation of penalty. If your payment arrives more than ten days late two times within a six-month period, the penalty rate will apply.

** The Prime Rate used to determine your APR is the rate published in the *Wall Street Journal* on the 10th day of the prior month.

Source: "Choosing a Credit Card." Federal Reserve Board http://www.federalreserve.gov/pubs/shop/

TOPIC LINKS

FRB credit card survey and
the Bankrate Monitor

kets. The U.S. Public Research Interest Group reports that a significant percentage of card-holders who called their credit card issuer to complain of high rate were successful in getting the interest rate reduced. In addition to interest charges, the cost of using a credit card will include maintenance fees and other specialized charges. Do not ignore these fees. They generate as much as one-third of the credit card companies' revenues and represent a significant burden on those who do not use credit wisely.

The best credit card for you will depend on your credit practices. If you intend to pay off the entire balance each month, a card with a grace period and a low annual membership fee would be favored. Given the high cost of finance charges on credit cards and the relatively lower cost of credit from other sources, this is probably the best strategy for most people. However, if you do intend to incur finance charges on your credit card, then you may be better off by paying a higher annual membership fee in exchange for a lower APR. For example, if your average outstanding balance is $1,000, then a 1 percent reduction in the APR would save you $10 a year. Therefore, if the annual membership fee on this card is no more than $10 above the fee on a card with a higher APR, it could be your best choice.

Many credit cards come with benefits and incentives that can range from frequent flyer miles to a cash rebate on purchases. Do consider these incentives, but be careful not to overemphasize them. There may be significant restrictions on how you may use such incentives as frequent flyer miles or hotel rebates.

Credit Cards for College Students

Given the financial characteristics of the typical college student, you would probably think that he or she would find it difficult to get credit. Many college students have no employment and a limited credit history. To overcome these seeming obstacles, some issuers use a special credit scoring formula for college students that minimizes these factors. In fact, the U.S. General Accounting Office reports that college students represent a prime market for credit card issuers. Both mail solicitations and on-campus presentations are commonplace. College students are viewed as good and responsible customers who will continue to have a lifelong need for credit. The issuers anticipate retaining these students after graduation when these accounts will become more valuable. Some universities have entered into financial arrangements with card issuers to provide an affinity card that bears the logo of the university in return for a payment. A survey by **Bankrate.com** showed that credit unions have the most consumer favorable terms for students.

TOPIC LINKS

Download a payback
spreadsheet.

Students who run up excessive debt or make late payments can impair their credit card rating in the future. However, the majority of these students seem to pay off their balance in full. Only about 5 percent of college students have an outstanding balance of $3,000 or more. Unfortunately, those students with large outstanding balances will have their financial problems compounded by interest charges. At a minimum monthly payment of $60, a $3,000 balance could take 100 months to pay off and generate about $3,000 in additional interest payments at a 19 percent APR (see Figure 6.4).

Protection Against Credit Card Fraud

The Federal Trade Commission recommends that you avoid credit card fraud protection and loss insurance. As we previously mentioned, the Truth in Lending Act limits your losses from unauthorized uses of your credit cards to $50 per card; but, if your purse or wallet is stolen and if it contains several cards, your loss can be more than trivial. So it pays to be careful with them. The following suggestions can help in this effort:

- Immediately sign a new credit card when it arrives. Record card numbers, expiration dates, and phone numbers and addresses for each card company and keep this information in a safe place.

Figure 6.4
*Payback Period on Credit
Card Debt of $3,000 at a 19
Percent APR*

Monthly Payment	Number of Months	Total Interest
$ 60	100	$ 2,991
75	64	1,790
100	42	1,102
125	31	804

Minimum payments are typically 2 percent of the outstanding balance or $10, whichever is higher.

- Don't leave blank lines above the total on a credit card slip. Draw a line through any blank line above the total. Make sure the sales check you sign is completed correctly, including the addition of separate line items; then save your receipts, compare them with your monthly bill, and report any discrepancy immediately.
- Watch clerks carefully while they are using your card to make sure they do not run impressions on other sales checks. Of course, ask the clerk to return your card immediately after it has been used.
- Destroy old bills and receipts. Also destroy all credit cards you do not use. Be extra careful in giving your number over the phone unless you initiate the phone call and want to charge the purchase. Any calls purporting to be "conducting a credit card survey" should be completely avoided.
- Don't provide your credit card number, bank account information, or Social Security number over the phone or on the Internet, unless you know you are dealing with an honorable business.
- Don't pay for credit preapproval on a loan. It is against the law for anyone to ask you to pay before your loan or credit is approved.
- Don't lend your credit card to anyone. Your credit history is too important.
- If your cards are stolen or lost, contact each issuer immediately. This means keeping a list of addresses and phone numbers in a convenient and safe place; but remember that accidents such as these often happen on vacation, and your list will not do much good if it is at home. Although getting ready for a vacation is hectic enough, try to remember the list, and don't store it in your wallet or purse, because that is what is usually lost or stolen.

Correcting Credit Card Mistakes

Despite the care taken by you or the credit issuer, mistakes do occur. It is important for your sake that they are corrected immediately, not only to save money if it's an overcharge but also to protect your good credit rating. Both the Truth in Lending Act and the Fair Credit Billing Act give you considerable legal protection against mistakes on open-end accounts. Since it is very important that you understand what your protections are, some of them—billing errors, defective goods, prompt payment, and credit blocking—are discussed next. This material is adapted from the *Consumer Handbook to Credit Protection Laws,* published by the Board of Directors of the Federal Reserve System.

TOPIC LINKS

Consumer Handbook to Credit Protection Laws

Correcting Billing Errors

If your credit card statement contains a billing error, notify the creditor *in writing* as soon as you discover it. You may want to call the card company to correct the problem, but phoning is not sufficient to cover your legal safeguards. Compose a letter similar to that shown in Figure 6.5 and send it by certified mail with return receipt requested.

Pay all parts of the bill that are not in dispute. The creditor should acknowledge your letter within a month or two, but in no case more than 90 days. If the creditor made a mistake, you do not have to pay finance charges on the disputed amount. If the creditor disagrees with you, the creditor must explain the basis for the disagreement.

A creditor may not threaten your credit rating while you're resolving a billing dispute. Once you have written about a possible error, a creditor is prohibited from giving out information to other creditors or credit bureaus that would damage your credit reputation. And, until your complaint is answered, the creditor may not take any action to collect the disputed amount.

After the creditor has explained the bill, you may be reported as delinquent on the amount in dispute, and the creditor may take action to collect if you do not pay in the time allowed. Even so, you can still disagree in writing. The creditor must report that you have challenged your bill and give you the name and address of each person who has received information about your account. When the matter is settled, the creditor is required to report the outcome to each person who has received information. Remember that you may also place your own side of the story in your credit record.

Defective Goods or Services

Chargeback A disputed amount charged back to the merchant by the credit card company.

Under most circumstances you may withhold the remaining payment on any damaged or shoddy goods or poor-quality services purchased with a credit card. However, you must first make a real attempt to solve the problem with the merchant. Withholding of payments results in what is called a **chargeback**, whereby the card issuer charges the disputed amount back to the merchant. At this point the merchant can dispute the chargeback. The

Figure 6.5
Sample Dispute Letter

Date

Your Name
Your Address
Your City, State, Zip Code

Complaint Department
Name of Credit Reporting Agency
Address
City, State, Zip Code

Dear Sir or Madam:

I am writing to dispute the following information in my file. The items I dispute also are encircled on the attached copy of the report I received. This item (identify item(s) disputed by name of source, such as creditors or tax court, and identify type of item, such as credit account, judgment, etc.) is (inaccurate or incomplete) because (describe what is inaccurate or incomplete and why). I am requesting that the item be deleted (or request another specific change) to correct this information. Enclosed are copies of (use this sentence if applicable and describe any enclosed documentation, such as payment records, court documents) supporting my position. Please reinvestigate this (these) matter(s) and (delete or correct) the disputed item(s) as soon as possible.

Sincerely,
Your name

Enclosures: (List what you are enclosing)

card issuer must then decide whether to reissue the bill to you or to proceed against the merchant for repayment.

Prompt Credit Payments and Refunds for Credit Balances

To avoid finance charges on your account within a certain period of time, it is obviously important that you receive your bills, and get credit for paying them promptly. If your account is one on which no finance charge is added before a certain due date, creditors must mail their statements at least 14 days before payment is due.

Creditors are required to credit payments on the day they arrive, as long as you pay according to payment instructions. Stores often give you a credit on your bill instead of cash when you return a purchase. If this results in a credit balance on your account, a store must make a refund in cash if you request it.

Credit Blocking

If you were ever in the embarrassing position of having a purchase denied because you had exceeded your credit limit, you may have been a victim of **credit blocking**. This is a perfectly legal practice. It can happen when you use your credit card to check into a hotel or to rent a car. The clerk will contact the card issuer with the estimated cost. Your line of credit is then reduced by this amount with what is termed a "block" or "authorization." When you pay your bill with the same credit card, the block is typically removed in a few days. However, using a card different from the one you used to initiate the transaction could create a credit problem. The credit limit on the first card might remain blocked for as long as 15 additional days. Consequently, if you use a different card to pay the bill, be sure to tell the clerk to unblock the first card.

Credit blocking Credit limit is reduced by the amount of the expected purchase.

Credit Cards Contrasted with Debit Cards

A credit card should not be confused with a **debit card** even though they may look identical. In fact, some cards are dual cards, which can function as a credit card or a debit card. When you swipe the card through a card reader you can select either the debit button or the credit button. The button you choose will have a unique impact on your cash flow and on the protection you have under federal law. You can use a debit card at an automated teller machine (ATM) or point-of-sale terminal. Whenever you use the card, your bank deposit is reduced immediately. By contrast, a credit card transaction puts you in debt to the bank; you reduce the debt later by paying your monthly statement. A debit card is actually a form of checking, which is how you should view it when considering its use.

Debit card The price of a purchase is deducted immediately from your bank deposit.

Over the last decade, there has been tremendous growth in debit card transactions. They are convenient for the consumer because using them reduces trips to the bank or money machine and time at the checkout counter. The convenience, however, comes at the cost of giving up some of the benefits related to credit card use. Most credit cards have a grace period over which no interest is charged. Depending on when the purchase is made and when the bill comes due, this grace period can provide the consumer with up to a month's free credit. Electronic transfers clear immediately. On the other hand, for consumers who have had trouble controlling their expenditures, replacing a credit card with a debit card can be a plus. Available funds must exist before the purchase is made.

ATM cards sometimes function as debit cards. Unlike credit cards, losses resulting from lost or stolen ATM and debit cards are regulated by the Electronic Fund Transfers Act. With an ATM or debit card, your losses are limited to only $50, if you report the loss within two days. If you fail to notify the debit card issuer within two business days after learning of the theft, you can lose up to $500. Furthermore, if you wait until 60 days or more after a bank statement has been mailed, your losses may be unlimited. This is greater than your potential loss on a credit card, which is limited to a $50 maximum under the Truth in Lending Act. Given a choice between using a debit or credit card, it is hard to see why you shouldn't always choose the credit card.

Use Your Credit Card Wisely

If you follow these few simple rules, using your credit card can save you money:

* Use credit instead of cash whenever you can.
* Use a credit card with a low or zero annual fee and a grace period.
* Keep a running balance of your charges so that you are not surprised by your monthly statement.
* Pay off your outstanding balance each payment period.
* Compare your credit card statement with your own list of charges each month.
* Immediately report and challenge any billing errors.

You must, however, follow all of these rules. If you don't pay off your balance each month, then a card with a low annual fee, but a high interest rate on the outstanding balance may not be a wise choice.

By using the zero interest credit during the grace period, you can keep additional financial assets in an interest earning account. If you can shift $1,000 out of cash into a financial asset earning only 5 percent, you can earn an extra $50 a year. With compounding, that would add up to an extra $629 after 10 years. That may not sound like a lot of money. But by making a number of sound financial choices on how you handle your credit, the financial benefits can add up.

Compare this virtuous cycle to the vicious cycle with a growing outstanding balance and late payments. Running a $1,000 outstanding balance on your credit card will cost you finance charges and may lower your credit score. Moreover, at a high interest rate, that outstanding balance will rapidly grow. At a 16 percent APR, that outstanding balance will double in less than four and one-half years.

Using your credit card wisely and paying off your monthly balance can improve your credit score and result in lower interest rates on car loans and home mortgages. In addition, a good credit score can even lower your insurance premiums and increase your chances of employment.

Cash Credit

Cash credit Credit extended in the form of cash.

Cash credit simply means borrowing money; as we have seen, sales credit involves borrowing in connection with buying something. The distinction is not always clear, since in most cases cash borrowed is also used to make purchases. The major difference between sales and cash credit is the way you repay the debt. Cash credit is repaid either with a single payment at the end of a period of time or by a series of uniform payments called installments.

You might remember that earlier we said that the retail installment account is a form of sales credit. This account is virtually identical to an installment cash loan, which is why it is explained now rather than before. Over the last few decades, the use of revolving charge accounts has displaced a large percentage of installment sales of consumer durables such as furniture and appliances. Installment sales are now reserved for the more expensive items on which you desire to spread out payments over time such as a car or a swimming pool.

The Contract

The agreement between you and a person selling an item is called a **retail installment contract**. If you purchase the item by obtaining a cash loan from a bank, savings and loan, consumer finance company, or credit union, the agreement is called a **promissory note**. Although promissory notes can be unsecured—and in fact, many are—their use in consumer credit is almost always on a secured basis, with the purchased item serving as collateral. The retail installment contract is always on a secured basis. The creditor obtains a security interest in the property with the **security agreement**, which is a separate instrument.

Retail installment contract A contract establishing a periodic repayment of the amount borrowed.

Promissory note A contract binding a borrower to future repayment of the amount borrowed.

Security agreement Establishes the creditor's security interest in the good.

Information That Must Be Provided

The Truth in Lending Act requires that each credit contract gives you the following information:

- The amount financed
- The total number of payments, the amount of each payment, and due dates
- Finance charges expressed both as a dollar amount and as an annual percentage rate
- The date when finance charges begin if that date is different from the transaction date
- An itemized list of all charges not included as part of the finance charge
- The charges for late payments or default
- A description of security held by the creditor
- How finance charge refunds are determined in the case of prepayments
- A description of prepayment penalties, if any

Creditors are also required to supply the following additional information when merchandise is purchased on time:

1. A description of the merchandise
2. The cash price
3. The deferred payment price
4. The down payment, including any trade-in

How Interest Charges Are Determined

Although the Truth in Lending Act requires lenders to state in writing the interest you must pay on a loan—both in dollars and as an annual percentage rate (APR)—it is still important that you know how these calculations are made. Three approaches are in general use: the simple interest method, the discount method, and the add-on method. These are explained next.

TOPIC LINKS

Read "The ABCs of Calculating Interest."

Simple Interest Method

Under the **simple interest method**, the interest payment is computed by applying a percentage rate to the outstanding loan balance during each payment period. This is the usual method for calculating a finance charge on a revolving credit account like that discussed earlier. It is also used by many banks and credit unions for computing the interest due on automobile installment loans and home mortgages.

Suppose you have a $1,000 loan with monthly payments and an annual percentage rate (APR) of 12 percent. Monthly interest charges are equal to 1 percent (12 percent/12 months) of the outstanding balance. You could pay off this loan in 12 equal monthly payments of $88.85. The formula for estimating the monthly payment is complicated.

Simple interest method The interest is computed by applying the APR to the outstanding loan balance.

Thankfully, you can easily calculate the needed payment with a handheld or online financial calculator by entering $1,000 for the amount borrowed, 12 for the number of periods, and 1 percent for the periodic interest rate.

How interest accrues and the balance is reduced over the loan's 12-month duration is illustrated in Figure 6.6. Using the simple interest method, the monthly finance charge in column 3 is equal to the outstanding balance in column 1 times the monthly interest charge of 1 percent. The excess of the monthly payment in column 2 over the finance charge in column 3 serves to reduce the outstanding balance. You should notice that as the loan is repaid, the finance charge in column 3 declines. You should also notice that, given the equal monthly installments and the declining monthly finance charge, a larger portion of each subsequent monthly installment is devoted to loan repayment. Thus, the loan is paid off more rapidly toward the end of the monthly payments.

The proportion of the monthly payment representing your finance charge does not change significantly over a loan that is repaid in only one year. However, on a longer term loan, such as a home mortgage, interest charges will make up a large percentage of your first monthly payments. Alternately, the final debt payments will go mostly toward reducing your outstanding balance.

Discount Method

Discount method The interest payment is deducted from the credit extended at the beginning of the loan.

The discount method is far more likely to be used by finance companies that make agricultural loans rather than consumer loans. Under the **discount method**, the lender deducts the interest to be paid from the credit extended to you at the beginning of the loan. Therefore, the face amount of the loan will exceed the amount you want to finance. To finance a purchase of $1,000, you have to borrow more than $1,000. On a one-year loan, your total payments are determined by the following formula:

$$\text{Total Payments on discount loan} = \frac{\text{amount financed}}{1 - \left(\text{discount rate} \times t\right)}$$

$$\$1,136.36 = \frac{\$1,000}{1 - \left(0.12 \times 1\right)}$$

Figure 6.6
A 12-Month Installment Loan with Annual Simple Interest of 12, or 1 Percent Monthly

Month	(1) Outstanding Balance	(2) Monthly Payment	(3) Monthly Finance Charge	(4) Monthly Loan Repayment
1	$1,000.00	$ 88.85	$10.00	$ 78.85
2	921.15	88.85	9.21	79.85
3	841.51	88.85	8.42	80.43
4	761.08	88.85	7.61	81.24
5	679.84	88.85	6.80	82.05
6	597.79	88.85	5.98	82.87
7	514.92	88.85	5.15	83.70
8	431.22	88.85	4.31	84.54
9	346.68	88.85	3.47	85.38
10	261.30	88.85	2.61	86.24
11	175.07	88.85	1.75	87.10
12	87.97	88.85	0.88	87.97
Total		$1,066.20	$66.19	$1,000.00

where t is the term of the loan in years. Thus, to finance a $1,000 purchase for one year at a discount rate of 12 percent, you must repay $1,136.36. If this were a 12-month install-ment loan, you would owe $94.70 ($1,136.36/12) per month. The true interest rate on this discount installment loan would be much higher than 12 percent because you would not have the full use of $1,000 during the entire year. As indicated in the cost comparison shown in Figure 6.7, the annual percentage rate on this loan is 24.28 percent, about twice the discount rate.

Add-On Method

The add-on method is by far the most widely used method for determining finance charges on consumer loans. Under the **add-on method**, the lender adds the interest to the value of the purchase you are financing to determine your total payments using the following for-mula:

$$\text{Total payments on add-on loan} = \text{amount financed} \times \left[1 + \left(\text{add-on rate} \times t\right)\right]$$

$$\$1,120 = \$1,000 \left[1 + \left(0.12 \times 1\right)\right]$$

> **Add-on method** Interest is added to the amount financed in order to determine total payments.

If the add-on rate is 12 percent per year and you intend to borrow $1,000 for one year, the interest charge of $120($1,000 × 0.12 × t) is the term of the loan in years, is added to the original principal of $1,000 to determine total repayments of $1,120 ($1,000 + $120). The monthly payments would equal $93.33 ($1,120/12). You should notice that an add-on rate of 12 percent is more costly than a similar loan with a simple interest rate of 12 per-cent. The monthly payments of $88.85 on the simple interest loan are $4.48 less per month than the $93.33 monthly payment for a comparable add-on loan.

As with the discount loan, the true interest rate on an add-on loan is far greater than the add-on rate of 12 percent. Again, you are being charged as if you had the full use of $1,000 for the entire year. However, you have the use of a full $1,000 only for the first month. Since you repay principal with each payment, the total amount borrowed declines with each payment. In the current example, an add-on rate of 12 percent would entail the same monthly payments as a simple interest rate of 21.46 percent. That is a significant dif-ference.

Annual Percentage Rate

Regardless of how the lender determines the interest charge, the government requires that the lender provide the borrower with the information on the true interest rate, or what is officially termed the annual percentage rate. The **annual percentage rate (APR)** is the ratio of the finance charge to the average amount of credit extended to you over the life of the contract, expressed as a percentage rate per year. Since the simple interest charge is also based on the amount of credit extended in each period, the annual simple interest rate and the APR are the same.

> **Annual percentage rate (APR)** The ratio of the finance charge to the average amount of credit extended over the life of the loan expressed as a rate.

Method	Contract Rate	APR	Monthly Payment	Total Interest Paid
Simple interest	12%	12.00%	$88.85	$ 66.19
Discount interest	12%	24.28%	94.72	136.36
Add-on interest	12%	21.46%	93.33	120.00

Figure 6.7
Comparative Interest on Credit of $1,000 to Be Repaid in 12 Equal Monthly Installments

There is nothing simple about calculating the APR on installment loans. However, inexpensive financial calculators will provide either the APR or monthly payments given the amount and term of the loan. In addition, interactive calculators on the Internet and software that can run on your personal computer are readily available.

The APR is the rate you should use to judge the relative cost of credit. As indicated in Figure 6.7, identical contract rates can result in widely different interest payments and annual percentage rates. If you are comparing loans for identical amounts of credit and identical maturities, the loan with the lower APR will also have the lower finance charge.

Areas of Special Concern

In addition to recognizing how the finance charges are computed, it is important that you read the entire credit agreement carefully and understand each of the several clauses that may be included in the contract. There may be late penalty fees for missing a periodic payment. In addition, a late payment may trigger special clauses, such as the following, in the loan contract.

Prepayment and the Rule of 78. Credit agreements will include a statement indicating how interest is to be calculated if you decide to repay the loan at any date that is earlier than scheduled. Agreements that utilize the add-on method for computing installment payments usually determine your interest refund by the so-called **rule of 78**. This method for computing the interest refunded upon early repayment depends on a difficult calculation that is favorable to lenders, because it penalizes early loan repayment.

The Acceleration Clause. If you miss just one payment on a loan, the **acceleration clause** makes the entire unpaid balance due immediately. If you can't pay this entire amount, you stand a chance of having the loan collateral repossessed. Repossession is guided by state law, but it usually means the lender is free to sell the item for its best market price. From this amount are deducted any expenses connected with the sale, and the difference is applied to the credit balance. If it is greater, the lender remits the difference to the borrower; if it is less, the borrower is still required to pay the difference. Your main concern here is the price the lender receives in selling the repossessed item. Under forced sale conditions, it could be very low, and you would bear the loss. Lenders do not usually apply the acceleration clause immediately, preferring instead to rely upon penalties for late payments, but it is not a factor to take casually.

The Add-On Clause. Suppose you purchase some kitchen appliances from an appliance dealer and finance the deal with an installment loan for one year. Six months later you return to the same dealer and purchase a television set and tape recorder as part of an add-on to your earlier agreement. This means it is added to the outstanding balance on your original loan. Eight months after that purchase, financial problems set in and you stop making payments on the loan. With an **add-on clause**, the dealer can repossess all the appliances he or she sold you, even though your total payments may have been more than enough to have paid for the earlier purchase. Fortunately, this clause is prohibited in some jurisdictions and in others the courts seldom enforce this clause.

The Balloon Payment. The **balloon payment** is usually the last installment payment, and it is for an amount much greater than the other monthly payments. The problem with the balloon is that borrowers may not prepare sufficiently to make the payment and so may require new financing when it is due or may have the item repossessed. Balloon clauses sometimes were used in the past as a means of defrauding borrowers, and this abuse led some states to make them illegal.

Rule of 78 A method for computing the interest refunded upon early repayment that is highly favorable to lenders.

Acceleration clause: Given a late payment the lender can demand immediate repayment of the loan balance.

Add-on clause Allows the lender to repossess all goods financed under the agreement in the event of a missed payment.

Balloon payment An amount larger than other periodic payments that is due as the last installment payment.

Obtaining Credit and Resolving Credit Problems

Once you understand how credit works, the next step is to select a lender. After successfully arranging credit, the final step is to use it properly to avoid credit problems. Unfortunately, even the most financially prudent people will find themselves overextended because of unforeseen contingencies. Therefore, you need to be prepared to deal with creditors when the unexpected happens.

Sources of Credit

There are many suppliers of credit, ranging from commercial banks at the top of a list to friends and relatives at the bottom. The discussion that follows will not attempt to explain detailed features of each but will focus instead on their most important characteristics. Comparative shopping is important in the credit market. We are in an era of volatile interest rates, and although it is true that similar lenders tend to charge about the same rates for similar loans, differences can exist. And don't underestimate the importance of saving 1 or 2 percent on the loan. For example, a 48-month installment loan for $5,000 will cost about $250 more at 16 percent than at 14 percent.

Interest rates charged on consumer loans in a recent period are illustrated in Figure 6.8. Current rates are probably different, but relative costs are likely to be similar. Rates on credit cards are typically above other types of personal loans. Highly collateralized loans, such as car loans, tend to be significantly lower. Over this recent period, there was almost a six-point differential between credit card rates and the rates on new car loans. Before you run up that balance on your credit card, it would be wise to check out less expensive sources of credit.

Be sure you consider the following dos and don'ts before you take out a loan:

Loan Dos

- Shop around for a loan
- Read the loan application form
- Get copies of all forms you sign

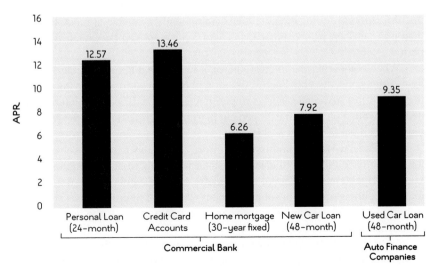

Figure 6.8
Interest Rates on Consumer Loans (May 2007)

Source: Federal Reserve Bank..

Loan Don'ts

- Be talked into falsifying information on a loan
- Accept larger monthly payments than you can afford
- Accept last minute changes in the terms of the loan
- Sign a blank form

Personal Lines of Credit and Banking Institutions

Commercial banks, savings and loan associations, and credit unions all compete for your consumer credit dollar with similar offers. In addition to credit cards, these institutions generally provide revolving credit at lower interest rates in the form of overdraft protection credit lines, unsecured personal credit lines, and home equity credit lines.

Overdraft protection credit line Credit is automatically extended to cover excess withdrawals from a checking account.

The financial institution where you have a checking account may offer you an **overdraft protection credit line**. If you write a check for an amount that exceeds the funds available, the bank automatically extends you a loan to cover the excess amount up to some predetermined credit limit. In addition to providing you with a convenient source of credit, the overdraft protection credit line has the advantage of saving you the embarrassment and cost of a bounced check.

Unsecured personal credit line An unsecured credit line upon which you can withdraw cash.

An **unsecured personal credit line** is separate from your checking account. You must apply for it by submitting a loan application. After you are approved for an unsecured personal credit line, you access the credit line by writing specially issued checks or utilizing a special credit card. Each month you receive a statement indicating the amount you owe, the amount of credit still available, your finance charges, and your minimum monthly payment.

Home Equity Loans

Home equity loan A loan secured by the ownership in your home in the form of a second mortgage.

With a **home equity loan**, your credit is secured by your ownership in your home. Banks typically let you borrow up to 75 to 80 percent of the equity in your home. Home equity loans come in two forms: closed-end credit and open-end credit. With an *open-end home equity line of credit,* you can borrow up to a predetermined credit limit on a revolving charge account. A *closed-end home equity loan* is the same as a second mortgage on your home. You borrow a fixed amount for a set period of time.

Home equity loans have become extremely popular because interest charges on home equity loans up to $100,000 for a married couple may be taken as an itemized deduction on federal income tax returns. Interest payments on all other consumer loans are nondeductible. Moreover, home equity loans are typically available at much lower interest rates than other unsecured consumer loans, and repayment can be stretched out over a longer period.

When comparing the interest rate on a loan with a tax deductible interest rate with a loan with a nondeductible interest rate, it will help if you first adjust the deductible rate for the related tax advantage. For example, if you have a 10 percent interest rate that is tax deductible and you are in the 28 percent marginal tax bracket, then the real cost of credit is only 7.2 percent (= $10 \times (1 - .28)$).

The Federal Trade Commission enforces a three-day cancellation rule on home equity loans. You have the right to cancel the loan within three days of signing the contract on your principal home. Beware of home equity scams listed in Figure 6.9. Predatory lenders may target home owners for subprime loans. These are high-risk loans at high interest rates to borrowers with minimal debt repayment capacity. Such loans have been used to fund shoddy or nonexistent home repairs.

Used wisely, paying off higher-interest-bearing debt with funds from a low-interest, tax-advantaged home equity loan could be a good decision. On the negative side, home

Figure 6.9
Home Equity Scams

Source: FTC Consumer Alert,
"Avoiding Home Equity Scams."

Equity Stripping: The lender gives you a loan based on the equity in your home, not on your ability to repay based on your income. If you can't make the payments, you could end up losing your home.

Loan Flipping: The lender encourages you to repeatedly refinance the loan and often to borrow more money. Each time you refinance, you pay additional fees and interest points. That only serves to increase your debt.

Credit Insurance Packing: The lender adds credit insurance to your loan, which you may not need.

Bait and Switch: The lender offers one set of loan terms when you apply, then pressures you to accept higher charges when you sign to complete the transaction.

Deceptive Loan Servicing: The lender doesn't provide you with accurate or complete account statements and payoff figures. That makes it almost impossible for you to determine how much you have paid or how much you owe. You may pay more than you owe.

equity loans may entice some consumers into making long-term payments on purchases that provide short-lived satisfaction and may place home equity at risk. If you can't repay your home equity loan, there could be stiff repayment penalties and you could lose your home.

Consumer Finance Companies

There are two types of consumer finance companies: those that offer specialized loans, such as GMAC on General Motors automobiles, and those that offer general-purpose loans, both secured and unsecured. The specialized lenders are dominant forces within their particular areas, and they usually offer interest rates at or below bank rates. Sometimes they are substantially below bank rates when they are part of auto dealers' sales promotion programs. Of course, the question then is whether you are getting the best price on the item purchased. Try to bring financing into the discussion as a separate topic after the price has been agreed upon. The objective is to get the best price *and* the best financing.

The general-purpose consumer finance companies are more willing to loan to first-time borrowers and to make loans on unsecured terms. Their administrative costs tend to be higher because they make many small loans, and their delinquency costs are also higher because of the poorer quality of the loans they make. As a result of these factors, you can expect their interest rates to be higher on these kinds of loans.

Student Loans

Credit cards should only be used to finance your short-term credit needs. Obviously, it is the wrong source of credit for a college education, which provides delayed long-term benefits. A prolonged outstanding balance on a credit card should signal the need to rethink your budget. You could work part-time or transfer to a less expensive school. If you are still short of funding, student loans available through government programs and through private lenders are the preferred source for funding your education.

About 42 percent of federal education loans come through the Stafford Loan Program, which provides both subsidized loans and unsubsidized loans. On subsidized loans the government pays the interest while you are in college; however, on unsubsidized loans you pay all the interest. Both loans are based on financial need and both loans are guaranteed by the federal government. Consequently, they are financed at favorable rates of interest that are likely to be significantly less than on other types of credit. For those in significant need, Perkins loans may be available through the school financial aid office. The interest on these loans is also subsidized while the student is in school. In addition, some of or the entire loan may be forgiven for employment in public service.

Parents can help finance their children's education through the PLUS loan program. The funds are sent directly to your school and the first payment including principal and interest is due 60 days after the loan is fully disbursed. These are less attractive than Stafford loans and the parent is responsible for repayment. Borrowers are charged a fee up to 4 percent of the amount disbursed to pay for repayment insurance. Since 2006 rates on Stafford and PLUS have been fixed at the rates shown in Table 6.2. These are maximum rates, lending institutions can charge less. You can check with **SallieMae.com** and other lending institutions for the current rates. Congress has passed reductions in the fixed rates on federal subsidized loans that will be phased in over future years.

Only after you have maximized your eligibility for federally subsidized loans should you consider private sources. Private student loans financed by banks and other financial institutions carry higher interest rates because they are not subsidized. The rates are tied to your credit score. Private student loans may be arranged through the school's student aid office or by direct to student financing. Your school may offer a preferred lender list. Don't assume that these are the lowest cost lenders. Recently, it has been discovered that some schools have received kickbacks from lenders placed on this list. Several have had to settle claims for deceptive practices. Conflicts of interest should be disclosed with the preferred lender list. Be sure to ask your institution if it receives any special benefits or treatment from lenders on this list.

Try to limit your borrowing. The more you borrow, the greater is your chance of defaulting on repayments. Data from the National Center for Education Statistics indicate that almost one-half of full-time undergraduates borrow to finance their education and the average annual amount borrowed is about $5,000 or $20,000 for four years. At a 6 to 8 percent APR and a 10-year prepayment schedule, $20,000 in student loans generates monthly payments of $222 or $242. They may not sound like a lot, but it will be added on to all of the other debt you are likely to accumulate after you graduate from home mortgages and car loans.

You are responsible for repaying your student loans even when you do not graduate or find a job. Moreover, student loans generally cannot be discharged in bankruptcy. If you default on your student loan by not making payments for 270 months, you could be in for a costly surprise. You will be liable for penalties, court costs, and attorney fees. Your wages and Social Security benefit payments can be garnished and on government loans your income tax refunds may be intercepted. If you are having trouble meeting monthly payments, discuss your situation with your lender. It may be possible to avoid default by deferring payments or lowering your monthly payment by extending your repayment schedule or considering loan consolidation strategies. You may also benefit from the recently enacted College Cost Reduction and Access Act of 2007. It provides monthly payment caps and loan forgiveness on federal direct loans, such as Stafford loans for low-to-moderate income earners. There is a complicated formula used to determine who is

Table 6.2
Illustrative Rates on Student Loans

Perkins loans	5.0%
Stafford loans	6.8%
PLUS loans	8.5%
Private loans*	7.6–15.3%

* Approximate rates for credit scores from excellent to fair
Source: Sallie Mae, May 2008

eligible, but essentially you should not have to devote more than 15 percent of your discretionary income to repayments. For those that satisfy the income constraints, monthly payments may be reduced and capped, and after 25 years of loan repayment on the outstanding principal may be forgiven. The Act also includes loan forgiveness for qualifying employees after 10 years of service in government agencies and nonprofit organizations.

Repayment of outstanding student loans should also be a part of your credit management strategy. High cost credit should always be paid off first. Credit cards and personal loans are likely to have higher interest rates than student or home equity loans. In addition, interest on student loans and home equity loans may be tax deductible, whereas interest charges on personal credit are not. The student loan must be for what the IRS terms "qualified educational expenses" and the deduction is phased out for upper income earners. It may be taken out to finance you, your spouse, or a dependent's education. Since the deduction is an adjustment to gross income, you don't have to itemize to receive the benefit. Check out IRS Pub. 970 "Tax Benefits for Education" for details on the tax advantage.

Other Sources

Some sources are not typical lenders to consumers but are nevertheless important. You can borrow on your ordinary life insurance policy up to its loan value, usually at a rate that could be far lower than any other available rate if the policy is older than, say, 10 years. These loans are exceptionally easy to make, requiring you to do nothing more than write a

FINANCIAL PLANNING *for*
young adults 6.3

Student Loan Consolidation

You just graduated with student loans and your mailbox is stuffed with loan consolidation offers. A consolidation loan is a new loan that refinances one or more previous loans. The old loan is paid off and a new loan is originated. You generally have to start paying back your initial student loans six months after leaving school. These loans generally have a maximum repayment term of 10 years. By arranging a loan consolidation, you can typically extend the repayment period to 30 years at a fixed rate. This can significantly lower your monthly payments. For example, on a 5 percent loan, this can cut your monthly payments almost in half. If you are just starting out with relocation expenses and initial household expenses, smaller monthly payments can reduce the strain on your budget. Of course, your total interest payment on the loan will be greater over the extended period. However, you should have the option of making larger monthly payments in the future and paying off your loan earlier than scheduled.

Generally, the interest rate on the consolidated loan is about equal to the weighted average of the rates on your separate loans. For example, when a $40,000 loan at 4 percent is consolidated with a $10,000 loan at 5 percent, the consolidated $50,000 loan will have a rate of about 4.2 percent (40/50*4% + 10/50*5%).

Both the government and private lenders offer loan consolidations. In addition to an extended term of repayment, lenders may offer other repayment options. These may include a graduated payment plan (payments are set to increase over time), an income-sensitive program (payments are tied to the size of current income), and an income-contingent program (payments are tied to your future income). You should analyze how each of these options affects the loan forgiveness provisions in the College Cost Reduction and Access Act of 2007, which provide loan forgiveness on federal direct student loans for eligible employees after 10 years of repayment and others after 25 years of repayment.

If you are out of school, in school but attending classes less than half-time, or in school with direct federal loans, you probably qualify for a loan consolidation. In many cases you don't even have to have more than one loan to consolidate. If you are thinking of entering graduate school, you may be able to consolidate your undergraduate loans while continuing your education.

Web sites with additional information:

Direct Consolidation Loans	loanconsolidation.ed.gov
College Funding Services	www.cfsloans.com
Federal Consolidation.Org	www.federalconsolidation.org
Sallie Mae	www.salliemae.com

letter. Although you never have to repay them, if you die, your beneficiaries will receive only the face value of the policy less the amount of the loan outstanding.

If you own stocks or bonds, you can consider using them as collateral for a loan. A bank will accept securities as collateral, or you can open a margin account with a stock-brokerage firm. In either case, you can usually borrow up to 50 percent of the market value of the securities pledged. The interest rate on such a loan will probably be one to two points above the prime rate (the rate a bank charges its most creditworthy customer). This arrangement can be risky in a volatile market. Should the market price of the stocks fall, you may get a call for additional collateral. If you fail to provide the requested funds, the broker may force the sale of your stocks at a market low.

If you are really desperate and have something of value, consider a pawnshop. Pawnbrokers are willing to make loans on practically any item they feel can be resold if you fail to reclaim it after a specified period of time, usually 60 to 90 days. You will be able to borrow only a fraction of the item's market value and can expect to pay the very highest interest rates allowed. They are bad places to borrow, but pawnshops can be good places to buy if you are willing to take some risks on product quality and service.

As a last (or maybe first) resort, friends and relatives might extend credit to you. Before taking this alternative, bear in mind that credit misunderstandings have ended many friendships. The best advice if you do borrow (or lend) is to put the arrangement in writing, complete with all pertinent details that are found on other credit contracts. A "pay-me-back-when-you-can" loan is bad for both the borrower and the lender, because neither knows how to budget for the loan. Also remember that if either borrower or lender dies, heirs will be left to resolve the loan. Although the two parties involved may know and trust each other, their heirs may not.

Another option is to have a creditworthy friend or relative cosign a loan for you. However, should you default on the loan, the individual who cosigned the loan will be financially responsible for the remaining payments and any penalties or collection charges. In most states, the lender has the same rights to collect from the cosigner as the initial borrower. This means the lender can collect from the cosigner without first attempting to collect from the borrower. If you are asked to cosign a loan, remember the reason the borrower needs a cosigner is that he or she has been deemed a poor credit risk.

A Credit Management Strategy

Credit management is similar in many respects to cash management, discussed in Chapter 5. There the objective was to maximize the return on short-term investments while achieving a reasonable degree of liquidity. Here the objective is to minimize the cost of credit while simultaneously achieving both the target amount needed and a reasonable level of shopping convenience. Since we differ in how much credit we want and in our attitude toward convenience, our strategies for managing credit will also differ, but the following guidelines apply in most cases:

1. Use as much of the grace period as you can, but be sure to avoid late payment penalties. You can thus keep your money in an interest-earning account longer than if you pay bills with cash.
2. Use revolving charge accounts, as a 30-day account. We mentioned previously that most often this is expensive credit, and it should be used only if other credit is unavailable.
3. Take a broad view toward credit; that is, do not think in terms of borrowing here to buy this or borrowing there to buy that, but think instead of a total borrowing requirement. Then search for the cheapest sources of credit to meet this requirement. For example, you might take a home equity mortgage to buy a car, send your kid to summer camp,

and enjoy a vacation. The after-tax interest on this loan could be far less than an installment loan on the car and personal loans for the other two activities—and no riskier.

4. Be careful of variable-rate loans if you think that interest rates may rise. The initial interest rate on a variable-rate loan is lower than on a fixed-rate loan. The variable rate, however, is indexed to other market rates of interest and automatically rises as they do. Under all circumstances try to avoid a vicious credit cycle In which interest payments on the debt become a burden, forcing you to search for other sources of credit just to repay the previous debt. Keeping track of your personal debt ratios can help you avoid this trap.

Resolving Personal Debt Problems

It's best to avoid credit problems by limiting your credit to an amount your income can support. Credit counselors often feel this limit is about 20 percent of your take-home pay, not including your home mortgage. The 20 percent is applied in two ways: First, your monthly credit payments should not exceed 20 percent of your monthly take-home pay; and second, your total consumer credit should not exceed 20 percent of your total take-home pay for the year. If you exceed either one of these limits, you are courting financial danger. You can keep credit within the 20 percent limit by always figuring the impact of any new credit arrangement on your budget *before* you take out a loan.

TOPIC LINKS

Consumer handbook to consumer regulations

 saving money 6.4

Avoid Payday Loans

The payday loan business is booming. You probably noticed new locations for payday loans in your city with flashing neon signs. The loans go by various names: payday loans, cash advance loans, check advance loans, post-dated check loans, or deferred deposit check loans. They are all small short-term loans at horrendous interest rates.

You write the lender a post-dated check for the amount borrowed plus a fee, or alternatively, you authorize an electronic withdrawal on the due date. If you don't have the required funds in the account, you may incur charges for a bounced check. The money paid the borrower equals the amount of the check less the fee. The lender may be reluctant to tell you just how much this loan costs, but thanks to the Truth in Lending Act you must receive the annual percentage rate (APR) on the loan.

Suppose the lender charges a fixed fee of $15 on a $100 14-day loan. You write a check for $115 to borrow $100 for the 14 days until you receive your pay check. The lender agrees to hold your check before depositing it 14 days from now. You pay the $15 fee for each 14-day extension. If you delay paying back the principal on the loan for an entire year, your fee totals $390. That's a 390 percent APR on the amount borrowed. That might be called legal robbery. Some state laws limit the number of times the loan can be extended and the maximum APR for the year. Even state imposed limits, however, are likely to be much higher than rates on other types of loans.

If you get caught in a financial emergency, consumer agencies have listed the following alternatives to payday loans:

- Check the rates on personal loans from your bank or credit union and compare the APR
- Check out the rate on a credit card cash advance
- Check out the cost of overdraft protection on your checking account
- Check with your employer for a possible cash advance
- Check with a current creditor to see if you can skip or delay a payment. The fee for the skipped payment may be less than the fee for a payday loan
- Get a little help from friends and family

You are, of course, much better off if you can avoid the need for a short-term loan by doing the following:

- Keeping a budget and monitoring your expenses
- Keeping an emergency fund in a savings account. Even a small amount might eliminate the need for a payday loan.
- Working a second job

If you find yourself always running out of funds before the next pay check, you may need the help of a credit counseling service. Your employer, credit union, or local government may help you locate a free or low-cost counseling program.

Despite all precautions, you may still run into credit problems. As indicated in Figure 6.10, medical institutions initiated over half of the collection actions for bad debts. No doubt most of these problems resulted from unexpected circumstances and inadequate health coverage. However, the National Foundation for Credit Counseling reports that the number one reason people gave when filing for bankruptcy was poor money management and excessive spending.

If you find yourself confronting a financial crisis, the first step is to contact the creditor. You cannot resolve a credit problem by avoiding creditors. Explain the reasons for your temporary difficulties and try to work out a modified payment plan that fits your budget. Most lenders prefer being paid in full, even if extra time is needed. In bankruptcy they may only collect a fraction of the amount due. Also, the Fair Debt Collection Practices Act protects you from lender harassment at all times. If you are unable to obtain relief from the lender, seek credit counseling. A personal bankruptcy should only be considered after all other attempts to resolve your problem have failed.

Credit Counseling

Beware of advertisements promoting debt relief. Some companies may be selling debt consolidation in a single high-interest loan or may be offering bankruptcy services. You cannot change your credit history, only your future.

The Federal Trade Commission warns you to beware of companies that

- Want you to pay for credit repair services before any services are provided
- Do not tell you your legal rights and what you can do yourself for free
- Recommend that you not contact a credit bureau directly
- Suggest that you try to invent a new credit report by applying for an Employer Identification number (EIN) to use instead of your Social Security number
- Advise you to dispute all information in your credit report or take any action that seems illegal, such as creating a new credit identity

If you have a credit problem, contact the Better Business Bureau or the Chamber of Commerce in your town and inquire about credit counseling assistance. Avoid any private credit counselor who supposedly specializes in working out your credit problems. The fee for this service can be as high as 35 percent of your total debt.

Recognizing their common interest in helping troubled borrowers, many lenders support the activities of **credit counseling** services sponsored by the National Foundation of Consumer Counseling. These counseling centers provide two levels of service. First, they

TOPIC LINKS

National Foundation of Consumer Counseling

Credit counseling Helps consumers with credit problems by rescheduling loans and eliminating negative behaviors.

Figure 6.10
Collection Actions by Type

Source: "An Overview of Consumer Data and Credit Reporting," Robert B. Avery, Paul S. Calem, and Glenn B. Canner, Federal Reserve Bulletin, February 2003.

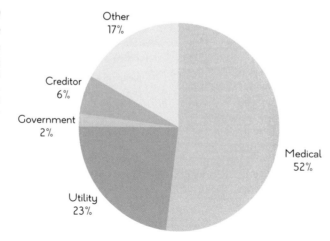

Other 17%

Creditor 6%

Government 2%

Medical 52%

Utility 23%

work with the borrower to develop a reasonable plan for repaying debts. This plan often includes a budget. Second, if this budget indicates that income will not be sufficient to meet both living expenses and the existing debt repayment load, the counselor will attempt to negotiate a more reasonable repayment plan with lenders. The borrower then gives the counselor a certain percentage of each week's income, and this in turn is given to the lenders. This service is essentially free to borrowers, regardless of their income, as are other counseling services.

Bankruptcy

Many people continue to regard bankruptcy as a calamity to be avoided at any cost. Others view it as an easy way to avoid all the bills that result from an enjoyable buying binge. Regardless of your viewpoint, bankruptcy is a serious step. The Bankruptcy Abuse Prevention and Consumer Protection Act of 2005 (BAPCPA) requires that debtors participate in financial counseling with an approved nonprofit budget and credit counseling agency prior to filing for bankruptcy. They must also complete a course in personal financial management before their debts can be discharged.

You can file for bankruptcy under Chapter 7 of the bankruptcy code, which is called a straight bankruptcy; or under Chapter 13 of the bankruptcy code, which is called a wage earner plan. In most instances, neither can be used to avoid payments for alimony, child support, fines, taxes, or recent student loans.

A Chapter 7 bankruptcy discharges all of your debts and thus provides you a fresh start. A **straight bankruptcy** may require you to sell off most of your assets. However, you are not left a complete pauper, and in most cases few assets are actually sold. Under federal exemptions, which may be more or less generous than state laws permit, you may keep from creditors a portion of home owner's equity or personal property and additional amounts of specific assets. The BAPCAP requires that you must pass a means test that depends on the median income in your state in order to file under Chapter 7. Filers with higher incomes who do not pass a means test may consider an alternative wage earner plan.

Straight bankruptcy A Chapter 7 bankruptcy in which most assets are sold off, most debts are discharged, and a fresh start is provided.

Debtors who have been through a straight bankruptcy cannot file again for another eight years, and the record of the bankruptcy remains on a credit report for 10 years. During this period it may be difficult to obtain credit or enter into normal everyday contracts such as rental agreements or purchase contracts. It may even hurt employment prospects if potential employers access credit records.

Under a Chapter 13 filing, the court creates a **wage earner plan**. This is a court approved and administered repayment schedule for employed persons with regular income. This allows debtors to retain most of their property and to repay all or part of their obligations over a five-year period with protection from creditors. It will remain on your credit report for seven years. On the plus side, it indicates that by filing under Chapter 13 rather than Chapter 7, you made a sincere attempt to repay your debts.

Wage earner plan A repayment schedule established under Chapter 13 bankruptcy that allows debtors to retain their property while repaying all or part of their obligations.

Bankruptcy is a financial tool of last resort. It should only be entered into when all else fails. Since it is likely to come to the attention of both future creditors and employers, it can hinder your attempts to obtain future sales credit, a mortgage, insurance, and even employment. In addition, income taxes, child support payments, alimony, student loans, debts incurred in anticipation of bankruptcy, and court awards may all survive a bankruptcy.

TOPIC LINKS

Association of Independent Credit Counseling Agencies

Protection from Lender Harassment

The **Fair Debt Collection Practices Act** entitles borrowers to be treated fairly by debt collectors. You are entitled to a written notice from the debt collector describing your debt in detail and what to do if you feel you do not owe the debt. You then have 30 days to send a letter to the debt collector denying the debt. The debt collector cannot continue collection

Fair Debt Collection Practices Act Regulates permissible tactics for collecting overdue loans.

efforts until you receive a written verification of the debt. Among other things, the debt collector cannot use abusive language, threaten you, harass you at work, or attempt to collect the bill through trickery. Finally, you can keep a debt collector from communicating with you by providing written notification that all contacts must cease. This does not eliminate the debt and you can still be sued. Report any problems you have with an abusive debt collector to your state Attorney Generals office and the Federal Trade Commission.

key terms

acceleration clause (p. 164)
add-on clause (p. 164)
add-on method (p. 163)
adjusted balance method (p. 152)
affinity card (p. 154)
annual percentage rate (APR) (p. 163)
average daily balance method (p. 153)
balloon payment (p. 164)
bank credit cards (p. 154)
cash credit (p. 160)
chargeback (p. 158)
closed-end account (p. 149)
credit blocking (p. 159)
credit counseling (p. 172)
debit card (p. 159)
discount method (p. 162)
Equal Credit Opportunity Act (ECOA) (p. 147)
Fair Credit Reporting Act (FCRA) (p. 148)
Fair Debt Collection Practices Act (p. 173)
grace period (p. 153)
home equity loan (p. 166)
individual credit account (p. 147)

joint credit account (p. 147)
open-end account (p. 149)
overdraft protection credit line (p. 166)
previous balance method (p. 152)
private-label cards (p. 155)
promissory note (p. 161)
regular charge account (p. 149)
retail installment contract (p. 161)
revolving credit account (p. 149)
rule of 78 (p. 164)
sales credit (p. 149)
secured credit card (p. 149)
security agreement (p. 161)
service credit (p. 143)
simple interest method (p. 161)
straight bankruptcy (p. 173)
travel and entertainment (T&E) cards (p. 154)
Truth in Lending Act (TILA) (p. 145)
two-cycle average daily balance method (p. 154)
unsecured personal credit line (p. 166)
wage earner plan (p. 173)

follow-up on the Steele family

Reread the chapter-opening vignette.

1. What are the pros and cons of borrowing on a credit card to pay for the necessary auto repairs?
2. What are the pros and cons of borrowing on home equity to pay for the necessary auto repairs?
3. How would you advise the Steeles to finance the auto repairs? What alternative sources of financing might you consider? Does selling off some stock holdings seem like a good idea?

problems and review questions

1. Explain how credit serves as
   a. a shopping convenience
   b. a means to increase total consumption benefits
   c. a hedge against inflation
   d. a source of emergency funds

2. What are several disadvantages of credit?

3. Describe the three Cs of credit and why lenders feel they are important in evaluating a loan request. Then list five steps you can take to begin a credit record.

4. What function does the credit bureau perform in the lender's evaluation of your credit application?

5. What is a FICO score? How do you improve your FICO score?

6. What is the difference between an open-end credit account and a closed-end credit account?

7. What is a revolving credit account? How does it differ from an installment loan?

8. Which method for determining the outstanding balance on a revolving credit account is likely to determine the lowest outstanding balance? Which method is likely to determine the highest outstanding balance?

9. What are some important considerations when choosing a credit card? Under what circumstances would you decide to obtain a credit card with a lower APR but a higher annual maintenance fee?

10. List steps you can take to protect yourself against credit card fraud. What is your liability limit on a lost or stolen credit card?

11. Suppose you review your monthly statement of credit card activities and discover that you have been charged for an item you didn't buy. What should you do?

12. What is credit blocking? How might it affect you?

13. How does a credit card differ from a debit card? Explain.

14. Describe the information a lender must provide you on a credit contract.

15. Why is the APR less than either the discount interest rate or the add-on interest rate?

16. Why should you be particularly concerned about the following items?
    a. the rule of 78
    b. the acceleration clause
    c. the add-on clause
    d. a balloon payment

17. Explain several steps you can take to avoid credit problems. Indicate the actions you should take if you are denied credit or employment because of an unfavorable credit report.

18. Explain why home equity loans have become an important source of consumer credit.

19. If a good friend of yours has had serious financial misfortunes lately and is unable to meet her debt payments, what advice can you give? Be sure to include the topic of bankruptcy, since she has heard that it will eliminate all her credit problems. In your discussion, distinguish between straight bankruptcy and a wage earner plan.

Helen received a $5,000 cash gift from her grandparents as a graduation present. She has no immediate need for these funds. Therefore, she plans to either invest the funds or use them to reduce some of her outstanding debt. Her debt includes an outstanding balance on her credit card, a used car loan, and a student loan. All of these loans are at current average market rates.

case 6.1

Helen's Debt Repayment Choices

Questions

1. Given Helen's three sources of debt, which is likely to carry the highest APR and which is likely to carry the lowest APR?

2. Which of these debts should she consider paying off first? Why?

3. Helen has to decide whether it is best to use these funds for debt repayment or investment. What factors should she take into consideration?

4. Are there special strategies she should consider with regard to her student loan?

case 6.2

Evaluating Nancy Tai's Revolving Account

Nancy Tai has recently opened a revolving charge account with MasterCard. Her credit limit is $2,000 but she has not charged that much since opening the account. Nancy hasn't had the time to review her monthly statements promptly as she should, but over the upcoming weekend she plans to catch up on her work.

In reviewing October's statement she notices that her beginning balance was $600 and that she made a $200 payment on November 10. She also charged purchases of $80 on November 5, $100 on November 15, and $50 on November 30. She can't tell how much interest she paid in November because she spilled watercolor paint on that portion of the statement. She does remember, though, seeing the letters APR and the number 16 percent. Also, the back of her statement indicates that interest was charged using the average daily balance method, including current purchases, which considers the day of a charge or credit.

Questions

1. Assuming a 30-day period in November, calculate November's interest. Also calculate the interest Nancy would have paid with: (*a*) the previous balance method, (*b*) the adjusted balance method.

2. Going back in time to when Nancy was just about to open her account, and assuming she could choose among credit sources that offered the different monthly balance determinations, and assuming further that Nancy would increase her outstanding balance over time, which credit source would you recommend? Explain.

3. In talking with Nancy, you have learned that she can also get credit through her credit union. An advertisement from the union shows that Nancy could take a personal cash loan at 14 percent on a discount basis or an installment loan at 12 percent add-on. Each is a one-year loan. Would you advise Nancy to use one of these to pay off her November balance with MasterCard? (Assume the 14 and 12 percents are not APRs.) Nancy doesn't believe she will have enough funds to reduce the November balance until the end of next October.

working out on the Web

Exercises to Strengthen Your Use of the Internet
(Internet links for the following exercises can be found at www.prenhall.com/frasca.)

Exercise 6.1 Obtain a Credit Report

You can link to TransUnion (www.transunion.com), Experian (www.experian.com), Equifax (www.equifax.com) and AnnualCreditReport.com for information on obtaining your credit report.

Q. Where and how can you obtain a credit report? How much will it cost you?

Exercise 6.2 Comparing Credit Card Offers

BankRate.Com (www.bankrate.com) provides information on numerous credit card offers. Select the "Credit Card" link. Select two credit cards and examine the terms and conditions?

Q. Given your expenditure habits, which is the preferred choice for you?

Exercise 6.3 Should You Prepay a Loan?

BankSite.Com (www.banksite.com) has calculators for personal loans. In the calculator section on Trusts and Investments there is a Prepayment vs. Investment Calculator. It determines when you benefit from making early payments on a mortgage. However, the results can be extended to any installment-type loan with simple interest payments.

Q. Using your best estimate of current interest rates, is it better to prepay your loan or invest in a money market fund? How about prepaying your loan versus investing in risky stocks? What part does risk play in your decision?

Exercise 6.4 How the Interest Rate Affects Your Debt Repayments

The interest rate can significantly influence the size and term of your debt repayments. This can be illustrated with the aid of several financial calculators on the Internet. The most appropriate one for this project is the Unknown Loan Variables Calculator from Bank 2000 (www.bank2000.com). Go to the link for "more" calculators on the home page and find the Unknown Variables Calculator. The program will calculate the value for the field you leave blank. Assuming compounding with simple interest, this program can calculate the number of periods needed to pay off a loan given the monthly dollar payments. You can also calculate the monthly dollar payment needed to pay off a loan in a given number of installments.

Q. Calculate the monthly payment on a 24-month installment loan of $5,000 at both an 18 percent annual rate of interest and a 15 percent annual rate of interest. At the lower interest rate, how much do you save on monthly payments and total interest payments?

Q. Calculate how long it would take to pay off a $5,000 loan balance with monthly payments of $100 at both 18 percent and 15 percent annual rates of interest. How much longer does it take to pay off the loan at the higher interest rate, and how do interest payments differ?

Exercise 6.5 Interest Rate Comparisons

Using the BankRate.Com (www.bankrate.com) Home Equity Loan page, find the lowest rate on a home equity loan in the closest geographic market. Compare this with the lowest rate on a credit card in the same geographic market from the BankRate.Com Credit Card page.

Q. Which is the better deal?

Exercise 6.6 Changes in Interest Rates

The Federal Reserve Bank publishes data on the types of loans listed in Figure 6.8. These are placed on the Internet at the Board of Governors Web site for the Federal Reserve Bank (www.federalreserve.gov/releases). Compare data on the most recent rates with those listed in Figure 6.8.

Q. Does the comparison indicate an increasing or a falling trend in interest rates? Given the historic trend in interest rates, how do you expect interest rates to change in the future?

Exercise 6.7 The Card You Pick Can Save You Money

Every six months the Federal Reserve System collects data on credit cards offered by major financial institutions and publishes the "Survey of Credit Card Plan" (www.federalreserve.gov/Pubs/shop/survey.htm). The survey reveals a variety of offers over a wide range of interest rates and annual fees.

Q. What are the highest and lowest interest rates in the latest survey? What are the highest and lowest annual fees in the latest survey?

part 3

Buying Now and Paying Later

managing your long–term liabilities

The previous section concentrated on management of short–term assets and liabilities. Liabilities that last longer than a year are long-term liabilities. Some of the techniques discussed in Chapter 6 can be applied to the management of long-term assets. For example, installment loans often last more than a year. Such loans are typically used to finance the purchase of consumer durables. A consumer durable is any good that provides benefits lasting more than one year.

Consumers often incur long-term liabilities to purchase consumer durables such as home furnishings. The logic of purchasing consumer durables with long-term credit is that you match the future stream of benefits with a future stream of financial obligations. Using long-term financing to purchase goods that offer only immediate and short-term benefits is unwise in most instances. It locks you into continuing payments that extend way beyond any enjoyment you may have derived from the product. Consumers that use long-term credit to finance temporary pleasures may find themselves on a financially disastrous treadmill. They become immersed in ever-increasing amounts of debt to sustain an overly high standard of living.

In this section we focus on two major lifestyle purchases that provide long-term benefits; the family car and the family home. First we discuss the new expanding electronic marketplace and your rights as a consumer in Chapter 7. Then we look at strategies for selecting the family car and weigh the relative benefits of leasing versus purchasing.

Chapter 8 examines the most long-lasting and expensive asset you are likely to own, the family home. Where you live should complement your desired lifestyle, but it also must be constrained by how much you can afford. This will depend on the cost of the home and the cost of financing. Accordingly, you must know how to shop for a home and shop for financing. The home mortgage market offers a wide selection of mortgage formats. Mortgages can have fixed or variable interest rates and the payments can be structured over various time frames. After reading the chapter, you should be able to assess your buying and borrowing opportunities intelligently.

Consumer Durables
the personal car

Steele family

Given the recent problems with Sharon's car, the Steeles now expect they may have to replace it sooner than they had planned. They are wary of buying a new car and committing themselves to large monthly payments. They could purchase a slightly "newer" used car, but they worry that might result in taking on someone else's problem.

At work, Sharon uses one of the company cars to visit clients. Every few years the company vehicles are replaced with the latest models. When she asked her boss about the cost, he said that the company leases rather than purchases its fleet of cars. She was shocked to learn that the monthly payments on these leases were substantially less than she and Arnold were paying on their car loans. Sharon wonders whether they should consider leasing their next car as a way of holding down monthly expenses. The morning paper contains numerous ads by car dealers listing leasing arrangements requiring little money down and low monthly payments.

After the family home, your car is probably the next most expensive purchase. The car is one member of a class of products called **consumer durables**. These are defined as goods that provide consumer benefits lasting at least one year. Purchasing decisions regarding consumer durables deserve more attention than do the decisions made when purchasing everyday consumables. The negative impact of making a wrong decision when buying a consumer durable probably will be more expensive and long lasting. Such goods make possible our high standard of living; however, they also make significant demands on both our financial resources and our available time.

Consumer durables
Consumer goods that provide benefits that last at least one year.

About 10 percent of consumer expenditures are devoted to household furnishings, appliances, and automobiles. When you consider the ongoing costs of operations and maintenance for these items, their proportionate impact on the household budget is even greater. In one way or another, $1 out of every $4 that consumers spend is somehow related to the purchase of consumer durables or the operation and maintenance of them.

Consumer durables give rise to multiple entries on the household budget. A product that is purchased with savings is listed as an expense at the time of purchase. If it is financed through borrowing, however, it will create inflexible future expenses until the loan is repaid. The continuing outflow required for maintenance and operations must also be budgeted. Moreover, additional expenses will most likely show up in separate household accounts for utilities and fuels. And finally, when they unexpectedly break replacement costs place a strain on our emergency funds.

Given our large discrete expenditures on consumer durables and their interrelatedness with other household expenditures, it's easy to see that consumer durables create special budgeting problems. Without adequate planning, repair or replacement is likely to be an unexpected event that creates havoc with the household budget.

Using your own funds to finance your purchases will save finance charges. You can budget for these expenditures by creating replacement funds for goods that are on a regular replacement cycle, such as the roof on your home or the family car. An emergency fund can be used to pay for unexpected replacements. Don't assume the use of your own money is costless. You are giving up interest income you could have earned on these funds. In addition, money in replacement funds may be limited to short-term, lower-yielding investments.

On products that have a trade-in value, you may want to calculate **net replacement cost**. This is equal to replacement cost less the market value of the trade-in. Consumer durables depreciate in market value over time because of wear or simply because the product no longer embodies the latest technology or fashion. Some consumer durables, such as cars, experience a rapid decline in market price after the initial purchase. Others, such as computer equipment, may be greatly affected by changes in technology.

Net replacement cost
Replacement cost less trade-in value.

Most of this chapter is devoted to the most expensive consumer durable you probably will purchase—a car. You must decide what kind of car best fits your needs and how much you can afford. You have a choice of leasing the car or financing a purchase. To avoid unexpected surprises, you must then budget for the maintenance and operation of the vehicle. Before we take a closer look at those decisions, we want to review some concerns that apply to all major household purchases and the new electronic market.

Major Household Purchases and the Electronic Market

An efficient selection process must include gathering and evaluating information. Information can be gained from talking to friends, visiting retail outlets, and reading consumer-oriented magazines such as *Consumer Reports* and *Consumer Research* or one of the numerous buyers' guides. Today the Internet is an important tool for researching prices and products. There are numerous shopping robots on the Web that will summarize prices at multiple online stores and provide buyer's guides on products. In addition, manufacturer's Web sites often provide additional information on technical specifications, instruction manuals, and warranties.

The Internet has significantly lowered the cost of comparison shopping. Most major chains and many local stores list their prices on Web sites. Shopping services by all the major Internet portals, such as Yahoo! and Google, provide instant price comparisons on products and retailers. It's likely that the ready availability of pricing information has made the entire retail sector more competitive.

There are many Internet sites that specialize in product reviews. Individuals who previously purchased the product or dealt with a particular merchant post reviews. The product reviews can be helpful in judging the product's qualities. On the other hand, you must be careful not to place too much weight on the experiences of a small number of customers. It is unfortunate that the Internet has also created numerous opportunities for criminals. Figure 7.1 lists the top 10 Internet frauds.

Electronic Purchases

The first rule you should adhere to when shopping on the Internet is to know with whom you are dealing. Several sites rate online retailers on honesty, convenience, and on-time delivery. Merchant reviews are essential when dealing with a new online store that is not backed up by a brick-and-mortar site. CNET (**shopper.cnet.com**), BizRate.com (**www.bizrate.com**), and Nextag (**www.nextag.com**) all provide information on online merchants and rate customer service. Local stores are likely to work with you to correct mistakes and ensure customer satisfaction. Although it may be more convenient to shop electronically, it may be much less convenient to return unsatisfactory merchandise. For both local and online merchants, be sure to check out return policies. Some may refuse to accept returned merchandise and others may charge a hefty restocking fee on returns.

The **Mail Order Merchandise Rule** was initially issued by the Federal Trade Commission to cover telephone and catalog sales. This regulation is now applied to all electronic sales, including purchases made on the Internet or by fax. Unless the seller states otherwise, the "30-day rule" applies. After accepting your order, the retailer must ship the product within 30 days or obtain your consent to delay shipment. This may be extended to 50 days if the retailer is providing a new line of credit. Should the retailer not obtain your consent to a delayed shipment, the seller must promptly refund your money, including all related sales charges. This rule covers merchandise only; it does not cover services such as photo finishing. If you receive merchandise you have not ordered, legally you may consider it a gift.

Online fraud and deception account for more than 25 percent of consumer complaints received by the Federal Trade Commission. The top complaint is identity theft. This is when someone uses your identity to run up fraudulent purchases. Crooks don't need the Internet to steal your identity. They can rob you of your wallet or go through your garbage. Unfortunately, increasingly criminals are using the Internet as a source to obtain personal information. As shown in Figure 7.2, the best advice is to follow the Federal Trade Commission's rules for "paying safe."

Online Auctions and Electronic Payments

The Internet Fraud Watch reports that about 34 percent of all Internet-related fraud complaints were about online auctions. Eighty percent of the online auction complaints

TOPIC LINKS

Product review and price comparison Web sites

Mail Order Merchandise **Rule** Protects customers against the untimely shipment of products.

TOPIC LINKS

National Fraud Information Center and FTC online fraud sites

Figure 7.1
Top 10 Internet Frauds

Source: National Fraud
Information Center, Trends
January–December 2005.

Scam Category	% of All Complaints	Average Loss
Auctions Goods never delivered or misrepresented	42%	$1,155
General Merchandise Sales not through auctions, goods never delivered or misrepresented	30%	$2,528
Nigerian Money Offers False promises of riches if consumers pay to transfer money to their bank accounts	8%	$6,937
Fake Checks Consumers paid with phony checks for work or items sold, instructed to wire money back	6%	$4,361
Lotteries/Lottery Clubs Requests for payment to claim lottery winnings or get help to win, often foreign lotteries	4%	$2,919
Phishing E–mails pretending to be from well–known source asking to confirm personal information	2%	$612
Advance Fee Loans False promises of personal or business loans, even if credit is bad, for a fee paid upfront	1%	$1,426
Information/Adult Services Cost and terms of services not disclosed or misrepresented	1%	$504
Work-at-Home Plans Kits sold on false promises of big profits from working at home	1%	$1,785
Internet Access Services Cost of Internet access and other services misrepresented or services never provided	1%	$1,262

involved the use of money orders and checks. Only 6 percent involved credit cards. A survey sponsored by the National Consumers League indicated that 41 percent of buyers who purchased through online auctions encountered a problem. A startling 10 percent received damaged items and another 10 percent never received the item won.

Auctions can be divided into "business-to-person" auctions and "person-to-person" auctions. In the "business-to-person" format, the auction site has control of the merchandise and ensures that it is delivered to the buyer. It is the latter category of auctions, "person-to-person" auctions that have been the source of most consumer complaints.

Internet auction sites for person-to-person auctions claim they are not responsible for the quality of the merchandise or the representations made by sellers. However, as an aid to consumers, most sites post feedback on a seller's previous transactions. You should review the posted comments and examine the seller's track record. However, be aware that shills can manipulate these posts and a dishonest seller can generate a good track record before cashing in on a major scam. Some auction sites offer buyers fraud insurance protection.

When you make purchases online, make sure your transactions are secure, your personal information is protected, and your fraud sensors are sharpened. Although you can't control fraud or deception on the Internet, you can take steps to recognize it, avoid it, and report it.
Here's how:

· Use a secure browser—software that encrypts or scrambles the purchase information you send over the Internet—to guard the security of your online transactions.

· Keep records of your online transactions. Read your e-mail—merchants may send you important information about your purchases.

· Be prompt about reviewing your monthly bank and credit card statements for any billing errors or unauthorized purchases. Notify your credit card issuer or bank immediately if your credit card or checkbook is lost or stolen.

· Read the policies of Web sites you visit—especially the disclosures about a Web site's security, its refund policies, and its privacy policy on collecting and using your personal information.

· Keep your personal information private. Don't disclose your personal information—your address, telephone number, Social Security number, and e-mail address—unless you know who's collecting the information, why they're collecting it, and how they'll use it.

· Give payment information only to businesses you know and trust and only in appropriate places such as order forms.

· Never give your password to anyone online, not even to your Internet service provider.

· Do not download files sent to you by strangers or click on hyperlinks from people you don't know. Opening a file could expose your system to a computer virus.

Figure 7.2
Paying Safe

Source: Federal Trade Commission, "Guide to Online Payments."

The maximum payout on fraud protection is usually limited to modest amounts after a small deductible.

To protect market participants, auction payments are increasingly being completed through a financial intermediary such as PayPal. A financial intermediary accepts credit card payments from buyers and makes cash payments to sellers. The service is paid for by about a 3 percent deduction from the amount paid to the seller. PayPal protects you from credit card fraud by ensuring that your financial information is not disclosed to the seller. An intermediary that functions as an escrow service may provide additional protection for both buyers and sellers. The escrow service holds the buyer's payment until the goods arrive and the buyer approves the transfer. If problems occur, the escrow service attempts to negotiate a compromise. The service is paid for with a fee that may range from 2 to 5 percent of the purchase price.

Warranties

Whether you make an online purchase or a store purchase, it's important that you check the product's warranty. Most consumers don't bother to read warranties, but they should, because the terms of a warranty can often provide sufficient reasons for selecting one product over another. **Warranty** and **guarantee** mean the same. They represent the seller's assumption of responsibility for the quality, character, or suitability of the goods sold. In a world of imperfect information, the buyer cannot know everything about the product being purchased. Therefore, the consumer requires some protection in the event the product does not perform as expected. It is the warranty that provides the needed protection.

Warranty or guarantee The seller's assumption of responsibility for the quality, character, or suitability of goods sold.

Implied and Express Warranties

"As is" The seller bears absolutely no responsibility for the quality or performance of the good.

All products, except those sold **"as is"** carry implied warranties. An implied warranty is imposed upon the seller by law. In other words, the law sets down certain requirements that the seller must live up to. The **implied warranty** consists of a warranty of merchantability and a warranty of fitness for purpose. *Merchantability* means that the buyer has the right to expect that the good is generally of the same quality as similar goods in its class and that it does what it was built to do. A buyer has the right to expect that a washing machine washes clothes. *Fitness of purpose* means that if the buyer is relying on the seller to select a good for a particular purpose, and the seller has reason to know of that purpose, the good should prove suitable. For example, if the seller knows that the buyer wants a washing machine to wash rugs, then the machine should be able to handle difficult tasks such as cleaning heavy rugs.

Not all products carry an **express warranty**. An express warranty is contractual; that is, it depends on the written or oral agreement between the buyer and seller. An express warranty need not be in writing, nor is it even necessary for the seller to intend to guarantee the item for an express warranty to exist. Statements of fact and promises expressed by the sales agent or manufacturer either at the time of the sale or in previous advertisements can form the basis for an express warranty. However, you must carefully distinguish statements of fact from what is called **puffery**. This is typical sales talk meant to persuade the customer by overly praising the good. Statements such as "This is a good buy" are mere puffery and do not carry an express warranty.

The **Magnuson-Moss Warranty Act of 1975** regulates express written warranties. Before passage of this act, many written warranties contained clauses that relieved the seller of an implied warranty. Consequently, some consumers would have been better off without an express warranty. One of the purposes of this act was to make such clauses ineffective by prohibiting written warranties from limiting the implied warranty to a shorter period than that covered by the written warranty. However, the seller can still avoid an implied warranty by selling the product "as is."

Full and Limited Warranties

Another purpose of the Warranty Act was to set down requirements for full and limited warranties. It is now necessary that all written warranties be labeled either *limited* or *full*.

The **full warranty** label means that consumers are entitled to full remedies for a specified period of time. They may even request a replacement or refund if the warrantor has been given a reasonable number of attempts to fix the product and has been unsuccessful. This provision is termed **lemon protection**, and it is included only in full warranties. The *full* label also means that, during the period specified, consumers will not be charged for parts or labor, or associated transportation and travel. In addition, a full warranty cannot disclaim or limit the duration of implied warranties, be limited to the original owner, require a registration card to provide the date of purchase, or impose an unreasonable requirement as a condition of warranty coverage. Any warranty that does not meet these standards must be labeled a **limited warranty**.

Many products will carry both limited and full warranties. For example, the first year of ownership may be covered by a full warranty, with coverage reduced to a limited warranty in subsequent years. It is also possible that some components will be covered by a full warranty, while others will have limited coverage or none.

Should You Purchase a Service Contract?

When you purchase a major home appliance or a car, the salesperson will usually try to sell you a **service contract** (also called an **extended warranty**). This is because service contracts have proved to be highly profitable for sellers and not so profitable for buyers. Unless you are particularly hard on the products you use, the expected cost of repairs is typically much less than the cost of the service contract. For example, an MIT study for the National Science Foundation revealed that the cost of a service contract for a television

Implied warranty A warranty created by the operation of the law when no express warranty exists.

Express warranty An oral or written agreement between buyer and seller concerning the character or performance of the good.

Puffery Persuasive sales talk overly praising the good.

Magnuson-Moss Warranty Act of 1975 Federal law regulating the conditions and limitations contained in express warranties.

Full warranty During a specified time period, purchases are entitled to full protection, including lemon protection and all repair-related costs.

Lemon protection If the merchandise cannot be repaired after a reasonable number of attempts, the customer can elect to receive a replacement or a refund.

Limited warranty An express warranty that does not meet all of the necessary conditions for a full warranty.

Service contract or extended warranty For an initial fee, the seller agrees to repair the merchandise, either free of charge or for a set charge, for a period beyond the initial warranty.

finance news 7.1

The No-Call List and Your Cell Phone

The Federal Trade Commission (FTC), the national consumer protection agency, instituted the Do-Not-Call Registry after receiving numerous complaints from consumers who were bothered by repeatedly annoying calls from telemarketers. You can subscribe to the Do-Not-Call list at **www.donotcall.gov** or call 1–888–382–1222 from the number you wish to register. You can also register for a state list that covers local companies. Registration is free and is good for five years after which you must reregister. The program originally required re-registration every five years, but it now appears that Congress may make the initial registration permanent.

After registration, you must wait 31 days before logging a complaint against a caller. Registration will stop most, but not all, telemarketing calls. Political parties, charities, telephone surveyors, and people with whom you have an ongoing business interest are exempt and can still call.

Other related rules require that the following:

- Telemarketers may not block their caller ID.
- Telephone solicitation calls before 8 A.M. and after 9 P.M. are prohibited.
- Telephone solicitors must provide their name, the name of the entity on whose behalf the call is being made, and a telephone number or address at which you may contact that entity.

The registry appears to have been an amazing success, with surveys indicating that consumers have experienced a significant drop in annoying phone calls. Violators are subject to a fine of up to $11,000. In the first case filed under the federal rule, consumers who filed complaints received up to $200 each for the inconvenience. Information on filing a complaint can be found at **www.donotcall.gov**.

It would be great if the FTC could create a "Do Not Email" list to eliminate unwanted spam. Currently, however, no one has figured out how to enforce a prohibition against spam. In fact, if such a list were constructed, it, too, might become a source of spam.

You might have received an e-mail warning you that you have to list your cell phone number on a special do-not-call list for cell phones. This is a phishing scam that steers you to a fake Web site that collects your personal information. If you want you can register your cell phone at **www.donotcall.gov**. However, there really is no need to do this because it's illegal for businesses to call cell phone numbers with automatic dialers.

was almost 10 times the expected cost of repairs, and for a refrigerator it was about 16 times the expected cost of repairs. This is why retailers pressure you to purchase an extended warranty. Industry analysts estimate that at least 50 percent of profits at electronic retailers come from extended warranties.

A service contract is, in effect, the same as an insurance policy. You are insuring yourself against repairs on your consumer durables. The manufacturer or retailer is betting that the equipment won't break down, and you are betting that it will. In subsequent chapters we will discuss the basic principles of insurance protection. One such principle is that you should concentrate on insuring yourself against major financial calamities and bear any small risks yourself. The breakdown of the washing machine may seem major at the time it happens, but it is really minor relative to other financial losses you may suffer.

Selecting a Car

The decision to buy or lease a car will lock you into future finance, maintenance, and insurance payments. Finding the right car takes more than just finding the best buy. You must decide which car best fits your needs. You can buy an expensive car that impresses your friends but drains your bank account, or you can more modestly satisfy your needs.

This section includes information about making the purchase versus lease decision and how to correct problems after a purchase. Selecting a car and selecting auto insurance are not separate decisions. Consequently, you might also want to read Chapter 13 on property and liability insurance before you purchase your next car.

TOPIC LINKS

Car guides on the Internet

Pricing Information

Current practices accompanying automobile sales seem to have evolved from horse trading. A car is one of the few purchases that still involves haggling over price. In such market encounters, the person with the best information will usually have the advantage. If you don't do some comparative shopping, you give the seller the advantage.

New Cars

Each new car must have a **Monroney sticker price** on a side window. This shows the base price, the manufacturer's installed options with the manufacturer's suggested retail price, the manufacturer's transportation charge, and the fuel economy. The **base price** is the cost of the car without options but includes standard equipment and the factory warranty. Some new cars may also have a **dealer sticker price**. This includes extras such as dealer-installed options, additional dealer markup (ADM), dealer preparation, and undercoating. Dealers rarely sell cars at the sticker price.

Monroney sticker price Legally required price information applied to the windows of all new cars.

Base price Price of the car without optional features.

Dealer sticker price Monroney sticker price plus dealer add-ons.

Invoice price The price the manufacturer charges the retailer for the car.

The most important piece of information you can have when bargaining with the dealer is the **invoice price**. This is the price the manufacturer charges the dealer for the car. However, on some cars the invoice price may be greater than the dealer's final cost. This is because the dealer may receive rebates, allowances, discounts, and incentive awards from the manufacturer.

Invoice costs and a wealth of other data are available at no charge on the Internet. You can even get a price quote from a regional dealer. If you use invoice cost as a bargaining chip in the showroom, it is suggested that you first ask the salesperson for the minimum markup over invoice that is acceptable to the dealership. If this markup is favorable relative to other dealers you have visited, add it to the indicated invoice cost and make a firm offer. Don't waiver from your initial offer. If your money doesn't talk, be ready to walk.

The salesperson is likely to offer you an extended warranty for an additional charge. For the same reasons stated previously, it is usually not a good buy. Moreover, to a considerable degree the extended warranty may cover repairs already provided for under the regular warranty. A four-year, 48,000-mile extended warranty on a car that has a manufacturer's three-year, 36,000-mile regular warranty extends coverage by only one year and 12,000 miles. The limited additional coverage, however, has not deterred dealers from charging exorbitant prices. The New York attorney general's office found that over half the consumers in that state who purchased extended warranties were charged more than the manufacturer's suggested retail price.

Used Cars

If you are considering buying, selling, or trading in a used car, the two most commonly used sources of pricing information are the *National Automobile Dealers Association Official Used Car Guide* (**www.nada.com**) and the *Kelley Blue Book Used Car Guide* (**www.kbb.com**). These are available at most libraries and at banks where car loans are offered. In addition, online versions are available. They contain the average trade-in or wholesale price and the retail price for many different makes of used cars. Also included are estimated prices for optional equipment.

TOPIC LINKS

Used Car Pricing Guides

Your best buy is typically a two- to three-year-old used car. This is because the annual percentage depreciation in price is greatest over the first few years. Before selecting a model, you should consult the *Consumer Reports* readers' survey on frequency of repair records published annually in the April issue. Obviously, try to avoid makes and models that are not included on their recommended list.

At a dealership, a used car should have a large sticker called the "Buyers Guide" posted in the window. This indicates whether the car is covered by a warranty, and if so, what the warranty includes. About one-half of used cars are sold "as is," meaning there is no warranty. When you purchase a car "as is," you are fully responsible for any needed repairs. For those cars that are sold with a warranty, the previous discussion on warranties applies. If the car is still covered by an unexpired manufacturer's warranty, then the manufacturer, not the dealer who sold you the car, is responsible for fulfilling the terms of this warranty. If you have any questions concerning warranty coverage, be sure to ask the dealer to explain the terms of the contract. Also be sure that all the dealer's promises are included in the written warranty.

If you find a used car you like, have it checked out by an independent mechanic. You can also purchase a vehicle history report from a company like Carfax (**www.carfax.com**) for about $25. The report provides ownership history, accident reports, and title fraud. Carfax attaches vehicle advisories to cars that were registered in states that have suffered serious hurricane damage. It's possible that a flooded car may still have a clean title. If you purchase a used car from one of these states, be sure to have it inspected for water damage.

Rebates and Dealer–Supplied Financing

Manufacturer's rebates and low-interest dealer financing are widely used advertising gimmicks. Once in the showroom, the consumer often finds that these items are being offered in place of the typical dealer discount. The true cost of the car may be unchanged or may be even greater.

A Federal Trade Commission investigation of promotions for dealer financing turned up numerous examples of unethical and possible illegal activities. In some cases consumers were offered the low rate on only a few cars and only if they made an unusually large down payment. In other cases the typical cash discount was unavailable, and the car was loaded with high-cost options. The latest promotional strategy is to apply the low advertised rate only on loans of very short duration. Watch out for last-minute changes in what you were previously promised. It is a sure sign you are being taken for a ride.

BankRate.com can provide information on interest rates in your area. Using Table 7.1 or a financial calculator, you can calculate your total payments at alternative interest rates. You can then judge any trade-offs between a lower interest rate and a higher purchase price. Remember: If you trade in the car before the loan matures, you lose the subsequent benefits of a lower interest rate.

A word of caution: Sometimes a lender will offer a loan at an attractive interest rate and then tack on to the monthly payment a charge for credit life insurance. This insurance will pay off the remaining principal on the loan in the event of your death. In some states it is illegal to require that the borrower accept the **credit life insurance**. Often, it is unnecessary, high-cost insurance—the purpose of which is actually to increase the interest return to the lender. If credit life is being forced upon you, be sure to compare loans according to total monthly payments, including the credit life premium.

Credit life insurance Pays off the remaining loan balance upon the owner's death.

Annual Percentage Rate	Term of Loan (Months)			
	24	36	48	60
3%	$42.98	$29.08	$22.13	$17.97
4%	43.42	29.52	22.58	18.42
5%	43.87	29.97	23.03	18.87
6%	44.32	30.42	23.49	19.33
7%	44.77	30.88	23.95	19.80
8%	45.23	31.34	24.41	20.28
9%	45.68	31.90	24.89	20.76
10%	46.14	32.27	25.36	21.25
11%	46.61	32.74	25.85	21.74
12%	47.07	33.21	26.33	22.24
13%	47.54	33.69	26.83	22.75

Table 7.1
Monthly Payments on Each $1,000 Borrowed

TOPIC LINKS

View current interest rates.

saving money 7.2

Use Your Home Equity to Finance Your Car

Rates on home equity loans are about the same as on car loans. However, there is one big difference—the tax advantage. Interest on home equity loans up to $100,000 is tax deductible. If you itemize your deductions (if you have a home, you probably do), this can be a substantial savings. To decide which is the better deal, compare the interest rate on the car loan with the after-tax rate on the home equity loan. If there is a loan processing fee on the home equity loan you should also take that into account.

A home owner can take out a loan by borrowing against the equity in the home, the difference between the market value on the home and the remaining balance on the mortgage. Of course, if you default, you can lose your home. Defaults on home equity loans, however, are low. This is why lenders can offer attractive rates.

One important concern is that you don't trade off long-term home equity debt for short-term enjoyment. With most car loans the outstanding balance is typically less than the market value of the car. When you use a home equity loan, the repayment schedule is not necessarily tied to the life of the car. Unless you monitor both your loan balance and the value of the car, you could find yourself in an ever-increasing financial quagmire. You may be burdened with debt on a car you no longer own.

In the past, lenders would not make a home equity loan if your total "loan-to-value" ratio was above 80 to 85 percent. This value provided the lender with a cushion in case you were unable to repay your loan. Home prices could fall 15 to 20 percent in a declining market without endangering the loan collateral. Before the subprime crisis lenders were making home equity loans that take total outstanding loans up to 100 percent of the appraised value of the home. The catch is that these loans carry a higher interest rate to offset the greater risk of default.

Given the following rates and a 25 percent marginal tax bracket, the after-tax rate of 6.2 percent (.75 × 8.27) on the home equity loan is slightly below the average rate on a new car loan.

Representative Loan Rates (mid-2007)	
New car loan (36-month)	6.90
Used car loan (36-month)	7.45
Home equity loan (30K)	8.27

The Costs of Owning and Operating a Car

When deciding whether to purchase a car, and when planning your household finances, you will need information on the cost of ownership and operation. Runzheimer International, a management consulting firm, specializes in the collection of data on travel and living costs. Its estimates for the cost of owning and operating selected vehicles are given in Figure 7.3. For the owner who purchases a new car and trades it in after 36 months and 60,000 miles, the cost of owning and operating a car is a significant expense. As indicated in Figure 7.3, the owner of even a modestly priced new car would incur almost $8,000 a year in expenses. For budgeting purposes, these expenses may be separated into the fixed cost of ownership and the variable cost of operation.

Figure 7.3
Projected Ownership and Operating Costs for Selected 2008 Cars, Standard City, USA

Make & Model	Annual Costs			Costs Per Mile*		
	Operating	Ownership	Total	Operating	Ownership	Total
Cadillac STS	$5,130	$14,407	$19,537	$0.26	$0.72	$0.98
Lexus LS 460	4,750	14,622	19,372	0.24	0.73	0.97
Mercury Grand Marquis GS	4,610	8,499	13,109	0.23	0.42	0.66
Honda Accord LX	4,170	6,820	10,990	0.21	0.34	0.55
Toyota Camry LE	3,620	5,812	9,432	0.18	0.29	0.47
Ford Focus SE	3,240	5,709	8,949	0.16	0.29	0.45
Chevrolet Cobalt LT	3,450	5,467	8,917	0.17	0.27	0.45
Toyota Corolla CE	2,980	4,953	7,933	0.15	0.25	0.40

All costs assure vehicles are equipped with auto transmission with overdrive, air conditioning, AM/FM radio with cassette or CD, speed control, rear window defogger, tilt steering wheel, and anti–lock brakes.

Costs include operating expenses (fuel, oil, maintenance and tires), fixed expenses (insurance, depreciation, financing, taxes, and licensing) and are based on three years of ownership with an annual usage of 20,000 miles.

Source: Runzheimer International. This data presented with the permission of Runzheimer International, the Rochester, Wisconsin–based management consulting firm.

The Cost of Ownership

Ownership costs are fixed; that is, they do not vary with usage. No matter how much or how little you use the car, these expenses will remain relatively constant. Each of the following is considered a **cost of ownership**: auto insurance, license, registration, taxes, depreciation, and finance charges.

Cost of ownership Fixed costs that do not vary with usage.

Insurance

The cost of insurance will depend upon the amount and type of coverage. For a detailed discussion of auto insurance, see Chapter 13.

License, Registration, Taxes

The state in which you live imposes these fees. Each state has its own formula for determining the cost of a license. This cost varies depending on the vehicle's weight and type and your intended use of the motor vehicle.

When you purchase a car you should receive a **certificate of title**. This authenticates your ownership of the car and should be kept in a safe place. Never leave it in the car, since the car may be stolen. Another important document is the **certificate of registration**, which indicates that the vehicle has been properly registered with your state motor vehicle department. This document should remain in your car.

Certificate of title Legal evidence of your ownership of a motor vehicle.

Certificate of registration A document indicating that your car is properly registered with the state motor vehicle department.

Depreciation

Depreciation is the reduction in the market value of the vehicle due to passage of time, mechanical and physical condition, and number of miles driven. The market value of the car at the beginning of the year less the car's market value at the end of the year is your annual depreciation. Although depreciation varies with usage, it depends primarily upon time for cars; therefore, it can be considered a fixed cost for any given year.

Depreciation The reduction in the market value of a motor vehicle.

Your average annual depreciation will depend on the age of your car and your holding period. If you purchased a new car each year for $20,000 and traded in the old car each year for $15,000, your average annual depreciation would be $5,000. Alternatively, if you purchased a new car every other year for $20,000 and traded in the two-year-old car for $12,000, the depreciation over the two-year period would be $8,000. After the total depreciation is divided by 2, the length of the holding period, the average annual depreciation is $4,000. The difference between average annual depreciation of $5,000 and average annual depreciation of $4,000 represents a yearly savings of $1,000. This is the dollar advantage of having a two-year holding period rather than a one-year holding period. The longer you hold the car, the smaller is your average annual cost of depreciation.

Finance Charges

Estimates of finance charges included in Figure 7.3 assume that each car is purchased with a 20 percent down payment and financed with a 36-month loan at a competitive market rate. If you purchase the car out of savings, you can eliminate these explicit finance charges; however, you give up the interest income you could have earned on those savings. This lost interest also represents a cost of ownership. Consequently, whether or not you intend to finance the purchase with borrowed funds, you should consider the Runzheimer estimate of finance charges as a real cost of ownership. Runzheimer estimates that depreciation and finance charges make up more than 50 percent of car costs.

Other Costs of Ownership

Any additional fixed costs that are incurred because of car ownership should also be considered. For example, if you rent a garage to house your car, the rental payments should be included in the cost of ownership. On the other hand, if you would normally live in a home with a garage, whether or not you own a car, then the additional or marginal cost of storage would be zero.

The cost of accessories may also be included. These may consist of such things as extra wheels for snow tires, radios, and trailer hitches. Items that have an effect on mechanical operation can be included under the maintenance component of operating expenses.

The Cost of Operation

Cost of operation Variable costs that are directly related to usage.

Costs that are related directly to usage are called *variable costs*. The **cost of operation** includes all variable costs. Your cost of operations will be directly related to how much you use your car.

Gasoline and Oil

After the cost of depreciation, this is likely to be your next largest vehicle expense. Your costs should be based on your regional cost of fuel and your car's fuel economy. With the cost of gasoline above $4 a gallon in 2008, you can estimate how much you can save by purchasing a more fuel efficient car.

$$\frac{\text{annual miles driven}}{\text{miles per gallon}} \times \text{price per gallon} = \text{annual fuel expense}$$

If you drive 20,000 miles a year in a car that gets 20 miles to the gallon, it will cost you $4,000 for fuel at $4 per gallon. By driving a more fuel efficient car that gets 25 miles to the gallon, your fuel expense drops to $3,200. This is a saving of $800 a year. Over a five-year ownership, the more fuel efficient car will save you $4,000, a significant amount.

Maintenance and Tires

The owner's manual or your local mechanic should be able to recommend a maintenance schedule based on the miles you typically drive. Maintenance and tires are not generally covered under an automobile warranty and therefore should be included in the household budget. For older cars on which the warranty has expired, unscheduled repairs and parts replacement should also be given consideration when estimating expenditures.

On the side of each tire you will find some important consumer information. All passenger tires must be rated according to governmentally set Uniform Tire Quality Grading Standards. The tires are rated for treadwear, traction, and temperature resistance. Treadwear is rated with a number. A tire rated 400 is projected to go twice as far as a higher rated 200. Letters are used to rate traction and temperature resistance, with an "A" signifying the highest rating.

Other Operating Costs

Metered curb parking, fees charged for parking lots, and toll charges for highways, tunnels, and bridges may all represent additional operating costs. In an urban environment these costs should not be overlooked; they can represent a significant cost of commuting.

The Total Cost of Ownership and Operation

By adding the fixed cost of ownership to the variable cost of operation, you can calculate the total cost of the family car. The cost of ownership generally represents a larger portion of total car expenditures than the cost of operation.

On a per-mile basis, the total cost per mile for the cars listed in Figure 7.3 is $0.61. This consists of $0.21 per mile in operating costs and $0.40 per mile in ownership costs. At 20,000 miles per year, ownership cost represents about two-thirds of your car-related transportation expenses. However, if the car is driven an additional mile, the variable cost of operations will increase by only approximately $0.21, while the fixed cost of ownership will remain relatively stable with only a slight decline. This means that as the car is used more often, the cost of ownership will become relatively smaller.

The Mass-Transit Alternative

In highly congested New York City, about 55 percent of the workforce uses public transportation to get to work. In less densely populated Indianapolis, only about 3 percent of the workforce uses public transportation. This difference can be explained in terms of relative availability, relative cost, and relative convenience of mass transit in each of these cities. If you have a mass-transit alternative in your city, you should compare the costs of using a private car with those of using public transit.

When judging the relative merits of public transit, first you should decide whether you could do without owning a motor vehicle. If you can rely solely on mass transit, you may weigh the cost of public transit against the total cost of ownership and operation. Alternatively, if you find you need the car anyway, then you should weigh the cost of public transit only against the cost of vehicle operation. This is because the cost of ownership is a **sunk cost**: It is something you have to pay whether or not you use the car. Therefore, if you own the car, you need consider only the **marginal**, or additional, **cost** you will incur when you drive your car another mile. In most circumstances, the least costly alternative will depend upon the necessity of car ownership. It's likely that the total average cost per

Sunk cost An historical cost that cannot be changed.

Marginal cost Additional or incremental cost that will be incurred.

FINANCIAL PLANNING *for*
young adults 7.3

First Job, Time to Buy a New Car?

You have just graduated college and landed that job you have been searching for. You are also part of a group targeted for advertising by car manufacturers. You have a little extra money in your pocket, and you deserve something in return for all your hard work. It's time to buy a new car, right? Well, maybe not. Think twice before you commit yourself to fixed payments for the next three or four years. You probably can save at least $5,000 buying a used car that is a few years old.

Edmunds.com (**www.edmunds.com**) lets you calculate the "True Cost to Own (TCO)." This includes both the cost of ownership and operations for specific manufacturers, models, and

years. The TCO is calculated over a five-year period. For example, a 2008 Ford Escape Hybrid with an initial cash price of $26,386 will have a TCO of $37,858. A good part of that expense consists of $17,617 in depreciation. Almost one-third, $5,423, occurs in the first year of ownership. This is an amount you could be easily saved by buying a slightly used car.

Remember, after five years you do own the car, but what you own is a five-year-old car worth approximately $11,769. A used car will also depreciate, but at a much slower rate. The savings on depreciation and finance cost could make balancing the household budget a whole lot easier and give you the peace of mind that large monthly payments will not. Time to buy a new car? Well, maybe not.

mile of using your private car is greater than that for mass transit, but that the marginal cost of private usage is less than the marginal cost of mass transit in most cities.

The Leasing Alternative

If you find that you need a car, but only for an infrequent trip, you might consider an occasional rental as a practical alternative to ownership. By renting you avoid the high fixed cost of ownership, an exorbitant expense for a car that is seldom used.

You might consider leasing, if you need a car for longer periods of time but wish to hold down the high initial cost of ownership, Your current expenses and your periodic payments will be less than if you purchased the same car on credit. When you lease a vehicle, you are paying rent only for the car's long-term use. Your payments are determined primarily by the difference between the initial price of the car and the resale value of the car at the termination of the lease. On the other hand, if you finance a purchase you are building equity as you pay off the loan principal. When you complete your car loan payments, you own the car. If you sell the car before all the loan payments are completed, you receive the resale value less any remaining balance on the loan.

A vehicle lease is a contract between the lessor (the property owner) and the lessee (the user) that sets out the terms and limitations on the use of the vehicle and the payment. There are two types of leasing contracts: closed end and open end. Both are covered by regulations specified in the Consumer Leasing Act of 1977 and by the Federal Reserve Board under Regulation M. Some of these regulations may not apply if the car is for business use or if the contractual obligation exceeds $25,000. Figure 7.4 contains a sample disclosure statement issued by the Federal Reserve Board. It requires the leasing company (the lessor) to disclose in writing specific information about a consumer lease before you (the lessee) sign the lease agreement.

The Closed-End Lease

Closed-end lease Your costs are determined at the time you lease the car .and you generally are not responsible for the value of the car at the end of the lease.

The **closed-end lease** is also sometimes called the *net* or *walkaway* lease. You make fixed periodic payments based on your estimated usage. When your lease expires, you simply return the car and pay a surcharge for mileage in excess of your estimate. Unless you have seriously damaged the vehicle, given it more than normal wear, or driven it more miles than the lease permits, you are not responsible for the value of the vehicle at the end of the lease term. Because the lessor is taking the risk as to what the value of the car will be when you return it, your lease payments generally will be higher than they would be under an open-end lease.

It's possible that the car will be worth more at the end of the lease than was originally estimated. If so, you will have made excessive monthly payments. A purchase option in the contract protects you against overestimated depreciation. If you can resell your car for more than the purchase option price, you should exercise the option.

The Open-End Lease

Open-end lease The total cost of the lease is unknown until the estimated resale value of the car is determined.

The **open-end lease** also has fixed periodic payments; however, the total cost remains unknown until the end of the leasing period. This is because the periodic payments are based on the estimated resale value on the returned car, sometimes called the estimated *residual value*.

Figure 7.4
Federal Consumer Leasing Act Disclosures

Federal Consumer Leasing Act Disclosures

Date ___00100100___

Lessor(s) ___Dealer or Leasing Company___   Lessee(s) ___J. Smith___   ❶

| Amount Due at Lease Signing or Delivery (Itemized below)* ❷ $ __4,241.94__ | Monthly Payments Your first monthly payment of $ __256.94__ is due on __00100100__ , followed by __47__ payments of $ __256.94__ due on the __1st__ of each month. The total of your monthly payments is $ __12,333.12__ ❸ | Other Charges (not part of your monthly payment) ❹ Disposition fee (if you do not purchase the vehicle) $ __400.00__ _____ — Total $ __400.00__ | Total of Payments (The amount you will have paid by the end of the lease) $ __16,368.12__ ❺ |

* Itemization of Amount Due at Lease Signing

Amount Due At Lease Signing:

Capitalized cost reduction	$ __3,500.00__
First monthly payment	256.94
Refundable security deposit	350.00
Title fees	75.00
Registration fees	60.00
_____	—
Total $	4,241.94 ❻a

❻ How the Amount Due at Lease Signing will be paid:

Net trade-in allowance	$ __2,500.00__
Rebates and noncash credits	—
Amount to be paid in cash	1,741.94
Total $	4,241.94 ❻b

❼ Your monthly payment is determined as shown below:

❽ **Gross capitalized cost.** The agreed upon value of the vehicle ($ __21,500.00__) and any items you pay over the lease term (such as service contracts, insurance, and any outstanding prior loan or lease balance) .... $ 22,300.00

If you want an itemization of this amount, please check this box. ☑

❾ **Capitalized cost reduction.** The amount of any net trade-in allowance, rebate, noncash credit, or cash you pay that reduces the gross capitalized cost .... − 3,500.00

Adjusted capitalized cost. The amout used in calculating your base monthly payment .... = 18,800.00

Residual value. The value of the vehicle at the end of the lease used in calculating your base monthly payment .. − 12,350.00

Depreciation and any amortized amounts. The amount charged for the vehicle's decline in value through normal use and for other items paid over the lease terrn .... = 6,450.00

❿ **Rent charge.** The amount charged in addition to the depreciation and any amortized amounts .... + 5,295.00

Total of base monthly payments. The depreciation and any amortized amounts plus the rent charge .... = 11,745.00

⓫ **Lease payment.** The number of months in your lease .... ÷ 48

Base monthly payment .... = 244.69

⓬ **Monthly sales/use tax** + 12.25

+ —

⓭ **Total monthly payment** .... = $ 256.94

⓮ **Early Termination.** You may have to pay a substantial charge if you end this lease early. *The charge may be up to several thousand dollars.* The actual charge will depend on when the lease is terminated. The earlier you end the lease, the greater this charge is likely to be.

⓯ **Excessive Wear and Use.** You may be charged for excessive wear based on our standards for normal use [and for mileage in excess of __15,000__ miles per year at the rate of __.15__ per mile]. ⓰

⓱ **Purchase Option at End of Lease Term.** [You have an option to purchase the vehicle at the end of the lease term for $ __12,350.00__ [and a purchase option fee of $ __150.00__ .

Other Important Terms. See your lease documents for additional information on early termination, purchase options and maintenance responsibilities, warranties, late and default charges, insurance, and any security interest, if applicable.

When you return the vehicle, the lessor will appraise it and compare the appraised value at the end of the lease, termed the realized value, with the residual value stated in the lease. Under the Consumer Leasing Act, you have the right, at your expense, to obtain an independent appraisal by someone agreed to by both you and the lessor. If you get an independent appraisal, you and the lessor are bound by it.

When the appraised value of the car is the same as, or greater than, the residual value specified in the lease disclosure, you owe nothing. (Your contract will determine whether you get a refund for any excess value. You can ask the lessor to include the right to a refund in your contract.) Alternatively, if the appraisal indicates that the vehicle is worth less than the specified amount, you may have to pay all or a portion of the difference. This cost is often called an *end-of-lease payment*. However, the contract should include a reasonable residual value. Given average wear the residual value may be unreasonable if it exceeds the realized value by more than three times your base monthly payments. A higher end of lease payment can be collected if you specifically agreed to pay a greater amount, there was unreasonable wear or excessive use, or the lessor wins a lawsuit seeking a higher amount.

Evaluating a Car Lease

Leases are difficult for even professionals to competitively evaluate. Therefore, it is no wonder that consumers with little training in finance can often find leases confusing. Of course, buyer confusion provides profit opportunities for unethical dealers. The best way to think about leasing is that you are taking out a loan, but instead of borrowing money, you are borrowing a car. You are paying for the use of the car in three ways. First, there are prepayments that are made at the time of the loan; second, there are monthly installments; and third, there is a balloon payment, which is a much larger payment at the end of the loan. The balloon payment is the end-of-lease payment.

Unfortunately, federal statutes do not treat a lease like a loan. Accordingly, the lessor does not have to reveal an APR. In addition, the language in leases may be difficult to understand. The "Keys to Vehicle Leasing" contains a helpful glossary and the sample leasing form in Figure 7.4. Leases, however, may contain terms for which there are no standard definitions. The terms *lease rate* or *money factor* should not be confused with an interest rate. These are just proprietary numbers that the lessor uses to calculate your monthly payment.

The **gross capitalized cost** (Figure 7.4, entry 8) is the negotiated price for the car, including all other items you finance over the term of the lease, such as taxes, fees, service contracts, insurance, and any prior credit or lease balance. Be sure to check the appropriate box to get an itemized listing of the specific components of gross capitalized cost. The **adjusted capitalized cost** is equal to the gross capitalized cost less any up-front payments included in **capitalized cost reduction** (Figure 7.4, entry 9). Capitalized cost reduction can consist of cash payments, a net trade-in balance, and rebates. In the current example, the capitalized cost reduction of $3,500 includes a $2,500 trade-in and a $1,000 cash payment. Note that the amount due at delivery will exceed the capitalized cost reduction (Figure 7.4, entry 6b). It may include several other items, such as the initial monthly payment, title and registration fees, a security deposit, and insurance premiums.

A capitalized cost reduction is, in effect, an advance payment on the lease. It may or may not be required by the lessor. If you trade in your old car, the capitalized cost reduction may be set equal to the value of the trade. The more you pay down initially, the lower your periodic payments will be. However, if you make a high initial payment in order to reduce your periodic payments, you lose one important advantage of leasing—the lower initial cost.

TOPIC LINKS

"Keys to Vehicle Leasing"

Gross capitalized cost The cost of the car and other items included in the leasing contract.

Adjusted capitalized cost Gross capitalized cost less up-front payments.

Capitalized cost reduction Up-front payments including cash, trade-in, and rebates.

The adjusted capitalized cost will be paid back over the life of the lease or at the end of the lease. At the end of the lease you give back the car and the lessor recaptures the residual value in the car. The **residual value** is equal to the car's initial market value less the depreciation in market value that occurs over the term of the lease. The depreciation and any other amortized amounts will be paid off uniformly over the term of the lease. In addition to these costs, you will have to pay for financing the carrying cost on the vehicle. This is similar to finance charges on a loan and is listed as a rent charge (entry 1D). However, you should not confuse the two. With a loan, you are building equity in a vehicle. With a lease, you own nothing at the end of the lease.

Residual value The car's market value at the termination of the lease.

Be sure you understand how early termination (entry 14) and end-of-lease charges (15 and 17) will be determined. The Consumer Bankers Association reports that about 43 percent of car leases are terminated early. In addition to simply desiring a new car, early termination can be triggered by theft or accident. Regardless of the reason for termination, you may be responsible for depreciation in the market value of the car and for additional special charges upon breaking the lease. Be sure you understand just how much you will owe if you decide to return the vehicle before the scheduled expiration of the lease. With an open-end lease it is important that you know how the residual value will be determined and whether it is a wholesale or resale price.

TOPIC LINKS

Read the "Keys to Vehicle Leasing" by the Federal Reserve.

A Lease/Buy Comparison

Given this array of numbers, it is difficult to figure out just how much this lease is costing you. This would be a nice number to have, if you want to comparison shop leases or make a lease/buy comparison. Let's concentrate on the numbers listed on the disclosure statement and assume that other expenses such as maintenance and insurance would be similar under either decision. Figure 7.5 contains a worksheet for examining the lease/buy decision. Costs are separated into three distinct categories: initial expenses when the lease or purchase is initiated, continuing periodic monthly expenses during the lease or loan, and final expenses when the lease is terminated or the loan paid off.

TOPIC LINKS

Download this worksheet or use a lease/buy calculator.

The data from the disclosure statement have been used to complete the leasing side of this worksheet. On the buy side, it is assumed that an identical dealer package can be purchased for $22,300. Initial expenses on the purchase decision will consist of a $5,000 down payment ($2,500 trade-in and $2,500 cash) and other related sales expenses. Given the large down payment and the up-front sales tax, the initial expenses of buying will exceed that of leasing.

The buy decision assumes the purchaser can finance the remaining cost of the car ($17,300) with a 48-month loan at an APR of 8.5 percent and monthly payments of $426.42. Accordingly, the payments on the loan will cost $169.48 ($426.42 – $256.94) more per month. It is obvious that the lease will entail significantly lower monthly expenses. This and the lower initial payment are what often make leasing an attractive alternative to buying for many consumers.

There are various ways that final expenses could have been handled. The worksheet analysis assumes that at the end of the lease the car is turned in resulting in a $400 disposition fee. For simplicity, it is assumed that the security deposit is returned and there are no other adjustments for excessive wear or residual value. At the end of the lease you own nothing. At the end of the loan you own the car. On the buy side it is assumed that the owner sells the car and nets the residual value ($12,350) less selling costs ($400).

If you total up all explicit, out-of-pocket expenses, it appears that the consumer saves $1,640 ($16,368 – $14,728) by buying rather than leasing. However, this does not take into account the time value of money. If you leased, you could have invested the savings on ini-

Figure 7.5
A Lease/Buy Comparison
Worksheet

Leasing	
Initial Expenses	
Capitalized cost reduction	$3,500.00
First monthly payment	$256.94
Refundable security deposit	350.00
Title fees	75.00
Registration fees	60.00
Sales taxes	—
Total explicit initial cost	$4,241.94
Monthly Expenses	
Base monthly payment	$244.69
Monthly sales/use tax	12.25
Total monthly payment	$256.94
Months	47
Total continuing explicit costs	$12,076.18
Final Expenses	
Excessive mileage charge	—
Excessive wear and tear	—
Adjustment for overestimated residual value	—
Security deposit	(350.00)
Disposition fee	400.00
Miscellaneous items	—
Total explicit final costs	$50.00
Total Explicit Expenses	
Initial Expenses	$4,241.94
Monthly Expenses	12,076.18
Final Expenses	50.00
Total explicit costs	$16,368.12

Buying	
Initial Expenses	
Down payment and trade-in	5,000.00
Title fees	75.00
Registration fees	60.00
Sales tax	1,075.00
Total explicit initial costs	$6,210.00
Monthly Expenses	
APR	8.5%
Initial amount financed	$17,300.00
Monthly loan payment	$426.42
Months	48
Total continuing explicit costs	$20,467.95
Final Expenses	
Loan payoff	—
Estimated residual value	(12,350.00)
Sales costs	$400.00
Total explicit final costs	($11,950.00)
Total Explicit Expenses	
Initial Expenses	$6,210.00
Monthly Expenses	20,467.95
Final Expenses	(11,950.00)
Total explicit costs	$14,727.95

Implicit Cost of Purchasing		
After-tax interest rate	6%	
Excess up-front cost of buying	$1,968.06	
Lost interest income		$532.34
Excess monthly payment	$169.48	
Lost interest income		988.66
Total lost interest income		$1,521.00
Total relevant cost of buying		$16,248.95
(Total explicit cost plus total lost interest income on purchase alternatives)		

tial expenses ($1,968) over the 48-month period. At a 6 percent after-tax annual interest rate, this would have generated compound interest income of $532. Moreover, you could also have invested the monthly differential of 169 over 47 months, providing an additional $989 in interest income. This implicit interest income could either be subtracted from the leasing alternative as an implicit benefit of leasing or added to the cost of purchasing as an implicit cost of purchasing. In the worksheet it has been added to the cost of purchasing. In this example, buying is still the better alternative, but by a smaller amount.

Economists like to say there is no such thing as a free lunch. If you cannot afford to purchase a new car, you probably should not be leasing it. You are going to pay for the cost of using the car; it is just a matter of how. The real problem with leasing is that the lower up-front and periodic payments tempt us to drive a more expensive car. Over the long run we may end up spending a lot more on depreciation and finance charges than we would have if we had purchased a more reasonably priced car.

Additional information on leasing can be found in a pamphlet published by the Federal Reserve Board entitled "Keys to Vehicle Leasing." Copies are available on the Internet. If you plan to lease, be sure to avoid high-pressure sales tactics. You need to consider all of the costs outlined here carefully and review your buying alternative. The Federal Reserve suggests that you follow a five-step process:

1. Don't directly enter into negotiations on a lease. First, identify the lowest price that the dealer will accept for the car. This will represent the capitalized cost.

2. After you have determined the best price you can get, then separately negotiate the value on any trade-in you may have. Given your anticipated down payment and trade-in, you can then estimate net capitalized cost.

3. Check all sources of financing to determine the best interest rate and your needed monthly payments under the purchase option.

4. Check out the resale value from industry publications.

5. Finally, enter into negotiations for the lease. You should now have all the information you need to use the lease/buy comparison worksheet and make an informed decision. Be wary of last-minute changes in the deal that don't leave you time to recheck your calculations. This is when consumers are most susceptible to high-pressure sales techniques that result in wasted dollars.

What If You Bought a Lemon?

Your chance of purchasing a new car with serious problems is about one in 800. Your chance of purchasing a car with at least a few defects is apparently much higher. Most of the complaints in the first year should be covered by the new-car warranty. To ensure that they are corrected, you should be prepared to deal with new-car defects and know how to seek remedial action.

The suggested procedure is to discuss the problem with the dealer first, allowing the firm an adequate opportunity to repair the defect. If the dealer is unwilling to honor the warranty or is taking an unreasonable amount of time to correct the problem, contact the manufacturer. At the car company, the person to contact first is often called the *zone representative* or the *area service manager*. If you still do not receive satisfaction, your next step is to contact the consumer representative at the company's headquarters. You may consider going to small claims court, entering arbitration, or hiring an attorney, if neither the dealer nor the manufacturer responds to your request.

Whichever alternative you choose, be prepared to supply adequate records on all your attempts at repair or replacement. Accordingly, be sure you receive a repair slip each time you return the car for service. The receipt should be legible and should contain an accurate statement of your complaint, the date of service, and the attempted repairs. If the dealer suggests you do not need a repair slip because the car is under warranty, insist on your right to receive one. Also retain copies of all relevant correspondence and a diary recording each related conversation, including the date, the name of the person with whom you discussed your problem, and a summary of what was said.

Secret Warranties

Warranties were examined previously in the section on the electronic market. Everything stated there holds true for automotive warranties as well. One additional item, however, commonly known as the **secret warranty**, seems to be unique to the automotive industry.

TOPIC LINKS

Run a lemon check.

TOPIC LINKS

Manufacturer's contacts

TOPIC LINKS

Check for safety recalls.

Secret warranty or **policy adjustment:** An understanding between manufacturers and retailers that certain defects will be repaired at no cost only when confronted with strong consumer complaints.

It takes effect after the written warranty has expired. Under a secret warranty, the manufacturer repairs certain defects only when customers complain. Other, more docile, customers are not told about this policy and are unfairly charged for repairs.

The industry prefers the term **policy adjustment** or *after-warranty assistance* to *secret warranty*. Given the way the auto industry treats customers, it's a good idea to complain whenever you think your problem results from faulty workmanship or design. You should ask the zone representative whether policy adjustments have been made on similar problems and whether a policy adjustment would cover your current defect. The Center for Auto Safety collects information on policy adjustments. It may be able to supply information on how a manufacturer has previously dealt with similar defects.

TOPIC LINKS

Contact the Center for Auto Safety and review the NHTSA complaints database.

Alternative Dispute Resolution

If you have a problem with a new car and do not receive satisfaction from the dealer or the manufacturer's representative, or if you are dissatisfied with repairs made on a used car, your next step is to consider an alternative dispute resolution program. Most of the car manufacturers cooperate with the Better Business Bureau's (BBB) Autoline program or the Automobile Consumer Action Program (AUTOCAP), which is managed by the National Automobile Dealers Association.

Most consumer protection agencies, such as the Better Business Bureau, will first attempt to resolve the disagreement through mediation. In **mediation**, an attempt is made to have the parties to the dispute reach their own agreement. If that doesn't work, arbitration may be entered into. **Arbitration** is a formal process for settling disputes in which an impartial third party listens to arguments made by both sides and suggests a remedy that may be binding or nonbinding. In consumer-related disputes, the Federal Trade Commission sets down rules to ensure that the arbitration procedure is, in fact, impartial. In the BBB Autoline program the arbitrator's decision is binding on the manufacturer but not on the consumer. If you accept the decision, you waive your right to sue the manufacturer in court.

Mediation Parties to the dispute attempt to reach their own agreement.

Arbitration A process for settling disputes with third party mediation and a binding or nonbinding remedy.

Entering arbitration has two significant advantages over using the court system: The process is relatively speedy, and there is little or no cost to the individual. However, there are also some disadvantages. The arbitrators need not be lawyers or knowledgeable mechanics. Thus, they may not fully understand your problem or your rights as a consumer. Furthermore, they will not award punitive damages or compensatory damages related to such incidentals as lost wages or medical bills resulting from a defective car. Without your own lawyer, you may not know whether you would be entitled to such payments in the regular court system. In addition, by entering arbitration you may be accepting a potential decision that is legally binding. You should realize that your chances of coming out of arbitration with a better offer than that provided by the dealer or manufacturer's representative are only about 50–50.

TOPIC LINKS

Arbitration programs

Lemon Laws

Nearly all states have lemon laws to protect buyers of new cars. A few states even have lemon laws regulating the sale of used cars. In general, lemon laws declare that if a car dealer does not repair substantial defects covered by the new-car warranty within a reasonable period of time, the owner may be entitled to a comparable new car or a refund. A reasonable time is usually defined as four trips to the repair shop for the same problem or a total of 30 days in the repair shop. If the manufacturer or dealer does not supply a new car, the customer may go to court after attempting to arbitrate the matter. If your state does not have a lemon law, you can still go to court to enforce performance of express and implied warranties under the Magnuson-Moss Warranty Act, discussed earlier in this chapter.

TOPIC LINKS

Know your state's lemon laws.

adjusted capitalized cost (p. 196)
arbitration (p. 200)
"as is" (p. 184)
base price (p. 187)
capitalized cost reduction (p. 196)
certificate of registration (p. 191)
certificate of title (p. 191)
closed-end lease (p. 194)
consumer durables (p. 181)
cost of operation (p. 192)
cost of ownership (p. 191)
credit life insurance (p. 188)
dealer sticker price (p. 187)
depreciation (p. 191)
express warranty (p. 185)
extended warranty (p. 185)
full warranty (p. 185)
gross capitalized cost (p. 196)
guarantee (p. 184)

implied warranty (p. 185)
invoice price (p. 187)
lemon protection (p. 185)
limited warranty (p. 185)
Magnuson-Moss Warranty Act of 1975
   (p. 185)
Mail Order Merchandise Rule (p. 182)
marginal cost (p. 193)
mediation (p. 200)
Monroney sticker price (p. 187)
net replacement cost (p. 181)
open-end lease (p. 194)
policy adjustment (p. 200)
puffery (p. 185)
residual value (p. 197)
secret warranty (p. 199)
service contract (p. 185)
sunk cost (p. 193)
warranty (p. 184)

Reread the chapter-opening vignette.

1. When the Steeles decide to replace the family car, what factors should they consider when deciding whether to purchase a new or a used car?

2. Why are the monthly lease payments typically lower than the monthly loan payments on a comparable car? How would leasing affect the Steeles' financial plans?

3. What factors should the Steeles take into consideration when weighing the lease/buy decision?

1. What special characteristics and budgeting problems do consumer durables present?

2. How is net replacement cost defined?

3. How do you protect yourself against online fraud?

4. What is the Merchandise Mail Order Rule?

5. Why should you be cautious about entering into person-to-person auctions on the Internet?

6. What is the difference between an express and an implied warranty?

7. Does an item sold "as is" carry an implied warranty?

8. What requirements must a warranty satisfy before it can be labeled *full*? How do these differ for a limited warranty?

9. You purchase a stereo system from a local department store on the basis of the salesperson's assurance that this system is a "good buy." You later find out that it wasn't such a good buy. The same product is being sold elsewhere at a much lower price. Does the salesperson's statement constitute an express warranty? What action do you now take?

10. Suppose you purchase a CD player and later find that it does not play mp3 files. The sales clerk assured you it would. What can you do?

11. What is the single greatest cost associated with owning and operating a car? How do you distinguish an ownership cost from an operating cost?

12. What is the difference between a closed-end lease and an open-end lease?

13. What is a capitalized cost reduction? What role does it play in determining the adjusted capitalized cost?

14. You commute 20 miles each day in your own car, and the estimated operational cost per mile is $0.15. If you used the mass-transit system, the same trip would cost you $2. Should you leave your car at home and use public transport?

15. Your new station wagon has 14,000 miles on the odometer. The new-car warranty expired at the 12,000-mile mark. Yesterday, while you were driving the car to school, the rear axle broke. The dealer tells you it will cost more than $1,000 to have the problem fixed because the warranty has expired. What do you do?

16. Explain secret warranties and lemon protection.

case 7.1

Ann Barnard Considers Alternative Holding Periods

Ann Barnard typically buys a new car and trades in her old one every four years. Because new cars are so expensive, recently she has considered changing her buying habits. She would like to know how much she might save in depreciation costs if instead she purchased a new car every five years.

Questions

1. Using a new-car price of $20,000 and assuming the market value will depreciate by 50 percent over the next four years, calculate the annual cost of depreciation given her present buying habits. Now calculate the annual cost of depreciation under the proposed change. Assume the market value will depreciate by 55 percent over the next five years. What is the annual cost savings? What is the cost savings over the five-year holding period?

2. What other factors should Ann Barnard consider before she changes her buying behavior?

case 7.2

The Reeds Examine the Lease/Buy Decision

The Reeds are considering the purchase or lease of a $20,000 car. They have used the worksheet shown in Figure 7.4 to evaluate the relevant costs. They estimate that the initial expenses for leasing are $1,000 and the initial expenses for purchasing are $5,000. They could lease the car for 48 months for a total monthly expense of $200. If they purchase, they could obtain a 48-month loan at an 8 percent APR with monthly loan payments of $366.19. The final expense on the lease side of the ledger is zero. The returned security fee just offsets the disposition fee. If they sell the car, the net residual value after selling costs is $13,000. Over the next few years they expect to earn a 5 percent after-tax return on their investments.

1. Before considering the time value of money, is it better to lease or buy?
2. After considering the time value of money, is it better to lease or buy?

Exercises to Strengthen Your Use of the Internet

(Internet links for the following exercises can be found at **www.prenhall.com/winger.**)

working out
on the Web

Exercise 7.1 How Much Is My Car Worth?

The Kelly Blue Book (**www.kbb.com**) contains estimates on the market price of used cars. The Web site provides price estimates on both new and used cars. It contains price information on almost every make of car and every price option you can think of. Best of all, it is free.

Q. Select a make and model that hasn't changed much over the last five years, such as the Toyota Camry. Using today's pricing data from the Kelly Blue Book, estimate how a new car is likely to depreciate over the next three years. Assume you drive the car 20,000 miles a year and that you keep it in good condition.

Exercise 7.2 Which Is Better: A New or Used Car?

At Kiplinger.Com (**www.kiplinger.com**) you will find a link to "Tools and Calculators. Go to the "Which Is Better, New or Used Car?" under "Spending Wisely Tools." Compare the annual cost of depreciation, maintenance, and finance costs on a new car versus an old car. Assuming a three-year holding period, compare the average annual cost of a new car and a one-year-old car. You may enter your own estimates for maintenance costs and finance charges.

Q. What is your annual savings from driving a three-year-old car?

Exercise 7.3 Find the Monthly Cost of a Car Lease

The "Should I Lease or Purchase an Auto?" calculator at the Yahoo! Finance (finance.yahoo.com) lets you compare the annual cost of ownership and leasing. You can find the link to a page of "Calculators" by first visiting the "Personal Finance" Web page.

Q. Enter the sample data from Figure 7.5. Do the results differ? If so, can you determine why?

Exercise 7.4 Check Out Vehicle Recalls

Autosite (**www.autosite.com**) has an online database that helps you track down manufacturer's recalls on most cars. You can find the link to "Automotive Recalls" at the bottom of the home page. When safety-related recalls are necessary, manufacturers will try to locate present owners and their vehicles. However, with a public that is always on the move, it is possible to lose track of owners of even recently purchased vehicles.

Q. Are there any recalls on your family car?

Exercise 7.5 Checking Out the BBB Autoline

The Better Business Bureau (**www.bbb.org**) runs the Autoline Program that helps manufacturers and consumers resolve disputes through mediation and arbitration. The link to "BBB Auto Line" is found on the home page. Check to see if your car or your family's car is covered by this program. At this site you can also electronically file a complaint against a manufacturer.

Q. What kinds of disputes are handled by BBB Autoline?

Exercise 7.6 Does Your State Have a Lemon Law?

BBB Autoline (see above) provides information on state-specific lemon laws. You can find out whether your state has such a law. If it does, you can get information on how the law is applied and under what conditions you may be entitled to full reimbursement.

Q. Is there a lemon law in your state? If so, what's covered and how is it applied?

Housing

the cost of shelter

Objectives

1. To determine how much you can afford to spend on housing
2. To estimate whether it is financially more attractive to buy or to rent
3. To explain the real estate transaction from appraisal to closing
4. To understand the many kinds of home mortgages
5. To know how to handle a potential foreclosure

Steele family

Arnold and Sharon are currently carrying a 30–year adjustable rate mortgage on their home with a current rate of 7 percent. The Steeles have an adjustable rate mortgage with a 1–year adjustment period and periodic adjustment cap of 1 percent. With the recent uptick in mortgage rates they expect the interest rate on the mortgage will soon rise to 8 percent. This will increase the monthly payment from $1,331 to $1,453. The extra $122 a month on mortgage payments will not significantly upset their current budget. However, they are worried that rates might go higher, possibly reaching the overall aggregate cap of 12 percent. At 12 percent, their current monthly payment would be $1,983.

They have discussed the possibility of refinancing with their present lender. For $500 in loan origination costs and $2,000 in points, the bank is willing to refinance the outstanding loan balance at a fixed rate 7.5 percent with monthly payments of $1,391. They like idea that the fixed rate would reduce future interest rate risk.

However, the refinancing costs would require some additional immediate expenditure. Given the uncertainties in the present housing market they are not sure whether this is a good strategy. Their neighborhood has experienced a modest decline in housing prices as a result of the recent crisis in the subprime mortgage market and the economy may be headed for a recession and higher inflation.

The Steeles are not sure how long they will live in the present house. They have no desire or need to move to another home, but they know that things could change. They could use a larger house if they had another child or Arnold could change employment. There is a small possibility that Arnold may have to relocate to corporate headquarters in another city in about five years. Is it worth even considering refinancing if they are not likely to remain in their present home more than another five years?

TOPIC LINKS

Follow the **Topic Links** in each chapter for your interactive Personal Finance exercise on the Web. Go to: **www.prenhall.com/frasca**.

Housing decisions, because they have a significant impact on the household budget, can often be difficult ones. This is especially so if you are a first-time buyer or seller. So much rides on the correct decision that it's important to familiarize yourself thoroughly with both the housing market and the home lending market. The recent crisis in the subprime mortgages, consisting of loans to less credit worthy borrowers, is the result of mistakes that were made by both borrowers and lenders. The expectations were that with rising housing prices and easy credit, subprime borrowers would be able to refinance and meet their mortgage obligations. The expectations were overly optimistic. The Mortgage Bankers Association reports that delinquencies on mortgage payments in the first quarter of 2008 were the highest they had been since 1985.

Every period has its economic uncertainties. Each generation thinks that it is living in the most unsettling of all times. Unfortunately, clarity only accompanies historical hindsight. With rising oil prices and skittish financial markets, the future does not appear clear. In addition to these factors, housing markets will be affected by many other variables, such as regional migration, the age structure of the population, and consumer tastes. A home is probably the largest single investment you will make. With so much uncertainty and with so much at stake, it is essential that you investigate before you buy.

The National Association of Realtors® publishes the **Housing Affordability Index** presented in Figure 8.1. When the median family income is enough to qualify for a conventional loan on an existing median-priced home, the index assumes a value of 100. When the index rises, more families find it easier to purchase and finance the typical home. For example, when the index rises to 110, those earning about 90 percent of the median family income will now qualify for a loan on a median-priced home.

Housing Affordability Index Published by the National Association of Realtors®, it is related directly to the ability of a median-income family to purchase a median-priced home.

The Housing Affordability Index (HAI) reached a low point at the beginning of the 1980s. Since then, the trend was generally upward, until a sharp drop in 2004. This decline in housing affordability reflects the recent turnaround in interest rates illustrated in Figure 8.2. As seen in Figure 8.3 there has been a significant departure from the upward trend in housing prices in the recent period. A median-priced home is the one that separates the bottom 50 percent from the top 50 percent. The statistical median house is about the same age each year. Consequently, the sales price of an actual home that ages from year to year would rise by less than the statistical median. Reflecting troubles in the housing and mort-

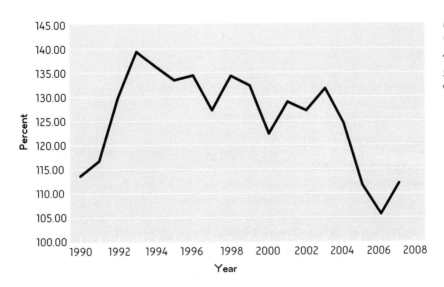

Figure 8.1
Composite Housing Affordability Index

Source: National Association of Realtors®.

Figure 8.2
*Effective Mortgage Rates
on Conventional Single-
Family Home Mortgages*

Source: Federal Housing
Finance Board

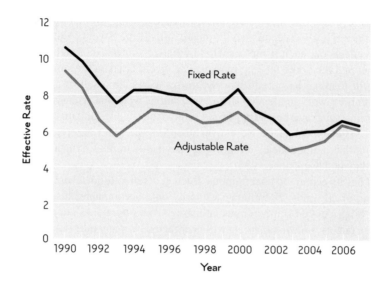

Figure 8.3
*Median Sales Price of
Existing Single-Family
Homes*

Source: National Association of
Realtors®. Inflation-adjusted
dollars calculated by authors.

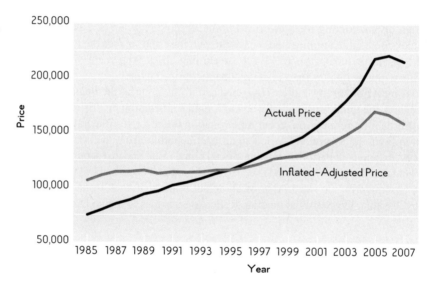

TOPIC LINKS

Find the latest data on the HAI.

gages markets, the median-priced home declined from a high of $221,900 in 2006 to $217,800. This was the first annual decline in at least four decades. It was accompanied by a 13 percent drop in the sales of previously owned homes, the biggest decline in a quarter century.

As rates on home mortgages reached record lows in the early part of this decade, banks increased lending to subprime borrowers—borrowers with poor credit history or poorly documented income. This lending helped support the upward trend in home prices. Mortgage lenders provided these borrowers adjustable rate mortgages with low initial rates that would then rise to higher levels after the first few years. The low initial rate held down monthly payments and allowed subprime borrowers to qualify for a home that they might not have otherwise qualified for. Banks and other mortgage lenders also eased lending requirements in the subprime market.

Interest rates on adjustable rate loans are periodically adjusted to reflect changes in credit markets. When they rise borrowers must make a larger monthly payment. The recent rise in mortgage rates has significantly increased the monthly payments on subprime loans. So much so, that there has been a substantial rise in delinquent payments. This crisis in the subprime market has reverberated throughout the mortgage and housing market, affecting more credit worthy borrowers. Mortgage lenders have since adopted more stringent lending standards that have had a negative impact on home prices and sales. What impact this may have on long-term housing prices is uncertain. It is clear, however, that buying a house in today's market requires some careful consideration. Consumers must fully weigh the benefits, costs, and risks of home ownership. If interest rates continue to rise, housing prices can fall.

Nationwide statistics, however, do not reveal the great variability in regional and local markets. Local markets may not mirror the movement in the national market. When you purchase a home you are also buying into a community that provides local resources. It is surprising how much in price the same home in different communities can differ. Purchasing a home may still be a wise decision, but prospective home buyers should carefully examine both national and local market conditions.

Rent or Buy?

We all need shelter. However, the ways we satisfy that need are practically unlimited. Like most decisions, this one must take into account your preferred lifestyle and your financial constraints. You can decide on a rental that places minimal demands on your time or finances. You can purchase a single-family home, thus taking on all the responsibilities of maintenance and a home mortgage. Or you may prefer to purchase a condominium or a cooperative, with characteristics falling somewhere between those of a rental unit and those of a single-family home. Obviously, your choice will, and should, depend on what makes you feel most comfortable. All we can do is point out the various advantages and disadvantages concerning your choice.

Figure 8.4 outlines some of the lifestyle considerations surrounding choice of renting or buying. The following discussion will be concerned with the financial considerations. We do not mean to imply that the financial decision is the most important one. The financial decision is an objective one that we can help you analyze. A preferred living arrangement is a personal choice.

To determine if you are a candidate for home ownership, you must first estimate how much you can afford. This largely depends on your income and your non-mortgage debt. Given this information, you can then examine housing within your price range. Once you understand what the market has to offer, you can decide whether it is financially more advantageous to buy or to rent.

TOPIC LINKS

Check out the latest housing market conditions.

Determining What You Can Afford

The following formulas and related worksheets indicate the highest-priced home you can afford. They do not intend to suggest that you should borrow the maximum amount a bank will lend you. When buying a home, you are committing yourself to fixed future expenses and future maintenance. While shopping, be sure to get information on what current owners are paying for utilities and property taxes. Then you can estimate the future expenses you will be locking in. Given these expenses, prepare a sample budget. You may find that even though you can afford a particular home, you may not want to cut back on the other expenditures that enrich your lifestyle.

The general rule of thumb for determining how much you can afford to rent or purchase is that you spend no more than 25 percent of your after-tax income on housing

Figure 8.4
Rent Versus Buy: Personal
Considerations

Renting	Buying
Lifestyle Choices	
Landlord may place restrictions on pets, guests, and children. There also may be restrictions on how you may redecorate your rental unit.	For condos and co-ops, similar restrictions may exist in the bylaws. The single-family home provides the most freedom in choice of lifestyle. You need only abide by city zoning ordinances.
Privacy	
You may be bothered by both other tenants and the landlord. The landlord will have rights to inspect the premises and to show the unit to prospective tenants.	You can have as much or as little privacy as you want, depending on the type of home ownership you choose.
Maintenance	
Maintenance costs will be included in your rental payments. With a responsible landlord, you will be free of maintenance concerns. With an irresponsible landlord, your only remedy may be to move.	You alone are responsible. You must budget for maintenance expenses and be prepared to do it yourself or hire a capable person.
Mobility	
At the end of the leasing period you simply pack up and leave. If you must move before the lease is up for renewal, you usually can negotiate a mutually agreeable termination.	Selling costs may be considerable, including sales commissions and fixing-up expenses. You are at the mercy of the marketplace. If home demand is down, you must either accept a lower price or incur carrying costs until the market improves.
Financial Risk	
The only risk you face is the possible loss of your personal property in the rental unit. This risk can be covered by renter's insurance.	Your home is also an investment. You can insure it against natural disasters and most other risks. However, you cannot insure against a forced sale at below market price resulting from the loss of your job.

expenses. For buyers, this usually implies a home purchase price of about two and one-half times after-tax income. This is only a rule of thumb; the actual guidelines used by lending institutions can be a lot more complicated.

A worksheet incorporating the housing expense and repayment test set down by the Federal Home Loan Mortgage Corporation, an agency that purchases and resells home mortgages, is contained in Figure 8.5. You begin by entering your monthly gross income on line 1. This includes all before-tax income from normal and regular sources.

Next, multiply the housing expense-to-income ratio on line 2 by your monthly gross income on line 1, and enter the result on line 3. This indicates the total amount you may devote to housing expenses. A maximum housing expense-to-income ratio of 0.28 is used in the example.

The Federal Home Loan Mortgage Corporation (popularly called Freddie Mac) recommends that your monthly housing expenses not exceed 28 percent of gross monthly income, the amount you earn before taxes. Furthermore, it suggests that your total monthly debt payments, including housing expenses, not exceed 33 to 36 percent of your gross monthly

TOPIC LINKS

Worksheet at Freddie Mac

Figure 8.5
How Much House Can You Afford?

1. Total monthly gross income	$6,300.00
Housing Expense Test	
2. Housing expense-to-income ratio	×0.28
3. Allowable housing expenditure (multiply line 1 by line 2)	$ 1,764
Nonmortgage housing expenses	
Homeowner's insurance	$ 40
Property taxes	300
Other	—
4. Total nonmortgage housing expenses	340
5. **Affordable monthly mortgage payment under housing**	$ 1,424
Debt Repayment Test	
6. Debt repayment-to-income ratio	×0.36
7. Allowable debt payment (multiply line 1 by line 6)	$ 2,268
Monthly installment debt and alimony	
Auto loan	$ 474
Student loan	—
Credit card debt	—
Alimony	—
Other	—
8. Total monthly installment debt and alimony	$ 474
9. Total nonmortgage expense and installment debt repayment (line 4 plus line 8)	−814
10. **Affordable monthly mortgage payment under debt repayment test** (line 7 less line 9)	$ 1,454
Your Affordable Home Purchase	
11. Affordable monthly mortgage (lesser of line 11 or line 6)	$ 1,424
Contract rate on home mortgage	0.08
Duration of loan (months)	360.00
12. Monthly payment per $1,000 mortgage	$7.34
13. Your affordable mortgage	$ 194,068
14. Fractional amount borrowed	÷0.80
15. **Your affordable home purchase**	$ 242,585

income. Most lenders will attempt to abide by these ratios. However, you may find a few who are willing to surpass the recommended ratios if you have proven yourself credit worthy. FHA-insured mortgages, discussed later in this chapter, limit housing expenses and debt payments to, respectively, 29 percent and 41 percent of gross income. The existing debt ratios for home owners (see Figure 8.6) are much lower than the maximum ratios.

Line 4 includes all your non-mortgage housing expenses. These consist of mortgage insurance premiums, property insurance, real estate taxes, and, when applicable, home owners' association or condominium maintenance fees. Subtracting nonmortgage housing expenses (line 4) from line 3 indicates your affordable monthly mortgage payment under the housing expenses test (line 5).

The debt repayment test is used to ensure that other claims on your paycheck do not interfere with your ability to meet your mortgage payment. An allowable debt-to-income ratio of 0.36 is used in the example. If you plan to place 10 percent or less down on the purchase price, use the lower limit of 0.33. Multiplying this ratio by your monthly gross income indicates the maximum amount you should be spending on debt repayment (line 7)

Figure 8.6
U.S. Household Debt
Ratios

Source: Federal Reserve Board,
First Quarter 2007,
http://www.federalreserve.gov/
releases/housedebt

Household Debt Service Ratio

The household debt service ratio (DSR) is an estimate of the ratio of debt payments to after-tax income. Debt payments consist of the estimated required payments on outstanding mortgage and consumer debt.

All Families	14.33%

Financial Obligations Ratio (FOR)

The financial obligations ratio (FOR) is a broader measure than the debt service ratio. The FOR includes automobile lease payments, rental payments on tenant-occupied property, homeowner's insurance, and property tax payments.

All Families	19.18%
Home owners	18.01%
Home owners—mortgage debt only	11.65%
Home owners—consumer debt only	6.36%
Renters	25.10%

including your potential mortgage payment. On line 8 include all installment debt with more than 10 payments remaining, in addition to any other regular claims on your income, such as alimony payments. Adding in nonmortgage expenses and subtracting the total (line 9) from the allowable debt payment (line 7) provides your affordable monthly mortgage payment under the debt repayment test.

You must satisfy both the home expense and debt repayment test; therefore, your affordable monthly mortgage will be equal to the lower of the values on line 5 and line 10. The next step is to determine how much you can borrow, given your ability to cover the monthly mortgage payments on line 11. To estimate this, first you need to know the current initial interest rates on home mortgages. You will find that interest rates differ by lending institution, type of mortgage, and size of down payment. However, after a few calls to local financial institutions or surfing the Internet, you should have an estimate of the likely mortgage rate. Given this rate and your affordable monthly payment, you could use a financial calculator to determine your maximum mortgage. Alternatively, you could complete Figure 8.5. Use your likely interest rate to find your monthly payment per $1,000 of mortgage loan in Table 8.1. Enter this value on line 12. In the example, it is assumed that the annual interest rate on an expected 30-year loan with a 20 percent down payment is 8 percent. This produces the monthly payment per $1,000 of $7.34 on line 12. Divide line 11 by line 12, and then multiply the result by $1,000 to obtain an estimate of your affordable mortgage on line 13.

The home purchase price will be equal to the amount borrowed plus the down payment. Given a 20 percent down payment, the mortgage will equal 80 percent of the selling price, and the affordable home purchase price on line 15 is $242,585.

TOPIC LINKS

Use an online monthly payment calculator.

Types of Housing

Since World War II, the U.S. Congress has pursued a policy of fostering home ownership through subsidies and tax breaks. That policy has largely succeeded. About two-thirds of housing units are now owner-occupied. Home ownership varies directly with age, income, and net worth according to data from the U.S. Census. In households with adults under age

Contract Interest Rate (%)	Duration of Loan (Years)					
	5	10	15	20	25	30
12	22.24	14.35	12.00	11.01	10.53	10.29
11 1/2	21.99	14.06	11.68	10.66	10.16	9.90
11	21.74	13.78	11.37	10.32	9.80	9.52
10 1/2	21.49	13.49	11.05	9.98	9.44	9.15
10	21.25	13.22	10.75	9.65	9.09	8.78
9 1/2	21.00	12.94	10.44	9.32	8.74	8.41
9	20.76	12.67	10.14	9.00	8.39	8.05
8	20.28	12.13	9.56	8.36	7.72	7.34
7	19.80	11.61	8.99	7.75	7.07	6.65
6	19.33	11.10	8.44	7.16	6.44	6.00
5	18.87	10.61	7.91	6.60	5.85	5.37

Table 8.1
Monthly Payment per $1,000 of Mortgage Loan

35, 42 percent of households own the home in which they are living. By age 55 to 64, ownership rises to about 80 percent. Household income and net worth both increase with age, so housing becomes both more affordable and more tax advantageous, because of federal income tax deductions for mortgage interest and property taxes.

The typical family starts out in a rental unit. With an increase in income and the accumulation of the necessary down payment, families tend to purchase their first home when the head of the household is around age 30. And when they do purchase, the overwhelming choice is the traditional single-family home. Your household, however, need not be typical. Choose the types of housing and the type of occupancy that best fits your lifestyle and financial plan.

Apartment Housing

Although any style of living unit can be rented, it is usually the apartment we think of first. Large apartment complexes may offer attractive amenities such as swimming pools, tennis courts, and clubhouses. Outside of a cooperative or condo, such amenities would be difficult for the average home owner to afford.

For mobile individuals demanding minimal responsibilities and an environment in which social relationships are nurtured, a large apartment complex may be desirable. This group seems to be the one to which new apartment construction is designed to appeal.

Condominium Housing

Condominium housing can offer the extras of apartment living along with the rewards of home ownership. Strictly defined, **condominium** does not refer to a particular type of housing. It stands for a unique type of ownership where part of the property is individually owned and part is owned in common with other members of the condominium complex. You own your living unit and have a shared interest in other areas of the condominium site, such as recreational and maintenance areas. You are responsible for the financing and upkeep of your individual unit and you are assessed charges for the financing and upkeep of the common areas. Before you purchase, you should fully understand what these charges are and how fees set by the condominium association will be determined in the future.

As an owner, you are a member of the condominium association and will be able to vote for directors in whom most of the governing powers will be vested. Condominiums

Condominium A form of ownership in which there is an individual ownership interest in the living unit but a shared ownership unit in the common areas.

are created by the laws of the state where they are located. The laws provide a legal framework for the operations of the directors and for the conditions and restrictions imposed on a property. Although this framework will differ from state to state, in all states you have a right to receive copies of the basic documents in which the legal and economic rules of the condominium are set out.

Cooperative Housing

Cooperative A corporate form of ownership in which individuals own stock giving them exclusive use of a dwelling unit.

As in a condominium, in a cooperative, several owners share an undivided interest. However, a **cooperative** has a corporate form. Instead of purchasing the individual living unit, you purchase stock in the corporation and then lease the living unit from the corporation. The corporation owns the living units and carries the mortgage on them. Its expenses are covered by the rents set in the lease agreements. As a stockholder, you can vote for the board of directors. One major problem associated with cooperatives is that you must receive the consent of the board of directors before you can transfer your stock and lease.

Single-Family Housing

When you purchase a single-family home, you take on all the responsibilities of finance and maintenance that go with it. You are your own landlord and maintenance person and you must budget your money and time accordingly. When something needs to be fixed, you must be ready to do it yourself or have the funds to hire someone.

Multifamily Housing

If you are considering purchasing a multifamily dwelling, you are looking for an investment that also satisfies your own need for shelter. The financial considerations concerning investment in real estate are not covered in this text. A specialized course in real estate can provide you with the needed financial tools.

Mobile Homes

Over 90 percent of mobile homes are not very mobile. They travel only from the manufacturer to the dealer and finally to a housing site, where they usually remain permanently affixed. For this reason, the industry prefers the term *manufactured home*. Because the homes are constructed at the factory, the cost per square foot of living space is considerably less than for homes constructed on-site.

The mobile home may be placed on a solitary plot or within a mobile home park. Often, parks have common recreational areas and offer many of the conveniences of large apartment complexes. Typically, mobile home parks rent sites using long-term lease agreements. However, there are a few condominium mobile home developments where you purchase the site and then pay a monthly maintenance fee to cover the cost of the common areas.

Because the market price of mobile homes has typically depreciated with age, financing has been a problem. Mobile homes are usually financed with a 20 percent down payment, a personal property loan of 10 to 15 years duration, and an interest rate a few percentage points above that on conventional home mortgages. For those who qualify, federally insured mortgages for longer durations and with lower down payments are available through the Federal Housing Administration (FHA) and the Veterans Administration (VA).

A Cost Comparison

When you purchase a home, you are undertaking a sizable investment of your own money. The financial question is: Would you be better off renting and investing your funds else-

finance news 8.1

The Subprime Crisis Tightens Credit Markets

You have a poor credit history, a FICO score below 620, and you either want to buy a home or borrow funds on your existing home. In the mortgage market you are known as a subprime borrower. Subprime loans are loans made to borrowers with a less than satisfactory credit history. Lately the government has been concerned with a rising number of mortgage foreclosures in the subprime market based on falling housing prices and rising interest rates. Banks have responded by tightening credit requirements on all borrowers, not just those in the subprime market. A 2008 Federal Reserve survey of financial institutions indicated that 55 percent of all respondents have tightened requirements on prime mortgages and 60 percent have also imposed stricter standards on home equity loans.

Subprime loans are at higher interest rates with prepayment penalties. These are not necessarily predatory loans, although some subprime borrowers may be offered predatory loans. Predatory loans are designed to cheat or deceive borrowers into losing the equity in their homes. Subprime loans carry higher financial costs because of the increased risks of lending to subprime borrowers who are more likely to default on their home mortgages.

Most subprime mortgages are adjustable rate loans that have a low fixed teaser rate for an initial period after which the contract rate rises and changes based upon an interest rate index. In the past, subprime borrowers have qualified for these loans based upon the low initial monthly payments during the initial teaser rate period. Many could not have qualified at the typical home mortgage rate. Unfortunately, some borrowers who do not understand how future monthly payments will be adjusted may be subject to mortgage payment shock after the initial teaser rate ends.

Adjustable rate mortgages known as "2/28" loans have a fixed rate for two years and then adjust to a variable rate for the remaining 28 years. There are also other variants such as "3/27" loans that have an initial fixed rate for three years. The idea is that consumers have the opportunity to repair their credit ratings during the initial fixed rate period. They would then be able to refinance at a more favorable rate after paying a significant prepayment penalty. The spread between the initial fixed interest rate and the fully indexed interest rate typically ranges from 2 to 6 percent. Generally, the adjustable rate can go up 2 percent a year after the initial fixed rate period for a maximum 6 percent increase over the life of the loan. On a $200,000 initial 2/28 mortgage financed at 5 percent, initial monthly payments would be $1,074. After two years the monthly payments could rise to $1,359 and after five years that could rise to a maximum

monthly payment of $1,976, an 84 percent increase over the initial monthly payment.

The recent surge in foreclosures reflects the inability of borrowers to make monthly payments after the rates are reset. Delinquency rates on single family residential mortgages almost doubled from a low of 1.4 percent in the first quarter of 2005 to 2.7 percent in the third quarter of 2007. Moreover, it does not appear that this problem will be resolved quickly. The Federal Reserve reports that about one-and-a-half million adjustable rate subprime mortgages will be reset in 2008, with an additional one-half million reset in 2009.

Rules adopted in 2007 by the Federal Reserve now require that borrowers must qualify at the fully indexed rate and not the initial teaser rate. This will eliminate some borrowers who would have had difficulty managing the monthly payment after the initial fixed rate period. Additional new regulations on subprime mortgages include the following:

- Creditors are prohibited from engaging in a pattern or practice of extending credit without considering borrowers' ability to repay the loan.

- Creditors are required to verify the income and assets they rely upon in making a loan.

- Prepayment penalties are only to be permitted if certain conditions are met, including the condition that no penalty will apply for at least sixty days before any possible payment increase.

- Creditors must establish escrow accounts for taxes and insurance.

In addition, the Federal Reserve enacted new regulations that affect all mortgages, not just subprime mortgages.

- Lenders are prohibited from compensating mortgage brokers by making payments known as "yield-spread premiums" unless the broker previously entered into a written agreement with the consumer disclosing the broker's total compensation and other facts. A yield spread premium is the fee paid by a lender to a broker for higher-rate loans. The consumer's written agreement with the broker must occur before the consumer applies for the loan or pays any fees.

- Creditors and mortgage brokers are prohibited from coercing a real estate appraiser to misstate a home's value.

- Companies that service mortgage loans are prohibited from engaging in certain practices. For example, servicers would be required to credit consumers' loan payments as of the date of receipt and would have to provide a schedule of fees upon request.

where? The answer will depend on expected future housing prices, the expected return on financial investments, the length of time you expect to stay in one location, and the expected tax advantage from home ownership.

The Tax Advantage

TOPIC LINKS

IRS on Home Mortgage Interest Deduction

Several immediate and long-term tax advantages are associated with buying a home. If you itemize deductions—and you probably should if you have a home mortgage—the state and local taxes you pay on the property and the interest you pay on the mortgage may be deductible from your adjusted gross income when you calculate your federal taxable income. This means that if you are in the 28 percent marginal tax bracket, each dollar you pay in property taxes and interest saves you $0.28 in federal income taxes. Naturally, the higher your marginal tax rate, the greater is the income tax advantage. As a renter, you may find these items included in the price of the rent, but you cannot take them as a deduction on your income tax return.

Mortgage interest is fully deductible only on first and second homes, if total home mortgages for couples filing a joint return do not exceed $1 million. Special tax treatment accorded capital gains provides an additional long-term tax advantage. You may exclude up to $250,000 ($500,000 if filing jointly) of the gain on your main home from your taxable income. This exclusion may be applied to each sale of a home so long as you owned the home for two years and used it as your main home for two of the last five years. The exclusion is proportionately reduced for shorter periods of ownership. Even if you held the house for less than two years, you may still exclude the gain if you had to sell because of a change in your place of employment or for certain unforeseen circumstances such as divorce or death. For additional information see IRS Publication 523.

TOPIC LINKS

IRS rules on buying and selling your home

Finally, there is a hidden tax advantage that is often overlooked. Suppose you could rent your present home for $500 a month; this is the market worth of the shelter that you are receiving. This value is part of the return from the investment in the home and may be thought of as an implicit rent paid to and received by you. However, payments to yourself are not considered income for tax purposes. Thus, the implicit rental income accompanying home ownership remains tax free.

Buying Versus Renting

TOPIC LINKS

Download worksheet.

Figure 8.7 shows a worksheet for comparing the relative costs of buying and renting a home. The worksheet contains entries for a one-year comparison and a five-year comparison. Both periods are considered because it is most likely that the best choice depends on the length of time spent at one location. The sample data are based on a home that could be purchased for $110,000 or rented for $700 per month plus utilities. If purchased, it is assumed the buyer would place 20 percent down and borrow $88,000, to be paid back over 30 years at an annual percentage rate of 6 percent. It is also assumed that all prices, including the market price of the home, will rise at 3 percent a year.

To calculate the gross gain or loss from buying in Figure 8.7, first we estimate the appreciation in the value of the home over the holding period. Looking at the first-year comparison, the assumed appreciation rate of 3 percent is equal to $3,300. The capital gain or loss at the sale of the home is equal to the appreciation less selling expenses. These selling expenses include commissions, advertising fees, legal fees, and loan charges paid by the seller. The largest selling expense is likely to be the sales commission. In Figure 8.7, selling expenses are 7 percent of the selling price.

The gross gain or loss on the sale of the home will be equal to the capital gain or loss less capital gain taxes and the after-tax closing costs you incurred when you purchased the home. Losses on the sale of your home are not deductible and, as previously discussed, there is generally no tax on the appreciation. The exceptions include a gain on a home held less than two years and a gain exceeding the exemption. Therefore, it is likely that the capital gains tax is zero. The initial closing costs you incurred at the time of purchase will also reduce your realized gain. Some of these initial expenses, such as property taxes and mortgage points, may be tax deductible. Therefore, these expenses may be reduced for tax adjustments.

The gross gain from renting is based on the assumption that if you did not buy, the $22,000 down payment and the initial closing costs of $2,500 would remain in an investment fund paying an annual interest rate of 6 percent. This investment would provide inter-

Figure 8.7
Buy Versus Rent: Cost Comparison (Page 1 of 2)

Givens:

Buying		Renting	
Home purchase price:	$110,000	Rent:	$700 a month plus utilities
Mortgage:		Renter's insurance:	$50 a year
Principal:	$88,000		
Term:	30 years		
Interest rate:	6% APR		
Monthly payment:	$527.60		
Selling expense:	7% of selling price	**Common Factors**	$527.60
Closing costs after taxes:	$2,500	Annual fuel and utilities:	$2,400
Annual property taxes	$2,100	Marginal tax rate:	28%
Annual home owners repair		Taxes on capital gain:	$0
and maintenance:	1,200	Before-tax return on investment:	6%
Annual homeowner's insurance:	$500	Inflation rate:	3%

One-Year Comparison

	Buying	Renting
Gross gain or loss		
Buying		
Appreciation:	$ 3,300	
Selling expenses:	(7,931)	
Capital gain or loss:	($ 4,631)	
Taxes on capital gain:	0	
Initial closing costs after taxes:	(2,500)	
Renting		
Interest earned after taxes:		$ 1,058
Total Gross Gain (1)	($ 7,131)	$ 1,058
Annual Expenses		
Buying		
Mortgage interest after taxes saved	($ 3,780)	
Property taxes after taxes saved	(1,512)	
Repair and maintenance	(1,000)	
Renting		
Rent		($ 8,400)
Common expenses		
Fuel and utilities	(2,400)	(2,400)
Insurance	(500)	(50)
Total Annual Expenses (2)	($ 9,192)	($10,850)
Total Gain or Loss (Gross gain (1) + annual expenses (2))	($16,323)	($9,792)

You save $6,531 by renting.

Figure 8.7
Buy Versus Rent: Cost
Comparison (Page 2)

	Five-year Comparison	
	Buying	**Renting**
Gross gain or loss		
Buying		
Appreciation:	$17,520	
Selling expenses:	(8,926)	
Capital gain or loss:	$ 8,594	
Taxes on capital gain:	0	
Initial closing costs after taxes:	(2,500)	
Renting		
Interest earned after taxes:		$ 5,769
Total Gross Gain (1)	$ 6,094	$ 5,769
Annual Expenses		
Buying		
Mortgage interest after taxes saved	($18,392)	
Property taxes after taxes saved	(8,027)	
Repair and maintenance	(5,309)	
Renting		
Rent		($44,597)
Common Expenses		
Fuel and utilities	($12,742)	(12,742)
Insurance	(2,655)	(265)
Total Annual Expenses (2)	($47,125)	($57,604)
Total Gain or Loss (Gross gain (1) + annual expenses (2))	($41,031)	($51,835)
	You save $10,804 by buying.	

est income of $1,470 before taxes. However, with an assumed marginal tax rate of 28 percent, interest earned after taxes is $1,058 = ($1,470 × (1 − 0.28)).

The related expenses of home ownership and renting are listed next. Mortgage interest payments can be taken from an amortization schedule prepared by your lender or any of the many online calculators on the Internet. This schedule will specify your yearly repayments on the loan and your yearly interest payments (for an example, see Table 8.2). On the present loan, mortgage interest payments for the first year are $5,251. Assuming you itemize deductions, the actual interest expense after taxes is $3,780 = ($5,251 = (1 − 0.28)). A similar tax adjustment should be made for property taxes.

The five-year comparison employs the same basic assumptions as the one-year comparison. The annual mortgage rate is 6 percent, and all prices, including fuel, insurance, maintenance, taxes, and rent are assumed to rise at a 3 percent annual rate.

Such analyses, including this example, commonly show that renting appears to be the better alternative over the short run, whereas ownership is cheaper over the long run. The high turnover cost of buying and selling a home makes renting the better short-term choice. On the other hand, inflation protection and tax advantages make buying the optimal long-term choice.

Table 8.2
Amortization Schedule for
a Fixed Rate Mortgage

Loan amount:	$88,000
Annual contract rate:	6%
Term (years):	30
Monthly payment:	$527.60

Year	Principal Repayment	Interest Payment	Ending Principal Outstanding
1	$1,081	$5,251	$86,919
2	$1,147	$5,184	$85,772
3	$1,218	$5,113	$84,554
4	$1,293	$5,038	$83,261
5	$1,373	$4,958	$81,888
6	$1,458	$4,874	$80,430
7	$1,548	$4,784	$78,883
8	$1,643	$4,688	$77,240
9	$1,744	$4,587	$75,495
10	$1,852	$4,479	$73,643
11	$1,966	$4,365	$71,677
12	$2,087	$4,244	$69,590
13	$2,216	$4,115	$67,374
14	$2,353	$3,978	$65,021
15	$2,498	$3,833	$62,523
16	$2,652	$3,679	$59,871
17	$2,816	$3,516	$57,055
18	$2,989	$3,342	$54,066
19	$3,174	$3,158	$50,893
20	$3,369	$2,962	$47,523
21	$3,577	$2,754	$43,946
22	$3,798	$2,533	$40,148
23	$4,032	$2,299	$36,116
24	$4,281	$2,051	$31,835
25	$4,545	$1,786	$27,291
26	$4,825	$1,506	$22,466
27	$5,123	$1,209	$17,343
28	$5,439	$893	$11,904
29	$5,774	$557	$6,130
30	$6,130	$201	($0)
Totals	$88,000	$101,938	

All other things remaining the same, the following changes will make owning a home more attractive:

- A reduction in mortgage interest rates
- An increase in the expected future price of housing
- An increase in your marginal tax rate
- An increase in rents
- A decrease in the rate of return on financial investments

The Real Estate Transaction

A home is most likely the largest single purchase you will make. It is also the largest single asset you are likely to own. According to the U.S. Census Bureau, the equity in the family home accounts for a surprisingly large 44 percent of household net worth. Because it is so important, and because few of us buy and sell homes often enough to become experts on the subject, you should seek the advice of experienced professionals before you become a home owner. Both the buyer and the seller will need to know current market prices, which can be verified by a home appraiser. The seller may have to rely upon a real estate agent to market the home and the buyer will have to retain home inspectors to assess any hidden problems. To ensure that there is a valid sale with no legal problems, both the buyer and the seller may want to seek the advice of a real estate attorney.

The Appraisal

As a buyer or a seller, you need information on market price. Housing prices depend on many factors, the principal ones being size, construction, age, and location. The last factor should not be underestimated. There may be a wide spread in the selling price of identical houses in two different locations. Remember, you are really buying more than a home. You are buying into a neighborhood, a score of community services, and a school system. Only someone very familiar with the local housing market may be able to appraise all these and other relevant factors.

Professional appraisers may be located at **AppraisalInstitute.com** or searching Yahoo! Local (**local.yahoo.com**) for "Real Estate Appraisers." Mortgage lenders can also provide you with a list of competent appraisers. In all cases, ask for credentials and references. The appraiser should be state licensed or certified.

Mortgage lenders will conduct an appraisal, but you should not rely on this procedure to determine the market value of your potential home. The lender's interest and yours are not the same. The lender wants to determine if the value of the house exceeds the amount borrowed by some safety margin. An independent appraisal may be necessary, because as a buyer or a seller, you need to know that you are paying or receiving current market value.

The Real Estate Agent

Unless you as a buyer have a special agreement with the real estate agent, the agent typically represents the seller. Many people fall into a comfortable relationship with the agent who is showing them homes and, in the course of casual conversation, reveal too much about what they are willing to pay. Because the seller agent's interest must be with the seller, this information may be later used to undermine the buyer's negotiating position.

If you, a buyer, would like someone to represent your interest, you can contract with a buyer's agent. The National Association of Exclusive Buyer Agents comprises agents that work exclusively for the buyer. An exclusive buyer agent works for a firm that does not take listings or represent sellers. Nonexclusive agents or dual agents may represent both buyers and sellers and may have conflicting interests. A buyer agent can help you select a home by providing information on relative home values and the local community. There is no set method for paying a buyer agent. Payment may be a flat fee, an hourly fee, or a percentage of the purchase price. Be sure you understand how the agent is to be compensated.

As a seller you can choose to use a real estate agent or not. The National Association of Realtors reports that only about 13 percent of all house sales are made without an agent

TOPIC LINKS

Review an appraisal form.

TOPIC LINKS

Check out the Neighborhood Explorer® for socioeconomic data on your neighborhood.

TOPIC LINKS

National Association of Exclusive Buyer Agents

and about one-third of the sales conducted without an agent were between parties that knew each other before the sale. An agent's commission is typically about 6 to 7 percent of the sale price. With the average existing home selling for over $200,000 and generating more than $12,000 in commissions, selling the home yourself can appear to be an attractive alternative. To make the best decision, think in terms of earning the commission rather than saving it. You will have to take on the work of advertising and showing the home and dealing directly with potential buyers. This work can be both time consuming and, for some people, emotionally draining.

Be sure that the agent you choose to sell your home is a member of the Multiple Listing Service (MLS). This will provide information on your home to all other real estate agencies in your area who are also members of the MLS. Because of fee-splitting arrangements among MLS members, every agent has an interest in selling your home.

The Listing Agreement

As a seller, you will be asked to sign a **listing agreement**, which is a contract between you and the real estate agent. It provides the agent with authority to act as your salesperson in return for a commission on the sale of the home. Important items on the contract will consist of the listing price, commission, description of the property, terms and conditions for sale, duration of the listing, and exclusivity of the listing. The last item will determine whether you have the right to retain other sales agents during the term of the listing agreement.

There are three basic types of listing arrangements: the exclusive right to sell, the exclusive agency, and the open agreement. The **exclusive right to sell** entitles the agent to a commission regardless of who sells the property. Even when you find a buyer, you still owe the agent a commission. With this agreement you should receive the full range of promotional services offered by the agent. Under an **exclusive agency agreement**, the seller agrees to retain one agent who typically provides more limited services than under an exclusive right to sell. The agent has an exclusive right to market your home. However, the agent collects a commission only if he or she finds a buyer. If you locate a buyer, you don't pay a commission. In both of the foregoing agreements the agent can co-broker the property, offering to split the commission with any other agent who can help find a buyer. With an **open listing agreement**, the agent receives a commission only if he or she discovers a buyer. If you or another agent sells the home, you don't owe a commission to the agent who listed your home.

Beware of clauses that automatically extend the listing period, prohibit recording (public notice) of the listing agreement, or contain a net listing agreement. Each of these can result in serious problems for the seller. Automatic extensions beyond the typical 90-day period reduce the agent's incentive to sell your home in a timely manner. Public notice may be required to avoid misrepresentation. A **net listing agreement** provides the seller with a predetermined net price from the sale of the property. The real estate agent receives the difference between the actual sale price and the net price promised the seller as commission.

Some real estate agencies will offer special inducements in an effort to get your home listing. These may turn out to be less valuable than first appearances would suggest. For example, some agencies will agree to buy your home if it cannot be sold by a specified time. Unfortunately, the price at which they are willing to purchase the home may be substantially below the price at which they are listing it. In addition, you may be still charged a commission, even though the home was purchased by the real estate agency at a low market price. Finally, the agreement may bind you to purchase a new home through this same agency, which will, of course, collect a commission on that transaction.

TOPIC LINKS

Check out sales on your street.

TOPIC LINKS

View a sample listing agreement.

Listing agreement A contract between the seller and the real estate agent providing the agent with authority to represent the seller in return for a commission on the sale.

Exclusive right to sell Entitles the agent to a commission no matter who sells the property.

Exclusive agency agreement The agent has an exclusive right to broker the property but may agree to share the commission with other agents. If you locate the buyer yourself, you don't pay a commission.

Open listing agreement Any agent can broker your home. The commission goes to the agent who locates a buyer. If you sell your home, you don't pay a commission.

Net listing agreement Provides the seller with a predetermined amount of money from the sale of the property.

The Purchase Contract

Verbal offers to purchase real estate are not binding. The offer to purchase a home is made on a document entitled *Contract to Purchase*, *Purchase Agreement*, or *Deposit Receipt*. There is no standard contract. When both the buyer and the seller have agreed to all the conditions in the purchase contract, it becomes a binding agreement that creates rights and obligations for both parties. Consequently, request a blank copy before you sign and have an attorney review it. Most real estate transactions are closed, however, without the aid of an attorney. Unfortunately, too many people consult an attorney only when they want to get out of a disagreeable contract. Such remedial action can be very costly.

Reviewing the Contract

You and your attorney should carefully examine the purchase contract to make sure it contains the following:

- The purchase price, the down payment, and the type of financing. Beware of an "escalator" clause that permits the builder to increase the price because of future cost increases.
- The anticipated closing costs and prepaid items and who will pay them.
- A description of the property and a list of all items being sold with the house. For new construction, plans and specifications should be included, and you should carefully review these with your architect and home inspector.
- A statement as to who is responsible for the property from the date of the contract to the date the property is conveyed to you.
- The amount of the deposit and the conditions under which the buyer or the seller might void the contract. For example, failure to buy or sell another house, inadequate financing, an unsatisfactory inspection report, or failure to obtain a marketable title may all be good reasons for voiding the purchase contract.
- A stated date after which the offer lapses if not accepted.

The process leading to the sale of a home begins when the buyer makes an offer to purchase, with a signed purchase contract and a commitment of earnest money. The seller may then accept the offer, reject the offer, or make a counteroffer by altering some or all of the terms on the purchase contract. Likewise, the buyer may then accept the counteroffer, reject it, or make another counteroffer. This process continues until the two sides either terminate negotiations or agree upon a sale.

The buyer's deposit of **earnest money** demonstrates that the offer is made in good faith. If the offer to purchase is not accepted or lapses, the earnest money should be returned to the buyer. If the seller accepts the offer to purchase, a third party—either a broker, a title company, or an escrow agent—will hold the money in a trust account until the sale is closed or the contract is broken. Should the buyer fail to purchase the home as indicated in the contract, the seller can keep the earnest money. On the other hand, if the seller breaks the contract, the deposit is returned to the buyer. When the sale goes through, the deposit is applied to the buyer's down payment on the purchase.

The Home Inspection

The home inspection is usually conducted right after the contract is signed. Your rights to home inspections and the potential remedies for problems should be specified in the purchase contract. To ensure your interests are protected have a real estate attorney review the contract before you sign.

TOPIC LINKS

View a sample purchase contract.

Earnest money Money deposited by the buyer, to be kept by the seller if the buyer does not abide by the terms of the offer to purchase. It demonstrates the buyer's good faith in the offer.

What looks like your dream home may actually be a house of horrors with a shaky foundation, termites, and a leaky roof. A thorough inspection by a qualified housing inspector should uncover problem areas that would otherwise go unnoticed. A home inspection will cost about $400, but this will vary by the extent of the inspection. For this amount, you should receive a written report stating the condition of the home and its component systems.

The American Society of Home Inspectors (ASHI) trains and certifies qualified individuals. They may be found in the Yellow Pages under *Building Inspection Services, Inspection Bureaus, Engineers,* or *Real Estate Inspectors* and at **www.ashi.org**. Be sure the inspector you hire has nothing to gain from your purchasing the home. The inspector should not, for example, run a remodeling firm or depend on a real estate agency for support. Ask for the names of previous customers and insist on being present during the home inspection. The person you hire should be able to answer all questions concerning the inspection.

TOPIC LINKS

Get "A Consumer Home Inspection Kit" from Freddie Mac.

TOPIC LINKS

Find an ASHI member.

The Title Search

The **deed** is a written document that transfers title, or ownership, to the buyer. However, the deed does not show who else might have rights to the property. In the **title search**, an attorney examines the public records to determine if others may have enforceable claims on the property. At the completion of the search, the attorney will render an opinion as to whether **marketable title** exists. A marketable title is free of all claims from other parties such as a hired contractor who may not have been paid.

The mortgage lender will conduct a title search. However, the fact that you are granted a loan does not necessarily mean the title is free of all defects. A loan may still be granted if the lender feels assured that the full value of the loan can be repaid in spite of minor defects in the title. In addition, if the search is deficient, you may have no claim against the attorney. The attorney is financially responsible only to the client. If the lender ordered the search, the lender is the client and not you. For this reason you need an independent examination.

The mortgage lender will require that you purchase **title insurance**. This insures the bank, not you, against a defective title. To protect your interest in the title, you can obtain owner's title insurance. You will save money by purchasing this coverage at the same time you buy the lender's policy. As with all insurance, coverage can vary. Read the insurance contract carefully to be sure it covers all defects in title, both in and out of the public record.

Deed A written instrument transferring title of real estate to the buyer.

Title search An examination of public records in order to determine who may have enforceable claims on the property.

Marketable title Legal evidence of a right to property that is free of claims from other parties.

Title insurance Protects the insured against defective title.

The Closing

Immediately before you are about to complete your home purchase, you should schedule a final walk-through to ensure that everything is acceptable. The meeting at which the purchase and the mortgage are finalized is called the **closing**. At the closing, the seller receives payment and the buyer undertakes the mortgage and receives the deed. By mutual agreement between the buyer and the seller, actual possession of the property may take place at this time or at some later date. Whoever closes the sale is required to report the terms of the sale to the IRS to ensure compliance with tax law. Costs due at this time are called **closing** or **settlement costs**. These typically add up to between 2 and 4 percent of the purchase price. A sample list of these costs is given in Figure 8.8.

Closing: The meeting at which the sale is finalized and the title is transferred.

Closing or settlement costs: Payments due at closing.

TOPIC LINKS

Sample closing costs

Government Charges

At the date of the closing, property-based taxes will be prorated to the buyer and seller over the current tax period. In addition, there may be various state and local charges on the

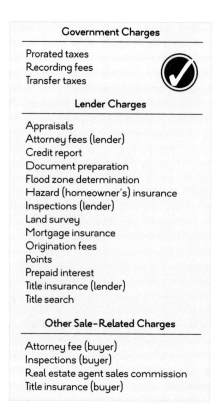

Figure 8.8
A Checklist of Potential
Closing Costs

transfer and the recording of the transfer. These charges are usually modest, but in some states these fees can run as high as 1 percent of the sale price.

Lender's Charges

The buyer generally pays lender's charges. They include the lender's cost of processing the loan, plus related costs such as property appraisals and inspections. Title charges include the costs of title search, title insurance for the lender, and document preparation. A single premium paid at this time will keep the policy in force until the house is sold again.

The Real Estate Settlement Procedures Act requires that the lender give you a good faith estimate of your closing costs within three days of receiving your loan application. The origination fee to start processing your loan cannot be more than 1 percent of the mortgage amount. Other fees they may charge include appraisal fees, inspection fees, and attorney fees.

Points Prepaid interest; one point is equal to 1 percent of the amount borrowed.

Points, also called discount points, may be included. Points are considered prepaid interest and are charged when the interest rate is below the yield required by lenders that buy mortgage securities. One discount point is equal to 1 percent of the amount borrowed. For example, on an $80,000 mortgage, $1\frac{1}{2}$ discount points are equal to $1,200. This has the effect of reducing the amount borrowed from $80,000 to $78,800. You still, however, owe the bank the unpaid balance of $80,000. Consequently, paying points raises the annual percentage rate (APR) on the loan above the **contract rate**, the rate applied to the unpaid balance for calculating your monthly mortgage payments. This difference arises because the APR calculates payments as a percentage of $78,800 (amount borrowed), whereas the contract rate calculates payments as a percentage of the amount owed ($80,000).

Contract rate The interest rate applied to the unpaid balance on the home mortgage.

Mortgage		$80,000
Points (1½)	(1.5%) × ($80,000) =	$1,200
Amount borrowed	($80,000 − $1,200) =	$78,800
Contract rate		6.00%
Interest payment	($80,000 × 6.00%) =	$4,800
APR	($4,800/$78,800) × 100 =	6.09%

Lenders may offer mortgages with identical APRs but with different contract rates. The loan with the lower contract rate would have more points up front. Should you prefer one mortgage over the other? The answer may depend on how long you intend to hold the home. Points push the interest payments to the front of the mortgage. If you are planning to move in a few years, you may prefer to defer interest into the future when you no longer own the home.

If the loan is closed before the last day of the month, the lender will want the borrower to prepay the balance of that month's interest. The lender may also require the borrower to prepay mortgage and hazard insurance. On some loans, particularly those with low down payments, the lender requires the borrower to set up and periodically fund a reserve account for paying insurance and property taxes. This account, called an *escrow account,* ensures that these payments will be made on time.

Other Sale-Related Charges

These may include the cost of your attorney, title insurance coverage for the buyer, and any home inspections arranged by the buyer or seller. The seller typically pays the broker's commission on the sale of the home. It currently runs about 6 or 7 percent of the sales price, but the exact percentage is negotiable.

Warranties

Homes, like other goods, will be covered by unwritten implied warranties set down by state law. Written warranties may also accompany the sale. These warranties fall into two categories: builders' warranties on newly constructed homes and home buyers' warranties on the resale of existing homes. Neither of these warranties relieves you from the duty of conducting a full and adequate home inspection before you buy.

Builders' warranties are meant to assure the buyer that the new home is structurally sound. The warranty can be backed by the builder or an independent third-party. For homes purchased with FHA or VA loans, insurance must be guaranteed by a third party. The buyer usually receives a 10-year warranty covering a list of defects that decrease in number as the home ages. During the first year almost all defects in workmanship and materials are covered. In the second year the list of guaranteed items is substantially shorter, and in the remaining eight years only major structural defects that make the home a danger are covered.

There have been problems with builders' warranties. Consumer groups have been highly critical. They charge that policies have been issued on poorly built homes. Moreover, the claims process may be complicated and lengthy, often forcing the consumer to deal with the original builder who was responsible for the faulty construction.

The second type of warranty, the warranty on the resale of an existing home, is similar to an extended service contract. Rather than covering the structural integrity of the home, it insures the major home appliances included in the sale. Typically, it lasts for only six months to a year. This provides the buyer with some assurance that he or she will not have to incur the cost of a new furnace or water heater soon after purchasing the home. Be warned that most policies include high deductibles on service calls and may even exclude preexisting mechanical problems. There is no standard format for resale warranties; therefore, policy coverage may vary widely.

Financing the Purchase

You can shop around for a home mortgage at a variety of financial institutions, including commercial banks, mutual savings banks, mortgage companies, and savings and loan associations. You can contact the lending institutions directly or you can employ a mortgage broker to shop for you. The broker may charge a fee at closing or the broker's cost may be included in a higher APR. Be sure to contact several lenders and mortgage brokers. A small reduction in the interest rate can result in significant savings. On a $100,000 30-year mortgage, a ½ percent reduction in the contract rate can reduce your future interest payments by more than $12,000.

Today's mortgage market is highly competitive. Lenders offer both fixed and adjustable rate loans and several ways in which each of these loans may be structured. Ask the loan officer to explain each of the loan options and discuss how each might fit your financial situation. The decision is an important one. A typical mortgage will commit you to interest payments that, over the life of the loan, can equal as much as three times the original amount borrowed.

The larger the down payment, the lower the interest rate, and the longer the term of the loan, the smaller is the monthly mortgage payment. The typical home buyer makes a 20 percent down payment on a 30-year mortgage with a fixed rate. However, with mortgage insurance you may obtain a home mortgage with as little as 5 percent down.

The annual percentage rate (APR), explained in Chapter 6, is the most important disclosure. It takes into account the interest rate and other credit charges, such as mortgage insurance, points, and loan origination fees, into a uniform measure of cost. Unfortunately, the published APR on adjustable rate loans must be based upon the initial interest rate. Since the future interest rate on the loan may differ from the initial interest rate, the APR in the mortgage contract will not likely reflect the interest costs you actually incur. Therefore, on adjustable rate loans, the lender is also required to describe the circumstances that will lead to rate changes and to give an example of the payment changes that can occur. For such loans, the circumstances under which rates may change are as important as the APR.

Realistically, it's impossible to present every repayment scenario for many adjustable rate loans. Loan officers will ordinarily try to be helpful, but time constraints may prohibit them from providing you with a complete examination of the proposed loan. Therefore, some previous knowledge of mortgage instruments may greatly aid you in the search for a home mortgage. The mortgage comparison checklist shown in Figure 8.9 should prove helpful when reviewing the characteristics of the available mortgages.

TOPIC LINKS

Obtain the latest rates on home mortgages.

TOPIC LINKS

Download a comprehensive checklist from the FED.

Fixed Rate Mortgages

As seen in Figure 8.10, most homes are financed with fixed rate mortgages. **Fixed rate mortgages** have an interest rate and monthly payments that remain constant over the life of the loan. For example, if you borrowed $88,000 at 6 percent for 30 years, you would have level monthly payments of $527.60 over the entire 30-year period. Part of each monthly payment will go to the repayment of **principal**—the amount owed—and part will go toward payment of interest on the principal.

Fixed rate mortgages Home mortgages on which the interest rate and monthly payment remain constant over the life of the loan.

Principal The remaining balance on the amount borrowed.

Lender

Loan type (fixed or adjustable)
Annual percentage rate
Duration (years)
Percentage down payment
Application fee
Points
Title insurance
Prepayment penalty
Other closing fees
Mortgage insurance
Initial interest rate
Initial monthly mortgage payment
Balloon payment

Additional Information on Adjustable Rate Loans

Interest adjustment index
Adjustment period
Periodic rate cap
Aggregate rate cap
Periodic payment cap
Negative amortization (Y/N)
Adjustable duration (Y/N)

Figure 8.9
Mortgage Comparison Checklist

Type of Payment Plan	Percent of Total
Fixed rate and payment	81.15%
Adjustable rate mortgage	5.30%
Adjustable term mortgage	0.35%
Graduated payment mortgage	1.12%
Balloon	1.12%
Other	0.05%
Combination of the above	1.03%
Not reported	9.88%

Term of Primary Mortgage at Origination or Assumption	
Less than 8 years	3.45%
8 to 12 years	3.58%
13 to 17 years	18.13%
18 to 22 years	5.80%
23 to 27 years	2.20%
28 to 32 years	64.95%
33 years or more	1.89%
Median term 29 years	

Figure 8.10
Characteristics of Home Mortgages, 2005

Source: American Housing Survey National Tables, U.S. Census Bureau

With a fixed rate mortgage, you are protected against future increases in mortgage rates. Rising mortgage rates are likely to happen during periods of increasing inflation. However, less risk for you means more risk for the lender. Lenders offset this risk by charging a higher rate on fixed rate mortgages than the initial rate they charge on adjustable rate mortgages. Fortunately, a fixed rate mortgage does not necessarily lock you

FINANCIAL PLANNING *for* young adults 8.2

Where Do You Get the Down Payment?

The biggest obstacle to purchasing a home is the down payment on your first home. If you are purchasing a starter home, you are most likely eligible for an FHA insured loan. It carries a higher insurance premium than private mortgage insurance, but it will let you buy a home with only a 5 percent down payment. In addition, the debt-to-income test is less strict than for conventional loans and it lets you include closing costs in the amount you borrow.

Most of your down payment will likely come from traditional savings, but you should also consider other sources of funds.

Retirement Accounts

If you have an IRA, you may be able to make a penalty-free withdrawal if you are a first-time homebuyer. Typically, withdrawals before age 59 1/2 are subject to a 10 percent withdrawal penalty. The requirements for a penalty-free withdrawal are in IRS Publication 590, "Individual Retirement Accounts."

Basically, you can withdraw up to a lifetime maximum of $10,000. Surprisingly, you do not even have to be the buyer to qualify for a penalty-free withdrawal. The first-time buyer can be the IRA owner, his or her spouse, children, or grandchildren. Thus, parents may help their children with a penalty-free withdrawal.

Low-Income Programs and Grants

Some cities and states provide grants to low-income first time buyers. In addition, reputable private institutions have special programs to help those in public interest occupations. The Neighborhood Champions program by Bank of America is designed to help teachers, police officers, firefighters, medical workers, and workers in related professions overcome the high cost of home ownership.

Bridal Account Registry

Couples with a future wedding can set up a bridal account registry at a local bank. You aren't committed to using the fund for a home mortgage, but it makes your priorities known to potential gift givers.

---

into a high rate when market rates are falling. On most fixed rate loans, you can pay off the remaining balance on the loan at any time without penalty. If there is a prepayment penalty, it should be stated in the mortgage contract.

Amortize To satisfy an obligation by periodic payments of interest and principal.

When you repay a loan by periodic payments, you are said to **amortize** your debt. Table 8.2 contains an amortization schedule for a fixed rate loan. During the first years of the loan, most of the mortgage payment will go toward paying interest on the principal. As the amount owed declines, a larger percentage of each mortgage payment will go toward paying off the principal. Near the end of the loan period, almost the entire mortgage payment will serve to reduce the outstanding principal.

Adjustable Rate Mortgages

Adjustable rate loans Home mortgages on which the interest rate is periodically adjusted over the term of the loan.

The distinguishing feature of **adjustable rate loans** is that the interest rate on the loan is not fixed over the entire life of the loan. This feature is about the only common characteristic of adjustable rate loans; there are almost as many types of them as there are homes. To add to the confusion, they come under various names—such as variable and flexible rate loans. Given the multitude of possibilities, only the common formats are discussed in this text.

Adjustable rate mortgages carry an initial interest rate below the rate offered on a standard fixed rate mortgage. The difference between the initial rate on fixed and variable loans can vary widely as credit market conditions change. As Figure 8.2 indicates, the differential has fluctuated between 1/2 and 2 percentage points in recent years.

The Federal Trade Commission suggests you examine all of the following when shopping for an adjustable rate mortgage:

- The initial interest rate
- How often the rate may change
- How much the rate may change
- The initial monthly payments
- How often payments may change
- How much payments may change
- The mortgage term
- How often the term may change
- The index to which rate, payment, or term changes are tied
- The limits, if any, on negative amortization

Interest Rate Adjustment Period and the Adjustment Index

The interest rate on the remaining loan balance may be changed after a specified period. The period between one rate change and the next is known as the **interest rate adjustment period**. The majority of adjustable rate loans have an adjustment period of one year. The change in the rate is tied to the change in an **interest rate adjustment index** that tends to mirror the general movement in interest rates throughout the economy.

Several different interest rate adjustment indexes are commonly included in mortgage contracts. You can check out the history and volatility of the most used indexes at HSH Associates (**www.hsh.com**). Financial analysts tend to favor the use of the National Average FHLB Mortgage Contract Rate as an interest rate index, because it seems to be less volatile than the other indexes.

To determine the contract interest rate on the outstanding mortgage balance, lenders add a few percentage points, called the **margin**, to the index rate.

Interest rate + margin = contract interest rate

For example, suppose an index rate such as the National Average FHLB Mortgage Contract Rate was 7.5 percent at the time of adjustment and the margin was 2 percentage points. The contract rate applied to the outstanding loan balance would be 9.5 percent. The margin may differ from one lender to the other, but it is usually constant over the life of the loan.

At periodic dates specified in the mortgage contract, the contract rate will be recalculated to reflect changes in the indexed rate. Using the current example, assume the index rate fell from 7.5 percent to 7.25 percent at the next rate adjustment. With a 2 percent margin, the contract rate will decline from 9.5 percent to 9.25 percent. Lenders have been known to determine the interest rate readjustment incorrectly; therefore, you should locate information on the index and check the lender's calculation.

A few lenders offer **teaser rates**, which are a promotional gimmick. Over some initial period a reduced margin is used to calculate the adjustable rate. When this period ends, a higher margin is used to compute the rate over the remaining term of the loan. This produces an upward adjustment in the flexible rate independent of any change in the interest rate adjustment index.

Rate Cap

Some loans may have rate caps that limit the movement in your interest rate. These typically limit rate increases but may also limit decreases. A **periodic rate cap** limits changes

---

TOPIC LINKS

FRB Mortgage Shopping Worksheet

Interest rate adjustment period The time between potential adjustments in the interest rate applied to the outstanding loan balance.

Interest rate adjustment index The index to which changes in the mortgage interest rate are related.

TOPIC LINKS

Examine data on interest rate indexes.

TOPIC LINKS

ARM Check Kit from HSH Associates

Margin The amount added to the index rate in order to calculate the interest rate on the mortgage contract.

Teaser rate An abnormally low initial interest rate meant to attract borrowers.

Periodic rate cap Limits the movement on changes in the interest rate during any one interest rate adjustment period.

during any one adjustment period. Suppose you had a $1\frac{1}{2}$ percent periodic cap, and the underlying index rate rose by 2 percent. The adjustable rate applied to the outstanding loan balance would be limited to a $1\frac{1}{2}$ percent increase during this adjustment period. However, the unused $\frac{1}{2}$ percent may be applied during the next adjustment period.

Aggregate rate cap Limits the total change in the interest rate over the entire term of the loan.

An **aggregate rate cap** limits changes over the entire life of the loan. If you have a 5 percent aggregate cap on your mortgage rate, then no matter how high the financial index increases, a mortgage with an initial rate of 7 percent could never go above 12 percent. By federal law, all adjustable rate mortgages must have a lifetime ceiling on the contract rate. There is no federal limit on how high the cap may be, although most states set limits.

Payment Cap

Payment cap Limits changes in the monthly mortgage payment.

A **payment cap** limits changes in your monthly loan payments. Under a payment cap, it's possible for the interest rate on your adjustable rate loan to increase while your monthly payments either remain unchanged or do not increase as much as required by the interest rate adjustment.

Don't assume you will not have to pay the higher interest. Suppose you take out a 30-year, $88,000 mortgage at an initial interest rate of 8 percent and an annual adjustment period. At the 6 percent rate your initial monthly payments are $527.60. If, at the end of the first year, the interest rate rises to 8 percent, the monthly payments would ordinarily increase to $645.71. However, if the yearly adjustment under the payment cap is less than $118.11 ($645.71 − $527.60), then the monthly payments will not increase to the level required to discharge the loan completely in the remaining 29 years. The difference between your monthly payment under the cap and the required payment may be made up in one of several ways. The term of the loan can be lengthened beyond the initial 30-year agreement. Alternatively, the term might remain unchanged, but the lending institution might require an additional lump-sum payment at the time the mortgage is to be paid. Still another method is for future monthly payments to be increased. The lending institution should specify in the mortgage contract the method it plans to use.

Negative amortization The resulting increase in the amount owed when the monthly payment is less than the interest due on the previous balance.

In the current example, the amount outstanding on the mortgage at the end of the first year will be $86,919.35. At an annual percentage rate of 8 percent, interest payments alone amount to $579.46 per month. If the payment cap keeps the monthly payment from rising up to $579.46, **negative amortization** will result. This term simply means that instead of your debt getting smaller over time, it will get larger. You will owe the lending institution more at the end of the year than you did at the beginning. Obviously, this situation can create problems for both you and the lending institution. For this reason, only a small percentage of mortgage contracts permit negative amortization. In all other cases, the payment cap cannot hold monthly payments to less than the interest owed on the outstanding loan balance.

Convertible Features

Convertible mortgage An adjustable mortgage contract that permits the borrower to convert to a fixed rate contract at some point during the term of the loan.

Some lenders offer **convertible mortgages**. These are adjustable rate mortgages that can be converted into fixed rate mortgages during a specified time period, usually between the 13th and 60th months of the loan. The fixed rate will be determined by rules set down in the mortgage contract. If you elect to make the conversion, the lender will charge a fee that, most likely, will be equal to either a stated dollar amount or a percentage of the outstanding loan balance.

The rate on the fixed rate loan may depend on the value of the interest adjustment index at the date of the conversion. If you believe that interest rates will decline, then a convertible mortgage would allow you to get the benefits of an adjustable rate loan today and the expected benefit of a lower rate on a fixed rate loan at a future date.

You should be careful not to place too much value on the conversion feature. Adjustable rate loans rarely carry penalties for paying off a loan before it is due. Therefore, even with an ordinary adjustable rate loan, you always have the choice of paying it off and refinancing with a fixed rate loan. If you refinance, however, you will be charged closing costs and points on the new loan. The real value of the conversion feature is, consequently, the difference between the conversion fee and traditional refinancing charges.

2/28 and Option Adjustable Rate Mortgages

2/28 mortgages have contributed to the current crisis in the subprime mortgage market. Consequently, lenders may be reluctant to provide these loans to new borrowers. During the first two years of the loan the contract rate is kept artificially low. After that the interest rate adjusts based on a margin that raises the adjustable rate above that on a typical ARM loan. The lender expects to receive higher payments during the adjustment period that more than offset the lower payments during the fixed rate period.

Previously, prospective home owners were allowed to qualify based on this low initial rate. Many, who just barely qualified at the initial rate, could not make payments when the adjustable rate kicked in and therefore defaulted on their home mortgages. New rules require that borrowers qualify based on the adjustable rate and not the initial fixed rate.

Option ARMs also have a low initial fixed rate during the first few months of the loan. This determines your minimum monthly payment. The interest rate then adjusts during subsequent periods. If your monthly payment on the fully amortized loan given the adjustable rate or an interest only monthly payment is greater than your minimum monthly payment, you have the choice of continuing the minimum monthly payment for some initial term. Payments at less than the interest only option result in negative amortization. Home owners who continue minimum monthly payments are likely to be shocked by the subsequent rise in required monthly payments after the allowable term for minimum monthly payments ends.

Business Week has called these "nightmare mortgages." Both 2/28 and Option ARM contain time bombs that can cause financial disaster without proper financial planning. On the other hand, when used by knowledgeable borrowers who realize the responsibilities they are taking on and who plan for future increases in monthly payments, they can enable home owners to qualify for homes today that will meet their future needs.

Specialized Mortgage Formats and Creative Financing

Most borrowers will end up with either a basic fixed rate or adjustable rate mortgage. During times of tight credit and high interest rates, however, both lenders and borrowers have demonstrated an increasing willingness to experiment with new financial instruments. Two of the less common formats that can be found in the market are graduated payment mortgages and shared appreciation mortgages.

With a **graduated payment mortgage (GPM)**, monthly payments rise gradually (usually over 5 to 10 years) and then remain level for the remainder of the loan. The lower initial monthly payments allow individuals to borrow larger amounts than they ordinarily would. The government offers FHA insurance on GPMs to aid young low-income families who expect their income to rise in the future. Unfortunately, the low monthly payments in the early years can result in negative amortization. This can create a financial problem if you have to relocate in the first few years after your home purchase. In addition, a graduated payment mortgage will have a slightly higher interest rate than a comparable-level payment loan, generating greater interest payments over the life of the loan.

Graduated payment mortgage (GPM) A mortgage with scheduled increases in monthly payments over the term of the loan.

TOPIC LINKS

GPM calculator from HUD

Shared appreciation mortgage (SAM) In return for lower monthly payments the lender shares in the home's appreciated market value.

With a **shared appreciation mortgage (SAM)**, you get a below-market contract rate on a loan that lets you qualify for a larger mortgage on a larger home than you would with a traditional mortgage. However, the bank becomes your partner on any future appreciation in the market value. Typically, the lender receives between 30 to 60 percent of the home's appreciation. If the home goes down in value, the bank gets none of the equity. Increases in the home's value due to significant improvements are not shared, nor are the selling costs incurred by the home owner. If you have not sold the home by the end of the mortgage, you still have to come up with the money to pay for the lender's share in the home's appreciation. With the recent weakness in the housing market, shared appreciation loans may be no longer available.

Reading the Fine Print

In addition to understanding the economic characteristics of the loan, you must also understand the legal ramifications. This means reading the fine print, understanding the late payment penalty and carefully examining each clause.

Acceleration clause The loan repayment is accelerated if you miss a payment.

The **acceleration clause** will allow the lender to speed up the rate at which the loan comes due if you miss a payment. Be sure you understand how and when this clause becomes operative. Also be wary of an acceleration clause that permits the lender to foreclose on the loan "without notice."

Due-on-sale clause The outstanding balance on the loan must be repaid when you sell the home.

A **due-on-sale clause** requires immediate repayment of the loan when the property changes hands. Such clauses are common and have been enforced by the courts. If you do not have a due-on-sale clause, then you may have an **assumable mortgage**. This mortgage may be transferred to the buyer at the time of sale. However, a credit review of the buyer and a fee may be required by the lender. In a tight credit market, an assumable mortgage at a relatively low contract rate can attract buyers.

Assumable mortgage The buyer replaces the seller as the borrower on the existing mortgage contract.

The prepayment clause indicates how early payment on the loan will be handled. The loan contract could impose a **prepayment penalty** if you repay the loan early for reasons other than the sale of the home. This clause is generally not permitted on adjustable rate loans.

Prepayment penalty A penalty incurred by the borrower if the mortgage balance is prepaid for any reason other than the sale of the home.

On some loans, the lending institution adds to the monthly mortgage payment an amount to cover home insurance or property taxes. The lender accumulates these funds in what is called an **escrow account**. When the insurance or property taxes become due, the lender will pay these bills out of the funds in the escrow account. By doing so, the lender ensures that these obligations are being met.

Escrow account An account held by the lender into which the borrower deposits funds in order to ensure that the home owner's expenses will be paid.

An escrow account is required when the mortgage is insured by the Federal Housing Administration or the Veterans Administration or when the loan is for 90 percent or more of the value of the house. In all other situations, the need for an escrow account is negotiable between the borrower and lender.

If possible, you should avoid setting up an escrow account. In most places the lending institution will pay no interest on the funds held. In the 14 states where lenders are required by law to pay interest on escrow accounts, the rate paid is typically less than the rate on a passbook savings account. You can do better by holding these funds in your ordinary savings account and paying your taxes and insurance directly. If you have an escrow account, you should contact the lending institution to see if it can be closed.

Beware Predatory Lending

The growth in predatory lending has come to the attention of state and federal authorities over the last few years. Predatory lenders target the old and the poor. Through fraud and deception, predatory lenders entice home owners into highly unfavorable second mortgages. This is often done in conjunction with the sale of home repairs that are either never or shoddily performed.

Subprime loans are not necessarily predatory loans. However, predatory lenders take advantage of borrowers in this market by overextending high interest rate loans to low-income borrowers with poor credit histories and low credit scores.. Predatory lenders hide from consumers the facts they need to make an informed decision. According to the Federal Trade Commission, predatory practices have included the following:

- Loan flipping The borrower's loans are repeatedly refinanced over a short period of time with no gain to the borrower
- Equity stripping The loan is designed to fail because it is based on the equity in the property and not the borrower's ability to pay
- Packing Adding credit insurance or other "extras" to increase the lender's profit on a loan

Don't be pressured or harassed into taking out a home loan. If you feel that you or a relative has been a victim of any of these predatory lending practices, contact your state Attorney General's office or the Federal Trade Commission.

Insured Mortgages

The term *conventional financing* is used for mortgages that are neither government insured nor government guaranteed. Conventional mortgages may have **private mortgage insurance** on high-risk loans to protect the lender in the event you default on the loan. If you take out a conventional home mortgage with less than a 20 percent down payment, private mortgage insurance is a required addition to your monthly mortgage payment. The insurance protects the lender from losses resulting from a defaulting borrower. Thus, private market insurance enables lenders to extend loans to individuals who do not have the necessary funds for the typical down payment.

> **Private mortgage insurance** Protects the lender when borrowers default on the mortgage.

> **TOPIC LINKS**
> MICA Insurance Cancellation Calculator

The cost of this protection is not cheap. The fee varies depending on the down payment and the size of the mortgage but typically ranges from $240 to $1,200 annually. Understandably, borrowers prefer to see these premiums end as soon as possible.

Typically, there is no need for private mortgage insurance when your equity in the home reaches 20 percent. However, many home owners do not know that they may request cancellation of the insurance when home equity reaches this level. In addition, lenders have been slow to honor such requests.

Given the high cost of private mortgage insurance, you would be better off to avoid it. You might consider putting off a purchase until you have the 20 percent down payment or even consider a temporary personal loan at a higher interest rate in order to fund a 20 percent down payment.

Mortgage insurance may also be arranged through either the Federal Housing Administration (FHA) or the Veterans Administration (VA). These programs make non-conventional mortgages available to individuals who might otherwise be considered poor credit risks.

Federal Housing Administration (FHA)

FHA mortgages are not government loans. **FHA mortgage insurance** protects the lender against loss on the mortgage, thereby permitting the lender to offer more liberal credit terms to families who could not otherwise afford a home.

The FHA insures mortgages when both property and borrower meet certain standards. Information on current requirements can be found by contacting the FHA or lenders that

> **FHA mortgage insurance** Federally backed insurance protecting lenders against nonrepayment of mortgage.

TOPIC LINKS

Check current FHA insurance limits.

TOPIC LINKS

Get the latest limits on VA loan guarantees.

TOPIC LINKS

Payback Worksheet

TOPIC LINKS

Download a calculator for biweekly mortgages.

provide FHA-insured loans. If you are eligible, you may borrow up to a government-set maximum with a relatively low down payment of no more than 5 percent of the purchase price.

Veterans Administration (VA)

All veterans and current members of the Armed Services are entitled to loan guarantees through the Veterans Administration. The stated purpose of the program is to help veterans finance the purchase of reasonably priced homes at favorable rates of interest. With a VA loan you do not need a down payment and there is a high maximum debt repayment-to-income ratio of 41 percent. The guarantee encourages lenders to make bigger loans with a smaller down payment than they otherwise could, because the government guarantees repayment of up to 50 percent of the loan and a legislatively set dollar maximum.

Refinancing

If you took out a mortgage at a high interest rate, and rates have since come down, you should consider the possibility of refinancing the loan. Your first step is to contact your current lender concerning refinancing. If you have been a good customer, the lender may be willing to reduce some of the up-front closing costs associated with refinancing. Your up-front expenses will consist of a possible prepayment penalty on the old loan and points and origination costs on the new loan. Your future savings will consist of lower monthly mortgage payments. To determine whether you should refinance, you must estimate your payback period, that is, the length of time required for your future savings to cover your up-front expenses. With the average family moving once every seven years, you most likely should not refinance if the payback period is longer than seven years.

Because loans may be written in so many ways, the proposed new loan is likely to differ by more than just the interest rate. You must also weigh these additional factors into your decision to refinance. For example, you may be considering giving up a high fixed rate mortgage for a currently low adjustable rate mortgage. This exchange may be profitable if rates stay low. Whether such an exchange is attractive to you depends on how much risk you are willing to accept.

Figure 8.11 contains a worksheet for calculating the approximate payback period. To calculate your monthly savings at the lower interest rate, the new monthly payment should be based on the outstanding loan balance and the remaining term on the old loan. Given a refinancing cost of $1,987 and savings on monthly mortgage payments of $97.92, the reduction in mortgage payments would pay for the cost of refinancing in about 21 months. This is only an approximate payback period, because it does not consider the differential tax treatment for mortgage interest and closing costs or the different rates at which low- and high-interest mortgages pay back principal.

You should recognize that the tax treatment of points differs for refinancing. On the initial home mortgage, the IRS has decided you can deduct all points representing prepaid interest in the year the loan is taken out. For refinancing, however, the deduction must be spread out over the term of the mortgage. In the current example, you would have an annual itemized deduction of $39.35 = $787/20 years. Of course, if you sell the home before the mortgage is fully paid, any remaining nonitemized points may be deducted in the year of the sale.

Refinancing can be used to get at the equity in your home. With "cash out" refinancing you refinance you original mortgage for more than you owe. The cost of refinancing must be compared with the cost of a home equity loan. It is likely the home equity loan would be at a higher interest rate; however, mortgage refinancing entails closing costs which generally don't accompany a home equity loan.

Figure 8.11
Refinancing: Calculating the Approximate Payback Period

Current Loan

Amount borrowed	$ 88,000
Outstanding balance	$ 78,698
Original term (months)	360
Remaining term (months)	240
Annual contract rate	9.00%
Present monthly payment	$708.07

New Loan

Initial balance	$ 78,698
Term (months)	240
Annual contract rate	7.00%
New monthly payment	610.15
Monthly savings	$ 97.92

Initial Cost of Refinancing

Origination fee	$ 100.00
Closing costs	1,100.00
Points (1%)	786.98
Total initial costs	$1,986.98
Divided by monthly savings	÷ 97.92
Approximate payback period (months)	20.29

What If You Can't Meet Your Mortgage Payments?

Unexpected things happen. You can lose your job, or your business can experience troubled times. Whenever the possibility exists that you may be unable to meet your future mortgage payments, the first step is to contact the lending institution. If you do not meet your scheduled payments, the lender probably has the right to demand immediate payment on the remaining loan balance. Failure to meet this demand may result in **foreclosure**. This legal process terminates your rights to the property and forces its sale. You receive any excess of the sale price over the amount needed to discharge the loan. Of course, because of the immediacy surrounding the sale, the price may be relatively low, leaving you with little or nothing in return. This process also involves costs and risks for the lending institution; therefore, you may both benefit by avoiding foreclosure. This is why you should contact the lending institution before you actually miss payments. It's possible that through a renegotiation of the loan, the monthly payments can be reduced. This can be accomplished by stretching out the term of the loan, postponing repayment of principal, or even negative amortization.

Foreclosure A legal process that terminates your rights to a mortgaged property and forces its sale.

The S&P/Case-Shiller Index showed that housing prices in 10 major metropolitan areas fell 8.9 percent in the fourth quarter of 2007 from the previous year. Furthermore, 2.2 percent of all prime mortgages were more than 60 days past due, the highest rate since 1998. Selling a home in a declining housing market like this can be a serious problem for borrowers with low down payments. The potential sales price may be less than the outstanding mortgage balance. In this case, the lender may be willing to enter into a *compromise* or *short sale,* in which the lender agrees to receive less than the full value of the mortgage. This permits the mortgager to sell the house for less than the original loan amount.

saving money 8.3

Biweekly Mortgages

Most mortgages require that you repay the loan in monthly installments. You may have the choice, however, of obtaining a biweekly mortgage, on which you make a repayment once every two weeks. If you decide on a biweekly mortgage, you will end up making 26 biweekly payments during the year. When the biweekly payment is set equal to one-half the monthly payment, the total annual value of the biweekly payments will equal 13 monthly payments instead of the traditional 12.

With the extra monthly payment you will reduce the term of the mortgage and eliminate a good chunk of your future interest payments. The accompanying table shows that the higher the interest rate on the loan, the more interest you save and, therefore, the earlier you pay off the loan. On a 30-year, $100,000 mortgage with an annual contract rate of 7 percent, a biweekly loan with a periodic payment of one-half the monthly mortgage payment would pay off after about 24 years; at a 9 percent rate it would pay off after about 22 years. The corresponding interest savings range from $46,299 to $60,417. At first glance, a biweekly mortgage looks like an excellent idea.

Are these savings really a net benefit? Your interest expense is less because you are paying off the mortgage at a faster rate. By using these dollars to pay off your mortgage at an earlier date, you give up the option of either investing these funds elsewhere or using them to reduce higher-cost debt. The optimal strategy will depend on which alternative provides the greatest after-tax savings or return. You are only really better off by the difference between mortgage interest not paid and what these funds could have earned in an alternative investment. If your returns are higher elsewhere, the correct strategy is to extend your mortgage payments.

Surprisingly, you don't need a biweekly mortgage to pay off your loan balance at a faster rate. Most traditional mortgage contracts allow you to make partial prepayments of principal at your discretion, thus providing you with greater flexibility than a similar biweekly loan. You probably already have the choice of making or not making a thirteenth monthly payment.

Annual Contract Rate (%)	Monthly Payment*	Biweekly Payment	Total Number of Payments	Term of Biweekly Mortgage (years)	Total Interest on Monthly Mortgage	Total Interest on Biweekly Mortgage	Interest Saved?
9.00	$804.62	$402.31	569.83	21.92	$189,664	$129,247	$60,417
8.00	733.76	366.88	593.81	22.84	164,155	117,857	46,299
7.00	665.30	332.65	616.40	23.71	139,509	105,046	34,463

*Monthly payments on a 30-year $100,000 mortgage.

When your lending institution appears uncompromising, you may still be entitled to some special help if you have a federally insured FHA or VA loan. If a potential foreclosure seems likely, you should consult an attorney. Under the bankruptcy code you may be able to force the lending institution to accept a proposed repayment plan or at least delay the forced sale until you can sell the property at a favorable price.

key terms

acceleration clause (p. 230)
adjustable rate loans (p. 226)
aggregate rate cap (p. 228)
amortize (p. 226)
assumable mortgage (p. 230)
closing (p. 221)
closing costs (p. 221)
condominium (p. 211)

contract rate (p. 222)
convertible mortgage (p. 228)
cooperative (p. 212)
deed (p. 221)
due-on-sale clause (p. 230)
earnest money (p. 220)
escrow account (p. 230)
exclusive agency agreement (p. 219)

exclusive right to sell (p. 219)
FHA mortgage insurance (p. 231)
fixed rate mortgages (p. 224)
foreclosure (p. 233)
graduated payment mortgage (GPM)
   (p. 229)
Housing Affordability Index (p. 205)
interest rate adjustment index (p. 227)
interest rate adjustment period (p. 227)
listing agreement (p. 219)
margin (p. 227)
marketable title (p. 221)
negative amortization (p. 228)
net listing agreement (p. 219)

open listing agreement (p. 219)
payment cap (p. 228)
periodic rate cap (p. 227)
points (p. 222)
prepayment penalty (p. 230)
principal (p. 224)
private mortgage insurance (p. 231)
settlement costs (p. 221)
shared appreciation mortgage (SAM)
   (p. 230)
teaser rate (p. 227)
title insurance (p. 221)
title search (p. 221)

follow–up on the
Steele family

Reread the chapter-opening vignette.

1. The Steeles are considering substituting a fixed rate loan for the adjustable rate loan they presently have. What factors should the Steeles consider before exchanging one type of loan for another?

2. How long must the Steeles remain in their present home if they are to break-even on the refinancing?

3. Help the Steeles in their decision making by drawing up a list of the potential benefits and the potential costs of mortgage refinancing.

problems
and review
questions

1. What is the relationship between market rates of interest and affordable housing?

2. If your income after taxes is $28,000 per year, and you expect to pay about $100 per month for utilities, about how much can you afford to spend on monthly rental payments?

3. Given an affordable monthly mortgage payment of $650, and a mortgage interest rate of 9 percent on a 30-year loan, what is the size of the affordable mortgage? Given this affordable mortgage, and a 10 percent down payment, what is the affordable purchase price?

4. How does a cooperative differ from a condominium? Can you think of any factors that might make you prefer one form of ownership over the other.

5. Suppose you had $6,000 in mortgage interest payments during the year and you were in the 28 percent marginal tax bracket. What is the real cost of the mortgage interest payments after tax considerations? Suppose you had $6,000 in rental payments during the year and you were in the 33 percent marginal tax bracket. What is the real cost of the rental payments after tax considerations?

6. Suppose housing prices rise at a 5 percent annual rate over the next five years. If a house now costs $100,000, how much will it bring after five years and the payment of a 6 percent sales commission?

7. What are the tax advantages attached to home ownership, and under what conditions will long-term capital gains on the sale of a residence be tax free?

8. What occurs at *closing?* Give three items that would be included in closing costs.

9. A lender is offering an 11 percent fixed rate mortgage, requiring a down payment equal to 20 percent of the home's purchase price. The lender estimates that closing costs should be equal to $500 plus four points. How much will closing costs be on a $120,000 home?

10. What are the relative advantages of fixed and adjustable rate loans?

11. What are some important characteristics of adjustable rate loans that you should examine carefully?

12. An adjustable rate mortgage has a yearly interest rate adjustment cap of 1 percent. If the indexed rate moves up by 1½ percent in the first year, and ½ percent in the second year, how much can the interest rate on the remaining loan balance move up after the first year, and after the second year?

13. Suppose you expect your income to increase significantly over the next few years. You would like to purchase a home that more closely fits your future income status rather than your present circumstances, thereby avoiding relocation expenses in a few years. What types of mortgages might be of interest to you?

14. You are thinking of retiring in about 15 years. You would like to purchase a home now but would like to have it paid off before retirement. You plan to live on reduced income during retirement, so the tax deductions on mortgage interest would not be significant at that time. What types of mortgages might be of interest to you?

15. What does the term *conventional financing* mean? What government programs exist for nonconventional financing?

16. Whom does private mortgage insurance protect, and why is it sometimes required?

17. Name two government organizations that can help you obtain a home mortgage with a relatively small down payment.

18. Why does the lender obtain title insurance?

19. What is the distinguishing feature of a convertible home mortgage?

20. What is foreclosure, and how might you avoid an impending foreclosure?

21. What is the subprime market? Why are loans in the subprime risky?

case 8.1

How Much House Can Kim and Dan Bergholt Afford?

Kim and Dan Bergholt are government workers. They are considering purchasing a home in the Washington, D.C., area for about $280,000. They estimate monthly expenses for utilities at $220, maintenance at $100, property taxes at $380, and home insurance payments at $50. Their only debt consists of car loans requiring a monthly payment of $350.

Kim's gross income is $55,000 per year and Dan's is $38,000 per year. They have saved about $60,000 in a money market fund on which they earned $5,840 last year. They plan to use most of this for a 20 percent down payment and closing costs. A lender is offering 30-year variable rate loans with an initial interest rate of 8 percent given a 20 percent down payment and closing costs equal to $1,000 plus three points.

Before making a purchase offer and applying for this loan, they would like to have some idea whether they might qualify.

Questions

1. Estimate the affordable mortgage and the affordable purchase price for the Bergholts.

2. Suppose they do qualify. What other factors might they consider before purchasing and taking out a home mortgage?

3. What future changes might present problems for the Bergholts?

The real estate agent tells the Bergholts that if they don't care to purchase, they might consider renting. The rental option would cost $1,400 per month plus utilities estimated at $220 and renter's insurance of $25 per month.

The Bergholts believe that neither of them is likely to be transferred to another location within the next five years. After that, Dan perceives that he might move out of government service into the private sector. Assuming they remain in the same place for the next five years, the Bergholts would like to know if it is better to buy or rent the home. They expect that the price of housing and rents will rise at an annual rate of 3 percent over the next five years. They expect to earn an annual rate of 5 percent on the money market fund. All other prices, including utilities, maintenance, and taxes are expected to increase at a 3 percent annual rate. After federal, state, and local taxes, they get to keep only 55 percent of a marginal dollar of earnings.

Questions

1. Given the information in this and Case 8.1, estimate whether it is financially more attractive for the Bergholts to rent or to purchase the home over a five-year holding period. (Assuming the contract interest rate of 8 percent, monthly interest payments over the five-year period would total $87,574.)

2. Suppose it turns out that they have to relocate after one year. Which is the preferred alternative after one year? (Interest payments over the first year would equal $17,852.)

Exercises to Strengthen Your Use of the Internet

(Internet links for the following exercises can be found at **www.prenhall.com/frasca**.)

Exercise 8.1 How Much House Can You Afford?

BankRate.Com (**www.bankrate.com**) has several calculators to help you with your housing decision. You can find a housing affordability calculator at this site or at **CNNMoney.Com** under the "Real Estate" link.

Q. Enter sample data and vary the interest rate from 6 to 9 percent. How does the affordable home price change as the interest rate changes?

Exercise 8.2 Rent or Buy?

Ginnie Mae (**www.ginniemae.gov**) bundles federally insured home mortgages for sale in financial markets. You will find a link to a "Buy v. Rent" calculator on their home page.

Q. Use the sample data to determine about how many years would you have to live at the same location for you to be financially indifferent to buying versus selling?

Exercise 8.3 Evaluating the Neighborhood

The market value of a home depends on more than just the number of rooms. To a large extent, the price of a home depends on the community in which it's located. Coldwell Banker (**www.coldwellbanker.com**) has a nationwide chain of real estate firms. In addition to providing online listings of homes, it also provides summary data on neighborhoods to help you evaluate the community.

Another convenient site for finding socioeconomic information on a neighborhood is the American Factfinder (**factfinder.census.gov**) provided by the U.S. Census Bureau.

Q. Using either of these online sites, compare the socioeconomic data on your own neighborhood with that from zip code 90210, the famous Beverly Hills community.

Exercise 8.4 Generate an Amortization Table

The mortgage calculator from Bloomberg.com (**www.bloomberg.com/invest/calculators**) generates an amortization table indicating the remaining balance on your loan after each mortgage payment. It also indicates how much you must increase your monthly payment for you to pay off the mortgage earlier. A $100,000, 30-year mortgage at 7.5 percent APR would require monthly payments of $699.21.

Q. How much more would you have to pay per month if you wanted to repay your mortgage in 20 years? How much interest would you save by paying off the mortgage in 20 rather than 30 years? (Go to the full table.)

Exercise 8.5 Comparing Monthly Payments on Fixed and Adjustable Rate Loans

Bankrate.Com (**www.bankrate.com**) publishes the national averages for 30-year fixed and one-year adjustable rate loans. Use these rates to calculate the monthly payment on a $100,000, 30-year mortgage with a mortgage calculator. Enter the average current contract rate on 30-year fixed rate mortgages and one-year adjustable rate mortgages.

Q. How would monthly payments on a $100,000 loan differ for fixed rate and adjustable rate mortgages given current market rates? If adjustable rates remained unchanged, how much would this save you in interest payments?

Exercise 8.6 Interest Savings on a Biweekly Mortgage

HSH Associates (**www.hsh.com**) provides helpful information on the home mortgage markets. Their "Amortization Calculator" can also be used to calculate the payoff on a biweekly mortgage.

Q. Given the 30-year fixed rate mortgage you used in the Exercise 8.5, how much sooner would you pay off this mortgage with biweekly payments? How much would you save in interest payments?

Exercise 8.7 Calculating a Rate Adjustment

HSH Associates (**www.hsh.com**) also provides timely information on ARM indexes.

Q. Which mortgage would have a lower contract rate: one using the weekly rate on the 10-year Treasury security with a two-point margin, or one using the National Mortgage Contract Rate with a one-point margin? The answer is likely to vary with the most recent economic conditions.

Exercise 8.8 Comparing Future Payments Under Fixed Rate and Adjustable Rate Mortgages

The fixed rate versus adjustable rate calculators, such as the one at SmartMoney (**www.smartmoney.com/home**) are great for comparing the worst-case and best-case outcome for an adjustable rate mortgage versus what would occur with a fixed rate mortgage.

Q. Compare a 30-year fixed rate mortgage at 8.75 percent and a 30-year annually adjusted mortgage with an initial rate of 4.75 percent, an annual cap of 2 percent, and a lifetime cap of 6 percent. Assuming you plan to remain in the house for 15 years, which is the better deal?

part 4

Investing for the Future

growing your financial resources

The next four chapters deal with investments. They explain different investment alternatives, discuss investment strategies, and describe important aspects of the investment process. Above all, they continuously alert you to the trade-off between the return you can expect from an investment and the degree of risk you must take to earn it. According to many financial advisors, failure to understand this trade-off is the single most important reason investors lose with their investments—and these losses are often catastrophic in relation to the investors' net worths. To succeed as an investor, you need to understand investment risk and realistic expectations of investment return.

Along with considering investment risk and return, you must also ask whether or not you should invest in the first place. Of course, the answer depends on how broadly we define *investment*. If it includes assets held for liquidity or to accommodate your lifestyle, the answer is you should be investing immediately and constantly. On the other hand, if we follow a narrower definition and include only those assets we hold for the specific purpose of increasing our net worth, then investment should come *only after* we have provided for adequate liquidity and have enough insurance to protect us against unexpected losses.

A key to successful investing is to understand *why* you are investing. Is it to provide for retirement? To educate your children? To buy a new car three years in the future? Or are you simply looking for a way to lower your income taxes? The answers to these questions help to determine the type of investment vehicles you should choose. This notion of linking specific investments to specific savings goals was introduced in Chapter 2 in the discussion of planned savings. Throughout Part 4, we will continue to stress the importance of having clearly defined investment objectives.

9 Financial Markets and Institutions

learning the investment environment

Objectives

1. To identify the basic investment alternatives
2. To understand the nature of securities markets, distinguishing between organized exchanges and the over–the–counter market
3. To recognize important legislation that protects investors
4. To learn how to select a stockbroker and how to choose an investment account
5. To know how to take an investment position and how to place investment orders
6. To recognize and use various sources of investment information

Steele family

Arnold and Sharon Steele have become deeply concerned about their ability to accumulate sufficient funds for Nancy and John's education and for their eventual retirement. They realize that successful investing will play an important role in achieving their goals but, unfortunately, they do not have a strong background in investment fundamentals and techniques.

Presently, the Steeles' investment portfolio consists of 400 shares of InChemCo common stock, which Arnold has acquired through the company's stockpurchase incentive plan (InChemCo is Arnold's employer) and 200 shares of Fidelity Fund (a mutual fund). The Steeles had almost doubled their money in InChemCo until the company cut dividends because of poor earnings and they were up over 50 percent in the mutual fund until problems in the subprime market hit the housing industry. Their investments lost most of the previous gains and have shown little recovery since then. Although they still have some profit, the amount is quite small and is probably no more than the Steeles could have earned by putting their money in savings accounts. In fact, Arnold and Sharon are wondering if switching their funds into such accounts might be their best step.

Before making any move, though, the Steeles want to know much more about the investing process. Should they use a stockbroker? If so, what kind—full service or discount? How frequently should they trade? Should they trade on the Internet? Are stocks better investments than bonds? Is a mutual fund a better alternative than owning stocks or bonds directly? What type of mutual fund might best meet their investment objectives? The list of questions is extensive.

TOPIC LINKS

Follow the **Topic Links** in each chapter for your interactive Personal Finance exercise on the Web. Go to: **www.prenhall.com/frasca**.

The Steeles are first-time investors, clearly amateurs in a game that is supposedly dominated by professionals. Perhaps you too are a first-time investor; if so, you might find the investment process bewildering and fearsome. Reading news items in the *Wall Street Journal* or watching *CNBC News* on cable convinces us that finance people speak a foreign language. Worse yet, there seems to be no logic in their stories. For example, a reporter announces, "The government's most recent employment figures hint strongly that a recession is coming." This must be bad news, right? Wrong. She then goes on, "Encouraged by the recent data, the stock and bond markets soared to new highs."

Fear not. The language isn't that hard to learn, and, believe it or not, there really is some sense in most investment news. This chapter will get you started by describing investment alternatives and by explaining important investment markets and institutions. Although you won't be an investment professional four chapters later, you certainly will know enough to make sound investment decisions.

Goals and Investment Alternatives

Our investment goals differ. If you are a young person starting a career, you may want to achieve a goal different from that of people preparing for retirement. You are concerned with building an estate; they are concerned with preserving what they have. You may be willing to sacrifice current income; they might depend on it to meet living expenses. Obviously, an investment that's good for you may be totally inappropriate for them. Before starting an investment program, define your goals as clearly as you can, then indicate specifically how an individual investment is related to those goals. Goal definition is made easier when you understand yourself better: that is, when you are aware of your investment needs. Then you can look at the basic investment alternatives.

TOPIC LINKS

Review investments at Yahoo! Finance.

What Are Your Needs?

Surprisingly, perhaps, earning a return on an investment is not the only need many people try to satisfy from investing. The pleasure associated with many investments derives from your using them (your home) or simply owning them (your antiques). Also, if you are looking for a dollar return, this goal has to be further defined to state whether you want more now or more later; that is, a current versus a future return. And people are quite different in their tax situations and attitudes toward risks.

Tangible and Intangible Investments

The first major classification of investments is based on whether an asset is tangible or intangible. Tangible assets, also called hard assets, are things you can (but don't necessarily) use or enjoy while owning them. Houses, antiques, gold coins or bullion, diamonds and other precious stones, land, and even certain automobiles are examples of **tangible investments**. Some people might object to referring to some of these as investments, since your main reason for buying them is not to earn a return, but that's not an important distinction. Anything that has the potential to increase in value over time is an investment, regardless of its other characteristics. If you can sleep on it, drive it, and enjoy looking at it, all the better. In fact, many Americans have found over the years that their most profitable investments were the tangible ones, particularly their homes. During the 1970s, you would have done much better owning the average home than the average common stock, but in the 1980s and 1990s, the situation was exactly the reverse. Another factor important

Tangible investments Investments that can provide enjoyment in use as well as an investment return.

to some people is the greater personal control they have with tangible investments. If you invest in an apartment complex, for example, you can decide what the rents will be or how much upkeep to provide. If you invest in an apartment complex indirectly, say, through a limited partnership or a corporation, someone else makes those decisions for you. If you like to control things, you have a mental disposition for tangible investments.

Intangible investments
Financial assets that provide claims to tangible assets or the earnings they provide.

   Intangible investments, also called financial or paper assets, are actually claims to tangible assets or the earnings those assets produce. For example, a share of common stock is a claim against the issuing corporation's assets and an entitlement to any dividend or other distributions the corporation might make.

Current Versus Future Return

Some investments offer a return the moment you invest in them—a savings account, for example. Others pay a return less frequently. Most bonds pay interest twice a year, and most stocks that pay dividends usually do so four times a year. Dividends, interest, or any other type of asset income you receive on a regular basis during a year is called a **current return**. Many people prefer owning investments that offer current return, since it supplements their other income. Retirees, for example, often depend on current investment income to meet living expenses.

Current return Dividends, interest, or other types of asset income received on a regular basis.

   Some investments, however, offer no current return whatsoever. Your only return comes about if you can sell the investment to someone else (or have it redeemed by the issuer) at a price greater than what you paid for it. Since this exchange takes place in the future, it is called a **future return** or simply a capital gain. The common stocks of many growth companies have never paid dividends and probably will not for some time in the future. Investors buying these stocks realize that their only return will be from price appreciation over time. These kinds of investments appeal to investors who do not want or need current return but instead are investing to achieve future goals. The Steeles fall into this category.

Future return A return expected in the future resulting from the potential sale of an asset that has appreciated in value.

   Some investments offer both current and future returns. For example, if you buy a share of IBM common stock for, say, $100, you will receive a yearly dividend of $1.70, giving you a 1.70 percent current return on your investment. Obviously, you would be looking for a better return than this in buying IBM, and you would hope to get it through price appreciation. Your target might be 11 percent a year. An investment's **total return** is the sum of its current and future returns, and, in the IBM example, this would be 12.70 percent. Before making an investment, then, you should decide what proportion of total return you want as current return and what proportion as future return.

Total return Sum of current return and future return.

Your Income Tax Situation

Having read Chapter 4, you know the importance of income taxes in overall financial planning. As you move into higher tax brackets, you have a greater incentive to choose investments that avoid or defer taxes. For example, interest on municipal bonds is not subject to federal income tax, but interest on a U.S. Treasury bond is. Suppose for a $1,000 investment you could earn $60 a year in the municipal bond or $80 in the Treasury bond. Which do you prefer? With no taxes to consider, your answer should be out in an instant—the Treasury bond. But suppose you are in a 28 percent tax bracket; now your choice is less clear. The Treasury bond would yield $57.60 after taxes, but the municipal bond would yield $60, clearly making it a better choice.

Risk averters Investors who prefer to avoid risk or at least expect adequate compensation for undertaking risky investments.

Your Attitude Toward Risk

Your attitude toward risk will also shape your investment horizons. Some of us are by nature **risk averters**. We feel extremely uncomfortable in risky situations and prefer to avoid them or at least expect adequate compensation for undertaking them. Going back to the choice between the two bonds above, it could be that an investor in a 28 percent tax bracket would still prefer the Treasury bond to the municipal, not on the basis of after-tax return, but simply because it is a less risky investment. He reasons that an issuing municipality has a far greater chance of defaulting on its interest or redemption obligation than does the U.S. Treasury, and to him, the after-tax greater return is not worth the added risk.

Just as there are risk averters, there are also **risk seekers**—but these aren't foolish people. Risk seekers also expect additional return for undertaking risky investments, although they don't demand as much as risk averters. To them, a marginally better return of 1 percent might be enough to buy the municipal bond. Both risk-seeking and risk-averting approaches can be satisfied in investment markets. In fact, investor differences help make these markets function as smoothly as they do.

TOPIC LINKS

The SEC on risk tolerance

Risk seekers Investors who will undertake risky investments for less compensation than that demanded by risk averters.

Basic Investment Alternatives

There are many different kinds of investments, and Table 9.1 summarizes their return and risk characteristics by five categories. The rankings assigned to each (A++ is the best and F– is the worst) reflect your author's opinions. Your instructor might have different rank-

 # finance news 9.1

Human Frailties: Why Smart People Make Dumb Investments

Is intelligence a guarantee of stock market success? Not hardly! Unfortunately, many investors' cranial capacities are often overshadowed by their emotions, perceptions, and downright bad habits. Following is a discussion of three serious character flaws that many of us share and that can have devastating effects on our portfolios.

We Never Learn

During the previous bull market all we heard was how things are different this time. Why? Because of the revolutionary changes forged by the Internet, fiber optics, and technology in general. Forget a company's earnings; if it's in technology, its stock price can go only one way—up. Gee, that's the same story (e.g., the Internet and fiber optics) we heard back in the early 1970s. The rage at that time was the "nifty fifty," 50 companies guaranteed to hit and stay in the stratosphere. For fun, take a look at where Xerox and Polaroid (two of the darlings) are today. For more recent humor, look at the price chart of almost any Internet or fiber-optic company.

We Have Unrealistic Perceptions

An absolutely amazing statistic is one found in a Consumer Federation of America/Primerica poll (October 1999) that many respondents felt that winning a state lottery (40 percent) was a more probable way of accumulating $500,000 during

their lifetimes than saving and investing (30 percent). How many of those respondents understood the true odds of winning a large lottery (10 million to 1)? Probably none, but even if they did it is unlikely that many would stop buying lottery tickets and start investing. The perception is that you can only get rich through some fortuitous event, such as winning the lottery. This same outlook extends to many investors, who hope to get rich by buying the next Microsoft at $2 a share and selling it (usually within a year) at $200.

We Binge on Excessive Optimism and Pessimism

The stock market is no place for emotional binges, yet that seems to be the order of the day on Wall Street. Few of us are immune from feeling good when the market is booming and becoming depressed when it tanks. However, how we feel should not affect how we invest, yet it often does. In recent years the cable news networks have provided additional drama for investors, who watch "breaking" news stories almost every hour. Unfortunately, too many investors then chase after certain securities that supposedly will thrive or perish by whatever events are reported in the stories.

What are investors to do then? Are we expected to act as machines when it comes to investing, removing all emotions from the process? The honest answer is "yes." Save emotions and feelings for your friends and family members where they are appreciated and do some good. When it comes to investing, be cold and calculating. In future years your friends and family members will be glad that you did.

Table 9.1
Investment Alternatives

| Investment | Dividends, Interest, Rents (Current Return) | Potential Price Appreciation (Future Return)[a] | Rank[b] | |
			Total Return	Total Risk
I Investments held primarily for liquidity: savings accounts, money market deposit accounts and mutual funds, U.S. Series EE and HH bonds, and certificates of deposit	Yes	No	C	A+
II Securities with long or no maturity				
Bonds and notes:				
U.S. Treasury issues	Yes	No	C+	A
Municipal and state government issues	Yes	No	B–	A–
Corporate issues	Yes	No	B	A–
Preferred stock	Yes	No	B–	B+
Common stock	Some	Yes	A–	B–
III Pooling arrangements				
Mutual funds:				
Income funds	Yes	No	B	A
Growth funds	Some	Yes	A	C
Balanced funds	Yes	Yes	B+	B
Investment trusts	Yes	Yes	B+	B
Limited partnerships	Some	Yes	B	C–
IV Contractual claims				
Warrants and rights	No	Yes	A+	D
Put and call options	No	Yes	A+	D
Commodity and financial futures	No	Yes	A++	F–
V Tangible assets				
Real estate:				
Personal residence	No	Yes	A	A
Others	Usually	Yes	B+	D
Gold and other metals	No	Yes	B+	D
Jewelry and collectibles	No	Yes	A–	F

[a]This does not consider price appreciation that is embedded in the investment, such as that sold on a discount basis; for example, U.S. Treasury bills, U.S. Series EE bonds, and zero coupon bonds. Nor does it include cyclical price variation arising from interest rate changes.

[b]Rank is based on a typical investment, but there are many variations within each class. Returns are ranked from low (C) to high (A), and risks are ranked in opposite order—low (A) to high (F).

ings. Reaching a ranking everyone agrees with is impossible; for one thing, it depends on the period of time you use to measure risk or return, and for another, the techniques one uses to measure each can differ. Table 9.1 simply provides a rough idea of these two characteristics. Also, the ranking is for a typical investment within the class, but there are many variations within each class. For example, a typical common stock is riskier than a typical corporate bond, but not every common stock is riskier than every corporate bond. A share of IBM common stock might be far less risky than a bond issued by Fly-by-Night Airlines or a bond backed by subprime home mortgages. A detailed discussion of each of these kinds of investments is presented in the next five chapters, but a brief overview of all is a helpful start.

Investments Held for Liquidity

Chapter 3 explained investments that satisfy your liquidity needs. Remember from that discussion that there are degrees of liquidity, ranging from checking and savings accounts that are almost perfectly liquid to certificates of deposit that have penalties for early withdrawal. Also, while we give these investments a return rank of only a C, bear in mind that they frequently have done far better than some of the other investments with higher ranks, particularly during high-inflation periods.

Securities with Long or No Maturities

By maturity, we mean the length of time you must wait before the issuer agrees to redeem the security. Corporate and government bonds, which represent creditorship claims—that is, the issuer borrows money from you and promises to repay it in the future—have maturities ranging from one to more than 30 years. Common stock and most preferred stock, which represent ownership claims—that is, you are a part owner of the business—have no maturities. The issuing corporations never redeem them, and the only way you can recover your cost is by selling them to someone else. Of course, there is no guarantee you will sell at the same price you paid for them; you might get more, you might get less. In Table 9.1 when we say that there is no appreciation with bonds and preferred stock, we mean that such appreciation is not what investors *expect* from these securities *when they are issued*, since the interest or dividends they pay are fixed and cannot grow. However, their prices do fluctuate with respect to changes in interest rates overall. Therefore, it is possible to have capital gains—or capital losses—with them.

Because of price volatility, bonds, preferred stocks, and common stocks are all considered risky, but common stocks are the riskiest of the three, and all can be very risky during unsettled economic times. None of these are suitable investments if there is a possibility you may need to sell them to raise cash. They are more appropriate for long-term investment.

Pooling Arrangements

A pooling arrangement allows you to achieve greater diversification for your investment dollar than if you attempt to buy individual securities. For example, one share of a mutual fund gives an ownership interest in perhaps as many as 100 different common stocks. Pooling arrangements also provide professional investment management. Not only do you reduce risk through diversification, you might also improve your return.

Contractual Claims

A contractual claim gives you a legal right or obligation to buy or sell something at a given price within a given period of time. Warrants and rights are issued by corporations, and they usually entitle you to buy a certain number of shares of the issuing corporation's common stock. Put and call options are similar to warrants and rights except that they are issued (written) by individuals. A *call* entitles buyers to buy, and a *put* entitles them to sell, shares of a corporation's common stock. People who buy options pay a price for them, since they are actually privileges, not obligations. If you buy an option entitling you to buy, say, 100 shares of General Motors stock at $60 a share, you are not forced to make the purchase; and if GM's stock price fell below $60, you would choose not to. So the most you can lose is what you paid to buy the option.

Commodity and financial futures are like options, but they differ in one important aspect. Rather than being a privilege to buy or sell something, they are an obligation to do so. If you enter into a futures contract on, say, 5,000 bushels of corn at a price of $3 per bushel, you are obligated to comply with that agreement regardless of what happens to the price of corn. Even if it falls to $2 a bushel, you must buy it at $3; thus, your losses with futures contracts are not limited as they are with options. Your potential future return with options and futures is extremely high—but so are your losses, and that is why we rank them highest in risk.

Tangible Assets

Only a few of the many tangible assets are listed in Table 9.1. We have singled out the personal residence from other real estate because it has been such a good investment for so many people. Perhaps our risk assessment is too favorable, especially given recent problems in the subprime mortgage market, but in many cases the prices of homes have not been as volatile as prices of common stocks or even U.S. Treasury bonds. Other real estate, particularly raw land, is another story.

The demand for gold, other metals, and jewelry and collectibles is highly erratic over time. All these kinds of investments are exceptionally risky. With some, such as collectibles, you need specialized knowledge to compete in their markets.

Securities Markets

On a normal day about 2 billion shares of stock are traded on the New York Stock Exchange. Assuming an average price of $40 a share means that about $80 billion worth of securities change hands on just this one exchange and just for common and preferred stocks and warrants. Add to this the combined total values of options, commodity futures, bonds, notes, and all short-term debt securities and you begin to see the magnitude of the securities industry.

Organized Exchanges

Organized exchange A physical place where securities are traded.

Facilitating the exchange process is the **organized exchange**, which is usually understood as a physical place where buyers and sellers—or their representatives—face each other in making transactions. Each exchange has a floor that is arranged to trade specific securities at specific locations. Only members of an exchange are authorized to make trades, and only securities listed on the exchange are traded. This traditional format is currently in transition with some of the major exchanges moving trades off the floor into electronic exchanges. In the future it is likely that all exchanges will occur electronically.

The New York Stock Exchange Euronext

New York Stock Exchange (NYSE) Largest organized exchange in the world.

The **New York Stock Exchange (NYSE)** is the largest organized exchange in the world. In mid-2007, NYSE Group, Inc. combined with Euronext N.V. to form NYSE Euronext. Together, they manage several exchanges in five countries, including the New York Stock Exchange. Most large U.S. corporations, as well as many large foreign companies, have their shares listed on the NYSE. To be listed, a company must meet certain requirements and pay rather stiff annual fees, but many firms are willing to do so since listing is often regarded as a sign of financial strength and prestige. More than 3,000 firms are listed on the NYSE with an aggregate market value of around $25 trillion (as of mid-2007).

Approximately 80 percent of the market value of all shares traded in the United States are traded on the NYSE; clearly, it earns its nickname—"the Big Board."

TOPIC LINKS

New York Stock Exchange

Order Execution on the NYSE

Organized exchanges are fascinating places to visit. What appears to be utter chaos is actually an efficient system for transferring billions of dollars' worth of securities each trading day. Figure 9.1 shows order execution on the NYSE and introduces its members who may be involved in the process. To be a member, you must buy or lease a "seat."

Commission Brokers **Commission brokers** are employed by stockbrokerage firms. Assuming you deal with Merrill Lynch and have placed a market order to buy 100 shares of Xerox, your representative will transmit the order to one of Merrill Lynch's commission brokers on the floor of the exchange. Suppose that, at the same time, someone else places an order to sell 100 shares of Xerox through her broker, Smith Barney. Both commission brokers would then go to the post where Xerox is traded. For an actively traded issue, such as Xerox, there will be a number of brokers and traders bidding to buy or sell shares. All of them will try to get the best possible price, either for their customers or for themselves. In effect, shares are auctioned to the highest bidders. (The NYSE and similar markets are thus called *auction markets*.) Perhaps the Merrill Lynch and Smith Barney brokers settle a trade at $10 a share. The entire transaction may be completed in less than 10 seconds.

Commission Broker An agent on the floor of an organized exchange who buys and sells shares for the brokerage house on commission.

Specialists **Specialists** play a number of critical roles in the trading process. They are expected to maintain an orderly and continuous market in the six or seven stocks assigned to them. To keep wide swings in price from occurring, they must buy or sell for their own accounts. For example, assume that when your commission broker arrives at Xerox's trading post, no other broker or trader is there to trade Xerox. Then it is the specialist's responsibility to trade. Another responsibility for the specialist is to maintain the limit books, which contain all limit orders clients have placed with their brokers. (Limit orders will be explained shortly.) Because of the inside information specialists have, it is possible for them to profit handsomely at the expense of outside investors. The NYSE, however, insists that customers' interests come first and specialists' second. This rule is monitored con-

Specialists Members of organized exchanges responsible for maintaining orderly and continuous markets.

Figure 9.1
A Trade on the New York Stock Exchange (NYSE)

stantly for compliance and enforced rigorously because the integrity of the specialist is critical to maintaining customer confidence in the system.

Floor Brokers and Floor Traders   **Floor brokers and floor traders** are not associated with any particular stockbrokerage firm but serve as independent operators. They assist commission brokers by executing orders on their behalf for a fee. They also serve stockbrokerage firms that do not own seats on the floor. Floor traders operate strictly for themselves, hoping their position on the floor will help them trade stocks profitably.

Floor broker Independent operators on the floor of an organized exchange who buy and sell shares for clients.

Electronic Communications Network

The NYSE, along with most other exchanges, has been moving some trades off the floor to an electronic communications network (ECN). In what it calls the "hybrid system" some trades are conducted hand-to-hand and others are completed electronically. On the electronic exchange the trades are made without specialists, where computer programs automatically match buyers and sellers. This increases the speed of the exchanges and reduces costs on over 80 percent of all trades. Opponents argue that by removing specialist from the process, an important check on disorderly markets is eliminated. The trend, however, is for electronic exchanges to continue eliminating the need for specialists. In the not too distant future, the hustle and bustle of the floor exchange may be gone.

The American Stock Exchange

The **American Stock Exchange (Amex)** is very similar to the NYSE in terms of physical layout and trading details, but it has easier listing requirements. The Amex has introduced its own hybrid system that combines electronic with human trades. Often called the "junior board," the Amex is younger than the NYSE and has less prestige. A good number of its listed securities are from relatively unknown companies nationally, and a fairly large percentage is energy oriented. The Amex has had considerable success with the introduction of exchange traded funds (explained in Chapter 12). These have become very popular.

American Stock Exchange (Amex) Another (smaller) organized exchange in New York City.

TOPIC LINKS

Amex

Regional Stock Exchanges

Along with the two major exchanges, there are regional stock exchanges, such as the National Stock Exchange and the Philadelphia Stock Exchange. Regional exchanges list securities of companies within their geographic areas, but very often these securities also are traded on the NYSE or Amex. In this respect they are duplicates, and it is hard to justify their existence. Consequently, many have merged with the major exchanges.

Organized Options and Futures Exchanges

Options are also traded on organized exchanges, such as the Chicago Board Options Exchange, the American Option Exchange (part of the Amex), the Philadelphia Option Exchange and the New York Stock Exchange. Options are traded in a manner similar to stock trading.

There are over a dozen organized commodity exchanges in the United States and Canada, and others throughout the world. Trading on commodity exchanges differs somewhat from trading on stock exchanges. In the past trades have been negotiated by public outcry and through a complicated series of hand signals. These are now being replaced by handheld computers as electronic trades also grow in the commodities markets.

Over-the-Counter Markets

Trading over the counter sounds like an illegal activity—but it's not. In fact, in terms of the number of different stocks traded, it is the largest securities market, surpassing the NYSE and Amex combined. In contrast to an organized exchange, the **over-the-counter (OTC) market** consists of a network of securities dealers who trade securities through an extensive communication system called **NASDAQ** (National Association of Securities Dealers Automated Quotations System). In addition to common and preferred stocks and warrants, all government and many corporate bonds are traded in the OTC market. Any securities dealer can buy or sell through NASDAQ, and many stockbrokerage houses make their own portfolio rather than acting as an agent of a customer. Most OTC stocks are of relatively small and unknown companies; however, some giant firms such as Microsoft and Intel trade on the NASDAQ.

On the NASDAQ you will see two prices quoted, a bid and an ask price. The ask price is always a little higher than the bid price. The buyer pays the ask price and the seller gets the bid price. The difference is known as the *spread* and it goes mostly to the market specialist to cover the cost of maintaining an orderly market.

Over-the-counter (OTC) market Securities trading via electronic communications.

NASDAQ Name of the electronic communications system used in the OTC market.

TOPIC LINKS

NASDAQ

Regulation of the Securities Industry

The nature of the securities industry has offered disreputable people considerable opportunities to defraud investors. Since 1933, important laws have been passed to protect investors; in addition, the industry has initiated reform through self-policing efforts. You have much greater protection now than in the past, but it would be a mistake to think fraud no longer exists or to believe losses you might suffer are the fault of your broker. It is important to know your rights and your obligations before you invest.

Federal Legislation

Federal laws form the backbone of investor protection. The important federal acts are explained in the following sections.

The Securities Act of 1933

The Securities Act of 1933 calls for full disclosure of new securities to be traded in interstate commerce. Such securities must be registered with the Securities and Exchange Commission (SEC, an independent agency of the Federal government), which approves their sale. To receive approval, the applicant must provide the SEC with economic and financial data relevant to the firm and the new offering. It does so in the form of a **prospectus**. After the SEC has determined that the prospectus represents adequate disclosure of all material information affecting the company's value and after the SEC has approved the registration, the company must provide the prospectus to any potential investor. Misrepresentation or fraud in preparing the prospectus can be the basis for lawsuits by investors and the SEC against the issuing corporation, its directors, stockbrokers handling the issue, and even public accountants who assisted in its preparation.

Prospectus Document describing a new security issue.

Stiff penalties and possible jail sentences have done much to provide investors with reliable and relevant prospectuses. However, SEC approval in no way assures the issues will be successful. Many new firms have prepared impeccably clean prospectuses and then gone into bankruptcy. The message is clear if you are considering investing: Obtain a prospectus; read it thoroughly, particularly the section explaining risk factors; and believe what it says. Some investors seem to think a prospectus is a mere formality; it isn't. It is a helpful document and should be regarded as such.

TOPIC LINKS

Review the SEC's Assistance and Complaints area.

The Securities Exchange Act of 1934

The Securities Exchange Act of 1934 extended regulation to securities that had already been issued. With this provision, it brought under government regulation almost all aspects of the security markets. It required all securities traded on organized exchanges and the exchanges themselves to be registered with the SEC (which it established). It outlawed fraud and misrepresentation by anyone engaged in the sale of securities, including stockbrokers and their representatives. It forbade price manipulation, and it required registered firms to file with the SEC both a detailed annual report (called a **10-K Report**) and quarterly financial statements. It stipulated that annual reports be provided to shareholders, and it also established guidelines for security trading by insiders, the intent being to prevent them from taking advantage of their privileged information.

The Maloney Act of 1938

The Maloney Act of 1938 required trade associations in the securities industry to register with the SEC. Only one—the National Association of Securities Dealers (NASD)—has been formed and registered. The NASD is the self-regulating arm of the securities industry. It establishes and enforces a professional code of ethics and is responsible for testing and licensing dealers.

The Investment Company Act of 1940

The Investment Company Act of 1940 brought regulation to investment companies, which we more frequently call mutual funds. Such companies are required to register with the SEC and provide shareholders with adequate information about the company's activities. A subsequent amendment to the act forbade paying excessive fees to fund advisors.

The Investment Advisors Act of 1940

The Investment Advisors Act of 1940 requires anyone providing advice to investors (for a fee or other compensation) to register with the SEC and indicate the methods employed for analyzing investments. As an investor, keep in mind that registration does not improve the quality of advice offered or in some other manner guarantee its usefulness. Some advisors advertise their registration, perhaps with the intent of impressing potential clients. Do not be impressed—virtually anyone with sufficient funds can pay the fee to register.

The Securities Investor Protection Act of 1970

The Securities Investor Protection Act protects investors from financial losses that might result from the failure of their broker. It created the Securities Investor Protection Corporation (SIPC), which insures an investor's account up to $500,000 for securities held and up to $100,000 in cash holdings. Most brokerage firms are members of the SIPC and contribute to its funding. It has been particularly helpful to discount brokerage firms in their efforts to overcome investor reluctance to deal with out-of-town brokers.

Some investors believe that the SIPC protection extends to any losses on securities they hold while a broker is in financial difficulty. This is not true. SIPC guarantees only that your securities eventually will be delivered to you or to another broker. Losses or gains during the time the failing firm's arrangements are being sorted out are the investor's. For example, SIPC only guarantees delivery of 100 shares of GM, if that is what you held with a failing broker; it does not guarantee a price for those shares. GM might have been worth $80 a share when your broker ceased to operate but be worth only $50 a share when you eventually have access to the shares.

The Sarbanes–Oxley Act of 2002

The Sarbanes-Oxley Act (SOA) is intended to curb a number of abuses that mushroomed during the boom of the late 1990s. The Act mandates a set of reforms to enhance corporate responsibility and financial disclosures, and to combat corporate and accounting fraud. It also created the Public Company Accounting Oversight Board, known as the PCAOB. The full impact of this legislation has yet to be determined, although early signs indicate it is significantly affecting the disclosure of information. On the negative side, some company owners complain that complying with the law is time consuming and potentially expensive, leading them to question the value of being a publicly traded company.

Among the provisions of SOA are those intended to make financial analysts more responsive to investors and less so to the companies that pay their salaries and bonuses, some of which often run into the millions of dollars. The Act requires brokerage firms and/or their analysts to disclose whether they own shares in the companies they are rating, or are involved (or expect to be involved) in investment banking of such companies. In short, if analysts stand to gain from favorable ratings, they must disclose the nature of their relationships. The securities industry has already paid over $1.4 billion to regulators to settle past grievances, and the penalties for future violations are expected to be steep.

State Law and Self–Regulation

State security laws actually predate federal law. Kansas passed the first "blue sky" law in 1911, and all states now have similar legislation. These laws attempt to keep investors from being defrauded by promoters selling securities worth no more than a piece of blue sky. State laws (patterned after the federal laws) apply to *intrastate* securities sales. Although federal laws apply to *interstate* sales, the SEC can be contacted for any expected fraudulent activity in securities trading.

In addition to federal and state regulation, the securities industry has its own internal regulatory process. Most of this is found in the National Association of Securities Dealers' Rules of Fair Practice, Code of Procedure, and Uniform Practice Code. These three documents cover a wide range of trading activities, specifying rules and appropriate conduct guidelines for NASD members.

An extremely important part of self-regulation is the process of **binding arbitration**. If you have a complaint against your broker for not handling a transaction properly, or for pressuring you to invest in securities totally inappropriate for your investment objectives, or for any suspected misconduct, you can appeal to any of the organized exchanges, the NASD, or the American Arbitration Association, for binding arbitration to resolve the problem. Recently, the arbitration programs of the NASD and the NYSE were merged under the control of the Financial Industry Regulatory Authority (FINRA). This new organization will also regulate several other exchanges.

> **Binding arbitration** A method of resolving disputes among stockbrokers and customers.

> **TOPIC LINKS**
> Learn how to file a complaint with FINRA.

Claims less than $10,000 are usually resolved quickly by one arbitrator, but claims above that amount involve more complicated procedures. As its name implies, binding arbitration decisions are final. When considered against the only alternative for seeking a resolution—hiring your own attorney and filing a suit—binding arbitration makes a great deal of sense, since it is much cheaper and faster. NASD reports that the customer win loss ratio was 42 percent in 2006.

Using the Services of a Stockbroker

Most financial investments are bought and sold with the assistance of a securities dealer, usually called a stockbroker, or broker for short. (Mutual fund shares, which are discussed in Chapter 12 are a major exception.) The first step is to select a broker and to choose either a cash or margin account. Then you must know whether to take a long or a short position. Finally, you need to distinguish among various types of orders.

Selecting a Stockbroker

Finding a stockbroker is not difficult. The number of brokers available has grown considerably since the industry was deregulated in 1974. In recent years, even commercial banks and savings and loans have entered the stockbrokerage business, and the chances are good that some of these institutions, along with traditional stockbrokers, are located in your community. Stockbrokers are described either as a full-service or limited-service (usually called a discount broker) firm.

Full-Service Stockbrokers

Full-service stockbroker A stockbroker who provides a wide range of services, including research and advice, but generally charges high commissions.

As the name implies, a **full-service stockbroker** provides a wide range of investment products—usually any you can think of—along with recommendations from its research department on which securities to buy or sell. Full-service firms, such as Merrill Lynch or Smith Barney, are probably the ones you recognize. The greatest benefit a full-service broker can offer you is advice on selecting stocks and managing your portfolio. As we shall soon see, you pay for these services through substantially higher commissions. If you fail to use them, you are, in effect, wasting your money.

You should know that a broker's sales representative (the person you probably call your "broker") is a salesperson first and an investment advisor second. This person may call you frequently to inquire about your investment needs. Of course, frequent calls can lead to frequent buying and selling, which, in turn, reduces your investment profits or adds to your losses. A conscientious full-service broker will discourage frequent transactions

saving money 9.2

Who Is Your Best Protector Against Dishonest Brokers? You!

Humberto Cruz, who writes a very timely and useful syndicated column on personal finance, noted recently a statement made by Arthur Levitt, Chairman of the Securities and Exchange Commission: "No group of regulators can possibly protect investors against their own inability, against their own unwillingness to protect themselves." No truer words could have been spoken.

Certainly Mr. Levitt does not mean that you shouldn't use the courts or regulators to seek restitution if you think you have been injured by a dishonest or incompetent broker or financial advisor; rather, his warning seeks to alert you that, even with all these protections, you still can suffer substantial financial losses. If you lose $10,000 to an incompetent who takes your money but winds up penniless, what consolation is it to you if he or she spends some time in jail but never repays your loss?

Mr. Cruz points out that if you are thinking of hiring an investment advisor, ask to see his or her Advisor Registration Form ADV, both Parts I and II. Advisors must provide you with Part II, which shows the advisor's qualifications and experience, but Part I is equally important because it shows the advisor's history of disciplines, convictions, or no-contest pleadings over the past 10 years. Be skeptical of anyone with a shady Part I regardless of how wonderful their qualifications appear or how successful they tell you they have been at managing other people's money. It goes without saying that you should never use a person who is not registered or who is reluctant to provide you with Part I. Also, after you have selected an advisor be prepared to regularly monitor his or her performance. If you ignore performance reports or tell the advisor to "go ahead and do what you think is best," you are asking for trouble.

You can search for an investment firm's Form ADV at an SEC website (**www.adviserinfo.sec.gov**). A free BrokerCheck Report is available at the Financial Industry Regulatory Authority (**www.finra.org**). The report contains an overview of his or her credentials, qualifications and previous employment. It also contains information on customer disputes and disciplinary actions.

(called "churning the account") and will, instead, become familiar with your investment objectives and help you arrange a portfolio to achieve them.

Discount Brokers

The advent of the **discount broker** after deregulation introduced important changes in the stockbrokerage business. The discounter emphasizes only one thing—low commissions. And, as Table 9.2 shows, these can be substantially below commissions charged by full-service brokers. As you can see, brokers' commissions vary widely, and you should ask for a commission schedule before opening an account. Also, many brokers will negotiate fees, depending on how often you trade and the dollar value of your account.

Discount broker A stockbroker who provides most services except research and advice and offers low commissions.

Internet Trading

The very hottest trend in the stockbrokerage business is trading securities over the Internet. While the discount brokers have pioneered this revolution, full-service brokers also offer this service to meet the competition. There are several reasons why many investors desire Internet trading. The first and undoubtedly the most important is very low commissions: some brokers offer rates as low as $8 a trade, regardless of the stock's price or the number of shares traded (up to some very high limit, such as 5,000 shares). Another attractive feature is easy account access to place orders and to review your holdings and the status of orders you have placed. Also, most of the Internet firms have excellent Web sites, which provide market data and news along with stock research. If you think you can manage your own investment portfolio, you definitely should have an Internet broker.

Round Lots and Odd Lots

The basic trading unit when placing orders is 100 shares. Orders for 100 shares, or multiples of 100 shares (e.g., 300 shares) are called **round lots**; orders for a fraction of 100 shares are called **odd lots**. So an order for 250 shares involves one round lot of 200 shares and an odd lot of 50 shares. There is no specific disadvantage in dealing in odd lots, although you should realize that most stockbrokers have a minimum commission amount, regardless of order size. So a trade with a low dollar amount will lead to a high commission as a percentage of the trade amount.

Round lots Orders for 100 shares or multiples of 100 shares.

Odd lots Orders for fewer than 100 shares.

Kinds of Accounts

Having picked a stockbroker, you should next open an account. This doesn't take much time. If you are married, it's a good idea to open a joint account, with each spouse having authority to initiate orders. Your account can be either a cash account or a margin account.

Transaction	Value of the Transaction	Commissions: Cost and Percentage of Value						
		Full–Service Broker		Well–Known Discounter		Internet Trades with a Smaller Discounter	
		$	%	$	%	$	%
10 shares @ $35	$350	18	5.1	35	10.0	8	2.30
200 shares @ $25	5,000	130	2.6	89	1.8	8	0.16
500 shares @ $18	9,000	225	2.5	107	1.2	8	0.09

Table 9.2
Illustrative Stockbrokerage Commissions: Common Stock Transactions

Source: Advertised rates and telephone inquiry.

FINANCIAL PLANNING *for* young adults 9.3

Investing over the Internet

Given a choice, young adults will use the Internet more than any other medium to undertake almost any activity, such as banking, planning vacations, or simply finding information. Investing over the Internet is no exception. However, this process has pitfalls along with benefits, so consider the following points before you invest.

- Opening a trading account online is rather simple. Most discount brokers have small minimum investments (usually $1,000), which you may charge to your credit card (probably a bad idea if you have to pay interest).

- Some brokers offer free trades for opening an account. While free is good, excessive trading because of "free" may not be good. A better strategy is to build a solid portfolio over time and not try to trade in and out of the market, trying to catch highs and lows.

- Be careful placing orders. While most sites have made order placing easy, it is still possible to make mistakes when

entering a stock's symbol or the number of shares you wish to trade. Be sure to click on the appropriate box to either buy or sell.

- You can choose to have your trade confirmations shown electronically, rather than through the mail. Since the broker might charge for mailed confirmations, choose the electronic option but make sure you print a copy for your tax records. The same advice applies to reviewing your monthly statement.

- A wealth of financial information is available over the Internet. Your broker will supply much of it at the Web site, but you can access other sources for even more. You may need to expand your background in finance to understand some of it and, of course, you must decide whether you wish to make the effort. If you choose not, you are well advised to limit your investing to shares of mutual funds, which, by the way, you may also purchase through your online broker.

Cash Account

Cash account A stockbrokerage account similar to a regular charge account.

A **cash account** is similar to a regular charge account used by many retailers, except you must pay for securities you purchase within three working days after the purchase is made. So, if you buy on Monday, you have three days to come up with the cash. The same time frame applies when you sell securities; that is, you must deliver shares sold within three working days. Some brokers will ask for an initial deposit before executing orders; others will not. If you wish, the broker can have your shares mailed to you, or you can choose to let the broker hold them. Holding your own shares prevents problems that might arise if the broker goes bankrupt or experiences other difficulties, but you must take steps to safeguard them, and a safe-deposit box is the only really safe place.

Actually, holding shares may not be possible in the future. Plans are currently in progress to do away with stock certificates, and your ownership interest would be shown only in so-called book-entry form.

Margin Account

Margin account A stockbrokerage account that allows borrowing from a stockbroker using securities as collateral.

A **margin account** sounds mysterious to the uninformed. Actually, it is nothing more than a loan the broker makes to you using your securities as collateral to support the loan. Here's how it works.

Initial margin requirement An amount that must be deposited when buying securities on margin; the current rate is 50 percent.

Say you open a margin account by depositing $3,000. (All brokers require a minimum deposit for a margin account, and the Board of Governors of the Federal Reserve System requires an **initial margin requirement** of 50 percent of the value of securities purchased.) Then you buy 100 shares of ABC stock at $50 a share. Thus, you bought $5,000 worth of stock, ignoring commissions, with a $3,000 deposit; obviously, the other $2,000 came from your broker. Now, what happens if the stock goes up or down in value? No problem, if it goes up. You can sell whenever you like and repay the $2,000 loan *plus interest* and pocket the difference. If it goes down, keep one simple fact in mind—the loss is all yours. You don't share it with the broker. So if ABC goes down to $30 a share and you then sell, the broker still gets $2,000 *plus interest* and you still pocket the difference—$1,000 in this case. You lose $2,000, which is $20 ($50 – $30) a share times the 100 shares.

Perhaps the mystique surrounding margin trading is the possibility of getting a margin call (this means your broker calls and asks for more money) if the price of a security falls below a certain level, called the **maintenance margin requirement**. This requirement varies among firms but cannot be less than the minimum of 25 percent of the market value of your securities set by the Board of Governors of the Federal Reserve System. If a broker had, say, a 30 percent requirement, this means the security in our previous example could go no lower than $28.57 a share before you would get a margin call. The way you get the above number is as follows:

Maintenance margin requirement A minimum equity required in an account to continue using a broker's loan.

Step 1   Divide the broker's loan by 1.0 minus the maintenance margin requirement; that is $2,000.00/(1.0 – 0.3) = $2,000.00/0.7 = $2,857.14.

Step 2   Divide your answer by the number of shares held: $2,857.14/100 = $28.57.

Since you still owe the broker $2,000, your equity at the maintenance margin is $857.14 ($2,857.14 – $2,000.00). As a check on your math, your equity should be 30 percent of the market value of your securities. In this example, 30 percent of $2,857.14 is $857.14, so our math is correct.

Using a margin account magnifies your gains or losses, as would any loan you use to buy securities. In the previous example, if you had used your own funds, you could have purchased only 60 ($3,000/$50) rather than 100 shares. Thus, if the price of the stock had gone up or down by $10, for example, your gain or loss would have been $600 rather than $1,000. A loan allows you to **leverage** your investment, which automatically increases the range of possible returns, which in turn is synonymous with more risk. Keep that in mind: Leverage always increases risk.

Leverage Using borrowed funds, such as with a margin account, to buy securities.

Kinds of Positions

After you open an account with a broker, the next step is to begin trading. Brokers refer to this as opening a position, and there are two kinds you can take: a **long position**, meaning you buy securities, and a **short position**, meaning you sell securities (that you don't own).

Long position A purchase of securities.

A long position is what you typically associate with investing: You buy, and then own, securities. A long position can be viewed as buying now and selling later. In contrast, with a short position, you sell now and buy later. This seems confusing, and certainly more mysterious than a margin account. How can you possibly sell securities you don't own? The broker helps you accomplish this by lending the securities to you. Here's how it works.

Short position Sale of securities you don't own.

Mechanics of a Short Position

Suppose you think KLM stock is overvalued at $40 a share and sure to go down in price over the next year (Figure 9.2). Your strategy is to sell 100 shares now at their high price and then buy them a year later after their price has fallen. You call the broker and tell him you wish to short-sell 100 shares of KLM. He will execute your order in exactly the same fashion as if you already owned the shares, and the buyer will receive 100 shares from your broker. Where did your broker get the shares? He probably borrowed them from other clients who own KLM shares and hold them in margin accounts. Is the broker adding risks to these clients by lending their shares? No, because the broker will insist that you deposit sufficient margin to cover potentially adverse price movements. In the above example, you would have to deposit at least 50 percent, or $2,000. You could deposit more if you wanted to, but it would be foolish to do so, since your deposit does not earn interest.

Figure 9.2
A Sample Short Transaction

The Opening Transaction (Market Price $40)

· You request your broker sell 100 shares of KLM stock short for $40 a share for a total sale price of $4,000
· Your brokerage account is credited with $4,000 from the sale of the stock
· You deposit $2,000 with your broker to cover the initial 50% margin requirement on the short sale
· Total amount in your account is $6,000 less interest on the borrowed stock

The Closing Transaction (Market Price $30)

· You purchase 100 shares of KLM stock for $30 a share for a total purchase price of $3,000
· You have $3,000 in your brokerage account
· You have a profit of $1,000 less interest on the borrowed stock

Brokerage account after opening transaction	$6,000
Stock purchase	–3,000
Brokerage account after closing trade	$3,000
Less margin contribution	–2,000
Net profit	$1,000

The Closing Transaction (Market Price $50)

· You purchase 100 shares of KLM stock for $50 a share for a total purchase price of $5,000
· You have $1,000 in your brokerage account
· You have a loss of $1,000 plus interest on the borrowed stock

Brokerage account after opening transaction	$6,000
Stock purchase	–5,000
Brokerage account after closing trade	$1,000
Return of margin	–2,000
Net profit	–$1,000

If you guessed correctly about KLM's price and it declines to $30 a share, you close out your short position by buying the stock and returning the borrowed shares to your broker. Your account was credited $4,000 when you sold them, and you need only $3,000 to buy them back. The $1,000 difference is your gain. If you deposited $2,000 to initiate the short sale, your account would now have $3,000 in it. If you guessed incorrectly about KLM and its price went up to $50 when you decided to close your position, you would lose $1,000 and your account would have only $1,000 left in it.

Short Position Risks

Is a short position any riskier than a long one? Probably so, because the long-run trend of stock prices has been upward, and you're betting against the trend with a short sale. Moreover, you lose all earnings potential on your margin deposit and you also must pay any dividends declared on stocks sold short. If KLM declared a $1 per share dividend while you were short, you would have to pay $100. (You probably are wondering if this means that two dividends are paid on the same stock—one by you and one by KLM. Yes, because the person who loaned the shares expects to receive a dividend, as does the person who bought them from you.)

Kinds of Orders

You place an order when you wish to buy or sell securities. Your order will be executed either through a major exchange or between brokers in the over-the-counter market. You can place three kinds of orders: a market order, a limit order, and a stop order.

Market Order

A **market order** instructs your broker to buy or sell securities at the best possible price. At the time you make a transaction, the broker will give you an up-to-the-minute price of a security. For example, you might call wishing to buy 100 shares of Alcoa. The broker will use his quotation terminal to find the last price paid for a share of Alcoa; assume it was $50. If you then instruct the broker to buy or sell Alcoa "at the market," you are placing a market order. Are you guaranteed a price of $50? No, even though your order may be executed in less than two minutes, Alcoa's price could change during that time.

Market order An order to buy or sell securities at the market price prevailing when the order is executed.

Limit Order

A **limit order** sets the price that you are willing to pay for a security. For example, if Alcoa's price is extremely volatile, you may fear that it could increase during the time it takes to execute a market order. If $50 a share is the top price you want to pay, you would use a limit order specifying that price. Limit orders remain in effect until they are either canceled or executed. Some investors do not want limit orders to remain "alive," so they place day orders, which are limit orders that are automatically canceled at the end of the day they are placed. Limit orders are not that important for actively traded issues such as Alcoa, since the large number of buyers and sellers usually keeps the stock's price from fluctuating widely within a short period of time. However, shares of less actively traded stocks are different. Perhaps as few as 200 or 300 shares trade each day, and substantial price changes are then possible. Limit orders are more appropriate here.

Limit order An order to buy or sell securities at a specific price.

SIMPLIFYING
financial planning 9.4

Your Broker—Your Banker

Let's suppose a minor financial emergency arises and you need to raise cash rather quickly. Should you see your local banker? You might, but a quicker route might be to tap into a margin account you establish with a stockbrokerage firm.

Many people are hesitant to have a margin account, since such accounts are used typically by aggressive investors as a source of funds to buy more securities. Used in this fashion, a margin account clearly adds risk to a portfolio. However, there is nothing preventing you from having a margin account without borrowing. Used this way, you establish a reservoir of readily available credit.

Suppose you have securities worth $5,000 in the account and no broker's loan against them. With a phone call you could arrange to borrow up to $2,500 and have the money almost immediately. Furthermore, the interest charged by the broker is usually at the prime rate plus 1 or 2 percent. Compared with other sources of consumer credit, that can be a steal. At this writing, the broker's loan cost about 8.5 percent versus about 14.5 percent on a bank credit card.

There are two problems to consider. Since you never have to pay off the principal on a broker's loan (barring a margin call), theoretically you can finance forever whatever it is that prompted the loan. If this is an item that decreases in value and needs to be replaced periodically, obviously, not reducing the loan in proportion to the depreciation value will keep you from accumulating enough funds to finance an eventual replacement. And there is the problem of a margin call. If the value of your securities falls appreciably, the broker will require a deposit of additional funds. As a hedge, you should consider borrowing less than maximum allowable—for example, never more than 30 percent of the total value ($1,500 in the foregoing example).

Stop Order

A **stop order** (often called a stop-loss order) is a market order that is triggered by the market price of a security. It is used to protect profits or limit losses. Suppose you bought Alcoa at $50 and its price subsequently increased to $80. You would have a nice profit but might not wish to sell, because Alcoa's price could go still higher. You could then place a stop-loss order on Alcoa at a price of, say, $75. If its price continued to rise, the order would be meaningless; but if its price fell to $75 (the trigger), the stop-loss order would become a market order. Again, you would not be guaranteed a $75 price, but only the best price your broker could get, which might be higher or lower, as is the case with all market orders. Stop orders are used by investors who do not wish to watch their securities closely or make frequent selling or buying decisions. (Stop orders can also be used to buy securities.) Also, some investors use such orders because they feel they lack adequate discipline to make correct decisions during emotionally charged periods. As a security's price falls, you are often tempted not to sell because you convince yourself it's bound to increase again. Consequently, you sit and watch as the price falls—perhaps back to the original purchase price, eliminating your entire gain. With a stop order, you make the selling decision without the emotional atmosphere created by a falling price.

Do Things on Paper First

Now that you have information about accounts, positions, and orders, should you begin investing immediately? We don't think so. It's often a good idea to have a trial period in which you make investments on paper. This is especially true if you plan to pick your own securities. This trial period, if you do it seriously, will familiarize you with the mechanics of investing and will give you firsthand experience with price volatility. Of course, you can always mimic a trial period by going back in time and selecting securities and then seeing how your selections would have fared, but this experience is often not the same as investing for future periods. In general, we have some background on the general market or specific securities, which is bound to influence our investment decisions. (Most of us like to cheat by picking known winners!)

You can track your stocks by creating an online portfolio at any one of several Internet sites. Three good interactive portfolio sites are Yahoo! Finance (**finance.yahoo.com**), Google Finance (**finance.google.com**) and CNN Money (**money.cnn.com**).

Keep Honest Records

The whole experience will be useless if you fail to keep honest records. It's surprising how much we wish to avoid admitting—even to ourselves—the mistakes we make. If you pick a stock and its price goes down, then measure your loss as carefully as you might measure a price increase. If the stock or bond pays dividends or interest, note that, too, along with the date it's received. In this dry run you would buy all the risky securities you might want to buy later. Include options and futures contracts in your portfolio if you are thinking of buying them. It is better to understand their enormous risks now rather than later, when it can cost you dearly.

Evaluate Your Performance

After a time, say, three months, you should designate a cutoff date and measure your performance for the period. A form or computer spreadsheet, such as the one illustrated in Figure 9.3, is helpful in doing this.

As you see, the investor (Cindy Lipton) narrowed her investment choices to five common stocks. Cindy assumed she had about $5,000 to invest and planned investing about

Name: _____Cindy Lipton_____

Reporting Period: _____1/1/05 – 3/31/05   (13 weeks)_____

Securities	(1) No. of Shares, Bonds, etc.	(2) Purchase Price per Unit	(3) Total (1) × (2)	(4) Commissions	(5) Total Invested (3) + (4)	(6) Closing Prices	(7) Total Closing Market Value (6) × (1)	(8) Gain or (Loss) (7) – (5)	(9) Dividends or Interest	(10) Total Gain or Loss (8) + (9)
1. Apple Computer	23 shares	$42.75	$ 983.25	$ 35.00	$1018.25	$49.00	$1127.00	$ 108.75		$ 108.75
2. Lucent	190 shares	5.25	997.50	35.00	1032.50	4.25	807.50	(225.00)		(225.00)
3. Hewlett-Packard	60 shares	16.50	990.00	35.00	1025.00	16.00	960.00	(65.00)		(65.00)
4. Exxon	22 shares	45.50	1001.00	36.00	1037.00	49.50	1078.00	41.00	11.00	52.00
5. IBM	8 shares	105.00	840.00	31.00	871.00	98.00	784.00	(87.00)	9.68	(77.32)
6.										
7.										
8.										
9.										
10. Money Market Fund										
			$ 4811.75	$ 172.00	$4983.75		$4756.50	$(227.25)	$ 20.68	$(206.57)

Supplementary Information:
A Interest on margin balance = $ _____—_____ (amount borrowed × margin rate)
B Dividends on stock sold short = $ _____—_____

Gain (Loss) This Period:
1 Dollar return = Column (10) – (A) – (B) = $ (206.57)
2 Rate of return = dollar return ÷ Column (5) = –0.0415 (–4.2%)
3 Rate of return annualized = rate of return for the period × 52/N (N = number of weeks held) = _____–16.8%_____

Figure 9.3
A Portfolio Summary Sheet

$1,000 in each security. When the quarter ended, she was somewhat surprised with the results and very glad she started investing with a dry run. As you see, she lost $206.57 for the quarter, and this figure doesn't include commissions she would incur if she actually wanted to sell out on March 31. Cindy was woefully underdiversified. Even though she bought five securities, three are in the computer industry—Apple, Hewlett-Packard, and IBM.

Note the relatively high total commissions in relation to the total amount invested: about 3.5 percent ($172/$4,983.75). This wouldn't be too bad if Cindy planned to hold the portfolio for some time, but it is very high if she plans to turn it over every quarter. If she did, the commissions alone would probably consume all her gains.

Cindy's quarterly rate of return of –4.2 percent indicates that if her performance remained the same, she would lose 16.8 percent (about 1/6) of her original investment in one year. Needless to say, this loss is considerable, and Cindy concluded that she needed more experience before investing on her own.

TOPIC LINKS

Set up a portfolio and track your favorite stocks on the Internet.

Finding Investment Information

Most investment decisions require some research. Even if you decide to limit your investing to mutual funds or other pooling arrangements, you still must evaluate the alternative funds available. And if you make your own investment decisions, your research must be ambitious. Information is the key to good research, and the sections to follow provide an overview of available sources.

Company Sources

TOPIC LINKS

Retrieve a 10–K Report or other SEC filing.

As noted earlier, companies are required by the SEC to provide shareholders with annual and quarterly financial reports. Companies must also provide 10-K Reports if they are requested. A 10-K Report is a detailed compilation of a company's financial performance for the previous year. It presents the same data found in a company's annual financial report but may include other information not found there, such as asset depreciation methods or officer compensation levels.

Considerable information can be found in company reports. In addition to financial data, these documents contain discussions of past results and plans for the future. The corporate officers who provide these statements want to present their company in its most favorable light. Thus, caution is necessary.

Investment Advisory Services

There are thousands of individuals registered with the Securities and Exchange Commission (the SEC). These people have licenses to offer (for a fee, usually) investment advice. But don't assume that their government licenses guarantee good advice. Some is good, but much isn't; or at least, it's no better than what you can find free at the library.

Library Sources

Most libraries contain three excellent investment services: *Moody's*, *Standard & Poor's*, and *Value Line*. Of course, you can also subscribe to each for home delivery or online access, but they are relatively expensive. Among other things, each offers a manual containing financial data for several thousand companies and a weekly newsletter that reports on economic trends and specific industries and companies. Each also recommends stocks to purchase or avoid. To become familiar with all their publications, you should visit your local or school library and ask the reference librarian to show them to you. Certainly, if you are doing any research on an individual company's securities or on an industry, include one of these publications.

Advisory Services You Pay For

There are many investment advisors who offer a weekly or monthly newsletter or e-mail update. Some also offer "hotline" connections that allow you to call for their up-to-the-minute advice, or they might contact you if there is an important change in their opinions. You pay handsomely for these services, and the logical question is, Are they worth it? It's difficult to answer that question. To begin with, you have to evaluate them on a risk-adjusted basis. Many tout that they beat the market, but it isn't clear that they do so, after considering risk. They tend to do well in bull markets (an expression meaning rising prices), but not so well in bear (falling-price) markets. Finally, unless you have sufficient funds to offset their advisory fees—which can be as high as $1,000 a year—their cost is simply too high in relation to the amount you invest.

Newspapers and Magazines

Many investors find a considerable amount of information in newspapers and magazines. This information includes investment stories and articles that might stimulate your interest as well as financial data. Most of the newspapers and magazines mentioned below are available at libraries.

The *Wall Street Journal*

The *Wall Street Journal* is a newspaper published each work day. Many investors subscribe to the *Journal* or read it at their offices or libraries. It is not exclusively investment oriented but rather covers a wide range of business and economic topics. Practically every issue has at least one story of relevance to most investors along with extensive price and trading information on a wide range of securities. It would be fruitless to attempt to describe this publication in detail; you simply must read an issue to appreciate its comprehensive coverage of investments. An interesting part of the *Journal* is its daily report on various market indicators, such as the Dow Jones Industrial Average (DJIA). The DJIA is perhaps the most widely watched market index in the United States because of its historical significance. Because it covers only 30 individual stocks, it's not considered a comprehensive market index. The S&P 500 Stock Index also has wide appeal, and it is far more representative of the overall market and differs in its method of computation.

All of this information and more is available to subscribers at the online edition of the *Wall Street Journal*. Plus, you can easily search the current and past issues for information on companies and markets. You can set up a computerized portfolio of stocks that is continually updated with the latest prices and download important data to your personal computer.

> **TOPIC LINKS**
>
> See the *Wall Street Journal*'s Interactive Edition; also, see its Classroom Edition.

Barron's

Barron's, a sister newspaper to the *Journal*, is published weekly and is exclusively investment oriented. It has regular columns dealing with different aspects of investing and a market laboratory section in each issue. In addition, it features stories on different companies, reports interviews with security analysts and other investment advisors, and offers refresher articles on different aspects of investing.

Investor's Business Daily

Investor's Business Daily (*IBD*) is a daily newspaper devoted exclusively to investment news. It provides full coverage of trading activity of stocks, bonds, options, futures, and mutual funds. *IBD* is similar to Section C of the *Journal* except that its coverage, in some respects, is more thorough. For example, it provides graphic displays of 30 stocks of interest on the NYSE, Amex, and OTC market each day; in addition, it highlights one company for extensive analysis, both graphic and in terms of the company's underlying fundamentals. If you are interested exclusively in investment news, you might consider *IBD* as an alternative to the *Journal*.

Magazines

A number of good magazines provide investment information and ideas. *Forbes* is exclusively investment oriented. Its stories and regular features usually are realistic in outlook, often forewarning investors of potential problems with various investments. Its annual survey of mutual funds is well worth the price of that issue.

Financial World is similar to *Forbes* but less extensive and perhaps less conservative in outlook. Although not a get-rich-quick magazine, it takes a more positive view than does *Forbes*.

Fortune magazine usually features in-depth articles on different companies or industries. These articles provide excellent background material but are not geared directly toward investing. Nevertheless, the articles are timely, as are the regular monthly columns.

Money magazine covers a wide range of financial planning topics, including investing. Its investment articles often provide personal investment stories—almost always of success—that are interesting and thought-provoking. After reading *Money*, you get the impression that becoming wealthy through investing is a simple task, involving little risk. More articles on investment failures would help temper that impression.

Internet Data Sources

There are so many excellent sources of investment information on the Internet that many investors use little else. We mentioned earlier that most brokerage houses offering Internet trading also offer market data and information on specific companies. But you don't need a brokerage account to access other great sites. Both Yahoo! Finance and Google Finance provide excellent tools for managing your portfolio and keeping track of the latest information on financial markets. In addition to stock quotes, each offers market news, company financial data, access to 10-K and 10-Q reports, price charts, company profiles, analysts' earnings forecasts, and other information. Another excellent site is FT.com. It has even more detailed information on international financial markets.

If you have never used an Internet site to obtain financial information, visit one of the preceding sites and explore by clicking and examining the various features. Both Yahoo and Google let you set up news alerts to have breaking news e-mailed to you. If you are "into" investing, you could spend the better part of a day reviewing the available data. In one sense, there is too much, which makes Chapters 10 and 11 so very important—you must learn how to interpret and understand the mass of information that is now so readily available.

TOPIC LINKS

Visit Yahoo! and FT.com.

key terms

American Stock Exchange (Amex) (p. 248)	market order (p. 257)
binding arbitration (p. 251)	NASDAQ (p. 249)
cash account (p. 254)	New York Stock Exchange (NYSE) (p. 246)
commission brokers (p. 247)	odd lots (p. 253)
current return (p. 242)	organized exchange (p. 246)
discount broker (p. 253)	over-the-counter (OTC) market (p. 249)
floor brokers and floor traders (p. 248)	prospectus (p. 249)
full-service stockbroker (p. 252)	risk averters (p. 242)
future return (p. 242)	risk seekers (p. 243)
initial margin requirement (p. 254)	round lots (p. 253)
intangible investments (p. 242)	short position (p. 255)
leverage (p. 255)	specialists (p. 247)
limit order (p. 257)	stop order (p. 258)
long position (p. 255)	tangible investments (p. 241)
maintenance margin requirement (p. 255)	10-K Report (p.250)
margin account (p. 254)	total return (p. 242)

follow-up on the Steele family

Reread the chapter-opening vignette. In common with thousands of beginning investors each year, the Steeles know virtually nothing about investing. Perhaps you are in a similar position, and perhaps after reading this chapter, your knowledge has expanded. Answer the following questions, playing the role of financial advisor to both the Steeles and yourself.

1. On a scale of 1 to 5 (5 representing the highest degree of risk aversion), where do you rank the Steeles? Where do you rank yourself?

2. The Steeles are contemplating opening a stockbrokerage account. Help them in the selection process. Is the type of broker you recommend for them the same as you would choose for yourself? Explain why or why not.

3. Should the Steeles open a cash account or a margin account? Explain and also discuss which type of account is the better choice for you.

4. Explain which of the three media choices—Internet, cable news (such as CNBC), or newspapers—is the best source of investment news for the Steeles. Assume they will devote no more than two hours a week to the task. Which source(s) do you like to use? How much time do you devote to the task? Is this amount too much or too little, in your view?

problems and review questions

1. How do tangible and intangible investments differ, and what investor needs can be satisfied with tangible investments?

2. What is an investment's total return? What type of investor prefers a current return? Who might prefer a future return?

3. Compare an organized exchange with the over-the-counter market.

4. Why are the organized exchanges moving to electronic trading?

5. What is NASDAQ?

6. Very briefly highlight the seven federal laws (discussed in this chapter) regulating the securities industry.

7. Explain a prospectus and a 10-K Report.

8. What are the differences between a full-service broker and a discount broker? Identify a round lot and an odd lot.

9. How does a cash account differ from a margin account?

10. What is an initial margin requirement? If its value is 0.50, and if you have $10,000 to invest, you can buy securities with a total market value of $_____.

11. What is a maintenance margin requirement? Assume that you bought 100 shares of Acme, Inc., at $100 a share. If the maintenance margin requirement is 0.30, at what price would your broker give you a margin call? What does a margin call mean?

12. Allen Gold thought Exxon's common stock was far overpriced at $45 a share; therefore, he executed a short sale on 100 shares. How did his stockbroker assist in arranging this short sale, and how much profit (ignore commissions) will Al make (or lose) if: (*a*) Exxon goes down to $40 a share, or (*b*) it goes up to $50 a share? Does Al have to put up any money for this short sale? Would you recommend short selling as a routine practice over the long run? Explain.

13. Explain market, limit, and stop orders. In what situations would investors use stop orders? Explain.

14. Identify three investment advisory services usually available at most libraries.

15. Identify three financial newspapers and four financial magazines.

case 9.1

Rose Geisler's Investment Plan

Rose Geisler, a college graduate in electrical engineering, has a good position with a major electronics firm. Her current annual salary is $65,000, and, since Rose is single with no financial obligations, she plans to invest all her savings (around $11,000) in common stocks. Rose has done some research on security selection, and she feels capable of picking her own stocks. At present, she likes the technology sector and also thinks companies in the auto industry will do well.

At the advice of her former personal finance instructor, Rose has decided to have a trial run before she actually invests. So she has selected three stocks—Intel, Microsoft, and GM—and has tracked their performances for six months. The results follow:

	Intel	Microsoft	GM
1. Purchase price per share	$60	$80	$40
2. Number of shares purchased	50	50	100
3. Commissions	$85	$85	$80
4. Closing prices	$50	$65	$50

Questions

1. Using a format similar to the one illustrated in this chapter, show the results of Rose's experiment.
2. Calculate the following: (*a*) the portfolio's dollar gain or loss, (*b*) the rate of return for the six-month period, (*c*) the annualized rate of return. Evaluate the portfolio's performance. Do you have any advice for Rose? Explain.

case 9.2

Should the Delaneys Open a Margin Account?

Pat and Ed Delaney are married and have two children. Both have professional positions, and their joint income is over $100,000 a year. Their net worth is well over $150,000, and they have excellent liquidity with very little short-term debt.

The Delaneys want to start an investment program by investing in growth stocks. They believe their situation calls for the services of a full-service broker who will guide their selections. One of the brokers they interviewed urged them to open a margin account, since the amount they wanted to invest initially—$10,000—was not enough, in her opinion, to achieve adequate diversification. She put together a list of 10 stocks and urged the Delaneys to invest $2,000 in each one.

Questions

1. Assuming the Delaneys would pay 12 percent a year on the broker's loan associated with the margin account, determine their net annual return (expressed as a percentage of the amount they invest) if their stocks paid a current dividend of 5 percent and increased in market value by 20 percent. Make a similar calculation assuming a current dividend of 5 percent and a decrease in market value of 20 percent. (Ignore commissions in both your calculations.) What advice do you have for the Delaneys about leverage?
2. Suppose the broker has a maintenance margin requirement of 30 percent. Ignoring dividends and commissions, how low could the market value of the Delaneys' holdings go before they would get a margin call? For simplicity in calculations, assume they bought 2,000 shares of only one stock at $10 a share.
3. What other advantage(s) might the Delaneys have with a margin account? Given their particular situation, do you recommend one for them? Explain.

Exercises to Strengthen Your Use of the Internet
(Internet links for the following exercises can be found at **www.prenhall.com/frasca**.)

working out
on the Web

Exercise 9.1 Investment Mistakes

The CFA Institute (**www.cfainstitute.org**) certifies financial analysts. At the home page click "About Us," and then "Investor Tools," and then "Find Out What Every Investor Should Know." There you will find several articles that should be of interest to investors, among which you will find "12 Common Mistakes Investors Make."

Q. What is the first error discussed in this section?

Exercise 9.2 Avoid Investment Scams?

The Financial Industry Regulatory Authority (FINRA) is a non-government regulator of securities firms. They provide resources for checking up on brokers and brokerage firms. FINRA (**www.finra.org**) also posts timely alerts to investment scams. On the home page you can find a link to "Investor Alerts."

Q. What is the latest investor alert.

Exercise 9.3 The NYSE Euronext (The New York Stock Exchange)

The New York Stock Exchange (**www.nyse.com**) has a useful site. Click through Home/About Us/Education/Educational Materials. There you will find an informative booklet entitled "A Guide to the NYSE Marketplace."

Q. What is the difference between a floor broker and a specialist?

Exercise 9.4 What's Happening to NASDAQ?

NASDAQ (**www.nasdaq.com**) maintains a lively market page that tracks trading activity during the day.

Q. Compare the NASDAQ Index to the DJIA. Are they moving in the same direction?

Exercise 9.5 Advice from the SEC

An important source of securities regulation is the Securities and Exchange Commission (SEC) (**www.sec.gov**). Visit its site for considerable information on investor protections.

Q. How can you file a complaint with the SEC?

Exercise 9.6 Trading over the Internet

Some firms specialize in Internet trading. See what E-Trade (**us.etrade.com**) offers. Click "Open An Account" and choose "Power E*TRADE."

Q. What is the minimum investment amount needed to open a margin account?

10 Investment Basics

understanding risk and return

Objectives

1. To grasp the nature of risk and its sources and to relate risk to investment return
2. To see the importance of diversification and to understand how it reduces investment risk
3. To understand how to accomplish adequate diversification, both among asset groups and within an asset group
4. To grasp the concepts of required return and expected return and to see how they are used in security selection
5. To become familiar with important methods and issues involved in establishing a portfolio and making changes over time

Steele family

Arnold and Sharon Steele are in the process of learning about investments. Their first attempts at investing provided new insights on the degree of risk associated with certain kinds of investments. Over a very short period of time, their small portfolio almost doubled in value and then very quickly gave back most of those gains. The Steeles aren't sure they can handle that much volatility, and they have no idea how much of a return might await them over time if they are willing to handle it. Put bluntly—is the return worth the risk? A good night's sleep shouldn't depend on how your stocks are doing!

The Steeles have met recently with a financial consultant who works for a large, full-service stockbrokerage firm. She has told them that they are poorly diversified and perhaps not invested in securities appropriate for their goals. She has offered to help them

design an investment plan and has encouraged them to open a margin account by transferring the InChemCo and Fidelity shares to her firm. She explained that such transfers are accomplished without paying commissions.

However, Arnold and Sharon are reluctant to follow her advice at the current time. The consultant made a number of investment recommendations, none of which were understood thoroughly by the Steeles. She felt that annual gains of 30 to 50 percent might be attained over the next several years by investing in good growth stocks, but profits of these magnitudes seem too good to be true. So, Arnold and Sharon want to learn more about returns and risks associated with both stocks and bonds. They also want to learn more about diversification. Finally, they would like to know how you judge a "good" investment from a "bad" one.

TOPIC LINKS

Follow the **Topic Links** in each chapter for your interactive Personal Finance exercise on the Web. Go to: **www.prenhall.com/frasca**.

Novice investors like the Steeles often find it difficult to select securities that are appropriate for them. Inexperience is partly to blame, but the core problem is an inability to recognize how much potential return a particular investment offers and the kind and degree of risk they must take to earn the return. You often hear people say, "Oh, I wouldn't put my money in common stocks—they're far too risky. I'll stick to conservative savings accounts." Keeping your money in a safe place might provide short-run security, but what do you give up in the long run? In 30 or 40 years, will these people accumulate a sufficient nest egg for retirement?

Investing is very serious business. It is not an activity that you should begin without preparation or with preconceived notions such as "stocks are too risky." Your goal is not to avoid risk altogether or to bet your life savings on one investment's performance; rather, you should attempt to create a portfolio of investments that connect suitably to all your investment goals and to your individual risk-tolerance level.

Risk and Return

Our review of investment alternatives in Table 9.1 reveals that investments with higher returns also have higher risks. Economists tell us there is no such thing as a free lunch, and in the investments arena that is certainly true. This positive direct relationship between risk and return can be called the **iron law of risk and return**, and it serves as a good forewarning: If you are seeking high returns, be prepared to undertake high risks.

Iron law of risk and return The strong positive correlation between higher investment return and greater risk.

What Is Risk?

You probably have an intuitive understanding of **risk** as the possibility of losing some or all of your investment. Games of chance are considered very risky because you can lose your entire bet. Most stocks and bonds are risky because their prices might decline after you buy them, and some may even go into bankruptcy, costing you practically your entire investment. This is the dismal side of risk, but there is also a bright side. You wouldn't invest in a risky venture unless you anticipated a high return. Therefore, an evaluation of risk must consider these high returns as well as losses, and it is actually better to view risk as a range of possible returns—positive and negative. The greater this range, the greater an investment's risk.

Risk Often thought of as a possibility of loss; but a better definition is variability of return.

An Example of Return Variability

The concept of risk as return variability is illustrated in Figure 10.1, which shows three hypothetical $1,000 investments. Investment A is a deposit in a savings account promising to pay 10 percent interest for the upcoming year. Assuming the deposit is FDIC insured, you are virtually certain of getting back $1,100 at the end of the year and earning a return of $100. Investment B is a U.S. Treasury bond that pays interest of $120. If you bought the bond for $1,000 and sold it for the same amount a year later, you would get back $1,120. But this result is not assured. Suppose instead that the bond's price could go up or down by $50 during the year. In the first case, your total return would be $170 ($120 + $50); in the second it would be $70 ($120 − $50). Investment C is a speculative common stock that pays no dividends. Your only return is through price appreciation. If its price increased by 30 percent over the year, you would make $300 on your $1,000 investment. If the price decreased by 10 percent, you would lose $100.

A is a risk-free investment since it has no range; that is, it has only one outcome. *C* is the riskiest investment, since it has the widest range of possible returns ($400). *B* has some risk, since its range of returns is $100. Estimating the range of possible returns provides a good approximation of risk, and it is often used for that purpose.

Risk and Time

It's often felt that investment risk is influenced by the passage of time, and there are two perspectives on the issue. First, the greater the time before an investment's return is expected, the riskier the investment—all things considered. The rationale is simple: We never know what the future holds, and the further we extend our projections, the more likely they are to be wrong. This principle implies greater variation in returns on long-term investments than on short-term ones.

The second perspective is somewhat different. Here, we ask the following question: Are we more likely to achieve an investment goal by holding an asset for a shorter or a longer period of time? Of course, the answer depends very much on the type of asset held. Consider a risky one, such as common stocks. Suppose that common stocks have shown an average yearly return of about 12 percent over the past 70 years or so. We would like to invest in them and hope to earn the average yearly rate in the future. Are we most likely to achieve this goal by holding stocks for one week, one year, or 10 years? You probably guessed the last choice—and you are right. The longer the investment horizon, the greater the odds of earning the average rate. This is why we realize that holding stocks for short periods of time is risky. This message was driven home very forcefully by "Black Monday"—October 19, 1987—when the stock market fell about 23 percent. The prospect of losing 23 percent of your portfolio in *one* day is indeed evidence of considerable risk, which is why financial planners urge us to hold common stocks only if we have relatively long investment horizons.

Sources of Risk

What factors make an investment risky, that is, widen its range of possible returns? The various sources of risk can be placed into two groups: those associated with changing conditions of the overall economy and those related to changing conditions of the issuers of the securities.

Changing Economic Conditions

Practically every investment's return is influenced by changes in economic conditions. First, many investments have **inflation risk**, which means that their returns may not keep pace with the rate of inflation. Any investment that pays a fixed number of dollars of return is subject to inflation risk because the purchasing power of your fixed return declines during inflation. Most government and corporate bonds fall in this group, explaining why investment advisors suggest not buying them if you expect inflation to increase.

Inflation risk The risk that an investment's return may fall short of the inflation rate.

Second, many investments are subject to **business cycle risk**. Economic growth seldom takes place in an even-keel manner. Usually, there is a period of rapid expansion followed by a period of recession. The profits of most businesses tend to follow these cycles, and so do the prices of their common stocks. The prices of real estate and other tangible assets also move in step with the economy, and their returns are similarly influenced by it.

Business cycle risk Fluctuations in an investment's return resulting from fluctuations in the business cycle.

Closely related to both inflation risk and business cycle risk is **interest rate risk**. This risk has to do with the relationship between the price of a fixed-return security that has already been issued and returns available on newly issued, similar securities. For example, suppose you bought a government bond for $1,000 that paid $100 a year in interest, a yield of 10 percent. What would happen, though, if a month later, because of tightened credit conditions, the government began issuing new bonds that yielded 12 percent? The bond you bought would still yield only 10 percent, but if you tried to sell it, nobody would be willing to give you $1,000 for it, since they could just as easily buy newly issued bonds paying $120 interest on $1,000. The buyer would expect the same percentage return on yours as he or she could get with any other bond of that type, so you would have to sell yours at a loss. At a price of $833, for example, your bond would also have a current yield of 12 percent, as calculated next:

Interest rate risk: The risk that the price of a fixed-return asset will decline if interest rates rise.

$$.012 = \frac{\$100}{\$833}$$

Thus, you would lose $167 ($1,000 − $833) by holding the bond during a period of rising interest rates. Interest rate risk has become increasingly important in recent years because interest rates have been so volatile.

Changing Conditions of the Issuer

Even in very good economic times, some firms go bankrupt; and in bad times, many do. You may buy the stock of a promising growth company anticipating a high return over time but then find that, because of poor management, the firm does not do well. In addition to this **management risk**, other sources of risk have to do with the issuer's condition. First, the company's line of business presents certain risks, usually called **business risk**. Making personal computers is inherently riskier than selling consumer perishables such as food. Another source of risk has to do with the way a company raises capital. Firms that borrow heavily are inherently riskier than those that issue mostly common stock. During periods of economic stress, the firm with a large amount of interest due its bondholders will be more vulnerable to bankruptcy than a firm without such payments. This risk is often called **financial risk**, and corporate financial managers attempt to minimize its impact, considering the firm's need for expansion capital.

Management risk Poor earnings performance of a firm associated with poor management.

Business risk Risk associated with a company's product or service lines.

Financial risk Risk associated with the use of considerable debt in a company's financing arrangement.

How Much Return Do You Need?

Having looked at risk, let's turn our attention to return. Suppose you are willing to undertake risk. How much return should you realistically expect to receive for doing so? The answer to that question for a specific investment is called the investment's **required rate of return**.

Required rate of return: A realistic estimate of the minimum return an investment must offer to be attractive, given its degree of risk.

FINANCIAL PLANNING *for*
young adults 10.1

Do Small Investors Have a Chance?

Do small investors have a chance? The answer is an emphatic "yes." In this age of insider information, computerized invest-ment strategy, and megabuck trading, you might think the small investor ought to call it quits and look for a comfortable mutual fund. Although many have taken that route, an equal number—if not more—have hung in there and are doing quite well, thank you.

Evidence of the small investor's success is usually hard to come by, but one indication is the performance of stocks selected by investment clubs affiliated with non-profit volunteer-driven Betterinvesting of the NAIC (National Association of Investors Corporation). Recently NASDAQ Stock Market, Inc. has joined with Betterinvesting to create the

Betterinvesting 100 Index and the Betterinvesting Total Return Index. Listed on major exchanges, the indexes track the top 100 companies held by Betterinvesting clubs according to an annual survey. This index has outperformed the Dow Jones Industrial Average since 2003 by more than 14 percent.

Why are the clubs, and the small investors who are their members, successful? There probably are a number of reasons, but the most important seems to be that they do considerable research before investing in specific securities. So, if you are investing $200 instead of $200,000, you can take heart that investment ante is less important than investment skill and hard work. As usual, doing your homework often leads to the higher grade. And, if you want the companionship of friends while doing homework, join an investment club. (You can get infor-mation from NAIC at its Web site: **www.better-investing.org**.)

But, if someone were to ask you what you think is a reasonable required return esti-mate for various financial assets, you might find it hard to answer. Should you earn 10 per-cent on common stocks, or 30 percent, or 5 percent, or what? While there is no completely satisfactory answer to the question, let's take a look at some relatively recent historical returns on two kinds of assets: common stocks as represented by the S&P 500 stock index and 90-day U.S. Treasury bills. Treasury bills are a cash like asset, mentioned in Chapter 5. Common stocks are covered in Chapter 11. Table 10.1 shows returns over the period from January 1, 1970 through December 31, 2006 (36 years).

While an actual return in any future year may be very different from an historical aver-age return, nevertheless, there is some evidence that the average annual return over many future years, say the next 36, will not be considerably different from the average of the past 36 years. However, there can be some difference. For example, as mentioned earlier, the arithmetic average return for common stocks over the past 75 years or so is around 12 per-cent. The average for the period covered in Table 10.1 is 11.53 percent, about 0.47 percent less.

The Returns

Even a cursory review of Table 10.1 shows why so many investors favor common stocks, particularly for long holding periods. Stocks earned 5.33 percent more than bills and 2.96 more that 10-year bonds. Many people find it hard to evaluate percentage rates of return in comparing investments. A far more forceful presentation is to show the accumulation of wealth, given the investments' returns. Note that $1,000 invested on 1/1/1970 would have grown in value to $50,838 for common stocks, and $8,724 for bills and $19,278 for bonds. We should note that for the accumulated amounts, calculations assume that any dividends and interest received on the investments were immediately reinvested when received. Clearly, common stocks dominate bills, almost to such a large extent that you wonder why investors ever invest in the latter. If you review other data in Table 10.1, you probably can make a guess.

Table 10.1
Returns and Wealth Accumulations from Stocks, Treasury Bills and Bonds, 1970–2006

Period	Stocks				Treasury Bills		Bonds (10-yr)	
	Annual Total Return (percent)	Annual Capital Gains (percent)	Annual Dividends (percent)	Stock Fund (total return)	Annual Total Return (percent)	Treasury Bill Fund (total return)	Annual Total Return (percent)	Bond Fund (total return)
Initial Investment: 1/1/1970				$1,000		$1,000		$1,000
1970 to 1979	5.88	1.60	4.20	1,771	6.48	1,874	5.94	1,781
1980 to 1989	17.55	12.59	4.40	8,920	9.13	4,489	13.01	6,050
1990 to 1999	18.21	15.31	2.51	47,523	4.95	7,277	8.02	13,086
2000 to 2006	1.13	−.49	1.63	50,838	3.07	8,724	6.67	19,278
Recent years								
2001	−11.89	−13.04	1.32		3.32		5.51	
2002	−22.10	−23.37	1.65		1.61		15.15	
2003	28.68	26.38	1.82		1.03		0.54	
2004	10.88	8.99	1.73		1.43		4.59	
2005	4.91	3.00	1.85		3.30		3.16	
2006	15.80	13.62	1.91		4.97		2.36	
36-year average return	11.53%				6.20%		8.57%	
Best 10-Year Return	17.75				4.12		11.37	
	(1958)				(1990)		(1991)	
Worst 10-Year Return	−3.81				1.03		−5.03	
	(1974)				(2003)		(1981)	
Return Range	21.56				3.09		16.40	

Source: Data on annual returns from Statistical Abstract of the United States 2008, Table 1181—Total Returns of Stocks, Bonds, and Treasury Bills: 1950 to 2006 and Global Financial Data (www.globalfindata.com).

The Risks

Clearly, common stocks are the riskier investment. Even given a 10-year holding period, the return range on stocks is about seven times that on bills. Moreover, the recent annual data shows that there were significant losses in 2001 (−11.89) and 2002 (−22.10). Losses of such magnitude attract investors to bills and other debt securities. But unless you have a very low risk tolerance level, you should seriously consider a portfolio heavily weighted with stocks—the longer your investment horizon, the greater the weight.

Risk Premiums

The difference between an investment's return and the return on Treasury bills is called a **risk premium**. Common stocks' risk premium as measured by the 36-year average in Table 10.1 is 5.33 percent (11.53 percent–6.20 percent). This number is very low in comparison to the risk premium calculated over a much longer period of time, which is about 8.0 percent (12.0 percent stock return average minus 4.0 percent Treasury bill return average). There are ongoing heated debates among financial experts as to the proper risk premium value to use in stock analysis. Some feel that a premium of 3 to 5 percent is appropriate, while others favor the long-run average of 8.0 percent. We will not develop these

Risk premium The difference between an investment's required return and the return on U.S. Treasury bills.

arguments here; however, we will use the 8.0 percent number later in this chapter and also in Chapter 11. Keep in mind that a lower value may change any conclusions that we reach about a stock as we will show.

The Rewards of Diversification

Portfolio A group of assets held at the same time.

The advice "Don't put all your eggs in one basket" is particularly applicable in the area of investments. By holding a **portfolio**, which is simply a group of assets held at the same time, certain risks can be avoided. In the short run, you might be lucky and do very well with one or two investments; but eventually luck reverses itself, and profits turn to losses. Unquestionably, an important part of a sound investment program is adequate **diversification**. Next, we explain diversification and show how it applies to investing in common stocks.

Diversification A portfolio attribute that can reduce investment risk.

Why Diversification Works

Diversification creates a synergistic quality in a portfolio in the sense that the portfolio's risk can be much less than the sum of the risks associated with all the securities it holds. In other words, you might hold two assets that by themselves are very risky but when held together create a very low-risk portfolio. The key to risk reduction is the correlation of returns between the two assets. We need an example.

An Example of Return Correlation

Figure 10.2 shows the returns from two hypothetical assets—A and B—over time. In each case, the return varies from 5 to 15 percent, and each asset has an average return of 10 percent. If you held either A or B, you would have a fairly risky asset since the range of returns (5 to 15 percent) is quite large. But look what would happen if, rather than investing all your money in one or the other, you allocated it evenly between the two.

You should see that whenever A's return is decreasing, B's return is increasing, and vice versa. Under the ideal arrangement assumed in our example, your return in the portfolio of A and B would always equal 10 percent. For example, when A's return is 15 percent, B's is 5 percent, and the average of the two is 10 percent. In effect, you have a no-risk

Figure 10.2
Returns over Time from Two Hypothetical Investments

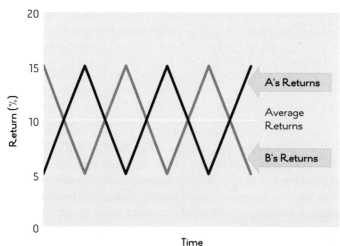

asset—the portfolio—that provides as good a return as the average return over time from either A or B, individually. If you are a rational investor, you should prefer holding the portfolio as opposed to holding only one of the assets.

Returns from assets A and B are perfectly, negatively correlated; that is why you can eliminate risk by holding the two together. Perfect negative correlation seldom, if ever, exists in the real investment world; nevertheless, significant risk reduction is achievable even if asset returns are simply *poorly* correlated. There are many examples of poor correlation.

When Diversification Is Less Effective

You probably already grasp the situation when diversification may not work effectively— when asset returns are highly, positively correlated. Indeed, if returns are perfectly, positively correlated, they are clones of each other and there is nothing to be gained by holding both. For example, suppose that every time gold's price increases, silver's price increases by a proportionate equal amount; and, the same correlation holds for price decreases. (Silver and gold returns are highly positively correlated but not perfectly so.) In this situation, if your interest in the metals is strictly one of investing for price appreciation, then there is no benefit to investing in both. Select gold or silver and look for another commodity with returns that correlate poorly with theirs.

Return Correlations Among Key Financial Assets

Statistical correlation studies have measured the degree of return correlation among the key financial assets—stocks, bonds, and Treasury bills. Their findings indicate rather poor correlations among the major groups, particularly between stocks and Treasury bills. These findings lend support to the conventional recommendations of financial planners that you should diversify among stocks, bonds, and bills (or other highly liquid assets). Although, compared with an all-stocks portfolio, such diversification lowers your average return over time and reduces your wealth accumulation, it adds far greater return stability.

Diversification Guidelines

Diversification is so critical to successful investing that certain guidelines should be followed. The objective is to achieve a reasonable portfolio return while simultaneously reducing return variability as much as possible.

Diversify Among Intangibles and Tangibles

Not only should you diversify among the key financial assets, you should further diversify between financial and tangible assets, such as real estate or commodities. For example, during the inflationary 1970s, common stocks did very poorly while gold showed excellent returns. Its price appreciated from around $35 an ounce early in the decade to over $850 in 1980. From the early 1980s to around 2000, the situation has reversed and gold fell to less than $300 by the end of the century. Since then gold has outperformed the stock market by rising to about $1,000 an ounce in 2008.

Diversify Globally

Recent investment studies clearly demonstrate the importance of investing on a global basis. Cross-country diversification reduces portfolio risk and frequently *increases* portfolio return. This is the best of both worlds. The explanation is that economies throughout the world do not expand and contract together. So there may be good times in the United States while Europe and Asia are lagging. This mix creates the negative correlations needed to reduce risk.

Moreover, certain parts of the world are growing much more rapidly than others: for example, South America and the Pacific Basin region compared with the United States. By investing in these parts of the world, not only do you diversify but also you pick up the higher returns that typically accompany rapid growth.

Diversify Within Asset Groups

This is perhaps the most important rule. Some people take the view that you should "put all your eggs in one basket and watch the basket very closely," but for most of us that is a prescription for poverty. Few investors are so clever that they can identify the specific assets that will boom in the upcoming period. Indeed, the majority of professional money managers fail to do as well as an unmanaged stock index such as the S&P 500. An old market pro was once asked how much diversification an investor should have. His answer: Keep diversifying until you can sleep at night. Not bad advice, but we'll be more precise in the next section.

Applying A Risk-Return Model

Although it's interesting (and sometimes even fun) to study financial theory and investment returns, it's far more profitable to be able to apply what we learn. In this regard, theorists have developed certain techniques that many practitioners have used successfully. One approach is derived from the so-called **capital asset pricing model** (**CAPM**, for short). The CAPM can be applied to investing in any type of asset, but it has been used most extensively in common stock investment. Our discussion will be limited to that area.

Capital asset pricing model An asset valuation model describing the relationship between risk and return.

Eliminating Random Risk

When you hold a limited number of stocks, you open yourself to all the risk factors discussed previously; that is, you take on risks associated with the overall economy as well as those associated with individual firms. A portfolio eliminates these latter risks. If you like the personal computer industry and put all your "apples" into Apple Computer, you rise or fall with this one stock. By putting half your money into Apple and the other half into, say, Dell you divide the risks associated with these two firms. If Apple fails in market acceptance, Dell might prosper. Of course, both might prosper or both might fail, but the probability is greater that one will prosper or fail.

Studies have shown what happens to risk as you increase the number of stocks in a portfolio. A fairly typical outcome is shown in Figure 10.3. This is a hypothetical, randomly constructed portfolio with individual securities drawn by chance from the S&P 500 Stock Index. What do you find interesting in the figure?

First, notice the extent to which risk can be reduced by holding only a few stocks in a portfolio. With only five, you can cut your risk almost in half. After 20, you have virtually eliminated all the risk that can be eliminated, which is called **random risk**. Second, no matter how much you diversify, you cannot eliminate all risk (individual stock returns are poorly, but not negatively, correlated), and that which remains is called **market risk**. In other words, even if you owned all the stocks in the S&P 500, you still could expect considerable return variation over time, as we have discussed.

Random risk Risk associated with any single asset; it can be reduced by holding the asset in a portfolio.

Market risk Risk associated with unpredictable movements of the overall market; it cannot be reduced by a portfolio.

Managing Market Risk

Since you cannot eliminate market risk, the next best step is to manage it. By managing risk, we simply mean that you receive sufficient return over time to compensate you for

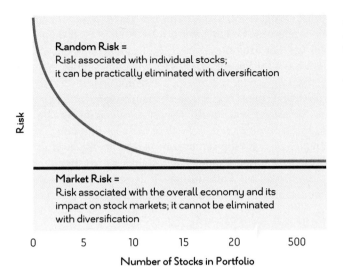

undertaking it. A general, but very, very important first rule is: *If you invest in stocks as risky as the overall market, you should receive a risk premium equal to that of the overall market.* Recall our discussion earlier about risk premiums, and how the overall market has averaged about an 8.0 percent risk premium over a long period of time. Now we put that information to use. Suppose you are contemplating investing in the overall market (either by selecting 20 stocks randomly or by buying a mutual fund that approximates the market).

SIMPLIFYING
financial planning 10.2

Are You Losing Sleep over Underdiversification?

If you have been losing sleep over underdiversification, there is a good explanation. Investment advisors constantly beat the drum for diversification, so there's no shortage of news stories in the popular investment media extolling its advantages. But you might find it comforting to know that you probably are better diversified than you think.

Many investors hear that, to hedge inflation, their portfolios should include tangibles, such as gold or silver. They worry, then, because they don't own any. But other tangibles are also good inflation hedges; one of the best is a home. If you own (or plan to own) a home, stop worrying about adding tangibles. If anything, your portfolio is probably too heavily weighted in tangibles and you need more in financial assets.

Another concern is global investing. We hear how important this is as a means of reducing wide swings in our portfolio's value. Again, sleep is lost because investors do not own foreign stocks. Although it is helpful to invest in foreign-based companies, you might be surprised to learn that many U.S. companies, such as Coca-Cola, Boeing, and Gillette, do as much or

more business abroad as they do at home. There are many truly multinational companies, and owning their shares automatically diversifies your portfolio globally.

Rather than worrying needlessly about global or tangibles diversification, investors should focus more on diversifying within their common stock holdings. Studies of individual investor accounts reveal the sad fact that most investors hold five or fewer stocks, often all in the same industry. This approach offers virtually no diversification benefits and frequently leads to disaster.

To keep things simple, follow this guideline: Invest in 20 companies, with 15 having foreign sales of at least 40 percent of total sales. (You can find this information in a company's annual report or in investment references such as *Value Line*.) Do not have more than two companies in the same industry. If you do not own a home, select five companies involved with natural resources (e.g., Exxon, Barrick Gold, Phelps Dodge, and Georgia-Pacific). Finally, never try to time buying or selling the shares. Use the company's dividend reinvestment plan (DRIP) to acquire more shares. Indeed, if a company doesn't have a DRIP, drop it and look for one that does.

What is your required return for one year? Step 1: Determine what the rate will be on risk-free, one-year U.S. Treasury bills. Step 2: Add the risk premium, and you have your answer. For example, if the U.S. Treasury bills rate is 5.0 percent, the required market return is 13.0 percent (5.0 + 8.0). Although simple, it's nevertheless a sound approach for estimating a required return. Assuming you invest, are you guaranteed the 13 percent return? Of course not. It could be much higher or much lower, as we saw in Table 10.1.

A second, and equally important rule in investment risk management is: *If you invest in stocks more or less risky than the overall market, you should expect a risk premium greater or less than the overall market premium in direct proportion to the greater or lesser risk taken.* Common sense tells us we should receive a higher return if we take greater risks, but, unfortunately, it doesn't tell us *how much* higher. More sophisticated—but not difficult to understand—techniques are needed to answer that question.

Estimating a Stock's Risk

Beta A statistic that measures the responsiveness of an asset's return in relation to changes in the overall market return.

The first step now is to determine the risk of an individual stock in relation to the overall market. This is done with a statistical figure called **beta**. A stock's beta measures the responsiveness of its return over time to that of the overall market. For example, if Apple Computer's beta is +1.5, it means that if the stock market goes up 10 percent, Apple's common stock goes up 15 percent; if the market goes down 10 percent, Apple goes down 15 percent. A beta value indicates relative risk, with higher betas meaning greater risk. Table 10.2 summarizes ranges of beta values and their meanings, and Table 10.3 shows a wide array of betas of companies, some of which might be familiar to you.

Betas are not difficult to calculate, although the method involves a type of statistical analysis that may not be familiar to you. Fortunately, betas are available from a number of sources, such as Yahoo! Finance (**finance.yahoo.com**).

TOPIC LINKS

Find Microsoft's beta.

Estimating a Stock's Required Return

After determining a stock's beta value, you can then estimate its required return. Considerable historical evidence shows that stock returns over time are related to their beta

Table 10.2
What Beta Values Mean

Range of Beta Values for a Stock	What It Means
Less than zero; that is, a negative beta	The stock's price moves in the opposite direction from the market; very few stocks have negative betas over extended periods of time.
Zero	The stock's return is independent of the market; this could be a risk–free U.S. Treasury security, where return is guaranteed regardless of the market's performance.
Zero to +1.0	The stock's price moves in the same direction as the market but not as much; stocks with betas less than 1.0 are considered conservative investments.
Equal to +1.0	The stock has the same risk as the market; if you bought all beta 1.0 stocks, your portfolio's return and risk would be the same as if you bought the overall market.
Greater than +1.0	The stock's price moves in the same direction as the market but by a greater percentage amount: buying these stocks increases your risk relative to the market.

Company	Ticker Symbol	Major Business	Beta Value
Southwest Airlines	LUV	Major airline	(0.31)
Avon	AVP	Cosmetics	(0.08)
Kellogg	K	Packaged foods	0.27
DPL	DPL	Electric utility	0.50
Barrick Gold	ABX	Gold mining	0.70
Citigroup	C	Global banking	0.78
Viacom	VIA	Communications	1.00
Google	GOOG	Internet	1.03
Exxon–Mobil	XOM	Oil refinery	1.22
Meadwestvaco	MWV	Packaging	1.47
Intel	INTC	Computer memory chips	1.62
International Business Machines	IBM	Computer services	1.66
Micron Technology	MU	Computer memory chips	1.76
Caterpillar	CAT	Construction equipment	1.78
Ebay	EBAY	Internet auction site	3.25

Table 10.3
Estimated Beta Values for Various Companies (2007)

values; specifically, risk premiums are shown to be directly proportional to beta values. The following equation expresses this relationship:

Stock risk premium (%) = stock's beta × market risk premium (%)

If a stock has a beta of +1.5, its risk premium should be 12.0 percent:

$$12.0\% = 1.5 \times 8.0\%$$

Stock's required rate of return = risk free rate + stock's risk premium

$$17.0\% = 5\% + 12\%$$

The total required return on a stock consists of the risk premium plus the expected return on risk-free Treasury securities. If this latter rate is 5.0 percent, the stock's total required return is 17.0 percent (5.0 + 12.0). The diagram shown in Figure 10.4, which incorporates the figures we have just used, is a convenient way to express and summarize the important relationship between required return and risk.

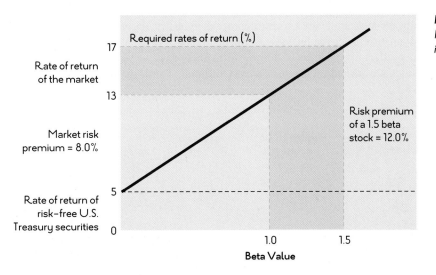

Figure 10.4
Required Rates of Return in Relation to Beta Values

The Importance of the Risk–Free Rate of Return

You should understand the important role played by the rate of return on U.S. Treasury bills. All required rates of return depend on it, and if it changes, so will these rates. For example, if this rate went up to 10.0 percent from 5.0 percent, all other rates would similarly increase by 5 percent; the market return will now be 18.0 percent, and a 1.5 beta stock will be 22 percent.

Making Stock Selections

Expected total return An actual return that investors expect to earn on a stock in an upcoming period.

Finding a stock's required return does not answer the question of whether the stock should be bought or sold. To make these decisions we need a stock's **expected total return**. This is a return that investors believe they will actually earn with the stock in the upcoming investment period. We will discuss this return in detail in Chapter 11; for now, let's work with it as a given.

Consider three investments—A, B, and C—shown in Table 10.4. They differ substantially in risk, as measured by their beta values, and in expected returns. How would you rank them in terms of appeal? Would you take C because it offers the highest return? Some investors might, but it would be a mistake.

Look for a Stock's Excess Return

Alpha A measure of a stock's appeal, calculated by subtracting required return from expected return.

Actually, A is the best investment. Why? Because it offers the highest **alpha** value, which is the difference between expected return and required return; that is,

$$\text{Alpha} = \text{expected return} - \text{required return}$$

Alpha values can be positive, as they are with investments A and C, or negative, as with investment B. Any stock with a negative alpha value should not be bought, and you might consider selling if you already own it. Stocks with positive alpha values are buying opportunities, with greater alphas indicating greater investment appeal.

Stock A with its 2.2 percent alpha value seems a good investment. Stock C's situation is not overwhelming; as noted in the table, you might flip a coin to make a choice here.

Is Selecting Stocks This Easy?

The answer to this question is a resounding "no." The CAPM technique is very simple, which makes it appealing; but there are several problems to consider. First, beta may not always measure a stock's risk appropriately, particularly when a company is undergoing dramatic changes in business or financial risk. A beta calculated from historical data may not reflect the riskiness of the new firm. Second, as we will see in Chapter 11, estimating a stock's expected total return is very difficult. Third, the 8 percent risk premium we are

Table 10.4
Selecting Stocks by Comparing Required Rates of Return with Expected Rates of Return

Stock	Beta Value	Required Rate of Return	Expected Rate of Return	Alpha Value	Decision
A	0.35	7.8%	10.0	+2.2%	Definitely accept, expected rate well exceeds required rate
B	1.50	17.0%	14.0	–3.0%	Definitely reject, expected rate is far below required rate
C	2.00	21.0%	21.0	0.0%	A borderline case, flip a coin to make your choice

using places a heavy risk burden on stocks B and C. Suppose we used a lower rate of, say, 4 percent. Then B's required return is only 11 percent [5% + 1.5 (4%)] and C's is 13 percent [5% + 2.0 (4%)]. Now, each should be regarded as solid buys.

Despite all the criticisms, though, the technique is useful if it does nothing more than force us to consider both risk and return in the investment selection process. Equally important, it highlights the need to earn higher returns if you take greater risks. If you invest your money in roller-coaster (high beta) stocks, you should at least get the thrill of the ride (a high return).

Building and Changing a Portfolio

Although the need to diversify in building a portfolio is important, there are other issues to also consider. First, assets selected must be suitable to meet the investor's objectives. You will understand this topic better after you have become more familiar with the wide variety of investments available; so our discussion of selecting assets is deferred to Chapter 12. But other issues can be addressed now. In the following sections, we discuss the topics of acquiring and selling securities over time.

Acquiring Securities

As funds become available to acquire securities, how should we do it? Two methods are often advised by financial planners—dollar cost averaging and routine investment plans.

finance news 10.3

Dogs of the Dow: Using a High-Yield Method to Select Stocks

Beating the market is not easy—just ask over half of all professional money managers who come up short each year. Surprisingly, one very simple method has a good track record and a rapidly growing number of converts. Even some mutual funds offer the method, if you prefer to avoid even the slight details of investing on your own.

What do you need to do? At the beginning of each year find the 10 (of 30) stocks in the Dow Jones Industrial Average (DJIA) with the highest dividend yield. You could use a copy of the *Wall Street Journal* or *Barron's* to find the 10 highest yielders, or make life easy and go to the "Dogs of the Dow" Web site (**www.dogsofthedow.com/**), which provides the names each day. It also provides performance results along with much other information. Actually, you can begin investing anytime; you don't have to wait until the beginning of a year.

Regardless of how you get the 10 stocks, invest an equal amount in each at the start of a year, then sit back and reap. From 1972 through 1995, this method has scored an average

annualized return of 17.7 percent versus only 11.9 percent for the overall DJIA. However, from 1999 through 2003, it underperformed the Index, 5.1 to 6.1 percent, but subsequently exceeded the DJIA by 9.9 to 8.7 percent from 2003 to 2006. This is a fairly good performance. Why does it do so well?

High-yielding stocks often represent so-called turnaround situations. A company, such as Sears at one time, may fail to keep up with its competitors in terms of market share or production efficiencies. As a result, the stock price plummets, but the company has ample cash and continues paying a decent dividend. So the dividend yield rises, and the company makes the top 10 list. Often these companies solve their problems—as Sears did—and their stock prices rebound sharply.

Would the high-yield method work in pinpointing other potential turnarounds? Sure, but be careful. Stocks in the DJIA are large blue chips that have the resources to make drastic operational changes. If you find a small company with a high yield, it may never turn around; instead, it may lower or cut its dividend altogether. Now, your high-yielder is a no-yielder, and its price might fall sharply. It is much simpler to limit your choices to the DJIA.

Dollar Cost Averaging

TOPIC LINKS

Review an example of dollar cost averaging.

Dollar cost averaging (DCA) is a mechanical method of investing in securities. Table 10.5 shows how it works. As you see, the idea is quite simple. You establish an investment plan calling for equal dollar investments at regular intervals. By following the plan, you then buy securities at a wide range of prices, and, over time, you will have an average cost somewhere between the highs and the lows. In this example, the average cost after six months is $8.89 per share. The mechanical nature of the plan keeps investors from using their own judgment to determine buying points or from buying a given number of shares (rather than investing a given number of dollars) at regular intervals.

A supporter of this plan believes that investors' judgments usually are wrong, because they are guided by emotions or incorrect assessments of the market situation. In the enthusiasm of a bull market (rising prices), we tend to invest too heavily; in the gloom of a bear market (falling prices) we don't invest at all. Following this approach, the average cost of purchased shares is much higher than the average with DCA.

Routine Investment Plans

TOPIC LINKS

Find DRIPS.

There are a number of ways to make investments on a regular basis. Many companies have **dividend reinvestment plans (DRIPs)** that enable investors to reinvest dividends they receive from a company's stock to buy more of the company's shares. Since dividends are paid at regular quarterly intervals, a DRIP accomplishes the same end as dollar cost averaging on a quarterly basis. A similar routine investment process arises if you own mutual fund shares and choose to reinvest dividends and capital distributions rather than receiving them in cash. Many mutual funds also encourage routine investing by offering plans that automatically transfer a certain amount of funds each week (or other period) from your checking account to the mutual fund.

All the preceding plans are effective primarily because they put savings and investment first, rather than last, in your budget. But they are not substitutes for sound investment selection in the first place. You don't want to dollar cost average with a poorly performing stock or use the DRIP of a company with no viable future. The downside of regularity in investing is that we might not review our holdings as often as we should.

Selling Securities

The decision to sell securities may be as difficult to make as the decision to buy them. There are a number of factors to consider. They are discussed next.

The Security Becomes Overvalued

Let's suppose that you bought stock A, which we discussed previously and showed to be a good value within the CAPM framework. Suppose that its price was $20 a share when you

Table 10.5
Illustration of DCA, Assuming $1,000 Invested Each Month

(1)	(2)	(3)	(4)	(5)	(6)	(7)
Date	Shares Purchased	Price per Shares	Total Shares Held	Total Cost	Average Cost (5)/(4)	Cumulative Profit (Loss) [(3) × (4)] − (5)
1/1	100.00	$10	100.00	$1,000	$10.00	$ 0
2/1	83.33	12	183.33	2,000	10.91	200
3/1	125.00	8	308.33	3,000	9.73	(533)
4/1	100.00	10	408.33	4,000	9.80	83
5/1	166.67	6	575.00	5,000	8.70	(1,550)
6/1	100.00	10	675.00	6,000	8.89	750

bought it, but it's now $50 a share. The CAPM might now indicate that it's overvalued and should be sold. Surely, one important reason to sell a security is if we believe that it is no longer attractive relative to other securities that could be purchased.

Selling for Tax Reasons

The tax law often encourages security sales. For example, suppose that you bought shares of GM stock, which subsequently declined in value. You now have a $3,000 loss. Should you sell? If you do, you might establish a loss that can be used to offset other income on your tax return, saving you taxes. The amount depends on offsetting gains and your marginal tax rate: At a 28 percent rate, you save $840 ($0.28 \times 3,000$).

Investment advisors say that you should not sell securities *simply* to save taxes; nevertheless, in certain situations it makes good sense. For example, you may think that Ford and Chrysler are just as attractive as General Motors; by selling the latter and buying one of the former, you will save enough in taxes to allow you to buy more shares. Changing investments for tax reasons is referred to as a **tax swap**. Swaps are very popular but more so with bonds than with stocks.

Tax swap Selling a security to establish a tax loss and then reinvesting funds in a similar security.

Your Investment Objectives Change

Over time, it is likely that your investment objectives will change. You might want more current income as opposed to price appreciation, or you might want less portfolio risk. Clearly, changing objectives require the sale of certain securities and the purchase of others.

TOPIC LINKS

Research MITTS at Yahoo! Finance.

 # saving money 10.4

Have Your Cake and Eat It, Too? Get a MITTS

Wouldn't it be great if someone invented a stock that would only go up in value and that would trade in the securities markets, so you could sell it if you didn't want it anymore? Well, somebody has. Actually a number of brokerage companies have created securities of this sort, going by names such as MITTS, SUNS, and TIERS. Since MITTS are the most popular, we'll confine our discussion to them.

MITTS stands for Market Index Target Term Securities, issued by Merrill Lynch. Actually, the security is a bond that pays no interest, like Series EE savings bonds issued by the Treasury. Also in common with savings bonds, at their maturity MITTS can be redeemed for a set price ($10 for a MITTS, the amount for a savings bond depends on how long you hold it). But MITTS offer something the savings bond does not—the opportunity to reap a much higher value. You see, MITTS are indexed to various types of stock indexes, such as the S&P 500, the NASDAQ 100, or the Nikkei 225. This means that if the index soars, the MITTS value will soar right along with it.

But what happens if an index tanks? Actually, nothing, if you are willing to hold the security until its maturity, which is usually

between two and seven years. Since MITTS are sold at $10 and mature at $10, you lose nothing. Nothing, that is, if you don't consider interest or dividends you could have earned investing elsewhere (MITTS pay no interest or dividends). You also pay an annual operating expense, ranging from 1.3 to 2.6 percent, which is taken as a reduction from the ending value.

Financial planners point out certain disadvantages with MITTS. The IRS considers these securities as bonds rather than as stocks, treating any gain as interest (fully taxable) as opposed to capital gains (reduced rates). Of course, you can overcome this disadvantage by holding MITTS in your tax-deferred accounts, such as an IRA. Planners also point out that the operating cost is quite stiff when compared to similar costs of mutual funds investing in the same indexes. These costs are often as low as 0.18 percent.

Still, MITTS are a pretty good deal for cautious investors who simply can't tolerate portfolio losses. But if you have a long investment horizon (say, over 10 years), you probably will be better off investing directly in the index that interests you. The dividends you will earn, coupled with much smaller operating expenses, add up to a considerable amount of money over time.

Economic Changes and the Portfolio

A frequently debated issue in portfolio management is whether your investment activities should ignore economic conditions or be managed in ways to exploit expected changes. The argument is referred to as buy-and-hold versus market timing.

Buy-and-Hold Strategies

Buy-and-hold strategy A method of portfolio management that does not attempt to trade securities over economic status.

As the name implies, a **buy-and-hold strategy** means you do not attempt to enhance your portfolio return by "trading with the investment cycle." People advocating the buy-and-hold approach argue that economic cycles cannot be forecasted. Since you can't forecast cycles, there is no way you can consistently benefit by trading in anticipation of them, and all you do is make your stockbroker wealthy by trying. Buy-and-hold advocates stress the importance of *carefully constructing* a well-diversified portfolio to begin with rather than continually *changing* one to improve performance.

The growing evidence that economic cycles cannot be forecasted certainly supports this view. Even the so-called experts have been consistently off their forecast targets, often by so much that any random forecasting device forecasted as well. If you like the idea of simply building and then holding a portfolio, there is no reason to be defensive about its simplicity.

Market-Timing Strategies

Market timing A method of portfolio management that changes a portfolio's composition in relation to expected market changes.

Market timing attempts to change a portfolio's composition in anticipation of expected changes in returns among different investments. Timing strategies range from the complex to some that are very simple. A simple one usually involves going back and forth between a common stock mutual fund and a money market fund. The simpler versions are growing in popularity, and certain advisors now specialize in offering timing advice or in managing portfolios based on their timing methods.

Since no evidence overwhelmingly supports even professional market timers, you should think twice before attempting your own timing techniques. If a formula appeals to you, our advice again is to try it on paper first and evaluate it critically. If it seems to work, then consider investing in a mutual fund family that allows you to switch among individual funds at little or no cost. (Fund switching is explained in Chapter 12.)

key terms

alpha (p. 278)
beta (p. 276)
business cycle risk (p. 269)
business risk (p. 269)
buy-and-hold strategy (p. 282)
capital asset pricing model (CAPM) (p. 274)
diversification (p. 272)
dividend reinvestment plans (DRIPs) (p. 280)
dollar cost averaging (DCA) (p. 280)
expected total return (p. 278)
financial risk (p. 269)

inflation risk (p. 269)
interest rate risk (p. 269)
iron law of risk and return (p. 267)
management risk (p. 269)
market risk (p. 274)
market timing (p. 282)
portfolio (p. 272)
random risk (p. 274)
required rate of return (p. 269)
risk (p. 267)
risk premium (p. 271)
tax swap (p. 281)

Reread the chapter-opening vignette. The Steeles have investment assets of $26,000 of InChemCo stock that Arnold purchased through his employer and $6,800 in a mutual fund, Fidelity growth fund. The retirement savings are in an employer-sponsored cash balance plan that is managed by his employer.

1. Do you agree with the financial consultant that the Steeles' portfolio is not adequately diversified? Explain your answer.

2. How likely is it for the Steeles to earn annual returns of 30 to 50 percent for the next *several* years? How likely are they to earn those returns *consistently* in the future? Discuss your answers.

3. Arnold and Sharon have been watching the financial news networks, such as CNBC. The commentators and guests generate a considerable amount of energy, which can be conducive to frequent trading. Explain if you feel the Steeles should be active traders, holding securities perhaps no longer than several months, or even several weeks.

4. Explain if you feel that dollar cost averaging and dividend reinvestment plans might be better alternatives to the frequent trading strategy discussed in Question 3.

1. How would you define risk to someone who doesn't have a grasp of investment fundamentals? Do you think the best definition is "Risk is the chance of losing money"? Explain.

2. Explain two views that you might take relating risk to time. Which is the more appropriate if you are a long-term (over 10 years) investor?

3. Drew Dugan is considering investing in one of three securities listed in the following table. Drew isn't familiar with return or risk and would like you to explain the data. Also, he would like your opinion on which security to invest in; he generally considers himself a risk-seeking individual.

	Securities		
	A	B	C
Highest expected return	50%	15%	30%
Lowest expected return	-30%	10%	-20%
Most likely return	20%	12%	22%

4. What sources of risk are associated with the overall economy? What sources are associated with individual issuers of securities? Explain two perspectives of the relationship of risk to time.

5. From 2001 through 2006, which financial investments—stocks, Treasury bills, or Bonds—were the most and the least risky? Explain and provide evidence for your answer.

6. What investment implications can you derive from the information in Table 10.1? Express your answer from the perspectives of a young investor (mid-20s) and an older investor (mid-50s) nearing retirement.

7. Explain an investment's risk premium. Is there some "set" number to use in stock analysis? Explain.

8. People often understand through common sense that diversification reduces risk. But explain *why* diversification works and when it works most effectively. Also indicate when it may not be effective.

9. Briefly explain three diversification guidelines.

10. How many securities must you hold for adequate diversification? Does diversification eliminate all risk, or does some remain? Explain.

11. What is meant by managing risk, and how is the beta concept used in this effort?

12. Dan Stramm thinks that if you invest in common stocks, you ought to get three times as much return as you would if you invest in Treasury bills. Do you agree with Dan? If not, explain how you would estimate a required return for common stocks.

13. How do you calculate a stock's alpha value? How do you use it to select stocks?

14. Explain dollar cost averaging and why it may be helpful for certain investors. What is a dividend reinvestment plan, and what advantage does it offer? Also briefly explain several other routine investment techniques.

15. Briefly explain three reasons for selling securities.

16. Explain a market-timing strategy, comparing it with a buy-and-hold strategy.

case 10.1

Selecting Stocks for Bart Parks

Bart Parks is a bachelor, 33 years old, with a good income and a reasonable net worth. Bart has about $20,000 invested in individual common stocks, most of them recommended by his broker, Buzz Bushkin. He's done well with Bushkin over the years, and he is particularly pleased that Bushkin always gives him a list of several stocks to choose from, instead of just one. Bart has saved another $3,000 for the market and has asked Bushkin for a new list, which follows. Bushkin recommends Alpha Dynamics, but Bart is concerned with this selection because he has heard that Alpha's latest product—an automatic envelope opener—has not met huge market acceptance.

Bart has turned to you for help, and in response you have gathered the following data on expected returns and betas.

Security	Current Price	Expected Return	Beta
Bushkin's alternatives			
Alpha dynamics	$ 10	25%	2.0
Beta depressants	18	5%	0.3
Gamma globulins	6	27%	3.1
U.S. Treasury bills	—	5%	0.0
A market index fund	16	13%	1.0

Bart doesn't consider himself either excessively risk averting or risk seeking, but he does expect a return commensurate with the degree of risk inherent in a security. Also, Bart's current holdings give him adequate diversification, so that need not concern him in selecting a stock now. Finally, Bart uses a market risk premium of 8 percent.

Questions

1. Calculating alpha values, explain if you agree or disagree with Bushkin's selection.

2. Should the information Bart has heard about Alpha's new product be a concern in his selection? Explain.

3. Assuming that Bart takes Bushkin's advice, calculate the commission he will pay and compare this with the commission he probably would pay to a discount broker.

Arlene Elton has been investing in LKV Aeronautics common stock over the past six months. She bought 300 shares initially at $25 a share. A month later, after a nice move by LKV, she bought another 300 shares at $35 a share. LKV then went into a tailspin over the next three months, and at the end Arlene considered selling all her shares at $15 a share. She's glad she didn't, though, because the stock rebounded in the last month and is currently selling at $30 a share. Arlene has saved some more money and is now thinking of buying 200 more shares. Before buying them, she has decided to talk to a friend, Mark Hatfield, who also invests in stocks. Mark uses dollar cost averaging. He thinks Arlene should also consider this technique. Indeed, he is convinced that dollar cost averaging almost guarantees successful investment results over time.

Questions

1. Assuming that Arlene goes ahead with her plan to buy 200 more shares of LKV, she will have invested $24,000 to buy 800 shares. Suppose that instead she had invested $4,000 each month over the six months and purchased shares at the following prices: $25, $35, $30, $20, $15, and $30. Set up a table that shows the number of shares purchased each month, the total value of her holdings, and her profit or loss after the purchase.

2. Compare Arlene's actual performance with the performance from dollar cost averaging. Calculate the average share cost each way, and use the values in your discussion.

3. Do you think Arlene is the type of person who should use dollar cost averaging? Explain.

4. Do you agree with Mark that dollar cost averaging guarantees good investment results? Explain.

Exercises to Strengthen Your Use of the Internet
(Internet links for the following exercises can be found at **www.prenhall.com/frasca.**)

Exercise 10.1 Learn More About Risk and Return

Go to the American Association of Individual Investors (**www.aaii.com**) home page and choose "Investment Basics" then choose "FAQs." If you scroll down to the bottom of this page you will find an article entitled, "Investor Classroom: Dividing Your Assets Between Stocks, Bonds and Cash." The article presents three portfolios that allocate your assets according to your risk preference.

Q. Which of the three portfolios is most compatible with your own risk preference?

Exercise 10.2 What's the Market Doing?

Many excellent Internet sites provide information on individual securities and the markets over all. One of the best is Yahoo! Finance (**finance.yahoo.com**). At the home page review the performances of the popular indexes throughout the day. Then click "S&P 500" to view an interactive graphic of this index. You can reload the performance graphic for longer time periods.

Q. What has been the highest value for the S&P 500 over the past five years?

Exercise 10.3 What's Intel Doing?

While at Yahoo! Finance (**finance.yahoo.com**) find out what Intel is doing by entering its symbol (INTC) in the search box. Along with the most recent price, other information appears.

Q. What are Intel's earnings per share and P/E ratio?

Exercise 10.4 Does P&G Have a Dividend Reinvestment Program (DRIP)?

DRIPS are very popular. You can find a list of plans at DRIP Advice (**www.dripadvice.com**).
Q. Check out the plan for IBM. How much is the dividend reinvestment fee?

Exercise 10.5 How Does Dollar Cost Averaging (DCA) Work?

DCA is a popular investment strategy that avoids the perils of "playing the market." Assuming you were investing in the S&P 500, MoneyChimp (**www.moneychimp.com**) lets you compare the results of DCA versus an initial lump-sum investment for a variable historic period. On the home page go to "Does Dollar Cost Averaging make volatility work for you"?

Q. Assume you could either invest in the S&P 500 or keep your funds in a money market account and that you could earn 3 percent annually on the money market account. Suppose you had $10,000 to invest in the S&P 500 in January of the previous year. Would you have done better by investing it all in January or averaging your purchases over the year? How about the year before?

Stocks and Bonds

your most common investments

Objectives

1. To identify basic shareholder rights and the means by which corporations make distributions to shareholders
2. To recognize the investment opportunities in various types of stocks, such as growth stocks or income stocks
3. To understand how to determine the investment appeal of a stock using various valuation techniques and the price–to–earnings approach
4. To understand corporate bondholders' rights and the payment characteristics of corporate bonds
5. To identify different types and payment characteristics of U.S. Treasury securities, U.S. agency securities, and municipal bonds
6. To know how to calculate a bond's current yield, yield to maturity, and present value
7. To understand default risk and interest rate risk associated with bond investments
8. To become familiar with preferred stock, recognizing its characteristics and investment quality

Steele family

After considerable deliberation, the Steeles have decided to manage their own investment program. They intend to direct most of their savings into mutual funds, although they also plan to build their own portfolio of common stocks, most likely through dividend reinvestment plans. Regardless of the specific investment approach they use, Arnold and Sharon are fully aware that they must increase their knowledge of the two most popular investment vehicles—stocks and bonds. At the present they know very little about each.

The Steeles don't understand fully the differences between a stock and a bond. Bonds seem to offer much better cash returns, and Arnold and Sharon wonder if perhaps they might be better investments than stocks. Then there is preferred stock; what makes it "preferred?" They have a general idea that common stocks are considered the best vehicle for growth, but surely not all common stocks can be considered "growth" stocks.

Arnold and Sharon want to learn enough about investing to achieve a basic understanding of how to evaluate most stocks. They don't hope to become experts, but they do want to be able to understand a company's relative strengths and weaknesses. Additionally, they want to know how to evaluate particular types of bonds. For example, should they buy corporate bonds or Treasury bonds? They have heard that municipal bonds are great for certain investors. Would they be in this category? Finally, should they buy bonds with short or long maturities?

TOPIC LINKS

Follow the **Topic Links** in each chapter for your interactive Personal Finance exercise on the Web. Go to: **www.prenhall.com/frasca**.

The Steeles have some work ahead of them. You do too, if you intend to be an active investor. The rewards, though, may be worth the effort. For one thing, you won't pay professional management fees and other expenses associated with a managed account, such as a mutual fund. And for another, you may show better investment returns. Often so-called "amateur" investors outperform the pros, not because they are smarter but because they bring simplicity to the process and tend to hold their investments for much longer periods of time. For example, many people still hold shares of Wal-Mart or Microsoft from the time these companies first went public. Some are now millionaires, thanks to these investments.

Of course, you can argue that these people were lucky—not informed investors. Sure, luck plays a role, just as it does in a poker game. But you wouldn't sit down at a poker table to test your luck unless you were very familiar with how to play the game. The same is true in investing, and this chapter will familiarize you with the most important "chips" in the investment game—stocks and bonds.

An Overview of Common Stocks

Common stock Shares that give you an ownership interest in a company.

Everybody likes to get in on the ground floor of an emerging growth company, such as Intel or Microsoft. To do this you must buy a company's **common stock**. Although it is riskier than bonds or preferred stock, it gives you a stake in the company's future—for better or worse. A $100 investment in Microsoft's shares in 1986 was worth over $31,000 in mid-2007! And it is safe to say that, with few exceptions, you should buy common stock only when you are willing to risk that its future price will exceed its current price; if you don't think that will happen, then you should invest in something else. Essentially, most common stocks are for the future, but in varying degrees; some are completely growth oriented, others are far less so. This chapter explains common stock investing. Perhaps it will help you find the next Microsoft; but even if it doesn't, it should make you a more informed investor.

Characteristics of Common Stock

Becoming an informed investor begins by learning common stock's basic characteristics. The important ones are explained in the following sections.

Shareholders' Rights

Suppose you were thinking of buying 100 shares of MeadWestvaco Corporation (stock symbol MWV), a packaging company, at around $31 a share in mid-2007. Along with receiving a stock certificate evidencing your ownership, you would have an interest of 0.0000005 (100/184,690,000 outstanding shares) in the company. Although your holding is a minuscule one, you are nevertheless an owner of MWV. And, although you have far less power than someone owning a million shares, you have identical privileges, which are explained below.

The Right to Vote. In most cases your voting right gives you one vote for each share of common stock you own, although some stock is classified as nonvoting. In contrast to voting in political elections, in a corporation you can assign your vote to someone else through a **proxy**. So if you can't make the annual stockholders' meeting where voting takes place, you can return it with your signature, either giving or not giving authority to vote your shares. It is hard to get excited over a voting right if you own 0.0000005 of a company. However, if you and several friends are contemplating going into business and

Proxy An assignment of your voting rights to someone else.

forming a corporation to do so, then be very careful about who owns how many shares and how these shares might be voted in controversial decisions. Hardly anything is more powerless than a minority interest in a corporation, even if that minority is 49 percent. Make sure in these situations to have an attorney's advice before the corporation is formed and shares are distributed.

The Preemptive Right. Your right to maintain a proportionate interest in a company is called the **preemptive right**. If MWV wanted to sell 20 million more shares of common stock to raise capital, you would have the right to buy 10 (0.0000005 × 20,000,000) more shares.

Preemptive right A right to maintain your proportionate interest in a company.

The Right to Share in Earnings or Asset Distributions. Your obvious intent for investing in a company is to receive a return. With common stock you have the right to participate (in proportion to the number of shares you own) in any distribution of earnings or assets. This right is limited, however. For example, most states prohibit any distributions that would impair the firm's capital and subject its creditors (usually bondholders) to greater risk. In addition, if the corporation has any preferred stock outstanding, any current or past unpaid dividends must be paid on it before any distributions are made to common stockholders. This means that, as a common stockholder, you come last in line, behind bondholders and preferred stockholders. You are said to have a **residual claim**; that is, you get what is left. Although this sounds dismal, actually, getting what is left is why you buy common stock in the first place. Bondholders and preferred stockholders have prior claims, but the amounts they are entitled to are fixed each year; that is, regardless of how well (or poorly) the company does, the amount they get is the same. In contrast, the amounts available to common stockholders vary in direct proportion to the company's profits. Figure 11.1 illustrates this relationship.

Residual claim The claim against assets or earnings of common stockholders; the claim comes after the claims of bondholders and preferred stockholders.

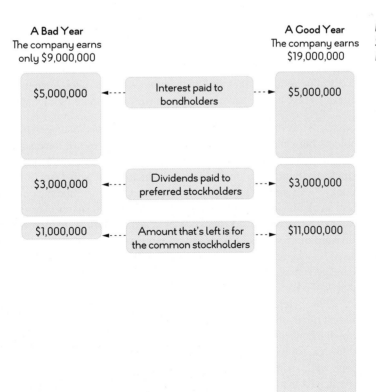

Figure 11.1
Sharing a Company's Earnings

The hypothetical company has bonds outstanding requiring $5,000,000 a year in interest and preferred stock requiring $3,000,000 a year in dividends. This represents $8,000,000 of fixed obligations that must be paid before any earnings are available to common stockholders. If the corporation has a bad year and earnings are only $9,000,000, common stockholders' claims will be $1,000,000. If the corporation has a good year and earnings are $19,000,000, the bondholders' and preferred stockholders' distributions will still total $8,000,000, but common stockholders' claims will now be $11,000,000. It should be noted that the corporation might not pay out all the common stockholders' claims in dividends. In fact, most companies retain a portion of the earnings and reinvest them in the business. For example, in the good year just described, perhaps $5,000,000 would be paid in dividends and $6,000,000 retained. In the bad year, it is possible that no dividends would be paid. However, many companies continue paying common stock dividends, even in very poor years.

Distributions to Shareholders

Although shareholders have a right to share earnings, this does not mean that the corporation pays its shareholders each year a cash amount equal to the annual earnings. Actually, there are various types of distributions corporations make, some in cash and some in shares of the company's stock.

Regular dividend Cash distribution made to shareholders on a regular basis, usually each quarter.

Cash Distributions. As the name implies, cash distributions are cash payments the corporation makes to its shareholders. By far the most common type of cash distribution is the **regular dividend**. Many corporations pay dividends on a regular basis. For example, MWV paid an annual dividend of $0.92 per share since 2002.

Periodic share repurchases Corporate repurchase of shares having a similar effect as cash dividends.

Although less popular, many companies have begun **periodic share repurchases** as a way of distributing cash to shareholders. These plans offer shareholders the right to sell shares back to the corporation at a set price, which is higher than the market price at the time the repurchase offer is made. In 2005 MeadWestvaco sold off its forestry division and used part of the proceeds from the sale in a stock repurchase. In effect, regular repurchases offer the same cash advantage to shareholders as regular cash dividends as long as they don't mind reducing their holdings in the company. (You have the option of selling shares or not.) There can be tax advantages as well with share repurchase.

Stock dividend A dividend paid by issuing additional shares of a company's stock.

Noncash Distributions. In many cases, corporations' managements want to reward shareholders but cannot do so because the business does not have sufficient cash. Frequently, noncash distributions are made, which include stock dividends and stock splits. With a **stock dividend**, you don't receive cash; instead, you receive shares of the company's stock. For example, if you owned 100 shares of MWV and the company declared a 10 percent stock dividend, you would get an additional 10 shares. Are stock dividends attractive? Not really, because every stockholder gets a proportionate increase in shares. All you then have are more shares of stock but no more assets or greater earning potential for the company. As a result, the day a stock dividend is paid, the price of the stock goes down by the same percentage as the percentage increase in the number of shares. Instead of having 100 shares of MWV at, say, $31 a share, you would have 110 shares at $28.18 a share.

Stock split Giving additional shares of stock to current stockholders.

Closely related to a stock dividend is a **stock split**. Here, a company simply gives you and all other stockholders more shares of stock. Two-for-one splits are the most common, which means the number of shares you own doubles. Are stock splits by themselves desirable? No, for the same reasons stock dividends aren't. Granted, many companies that have done well, such as Microsoft, sometimes split their shares to lower the stock's price and broaden its market appeal. But it's not the split that adds value, it's the underlying strength of the company.

Opportunities in Common Stocks

Your opportunities to earn a return with common stocks are as varied as the many different kinds of corporations that issue them. You can buy very conservative stocks with low risk, or you can find those that are extremely risky. The total return you can expect over the long run should reflect your willingness to assume risk—the more you take, the higher your potential return. The following are the different kinds of stocks most investors buy.

Growth Companies. The earnings and dividend-paying potential of a **growth company** are expected to grow at a rate faster than the growth rate of the overall economy. The price of its common stock should also grow rapidly in the future. Of course, there are all sorts of growth companies. Microsoft is one, Google is another. Microsoft represents less risk than Google because it has a good history of achieving growth, and its chances of continuing to do so in the future are very good. Google, on the other hand, is a relative newcomer, but it may have the more rapid growth. If you are interested in buying growth stocks, get as many recommendations as you can from brokers or other advisors, and narrow down the field to 10 or 15 companies that appeal to you.

Growth company A company with expected earnings growth greater than the growth of the overall economy.

Income Stocks. As their name suggests, **income stocks** pay high dividends in relation to their market prices and offer good current rates of return. However, they vary considerably in risk, so be sure to review that characteristic before investing. Because of their capabilities for paying regular cash dividends, public utilities are often considered the best income stocks. In recent years, their dividend yields have been in excess of 7 percent, and some also offer reasonable growth prospects. They are not without risks, though, as investors learned with public utilities that have not been permitted to use nuclear reactors.

Income stocks Stocks that pay high dividends in relation to their market prices.

Blue Chips. The popular expression **blue chip** really doesn't tell you much about a stock. It usually refers to low-risk stocks—those you can count on to deliver the dividend or growth you expected when you bought them. It also usually refers to what are called *high-capitalization stocks*, which means the issuing corporations are very large companies with many millions of shares outstanding. Being a blue chip doesn't guarantee success, however. The New York Central Railroad was the bluest of the blue in the 1920s and bankrupt in the 1960s.

Blue chip A low-risk stock that reliably provides investors with the expected dividend or growth.

Cyclical Stocks. **Cyclical stocks** are stocks that are more responsive to changes in the business cycle than are other stocks. Companies in the capital goods industries, such as the Caterpillar Corporation, are good examples of cyclical stocks. Investors like to "play" cyclical stocks by buying them in recession periods and then selling out as the economy improves. Sounds easy, but it isn't, because it is almost impossible to know when the stock's price is at the bottom of its cycle.

Cyclical stocks Stocks that are highly responsive to changes in the business cycle.

Special Situations. Anything can be a **special situation**, but the most common is when one company is expected to take over another. Almost always these takeovers result in a substantially higher price for the stock of the company taken over. For example, in 2008 Microsoft offered to purchase Yahoo! for a 62 percent premium over its market price. If you can get in on a takeover shortly before the event takes place, the profit opportunity is enormous. Naturally, the trick is to know if and when a takeover will occur. If you don't have inside information, you must rely on opinions of so-called experts in identifying takeover situations. Very often these opinions are no better than random guesses. Other special situations could involve changes in key managers, favorable or unfavorable legal opinions, granting of a license or patent, a new and unexpected invention, and many others. All these events can change a company's financial outlook dramatically and its stock price accordingly.

Special situation Any potentially profitable investment opportunity, but often referring to a possible takeover.

Stock Quotations

Stock quotations are reported in major financial newspapers, such as the *Wall Street Journal*, and in many local newspapers. Over the last decade, most papers have significantly cut back on reporting quotes in an effort to reduce cost. At a minimum, the quotes usually provide the stock's closing price (the price of the last trade of the day) and the number of shares traded (called "volume"). Additional information may include the highest and lowest prices of the day and of the previous 12 months, the change in price from today's closing price to the closing price on the previous trading day, the dividend yield, and the P/E ratio (explained shortly). Figure 11.2 illustrates a quote for MeadWestvaco in mid-2007.

TOPIC LINKS

Find a company's stock symbol and market price.

While newspaper quotes are still useful, investors today clearly use the Internet much more often to obtain quotes and much additional information about a stock. Moreover, these quotes are available throughout the trading today. As an exercise, you should access the Yahoo! (finance.yahoo.com) or Google (finance.google.com) Web site. Click "Finance" and then enter a stock symbol (say, MWV) in the "Quote" box. Then observe the rich amount of information available, both on the current page and on other options available from that page. If you are not sure of a stock's trading symbol, at Yahoo! Finance you can find it by clicking "Symbol Lookup" in the Quote box.

You probably will not understand many of the notations. Some are explained later in this chapter, but you can also access a glossary that defines a large array of terms and expressions. On the Yahoo! Finance page, access "Glossary" at the Education heading under Investing. As in most activities, practice will improve your skills. So, as we sug-

Figure 11.2
How to Read Stock Quotations

52 Weeks High	52 Weeks Low	Stock	Symbol	Div.	Yield %	P-E Ratio	Sales 100s	High	Low	Close	Net Change
19.42	11.01	McMoran	MMR	...	...	dd	10139	15.09	13.96	14.60	0.64
12.48	8.54	Meadowbrook	MIG	...	...	11	5486	9.05	8.59	9.03	0.26
36.50	24.76	Mead	MWV	0.92	2.9	51	17602	31.75	30.97	31.33	-0.31
47.93	19.70	Mechel	MTL	...	...	26	3952	40.77	38.00	40.23	0.24
86.71	47.08	Medco	MHS	...	...	27	28402	84.26	80.25	82.67	1.43
43.94	26.78	Media	MEG	0.92	3	14	7034	31.54	29.45	30.19	0.29
16.70	10.86	Medical	MPW	1.07e	8.8	15	10764	12.68	11.92	12.15	-0.34

36.50	24.76	Mead Corp.		0.92	2.9	51	17602	31.75	30.97	31.33	-0.31
①	②	③		④	⑤	⑥	⑦	⑧	⑨	⑩	⑪

1. The highest price paid per share in the past year, $36.50 for MeadWestvaco.

2. The lowest price paid per share in the last year, $24.76 for MeadWestvaco.

3. The company's name, which may be abbreviated.

4. The indicated regular dividend in the current year based on what the company has paid in the last quarter or six months. Some companies pay extra dividends in good earnings years, but these are not shown. MWV's regular dividend was estimated at $.92 per share. "dd" indicates a loss in the most recent four quarters.

5. The current yield, which is found by dividing the current year's regular dividends by the closing price of the stock. MWV's current yield is 2.9 percent.

6. The price–earnings ratio, which is the company's earnings over its last fiscal year divided by the closing price of the stock. MWV's ratio is 51.

7. The number of shares sold on that day, in hundreds. For example, 17602 means 1,760,200 shares of Mead stock.

8. The highest price paid for the stock that day. MWV's was $31.75.

9. The lowest price paid for the stock that day. MWV's was $30.97.

10. The last price paid that day. MWV's was $31.33.

11. The difference between the closing price that day and the closing price of the previous day. For example, MWV's closing price on the previous day was $.31 higher than the closing price on the reported day.

gested in Chapter 9, put together a simple portfolio and measure your success over some designated period of time. Actually, you can create a portfolio at either Google Finance or Yahoo! Finance that is automatically updated throughout the trading day. The site does all the work, but we see that as a disadvantage in your learning stage. After you gain expertise, delegate the work to the site.

Fundamental Analysis of Common Stocks

What is a stock worth? In mid-2007, MWV was selling at around $31. Was it worth that much, or was it worth more, or less? These are very difficult questions to answer, but investors must at least try; otherwise, securities could sell at any set of prices. You may choose not to undertake value analysis on your own, but even if you rely on professional analysts' opinions, you should be familiar with their techniques. We will consider two basic approaches—application of the CAPM (introduced in Chapter 10) and a price-to-earnings analysis. The section concludes with a discussion of book value. Much of the discussion uses information provided in Table 11.1, which compares MeadWestvaco with two other companies, Kellogg and Intel. All of the data were readily available from the Yahoo! Finance Web site.

TOPIC LINKS

Access fundamental data at Yahoo! Finance.

Application of the CAPM

In Chapter 10 we learned that a stock offers two pertinent returns: (1) a required return, which reflects its individual risk and a risk premium for the overall stock market, and (2) an expected return, which reflects what you as an investor believe the stock will offer in

Table 11.1
Selected Financial Data for Three Companies

Company Ticker Symbol	MeadWestvaco MWV	Kellogg G	Intel INTC
1. Current (mid-2007) stock price	$31.00	$53.00	$24.00
2. Dividends per share (DPS):			
(a) paid over previous 12 months	$0.92	$1.16	$0.44
(b) estimated over next 12 months	$0.92	$1.24	$0.45
3. Earnings per share (EPS):			
(a) earned over previous 12 months	$0.62	$2.70	$0.97
(b) expected over next 12 months	$1.58	$3.03	$1.12
4. Estimated five-year average annual EPS growth	11.0	8.3	17.7
5. Price/Earnings (P/E) ratio			
(a) based over previous 12-month EPS	50.00	19.63	24.74
(b) based on expected 12-month EPS	19.66	17.49	21.43
6. Book value per share	$19.33	$6.06	$6.82
7. Market price to book (line 1 divided by line 6)	1.63	8.74	3.52
8. P/E to growth (PEG) ratio (line 5b divided by line 4)	1.79	2.12	1.21
9. Beta value	1.47	0.27	1.62
10. Weighted average analyst's recommendations (Strong Buy) 1.0 – 5.0 (Strong Sell)	2.5	1.9	1.9

terms of a cash dividend or potential price appreciation. The required return concept was developed thoroughly in Chapter 10; now let's turn our attention to the expected return.

The expected total return, *TR*, is the sum of current return, *CR*, and future return, *FR*; that is,

$$TR = CR + FR$$

Current return (also called the "yield") can be expressed in ratio or percentage form. For example, if you expected to receive a $0.92 dividend on a share of MWV over the next 12 months, and if you paid $31 a share, your expected current return would be 3 percent, calculated as follows:

$$CR\% = \frac{\$0.92}{\$31} = .0297 \text{ or } 3.0\%$$

Earnings as a Source of Dividends

All dividends must come eventually from earnings. If a corporation's dividends exceed the sum of its current earnings and earnings it has accumulated in the past, then it is actually liquidating itself. It is relatively easy for potential investors to estimate a current dividend, because it is also relatively easy to estimate both a company's current earnings and the proportion of those earnings it is likely to distribute. Moreover, many companies indicate what the current dividend will be. But it is not so easy to estimate future earnings and future dividends. How much MeadWestvaco will earn per share in 2008 or 2009 is not an easily answered question. Nor is it easy to know the company's future policy with respect to dividend distributions. MWV might undergo a complete change in the nature of its business, and this change might demand more cash, forcing MWV to cut the proportion of its earnings it pays in dividends.

Expressing Future Return in the Total Return Equation

Bringing future return into the total return equation is done most easily by expressing it as a percentage return, and the most commonly used percentage is the company's expected annual growth in dividends (or earnings) in the future. So, if you thought MeadWestvaco's dividends would grow at an 11 percent annual rate each year in the future, this is its future return percentage. Add this to the current return percentage to arrive at the total return percentage; that is,

$$TR\% = CR\% + FR\% = 3.0\% + 11.0\% = 14.0\%$$

It makes sense to include the dividend growth factor since a stock with a growing dividend should be worth more than one without growth. Moreover, the growth factor allows you to make return comparisons among different stocks with different current return characteristics. For example, MWV's $0.92 dividend will grow to $1.55 in five years at Meadwestvaco's growth rate of 11 percent. But Intel's $0.44 dividend will almost double to $0.87 in five years given an expected growth rate of 17.7 percent. Of course, Intel's advantage grows larger each year thereafter.

Was MeadWestvaco Worth $31 a Share?

To answer this question, recall from the previous chapter the concept of alpha, which is calculated as follows:

$$\text{Alpha} = \text{expected return} - \text{required return}$$

Greater positive values of alpha signal greater investment appeal; conversely, negative alpha values indicate stocks that should not be bought and perhaps should be sold, if you already own them.

Figure 11.3 summarizes the evaluation of MWV. Short-term Treasury bills yielded about 4.5 percent when the analysis was undertaken. In Table 11.1, note that we use MWV's expected growth in earnings, because it generally is the best estimate of future dividend-paying capacity.

Figure 11.3 shows that MWV has a negative alpha value of –2.3 percent. MWV, then, was not a "buy" at the time of the analysis. Investment analysis is not an exact science, and it's quite possible that the estimate of MWV's 11 percent growth rate is too pessimistic.

Financial Analysts' Opinions

Line 10 in Table 11.1 summarizes the opinions of financial analysts who follow the three stocks. These are trained professionals who use a variety of analytical techniques to determine the investment quality of a stock. While their opinions are certainly worth reviewing, you shouldn't buy a stock simply because it has a high rating since the stock may not fit your investment objectives. Moreover, analysts tend to be somewhat optimistic in their growth projections. Also, be careful of a recommendation if it is made by only one or two analysts. It is better to have a weighted average of, say, six or more analysts. The weighted average recommendations in Table 11.1 reflect more than a dozen analysts for each stock. As you see, both Intel and Kellogg receive a higher recommendation than MeadWestvaco. While interpretations can differ, you might consider a 1.0 to 2.0 rating as a buy recommendation, a 2.0 to 3.0 rating as a hold (if you currently own the stock), and anything over 3.0 as a sell rating (if you own the stock).

Price-to-Earnings Analysis

A **price-to-earnings analysis** is a somewhat simpler and more direct approach than the CAPM method. Basically, analysts who follow this approach feel that the price of a share of a company's stock depends entirely on the company's future **earnings per share (EPS)**.

Price-to-earnings analysis A method of valuing common stocks based on a company's expected future earnings.

Required Rate of Return		Expected Rate of Return	
1. Market risk premium	8.0%	1. Current market price of stock per share	$31.00
2. Mead's beta weight	1.47		
		2. Expected dividend	$0.92
3. Mead's risk premium (line 1 × line 2)	11.80%	3. Current yield (line 1 × line 2)	3.0%
4. Risk-free rate on U.S. Treasury Bills	4.50%	4. Expected annual growth in dividends	11.0%
5. Required return (line 3 + line 4)	16.30%	5. Expected rate of return (line 3 + line 4)	14.00%

Difference (alpha) equals –2.3%. The decision is to not buy or sell MWV since its required rate of return is less than the expected rate of return.

Figure 11.3
Comparing MWV's Required Rate of Return with Its Expected Rate of Return, Mid August 2007

Earnings per share (EPS) A company's total earnings divided by the total number of shares of common stock outstanding.

EPS is simply the company's total earnings divided by the total number of shares of common stock outstanding.

Analysts also use a **price-earnings (P/E) ratio**, which reflects how much a stock is worth in relation to its EPS; that is,

$$\text{P/E ratio} = \frac{\text{stock's price}}{\text{EPS}}$$

Price-earnings (P/E) ratio The price of a company's stock divided by the company's earnings per share.

So if a stock earns $1.50 per share and if a P/E ratio of 12.0 seems appropriate for valuation purposes, rearranging the foregoing equation shows that the stock's price should be $18 a share:

$$\text{Stock's price} = \text{EPS} \times \text{P/E ratio}$$
$$\$18 = \$1.50 \times 12$$

A price-to-earnings analysis is only as good as the analyst's estimates of EPS and the P/E ratio. Further discussion of each is needed.

finance news 11.1

Financial Analysts: Do They Help or Hinder?

Financial analysts are professional people whose main function is to evaluate companies with respect to their financial strengths and weaknesses. The end product of their work is a research report that includes rating companies as to whether they are buys, holds (if you already own them), or sells. Some analysts are independent operators, but most are employed by large financial institutions, particularly large stockbrokerage firms. On balance, analysts do a good job and are an important component in the overall investment process. Certainly, their efforts make the process more efficient than it would be in their absence. However, in recent years problems have surfaced that should prompt investors to be cautious when following analysts' opinions.

Appearing before the House Financial Services Subcommittee, Chairperson of the SEC, Laura Ungar, testified that nearly 30 percent of analysts whom the SEC surveyed owned shares in companies they covered. On the face of it, this should not necessarily be cause for concern; indeed, you can make a case that "putting their money where their mouths are" makes analysts' opinions more credible. However, the SEC report also noted that some analysts made between $300,000 and $3.5 million trading against their own advice—selling their shares while telling us to buy. Surely, an ethical issue seems at play here.

Another study, involving four years of data, prepared by **Investars.com** (a subscription online investment service) showed that investors lost 53.34 percent by following the advice of analysts whose firms led or comanaged an IPO versus a loss of 4.24 percent by following nonaffiliated analysts. (IPO stands for initial public offering—the first time a company's shares are sold to the public.) Although the latter figure is hardly encouraging, the former is absolutely dreadful.

The securities industry has paid over $1.4 billion to settle claims arising from past abuses, and Congress passed the Sarbanes–Oxley Act in 2002 in an attempt to curb abuses in the future. Chief executives and chief financial officers personally must now certify that financial statements are complete and accurate, under penalty of jail time. How has Sarbanes–Oxley worked so far? While a full evaluation will take time, we do know that the distribution of analyst ratings has changed dramatically. In early May 2004, about 9 percent of all ratings were "sell" or "under perform"; in 2000, not even 1 percent was in these categories. Some indication remains, though, that investment banking clients are viewed more favorably than non-clients. Sarbanes–Oxley didn't prevent the subprime mortgage crisis in 2007 or previous stock option backdating scandals. Moreover, Professors Begley and Cheng of the University of British Columbia and Professor Gao of the University of Alberta find that Sarbanes–Oxley may have traded off reliability for less information, reducing the quality of forecasts by financial analysts.

If you are considering investing in a particular company, you should review not only the overall ratings for the company but determine if your broker's rating is in step with most others, and if the firm has any financial connections with the recommended company. You are entitled to that information and should ask for it.

Use Future (Not Past) EPS Amounts

Past earnings, though interesting from a historical perspective or in helping to forecast future earnings, are not integral in the valuation process. In a sense, past earnings have already been distributed or used by the company. So their impact on the company's value has already been felt. But future earnings can influence this value by being greater or less than past earnings. To use a sports example: You wouldn't pay a top price for athletes who are in the twilight of their careers, no matter how great they may have been in their prime. This seems a bit harsh, but the investment world is brutal. The moment a stock fails to live up to investors' expectations, its price falls dramatically as investors rush to "dump" the stock.

What Is an Appropriate P/E Value?

Determining a P/E ratio to apply to future EPS amounts is unquestionably the most troublesome task in using a price-to-earnings analysis. We must carefully distinguish between a calculated P/E ratio and an appropriate P/E ratio to use. For example, MWV's P/E ratio of 50.0 is based on past year's earnings (line 3a in Table 11.1). Similarly, the P/E ratio of 19.66 reflects the expected next year EPS amount. Both are calculated ratios. Now, analysts may use these P/E ratios in a comparative way to determine if a company is over or undervalued. For example, other packaging companies may show P/E ratios (based on next year's earnings) of, say, about 17. In this comparative sense, then, MWV's ratio is rather high.

Continuing the example, let us say that the other paper companies' P/E ratios have an average value of 17. If we think this average should apply to MWV, then we are using an appropriate ratio to value MWV, and we call the resulting number MeadWestvaco's **fundamental value**. In the example, it is $26.86. To reinforce the concept:

Fundamental value A stock value based on the underlying strengths of a company.

$$\text{Fundamental value} = (\text{appropriate P/E ratio}) \times (\text{next year's EPS})$$
$$= 17 \times \$1.58$$
$$= \$26.86$$

Since MWV is selling at $31 a share, it is clearly overvalued and should be sold. Of course, you can question if using the average is a reasonable approach. To the extent that there might be considerable manufacturing, marketing, and financial differences among the firms, using an average accomplishes very little. Still, if not the average—then what?

The PEG Ratio

Some analysts think that a company's future growth rate (expressed as a number rather than as a percent) should serve as a reasonable estimate of an appropriate P/E ratio. Applying this logic to MWV leads to a very low value of $17.38 (11 × $1.58), since MWV's growth rate is only 11.0. In common with most price-to-earnings approaches, this one also fails to consider a stock's riskiness. Two companies with equal earnings and growing at the same rate may have very different market values if they differ in risk.

Despite its shortcomings, analysts often compare a company's P/E ratio to its growth rate. This comparison is called the **PEG ratio**. MWV's PEG ratio is calculated next:

PEG ratio The ratio of a stock's P/E ratio to the expected annual rate of growth of earnings per share (EPS).

$$\text{PEG ratio} = \text{P/E ratio}/\text{growth}$$
$$= 19.66/11 = 1.79$$

All other things held equal, the lower the number, the more attractive the stock. The basic idea is not to pay too much for growth. For example, Kellogg's PEG ratio is 2.12 and Intel's is 1.21. Unfortunately, there is no simple answer to the question of what is "too much." While Intel's ratio is attractive, it also is the most risky of the three companies, as measured by beta.

Fundamental Value and Book Value

Book value A company's net
worth divided by the number
of common stock shares outstanding.

Investors often refer to a company's **book value**, which is determined by dividing a company's net worth by the number of shares of common stock outstanding. The net worth of
a business is measured in the same way that someone's personal net worth is measured;
that is, net worth equals total assets minus total liabilities. (Refer to Chapter 3 if you need
to review the concept.) Table 11.1 shows MWV's book value in line 6. As you see, MWV
had a book value of $19.33 at mid- 2007.

Book Value's Limitations

If MeadWestvaco's book value is only $19.33, why should anyone pay $31? The answer is
that book value often is a poor estimate of fundamental value. Book value reflects the his-

FINANCIAL PLANNING *for*
young adults 11.2

Is It Time to Begin a Self-Directed Stock Portfolio?

You have saved a little money and you want to try your hand at
picking stocks. Your desire to invest is spurred on by stories of
how others have made a killing on some recent prized stock.
Every office has a braggart who likes to impress others with his
or her stock market successes. Those same individuals, however, may be shy about sharing stories on the losing picks. Even
worse, stockaholics honestly forget losses, and only think of
wins.

Before you take on any added risks, make sure you have first
undertaken a comprehensive overview of your personal financial plan. That means reviewing the financial concerns discussed elsewhere in this book. For example, have you set aside a
sufficient emergency fund and do you have adequate life and
health insurance? If you can answer yes to those questions then
you might consider whether you have enough to invest in a
self-directed portfolio of stocks and bonds.

You don't need much to open an account with a broker.
Some require a $2,000 minimum, but you can find discount
brokers on the Internet that will establish a trading account for
much less than that. The downside is that if you only have a
small amount to invest, your returns may be eaten up with
trading fees and you are not likely to be adequately diversified.

Some investment advisors will tell you that you can achieve
adequate diversification with as few as 10 to 15 stocks. With less
than that you are accepting high levels of risk and you are gambling rather than investing. Experienced professionals such as
Professor Malkiel at Princeton University, who wrote the best-
selling book on the market, *A Random Walk Down Wall Street*,
will argue you need much wider diversification. Not only must

you diversify across industries, but you should also diversify
across stocks, bonds and real estate, both domestically and
internationally. Such diversification is difficult to achieve on a
limited budget with individually selected investments.

Young adults with limited amounts to invest should first
consider pooling arrangements like the mutual funds discussed
in Chapter 12. They can offer adequate diversification on minimal investments. Probably your best investment is a mutual
fund offered through your employer as part of a 401(k) retirement account. Many employers match employee contributions up to a specified percentage of salary. If your employer
adds $0.50 for every dollar you contribute, that's an immediate
50 percent return on your money. You will be hard pressed to
find a better return than that. In a 2006 study of defined contribution plans, including 401(k) accounts managed by the
Vanguard Group, about 89 percent of the plans included
matching contributions by employers. Unfortunately, younger
workers were much less likely to participate in these plans, forgoing a significant return on their investments. The participation
rate was 71 percent among those age 45–54, but only 27 percent of those younger than age 25.

We don't mean to discourage you from creating a self-
directed stock portfolio. Many individuals find this fun and challenging. In addition to having a better understanding of how
individual firms operate, you are also likely to gain a broader
appreciation for our market economy and political system.
However, it is best to start out slowly as you develop your
financial skills and appreciate the associated risk-return trade-
off. Starting out with investments in mutual funds and then
moving to an individually selected stock portfolio when you
have accumulated sufficient funds is a wise first move.

torical costs of a company's assets, which may be poor indicators of the current or replacement costs of those assets. Moreover, what a company paid for an asset may have little connection to the asset's ability to generate future cash inflows to the company. Also, perhaps the most valuable of all assets—a company's goodwill—is not even shown on its balance sheet. What is the brand name Coca-Cola worth? If you guess "a lot," you are correct; it's probably worth far more than all of Coke's other assets combined. Yet it is not listed on Coke's balance sheet. These limitations make book value a poor estimate of fundamental value in most cases.

Market-to-Book Ratios

However, it would be a mistake to conclude that book value has no use whatsoever. If, over time, the price of a company's stock increases (or decreases) more rapidly than its book value increases (or decreases), we might want to know why. If there is no underlying explanation, then perhaps the stock is being overvalued (or undervalued) in the market. So analysts often examine a company's **market-to-book ratio**, which is simply market price divided by book value. MWV's ratio is 1.63 as shown in line 7 of Table 11.1.

Market-to-book ratio The market price of a common stock divided by its book value.

Most stocks have market-to-book ratios greater than 1.0, and these values change considerably over time. For example, since 1960, the average ratio for the 500 stocks in the Standard & Poor's 500 Stock Average (the S&P 500) has varied from 1.13 (1982) to 6.98 (2000). In mid-2007 it was 3.77.

All other things being equal, analysts prefer low market-to-book values rather than high values. Indeed, some analysts feel that you will find more undervalued stocks if you limit your analyses to companies with low ratios. If you follow their advice you might be attracted to MeadWestvaco, and you probably would ignore Kellogg and Intel. Many other analysts argue that could be a big mistake. Their view is probably the correct one, since there is no reason to limit your perspective in searching for good investments. Try to apply the CAPM or price-to-earnings method to any company. Be careful, though, if a company seems terribly undervalued. Our introductory treatment of valuation cannot cover all possible problems. If you are going to make your own stock selections, you really should learn more about investments. Taking an investments course at a university would be very helpful.

Calculating Your Capital Gain or Loss

Successful investors must share their gains with the government. On the other hand, unsuccessful investors get a tax advantage by writing off their losses. You need to document both your gains and losses, so be sure to keep all documents indicating what stock you bought, when you bought it, and related commissions and fees.

Your capital gain or loss is the difference between your net sale price from the stock less the stock's cost basis. The cost basis is the purchase price of the stock plus any cost of purchase, including commissions, recording, and transfer fees. There are special rules for calculating the cost basis of stocks given as gifts or as part of a death estate. The net sale price is the sale price less commissions and other sales fees.

TOPIC LINKS

IRS on capital gains and losses.

Long-term and short-term gains and losses are reported separately. The short-term holding period is one year or less. The holding period for long-term gains or losses is more than one year. Net short-term gains are taxed at ordinary income tax rates; whereas, net long-term gains receive favorable tax treatment at reduced rates. If you have a net gain in one holding period and a net loss in the other, there are complicated rules for determining the tax treatment on your overall net gain. However, if you have an overall net loss you can deduct up to $3,000 against other ordinary income. Losses exceeding this amount may be carried over to the next tax year.

Corporate-Issued Bonds

Corporations raise far more money selling bonds to investors than they do selling common stocks. Think of a bond as an IOU; that is, a piece of paper proclaiming the fact that its issuer acknowledges owing you money and agreeing to repay your loan at some future date along with interest at periodic intervals. This idea seems simple enough, but there are numerous details that must be addressed, particularly with corporate bonds.

TOPIC LINKS

Find information on corporate bonds.

Your Rights as a Bondholder

Just as stockholders have certain rights, so do bondholders. Bondholders' rights are described clearly in a document that accompanies each bond issue—the **bond indenture**. The indenture is actually a contract between the issuing institution and the bondholders. In some respects it is similar to a loan agreement you sign when you borrow from a bank. Since it is impossible for the issuer to have an individual contract with each bondholder, the indenture acts as a comprehensive contract covering all bondholders. To see that the issuer lives up to its agreements in the indenture, a trustee (which is usually a large commercial bank) is appointed to represent bondholders.

Because of the risk of bankruptcy, many bond indentures contain **protective covenants** (restrictions) to strengthen the bondholders' position. Perhaps the best protection is provided by **mortgage bonds**, which are secured by collateral. In the event of bankruptcy, the bondholders' interest is protected by the pledged property, which does not have to be shared with other creditors or stockholders.

Bonds without supporting collateral are called **debentures**, and there are still other bonds that offer even less protection. These are called **subordinated debentures**. If you buy this kind of bond, your claim to assets in liquidation are subordinated to (meaning they come after) the claims of another issue.

Bond indenture Document accompanying a bond issue— a contract between the issuer and bondholders.

Protective covenants Restrictions placed on a bond issuer designed to strengthen the bondholders' position.

Mortgage bonds Bonds secured by collateral.

Debentures Bonds not secured by collateral.

Subordinated debentures Bonds with claims given to other bond issues.

Payment Characteristics of Bonds

Regardless of who issues them, bonds have many similar characteristics. The most important of these is the **fixed return**. Let's look at the return components in greater detail.

Fixed return A return of a specific dollar amount each year, characteristic of bonds and preferred stock.

Face Value

The **face value** of a bond is the amount for which the issuer agrees to redeem the bond at its maturity. When a bond is issued, it has a set life; for example, a 25-year bond means the bond may not be redeemed by its issuer until 25 years after the date it is issued.

Practically all corporate bonds sold to the public have the same face value—$1,000— although some (mostly those issued by various governments) have higher face values. When a bond series is issued, the issuer attempts to adjust its interest rate so that it can be sold *at par*, which means it is sold at the face value. However, bonds issued in the past and currently traded on bond markets may have market prices completely different from their face values, because interest rates may have increased or decreased since their issuance.

Face value An amount for which a bond is redeemed at maturity.

Semiannual Interest Payments

Most bonds pay interest twice a year and are referred to as **coupon bonds**. The amount of interest you receive is stated on the bond and expressed as a percentage of par value. For example, a 12 percent bond pays $120 a year ($1,000 × 0.12) in interest, or $60 each six months. This rate is often called the **coupon rate**. This term is a carryover from the past,

Coupon bonds Bonds that pay periodic interest.

Coupon rate Stated interest rate on a bond.

when most bonds were coupon bonds and you received interest by clipping coupons from the bond and presenting them to a bank for payment. Since all corporate bonds now are registered, rather than coupon bonds, the interest checks come directly to you, or to your broker if your certificates are held at a firm.

Zero Coupon Bonds

A **zero coupon bond** (zero, for short) pays no semiannual interest; you earn interest by buying the bond at less than face value and receiving face value at redemption. For example, you buy a bond for $940 today and redeem it for $1,000 one year later. The interest earned is $60 in this case, and the percentage return (yield) is 6.38 percent ([$60/$940] × 100). Zero coupon bonds have increased considerably in popularity in recent years, primarily because investors like to hold them for retirement funds.

Zero coupon bond A bond that pays no periodic interest; all interest is earned at the bond's redemption.

Zeros are issued in a wide array of maturities, some as long as 40 years. For any given yield, the longer a bond's maturity the bigger the difference between its price and its redemption value, called the discount. So, a two-year zero with a 6.38 percent yield would have a price of $883.60 and a discount of $116.40 ($1,000.00 – $883.60). We'll discuss valuation methods for both coupon bonds and zeros more fully later in this chapter.

Retirement Methods

Although many bond issues have long maturities, in reality most such bonds are retired (terminated) long before their maturity dates. There are three retirement methods: redemption at maturity or by a call from the issuer, through the operation of a sinking fund, or with a conversion of the bond into shares of the issuer's common stock.

Redemption at Maturity or Earlier

As previously mentioned, the issuer agrees to redeem your bond at its maturity. However, many corporate bonds (and some government bonds) can be redeemed earlier at the discretion of the issuer. These **callable bonds** allow the issuer an earlier redemption, and such redemption usually takes place at a price above face value. For example, a bond may be callable at $1,100. Corporations attach calls to bonds to give them greater flexibility in future financing. However, the call feature may be a disadvantage to investors, who should review the call situation before buying a bond.

Callable bonds Bonds that can be redeemed before their maturities.

Sinking Funds

Another retirement method involves the use of a **sinking fund**, which consists of reserving funds for the purpose of gradually retiring bonds before their maturity. Most sinking funds operate through a plan stipulating that a portion of the bonds in a bond issue be retired each year. This gradual retirement of an issue provides greater safety to bondholders as opposed to having all the bonds redeemable at one time.

Sinking fund A system for gradual retirement of a bond issue.

The Convertible Feature

A particularly attractive bond to potential common stock investors is the convertible bond. A **convertible bond** may be redeemed, but it may also be converted into shares of the issuing corporation's common stock. For example, a bond may convert into 20 shares of the company's common stock. Convertible bonds are quite different from conventional bonds. They offer potentially higher returns by virtue of their conversion privilege, but they are also riskier.

Convertible bond Bond that can be converted into shares of the issuer's common stock.

Investing in Corporate Bonds

After you have a reasonable understanding of bond valuation techniques, you might decide to be a corporate bond investor. At this point, you must become familiar with the mechanics of making your investments.

Trading Costs

The cost to trade corporate bonds can be quite high. First, you typically buy bonds through a stockbrokerage firm and, of course, pay a commission. The amount varies from one firm to the next, but expect to pay a cost of $25 to $40 per bond if you buy one bond. The cost per bond goes down substantially if you increase the size of your order.

Most securities, including bonds, are traded in the market at bid and asked prices. A bid price is the highest price a buyer is willing to pay to buy a bond; the asked price is the lowest price a seller will take to sell it. The asked price is always higher than the bid price, and the difference is called the *spread*. So if you buy a bond, you will pay the asked price, but you receive only the bid price when you sell. The trouble with bonds is that the spread often is large, sometimes as much as $50 per bond. Obviously, the spread adds to your trading cost and certainly discourages frequent trading. As with common stocks, if you invest in bonds you should have a long investment horizon.

Pooling Arrangements May Be Best

Along with the potential for high trading costs, bond investors must constantly be on guard to determine if their bonds have been called. Failing to meet a call does not mean you lose the value of your bond, but it does mean that you lose any interest payments that were scheduled to be made after the call date.

All things considered, investing in bonds should perhaps be left to investment professionals. Not only can they operate with much smaller trading costs and follow individual bond issues more closely, but they also are able to diversify far more effectively. We are better off by simply investing in a mutual fund, or other pooling arrangement, that invests in bonds. We'll cover these investment vehicles in Chapter 12.

Government–Issued Bonds

As previously noted, corporations raise huge sums of money each year by selling bonds, but government units raise even more. You have heard of the national debt, which the government is trying to reduce. We discuss the variety of government-issued bonds in the following sections.

U.S. Treasury Securities

U.S. Treasury securities are the most popular investment vehicles in the world. They are owned by investors throughout all parts of the world and are actively traded 24 hours a day. Treasury securities are issued in three forms: Treasury bills, with maturities of one year or less; Treasury notes, with maturities from 2 to 10 years; and Treasury bonds, with maturities from 10 to 30 years. Treasury bills are held for liquidity purposes as discussed in Chapter 5, so we will focus on bonds and notes. Also, the term *Treasury bonds* (T-bonds, for short, or simply Treasuries) is often used to describe both notes and bonds, and we will make no distinction between the two in our discussion. With the exception of maturity, notes and bonds are identical.

TOPIC LINKS
Access TreasuryDirect.

T-Bond Payments

T-bonds are issued only in coupon form, and they pay semiannual interest. As with corporate bonds, par value is $1,000, and interest payments depend on the coupon rate. For example, an 8 percent bond pays $40 interest each six-month period. The market price of the bond is determined at auction; consequently, it can vary from the par value. Since T-bonds have no default risk, their yields always are lower than all other comparable-maturity bonds. Table 11.2 shows a variety of bond yields in 2004 and 2007 and, as you see, Treasuries' yields are the lowest in each year with the exception of municipal bond yields. An income tax advantage explains this oddity, and we'll discuss it later.

Type of Bond	2004	2007
Corporate bonds: best quality	5.82%	5.73%
Medium quality	6.62	6.65
U.S. Treasury bonds	5.24	5.19
General obligation municipal bonds	4.51	4.71

Table 11.2
Various Bond Yields at Mid-August 2004 and 2007

SIMPLIFYING financial planning 11.3

Buy Treasuries Directly

Investors throughout the world consider U.S. Treasury-issued securities the bedrock of safety. Actually, from a safety perspective a Treasury security is the same as currency itself; the major difference is that one pays interest and the other does not. Despite the advantages, unfortunately, small investors seldom buy Treasuries, primarily because they are unaware of how easy it is through a government program called Treasury Direct.

That might change in the future, though, since buying Treasuries now can be done directly through the Treasury, eliminating the middleman and the usual buy/sell commissions. Over 1 million Americans are currently using the Treasury Direct program, and the number is growing rapidly. Government securities available through Treasury Direct include Treasury Bills, Notes, Treasury Inflation-Protected Securities (TIPS), Bonds and savings bonds.

It's simple to sign up at **www.treasurydirect.gov**. Treasury Direct does not provide paper account statements. All information is provided electronically. You can buy securities and manage your account online, transferring funds between your Treasury account and your bank account. You may even have an automatic payroll deduction sent electronically to your Treasury Direct account. Treasuries are sold at auctions, and you must be sure to submit the application before the auction day. Your application is referred to as a "noncompetitive tender," which means that you agree to accept the average yield that arises from competitive bidding at the auction.

Interest paid on the securities each six months will be forwarded from your Treasury Direct account to your bank, as will the redemption of the securities at their maturity. What could be easier? Here is a brief summary of Treasury securities:

Security Name	Maturity	Minimum Investment	Interest Information
U.S. Treasury bills	Up to 1 year	$1,000 (cashier's check)	Interest is earned via a discount from $1,000
U.S. Treasury notes	2–10 years	$1,000–$5,000 (personal check)	Interest is paid semiannually
U.S. Treasury bonds	10–30 years	$1,000 (personal check)	Interest is paid semiannually

U.S. Treasury Strips

Although the Treasury does not issue zero coupon bonds, it provides a mechanism that allows large brokerage firms to create such bonds, and these are called **U.S. Treasury Strips** (STRIPS, for short). The creation process is somewhat involved and of little concern to investors; however, they are indeed concerned that STRIPS also be free of default risk. And they are. As with zero coupon corporate bonds, but to a much greater extent, Treasury Strips are an appealing vehicle for retirement investments.

U.S. Treasury Inflation-Indexed Bonds

In 1996, the Treasury issued a new class of bonds, called **inflation-indexed Treasury bonds**. This bond is unique in that its redemption value will be adjusted each year to keep pace with inflation. For example, assume that on January 2, 2008, you bought one at its face value of $1,000. Suppose, then, that inflation for 2008 is determined to be 3 percent; then the redemption value of the bond is adjusted upwards to $1,030. Such an adjustment would occur each year until the bond's maturity. So, if inflation was 10 percent in 2009, the bond's redemption value would be increased to $1,133 ($1.10 \times \$1,030$).

The assurance that your investment's value will not be ravaged by inflation is clearly an advantage over traditional bonds with fixed redemption amounts. But, of course, there is a catch: The inflation-indexed bonds offer lower coupon interest payments than conventional Treasuries. The extent of the difference varies over time and was around 2.5 percent at mid-August 2007 on the 30-year bond.

U.S. Agency Bonds

Agencies of the federal government besides the Treasury also issue notes and bonds, which are referred to as **agency bonds**. There are two types of agency bonds—those that are virtually identical to Treasury bonds and those related to mortgage and other forms of lending. The former are referred to as conventional agency bonds, and the latter are called mortgage-backed bonds.

Conventional Agency Bonds

Conventional agency bonds have the same features as coupon Treasury bonds, and their prices are also reported in the financial pages. Although considered by most investors to be also free of default risk, these bonds usually offer a slightly higher yield. The difference is explained by poorer liquidity in the sense that there is less trading of agency bonds and greater bid-asked price spreads. Investors who do not trade bonds frequently perhaps can ignore this lack of liquidity and go for agencies' better yields.

Mortgage-Backed Bonds

Certain agencies of the federal government are involved in the credit industry. For example, you may buy a home and finance it with a mortgage loan from a local bank. Although you may never know it, the bank might sell the mortgage to the Government National Mortgage Association (GNMA), which buys many similar loans and holds them in what is called a "pool." GNMA then issues bonds to investors on the basis of the payments being collected in the pool. The cash collected by the pool is distributed (said to be "passed through") to the investors; in this fashion, the bonds are supported by the mortgages and so are called **mortgage-backed bonds**. Such bonds issued by the GNMA are called "Ginnie Maes." Although not a mortgage loan, your student loan has probably been sold by the lending bank to the Student Loan Marketing Association, which creates bonds (called

"Sallie Maes") that are supported by pools of student loans. The complexities of mortgage-backed bonds offer a strong incentive to invest in them through a mutual fund rather than on your own. The recent crisis in subprime mortgages may adversely affect some bond pools that have heavily invested in the low end of the housing market.

Municipal Bonds

Municipal bonds (referred to as munis) are bonds issued by state and local governmental units to finance their capital spending programs. An average of about $200 billion of municipal bonds is issued each year, and they are very popular with investors in high tax brackets. The easiest way to invest is through an exchanged traded fund discussed in Chapter 12, such as Standard & Poor's National Municipal Bond Index iShare (MUB) and Lehman Municipal Bond SPDR (TFI).

Municipal bonds Bonds issued by state and local governments.

TOPIC LINKS

Get information on the municipal bond market.

Types of Municipal Bonds

If a muni bond issue is supported by the full taxing authority of the issuing governmental unit, it is a **general obligation (GO) bond**; if it is supported only by the revenues that a particular capital project generates, it is a **revenue bond**. In general, GO bonds offer better protection than revenue bonds and, therefore, are safer investments. As you might guess, GO bond yields, such as those shown in Table 11.2, are a bit lower than revenue bonds.

    Munis are issued in coupon and zero coupon form with face values usually $5,000. You should realize that munis can have default risk even though they are issued by a government. It is not uncommon for municipalities to default on their bond issues.

General obligation (GO) bond A municipal bond supported by the full taxing authority of the issuing governmental unit.

Revenue bond A municipal bond supported by the revenues of a particular project.

The Income Tax Advantage

Any interest received from a municipal bond is free of federal income tax. Municipals issued by your state are probably also exempt from your state income tax. This is a major advantage for munis versus taxable bonds. The muni yields in Table 11.2 are the lowest of all shown. However, to put them on a comparable footing with the other bond yields, you need to adjust for the income tax differential. To do this, we calculate a muni's **pretax equivalent yield**, which is the yield a taxable bond must offer before taxes to have the same after-tax yield as the muni. The pretax equivalent yield (*PTEY*), considering a 28 percent investor's marginal tax rate (*MTR*), is calculated as follows:

Pretax equivalent yield A pretax yield a taxable bond must offer to have the same after-tax yield as a municipal bond.

$$PTEY = \frac{\text{muni yield}}{1.0 - MTR}$$

So the 4.51 percent muni yield in 2004 has the pretax equivalent yield of 6.26 percent (4.51%/[1.0 − 0.28] = 4.51%/0.72). A similar calculation for 2007 provides 6.54 percent (4.71%/0.72). When adjusted for taxes, the muni yields in Table 11.2 are among the highest each year.

Return and Risk Characteristics of Bonds

Clearly, there are reasons why bond investment is so popular. Although young people tend to favor common stocks, seeking their long-term growth, other investors are drawn to the more certain cash payments bonds offer. But there is substantial risk in bond investing, and informed investors of all ages must understand its sources and how it operates. The following sections explain both return and risk characteristics of bonds.

Expected Return from Bonds

If you bought a bond at its face value when it was issued and eventually redeemed it at its face value, then your return would consist exclusively of the semiannual interest payments you would receive each year. The preceding situation may not happen, however. You may buy the bond for more or less than its face value; doing that leads to a capital loss or gain if you hold it to maturity. Or you may sell the bond before maturity, and the price you receive will probably be different—perhaps quite different—from your purchase price. Therefore, just as with common stocks, a bond's return may consist of both a current return and a future return. Each must be considered in evaluating investment performance.

Current Return or Current Yield

Current yield A bond's annual interest divided by its market price.

The current return with a bond comes from the semiannual interest payments. This is often expressed in percentage form and is called the **current yield**. To calculate the current yield, all you need to do is divide the annual interest by the current market price of the bond. Suppose you have a bond that pays $120 a year interest: If its current market price is $1,000, then its current yield is 12 percent ($120/$1,000). If its price is $900, its current yield will be 13.3 percent ($120/$900). The formula is

$$\text{Current yield} = \frac{\$I}{\$P}$$

where

I = annual interest
P = current market price

If you refer to the financial section of many newspapers, you will notice that current yields are reported for corporate bonds. Although that information is helpful, you usually want to know more about a bond's return than the current yield. You also want to determine its yield to maturity.

Yield to Maturity

Yield to maturity A yield measurement that considers a bond's annual interest plus price appreciation or depreciation if the bond is held to maturity.

In addition to current yield, bond investors often are interested in a bond's **yield to maturity**, which may differ from current yield. A yield to maturity is the return you would earn by buying a bond today and holding it until it is redeemed by the issuer. A precise calculation of yield to maturity requires the use of a financial calculator or a computer spreadsheet, but a close approximation is possible using the following formula:

$$\text{Yield to maturity} = \frac{\$I + \left(\$1{,}000 - \$P\right)/N}{\left(\$P + \$1{,}000\right)/2}$$

where

I = annual interest
P = current market price
N = number of years remaining to maturity

It is assumed that the bond has a face value of $1,000. Let's return to the bond mentioned previously and assume that its market price is $900 and that it has five years to maturity. Its yield to maturity is 14.7 percent, as calculated next:

$$\frac{\$120 + \left(\$1{,}000 - \$900\right)/5}{\left(\$900 + \$1{,}000\right)/2} = \frac{\$140}{\$950} = 0.147, \text{ or } 14.7\%$$

Present Value of a Coupon Bond

Bond investors often determine a bond's present value. This task is performed quickly with a financial calculator, but it can also be accomplished with present value tables. Recall from Chapter 2 that a present value is simply a discounted future value. To review, if you expected to receive $1,000 one year from today, and if you felt you could earn 10 percent interest on your money, then the $1,000 has a present value of $909.10. You find this amount by multiplying the future value by the present-value-of-$1 factor from Table A.3 in the Appendix at the end of the text. Referring to that table, go to the 10 percent column and the period 1 row; you read 0.9091, and 0.9091 × $1,000 = $909.10.

Remember that discounting is simply the opposite of compounding. So if you invested $909.10 today to earn 10 percent for one year, your accumulation (compounded value) is $1,000 ($909.10 × 1.10 = $1,000).

Table 11.3 shows the present value calculation for the five-year coupon bond we are discussing, using a 15 percent interest rate. The bond has a present value of $899.46, which is approximately its price of $900. Notice that the bond provides two sources of cash inflow: (1) the annual interest of $120 for five years, and (2) the $1,000 redemption value at the end of the fifth year. For simplicity, we assume that the bond pays annual, rather than semiannual, interest. Also, interest is assumed to be paid at the end of each year.

A Quicker Method for Finding Present Value

Table 11.3 is used to illustrate the process of finding a coupon bond's present value. However, a quicker solution uses the present-value-of-$1 annuity table (Table A.4 in the Appendix at the end of the text). There are two operations. First, from Table A.4 find the present value of a $1 annuity for 15 percent and 5 years; it is 3.3522. Multiply this number by the annual interest to find the present value of the coupon interest cash inflows— $402.26 (3.3522 × $120). Second, find the present value of the future redemption value, which has already been done in Table 11.3. The value is $497.20. Add the two present values to arrive at the total present value of $899.46. This quicker method is very desirable if you are examining bonds with long maturities.

$$\begin{array}{rcl}
\text{present value of \$1 annuity factor} \times \text{interest payment} & & \\
3.3522 \times \$120 & = & \$402.26 \\
\text{present value of \$1 factor} \times \text{redemption value} & & \\
0.4972 \times \$1,000 & = & \underline{497.20} \\
\text{Bond's present value} & = & \$899.46
\end{array}$$

Present Value of a Zero Coupon Bond

Finding the present value of a zero coupon bond is very simple since there are no coupon interest payments to consider. The only cash inflow to discount is the future redemption value of $1,000. For example, the present value of a five-year zero discounted at 15 percent is $497.20. Once again, you find this value in Table 11.3.

Present Value and Yield to Maturity

If the bond's cash inflows are discounted by the bond's yield to maturity, the present value is the same as the bond's price. Indeed, the yield to maturity should be viewed as the precise discount rate that equates a bond's price to the sum of its discounted future cash flows. For most practical purposes, 15 percent can be considered the true yield to maturity on the coupon bond since $899.46 is almost $900. Also, we can see that the 14.7 percent estimate using the approximation method is a fairly close estimate.

However, a bond's future cash inflows can be discounted using any rate that the investor feels is relevant. For example, suppose that you are convinced that interest rates will fall in the future and that very shortly our example coupon bond will have a yield to maturity of only 9 percent. What will be its new present value? To find the answer, simply consult Table A.3 in the Appendix at the end of the text and obtain PV of $1 factors from the 9 percent column. Substitute these values for those in Table 11.3 and calculate the new present value. Your answer should be $1,116.65. So, if you are right in your assessment of future interest rates, this bond's price will increase by $216.75 ($1,116.75 – $900.00). But if you are wrong, its price will fall. This potential price volatility is unquestionably a serious risk element that deserves more attention.

Risks of Bond Investment

If you buy a bond, you face two major sources of risk. First, unless you are investing in Treasury or agency bonds, the bond's issuer may default on paying interest or redeeming the bond at maturity. Second, all bond prices, regardless of issuer, are sensitive to changes in the overall level of interest rates.

Default Risk

Default risk Probability of receiving bond interest and redemption payments.

Default risk has to do with the probability of actually receiving the promised interest and redeeming the bond at face value. If the probabilities of both of these happening are high, the bond is considered low risk; if the probabilities are low, the bond is risky. As we saw earlier in the chapter, default risk depends in large measure on the protections provided in the indenture. All things considered, a subordinated debenture is much riskier than a mortgage bond. But default risk also depends on the financial strength of the issuer. You probably would be safer with a Sears or Du Pont subordinated debenture than a mortgage bond issued by Fly-by-Night Airlines using a dilapidated hangar or vintage airplane as collateral.

Very frankly, very few investors are sufficiently skilled to do their own bond safety analysis; it is far better to rely on professional rating services. The major sources are Standard & Poor's and Moody's and their manuals can be found in most public libraries.

TOPIC LINKS

Ratings service companies

Interest Rate Risk

Interest rate risk Price volatility of a bond in relation to changes in market rates of interest.

After you purchase a bond, your investment will be subject to **interest rate risk**. This risk results from the fact that if credit conditions tighten or loosen after your purchase, interest rates in general will go up or go down. Along with these changes, the market price for your

Table 11.3
Finding the Present Value of a Bond

Year	Cash Inflow to Investor		PV of $1 Factor ($i = 15\%$)*	Present Value of the Cash Inflow
1	Interest $	120	0.8696	$104.35
2	Interest	120	0.7561	90.73
3	Interest	120	0.6575	78.90
4	Interest	120	0.5718	68.62
5	Interest	120	0.4972	59.66
5	Redemption 1,000		0.4972	497.20
			Bond's present value = total =	$899.46

*PV of $1 factors are found in Table A in the Appendix at the end of the text. Look in the 15 percent column.

bond will also change, as we have already demonstrated. The primary factor determining how risky a bond is in relation to interest rate changes is its maturity; the longer the maturity, the greater the price volatility and risk. This is seen best through the use of an example.

Let's assume that you are considering three different bonds each with a 12 percent coupon rate: One matures in one year, another in five years (our previous example bond), and the third in 20 years. Assume further that each is currently selling for $1,000, meaning each has a yield to maturity of 12 percent. Now assume that after you purchase each one, yields to maturity on identical new bonds (1) increase to 15 percent or (2) decrease to 9 percent. Let's see what would happen to the market prices of the three bonds. The new market prices can be calculated using the discounting techniques for finding present values that we just explained. Table 11.4 shows the results. As you see, if yields to maturity rise to 15 percent, your loss is greatest with the 20-year bond and least with the one-year bond; but if interest rates fall, you enjoy the biggest gain with the 20-year bond and, again, the least with the one-year bond. It should be clear that your greatest exposure to risk is with long-maturity bonds.

Preferred Stock

Preferred stock represents another type of fixed-income investment. It is often called a hybrid security because it has characteristics of both common stock and bonds. It is unfortunate the word *preferred* is used to describe this type of security because it suggests that in some way it must be superior to common stock. Although preferred stock is certainly different from common stock, it isn't necessarily preferable.

Preferred stock A hybrid security with characteristics of both common stock and bonds.

Characteristics of Preferred Stock

Most of preferred stock's characteristics make it similar to bonds, except one: By law it is considered a form of equity ownership. Therefore, preferred stockholders rank behind bondholders in terms of asset distributions in the event of liquidation. If a corporation files bankruptcy, all its creditors' claims must be settled before any payments can be made to preferred stockholders.

Dividend Features

Like common stock, preferred stock is paid a dividend, not interest. However, the dividend is usually a fixed amount, and it is often expressed as a percentage of par value (which is usually $100), similar to how interest is paid on bonds. For example, an 8 percent preferred stock would mean that an $8-a-year dividend is paid on each share of stock. Even though a preferred stock has a par (or face) value of $100, its price in the marketplace could be quite

Yield to Maturity	Market Prices		
	1-Year Bond	5-Year Bond	20-Year Bond
9%	$1,028	$1,117	$1,274
12%	1,000	1,000	1,000
15%	974	900	812
Change in Yield to Maturity	Change in Market Prices		
Down by 3%	$+28	$+117	$+274
Up by 3%	−26	−100	−188

Table 11.4
Changes in Market Prices of Three Bonds in Response to Changes in Interest Rates

saving money 11.4

No Reason to Settle for 90 Percent

If you are holding series EE (savings) bonds as a long-term investment, you probably should consider other Treasury bonds. To begin with, the return on five-year Treasuries is likely to average 1 to 2 percent less than the return on 20- or 30-year Treasuries; then, you receive only 90 percent of that return. On Series EE bonds issued through April 2005 the interest return was periodically readjusted to reflect current market rates. Series EE bonds now carry a fixed rate set each May and November. The return you receive is about the equivalent, on average, of what you might earn in very short-term Treasury bills. We shouldn't complain about receiving the Treasury bill yield if we are holding savings bonds for liquidity purposes, but this yield is not adequate for long-term bond investment.

Unfortunately, many families *do* hold savings bonds for long periods of time. For example, parents and relatives like to give them as gifts to small children with the usual warm feeling that the bonds can help much later in the recipients' lives. Then, too, the convenience of buying savings bonds leads many people to buy them for their retirement. Sadly, these long-term holdings will not produce the accumulations that other bonds could. Beginning in 2008, the Treasury has placed an annual limit of $5,000 on individual purchases of Series EE and Series I bonds.

True, savings bonds have other appealing features, such as federal income tax avoidance if they are used for certain educational purposes and if the owners meet certain conditions. But these other features do not apply to many investors, so they are worth nothing. If you want to hold Treasury bonds as a long-term investment, and if there are no unique advantages applicable in your case, then go after all the yield—not just 90 percent.

It's relatively easy to buy bonds directly from the Treasury without a commission through Treasury Direct or your broker can buy them for you in a flash. The broker's commission will be insignificant in the long run when it's compared with savings bonds' smaller yields. Also, there are a number of very good mutual funds specializing in Treasury bonds. Tell Grandma and Grandpa and aunts and uncles that opening a custodial mutual fund account for the kids (a five-minute task) will be as warmly appreciated as savings bonds.

---

different, depending again upon the overall level of interest rates. Some preferred stocks do not have par values; they simply state the dollar amount of dividend.

Cumulative, noncumulative Feature of preferred stock indicating if nondeclared dividends will (cumulative) or will not (noncumulative) carry forward to future years.

Preferred dividends can be **cumulative or noncumulative**. Cumulative means that if a dividend is not declared in one year, it accumulates and must be paid in a future year before any dividend can be paid on the common stock. With noncumulative stock, a missed dividend is lost forever. It's important to know that a corporation is not required legally to pay preferred dividends. In contrast to bond interest, which becomes a legal liability of a corporation the moment it's due, preferred dividends are not liabilities until they are declared.

Preferred Stockholders' Rights

As mentioned previously, preferred stockholders do not enjoy the same legal protections as bondholders do. However, there are similarities. For example, preferred stock is issued under an offering agreement, and many protective covenants are written into it. Some agreements go so far as to give voting rights to preferred stockholders (which they almost never have) if the common stockholders fail to live up to the terms of the agreement or are unable to manage the business profitably. However, these restrictions are rare. You are better advised to think of preferred stock as a considerably weaker instrument than a bond with respect to your protections in bankruptcy.

The Convertible Feature

Convertible preferred stock Preferred stock that converts into shares of the issuer's common stock.

A growing number of new preferred stocks are convertible. Just as in the case of convertible bonds, **convertible preferred stock** converts into a given number of shares of the company's common stock. In recent years, the convertible feature has replaced the participating feature as a "sweetener" to help sell the preferred.

Expected Return from Preferred Stock

The expected return from nonconvertible preferred stock is calculated in the same way as the expected return on bonds. You receive a fixed annual dividend (usually paid quarterly), which is the current return, and you may have a future capital gain or loss if you sell the preferred for a price more or less than your purchase price. It must be noted, though, that most preferred stock does not have a maturity date when the corporation must redeem it. It's said to be issued in perpetuity (forever). Therefore, you cannot calculate a yield to maturity, but you can calculate a current yield in the following way:

$$\text{Current yield} = \frac{\$D}{\$P}$$

where

    D = annual dividend

    P = market price of the preferred stock

A preferred stock paying $2 a year in dividends and having a market price of $18 would have a current yield of 11.11 percent ($2/$18). This is the same calculation we made to find a bond's current yield. Although the preferred stock may not have a redemption date, it may have a call option attached, allowing a corporation the right to call the shares if it wishes to. Finally, preferred stock has the same degree of price risk as bonds, given similar maturities.

key terms

agency bonds (p. 304)
blue chip (p. 291)
bond indenture (p. 300)
book value (p. 298)
callable bonds (p. 301)
common stock (p. 288)
convertible bond (p. 301)
convertible preferred stock (p. 310)
coupon bonds (p. 300)
coupon rate (p. 300)
cumulative (p. 310)
current yield (p. 306)
cyclical stocks (p. 291)
debentures (p. 300)
default risk (p. 308)
earnings per share (EPS) (p. 295)
face value (p. 300)
fixed return (p. 300)
fundamental value (p. 297)
general obligation (GO) bond (p. 305)
growth company (p. 291)
income stocks (p. 291)
inflation-indexed Treasury bonds (p. 304)
interest rate risk (p. 308)
market-to-book ratio (p. 299)

mortgage-backed bonds (p. 304)
mortgage bonds (p. 300)
municipal bonds (p. 305)
noncumulative (p. 310)
PEG ratio (p. 297)
periodic share repurchases (p. 290)
preemptive right (p. 289)
preferred stock (p. 309)
pretax equivalent yield (p. 305)
price-earnings (P/E) ratio (p. 296)
price-to-earnings analysis (p. 295)
protective covenants (p. 300)
proxy (p. 288)
regular dividend (p. 290)
residual claim (p. 289)
revenue bond (p. 305)
sinking fund (p. 301)
special situation (p. 291)
stock dividend (p. 290)
stock split (p. 290)
subordinated debentures (p. 300)
U.S. Treasury Strips (p. 304)
yield to maturity (p. 306)
zero coupon bond (p. 301)

follow-up on the Steele family

Reread the chapter-opening vignette.

1. Knowing the Steeles' financial background, particularly their financial goals, do you feel that most of their money should be invested in stocks or bonds? Discuss.

2. Suppose your preceding answer is "stocks." Indicate what types of stocks are most appropriate for the Steeles. For example, is MeadWestvaco a better choice than Intel or Kellogg? Discuss. (You might want to dig a bit more deeply into these three companies. From the Internet, find a price chart that goes back to 1998. How have the prices of these stocks done since then?)

3. Suppose your preceding answer is "bonds." What types of bonds are most appropriate for the Steeles? Recommend specific bonds, such as "a corporate bond with a 20-year maturity" or "a Treasury STRIP with a 10-year maturity." Explain your choice(s).

4. Assume the Steeles have done their research and subsequently invest in several companies. What financial information should they use to monitor their results? You can limit your answer to Internet sources. Indeed, you need go no further than financial data available through Yahoo!'s Finance company listings.

problems and review questions

1. Explain your rights and return potential as a common stockholder, bondholder, or preferred stockholder. Discuss whether one of these is better than the other two.

2. Suppose you and two friends are considering forming a corporation to produce and market computer software programs that each partner has written. Explain whether you think you should be concerned about voting rights and the preemptive right, assuming each shareholder receives 1,000 shares.

3. Magna Corporation has the following securities outstanding: 1,000,000 shares of common stock, 200,000 shares of $2.50 (annual dividend) preferred stock, and $10,000,000 of 15 percent bonds. Calculate earnings per share available to common stockholders if Magna earns the following:
   a. $5,000,000
   b. $2,200,000
   c. $1,000,000

4. Compare a regular cash dividend with a periodic share repurchase. Which has greater appeal to you? Explain.

5. Explain a stock dividend and further explain if you would prefer it to a cash dividend. What are stock splits, and how desirable are they?

6. Bartholomew Industries' common stock indicates a dividend of $2 a share next year, and its dividend has been growing at an annual rate of 15 percent. If its stock has a current market price of $40 a share, calculate your total expected return on the stock.

7. Bartholomew Industries' (see Question 6) common stock has an estimated beta of 2.2. Assuming you could earn 9 percent on U.S. Treasury securities and the market risk premium is 8 percent, should you buy the stock? Explain, using your answer from Question 6 here.

8. Tartan Corporation has the following 10-year data:

Number of common shares outstanding	1,000,000
Average annual earnings	$2,635,000
Average market price of the common stock	$20/share

   a. Securities analysts think Tartan will earn $5 million next year and have 1,200,000 common shares outstanding. What price do you expect for its common stock next year? Begin your answer by calculating a P/E ratio.

b. Calculate the market-to-book ratio using your answer to part (a) and assuming a book value of $10 a share.

c. If the price of Tartan's stock is currently $30 a share, explain if you think it's a good buy.

9. Explain the following stock quotation.

| 52 Weeks | | | | | | | | | |
High	Low	Stock	Dividend	Yield	P/E	High	Low	Close	Net Change
17.75	7.13	AAR	.44	3.1	18	14.13	14.00	14.13	0.13

10. Is a bond a loan? If it is, who is the borrower and who are the lenders?

11. What is a corporate bond indenture? Differentiate among a mortgage bond, a debenture, and a subordinated debenture.

12. Using a bond's face value and coupon rate, explain how the amount of semiannual interest is determined.

13. Indicate three ways that a bond may be retired.

14. Explain a convertible bond. Would you be inclined to buy such a bond if it were issued by a growth company? Discuss.

15. Why do U.S. Treasury bonds have the lowest yields of all bonds?

16. What is a U.S. Treasury Strip?

17. Calculate the yield to maturity for the following bonds (each has a par value and redemption value of $1,000):
    a. 8 percent coupon rate, 10-year maturity, $1,200 price
    b. 12 percent coupon rate, 20-year maturity, $800 price

18. Using appropriate tables found in the Appendix at the end of the text, determine the present value of the following bonds (each has a redemption value of $1,000):

Bond	Annual Coupon Interest	Maturity (Years)	Yield to Maturity
A	$120	10	8%
B	60	20	8
C	zero	20	10

19. Suppose the yields to maturity for bonds A and B increase to 10 percent. Calculate the new present value of each, and, comparing it with your answer to Question 18, discuss which bond has the greater interest rate risk.

20. What is meant by default risk, and how do investors usually determine how much a bond might have?

21. The following bonds have the same maturity and coupon rate. Also shown are four yields. Match the yields to these bonds.10 percent, 9 percent, 8 percent, and 7 percent:
    a. Municipal
    b. Treasury
    c. Corporate, best quality
    d. Corporate, medium quality

22. What feature of a municipal bond is particularly appealing? Suppose you have a marginal tax rate of 28 percent, and a municipal bond offers a yield of 5 percent. Would you prefer this bond to a similar quality corporate bond with a yield of 6.5 percent? Show why or why not.

23. What is a cumulative preferred stock?

24. If a preferred stock (issued in perpetuity) has a price of $20 a share and pays an annual dividend of $1.50 a share, what is its current yield? Can you calculate its yield to maturity? Explain. Could you experience a capital gain or loss with this stock? Explain.

case 11.1

Ed Driessen's
Stock Pick

Ed Driessen is in a management trainee program at Leyton and Leyton Company, a manufacturer of business forms and accounting systems. During his first month on the job (January 2008), Ed was assigned to the sales department to become familiar with its operations. In reviewing customer accounts, Ed noticed a substantial increase in orders from Antogen, Inc., a hospital supplies company with diverse interests in that area. Since most of these orders were for invoices, purchase orders, and other forms related to sales, Ed reasoned that Antogen might be on the verge of increasing its sales and profits rapidly. If this were to happen, its common stock might be a very good buy.

Before buying, however, Ed thought it would be a good idea to research the stock at the local library. One day during his lunch hour, he stopped there and gathered some data and made a photocopy of Antogen's price chart.

Data for Antogen, Inc.		
Current market price per share: $50	Dividends per share:	Average price/earnings (P/E) ratio:
Earnings per share (EPS):	Average annual growth 1998–2007: 10%	1998–2007 10
Average annual growth 1998–2007: 10%	2007 actual $1.00	2007 12
2007 actual $3.60	2008 estimated $1.20	Current beta estimate: 1.5
2008 estimated $4.30	2009 estimated $1.44	
2009 estimated $5.20		

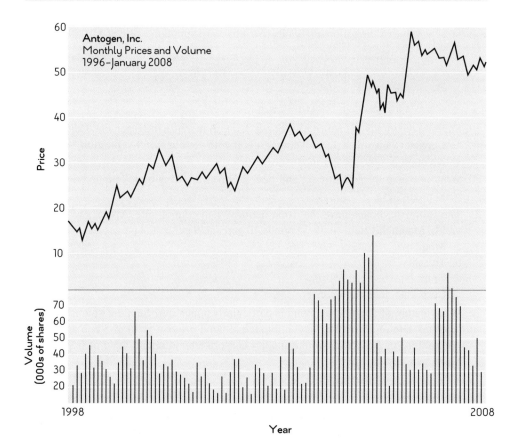

Antogen, Inc.
Monthly Prices and Volume
1996–January 2008

Ed isn't quite sure how to use all this information, but his friend indicates that it shows fairly good performance and that Ed's investment should work out well. Ed is ready to buy the stock but first he would like your opinion. He is single and has good insurance coverage, and his position with Leyton and Leyton seems very secure and promising for the future.

Questions

1. Assume that at the time Ed asks your advice, the rate of return on U.S. Treasury bills is 5 percent and that a market risk premium of 8 percent seems appropriate. Using the 1998–2007 dividend growth rate, do you think Ed should buy the stock? Explain your answer. Suppose you use the dividend growth rate indicated for 2008 and 2009 instead of the 1998–2007 rate; what is your answer then? Which rate do you feel is the more appropriate? Explain.

2. Rather than using a dividend approach, suppose you prefer to judge a stock's value by using a price-to-earnings analysis. Based on the available data, does this approach indicate the stock is a good buy? Explain your answer.

3. Does the stock's price chart help you in making a decision? Explain.

4. What do you think of Ed's hunch? Do you feel he has information that might not be available to investors in general? Does the information given suggest that other investors are not aware of Antogen's prospects for growth? Explain.

5. All things considered, do you think Ed should buy the stock? Defend your answer. (Assume that Ed already has adequate diversification.)

---

case 11.2

Brendan Hoyt Speculates About Bonds

Brendan Hoyt has been fortunate to accumulate about $50,000 of savings, currently held in a money market fund. Brendan is single and has a good position that pays over $80,000 a year. He has no serious financial obligations. He is reluctant to speculate in the stock market because he has a poor background in security analysis, but he believes he can forecast future interest rates with moderate success.

Brendan is convinced that interest rates will fall two percentage points very shortly. His friend, Tina Tobe, has told Brendan that if he really can forecast interest rates, he should speculate in the bond market. He can limit his bond selections to Treasuries, so he doesn't have to worry about possible defaults. Tina says that he should buy Treasury Strips with a 20-year maturity and a yield to maturity of 10 percent. Brendan likes the idea but fails to see why STRIPS are Tina's choice. He thinks he should select bonds with the highest yields to maturity, and right now those are 10-year bonds with a 14 percent coupon rate (coupon interest of $140 annually) and with a yield to maturity of 12 percent.

Questions

1. Brendan needs your help. Calculate the present value of the zero coupon bond and of the 14 percent coupon bond.

2. Assuming a $50,000 investment, how many of each bond type could he buy if he invested the entire amount in one or the other?

3. Assume that Brendan forecasts correctly and that each bond's yield to maturity declines by two percentage points. Determine the new present value for each bond and then further determine which bond provides the greatest profit opportunity.

4. Assume that Brendan guesses incorrectly and each bond's yield to maturity increases by two percentage points. Again, determine new present values and indicate which bond suffers the largest loss. What advice can you offer Brendan?

working out
on the Web

Exercises to Strengthen Your Use of the Internet
(Links for the following exercises can be found at **www.prenhall.com/frasca**.)

Exercise 11.1 How Are the Dogs of the Dow Doing?

Many investors rely on a company's dividend yield as a guide for selecting companies. Read about a popular approach called Dogs of the Dow (**dogsofthedow.com**). Click on "YTD Performance" to compare the approach to the overall Dow Jones Industrial Average.

Q. For the current year, are the Dogs of the Dow beating the overall market?

Exercise 11.2 How Is MeadWestvaco Doing?

A number of excellent sites provide both quotes and company data. Perhaps the best is Yahoo! Finance (**finance.yahoo.com**). Enter MeadWestvaco's symbol, MWV, in the request block and receive the price quote. Click "Headlines" to see if any news items occurred recently. Choose "Charts" to get a great price chart. Choose "Analysts Opinion" to find recommendations on securities analysts.

Q. What is MWV's average recommendation? Compare it to the industry mean.

Exercise 11.3 Help for the Bond Investor

You can find information about all kinds of bonds—corporate, Treasury, and municipal—with Bonds On Line, available at Yahoo! Finance (**finance.yahoo.com**). Choose "Bonds" under "Investing" and go to "Bond Screener." Find the answer to the following question, choosing "Corporate."

Q. Suppose you want a bond with a maturity between 10 and 20 years and a coupon rate of 5 to 8 percent with a AAA Fitch rating. Enter these data. What list of corporate bonds does the search suggest?

Exercise 11.4 How Can I Buy Treasuries Without Paying a Broker's Commission?

TreasuryDirect (**www.treasurydirect.gov**) provides information on purchasing government securities directly from the U.S. Treasury without paying a broker's commission.

Q. How do you open a TreasuryDirect account?

Exercise 11.5 What Are My Savings Bonds Worth Right Now?

At At TreasuryDirect (**www.treasurydirect.gov**) find the link to the "Savings Bond Calculator."

Q. What is the redemption value for a Series EE savings bond from issue date January 2001 (enter 012001 as the issue date in the calculator)? Choose $50 face value ($25 investment).

Mutual Funds and Other Pooling Arrangements

12

simplifying and (maybe) improving your investment performance

Objectives

1. To understand why pooling arrangements are important alternatives to direct investment
2. To identify the important characteristics of open–end and closed–end mutual funds
3. To be able to evaluate a mutual fund within a risk and return framework
4. To recognize the characteristics of unit investment trusts and real estate investment trusts and how each differs from mutual funds
5. To understand the basic framework of limited partnerships and why they appeal only to a limited number of investors
6. To learn the basics of portfolio construction and maintenance and appreciate why mutual funds simplify the process

Steele family

The Steeles invested in the Fidelity Fund several years ago, primarily on the recommendation of a friend. They were surprised and delighted at the ease of opening and maintaining their account. They chose to reinvest dividends and other cash distributions from the fund, and by so doing they have accumulated 200 shares of the fund, worth about $6,800. They like Fidelity's services and quarterly reports, but the fund's performance since their initial investment has been modest and, after doing some basic research, they now are unsure if they have invested in the right fund for their investment objectives.

Arnold and Sharon thought that mutual fund investing would be rather simple, but it hasn't turned out that way. They are amazed at the large number of funds available, even within narrow categories, such as *growth* funds. Moreover, many funds tout the superiority of past performances, making it difficult to separate the real winners from the losers. Also, the Steeles have learned that some funds' shares trade in the financial markets just as individual stocks do. Maybe these funds are better alternatives to the conventional ones, such as the Fidelity Fund. Finally, they noticed there are wide differences among funds in terms of commissions to buy or sell them, operating costs incurred in managing the funds, and the frequency of trading undertaken by fund managers. Perhaps some or all of these factors are important in selecting a fund.

In future years, the Steeles envision investing most of their available savings in mutual funds, primarily to ensure adequate diversification. Given the eventual size of this investment, they realize the importance of gaining knowledge to become sophisticated fund investors.

TOPIC LINKS

Follow the **Topic Links** in each chapter for your interactive Personal Finance exercise on the Web. Go to: **www.prenhall.com/frasca**.

As with the Steeles, many investors become overwhelmed in mutual fund investing. Also, like the Steeles, many find themselves in potentially inappropriate funds for their investment objectives. Some people harbor an illusion that mutual funds have little investment risk. Ignoring diversification advantages, mutual funds are as equally risky as the underlying securities in which the funds invest. When technology stocks tanked in the recent bear market, many technology funds showed similar losses. Although it may be virtually impossible to lose all your money in a good fund, it's not impossible to lose a great deal. Knowing more about mutual funds will help you make better decisions when choosing among the numerous funds.

The important characteristics of mutual funds and other pooling arrangements are explained in this chapter. Actually, the term *mutual fund,* or simply *fund,* is often used in a generic sense to describe any pooling arrangement. There are legal distinctions among the different arrangements, but our focus is on their investment differences.

Mutual Funds

Mutual fund An investment company that invests in securities issued by corporations or governmental units.

A **mutual fund** is an investment company that invests its funds in securities issued by other entities, such as corporations or governmental units. When you buy shares of a mutual fund, you are buying a proportionate interest in the fund's securities. As a simple example, if a fund owns 100 shares each of IBM, Exxon Mobil, and General Motors and if you own 10 percent of the fund's outstanding shares, then you effectively own 10 shares in each of those corporations. The value of a mutual fund share—called its **net asset value (NAV)**—depends on the values of its underlying securities; in the preceding example, those are IBM, Exxon Mobil, and General Motors. Suppose that, on a particular day, the following market values existed; then NAV is calculated as follows, assuming the fund has no liabilities:

Net asset value (NAV) The net value of one mutual fund share determined by the net market value of the fund's shares.

(1) IBM—$120/share × 100 shares	=	$12,000
(2) Exxon Mobil—$80/share × 100 shares	=	8,000
(3) GM—$70/share × 100 shares	=	7,000
(4) Value of the fund's portfolio	=	$27,000
(5) Number of shares outstanding in the fund	=	1,000
(6) Net asset value (NAV) per share = (4) divided by (5)	=	$27

Owning 10 percent of the shares outstanding means you own 100 shares and the value of your investment is $2,700 ($27 × 100). Surely, the first bit of information you want when considering a mutual fund's shares is its NAV per share.

Characteristics of Mutual Funds

To many investors, the single biggest advantage of a mutual fund—after diversification—is its professional management. As discussed in Chapter 11, determining which securities to buy and deciding when to buy and sell them are very difficult decisions—and time consuming if you take them seriously. By investing in a mutual fund, you transfer these problems to someone else, who may be better trained to handle them. Mutual funds charge for these services, but the charges are quite minimal and usually worth it. Before looking more closely at mutual fund selection, you should first understand some of their characteristics.

TOPIC LINKS

Information on mutual funds at the Investment Company Institute

Load Versus No-Load Funds

A **load fund** is one that charges commissions on the shares you buy; a **no-load fund** does not charge commissions. In a load fund, the price you pay for a share is called the offer price, and it is higher than NAV, the difference being commission. In a no-load fund, the price you pay is NAV. (We should point out that mutual funds typically have some liabilities outstanding at any point, and these are deducted from the funds' assets to arrive at *net* assets; however, these liabilities are inconsequential in comparison with assets.) Mutual funds' NAVs are reported in most newspapers, but it is more convenient to review funds and get the latest values at an Internet site like Yahoo! Finance.

Obviously, with commissions, you should be concerned with whether load funds outperform no-loads. On balance they do not. There have been spectacular performers on each side—but there also have been dreadful losers, and most studies show their average performances to be about the same, on a risk-adjusted basis. So why buy a load fund? There is no compelling reason to do so, unless you receive other advantages, such as investment advice. If you invest regularly, saving commissions gives you that much more money invested, and over the long run these extra amounts will produce a substantial addition to the value of your holdings.

In addition to the commission, or front-end load, some funds also have a redemption charge, or rear-end load. The Emerging Markets Fund (FEMKX), which typically invests 80 percent of its funds in emerging markets or investments related to emerging markets, has a 1.5 percent redemption charge for shares held less than 90 days. The increasing popularity of funds, coupled with their apparent success, prompted many funds to begin front- and rear-end loads. Also, redemption charges tend to discourage frequent trading in and out of the fund.

> **Load fund** A mutual fund that charges commissions on share purchases.
>
> **No-load fund** A mutual fund with no purchase commissions.

> **TOPIC LINKS**
>
> Visit Fidelity's and Vanguard's Web sites.

Open-End Versus Closed-End Funds

An **open-end fund** issues shares at their NAV to anyone caring to buy them and, equally important, is also willing to redeem shares at their NAV. For example, if you held shares in any of Fidelity's funds, you could have sold them back to the funds at any time. You generally buy or sell shares directly from or to the fund, rather than through a stockbroker. According to the Investment Company Factbook (**www.icifactbook.org**), there are over 8,000 mutual funds in existence, and more than 70 percent are open-end funds. Their greater popularity is due in part to the assurance investors have in always being able to sell their shares at NAV. They are also widely advertised, and the load funds are promoted by sales representatives.

A **closed-end fund** is different in a number of respects. First, it has a relatively fixed number of shares outstanding. Second, you buy these shares as you would buy shares of any other corporation; that is, its shares are traded on organized exchanges or in the over-the-counter market. Third, because the fund neither buys nor sells shares to the public, you must buy or sell them from or to another party, which further means you are not guaranteed their NAV as either a seller or a buyer. Finally, these funds are seldom promoted, so chances are good you won't know much about them unless you do research on your own. However, quite a few closed-end funds are available with a variety of investment objectives. You can review the variety of funds and market information on each at the Internet site for the Closed Fund Association (**www.closed-endfunds.com**).

> **Open-end fund** A fund that issues or redeems shares at their NAVs.

> **Closed-end fund** A fund with a relatively fixed number of shares outstanding that are purchased (or sold) in the open market rather than from (or to) the fund.

> **TOPIC LINKS**
>
> Review ratings and discounts (premiums) on closed-end funds.

Discounts on Closed-End Funds Enhance Their Appeal

A major point of interest about closed-end funds is the size of premium or discount, which is the difference between their market prices and their NAVs. Some are selling at premiums while others were selling at discounts. More often than not, these funds sell at discounts, which enhances their investment appeal. For example, suppose you can buy Adams Express at an 8 percent discount. To keep things simple, suppose Adams Express held securities that offered a 10 percent current return. If you invested $100 in these securities directly, you would get $10 in dividends or interest. But you need to invest only $92 in Adams Express to get a $10 return. Rather than a 10 percent rate of return, your rate is 10.87 percent ($10/$92). This is a sizable increase in return for no increase in intrinsic risk. You should realize, though, that the size of the discount varies over time, and it could increase after you invest. This means the market price of your shares declines relative to NAV, and if you then sell, you do so at a loss, or at a relatively smaller gain than would have been the case had the discount remained the same.

The Fund's Objectives

Prospectus A document describing a fund in considerable detail.

Shareholder report A statement showing how a fund has performed in the past and the securities it currently owns.

International fund, global fund: A fund that invests in foreign securities.

It is obviously important to select a fund that is attempting to achieve the same investment goal you are. For most funds you can download a **prospectus** and a **shareholder report** at their Internet site. The prospectus describes the fund in detail, and the shareholder report indicates how the fund has performed in the past and the securities it currently holds. Risks associated with investing in the fund are also discussed, and they should be read as thoroughly as material describing the fund's objective and its past performance.

Figure 12.1 indicates the more common fund objectives. As you see, there are a number from which to choose. While growth, income, and balanced funds are the most popular, many investors use the other funds also. **International funds** and **global funds** allow you to invest in foreign countries, where returns have often been higher than in the United

FINANCIAL PLANNING *for*
young adults 12.1

Want to Invest in a Mutual Fund? Just Do It!

The most popular investment vehicle over the past 10 years has been the mutual fund. From $135 billion invested in 1981, there was over $10 trillion invested in 2006. This is remarkable. Equally remarkable, though, is the number of people who feel that mutual funds are good investments but, for one reason or another, do not invest in them or who do so only through a broker. Why?

In a recent survey, some respondents indicated that they didn't know where to look to find a fund. Others didn't think the "hassle" of investing in a fund on their own was worth it, so they let their brokers find one for them. Many felt nervous about venturing into an unknown situation and, therefore, left their money in bank savings accounts.

What these people need desperately is more confidence in themselves and a "power of positive thinking" attitude. In short: just do it, and here are four simple steps to get started.

1. Two large fund families are Fidelity (**www.fidelity.com**) and Vanguard (**www.vanguard.com**). Each has an excel-

lent Web site. Use either to get started; when you become more knowledgeable, you might use the many other fund families that are available. If you want to start with a very small investment, you can find funds with low or no minimum with the Yahoo! Mutual Fund Screener (**screen.yahoo.com/funds.html**)

2. Call or download information on any three or four of their most popular funds (either no-load or loads less than 5 percent) that match your investment goal. Review them as well as you can and pick one. The application takes about three minutes to complete.

3. Regardless of how much money you have to invest, make a small initial commitment. The idea is simply to get in the game, not to find the ideal fund right at the start.

4. Invest regularly, which you can do in two ways. First, check the automatic reinvestment boxes on the application form, both for dividend and capital gain distributions. Second, arrange to have an amount automatically deducted from your checking or savings account and invested in the fund each month. Most fund families provide this service.

Figure 12.1
Types of Mutual Funds

Type of Fund	Objective	Primary Investment Securities
Growth	Price appreciation over time	Common stocks
Income	High current return	Bonds, preferred stocks
Balanced	Moderate growth plus moderate current return	Bonds, preferred and common stocks
Money market	High liquidity plus higher current return than bank savings accounts	Money market securities
Maximum capital appreciation	Exploit opportunities to earn high returns	Varies, depending on strategy
Sector	Invest in one industry	Common stocks
International	Earn returns in countries outside the U.S.	Common stocks
Global	Earn returns in both the U.S. and foreign countries	Common stocks
Index	Earn returns equal to a market index, such as the S&P 500	Common stocks or bonds; depends on the index

States. **Sector funds** make it possible to invest in one industry if you think that industry will do better than the overall economy. **Maximum capital appreciation funds** use a number of investment strategies in an effort to earn high returns. For example, some look for companies that might be acquired (at high prices) through takeovers. Some invest in distressed companies (even bankrupts) that are expected to recover.

A particularly interesting fund is an **index fund**. It invests in securities that constitute a market index, such as the S&P 500 Stock Index. Its sole objective is to earn the return the index earns. Beginning investors often feel they can do better than a simple index, which has no investment strategy or approach. In actuality, however, many investment professionals do not perform as well as an index. Studies indicate, for example, that fully two-thirds of equity mutual funds underperform the S&P 500 on a risk-adjusted basis.

A particularly popular fund is the **money market fund**. There are several reasons for its popularity. For one thing, these funds are known as dollar funds, which means you always buy or sell shares at $1 each. Actually, the fund is a form of checking account, allowing you to write checks against your account balance. You earn interest daily and can withdraw all funds credited to your account at any time. Withdrawals can be made by telephone or wire but are more frequently made by checks. The usual minimum withdrawal is $500, but some accounts allow checks for any amount. The big appeal is the earnings on the account. In contrast to some checking accounts that pay no or low interest, these funds usually offer rates that are about the same as those earned on liquid money market instruments.

Sector fund: A fund that invests in only one industry.

Maximum capital appreciation fund: A fund that uses a variety of strategies in an effort to earn high returns.

Index fund A fund that attempts to match the return on a market index.

Money market fund A fund that invests in money market instruments issued in large denominations.

TOPIC LINKS

Find information on mutual funds.

Important Mutual Fund Services

Along with a professionally managed and well-diversified portfolio, mutual funds offer other appealing features. Some of the more important services are described here.

Reinvestment Plans

Reinvestment plan An option a fund investor can choose to have cash distributions used to acquire more fund shares.

A **reinvestment plan** allows you to reinvest the fund's dividends and capital gain distributions into additional shares of the fund automatically. You choose the amount you wish to reinvest. It can be all or only a fraction of the total distributed. Many investors like to receive dividends in cash but prefer having capital gain distributions reinvested. When you fill out an application to buy shares, you indicate how you wish to handle reinvestment.

Transactions by Telephone or over the Internet

Once you have completed an application, you can buy or sell shares by calling a toll-free telephone number or by accessing your account over the Internet. You can also arrange to have funds wired to your bank, which eliminates delays with checks in transit. If you sell shares and have the funds wired, they can be in your interest-earning bank account the next day.

Fund Switching

Fund switching An option allowing fund investors to switch among funds within a fund family.

Fund switching allows you to withdraw money from one fund to reinvest in another, as long as the two funds are members of the same family (Fidelity, for example). If the fund is a no-load, this feature is particularly attractive for investors trying market-timing techniques. In general, switches up to a certain number can be made without charges; however, you will pay commissions on a load fund. Be sure to determine your fund's policy before you begin making switches.

Adaptability to IRAs

Most mutual funds make attractive IRAs (IRAs are discussed in Chapters 4 and 16). This is because of the wide range of investment objectives available and their relatively low administrative costs, which usually are less than $20 a year (some funds offer them free). To open an IRA, all you need to do is indicate your intent, and you will be sent a simple document for your signature. This document, along with the completed application form to the fund, automatically makes your investment an IRA.

Selecting a Mutual Fund

Once you have defined clearly your investment objective, you will find many funds available for your choice. Picking one or two is a difficult task. You can get started by looking at a fund's historical performance and comparing it with its risk. Use a beta value (if one is available) in this effort. Other steps to take include reviewing the fund's current holdings, comparing its expenses in relation to its earnings or to the market value of its securities, and seeing how often it buys and sells securities (called the fund's portfolio turnover). Yahoo! Finance (**finance.yahoo.com**) has a convenient fund screener that allows you to review funds according to several characteristics.

TOPIC LINKS

Screen mutual funds at Yahoo! Finance.

Evaluate Performance

A fund must indicate its past performance in its financial reports to shareholders. Figure 12.2 shows data for Fidelity Fund, a very large, open-end growth and income fund that is part of the Fidelity family. This report is typical of reports all mutual funds provide investors, although Fidelity's report is particularly useful in that it discusses how to evaluate performance.

Figure 12.2
Fact Sheet for the Fidelity Fund

Adapted from: Fidelity Investments (Fidelity.com): Choose investment products, then mutual funds, then Fidelity funds, then Fidelity (symbol FFIDX). Annual returns are found in the Prospectus.

I. Performance and Risk	Fidelity Fund	S&P 500 Index	Difference
A. Annual Total Returns (as of 2/29/08)			
1 Year	5.43%	-3.6%	9.03%
3 Years	8.99	5.37	3.62
5 Years	13.00	11.64	1.36
10 Years	5.12	4.07	1.05
B. Beta Statistic (as of 2/29/08)	1.06	1.00	
C. Growth of $10,000	$17,709		
(10 years ended on 2/29/08)			

II. Ratings as of 2/29/08

Morningstar (5 is best)   Lipper

★★★★★ 3 Years   1 Year #33 out of 1629 Growth & Income
★★★★ 5 Years   5 Year #212 out of 962 Growth & Income
★★★★ 10 Years   10 Year #175 out of 505 Growth & Income
★★★★ Overall Morningstar Ratings

III. Top 10 Holdings (21.8% of Aggregate Value)

Monsanto Co New   Hewelett–Packard Co
Microsoft Corp   Becton Dickinson & Co
Google Inc A   Honeywell Intl Inc
Verizon Communications Inc   Valero Energy Corp
Exxon Mobil Corp   Procter & Gamble Co

IV. Market Sectors (%) as of 1/31/2008

Consumer Discretionary	7.1
Consumer Staples	8.3
Energy	12.4
Financials	19.3
Health Care	11.9
Industrials	12.4
Information Technology	14.7
Materials	5.6
Telecommunication Services	3.5
Utilities	2.9

V. Other Data

Expense Ratio: as of 8/31/2007	0.57%
Lipper Growth & Income Avg. Expense Ratio	1.13%
Portfolio Turnover Rate as of 12/31/2007	63%

Average Annual Total Return (AATR). The average annual total return (AATR) is a difficult calculation and cannot be solved accurately without time-value-of-money techniques. Fortunately, fund reports provide the values. Fidelity's 5.12 percent average annual total return for 10 years is a uniform annual return that matches the total return over the 10 year period. This is a good return and, as you see, it was better than the return on the S&P 500 index.

Growth of a $10,000 Investment and Cumulative Total Return. Figure 12.2 shows that $10,000 invested in the Fidelity Fund over the 10-year period ending February 29, 2008, would have grown to $17,709, assuming that capital gains and dividends were reinvested. Most funds provide this information, sometimes in graphic form and year by year. Fidelity shows such a graph along with the numeric data. Some funds also provide the so-called cumulative total return percentage. The cumulative total return is calculated by dividing the ending value by the beginning value, subtracting 1.0 and expressing the result as a percentage. Fidelity's cumulative total return for the 10 year period is 77.09 percent ($17,709/$10,000 = 1.7709; 1.7709 – 1.0 = .7709; .7709 × 100% = 77.09 percent).

The Reinvestment Assumption. A key input in determining both the average annual total return and the cumulative total return is the assumption of immediate reinvestment of fund distributions. To illustrate the situation, let's look at the example for a hypothetical fund shown in Table 12.1. Although funds actually make quarterly distributions, we will assume that all distributions were made at midyear and then reinvested at the average NAV for the year. We also assume that one share was owned at the beginning of each year.

The cumulative total return can also be determined from the foregoing data. You had 1.043 shares of the fund at the end of year 2 for each share that you owned at the beginning of that year. Since you actually owned 1.111 shares at the year's beginning, you would have owned 1.158773 (1.043 × 1.111) shares at year-end. And the total value of those shares is $19.70 (1.158773 × $17.00). Your initial investment at the beginning of year 1 was $15.42, so your gain is $4.28 ($19.70 – $15.42). The cumulative total return over the two-year period is 27.76 percent ([$4.28/$15.42] × 100).

The year-to-year changes in returns shown in Table 12.1 reveal the riskiness of investing in the fund; clearly, going from a +29.2 percent return to a –5.2 percent return suggests quite a bit of risk. Risk is often incorporated into an analysis by determining a fund's beta value and using it to adjust the average annual total return (*AATR*), as shown in the following examples.

Risk–Adjusted Return. Professionals who evaluate mutual fund performance often make comparisons among funds using the risk-adjusted rate of return (*RAROR*). One very simple way to calculate this follows:

$$RAROR = \frac{AATR}{\text{fund's beta weight}} - \text{S\&P 500 return}$$

From Figure 12.2 we see that Fidelity Fund's beta was at 1.06, which means it was somewhat more risky than the overall market. Using Fidelity Fund's 10-year *AATR* and the S&P 500 10-year *AATR*, we have

$$\text{Fidelity's } RAROR = \frac{5.12}{1.06} - 4.07 = 4.83 - 4.07 = +.76\%$$

Table 12.1
Calculating a Fund's Average Annual Return

	Year 1	Year 2
(1) NAV, beginning of year	$15.42	$17.93
(2) NAV, end of year	$17.93	$16.30
(3) Average NAV = [(1) + (2)]/2	$16.68	$17.12
(4) Distributions during the year	$1.85	$0.74
(5) Shares acquired during the year = (4)/(3)	0.111	0.043
(6) Shares owned at year end	1.111	1.043
(7) Value of shares owned at year end = (2) × (6)	$19.92	$17.00
(8) Change in value during the year = (7) – (1)	$4.50	–$0.93
(9) Average annual total return = (8)/(1)	+29.2%	–5.2%

The +0.76 percent indicates the amount the Fidelity Fund outperformed the S&P 500. A positive number indicates a good performance; and the larger the positive number, the better the performance. Of course, a negative number indicates poor performance. We conclude, then, that Fidelity Fund's performance was well ahead that of the S&P 500 index.

Review the Fund's Current Portfolio

At this point, you should look at each fund's current holdings. If you invest in a number of different funds, you should be concerned with the specific companies in which the funds invest. This will help you determine the extent to which you are diversified. At an extreme, imagine that all your funds are invested in the same companies. In that case, it would make no sense to own all the funds since one fund would be sufficient. Furthermore, you probably would have much less diversification than you think you have. Reviewing the fund's portfolio will help you evaluate your degree of diversification. As Figure 12.2 shows, the Fidelity Fund held 10 investments that totaled 21.8 percent of the fund's aggregate value; altogether, the fund held about 140 different companies. On balance, the fund seems reasonably diversified; but you should be cautious to invest in a similar fund if its top 10 holdings were approximately the same as the Fidelity Fund's. You should also notice that the fund's assets were not concentrated in any single market sector.

TOPIC LINKS

A Morningstar review of the Fidelity Fund

Examine Expenses and Portfolio Turnover

Managing a mutual fund involves certain administrative expenses. The greater these expenses, the fewer resources the fund has to invest or make shareholder distributions. These expenses are usually related to the size of the portfolio and the frequency of security purchases and sales. This frequency is measured by a turnover percentage. (For example, if a fund replaced 10 percent of its holdings with new holdings, its turnover would be 10 percent.) It is important, by the way, to express expenses as percentages of average net assets because funds are quite different in size, and a large fund naturally has higher expenses than a small one. The ratio of expenses to average net assets for most equity funds is around 1 percent. Fidelity's ratio is well below that figure, indicating that management controls expenses rather well.

Review a Fund's Ratings

There are two excellent ratings services that evaluate fund performance—Morningstar (www.morningstar.com) and Lipper Analytical Services (www.lipperweb.com). Each has a Web site that you can review if you would like more information on how their ratings are derived. How they report ratings is simple in both cases. Morningstar assigns a number of stars with five indicating the best performance. Lipper shows the rank of the fund in relation to all others in its peer group. Figure 12.2 shows that Fidelity was an overall four-star performer according to Morningstar compared to an average rating of three stars. Its Lipper rank varies depending upon the time period over which returns are measured. The Fidelity Fund is ranked in the top half of all similar funds in all three periods. Actually, these ratings somewhat confirm the conclusion we reached using the *RAROR*—that the Fidelity Fund performs well as compared to the overall market.

Ratings are very helpful and you are well advised to use them before investing. However, you should not place excess emphasis on ratings based on short time periods. Many funds pursue investment strategies that produce high returns in certain economic environments, but very poor returns in other situations. If you chase after funds always showing the highest ratings, you might be investing at the end of the boom cycle. Naturally, you then are stuck with poor returns that often follow the good ones. Many financial planners favor long-run evaluations—three-year periods and longer.

saving money 12.2

Focus on Loads and Annual Expenses

You have $1,000 to invest and are considering mutual funds. Two have come to your attention. Fund A has an 8.5 percent load and typically incurs operating expenses at 2 percent of net assets; Fund B is a no-load fund with an expense ratio of 0.25 percent. If each fund manager earns, say, 12 percent each year before expenses, how much better off are you with Fund B? Answers are in the table that follows.

B's advantage is anything but trivial, but you probably think this example is stretched to make a point. It is somewhat, but not completely. There are funds with loads as high as 8.5 percent, and you certainly can find two funds with that much difference in expense ratios.

Saving money, then, is simple: First, ignore all load funds; second, select only those no-load funds with low operating expense ratios. But, as with all simple plans, there are a few hitches. First, by eliminating all load funds you cut out a few super performers and many of the better performers.

Second, many load funds are sold by stockbrokers who also provide investment and portfolio management advice. Notice in the table that the load has far less importance with long holding periods. Paying $820 over 20 years may not be an excessive amount if the broker provides useful advice.

The table clearly shows that operating costs are the real villain in the long run. Indeed, some studies have shown that selecting funds with low cost ratios is the most consistent method of selecting funds that are likely to perform well in the future. One mutual fund family, Vanguard, emphasizes low costs, and its funds typically have the lowest ratios in the industry. Not surprisingly, its funds—particularly its index funds—are consistently among the best performers.

| | Accumulation: | | | Advantage Due to: | |
Years After Investment	Fund A	Fund B	B's Advantage	No Load	Low Costs
1	$1,007	$1,120	$ 113	$ 95	$ 18
10	2,373	3,106	733	265	468
20	6,156	9,646	3,490	820	2,670

Select Mutual Funds

You can get help in selecting mutual funds from a number of sources, including financial advisory services that charge fees. More readily available sources, though, include the *Wall Street Journal*, *Barron's*, *Money*, *Business Week*, and *Forbes*. *Money* has a "Fund Watch" column appearing in each monthly issue. In addition, it ranks a large number twice a year, reporting each fund's 1-, 5-, and 10-year performance along with a risk rating. It also gives each fund's address and phone number, making it easy for you to get information. There are a number of Internet sites that provide fund data, including risk factors and performance results. Yahoo! Finance provides a complete review of a fund's performance, comparing it to performances of other funds with similar investment objectives.

Other Pooling Arrangements

Although mutual funds are clearly the dominant pooling arrangement, other forms have arisen to meet special considerations. We review four relatively popular arrangements: unit investment trusts, real estate investment trusts, limited partnerships, and investment clubs. Figure 12.3 summarizes the main characteristics of these funds.

Unit Investment Trusts (UITs)

Unit investment trust (UIT)
A pooling arrangement similar to an open-end fund; however, the investment portfolio is relatively fixed (unmanaged) over the fund's life.

A **unit investment trust (UIT)** is similar in some respects to an open-end mutual fund, but there are important differences. As Figure 12.4 shows, a UIT is formed when an originator,

Fund	Investor	Fund Management	Tax Consequences	Fees
Closed end mutual fund	Buy and sell on the open market at a price that may be greater or less than NAV	Fixed number of shares Shares trade on the public market Fund is not required to repurchase shares	Taxes on dividends Capital gains and losses when shares in the fund are sold	Management fees charged to the fund Brokerage commissions on buys and sells
Open end mutual fund	Buy or sell from fund sponsor at NAV Can automatically reinvest dividends	Variable number of shares that are typically actively managed	Taxes on dividends and capital gains that pass to investors Capital gains and losses when shares in the fund are redeemed	Management fee and cost of actively managing portfolio May be commissions on buy and sell May be an additional management fee on small accounts
Unit Investment Trust	Buy and sell shares directly from the UTF at NAV plus commission	Unmanaged fund of initial portfolio Termination date for fund	Taxes on dividends and capital gains that pass to investors Capital gains and losses when shares in the fund are redeemed	Low management fee Commissions on sales and purchases
Exchange Traded Funds	Buy and sell shares directly on public market	Manages the fund so that it tracts a specific Index (variable number of shares, fund can expand or contract)	Typically only dividends are passed on to investors Capital gain or losses when shares are bought and sold	Brokerage commissions when buying and selling shares Low management fees charged to fund
HOLDR	Buys and sells shares directly on public market	Buys a set portfolio of financial investments that does not change	Taxes on dividends that pass through to investors Capital gain or loss when shares are bought and sold	Brokerage commissions when buying and selling shares Very low management fee
REIT	Buys and sells shares directly on public market	Actively manages property or mortgages	Income passes through as taxable dividends Capital gain or loss when shares are bought and sold	Brokerage commissions when buying and selling shares Management fees can vary and can be significant

Figure 12.3

Comparative Characteristics of Pooling Arrangements

Figure 12.4
Formation of a Municipal Bond Unit Investment Trust

a large financial firm, such as First Trust Portfolios, creates a portfolio of assets and then sells trust units to individual investors. In most cases you can sell your units back to the trust at their NAVs, which may be quite different—higher or lower—from their original cost to you. Basically, this is how an open-end mutual fund works. The big difference is that the original portfolio of securities remains intact until they are redeemed or the trust is dissolved. The trust is, thus, an unmanaged fund, reducing administrative expenses considerably, but you do pay a commission (usually 4 percent) to the trust originators.

Exchange-Traded Funds and HOLDRs

Exchange-traded funds (ETFs) are a variation of the UIT model. The major difference is that trust units (more popularly referred to as shares) trade in the securities markets. In this respect they are similar to closed-end funds. However, in common with UITs and in contrast to closed-end funds, the portfolio of assets held by indexed based ETFs typically remains fixed. Each ETF attempts to mirror the performance of a specific market index. The portfolio is only changed to reflect changes in the composition of the index.

An ETF is initially issued in large blocks called "creation units." The initial investor sells shares in the creation unit that are traded on stock exchanges. To ensure that the market price does not get out of line with the value of the underlying assets, creation units may be redeemed for an in-kind transfer of the underlying assets. However, individual shares purchased in the secondary market may not be redeemed from the ETF.

The Investment Company Factbook reports that the number of ETFs has grown rapidly from 1 in 1993 to 357 in 2006 having a valuation of over $400 billion. This phenomenal growth is due to a variety of reasons:

1. Since they are market traded, investors can enter and exit positions very rapidly, intraday if they so desire. In contrast, most mutual funds settle only at the day's closing net asset value.

2. Investors can use margin to acquire the shares. This may not be possible with mutual funds.

3. They have very low expense ratios, often under 0.3 percent with some as low as 0.18 percent when compared to mutual funds with typical expense ratios at 1 to 3 percent.

4. They are more tax efficient. Mutual funds pass their capital gains to investors each year, adding to investors' tax liabilities. With ETFs, investors can choose to hold their

Exchange-traded funds (ETFs) Fixed portfolios of securities that trade in the securities markets.

TOPIC LINKS

Learn more about ETFs.

positions, thereby not incurring taxable gains. Over a long period of time, this deferral of taxes can significantly increase wealth.

5. Of course, investors incur brokerage commissions in trading ETFs. However, these commissions could be far less than a front- and/or back-end load on a mutual fund. Clearly, frequent trading usually diminishes wealth no matter what security is traded.

Most ETFs are designed either to track a broad market index; however, there are also sector-based ETFs that are tied to particular sectors such as housing, transportation or technology.

Broad Market ETFs

Broad market ETFs are by far the most popular. The first offered was one that tracked the S&P 500 stock index. Its trading symbol on the American Stock Exchange is SPY and it is referred to as a "spider" (SPDR, acronym for Standard and Poor's Depository Receipt). Shortly after spiders, an ETF tracking the Dow Jones Industrial Average—called a "diamond" (DIA)—was introduced. Although actively traded, diamonds have been far less popular than spiders. However, each has been eclipsed completely with the introduction of the ETF that tracked the 100 largest stocks traded through NASDAQ. Called the "Qs" (after their trading symbol, QQQQ), trading in these shares often averages over 80 million shares a day, making it perhaps the most popular stock traded.

In addition to the S&P 500 spider, the Amex trades other ETFs that track almost every major market index, such as those representing small and intermediate-sized companies. ETFs have been created also to track stock indexes in other countries, making global diversification possible for individual investors. Actually, with ETFs investors can create virtually any type of highly diversified stock portfolio they desire. Of course, the diversification exists only as to having an adequate number of individual stocks; for example, the 100 different companies in the Qs provide excellent company diversification. However, you still have an investment that is not broadly diversified among many different kinds of stocks. The 100 companies are largely technology oriented. Any decline in that market segment will mean similar declines in the Qs, as their owners well know from the previous market downturn.

Market Segment ETFs

Market segment ETFs are designed to track the performances of specific market sectors. For example, the S&P 500 index is broken down into nine sectors—consumer staples, consumer cyclicals, consumer services, basic industries, financials, utilities, energy, industrials, and technology—and an SPDR fund has been created for each one. In addition, Barclays Global Investors has created similar ETFs—called iShares—on over 30 different sectors, including real estate, health care, and chemicals.

HOLDRs

Merrill Lynch has created a somewhat different type of ETF, called "HOLDRs." The difference is that the owner of the HOLDR has all rights to the underlying stock. For a small fee a trust unit can be converted into a fixed number of shares of the companies included in the HOLDR. The trust unit actually consists of 100 shares of the HOLDR, and trades cannot be for less than 100 shares. The first fund consisted of 16 Internet companies, including Yahoo!, AOL, Amazon, and eBay. Initiated at the peak of the Internet frenzy, this ETF (symbol, HHH) quickly became a very popular way to diversify among leading Internet companies that were trading at extremely high prices. At its peak, the share price of HHH was about $175. A year or so later it traded at $27.91. Nevertheless, HOLDRs have

TOPIC LINKS

Review types of HOLDRs.

achieved some degree of popularity, and Merrill Lynch has now introduced 17 others, each tracking a different market segment. The biotechnology and semiconductor HOLDRs have become very popular.

Real Estate Investment Trusts (REITs)

Real estate investment trust (REIT) A pooling arrangement (similar to a closed-end mutual fund) that invests in real estate and real estate mortgages.

A **real estate investment trust (REIT)** is a type of closed-end investment company similar to closed-end mutual funds explained earlier. To be considered an investment company for tax purposes, the REIT must derive 70 percent of its income from real estate and distribute no less than 90 percent of its income as cash dividends. Many REITs are publicly held, which means that their shares are traded on organized exchanges or in the over-the-counter market. In effect, you buy or sell their shares as you would the shares of any other public corporation. This feature makes REIT shares very marketable but not necessarily liquid, since their prices are often as volatile as those of other stocks.

TOPIC LINKS

Learn more about REITS.

Differences Among REITs

Equity trusts REITs specializing in investing in real estate.

Mortgage trusts REITs specializing in mortgage lending.

REITs differ in a number of respects. First, some invest in buildings, shopping centers, warehouses, and many other kinds of properties. These are called **equity trusts**, and they earn income from renting space to tenants. Other REITs do not invest in properties but instead invest by lending funds to others; that is, they make loans (usually mortgage loans) to builders and developers. These are called **mortgage trusts**. A second difference has to do with the manner in which a REIT finances itself. Some are financed entirely with owners' equity, having no long-term debt whatsoever. Others make extensive use of borrowed funds, which increases their leverage.

Since REITs differ so much in both the kinds of investments they make and how they are financed, they also differ considerably in their expected return and risk characteristics. Some are extremely safe, while others are very risky. Before investing, you should research their underlying fundamentals, by either doing the work yourself or asking your broker for a research report and an opinion on which ones seem appropriate for your investment objectives.

The Return from a REIT

As noted earlier, 90 percent of a REIT's earnings must be distributed as dividends. The current return on many REITs is, therefore, fairly high but also volatile, a factor you should not overlook if a stable return is important to you. Similar to the NAV of a mutual fund, the equity per share (*EqPS*) of a REIT can be determined by dividing assets minus liabilities by the number of shares outstanding; that is,

$$EqPS = \frac{\left(\text{REIT assets} - \text{liabilities}\right)}{\text{REIT shares outstanding}}$$

EqPS is an important figure to investors who want to know if the market price of a REIT share is selling at a discount or premium to it. You should understand, however, that assets are measured at their book—rather than appraised—values. If a REIT acquired properties some years ago, there is a good possibility that book value will be substantially below appraised value. So it is important not to attach excessive importance to the *EqPS* figure.

Investment Appeal of REITs

Many financial planners feel that a portion of your portfolio should be invested in certain types of assets to hedge against inflation. Real estate has been particularly effective in this capacity, and people who buy homes not only achieve living space but also add an important asset to their portfolios.

Unfortunately, not all investors are home owners. REITs (of the equity trust variety) should be even more appealing to them. If you are a renter, consider seriously a REIT investment. A good place to begin your search for information is the National Association of Real Estate Investment Trusts (**www.nareit.com**).

Limited Partnerships

A **limited partnership** is a legal arrangement that combines features of a corporation and a general partnership. The formation of a limited partnership is illustrated in Figure 12.5; as shown, limited partnerships engage in a wide variety of business activities. However, owning and managing real estate is the most important.

A limited partnership is similar to a corporation in that most investors (called *limited partners*) are inactive in management of the business, preferring instead to turn over these responsibilities to a person called the *general partner*. It resembles a partnership in that profits or losses from the business are passed directly to the partners rather than being profits or losses of the business itself.

Limited partnership A pooling arrangement that combines features of a corporation and a general partnership.

Liquidity with Limited Partnerships

While some limited partnerships issue shares (such as the Boston Celtics basketball team) that trade in the securities markets, most limited partnership interests cannot be sold in any readily available markets. If partnership interests are held by the public and if the promoter is a large stockbrokerage firm, they might be able to find a buyer, but there is no guarantee. If the partnership is privately held, selling your interest may be extremely difficult. You might wait until the partnership is dissolved to recover your original investment plus any capital appreciation. Obviously, if liquidity is an important concern, then a limited partnership interest is not a suitable investment.

The Tax Situation with Limited Partnerships

The 1986 Tax Reform Act eliminated many of the tax advantages previously associated with limited partnerships. The act's loss limitation rules stipulate that any loss from a lim-

Figure 12.5
Formation of a Limited Partnership

ited partnership can be used to offset gains from other limited partnerships, but any combined net loss cannot be used to offset other forms of income, such as earned income or portfolio income. Obviously, if you intend to take part in a limited partnership you should discuss the tax implications with a tax accountant.

Investment Potential

The income tax situation seriously limits the investment quality of many real estate limited partnerships. Without any particular tax advantages to consider, you should evaluate this investment no differently than you would all other passive investments, such as stocks or bonds. However, evaluation might be more difficult since cash flows from the business, including its eventual liquidation, are difficult to estimate. In today's environment it's probably good advice to avoid all limited partnerships unless you are skilled at interpreting the materials they provide.

You can, of course, rely on a financial advisor, but be careful if that person receives a commission from the partnership in which you invest. At the very least, have the advisor explain (in writing) the return and risks you can expect and why the partnership is suitable for your investment objectives. Investment scams frequently take on the appearance of legitimate business activities, many cloaked in the mystique of the limited partnership. Put simply, you can't be too cautious. All things considered, small investors are well advised simply to avoid limited partnerships altogether.

 finance news 12.3

What's a Hedge Fund?

Average investors seldom hear about hedge funds. They wonder, then: "Are these the really good funds—the ones my broker reserves for his or her wealthy clients?" Well, hedge funds certainly are for the wealthy since investors must have a net worth of $1 million, or $200,000 to invest. You might think this excludes you from the hedge fund industry. It might directly, but not necessarily indirectly, since hedge funds are rapidly gaining popularity among institutional investors. So, your retirement fund, or even your university, might have some of its money in such a fund. Estimates at mid-2004 put the amount invested in hedge funds at $650 to $800 billion.

Hedge funds are very different from other types of funds. First, they are usually structured as limited partnerships. Another difference is that fund managers usually receive compensation in the form of a profit share (often 20 percent), which is typical of most limited partnerships. The rules for withdrawing cash from the partnership are more rigid than with mutual funds. Also, they do not have to register with the Securities and Exchange Commission (SEC) and are not required to make periodic reports to the SEC.

The term "hedge" suggests the funds pursue investment strategies designed to lower periodic investment risk, and many do just that. After the market crash in 2000, this feature began

to appeal to investors. However, some funds do not hedge; rather, they seek profits in certain market segments, such as fluctuating exchange rates. This single theme can make them very risky. Consider the case of Long Term Capital Management, a so-called leveraged fund. At one point it had $4 billion in assets and almost as much in borrowed money. Its managers, often called financial geniuses, thought they could predict future interest rates. The geniuses were wrong and resulting losses led to a $3.6 billion bail out by the Federal Reserve. This debacle, along with other abuses, has moved the SEC to propose strict new guidelines for the hedge fund industry, which has been virtually unregulated since its beginning in 1949.

As with the mutual fund industry, some hedge fund returns have been excellent while others have been dismal. *Barron's* reports regularly on fund performances should you be inclined to research them. Actually, you shouldn't feel too badly about being excluded from the market. If the fund does indeed hedge against risk, it probably will do so by forgoing potential return. As a young adult investor who, ideally, is investing for the long term, you should not seek a lower-return investment simply because it lowers periodic risk. Now, when you are ready to retire, you can weigh risk more heavily into the return-risk equation. By that time, you might also have the financial resources to meet the stringent financial requirements for entry.

Investment Clubs

For many people, an **investment club** is the ideal way to achieve diversification: It gives them an opportunity for fun and fellowship, along with a possibility of profit. Most investment clubs invest in common stocks, although you can find a range of investment objectives. Some of the clubs have excellent performance records, and their members take a most serious attitude toward finding good investments.

You invest in a club by paying monthly dues, usually in the $25 range, which are then used to buy securities selected by the membership. Most clubs reinvest dividends and capital gains. Securities are often recommended for purchase by members given the task of researching a specific company or industry, and this is perhaps the most enjoyable part of being a member. You can expect divergent opinions and robust discussion in any club in which members take their investments seriously. Information on forming an investment club can be found at Better Investing (**www.better-investing.org**).

Investment club A pooling arrangement characterized usually by a small number of members, monthly meetings and dues, and regular investment (and social) activities.

TOPIC LINKS

Find information on investment clubs.

Constructing and Maintaining Your Personal Portfolio

Now that we have examined the two most popular direct investments—stocks and bonds—and the popular pooling arrangements, it's time to put it all together by considering your personal portfolio. Investors share many common characteristics, but in a sense each investor is unique in terms of his or her risk attitude and financial goals. A portfolio suitable for you may be totally inappropriate for your parents.

Portfolio Construction

A portfolio should begin with a plan that considers your risk-tolerance level and your investment objectives. Then, specific investments are selected and combined to achieve the objectives within the risk tolerance specified. An important reason why many investors have so little success is that they do not specify concrete investment objectives. General goals, such as "making a lot of money," are too ambiguous to be of much help. We all want to make money—but over what period of time and subject to what degree of risk?

Figure 12.6 illustrates the portfolio construction process for three different types of investors. (Of course, other types are possible.) It's assumed that each investor owns a home and has adequate liquid assets and insurance. If any of these conditions are not met, then a different asset portfolio would be recommended. For example, if a home was not owned, then it would be desirable to allocate 30 to 40 percent to real estate (or some other form of investment with inflation-hedging capacity), possibly REITs, and cut back proportionately in the other asset categories.

Aggressive Investors

As an aggressive investor, you are likely to have a high risk-tolerance level and generally prefer future return to current return. We assume in this example that you have no specific future goals with high priorities; although that assumption could be relaxed with respect to a retirement goal. As you see, the recommended asset mix is one-third each for large company growth stocks, small company growth stocks, and international stocks. Many excellent mutual funds offer these kinds of stocks, and you should diversify by owning two or three funds in each category. It is very important to make sure of the fund's investment

Figure 12.6

Portfolios are designed to meet specific investment objectives. These differ, depending on circumstances and the investor's risk tolerance. Three cases are shown. The asset weights in each portfolio should be considered as broad approximations, since more exact amounts would require detailed information about specific investors. Also, it is assumed that the investor owns a home, has sufficient funds to meet liquidity needs, and has adequate life insurance.

	Aggressive Investor	Cautious Investor	Investor Who Needs Income
Risk tolerance	High	Low	Moderate
Return preference	Future return	Future return	Current return
Priority of specific future goals	Not strong	Very strong	Moderately strong
Candidates	· Persons with no dependents · Wealthy investors	· Anyone with dependents · Investor planning retirement · Investor planning a major purchase	· Retirees · Persons with dependents needing current support · Persons with no major future expenditures

objective. For example, the Fidelity Fund we have been reviewing would not be a good choice even though it has a good performance history. It is a growth *and income* fund, not simply a growth fund.

Although the recommended mix of assets will provide some degree of diversification, particularly with the international stocks, your portfolio still will have a high degree of market value volatility. However, if you hold the portfolio for a reasonably long period of time (say, 10 years or longer), you should show a good accumulation of value.

Cautious Investors

A cautious investor generally has a low risk-tolerance level but, more important, also attaches a high priority to accumulating sufficient sums of money to achieve certain future goals. If you are planning for a major expenditure in 5 years, or retirement in 10 years, and you want to be sure that sufficient funds are available to meet that target, then your portfolio must be constructed accordingly.

In our example, 70 percent of your funds are invested in assets with predetermined accumulation amounts—bank-issued certificates of deposit (CDs) and U.S. Treasury Strips. (Of course, the maturities of these investments would match the horizon dates of your goals. You could use mutual funds to acquire the Treasury Strips, or you could purchase them directly through a broker.

Even though you have a strong priority for achieving future goals, it often makes sense to put some of your funds into a growing asset, such as large company growth stocks, since you do not need current return. Clearly, this move adds an element of risk to your future accumulation amount, and you should not make it if your future plans are in a sense "set in stone." But such rigidity is not common with many investment goals. You might plan $10,000 for a nice vacation in four years, although any amount between $8,000 and $12,000 will do; adding a growth asset gives you a good shot at the higher amount but also brings a possibility for the smaller one.

Investors Who Need Income

If you need income from your investments, you must select vehicles that provide high current returns. Our example assumes that you have a moderate risk-tolerance level. So you could place half of your funds in high-quality corporate bonds and divide the other half between two moderately riskier investments—medium-quality corporate bonds and income stocks. This mix should provide a return of one to two percentage points more than if you invested in very safe bonds, such as U.S. Treasuries. Of course, if you have a very low risk-tolerance level, then the Treasuries would be more appropriate.

Mutual funds are definitely the best route for the recommended investments here. As we noted in Chapter 11, bond investment is somewhat complex and can be expensive when investing small amounts. You will have no trouble finding very good bond funds. Those offered by the Vanguard Group are particularly appealing because Vanguard features low operating costs and no front-end loads. Several studies have shown that performance differences among fixed-income funds are explained mostly by variations in fund expenses. Therefore, find funds with low expenses and you are likely to find funds with good performance potential.

SIMPLIFYING
financial planning 12.4

All in the Family: Selecting a Mutual Fund Family

A "fund family" is a group of mutual funds sponsored by the same organization. Keeping your investments within a fund family can save you time and money. Some mutual fund companies base annual fees on the aggregate amount invested in the fund family, regardless of how small your investment in any individual fund. Furthermore, you typically can exchange shares in one fund for shares in another fund within the same family at no charge or for a minimal fee. However, excessive trading between funds will lead to additional fees.

By investing in a fund family you save time because you can review all of your accounts at a single online site and receive consolidated reports. This can be especially helpful at tax time when you need to report taxable income on each fund. Remember, whenever you trade a mutual fund, even when they are members of the same fund family, you may owe taxes on any capital appreciation.

When selecting a fund family be sure to check out all of the relatives. Does the company offer a large selection of funds with a wide range of objectives? It should offer all of the fund types listed in Figure 12.1. If you are interested in allocating your funds by sector, make sure the company provides an adequate selection of no-load sector funds. Many companies offer both load and no-load funds. If you have initially invested in a no-load fund, don't assume that all of the other company's funds are also no-load. Check out the expense ratios on a range of the company's funds you might consider holding and whether loads are waived for in-family exchanges.

With any investment strategy there must always be some words of caution. While most of the major fund families, such as Vanguard and Fidelity, are highly respected and financially stable companies, unexpected events can shake our confidence. Investment company risk can be reduced by investing in more than one mutual fund family. In a recent article by Elton, Gruber, and Green in the *Journal of Financial and Quantitative Analysis*, "The Impact of Mutual Fund Family Membership on Investor Risk," the authors found that mutual fund returns were more closely correlated within than between mutual fund families. In other words, investors can gain some risk reduction by investing in more than one fund family.

Maintaining Your Portfolio

Over time, the values of assets in your portfolio are likely to change; some assets will increase in value while others decline, or increase less rapidly. Of the three investor types discussed above, fluctuations would be most likely for the aggressive investor. As the investment values change, the portfolio weights also change. For example, the aggressive investor's small company growth stocks might show substantial increases over several years and become, say, 50 percent of the portfolio's total value. Clearly, it may be necessary to rebalance the portfolio. Two rebalancing approaches are used—a constant ratio plan and a variable ratio plan.

Constant ratio plan A method of rebalancing a portfolio that restores each component to a preset percentage.

As the name implies, a **constant ratio plan** adjusts the portfolio back to its target weights—a third in each asset category for the aggressive investor example. So you would sell some of the small company growth stocks and reinvest in the large company growth stocks and the international stocks, assuming that each was less than 33 percent. To avoid excessive trading, you might do rebalancing only once a year or when one asset exceeds a predetermined limit, say 40 percent. Rebalancing might be done more often with mutual funds if switches among funds are free.

Some investment advisors feel that rebalancing your portfolio not only keeps the portfolio in line with your investment goals but also has the advantage of selling some assets that have appreciated (perhaps excessively) in value and buying those that have not fared well (but are hoped to do so in the future). If you like this idea, then why not carry it to a higher level?

Variable ratio plan A method of rebalancing a portfolio that places greater weight on underperforming assets in a restoration.

A **variable ratio plan** does just that; it rebalances, but it stacks the proportions in favor of assets that have performed poorly in recent periods. For example, you would reduce small company growth stocks to, say, 25 percent while increasing large company growth stocks and international stocks to, say, 37.5 percent each. You should see that this plan not only departs from your original plan but is also a form of market timing. Our discussion of market timing in Chapter 10 was not encouraging, and neither is our opinion of variable ratio plans.

Asset Allocation Mutual Funds

Asset allocation mutual funds Mutual funds that operate with certain portfolio component weight guidelines.

If you dislike the idea of constructing and maintaining a portfolio, you could consider investing in **asset allocation mutual funds** and let the fund managers make such decisions for you. These funds operate within certain guidelines as to component weights of their portfolios. For instance, Fidelity has a number of such funds, each having a different objective. Its Asset Manager fund, for example, seeks high total return with relatively low risk. Its target asset weights are 40 percent common stocks, 40 percent bonds, and 20 percent short-term securities, and it adjusts its portfolio to fluctuate around those weights. Although we don't know its actual strategy, it's likely to be a version of a constant or variable ratio plan.

TOPIC LINKS

Review Fidelity's Asset Allocation funds.

Asset allocation funds are appropriate for investors with broadly defined investment objectives, such as our above aggressive investor. Unfortunately, there is some evidence suggesting that their returns are not very good, when measured in a risk-return setting. Much of their poor performance arises from poor market-timing results, the very area in which they supposedly are better than the average small investor.

Mutual Funds Management in the 401(k) Retirement Plan

A typical 401(k) plan offered by many employers allows employees to invest in a wide array of mutual funds. While legal and operational details of such plans are discussed in

Chapter 16, it's helpful to discuss here the topic of managing mutual funds you might own in a plan. The topic is important because there is growing evidence that many employees are not managing their investments wisely. Some critical problems are addressed next.

Rejecting Participation in the Plan

Many employees choose not to enroll in 401(k) plans, even when employers agree to match, partially or wholly, their contributions. The Pension Protection Act of 2006 is supposed to remedy that situation by automatically enrolling employees in company plans. You still have the right to reject plan participation. If you turn down such an offer from an employer who wholly matches your contributions, in effect, you give up the opportunity to double your money immediately. No one can match that performance investing outside a plan. True, you can eliminate the 401(k) management problem by simply not participating, but it could be the worst retirement and investment decision you make.

Holding a Single Fund

Too many employees choose only one fund in which to invest. Often they select the fund based on its previous year's performance. Each of these actions can be a mistake. First, it is difficult for one fund to accomplish a variety of objectives. For example, even an index fund of, say, the S&P 500 stocks does not provide adequate significant international exposure or any exposure to small- and medium-sized businesses. So, even if you desire a 100 percent stake in common stocks, you should choose perhaps three or four different equity funds to gain broader diversification. Second, when you choose a fund, you should review a number of factors as we have explained in this chapter and not simply focus on what the fund did last year. Very often, last year's hot fund is this year's dud, particularly if the fund follows a narrow theme, such as investing in Internet stocks.

No Coordination Between In-Plan and Out-of-Plan Investments

Remember that your 401(k) investments are a part of your overall portfolio. Often it is helpful to coordinate the two areas and not treat each as a separate investing activity. For example, outside the plan you might have money invested in savings accounts, CDs, and other relatively safe vehicles, while you invest totally in growth stocks within the plan. It could be better from an income tax point of view to reverse the process. Since you defer taxes with in-plan investments, you can choose a good bond fund with a high current return; meanwhile, outside the plan you can buy growth stocks on your own or invest in growth funds that try to minimize taxes. In a sense, a good growth stock such as Microsoft has a built-in tax deferral since it pays no dividends, and you can avoid a capital gains tax by simply not selling. Putting Microsoft in your 401(k) accomplishes nothing by way of tax deferral.

An important operational rule is that you should choose retirement-directed investments based upon diversification considerations, your tolerance for risk, and your proximity to a retirement date. After you have constructed such a plan, then consider income tax or other implications of how the investments should be held.

Trying to Time the Markets

401(k) plans have created a whole new class of market players—individuals who think they can time the market. So, they rush to sell when the market sinks and then scramble to get back in when it rises. Regrettably, the ease of switching investments in a plan (often, you can do it over the Internet) without any income tax effects is conducive to a trading habit. But the evidence on how well traders perform these timing decisions indicates more failure than success. Market timing's primary risk to the young investor is that it too often puts you out of the market, usually at critical times when prices advance sharply.

Excessive Conservatism

Several studies of 401(k) investors have been revealing. Along with poor diversification, many investors choose ultraconservative investments such as fixed-income annuities. These are not older investors nearing retirement; rather, they are young investors with very long investment horizons. Moreover, these investors are not choosing annuities for tax reasons, as discussed above, since practically all of their investments are in the 401(k) plan.

Being too conservative can be the most tragic mistake you make in investing. If you have forgotten the power of compounding over long periods of time, you should review the section covering the topic in Chapter 2. And, if you ask people who have invested properly in a 401(k) plan for the past 20 years, they will tell you that compounding is not just a textbook lesson. Indeed, they already may have joined the ranks of 401(k) millionaires.

key terms

asset allocation mutual funds (p. 336)	money market fund (p. 321)
closed-end fund (p. 319)	mortgage trusts (p. 330)
constant ratio plan (p. 336)	mutual fund (p. 318)
equity trusts (p. 330)	net asset value (NAV) (p. 318)
exchange-traded funds (ETFs) (p. 328)	no-load fund (p. 319)
fund switching (p. 322)	open-end fund (p. 319)
global fund (p. 320)	prospectus (p. 320)
index fund (p. 321)	real estate investment trust (REIT) (p. 330)
international fund (p. 320)	reinvestment plan (p. 322)
investment club (p. 333)	sector fund (p. 321)
limited partnership (p. 331)	shareholder report (p. 320)
load fund (p. 319)	unit investment trust (UIT) (p. 326)
maximum capital appreciation fund (p. 321)	variable ratio plan (p. 336)

follow-up on the Steele family

Reread the chapter-opening vignette.

1. What type of fund (as to fund objective—such as growth, income, index) do you feel is appropriate for the Steeles, given their investment goals? Explain your answer.

2. What type of fund (as to fund structure—such as open-end, closed-end, exchange traded) do you feel is appropriate for the Steeles, given their backgrounds and willingness to manage their investments?

3. The stockbroker with whom the Steeles have had discussions is encouraging them to invest in several balanced funds sponsored by her firm. Each has a 4.5 percent front-end load and operating costs of 1.2 percent annually. Would you advise the Steeles to follow her suggestion? Explain and indicate any additional information you would like to have about the funds.

4. Refer to Figure 12.6. Of the three types of investors shown there, which is the most fitting for the Steeles? Explain. Also, if you feel that none of the three is appropriate in the Steeles' case, design a portfolio that you think is better.

1. What is a mutual fund? Define NAV, and explain how it is calculated.
2. What is the difference between a load and a no-load fund? Is one a better performer than the other?
3. What is the difference between an open-end and a closed-end fund? Which type might show a discount? Is a discount an advantage or disadvantage? Explain.
4. Kim Karnes is thinking of buying the following three mutual funds:

	NAV	Offer Price	Closing Price on NYSE
Alpha	10.50	N.L.	—
Beta	21.00	22.90	—
Gamma	30.75	—	$26.25

But Kim doesn't know what the preceding figures mean. Help Kim by explaining the differences among the three funds.

5. Identify nine different fund objectives. Explain which one appeals to you most.
6. Briefly explain four important services provided by mutual funds.
7. Distinguish between a fund's cumulative total return and its average annual total return over a given time period, say, five years.
8. Metro Fund had a cumulative total return of 150 percent over the past four years. If you invested $1,000 in the fund four years ago, how much is your investment worth today?
9. What roles do a fund's operating costs and portfolio turnover rate play in terms of fund evaluation? Explain.
10. You bought 100 shares of an open-end mutual fund one year ago at $10 a share. You received a $0.50 per share distribution six months ago when the fund's NAV was $12.50 a share. If the fund's NAV at the end of the year was $12 a share, calculate your rate of return on the fund for the year.
11. Provide a brief explanation of the following, indicating their advantages and disadvantages:
    a. unit investment trust
    b. exchange-traded fund
    c. real estate investment trust
    d. limited partnership
    e. investment club
12. Explain how your risk-tolerance level and investment objectives influence the construction of your personal portfolio.
13. Indicate the type of securities or mutual funds that you believe are suitable for an aggressive investor whose primary investment goal is capital accumulation over the long term. Contrast your advice in that case to the advice you would give a person with a low risk-tolerance level who seeks current income.
14. Explain constant and variable ratio plans. Which is actually a form of market timing? Explain.
15. Describe an asset allocation fund. What type of investor might be interested in such funds?
16. Maria Gomez has recently been hired by a major corporation with a 401(k) plan. She thinks she will not participate, though, because she believes she can earn better returns investing on her own. What insight can you offer Maria?

17. Is holding a single fund in a 401(k) plan a good strategy, particularly if that fund was a super performer last year?

18. Explain a situation highlighting the importance of coordinating investments within and out of your 401(k) retirement plan.

19. Helmut Bosh, a 22-year-old recent college graduate, has a low risk tolerance. He has signed up with his employer's 401(k) plan but has chosen to put all his money in an annuity guaranteeing a 5 percent annual return. Evaluate Helmut's strategy.

case 12.1

The Byron's Search for a Mutual Fund

Lorrie and Dave Byron are saving for their children's education. They estimate they will need about $10,000 a year for a six-year period beginning nine years from now. The Byrons have sufficient liquidity and will not need these investment funds until then. They have decided that mutual funds represent the best investment vehicle for them, and they are currently trying to select one for their first investment of $3,000.

Lorrie is impressed with the Sun Income Fund, which invests mainly in fixed-income securities. Lorrie notes that it has a good history of making distributions and that its rate of return last year (2007) was 17 percent. Dave disagrees with Lorrie's selection; instead, he favors the Ambrux Capital Appreciation Fund. It invests heavily in the common stock of growth companies, and it distributes very little each year, preferring rather to reinvest capital gains. He argues that since they will not need distributions, it doesn't make sense to invest in a fund that features them. He also notes that Ambrux's rate of return last year was 33.4 percent, a much better performance than Sun's.

Lorrie agrees that growth might be a better investment goal than high current income, but she thinks it doesn't matter how much a fund distributes, since they will elect to have all distributions reinvested in the fund anyway. Her preference for the Sun Fund rests mostly with her feeling that it is less risky—and she thinks the beta values for each support this view.

Questions

1. Using the data below, calculate the rates of return for each fund for 2006 and 2007. Your figures for 2007 should agree with the values given in Case 12.1. Calculate the average rate of return for the two-year period for each fund.

2. Show how much their $3,000 investment would be worth as of December 31, 2007, assuming it was invested in one or the other fund. Assume that distributions during the year were used to acquire additional shares at the average NAV for the year.

3. Assuming that each fund is no-load and that the two funds are similar in other important respects, which do you recommend for the Byrons? Explain the reason(s) for your choice. Be sure to comment on the issue of distributions from the funds.

4. Explain whether you think it might be a good idea for the Byrons to divide their investments between the two funds.

	Sun Income Fund	Ambrux Capital Appreciation Fund
NAV:		
December 31, 2005	$16.50	$12.50
December 31, 2006	15.00	11.00
December 31, 2007	16.00	14.00
Distributions per share:		
2006	$ 3.00	$ 0.50
2007	1.50	0.60
Current beta value	0.60	1.20

Cliff Swatner is single, 33 years old, and owns a condominium in New York City worth $350,000. Cliff is an attorney and doing well financially. His income last year exceeded $160,000, and he has sufficient liquid assets to supplement his condominium and other tangible assets. Several years ago, Cliff began investing in stocks and bonds. He made his selections on the basis of articles he read describing good investment opportunities. Some have worked well for Cliff, but others have not. Cliff has never taken the time to evaluate his portfolio performance, but he feels it isn't very good. Cliff currently has about $110,000 invested. He has been dating a woman who he hopes to marry in three years, at which time he will need $30,000 for wedding and honeymoon expenses. Cliff's only other objective is to accumulate funds for retirement, but he does not have a specific dollar target for this goal. Cliff feels that he has a moderate risk-tolerance level.

case 12.2

Evaluating Cliff Swatner's Portfolio

Questions

1. Explain some disadvantages of Cliff's current investment approach.

2. Construct a portfolio for Cliff, limiting your selections to mutual funds (assume that he sells his current stock and bond holdings). Make sure your plan indicates specific dollar amounts for each portfolio component.

3. Explain how Cliff should rebalance his portfolio periodically, indicating how frequently rebalancing should be done.

Exercises to Strengthen Your Use of the Internet
(Internet links for the following exercises can be found at **www.prenhall.com/frasca**.)

working out
on the Web

Exercise 12.1 Does Fidelity Have a Growth Fund?

Many mutual fund families, such as Vanguard's (**www.vanguard.com**), have Web sites. For another great site, visit the Fidelity Investment Center (**www.fidelity.com**). Click "Mutual Funds" and then click "Fidelity Mutual Funds" for comprehensive information, including performance measurements, on any Fidelity fund. "Browse All Funds" and use the "Fund Evaluator" to group funds by investment category. Click the fund that interests you.

Q. How many "large growth" funds does Fidelity offer?

Exercise 12.2 What Are Closed-End Funds?

The Investment Company Institute (**www.ici.org**) is a national association of U.S. investment companies that promotes the public understanding of mutual funds. Closed-end funds offer certain advantages and disadvantages in relation to open-end funds. Go to "Statistics and Research" and choose "Closed-End Funds Statistics."

Q. How many closed-end funds are there? How has the number of closed-end funds changed over the last decade? Are bond funds more numerous than stock (equity) funds?

Exercise 12.3 How Many Stars Does the Berger Select Fund Have?

Morningstar (**www.morningstar.com**) is a premier mutual fund evaluation service. You can browse the alphabetical index at no charge and find the Morningstar rating for many funds, but you will first have to register on the Web site.

Q. Of the "Highest Rated Growth" funds, which one had the highest YTD?

Exercise 12.4 How Are the Qs Doing?

Exchange-traded funds have become very popular. You can review a large list of ETFs at the Amex Market Site (**www.amex.com**).

Q. Click "ETF" and note the most active ETF. Enter QQQQ in the "Symbol Lookup" for the NASDAQ-100 Index Tracking Stock^{SM} and then click the name of the ETF. The "Tear Sheet" summarizes information on the stock's performance. What was the 1-year annualized return on the QQQQ?

Exercise 12.5 Where Can You Find a High–Performing REIT?

The National Association of Real Estate Investment Trusts (**www.nareit.com**) can help answer this question and also provide much more information about REITs. On the home page, click "Data Library," then "Performance Data," then "Performance by Property Sector." Open the latest "REIT."

Q. What is the average total return for the most current year for industrial/office REITs?

Exercise 12.6 Want to Join an Investment Club?

If your answer is yes, or if you simply want to learn more about investment clubs, or if you want to find some sound ideas on investing in general, visit the National Association of Investment Clubs site (**www.better–investing.org**).

Q. How can you find an investment club to join?

part 5

Protecting Your Wealth

insurance and retirement planning

Financial security is the major theme of this section. You want to be secure from uncertain financial losses, and you want to ensure that you are comfortable in your later years. To accomplish these goals you have to adopt a strategy that both preserves your current assets and plans their future growth.

Insurance is one area in which a wrong purchase is very easy to make. The objectives are complicated, the terminology is confusing, and the sales agent may not be working in your best interest. Moreover, if you buy without adequate forethought, your mistake will become apparent only after it is too late. What good does it do to realize you purchased the wrong kind or amount of insurance *after* an auto accident, a home fire, or a disabling illness? Insurance is purchased for many reasons. However, the basic and most important purpose of insurance is to protect you against financial catastrophe.

Part 5 begins with a brief review of insurance basics in Chapter 13. Property and liability insurance protects what you have today. Property loss coverage protects you from financial loss as a result of either nature's perils or human negligence. Health and disability insurance, examined in Chapter 14, protects you and your family from the disastrous financial consequences that accompany a major illness or injury. Life insurance provides support for dependents at the death of a household provider. In Chapter 15 you will estimate your life insurance needs. Life insurance can also serve as a vehicle for accumulating retirement savings and a means for the orderly transfer of a death estate. You will estimate your retirement needs and structure a plan for satisfying those needs in Chapter 16.

13

Property and Liability Insurance

protecting your lifestyle assets

Objectives

1. To review the foundations of insurance coverage
2. To understand the primary components of the homeowner's and auto insurance packages
3. To list and explain the standard formats for homeowner's insurance policies
4. To learn how to evaluate your auto and home insurance needs
5. To be able to find and fill any gaps in your homeowner's and auto coverage

Steele family

The evening news dwells on catastrophes. Floods, hurricanes, and tornadoes provide dramatic video and touch on our sympathies for those who must endure nature's perils. The Steeles feel lucky. The family is in good health. They have not had a serious auto accident or suffered significant damage to their home. A neighbor's tree fell against their house last year, but there was only minor damage to the rain gutter and fence. The cost of repairs was quickly reimbursed by their neighbor's homeowner's insurance.

Despite their relative good fortune, the Steeles know that bad things can happen. To protect themselves from financial harm, they have purchased the usual types of insurance coverage: home, auto, health, and life insurance. They know they are protected, but they are not quite sure what each policy covers. Over the past few years, the combined cost of this insurance protection has risen significantly and now is taking up a larger percentage of their budget. They would like to find ways of minimizing these cost increases while still providing adequate financial protection.

TOPIC LINKS

Follow the **Topic Links** in each chapter for your interactive Personal Finance exercise on the Web. Go to: **www.prenhall.com/frasca**.

Surveys by the National Association of Insurance Commissioners (NAIC) reveal that a large percentage of policyholders mistakenly believe they are protected against perils that actually fall outside the boundaries of their policy coverage. It's unfortunate that many people wait until after an accident or catastrophe to read the provisions in their property and casualty insurance coverage closely. Some will find that their homeowner's or auto policy covers more than they expected. Others may feel cheated, having less coverage than they thought or receiving less reimbursement than they expected. With a little forethought and financial planning, you can protect yourself from financial harm due to either the negligence of others or the vagaries of nature.

In this chapter we will examine both homeowner's and auto insurance. Each is a package of component policies covering disasters at home or on the road. Both can provide nonoverlapping protection against property loss and personal liability. **Property loss insurance** reimburses you for damage to your property due to accidental or natural circumstances or due to the negligence of others or yourself. By negligence we mean the failure to exercise the care expected of a prudent person. Property damage due to a faulty furnace or a violent storm should be covered by property loss coverage in your homeowner's insurance policy. **Personal liability insurance** provides protection from claims against you resulting from the financial harm your negligence may cause others. You drive carefully, but you know the unexpected can happen. One lapse in your attention at the wrong moment can have dreadful financial consequences. The liability coverage in your auto policy limits the financial risk of your inadvertent negligence.

Property loss insurance Reimburses you for damage to your property due to accidental or natural circumstances or due to the negligence of others or yourself.

Personal liability insurance Protects you from the financial harm your negligence causes others.

Fundamental Insurance Concepts

Many consumers are highly suspicious of insurance companies. They see themselves paying premiums and getting very little or nothing in return. That suspicion is fed by either news of needy people who are denied coverage or significant increases in annual premiums. In some cases, these suspicions may be well founded, but many times they arise from a misunderstanding of fundamental insurance principles. This is why we review some basic risk and insurance concepts before examining insurance policies and your needed coverage. Given this foundation in the principles of insurance, you may better understand how the information in this and subsequent chapters will help you avoid many of the worst financial catastrophes.

Risk

It's impossible and probably not even desirable, to eliminate all risk from your life. Every day brings you unexpected pleasures and unforeseen disappointments. Without them, life would be bland and unexciting. That new job can be rewarding or frustrating. The new car can provide hours of enjoyment or hours in the shop. Everything you do involves some risk.

You willingly undertake certain risks because they provide the possibility of financial gain. **Speculative risk** exists when both gain and loss are possible. In the stock and bond markets you accept speculative risks in the hope that you will receive a compensating return on your investments. This risk-return trade-off was emphasized in the chapters on investment. As a knowledgeable investor, you can adjust your speculative risk according to your personal risk preferences.

Speculative risk Exists when there is the opportunity for both gain and loss.

There are some risks, however, that you certainly could do without. These risks provide only the opportunity for loss, with no possibility of gain. Examples include the risk that your home might burn to the ground or that you might be injured in a car accident.

Pure risk The risk of loss from accidental circumstances.

Each represents a potential financial drain on your resources and is said to contain pure risk. **Pure risk** exists when only loss is possible and the loss is the result of accidental circumstances. You may undertake certain precautions to reduce these risks, such as keeping a fire extinguisher in your home and driving only in good weather. However, individual action may not be enough to significantly reduce pure risk. In some circumstances, group action in the marketplace may be necessary. It is pure risk we seek to protect against when we purchase insurance.

Pooling of Risk

All market insurance involves a pooling of risk. For each of us individually, the future is highly uncertain. However, when we combine many individuals, functioning under similar circumstances, future events affecting the group as a whole become highly predictable. It's difficult to forecast with any certainty whether you will have an auto accident on a given weekend. However, it is not too difficult to predict how many accidents will take place nationally on any weekend. This ability to forecast with great certainty the likelihood of events for large numbers of individuals allows us to join together and pool our risks.

If we can estimate total losses suffered by a given group of individuals, then we know the necessary amount of financial reserves that will reimburse these same individuals for their expected losses. When group members share the cost of this reserve by each paying what is termed a *premium*, they share the group's losses. Each member is committed to paying a certain premium but is also freed from the possibility of a larger financial loss. The premium represents the cost of the risk transfer.

The premium should be based on the average loss experience for the group as a whole. When using past loss experience to project future losses, insurance companies must be wary of adverse selection. **Adverse selection** is the tendency for those with higher than average risk to desire insurance coverage. If, over time, those at high risk either purchase insurance or continue coverage to a greater extent than those at low risk, then average losses must rise. The insurance company will then find that the premiums it has collected do not adequately cover the losses it had insured. If the insurance company is unable to meet its obligations, it is insolvent. This may result in widespread financial loss and great hardship for many policyholders who had paid premiums for nonexistent protection. It is certainly a tragedy to have suffered a loss, only to find that the insurance protection you were depending on is not there.

Adverse selection When those with higher than average risk seek or continue insurance coverage.

Underwriting Selecting and classifying risk exposure.

Underwriting is the process of selecting and classifying risk exposure. The person who does this is called an *underwriter*. It is the underwriter's responsibility to guard against adverse selection by denying coverage to those who are at greater risk than that of the insured group. This can lead to negative publicity for the insurers, who are often accused of being heartless because they deny coverage to those who need it most. In doing this, however, the underwriter is protecting not only the interest of the insurance company, but also is guaranteeing the continued protection of the many policyholders who are relying on this company to be there in time of need.

Obviously, if everyone in the group suffered a loss at the same time, the reserves could not cover all the losses. Consequently, we cannot successfully insure ourselves against risks that affect the group as a whole; we can only insure against risks that are personal in nature. For this reason, private market insurance does not cover losses resulting from wars, nuclear accidents, or floods. Where such insurance does exist, it is viable only when backed by a government with the power to levy taxes and print money.

In the marketplace, the insurance company manages the reserve pool of funds. In doing so, it incurs some transaction costs and some financial risks. The company must receive adequate compensation for processing and policing the many claims and for assuming the risk that the pooled reserves may not be adequate to meet all of the claims.

Consequently, insurance companies will receive more in premiums than they pay out in claims. This doesn't mean that insurance is a bad deal. It does mean there is an expected cost attached to using the marketplace. Therefore, you should decide whether the transfer of risk is worth the additional cost before purchasing insurance.

Insurable Interest

You may purchase insurance when you have an insurable interest. In order to have an **insurable interest**, you must be related to the insured event in such a way that if the event occurs, you will incur a financial loss. Without this requirement, you would be **gambling**, not purchasing insurance. For example, I cannot purchase insurance against loss of the space shuttle. I have no financial interest in the enterprise. If it were lost, I would not suffer any financial harm. An agreement whereby I would receive payment if the shuttle were unsuccessful would be a gamble rather than an insurance contract. However, companies having payloads aboard the shuttle can and do enter into insurance contracts dependent on the shuttle's success. The financial loss these companies would suffer if the shuttle mission were unsuccessful represents an insurable interest.

Insurable interest An interest for which you can purchase insurance protection.

Gambling Wagering on a risky event in which you have no insurable interest.

Indemnification

Another way in which insurance differs from gambling is that payment under an insurance contract should not exceed the value of the loss. At most, insurance is meant to provide **indemnification**; that is, a return to your financial status before the loss. You should not receive a net financial gain when an insurance policy pays off. For this reason, you should not insure an article for more than it's worth. Overinsurance is a waste of money, because an insurance company will not pay out more than the market worth of the loss.

    Of course, no fair market value can be placed on a human life. Consequently, the amount of life insurance we can take out on ourselves and our relatives is practically unlimited. The concept of indemnification, however, is important when we take out life insurance on our business associates. In business relationships, the amount of life insurance must be limited by the amount of financial harm.

Indemnification The restoration of the financial state that existed before a loss.

Risk Management

Risk management consists of identifying, evaluating, and determining how to handle your risks. Your health, property, and ability to generate income are constantly at risk from numerous sources. You need to enumerate these risks and determine how threatening each is to you and to your family's financial survival. There are four basic strategies you may adopt for managing risk: risk reduction, risk avoidance, risk transfer, and risk retention.

Risk management The process of identifying, evaluating, and managing risk.

Risk Reduction

You engage in **risk reduction** when you lower the probability of a loss by taking preventive action. Examples of personal risk reduction include the use of car bumpers, football helmets, seat belts, and smoke and burglar alarms. Each reduces the probability of major property damage, the probability of loss of life, or both.

Risk reduction Reducing the probability of loss through preventive action.

Risk Avoidance

Risk avoidance involves reducing or eliminating the probability of a loss by avoiding the cause of the loss. If you avoid smoking and the heavy use of alcohol, you avoid severe risks to your health.

Risk avoidance Reducing or eliminating risk through behavior modification.

Risk avoidance is termed a conservative strategy because it calls for a change in behavior. Sometimes, the cost of changing our behavior is just too high for us to accept. You could avoid the risk of flying by not flying, but this would limit both your business career and your vacation alternatives. Furthermore, you must be careful that the avoidance of one risk does not increase another. By not flying, you may be accepting greater risks by driving.

Risk Retention

Risk retention Accepting risk as the least costly, best course of action.

When the cost of eliminating the risk far exceeds the benefits of eliminating the risk, your best decision may be **risk retention**. This can be true for both major losses and minor losses. For example, it would be prohibitively expensive—if not impossible—to insure your property against loss to war or insurrection. Consequently, you must assume the risk.

You can insure against the cost of appliance repairs with a service contract. The expected cost of repairs, however, is typically much less than the cost of the service contract. In addition, when the appliance does need repairs, it's usually a minor inconvenience rather than a major financial catastrophe. Your optimal strategy is to retain small risks but transfer the large ones when possible.

Risk Transfer

Risk transfer Eliminating risk through the purchase of insurance.

By purchasing an insurance contract, you engage in **risk transfer**. With life, health, auto, and homeowner's insurance the associated risks of major financial loss are transferred from you and your family to the insurer. Transferring risk is an important tool for eliminating major risks that cannot be feasibly disposed of through risk reduction or avoidance. No matter how moderate and healthful your lifestyle may be, there is still the possibility of a disabling sickness or premature death. The resulting expense and loss of income could lead to drastic changes for both you and your family. For protection against significant risks such as this, transferring risk through insurance is the best risk management strategy.

Homeowner's Insurance

The Insurance Information Institute indicates that almost all home owners have homeowner's insurance. The typical home mortgage contract requires that borrowers purchase and retain homeowner's insurance. The lender wants assurance the loan will be paid back, if your house is destroyed. Even if you are not required to purchase homeowner's insurance, it would be courting disaster to do without it.

Over the years, homeowner's policies have evolved into a few standard formats that seem to serve adequately the needs of the typical home owner or renter. In order to fully understand the differences among homeowner's policies, you first must master some standard insurance terminology and the basic elements of a homeowner's policy.

TOPIC LINKS

Review the NAIC Home Owners Insurance Report.

The Terminology of Homeowner's Policies

Most homeowner's policies are written in a clear and straightforward style. In fact, if you can't understand your policy and your insurance agent can't provide an adequate explanation of your coverage, you may have sufficient reason for finding another insurer. However, even the best-written policies contain some points that require an explanation to help you fully realize what you have purchased and how you are protected.

All Risks Versus Named Perils Insurance

The policy should indicate whether you have **all risks coverage** or **named perils coverage**. The type of coverage need not remain the same throughout the policy. You may find that some items come under all risks insurance and others come under named perils insurance. All risks protection doesn't necessarily cover you against all risks. It does protect you against all risks that are not specifically excluded in the policy. Named perils insurance is just what the term implies: It covers only risks that are specifically stated in the policy. Therefore, with all risks protection you should see a list of circumstances not covered, whereas under named perils you should see a list of circumstances that will be covered.

> **All risks coverage** Insurance covers all risks that are not specifically excluded.
>
> **Named perils coverage** Insurance covers only risks that are specifically named.

The difference is important, because each places special obligations on the insurer and the insured. Under all risks coverage, the insurance company is responsible for showing that your loss was not due to one of the specific exemptions stated in the policy. Alternatively, under named perils coverage, it's your responsibility to demonstrate that your loss was due to one of the named perils.

Replacement Cost Versus Actual Cash Value

The policy should state whether you will be reimbursed for losses at replacement cost or actual cash value. When the insurance company agrees to pay **replacement cost** on damaged goods, you receive the amount needed to replace new for old, with no deduction for depreciation. Depreciation is equal to the decline in market value, the difference between the purchase price of a good and its current market value. For example, if the roof on your home is destroyed, replacement cost coverage will pay for the construction of a new roof, regardless of the age of the old one.

> **Replacement cost** The amount needed to replace new for old, with no deduction for depreciation.

Actual cash value is equal to replacement cost minus depreciation. If the typical roof lasts 20 years and yours is destroyed in the 10th year, under actual cash value reimburse-

> **Actual cash value** Market value equal to replacement cost minus depreciation.

finance news 13.1

Insurers Use Credit Report to Determine Risk Exposure

Insurers believe they have found a relationship between an individual's credit record and the likelihood of filing an insurance claim. Under the Fair Credit Reporting Act, insurers can access your credit reports before determining your risk rating. Your FICO score that reflects your credit worthiness was discussed in Chapter 6 on credit management. Using similar information, insurance companies calculate an insurance risk score to forecast the probability of future claims.

Several insurance companies use ChoicePoint as a source of information on your claims and credit history. ChoicePoint supplies information to these companies based upon two scoring models: one for home owners and one for auto owners. The accompanying report provides insurance agents with instant information on clients. Insurance companies use the risk score and your previous loss record to rate your claims risk. You can check your own scores and your claims history by ordering a

copy of your report from ChoicePoint. Information on these scores and how to correct an erroneous report can be found at **www.choicepointinc.com.**

You may not think that your ability to handle credit is linked to your ability to drive safely. Statistical models, however, show a positive link between good credit and low insurance claims. Insurance companies cannot see the future. The best they can do is lump individuals into categories with others having similar characteristics. If you share the characteristics of others who have had a poor claims record, you will have to pay more for insurance. The benefit of an insurance score based on a credit record is that unlike age and gender, it's something that you can control. Establishing a good credit record can show up in lower interest charges and lower insurance costs.

The use of credit scores for assessing property risk is not without controversy. In several states, consumer groups have successfully set limits on the practice, because they believe it penalizes low-income families.

ment you would receive only 50 percent of the funds needed to replace the roof. This could place you in a very unfortunate position if you do not have the additional funds needed to repair the structural damage to the home. Without a roof over your head, you would need to rent some place to live. In addition, you would still be responsible for the mortgage payments on the home. Failure to pay could wipe out a good portion of your remaining equity in the home. For this reason, most homeowner's policies provide for reimbursement at replacement cost for structural damage and reimbursement at actual cash value for the contents. Moreover, additional living expenses while the structure is being repaired may be partially or totally reimbursed.

Replacement Cost Provision

Coinsurance Home owner is a coinsurer when the home is insured for less than 80 percent of its replacement value.

Homeowner's policies contain a provision that requires the home owner to provide **coinsurance** when the dwelling unit is insured for less than 80 percent of replacement value. Replacement value is the cost of rebuilding the home from the foundation up. It should be approximately equal to the price of a similar new home minus the cost of the lot and foundation.

The following example shows how a coinsurance clause works. Suppose the replacement value of your home is $100,000. If your insurance coverage on the dwelling is at least $80,000, the insurer will pay the full cost of repairing covered damages to the dwelling, up to the face amount of the policy. However, if your protection is for less than $80,000, you will receive less than full replacement cost. You would, in effect, become a coinsurer by having to pay the difference when repairing the structure.

Let's look at a specific example. Suppose a fire in the kitchen causes structural damage that would cost you $10,000 to repair. If you carry $50,000 of insurance on a home with $100,000 replacement value, you fall below the 80 percent requirement. In this situation, the amount you would receive from the insurance company would be calculated under the following formula:

$$\frac{\text{Amount of dwelling protection}}{80\% \times \text{replacement cost of dwelling}} \times \frac{\text{cost of damage at}}{\text{replacement cost}} = \text{insurance payout}$$

$$\frac{\$50,000}{80\% \times \$100,000} \times \$10,000 = \$6,250$$

The payout is reduced by the ratio of your actual protection to the 80 percent requirement. Thus, you would receive only $6,250, less the deductible on the policy.

There is one important exception to the preceding analysis. If the actual cash value of the loss were greater than the $6,250 calculated under the coinsurance formula, the insurer would reimburse at actual cash value up to the policy limits. For example, if the actual cash value of structural damage to the kitchen, equal to replacement cost minus depreciation, is estimated at $8,000, you will receive $8,000 rather than $6,250. Notice that this reimbursement is still less than $10,000 replacement cost, the amount received by a comparable fully insured home owner.

Coinsurance may seem like a scheme designed to cheat home owners, but it actually serves a useful purpose. Most losses are for much less than the replacement value of the home. Without the coinsurance clause, some home owners might be tempted to reduce insurance costs by carrying less than full coverage on the home, leaving them with inadequate coverage in the case of total destruction.

Inflation Guard Endorsement

With rises in the general price level, the cost of replacing your home should also increase. This means that unless you periodically increase the face amount of dwelling protection, your coverage will eventually fall below 80 percent of the replacement cost of the home. To protect against this deficit, you can include an **inflation guard endorsement** that periodically increases the face amount of dwelling protection. The increase may either be set at an agreed-upon percentage or tied to an index of construction costs.

Be careful; the inflation guard endorsement does not necessarily mean you have the right amount of coverage. Even with the endorsement, it is still your responsibility to make sure that there is neither too much nor too little dwelling protection.

Deductible Clause

A **deductible clause** limits payments to damages that exceed a given dollar loss. For example, a $100 deductible means that payments will be made only for damages exceeding $100, and then the amount of the payout will be reduced by $100. Under a $100 deductible, you would receive $400 back on a $500 loss. By including a deductible, the insurer eliminates the cost of handling many small claims. This saving can be passed on to the home owner through lower premiums. Including deductibles in your policy is an excellent way of holding down your insurance costs.

Deductible clause Limits reimbursement to damages in excess of deductible.

Some policies contain a *disappearing deductible*. For example, the insurer might agree to pay 111 percent of the excess of any loss over $50, up to losses of $500. If you suffer a loss of $150, the insurer will pay you 111 percent of $100, or $111. If your loss is $500 or more, you will receive complete reimbursement.

Mortgage Clause

You will discover in the **mortgage clause** that payments for damages to the dwelling and surrounding structures are made to the mortgagee if the mortgagee is named in the policy. The mortgagee is the lender, not you. The lender may hold the money to pay for repairs or to pay off the loan if the house is not rebuilt.

Mortgage clause Insurance payments for structural damage are made to the mortgage lender.

Other Insurance and the Apportionment Clause

If you have more than one insurance policy, each will pay only for damages up to their proportionate share of coverage. The **apportionment clause** makes it impossible for you to collect more than 100 percent of your losses by having multiple policies.

Apportionment clause Apportions financial responsibility so that the insured cannot collect more than 100 percent of the loss.

Because of the significant cost advantage of having all your homeowner's protection under one policy, you are not likely to want dual coverage. This clause is important, however, when you have additional coverage on a business conducted in the home. In this situation it may be unclear whether a particular loss is to be covered under your homeowner's insurance or your business insurance. Whoever pays, the apportionment clause makes sure you will not collect more than 100 percent of the value of the loss.

Subrogation Clause

Most insurance policies, both homeowner's and auto, contain a **subrogation clause** that places your right to sue for recovery after the insurer's. If the insurer pays you for a loss, it can then seek to recover its payments from the party who caused the harm. You are entitled to sue for and collect only amounts that exceed those you have received from the insurer. Likewise, the insurer cannot sue for or collect more than you were paid under the insurance coverage.

Subrogation clause Places your right to sue after the insurer's.

Property Coverage

Homeowner's policies contain two sections: Section I on property coverage and Section II on liability protection. The first section includes a discussion of your coverage for losses to the dwelling unit and your personal belongings. It states the method for determining reimbursement and the types of losses covered. Subsections A, B, C, and D in Section I are organized by type of property loss and typically begin with a discussion of coverage on the dwelling.

Coverage A—Dwelling Protection

Dwelling protection Protects against structural damage to the home.

Dwelling protection generally protects you against damage to the structure resulting from fire, lightning, civil commotion, smoke, hail, vehicle damage, aircraft damage, riot, and explosion. Unless the dwelling has been unoccupied for the previous 30 days, you may also be covered for damage resulting from vandalism and malicious mischief. Loss from earthquake, flood, nuclear accident, and war are specifically excluded.

The face amount of your dwelling protection is the most important number in the homeowner's policy. As stated previously, to avoid coinsurance payments, you should set the face amount at or above 80 percent of the cost of rebuilding. The amount of dwelling protection is also important because most of your other property loss limits will be stated as a percentage of the amount of insurance carried on the dwelling.

Coverage B—Appurtenant Structures

Appurtenant structures Structures other than the dwelling unit.

Structures other than the dwelling unit are called **appurtenant structures**. They include the garage, the storage shed, and even the mailbox. These will usually be covered for losses up to 10 percent of the amount on the dwelling unit.

Coverage C—Contents

Unscheduled personal property Property not specifically listed in the policy.

The loss of **unscheduled personal property**—items that are not specifically listed in the policy—from theft or damage at the home will generally be covered for about 50 percent of the dwelling coverage. This coverage is not as generous as it sounds. First, reimbursement is usually set at actual cash value, and second, there are much lower limits on specific valuables. If your valuables exceed these limits, you can take out additional insurance coverage by attaching a personal property floater to your homeowner's policy.

Many policies cover computer equipment for up to $5,000 damage, regardless of whether it is used for business. Some companies, however, may refuse to pay for damage to business-related property such as computers, fax machines, and printers unless they are covered by an optional rider insuring a home business. In addition, coverage limits on portable computers away from home may be much less.

One aspect of a homeowner's policy that most people overlook is the protection it provides away from home. If you read this subsection, you will likely find that your personal property away from home is covered for at least 10 percent of the value of the personal property on the premises.

Coverage D—Loss of Use

This often unnoticed subsection on additional living expenses can prove extremely helpful in the event of serious loss. If a covered loss leaves your home uninhabitable, it will pay for the additional expenses necessary to retain your normal living standards. The limit on this might be expressed as 10 to 20 percent of dwelling protection prorated for the amount of time spent out of the house, or the limit might be stated as a period of time over which additional expenses will be paid.

Totaling the Coverage

It is unlikely that a single catastrophe would permit you to collect up to each of the previously stated limits. However, if such a disaster did occur, the total reimbursement could be considerably greater than the face amount of the homeowner's policy. On a policy with a face amount of $100,000 in dwelling protection, the maximum payout is as follows:

Dwelling	$100,000
Appurtenant structures (10%)	10,000
Unscheduled property on premises (50%)	50,000
Unscheduled property off premises (5%)	5,000
Additional living expenses (20%)	20,000
Total coverage	$185,000

In addition, you might also receive payment for the following incidentals:

- Theft of items from cars
- Credit card and check forgery
- Debris removal
- Emergency removal
- Fire department charges
- Necessary repairs after loss
- Damaged trees, shrubs, plants, and lawns

Exclusions on Property Loss Coverage

In most policies, the following classes of property are specifically excluded from contents coverage, either because they are nonpersonal in character or because they are more appropriately covered by other types of policies:

- Articles described separately in a personal articles floater or insured elsewhere
- Animals, birds, or fish
- Motorized land vehicles and electronic communication and sound devices attached to them
- Aircraft and parts
- Property of roomers, boarders, and tenants
- Property in an apartment regularly rented to others
- Property rented or held for rental to others
- Business records

Liability Coverage

Liability coverage, explained in Section II of the homeowner's policy, protects you and your family from the financial harm your **negligence** causes others. When you take the proper precautions against harming others, you are exhibiting *due care*. Due care is the type of behavior that is expected of a reasonable person. Due care standards are defined by court decisions and legislative statutes. If you violate those standards, you become liable for any harm you may cause.

Usually people become liable because either they do not understand what is expected of them or they have a temporary lapse in judgment. For example, you might not realize that you have a responsibility to protect neighborhood children from attractive hazards on your property, like a swimming pool. On the other hand, you may realize you have a responsibility, but you forget to lock the gate to the pool when you leave home. In either case, you are liable for the potential harm. The three components of liability protection in

Liability coverage Protection from the financial harm your negligence causes others.

Negligence The failure to exercise due care, the care expected of a prudent person.

your homeowner's policy consist of personal liability insurance, medical payments insurance, and insurance against physical damage to the property of others.

Specifically excluded from your homeowner's coverage will be liabilities incurred while driving your car. For that you will have to purchase auto insurance, which is discussed in the next section.

Coverage E—Personal Liability

The insurer will pay, up to the limits of protection, all legally obligated expenses for bodily injury or property damage, assuming you did not intentionally inflict them. In addition, the insurer will also pay defense and settlement costs if it decides to fight the payment in court. However, once the insurance company has paid up to the policy limits, it is no longer legally responsible for further damage payments or for your legal defense.

The generally recommended minimum is $300,000, but the standard limit under this section is $100,000. This is not much protection when your actions result in serious physical harm. For example, if you are sued for $150,000 and your liability coverage is for $100,000, the insurer might decide to pay $100,000 to the injured party, leaving you with the cost of defending against a potential $50,000 award. If you are sued for an amount that approaches your policy limits, you may need to retain a lawyer to ensure that the insurance company is operating in your best interest.

Coverage F—Medical Payments Coverage

Minor injuries that occur on your property are covered by medical payments insurance, regardless of who is at fault. Off your premises, it pays for minor injuries that are caused by you. It doesn't pay the medical bills for you or your family, only the medical bills of others.

Most policies limit payments to a relatively small amount, $500 to $1,000 per person. While this is not major dollar protection, nevertheless it serves a useful purpose by providing the means and incentive for timely medical treatment. This protects both you and the insurer. Immediate inspection and documentation of the injury may prevent the filing of larger claims resulting from exaggeration or delayed medical action.

Damage to the Property of Others

Similar to medical payments coverage, property liability insurance pays for minor property damage, regardless of who is at fault. The limits are typically $250 to $500 per occurrence.

Exclusions on Liability Coverage

The homeowner's policy doesn't cover slander or libel, nor does it protect you against business-related liabilities. Professional practices need special malpractice insurance, and this need is generally recognized. Where problems occur, they usually have to do with defining a business. For example, if you take on an occasional babysitting job, you may or may not be covered under your homeowner's policy. However, if you regularly take in the neighbor's children for a fee, you probably will not be covered. If there is any question that your activities might constitute a business, check with your insurance agent.

If your child works part time delivering papers or mowing lawns, be sure your policy covers those activities. Most homeowner's policies will state that the business exclusion does not apply to occasional and part-time business activities of an insured person who is under 21 years of age.

In general, your liability coverage will not extend to accidents in your automobile or aircraft. It will cover boating accidents on boats having less than a stated horsepower and less than a given length. For these exclusions you will need specialized insurance.

Policy Format

The present homeowner's policy achieved its standard form in the 1950s. Today there are established formats into which almost all policies can be categorized. The coverage under each is outlined in Figure 13.1. It's likely that your homeowner's policy can be categorized under one of these formats. However, insurers' policies can be unique and contain specific exceptions. It's important to read the fine print.

Basic Format (HO-1) provides the least coverage, insuring against the 11 most common perils on a named peril basis. Only a few of these policies are sold, because most home owners correctly demand more adequate protection.

Broad Form (HO-2) also provides named perils coverage for both dwelling and personal property. However, it is broader than HO-1, including seven additional named perils. It is the second most popular homeowner's insurance package.

Special Form (HO-3) is now the most widely purchased form and is highly recommended for most home owners. The NAIC estimates that about 84 percent of all homeowner's policies are in the HO-3 format. It provides all risks coverage on the dwelling and named perils coverage on the personal property. The typical excepted perils on all the risks coverage are flood, earthquake, war, and nuclear accident.

Contents Broad Form (HO-4) is for renters. The dwelling is not covered because it is the landlord's responsibility. Coverage on personal property is for the same named perils as under HO-2. There is also additional living expense coverage equal to 20 percent of the limit on personal property and protection on tenant improvements to the property equal to 10 percent of the personal property coverage.

FINANCIAL PLANNING *for*
young adults 13.2

A Property Insurance Protection Checklist for College Students

When you headed off to school did you check to see if you had everything you needed? It's likely that you overlooked an important item: your property insurance protection. You can remedy that oversight by answering a few simple questions.

1. Is your personal property protected under your parents' homeowner's policy?

   Most homeowner's policies cover the property of students away at college, but the coverage may not extend to off-campus housing. The easiest way to find out whether you are adequately covered is to discuss the matter with your family's insurance agent. If you are not covered under your parents' homeowner's policy, consider purchasing renters' insurance.

2. Do you have adequate overall property protection?

   Personal property coverage is typically 50 percent of dwelling coverage. However, the limit on property away from home may only be 10 percent of personal property
   coverage. On a home insured for $200,000, personal property coverage would be $100,000, and coverage of property away from home would be $10,000. In most cases, this should be adequate. However, if more protection is needed, an endorsement could be added to your family's homeowner's policy.

3. Have you taken a personal inventory?

   A descriptive list of the important items in your apartment, along with approximate values, should be compiled. Keep the list somewhere other than at school; typically, the family home is the best place. If the apartment is broken into while you are not at school, you will be able to supply the authorities with an accurate list of property that may be missing.

4. Do you exceed the limits on specific classes of property?

   Valuable property is more likely to be lost or stolen when it is away from home. Coverage for computers and related equipment is probably limited to $5,000. Jewelry typically has a lower limit of $1,000. Property that exceeds policy limits can be insured with a personal articles floater.

Figure 13.1
*Insured Perils Under
Homeowner's Policies*

Peril	Basic Format (HO-1)	Broad Form (HO-2)	Special Form (HO-3)	Contents Broad Form (HO-4)	Comprehensive Form (HO-5)	Condominium Form (HO-6)	Older Home Form (HO-8)
1. Fire or lightning							
2. Loss of property removed from premises endangered by fire or other perils							
3. Windstorm or hail							
4. Explosion							
5. Riot or civil commotion							
6. Aircraft							
7. Vehicles							
8. Smoke							
9. Vandalism and malicious mischief							
10. Theft							
11. Breakage of glass constituting a part of the building							
12. Falling objects							
13. Weight of ice, snow, sleet							
14. Collapse of building(s) or any part thereof							
15. Sudden and accidental tearing asunder, cracking, burning, or bulging of a steam or hot water heating system or of appliances for heating water							
16. Accidental discharge, leaking, or overflow of water or steam from within a plumbing, heating, or air-conditioning system or domestic appliance							
17. Freezing of plumbing, heating, and air-conditioning systems and domestic appliances							
18. Sudden and accidental injury from artificially generated currents to electrical appliances, devices, fixtures, and wiring (TV and radio tubes not included)			Dwelling Only				
All perils except flood, earthquake, war, nuclear accident, and others specified in your policy. Check your policy for a complete listing of perils excluded.							

Comprehensive Form (HO-5) provides all risks coverage on both the dwelling and personal property. It differs from HO-3 in that HO-3 includes only named perils coverage for personal property. The Comprehensive Form has the most protection and is the most expensive of all policies. In place of HO-5, some insurance companies provide HO-3 with Comprehensive Endorsement HO-15.

Condominium Form (HO-6) is similar to renters' form HO-4. Like the landlord, the condominium association usually provides insurance for the building and other structures. This may not cover, however, the condominium owners' additions and improvements to the dwelling unit. Therefore, the Condominium Form protects the owners' interest in additions to the dwelling unit at replacement cost up to a set limit. Furthermore, additional living expenses are typically paid for up to 40 percent of the coverage on personal property, instead of 20 percent. The policy also provides for endorsements in the event the owner is assessed for property or liability losses not covered under the association's insurance.

Older Home Form (HO-8) is for homes with actual cash value substantially below their replacement cost. This form provides coverage at actual cash value rather than replacement cost. Some older homes in declining neighborhoods sell for less than their replacement cost. Coverage at replacement cost on older homes would provide an incentive for arson, and carry exorbitant premiums.

Comprehensive Endorsement Form (HO-15) extends the coverage offered under HO-3 by providing all risks coverage on contents. In combination with HO-3, it provides the same coverage as HO-5.

Specialized Insurance

To close a gap in protection from either a standard exclusion or an insurance liability limit, you might consider some of the following additions to your homeowner's policy.

Endorsements

An **endorsement** is a paragraph that amends the original policy. It's added to make the standard policy more closely fit your individual needs. Endorsements may also be used to change the kind of coverage. Most policies agree to pay actual cash value on personal property damage. With an endorsement for "replacement cost coverage," you could change that. The perils insured against may also be changed with an endorsement. As previously mentioned, the standard policy excludes damage resulting from earthquakes. At additional cost, an endorsement can provide financial protection from this calamity.

Endorsement An amendment to the basic policy extending or changing the type of insurance coverage.

Coverage that exceeds standard policy limits on personal property may be included in an endorsement. In addition, a business pursuits endorsement could cover a small business in your home. Of interest to most home owners is an "inflation guard" endorsement. As housing values rise, this endorsement automatically increases your coverage. It's a worthwhile addition, ensuring that you will not get caught short under the coinsurance clause.

Floaters

The term **floater** is left over from the industry's early days, when it specialized in marine insurance. Like the cargo on a ship, your valuables can be insured with a *personal articles floater*. This can take the form of a separate policy or an endorsement to the original policy. Under the unscheduled property coverage, fairly low limits are set on payments for damaged or stolen valuables. If you need coverage beyond these limits, you can acquire it with a floater.

Floater Schedules property for specific coverage.

In a floater, the property is *scheduled*. This means it is described in terms of type and quality, and its value is supported by a report from a professional appraiser or bill of sale. Personal articles floaters usually cover all risks with no deductible.

An Umbrella Policy

Umbrella coverage Provides catastrophic protection that begins where basic coverage ends.

Umbrella coverage is written over an underlying homeowner's policy and a family auto policy. It takes over when the liability limits on these policies are reached. For example, if your homeowner's policy covers liability losses up to $100,000, an umbrella policy can protect you from losses in excess of $100,000, up to $1 million or more.

An umbrella policy is often written on a "following form" basis, meaning it will follow the form of the underlying coverage on which it was written. Consequently, you will be insured for the same perils as in the underlying policy.

Earthquake Insurance

Earthquake insurance may be purchased as an endorsement to the homeowner's policy. In earthquake-prone areas such as California, this insurance carries a high premium and a high deductible. Because of the high premiums and attempts by insurers to cut back their exposure in this market, fewer homes than you might expect carry earthquake protection. At most, only about one in four California homes is covered.

TOPIC LINKS

Check out the premium calculator at the California Earthquake Authority.

In California, where insurers have been reluctant to sell earthquake insurance, the legislature passed a law requiring insurers to offer earthquake insurance along with normal homeowner's policies. In response, some insurers withdrew from the homeowner's insurance market. To remedy this situation the state legislature created the California Earthquake Authority (CEA) to provide catastrophic earthquake coverage. By law it is required to sell policies to all customers of insurers within the state. Rates on CEA coverage can be obtained online.

Flood Insurance

An NAIC survey found that about one-third of policyholders incorrectly believe that their homes are insured against flood damage. Unfortunately, flood damage is a commonly excluded peril under homeowner's policies. You may be able to obtain flood insurance through the federal government's National Flood Insurance Program. Your community must participate in this program before individual home owners are eligible for government flood insurance. The federally guaranteed insurance is sold by participating private insurance companies. You can locate an insurer through your agent or by checking with FEMA (Federal Emergency Management Agency) at **www.fema.gov**.

When you apply for a home mortgage, a second mortgage, or a home equity loan, it is likely that your lender will require certification as to whether your home is in a Special Flood Hazard Area. If it is, you must acquire flood insurance before the loan can be closed. To ensure that your policy does not lapse from nonpayment, your lender can require that you deposit flood insurance premiums in an escrow account.

If your home is in an area no longer rated as a flood hazard region, then you can drop your flood insurance. But you might want to think twice about doing so; one-third of flood claims come from outside special flood-designated areas. Do not plan on obtaining flood insurance when you see the hurricane on the horizon. Unless the insurance is purchased when the property is acquired, there is a 30-day waiting period for coverage.

TOPIC LINKS

Locate a National Flood Insurance provider.

Coastal properties hit hard by hurricane Katrina suffered damage from wind and flood. Wind is a covered peril under a basic homeowner's policy, but flood is not. The Katrina's aftermath has generated numerous legal disputes between insureds who did not have flood insurance and their property insurers. The property owners claim that most of the damage was due to wind and therefore is covered; whereas, the insurance companies argue that most of the damage resulted from the rising waters. The cases are presently being litigated in state courts.

Renters' Insurance

A survey by the Independent Insurance Agents and Brokers of America (IIABA) found that 64 percent of respondents living in rental properties did not have property insurance. The most common reason was that they believed they were covered by their landlord's insurance. However, under most circumstances the landlord is not responsible for your property losses. If you add up the cost of your belongings, you might discover that an apartment fire or a burglary can leave you with significant uncovered property losses. In addition, if a visitor trips on your carpet and breaks a leg, you could be responsible for the medical bills. The IIABA reports that the average cost of a policy is $12 per month for about $30,000 of property coverage and $100,000 of liability coverage. Some insurers let roommates hold down total cost by sharing policy coverage.

The family homeowner's policy most likely protects the personal property of college students when living on campus. Students living off-campus should check to see if their personal property is also covered by the family policy.

Home Office

With the advent of Internet access and mobile communications, more people than ever are spending at least part of their workday in a home office. Many more take work from the office home. Over one-third of the adult population engages in some work at home. Unfortunately, homeowner's policies do not protect you from business-related liabilities. In addition, business property coverage typically is limited to $2,500. Moreover, there are policy limits on computers and electronic equipment. If you use that laptop away from home, the limit may be as low as $250.

A small business in your home might be covered by a business pursuits endorsement added to your current homeowner's policy. However, for anything substantial you will need a separate business insurance policy to cover all business-related losses. Professional liability insurance, also called errors and omissions insurance, provides coverage for malpractice in the provision of services.

Selecting Homeowner's Insurance

Now that you understand the basics of homeowner's coverage, you should be able to compare policies and insurers. The following points should aid you in your selection:

- Shop for coverage. Market studies have found a wide range in prices for similar policies. It's worthwhile to speak to several insurers before you select an insurer and the type of coverage that is right for you. Check the Web site for your state's department of insurance. Several states now compare prices on insurance products and publish the results on the Internet.
- Buy your homeowner's and auto insurance from the same insurer. Insurers often offer discounts for combined coverage.
- Select a high deductible. A high deductible can result in significant cost savings on premiums. You can self-insure the small risks.
- Periodically revise your coverage for increases in building costs. If you insure for significantly less than current replacement cost, you may be penalized under the coinsurance clause.
- Check out discounts. You may be able to lower your premiums by improving your home security and making your home more disaster resistant.

- Maintain a good credit record. A low credit score can result in higher premiums. It indicates to the insurer that you are not a responsible person.
- Review your limits on personal property. If the value of your personal property exceeds the limits on your policy, you might want to extend coverage with an endorsement.
- Insure for special circumstances. If you conduct part of your business at home, don't assume your business is covered by your homeowner's policy. Discuss your special circumstances with your agent.
- Check out the financial stability of the insurer. You want to feel secure that the insurer will be there when you need help.

TOPIC LINKS

See if your state's Department of Insurance has a rate comparison guide.

Making Sure You Collect on a Loss

Having adequate insurance coverage is not enough to ensure that you will receive appropriate compensation in the event of property loss. Policyholders with identical losses and identical coverage may receive different levels of reimbursement simply because they approach the claim process differently. Making good on a claim requires documentation, notification, and evaluation.

Documentation

The first step in filing a claim should be taken before the loss occurs. The loss must be documented. Of course, doing so is a lot easier while you still have your property in good condition.

When you apply for scheduled property coverage with a floater, you will be required to document the property's actual cash value. Be sure to update the appraisals whenever market prices change, including both upward and downward movements.

On unscheduled property coverage, evidence of worth need be supplied only after the loss. You are entirely responsible for documenting and describing your loss to the insurance company. Keep an inventory of your belongings, including a description of each item that indicates all identifying marks, the original purchase price, and the date of purchase. For the more expensive items you should include a copy of the bill of sale in your records. While taking inventory, check for items that might exceed the recovery limits on your homeowner's policy. Consider scheduling these goods with a floater. Take photos of every room in your house, or better yet, make a video tour of your home. Then take all of this documentation and store it in a safe place away from the home. If your house burns down, you don't want this destroyed with it.

Notification

When a property loss occurs, you should immediately contact the relevant civil authority, and then take whatever steps are needed to protect your property from further damage. Your failure to notify the police or a credit card company in the event of theft may invalidate your coverage. Next, contact your insurer. Your agent should be able to inform you immediately whether you are covered, in addition to supplying information on what you should do next. Insurance agents are used to dealing with tragedies. At a time like this, the support they can provide in seeking alternative shelter or assistance with repairs and debris removal can be invaluable.

Before anything is repaired or removed, be sure you have fully documented the loss. Take photos of the damage. If you followed the previous advice, you will now have a set of before and after snapshots. Also, request copies of any police or fire reports on the damage, and get the names and addresses of any witnesses to the mishap.

Evaluation

If the insurer feels your claim may be covered, an adjuster will be sent to verify the claim and determine the amount of loss. You should supply the adjuster with copies of all the evidence of loss you have collected. Under most circumstances, a settlement offer will be made promptly. Don't be too hasty to accept. Take the time to review your inventory of damaged items and to search out the replacement cost on these goods.

Let the adjuster make the first settlement offer, and request an explanation of how the amount was determined. If you feel the offer is too low or you are denied payment on what you believe is a covered loss, you may state your case to the adjuster and ask that the settlement offer be reconsidered. If you still can't agree, you can demand that the settlement be submitted to arbitration. You and the insurer will be required to split the cost of the arbitrators' fees.

One less costly but potentially less effective action is to write your state's insurance commission. They are not likely to take action on an individual complaint. But if yours is one of many, the state commission may decide to look into the problem.

You may be able to deduct any unreimbursed casualty losses on your personal income tax return. Only sizable losses, however, are likely to lead to any significant tax savings. The rules for reducing your taxable income by the amount of the loss are quite strict. (See IRS Publication 547, "Casualties, Disasters and Thefts.")

Frequency of Claims

The Insurance Information Institute reports that home owners file about 6.9 claims for every 100 homes. That is, about one claim every 14.5 years and an average claim of $5,974. Your claim will be included in the Comprehensive Loss Underwriting Exchange (CLUE). This is a shared industry-wide database that tracks claims. Filing a number of small claims can result in your insurer dropping your coverage or increasing your premiums. This is because it will affect your insurance risk score, which insurers used to assess your risk classification. This is another good reason for having a large deductible on your insurance policy. By avoiding a number of small claims you will hold down your risk score and your premiums.

Automobile Insurance

Automobile insurance is meant to protect you against three risks: (1) bodily harm and property damage to others from negligent operation of the vehicle; (2) personal injury to you, your family, and guests riding in your car; and (3) damage or loss of your car due to fire, theft, or collision. Of the three, the first has the potential for the greatest financial loss.

Who Needs Auto Insurance Coverage?

The simple answer is that if you drive a car, you do. There is a substantial chance of being in some kind of car accident over the next five years, and if you are an unmarried male driver under age 25, the odds are even higher (see Figure 13.2). In all states, liability insurance is mandatory. However, regardless of state requirements, it's just downright foolish to take a car on the road without adequate coverage. One accident can result in hundreds of thousands of dollars in claims against you and your estate.

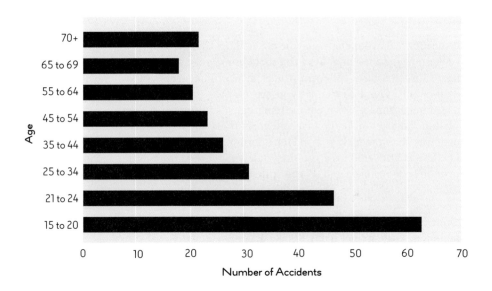

Coverage Under Your Auto Policy

Personal auto policy Provides standardized coverage for families and individuals.

The standard policy covers you and other family members living with you. It also protects others when driving one of your covered cars and you and your family when driving someone else's auto. The **personal auto policy** follows a standard format used by most insurers. Policy comparisons are fairly easy, because coverage is usually divided into identical parts listed in the same order. However, auto policies tend to be written in stilted language and are difficult to read. If your policy contains the terms *first party, second party* and *third party*, just remember that the first party is you and the second party is the insurer. If you collide with another car, the driver of that car becomes the third party. Claims by you or your passengers are first-party claims. Those by the driver or passengers in the other vehicle are third-party claims.

The personal auto policy follows a standard format that with only minor revisions has existed for several decades. The areas of coverage are divided into the following sections:

Part A	Liability Coverage
Part B	Medical Payments Coverage
Part C	Uninsured Motorists Coverage
Part D	Coverage for Damage to Your Auto
Part E	Duties After an Accident or Loss
Part F	General Provisions.

Part A—Liability Coverage

The most important component of your auto insurance is liability coverage. It operates much the same as liability coverage under the homeowner's policy, except that it applies only to damages resulting from an auto accident. It pays for bodily injury and property damage you cause to third parties. Part A excludes coverage for intentional acts. The harm must be accidental. Also excluded will be liability related to using your car for work.

Split liability limit Includes specific liability limits for a single individual, a single accident, and property damage.

On a policy with a **split liability limit**, you will see the liability limits presented in the following format: 100/300/10. The first number indicates the maximum amount the insurer will pay for bodily injury to a single person. The second number is the maximum amount the insurer will pay for all injuries sustained in a single accident, and the last is the insurer's liability limit for property damage in a given accident. For example, suppose there were two riders in the other car. One sustained $210,000 in bodily injury and the other $80,000 in bodily injury. The insurer would reimburse the first rider for $100,000 and the second rider for the full $80,000 sought, since total payments are under the $300,000 limit for a single accident. In addition, the insurer would pay for damage to the other vehicle up to $10,000. You would be responsible for the excess liability, which would include $110,000 to the first rider and any property damage exceeding $10,000.

Some policies have a **single liability limit**. This means the insurer will pay up to this limit for each accident, regardless of how this amount may be divided among the injured and for property damage. When the single liability limit on one policy is the same as the limit per accident on a split liability policy, the single liability limit provides the better coverage. In the previous example, a single liability limit of $300,000 would have left you with little or no excess liability.

In addition to damages up to your policy limits, the insurer will also cover the cost of defending you in a lawsuit. This coverage will include such supplementary costs as legal and defense fees, premiums on appeal bonds, and limited reimbursement for bail bonds and lost earnings. However, once the company has reached your liability limits, perhaps through an out-of-court settlement with the injured party, then further legal costs are all yours.

A liability limit of $300,000 may sound like a lot of protection. It actually isn't. The damages suffered by a severely injured person who is unable to work can easily exceed this figure. You might suggest you don't need this much insurance because you don't have $300,000 in assets to protect. But the higher your protection, the less likely it is that you will have any excess liability above your insurance coverage.

Part B—Medical Payments

Injuries to you, your family, and passengers riding in your car are insured under **medical payments coverage**, regardless of who is at fault. The coverage also applies when you or your family are riding in other vehicles or when one of your family members is hit by a car while walking. The typical limits on payments are low, between $500 to $5,000 per person. It's not meant to take the place of a good health insurance plan. In fact, if you have good health insurance, you should consider holding limits in this part to a minimum.

Some companies will include death and disability insurance under the medical payments section. A special life insurance or disability policy would take care of these contingencies with broader coverage than would a policy that covers only auto accidents.

Part C—Uninsured Motorists

Uninsured motorists coverage is worthwhile low-cost protection, about $11 per year for a policy with 25/50/10 limits. In most states, damage to your auto is not covered under uninsured motorists. It primarily covers bodily injury to you or your family members from either an uninsured driver or a hit-and-run driver. The coverage also applies when riding in other cars or walking. For the policy to pay off, the other driver must be at fault.

You may want to carry this protection even when your state requires auto liability insurance, since there is no way the state can ensure that every driver is financially responsible. The need for this coverage is apparent when you consider that about 14 percent of drivers do not carry auto insurance according to the Insurance Research Council. The states along the southern border have the highest percentage of uninsured drivers.

In many areas you may purchase supplementary **underinsured motorists coverage**. This operates in the same manner as uninsured motorists, except that when the other motorist is insured for less than the damages, your policy pays for the difference up to specified limits.

TOPIC LINKS

Find your state's mandated minimum liability coverage.

Single liability limit A single limit that covers all bodily and property losses incurred in a single accident.

Medical payments coverage Covers minor medical expenses for those riding in your car.

Uninsured motorists coverage Covers bodily injury to you or your family members from either an uninsured driver or a hit-and-run driver.

Underinsured motorists coverage Protects you when at-fault motorist is insured for less than damages incurred.

saving money 13.3

Holding Down Insurance Costs for Young Drivers

Away at School

If students attend school far from home (more than 100 miles) and drive the family auto only on vacations and holidays, most insurance companies will lower the premiums on student drivers by 12 to 33 percent.

Good Grades

Students with good grades have fewer accidents. Insurers recognize that fact by offering a discount of from 5 to 25 percent for students with at least a B average.

Sporty Car

Insurers target certain makes and models for higher premiums because these are more likely to be stolen or damaged. You can find out which autos carry higher premiums by contacting your insurer. Unfortunately, these are most often the same cars favored by younger drivers.

Family Auto Policy

Individual coverage is more expensive than insuring all the drivers in the home under a single family auto policy. New drivers purchasing an individual policy may be placed in an "assigned risk" pool, for which rates are much higher than on ordinary policies.

Young Driver, Old Car

In a multicar family, assign the youngest driver in the family to the oldest car. If the high-risk driver doesn't drive the luxury sedan, premiums should be lower.

Driver's Education

Your state may require a driver's education course before you are eligible for a driver's license. If it doesn't, your insurer may provide a discount if you take this course.

Part D—Damage to Your Auto

Collision coverage Pays for damage to your car in a collision, regardless of who is at fault.

Other than collision coverage All risks coverage on your car.

Part D consists of two separate components, collision and other than collision. An NAIC survey indicates that about 72 percent of car owners purchase collision coverage and about 77 percent buy other than collision coverage. **Collision coverage** pays for damage to your car in a collision, regardless of who is at fault. If the other driver is responsible for damages, your insurer will seek reimbursement and refund the deductible if it is successful. **Other than collision coverage**, also called comprehensive auto coverage, provides all risks coverage on your car. Specifically included are such perils as fire, theft, falling objects, windstorm, flood, earthquake, and collision with an animal. Both coverages carry deductibles, and under either, the insurer has the option of paying for repairs or paying the actual cash value of a similar auto.

Because the actual cash value on older cars is small, it's generally recommended that you not purchase property damage insurance on cars five years or older or when your car is worth less than 10 times the annual premium on collision and comprehensive coverage. The premiums do not justify the minimal benefits in case of loss. With newer cars, you can hold down your premiums by including higher deductibles. Again, the optimal strategy is to take on the small risks yourself and use the savings to transfer the big risks.

Part D will generally extend coverage to both your "covered car" and a "non-owned" vehicle, a rental car. If your car is in the shop after an insured event, the typical policy may reimburse you for "transportation expenses" up to a specified limit.

Part E—Duties After an Accident or Loss

You have a duty to report the loss to your insurance company in a timely manner and protect your property from further loss. Reasonable costs related to protecting your damaged car, such as notifying a towing company, will most likely be reimbursed by your insurer. You also have a duty to cooperate with civil authorities and assist the insurance company in its investigation of the loss by turning over all relevant record and submitting to medical examinations. If your actions harm the company's efforts to protect its rights, you could place your coverage in jeopardy.

Part F—General Provision

This section states the conditions which may trigger a change in your coverage or premiums. It should list the conditions under which your policy may be terminated. Your rights to recover payment from the company will be explained and the company's response to a fraudulent application for insurance.

General Exclusions

Most policies will exclude non-factory installed sound and CB equipment from theft coverage. The chances of such accessories being stolen are just too high. You might consider covering these with a floater on your homeowner's policy.

A few other common exceptions are important to your personal liability coverage. Some are clear-cut, and others are not so obvious. If you think you might be subject to any of the following exclusions, you should discuss the matter with your insurance agent:

- Using someone else's car without permission
- Using a nonlisted car you own, except for a grace period during a trade-in, usually about two weeks.
- Carrying passengers for a fee
- Driving a motorcycle
- Using a company car
- Driving a noninsured car of a live-in relative
- Driving a rental car unless the policy states otherwise

No-Fault Insurance

Many states have some form of no-fault insurance. A **no-fault insurance** plan is one that allows policyholders to recover financial losses for personal injuries from their own insurer, regardless of who is at fault. In return for receiving reimbursement from your own insurer, there may be restrictions placed upon your right to sue. There are many variations of no-fault insurance so that the rules vary by state. You typically retain the right to sue only when your physical injuries are severe according to a **verbal threshold** or your medical expenses exceed a **monetary threshold**. In addition, your right to sue for nonmonetary losses such as pain and suffering may also be restricted. By eliminating the determination of fault and reducing the types of damages that may be litigated, no-fault insurance is meant to hold down insurance premiums.

Although the required minimum amount of coverage varies, in all no-fault states you are required to carry **personal injury protection (PIP)**. This permits you to recover medical and hospital expenses, lost wages, and other injury-related expenses up to your policy limits from your own insurer, regardless of fault. However, because lawsuits are still possible, in most of these same states you also must carry residual bodily liability coverage.

In most states no-fault insurance does not cover the damage to your car or the damage you do to the property of others. If you are at fault, you may be sued for property damage. Therefore, you may also need property damage coverage.

No-fault insurance Policyholders recover financial losses from their own insurer regardless of who is at fault.

Verbal threshold Victims may sue for reimbursement for physical injuries that satisfy this definition.

Monetary threshold Victims may sue for medical expenses that exceed this amount.

Personal injury protection (PIP) Mandatory coverage in no-fault states that covers expenses for personal injury, regardless of fault.

Rental Coverage

Your personal auto policy may extend liability coverage to rental cars. It may even cover damage to a rental car. Your credit card may provide similar auto damage coverage. It's important to check before you rent. With this coverage you can avoid purchasing a **collision damage waiver (CDW)** when you rent a car. CDW looks like insurance, but it isn't. It's actually a waiver of the rental firm's right to charge you for damage to the rental. The cost of this limited protection can be very high, from $10 to $20 a day, which totals from $3,650 to $7,300 over a 365-day year.

Collision damage waiver (CDW) Waiver of the rental firm's right to charge you for damage to the rental.

Other Coverage

There are several supplemental coverages that some insurance companies make available. These are generally considered high-cost add-ons when they are not part of the basic policy, and most consumer groups advise against purchasing them. The most common is *rental reimbursement*, which covers a rental vehicle if your car is damaged or stolen. Insurance for *towing and labor* charges for road repairs can also be added. And if you really love your car, there is *auto replacement coverage* that insures that your car will be either repaired or replaced without adjustment for depreciation.

The Cost of Auto Insurance

The cost of your auto insurance will be greatly influenced by where you live. An NAIC survey indicates that average auto premiums in 2005 ranged from a high of $1,184 in New Jersey to a low of $554 in North Dakota. These differences can be largely explained by population density and the number of cars on the road.

The cost of auto insurance can also vary widely from one company to another. As with homeowner's policies, most auto companies sell a standardized policy, making it easy to compare features and price. Moreover, it may be wise to shop for both homeowner's and auto insurance at the same time, since some companies provide a multiple-policy discount when both are purchased. Be sure to request the potential discounts listed in Table 13.1. To help with your shopping, use a checklist like that shown in Figure 13.3, listing the kind, amount, and cost of each coverage.

Check with your state's Department of Insurance. Several states provide buyers' guides and rate reporting services on the Internet. They may also supply background information on insurers in your state. Moreover, before you buy, be sure to review the financial stability of the insurer with one of the rating services such as Best's or Standard & Poor's.

TOPIC LINKS

Find the average cost of auto insurance in your state.

Table 13.1
Typical Discounts Offered by Auto Insurers

Discounts Offered for Cars with the Following Features	Discounts Offered for Insureds with the Following Characteristics
Antilocking brake system	Away-at-school driver
Antitheft devices	Carpool driver
Automatic seat belts or air bags	Driver training
High-level brake light	Good driving record
	Good student record
	Mature driver
	Multicar household
	Multipolicy household
	Nonsmoking driver
	Retired driver

Company _____

	Limits	Deductible	Annual Rate
Liability	_____		_____
Medical payments	_____		_____
Personal injury protection			
(no-fault states)	_____		_____
Uninsured motorists	_____		_____
Underinsured motorists	_____		_____
Collision		_____	_____
Other than collision		_____	_____
Total Cost			_____

Discounts (see Table 13.1)

Type	Percentage Discount	Dollar Discount
1. _____	_____	_____
2. _____	_____	_____
3. _____	_____	_____
etc. _____	_____	_____
Total Dollar Discount		(_____)
Total Cost after Discount		══════

Figure 13.3
Auto Insurance Comparison Checklist

The Rate Base

The cost of your insurance policy will depend on your risk class. It's based on factors over which you have some control, such as your driving record and your zip code, and others over which you have no control, such as your age and gender. If other drivers in your age group are accident prone, you are going to be charged more, independently of how good or bad a driver you happen to be. This may sound discriminatory, and in a sense it is. However, an efficient system of insurance requires the assignment of probabilities to groups of events. The insurance company must be able to discriminate, on the basis of experience, between apparent high-risk groups and low-risk groups. Otherwise, we all end up paying higher premiums for the most negligent among us.

Individual auto insurance premiums are determined in a two-stage process. First, each state is divided into territories, and each territory is assigned a base rate dependent on risk factors and costs within that region. Next, the base rate is multiplied by a value that is determined by the risks associated with the personal characteristics of the insured. Your risk classification will take into account your age, sex, marital status, educational level, driving record, credit record, and even the kind of car you drive.

When discounts are offered (see Table 13.1), they are figured from the base rate, not from the individual auto insurance premium. A young male driver, for example, might receive a 10 percent discount for having taken driver education. If his base rate is $200 and his annual premium is $760, his discount will be $20, not $76.

Driving Record

One factor over which you definitely do have some control is your driving record. A charge-able accident (one that is your fault) or a serious driving violation will increase your premiums by 40 percent or more. A history of such behavior can cause your rates to double and may result in cancellation of your policy. You will then have to purchase very expensive insurance from a company specializing in high-risk drivers or from the *shared* market in your state. In this market, which is also called the *assigned risk market*, your policy is placed in a pool with those of other high-risk drivers. The insurance companies agree to jointly share the cost and risk of providing for the insurance needs of these drivers. In about half the states, these are known as FAIR (Fair Access to Insurance Requirements) plans.

Car Make and Model

It's obvious that a car requiring more expensive repairs will carry higher rates for property damage coverage than other vehicles. What is not so obvious is that certain cars will carry higher rates for liability coverage and collision because the chances of you, your passengers, and others being seriously injured in this particular car are greater.

The relative mix of age groups driving a particular car should affect that car's risk exposure. However, even after we consider that factor, some cars are just more accident prone than others. The insurance companies have responded by providing discounts for cars in low-risk groups and surcharges for cars in high-risk groups. The next time you think about buying a car, it's probably wise to check with your insurance agent to find out how your planned purchase ranks. The insurance saving on an alternative purchase might more than outweigh any saving on purchase price.

TOPIC LINKS

Check out auto loss data.

Before, At, and After the Accident

The odds are overwhelming that you will be involved in at least one auto accident. For most of us, these will be fender benders. But for an unlucky few, an auto accident will result in serious injury. It's important in these circumstances to follow some simple rules that are mostly common sense.

Before the Accident

Adequate liability protection is a must. You should periodically review your policy to make sure that your family has the right kind and amount of coverage. Auto insurance information, including your policy number, agent, and telephone number, should be kept in the glove compartment. Any preprinted insurance forms allowing you to report the particulars of any accident, including a sketch of the scene should also be placed there.

At the Accident

If you are driving, you must stop the vehicle immediately. Do not, however, leave it in a position that creates a traffic hazard and causes another accident. Give your name and address, insurance information, and the registration number of the vehicle involved, to the other driver, any injured persons, and the arriving police officer. Obtain similar information of all persons involved in the accident and witnesses to the accident. Furthermore, get the name of the arriving police officer, and request a copy of the officer's accident report (see Figure 13.4).

Make notes of the circumstances concerning the accident, including the position of the cars before and after the accident, traffic signs, road and weather conditions, and road obstacles. Step off the skid points to measure them, and locate the point of collision. If you have a camera with you, photograph the damage and the accident scene.

Assist the investigating officer by providing all factual information when requested. Do not offer any opinion on the cause of the accident or admit any guilt or blame. If others are injured, your first reaction may be to feel responsible. On calmer reflection, you might realize the fault was not yours. If you are arrested, ask to meet with your attorney before offering any explanation.

Figure 13.4
Auto Accident Checklist

1. Stop the vehicle immediately and remain at the scene until a police officer arrives.
2. Give your name and address, those of the vehicle's owner, and the registration number of the vehicle to:
    (a) Any injured person.
    (b) The owner, operator, or attendant of any damaged vehicle.
    (c) Any police officer at the scene of the accident.
3. Obtain the name and address of the driver of the other vehicle, all passengers, and witnesses.
4. Obtain license numbers of all drivers involved.
5. Make notes of all significant circumstances surrounding the accident.
6. If there are serious injuries, make the injured person comfortable and phone for medical aid immediately. Under no circumstances should you move the injured person.
7. If you or any passenger in your car is injured, consult with your doctor immediately and encourage others to do so.
8. Obtain copy of the police officer's accident report.
9. File all accident report forms required by the state or local government.
10. Report the accident to your insurance company as soon as possible.

Do not make any payments or accept any payments at the scene of the accident. A settlement offer should be considered only after you have discussed the matter with your agent and, possibly, an attorney.

If there are serious injuries, your first obligation is to seek medical aid. You may make the injured person more comfortable, but do not move the injured in any way that might aggravate a serious injury. Even if the accident was not your fault, if your actions contribute to the other person's injuries, you may be liable. If you think that you or anyone in your car might be injured, be sure to seek treatment immediately. You will be reimbursed under your medical payments coverage.

After the Accident

Report the accident to your insurance agent as soon as possible and file any written reports required under your state's motor vehicle statutes. Most policies require that you notify the company within one day of the accident. If you fail to satisfy this requirement, the insurer can later refuse to honor any claim resulting from the accident.

Keep track of all your accident-related expenses, including medical payments, lost wages, and additional traveling costs. These are all collectible damages when the other driver is at fault. If you think these losses may be sizable, seek the advice of an attorney. You may find that, in addition to the economic damages, you may also be able to collect for pain and suffering.

In a suit for damages, the plaintiff's attorney usually recovers a contingency fee; although, a few lawyers may be willing to work on an hourly basis. The contingency fee is normally 30 percent of the awarded damages, but the exact percentage is negotiable. This pays only for the lawyer. Whether you use an hourly basis or a contingency fee, there will be added expenses for such things as expert witnesses and depositions. These additional expenses must be paid whether you win or lose the case. Be sure to request that the lawyer first seek your approval before incurring any of these extra costs.

If the accident was your fault and it appears the damages awarded may exceed the liability limits on your policy, the insurer should inform you of this likelihood. You must then independently hire an attorney to take over when the insurer's participation ends and to make sure the insurance company has operated in your best interests.

key terms

actual cash value (p. 349)
adverse selection (p. 346)
all risks coverage (p. 349)
apportionment clause (p. 351)
appurtenant structures (p. 352)
coinsurance (p. 350)
collision coverage (p. 364)
collision damage waiver (CDW) (p. 366)
deductible clause (p. 351)
dwelling protection (p. 352)
endorsement (p. 357)
floater (p. 357)
gambling (p. 347)
indemnification (p. 347)
inflation guard endorsement (p. 351)
insurable interest (p. 347)
liability coverage (p. 353)
medical payments coverage (p. 363)
monetary threshold (p. 365)
mortgage clause (p. 351)
named perils coverage (p. 349)
negligence (p. 353)
no-fault insurance (p. 365)

other than collision coverage (p. 364)
personal auto policy (p. 362)
personal injury protection (PIP) (p. 365)
personal liability insurance (p. 345)
property loss insurance (p. 345)
pure risk (p. 346)
replacement cost (p. 349)
risk avoidance (p. 347)
risk management (p. 347)
risk reduction (p. 347)
risk retention (p. 348)
risk transfer (p. 348)
single liability limit (p. 363)
speculative risk (p. 345)
split liability limit (p. 362)
subrogation clause (p. 351)
umbrella coverage (p. 358)
underinsured motorists coverage (p. 363)
underwriting (p. 346)
uninsured motorists coverage (p. 363)
unscheduled personal property (p. 352)
verbal threshold (p. 365)

follow–up on the Steele family

Reread the chapter-opening vignette.

1. Given the Steeles' assets (outlined in previous chapters), what types of property insurance should they have?

2. The Steeles are interested in holding down their property insurance costs. What strategies might satisfy this objective?

3. Given the Steeles' financial position (discussed in previous chapters), how much auto liability insurance should they carry?

problems and review questions

1. How does gambling differ from purchasing insurance?

2. Explain the difference between all risks insurance and named perils insurance. List three perils not ordinarily covered under the basic homeowner's policy.

3. Which cost is greater: replacement cost or actual cash value? Why?

4. What items are typically insured for replacement cost?

5. What is the difference between unscheduled property and scheduled property? How is scheduled property insured?

6. Where would a home owner obtain flood insurance?

7. How does a home owner obtain earthquake coverage? Assess the pros and cons of obtaining earthquake insurance.

8. Larry recently started operating a mail-order business in the basement of his home. Unfortunately, a fire put an end to his dreams of success by destroying about $10,000 worth of goods that had been temporarily stored in his basement. Will his homeowner's policy cover the loss? Why or why not?

9. While on her newspaper route, Jane's daughter tosses a paper through a subscriber's front window, causing $300 in damages. Might Jane be covered by her homeowner's insurance?

10. Why is it important to insure your dwelling for at least 80 percent of its replacement cost? How does the coinsurance clause operate?

11. What is the most important component of your auto insurance coverage? Why?

12. Ruth had stopped for breakfast during a long morning drive to the ski slopes. While she was inside eating, someone broke into her car and made off with over $500 in ski equipment. What should she do? Under what policy might she be covered?

13. Last week Fred traded in his old junker for a new sports car. Not used to the fast response of a sports car, he accidentally drove it off a country road into a field, killing a cow. The car suffered extensive damage, and the farmer is demanding compensation for his cow. Fred had insurance on his old car. But he hadn't yet gotten around to informing his insurer of the trade-in. Will his old policy still cover him?

14. While riding to school on her bicycle, Ruth was run off the road by a hit-and-run driver. Except for a broken arm that is healing nicely, she was unhurt. Under which insurance policy and under what section of that insurance policy might her parents apply for reimbursement of medical expenses?

15. An engine fire destroys your car. Which coverage would reimburse you for the damage? What is the maximum amount you could collect under your auto policy?

16. While stopped for a red light on Main Street, Ralph's car was hit from behind by a negligent driver. Because he was in a state with no-fault insurance and since nobody was injured, he didn't think it was necessary to get the other driver's name and license number. Under what section of his auto policy is he covered?

17. Name several factors insurers consider when setting auto insurance rates. How might you hold down your auto insurance costs?

18. Peter is away at college and drives the family car only when he comes home on special occasions. How might Peter's family hold down the cost of their auto insurance?

19. Why is it wise to review your auto policy before you rent a car?

20. Why is uninsured motorists coverage sold in states that have laws requiring compulsory auto insurance?

---

case 13.1

A Fire at the Pages'

It was around midnight when the smoke alarm woke Peter and Barbara Page. The fire had started in the attached garage and was already flaming when the fire department arrived. By the time it was out, the Pages' home had sustained damages that would take $20,000 to repair. In addition, their Honda, with a market price of $8,000, was totally destroyed.

When the Pages purchased their home, they took out a homeowner's policy with $60,000 worth of dwelling protection. Since then they have received several letters from the insurance company suggesting they increase the dwelling coverage. For one reason or another they just never got around to responding. Now the insurer tells them that because their coverage was for less than 80 percent of the home's replacement value, as determined by the replacement cost provision, the insurance company probably will not pay the full cost of repairs. To avoid coinsurance payments, they should have been carrying at least $90,000 in dwelling protection.

Questions

1. Given the position of the insurance company, what is the smallest reimbursement the Pages can expect?

2. Is there any chance they can collect for the destroyed auto? How much and from whom?

3. Suppose the Pages disagree with the insurer's cost estimates. What course of action should they follow?

case 13.2

After the Accident

Bob Brown was recently involved in a minor auto accident. His car was hit from behind, and he, in turn, slammed into the car in front of him. He would like someone to explain his coverage and show him where in his auto policy each of his losses might be covered. Help him out by doing that for each of the following items:

1. The cost of a medical checkup for his passenger, Ruth
2. The front and rear damage to his car
3. The damage to the car in front of him
4. The damage to the car behind him
5. The total amount of liability protection for bodily harm and property damage

working out on the Web

Exercises to Strengthen Your Use of the Internet

(Internet links for the following exercises can be found at **www.prenhall.com/frasca**.)

Exercise 13.1 Check the Financial Stability of Property Casualty Insurers

In the event of a major catastrophe, such as hurricane Katrina, property casualty insurers must have adequate reserves to cover the liabilities. The Insure.Com (**www.insure.com**) provides Standard & Poor's ratings of property and casualty insurers and life and health insurers. You can find the ratings page by conducting an articles search for "financial strength ratings."

Q. What does a "CCC" rating mean?

Exercise 13.2 Does Your State Publish a Rate Comparison Survey?

The National Association of Insurance Commissioners (**www.naic.org**) provides a link to state insurance regulators on the home page. Go to the department of insurance for your state and review the helpful material at this site.

Q. Does your state provide a rate comparison survey of homeowner's insurance or auto insurance? What other useful information is available at this site?

Exercise 13.3 What Are the Minimum Liability Limits in Your State?

Each state requires car owners to purchase a minimum amount of auto liability coverage. This minimum amount is probably less than you should have. However, this may be what the other driver on the road has. Consequently, you should be aware of your state's minimum. This information can be found at Insure.Com (**www.insure.com**) at a link on the "Auto" page entitled "Minimum levels of required auto insurance." Similar information can also be found at Autopedia (**autopedia.com**).

Q. What is the minimum split liability coverage in your state? Explain how the split liability limit is applied to bodily injury and property damage.

Exercise 13.4 What Is the Cost of Auto Insurance and How Much Coverage Do You Need?

Insure.Com (**www.insure.com**) provides the average cost of auto insurance by state. See "More Interactive Tools" under "Insurance Shopping Tools' at the bottom of the home page. On the next page look for "The Best and worst states for auto insurance premiums."

SmartMoney (**www.smartmoney.com**) examines how much coverage you need. At the SmartMoney home page go to "Personal Finance/Insurance." On the insurance page you will find a link to "How Much Policy Do You Need?"

Q. What is the average cost of auto insurance in your state, and how much coverage do you really need?

Exercise 13.5 Vehicle Losses by Make and Model

The Highway Loss Data Institute and the Institute for Highway Safety (**www.iihs.org**) jointly publish information on economic losses associated with the ownership and operation of automobiles. On the "Research and Stats" page there are "Insurance losses by make and model." Vehicles that rank poorly are likely to have higher insurance premiums.

Q. What is the relative ranking of your family auto for injury, collision, and theft?

14

Health Care and Disability Insurance

protecting your earning capacity

Objectives

1. To describe the separate components of basic health care coverage
2. To discuss the need for major medical insurance
3. To list the important providers and insurers of health care
4. To compare and evaluate health care insurance plans
5. To list sources of disability income
6. To estimate your disability insurance needs

Steele family

Like most families, the Steeles are concerned about the rising cost of health care. They recognize the importance of having health insurance to protect them in the event of major medical emergencies. The Steeles obtain their health insurance coverage through Arnold's employer. Arnold has a choice of joining a traditional fee-for-service plan or a health maintenance organization (HMO). Arnold's employer covers the full cost of his individual coverage and for an extra $150 a month he receives family coverage. Over the past few years, the additional contribution for family coverage has risen significantly. The Arnolds hope that when Sharon returns to full-time employment, she may be able to obtain less costly family coverage.

The Steeles are members of the HMO but they have not utilized an optional flexible spending account. They have been gener-ally satisfied with the HMO; however, copayments for doctors' visits and drug prescriptions will increase significantly. Moreover, dental visits and eyeglasses are not covered. Combined expenditures for copayments and noncovered health expenditures, such as dental braces, are expected to be almost $2,500 next year.

Arnold's employer does not provide long-term disability income protection. If Arnold becomes ill, his short-term disability benefits would end after six months. Arnold and Sharon have discussed this possibility. They feel that if Arnold were permanently disabled, Sharon could return to full-time employment. Over all, the Steeles believe that they are prepared for all future medical emergencies.

TOPIC LINKS

Follow the **Topic Links** in each chapter for your interactive Personal Finance exercise on the Web. Go to: **www.prenhall.com/frasca**.

In terms of financial burdens, nothing is more devastating than a catastrophic illness. Serious illness or injury is difficult enough to deal with, even without the stress that medical bills and lost income can create. Having quality health and disability coverage can at least lessen the increasing financial hardship that accompanies injury and illness.

Over the past two decades, the price of medical care has risen at almost twice the rate of increase of other services. An increasing share of this rising burden has been covered by third-party payments through private insurance and government programs. In 1990, private health insurance covered only 50 percent of private health care expenditures. Over the past decade, this percentage has risen sharply and now covers about 74 percent of all private consumer health care expenditures. As indicated in Figure 14.1, this can range from a high of 92 percent for hospital care to a low of 22 percent for nursing home care. The Bureau of the Census reports that about 85 percent of all Americans have some type of private or public health insurance coverage. Most of the private coverage is group coverage related to the past or current employment of a family member. Because health insurance coverage is primarily work related, young adults aged 18 to 24 and retirees who don't yet qualify for Medicare are the groups most likely to be without health insurance protection.

Many people with insurance are inadequately covered because they have the wrong kind or amount of protection. Adequate protection includes reimbursement for major medical expenses through health care insurance and compensation for lost income through disability income insurance. Protection against loss of income due to illness or injury is even less adequate than health care coverage. Apparently, most people feel that the chances of becoming disabled are too small to require protection or that government programs will prove sufficient. As we will see, both assumptions are incorrect.

Health Care Insurance

Figure 14.2 illustrates the typical flow of expenditures for health care services. Families acquire health care insurance through employers or directly from health insurance companies. The policy premiums are used to fund covered medical services. Out-of-pocket payments make up the difference between the cost of medical services and insurance reimbursements. Depending on the type of coverage, uncovered expenses can be moderate or

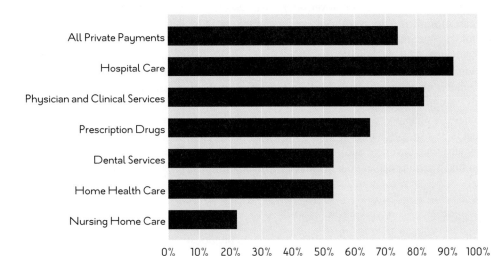

Figure 14.1
Health Insurance Reimbursement as a Percentage of Private Consumer Expenditures for Health Care, 2005

Source: Centers for Medicare and Medicaid Services,
U.S. Dept. of Health and Human Services,
http://www.cms.hhs.gov/ NationalHealthExpendData/dow nloads/nhe2005.zip

Figure 14.2
Health Insurance Payment Structure

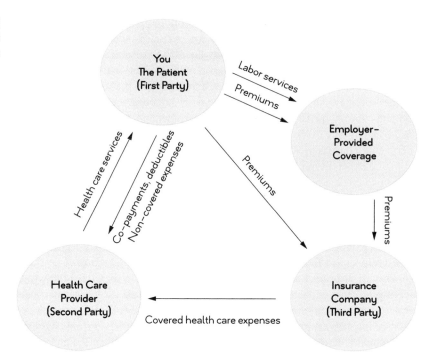

highly variable. The unexpected nature of these medical expenses has driven many individuals into bankruptcy. In the strange language of insurance, the insurance company is known as the third party. The health care provider is the second party and you are the first party. Insurance payments for covered services are termed third-party payments.

Employment-related health insurance is often a very attractive deal. First, because of lower administrative costs and because of lower health risks than exist for the whole population, on average, insurance companies will charge lower premiums for employer-sponsored health insurance. Second, more than half of the premiums are typically paid for by the employer. And finally, you and your family are probably eligible regardless of your physical condition.

You might think that most people have little need to consider health insurance. You simply accept what your employer offers. This assumption is incorrect. Today, many companies offer their employees a choice among two or more health care plans with differing employee premiums and schedules of benefits. And, in families where both spouses are employed outside the home, these choices are greatly compounded. Not only must couples compare the plans offered by their individual employers, but also they must consider whether it's better for them to join their respective group plans separately or to participate in only one, listing the other as a dependent. No doubt your company human resource representative will help you compare and contrast the available options, but the final decision on what is best for you and your family must be yours. You alone can determine the adequacy of your group coverage and select a supplemental individual or family nongroup policy if you find a serious gap in your health care protection.

Types of Coverage

Unlike auto and homeowner's policies examined previously, there are no standard formats for most health care policies. This means that most plans will not provide an explanation of coverage that is broken down into the discrete components discussed later. However, after you read the policies closely and discuss them with insurers' representatives, you should be able to reorganize the benefits provided into a more comparable format. Most policies include **comprehensive health insurance** coverage providing both basic health care benefits and major medical protection.

Basic Health Care Coverage

Three components—hospital insurance, surgical insurance, and medical insurance—make up **basic health care insurance**. Each can be purchased separately, but they are usually combined and sold as a basic health care package.

Hospital insurance will help pay for room and board and other medical expenses while you are in the hospital. It can take the form of indemnity coverage, expense coverage, or service benefit coverage. *Indemnity insurance* provides for specific dollar payments made directly to you for each day you are in the hospital, regardless of your actual expenses. *Expense insurance* provides for cash reimbursement either to you or to the provider of health care, based on expenses actually incurred.

Hospital **indemnity insurance** typically ranks as least preferable. This is the type of hospital insurance most often sold on television and in newspapers. Although receiving $100 to $200 a day for each day you are in the hospital may sound attractive, it's not likely to cover even your room and board. In addition, many of these policies do not begin payments until you have been in the hospital a set number of days. With the average hospital stay a little over six days at an average charge of over $8,000, don't plan on collecting much from an indemnity policy that commences payments after the fifth day. Furthermore, your likelihood of being admitted to a hospital has steadily declined over the last decade as more surgeries are performed on an outpatient basis.

More adequate benefits are generally provided by **hospital expense insurance**, which pays for room and board up to a set daily maximum. In addition, hospital expense insurance should pay for other hospital-related expenses, such as laboratory procedures, surgical materials, and X-rays—typically stating payments for these items as a percentage of the maximum payment for room and board. This is not a trivial supplemental benefit. On average, such items can double the cost of a hospital stay.

Surgical expense insurance should cover the fees of the operating surgeon and the anesthesiologist. An expense-type policy might provide a list of covered operations along with the maximum amount to be paid for each. A preferred policy agrees to pay all surgical costs as long as these are **usual, customary, and reasonable (UCR)** for your geographic area. If you have a policy with this provision, be sure to find out whether your physician will accept this amount as payment in full. If the doctor will not, find out how much extra he or she is planning to charge you. You physician may agree to an "assignment of benefits" under which the insurer pays the physician directly and the physician agrees to accept this reimbursement as full payment.

Service benefit coverage is the preferred approach to reimbursement for both hospital and surgical expenses. This type is provided by Blue Cross and many HMOs. For qualified and participating hospitals, full reimbursement for covered services is made directly to the health care provider. With service benefit insurance you don't have to constantly keep track of hospital costs in order to ensure adequate coverage. The one drawback is that you may have to stay in a qualifying hospital to receive 100 percent reimbursement.

Physicians' expense insurance, also termed *regular medical insurance,* provides payments for general nonsurgical physician care at the office or in the hospital. Traditional insurance has used an indemnity approach, paying you so much for each visit. Because you are likely to visit a doctor's office several times during the year, such insurance is relatively expensive. It has proved efficient, however, as one component of a comprehensive health care plan offered by a health maintenance organization (HMO). Under an HMO,

---

Comprehensive health insurance Provides both basic health care benefits and major medical protection.

Basic health care insurance Consists of hospital, surgical, and medical coverage.

Hospital insurance Provides coverage for room and board and other medical expenses while in the hospital.

Indemnity insurance Provides a specified dollar benefit regardless of actual cost.

Hospital expense insurance Pays actual cost up to a daily maximum.

TOPIC LINKS

Check online data on hospitals.

Surgical expense insurance Covers fees charged by operating surgeon and anesthesiologist.

Usual, customary, and reasonable (UCR) Typical fee charged for a specific good or service. Insurers will generally not provide reimbursement for expenses in excess of this amount.

Service benefit coverage Provides full reimbursement for covered services at UCR rates.

Physicians' expense insurance: Covers general nonsurgical physician care at the office or hospital.

Copayment: A payment by the insured covering the partial cost of the service.

Prescription drug coverage Specialized coverage for medically required pharmaceuticals.

TOPIC LINKS

Review physician's credentials.

Major medical insurance Provides protection after limits on basic health care coverage have been exceeded.

Coinsurance Percent of overage that must be paid for by the patient.

office visits may be fully covered, or you may be required to make a small copayment. A **copayment** is a dollar fee covering less than the full cost of the service. Its purpose is to limit unnecessary use.

Prescription drug coverage has become an increasingly important part of health insurance. Annual per person expenditure on prescription drugs is now over $450. As seen in Figure 14.1, private insurance covers about 65 percent of these expenditures. This percentage can vary significantly among households, with the elderly paying much more. For this reason, the government has recently created a drug prescription program for the elderly, which is discussed in the Medicare section of this chapter. Prescription coverage does not extend to drugs that can be purchased without a prescription such as common cold remedies.

Major Medical Coverage

The one component of health care insurance you should not do without is **major medical insurance**, because it eliminates the greatest risk to your financial health. Basic health care coverage may not pay all of your health care expenses, either because particular services are not covered or because you have exceeded the limits on coverage. Major medical is the backup you need when catastrophic illness strikes. If, after reimbursement under basic health care insurance, your health care expenses exceed a stated deductible, major medical will pick up part of the overage. Most policies have a **coinsurance** clause under which the insurer pays 80 percent of the overage and you pay the balance. The better policies put a dollar limit, perhaps $2,000, on your out-of-pocket expenses. Your payments after 20 percent coinsurance and a $2,000 limit are illustrated in Figure 14.3 In this example, health care costs total $9,200, of which basic health coverage pays $4,900, leaving a total overage of $4,300. After a deductible of $100 and a coinsurance payment of $840, your total out-of-pocket expenses would be $940. According to the terms of the illustrated policy, the amount you pay normally cannot exceed $2,000 per year.

Long-Term Care Coverage

With recent attempts by government, hospitals, and insurers to reduce the average hospital stay, nursing or rehabilitative care at home or in a skilled nursing facility is becoming

Figure 4.3
Sample Illustration of Major Medical Coverage

	Cost	Basic Health Payment	Overage
Hospital bill	$5,200	$3,000	$2,200
Physician services (office visits)	840	—	840
Surgical services	2,400	1,900	500
Prescription drugs	760	—	760
Total	$9,200	$4,900	$4,300
		Minus individual	
		deductible	−100
			$4,200
			× .20
		Coinsurance	$ 840

You pay the lesser of the deductible ($100) plus the coinsurance ($840) or $2,000.

increasingly important. Where traditional coverage for such services does exist, it applies only to services absolutely required by the illness or injury. Insurers will not typically pay for care that is primarily personal or custodial. Medicare and most traditional health care insurance limit nursing care to a fixed number of days in a skilled care facility. Out-of-pocket expenses for custodial care would be a much larger percentage of private expenditures than indicated in Figure 14.4.

A 2006 survey by Metlife found that the average annual cost of a nursing home stay was $75,190. It should be obvious that an extended stay can easily deplete your life savings and force you to rely on the health care provider of last resort—Medicaid. The insurance industry has responded by offering specialized long-term care policies. In addition, the government has provided tax preferences for long-term care premiums and policy payouts.

Long-term care policies sold by commercial insurers are typically indemnity policies that pay up to a set daily limit for nursing home expenses and home health care. To qualify for custodial care under these policies you must demonstrate that you can no longer care for yourself. This is usually defined in terms of "activities of daily living," or ADLs. This includes bathing, continence, dressing, eating and mobility. Although policies differ, you may qualify for benefits if you cannot do at least two or three of these tasks.

Long-term care policies
Covers long-term custodial care.

Long-term care policies are expensive, especially for the aged. The older you are when you first purchase long-term care coverage, the more the policy costs because your chances of needing benefits are greater as you age. Moreover, even high premiums are no guarantee that you will get the anticipated benefits. Some insureds have mistakenly thought their policies covered custodial care, whereas the contracts covered only the more restrictive skilled or intermediate care.

Dental Insurance

Dental insurance is a valuable fringe benefit if it's included in your group plan and paid by your employer. Dental insurance, which is similar to other kinds of health insurance, is one of the fastest-growing forms of insurance. Many plans require a deductible, have maximum reimbursement limits, or have copayments. One major difference is that dental insurance covers the cost of preventive care, usually paying all of the fees for routine checkups and cleanings, but only partial payment for corrective care.

Dental insurance Primarily covers cost of preventive care, with coinsurance on nonroutine dental work.

Figure 14.4
Sources of Payment for Long-Term Health Care, 2005

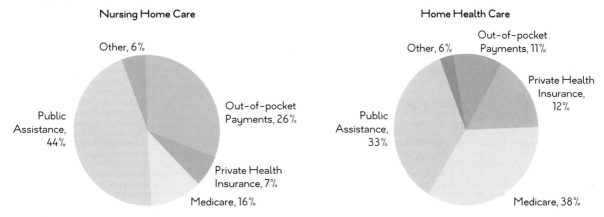

Nursing Home Care

Other, 6%
Out-of-pocket Payments, 26%
Public Assistance, 44%
Private Health Insurance, 7%
Medicare, 16%

Home Health Care

Other, 6%
Out-of-pocket Payments, 11%
Private Health Insurance, 12%
Public Assistance, 33%
Medicare, 38%

Source: Centers for Medicare and Medicaid Services, U.S. Dept. of Health and Human Services, http://www.cms.hhs.gov/NationalHealthExpendData/downloads/nhe2005.zip

If your dental insurance is not part of your overall health insurance plan, it may not be cost-effective to buy the insurance on your own. You should be able to plan for these expenses in your yearly budget. Moreover, expensive dental surgery to correct birth deformities or injuries is in most cases already covered under the surgical expense component of the basic health care package.

Specific Disease and Accident Insurance

Widely sold through the media, specific disease insurance is one policy you definitely should not purchase. Not only is it likely to be expensive, but also it makes no sense. Why would you want a policy that covers you if you have cancer but pays nothing if you have a heart attack? You need broader coverage that pays regardless of the cause of illness. Companies offering such policies are playing on our fears of a dreaded disease.

Although accident insurance is often sold by reputable major insurers, the reasons against purchasing it are much the same as those for not purchasing specific disease insurance. The purpose of health care insurance is to reduce your financial risks. Gambling on the cause of future illnesses and injuries does not serve that purpose.

Important Provisions

No matter what type of health care coverage you have, certain provisions will indicate the quality of your insurance coverage. In general, those with shorter waiting periods, fewer exclusions, and higher policy limits offer better protection.

Preexisting Conditions Clause and Waiting Period

Preexisting conditions clause Excludes coverage for certain medical conditions that existed before the initial date of coverage.

Waiting period (health care): Period after which preexisting conditions are covered.

All individual policies and some group policies will contain a **preexisting conditions clause**, which excludes from coverage certain types of injuries and illnesses that began before the policy was issued. These conditions may later be covered after a specified **waiting period**.

This clause is a common means of denying payment. You may be better off keeping a less-than-satisfactory policy rather than waiting the necessary time before you are fully covered under a new policy. Also, beware of policies that do not waive the preexisting conditions clause after a given period of time.

Guaranteed Renewability

Guaranteed renewability: Guarantees coverage up to specified age upon payment of premiums, although future premiums may increase.

Unless you are purchasing temporary coverage to bridge a gap between group insurance policies, you should consider purchasing insurance that is guaranteed renewable until age 65. **Guaranteed renewability** means that no matter what your health, your coverage will continue so long as you pay the premiums. The company can increase rates for a given class of insureds, but cannot increase your individual premium for any reason.

Policy Limits

The maximum amount the insurance company will pay out is particularly important on the major medical portion of your coverage. The limit may hold for each benefit period, usually a calendar year, over a lifetime, or for each illness or accident. Never purchase a policy with a limit of less than $250,000 on hospitalization payments for a given illness or accident per benefit period or less than a lifetime maximum of $500,000. The likelihood of huge medical expenses, although small, does exist.

Waiver of Premium

This clause waives your premium payment should you be unable to work because of illness or injury. If your health insurance policy does not contain this provision, you must plan for these payments under your disability income protection.

Exclusions

Some injuries and illnesses will not be covered even when there is no medical history of them. For example, intentionally self-inflicted injuries, injuries covered by workers' compensation, mental illness, or injuries resulting from war or military service are typically excluded. Such elective procedures as cosmetic surgery and dental treatment may be covered only if the condition being treated results from birth defects or accidental injuries.

Some policies will cover maternity expenses, and others will exclude them. Under the Pregnancy Discrimination Act, employer-provided health insurance must cover pregnancy expenses on the same basis as other medical costs. Although a maternity plan may be helpful if you are planning a family, it's not necessary financial protection. After all, you should be able to budget adequately for these expenses over at least a nine month period. Of much greater importance is how your policy handles the costs of childbirth complications and the costs of treating birth defects.

For most types of policies the Newborns' and Mothers' Health Protection Act of 1996 (NMHPA) prohibits health insurers from restricting a hospital stay for childbirth to less than 48 hours after a vaginal birth and 96 hours after a caesarian birth. You can be forced to leave earlier if the attending provider agrees. The act, however, does not require that your insurer offer maternity coverage. It only ensures that you have a prescribed time for recuperation when it is covered by your policy.

finance news 14.1

Mandatory Health Insurance

All states require that drivers have some auto liability coverage. Depending on the state in which you live, you may be required to purchase equally important health insurance. Under a bill passed by the Massachusetts legislature in 2006 all of the state's citizen's must purchase health insurance or face penalties. Other states are considering similar laws. To ensure that those at the bottom of the financial scale can satisfy the new law, the state has expanded the Medicaid program and has subsidized insurance for the poor. Those who cannot afford health insurance will not be penalized.

The Massachusetts law establishes the Commonwealth Health Insurance Connector. It is a state agency that connects individuals who need insurance with insurers that provide a wide range of insurance plans from basic to comprehensive coverage. Those with low to moderate incomes are eligible for the Commonwealth Care Health Insurance Program, which con-

nects low income families with approved health care plans and subsidizes their payments. If your family is below the poverty line you may be eligible for free health insurance, called Commonwealth Care. For others, the program applies a sliding scale of affordability that determines just how much you are expected to contribute. If you cannot find insurance at the affordable price, you will not be penalized.

The new law will probably increase the number of workers who sign up for employer-subsidized health care, increasing the burden on employers. Employers are not required to provide health insurance coverage. However, employers will be required to pay part of the cost of their employee's health insurance if they do not sponsor a health insurance plan. The law creates a "Fair Share Contribution" that these employers must contribute toward the cost of the employee's individually purchased insurance. The employer may also have to pay a surcharge if a non-insured employee receives free health care.

Insurance Providers and Service Networks

There are three major categories of private health care insurance: commercial insurers, Blue Cross and Blue Shield and health maintenance organizations (HMOs). The commercial companies are for-profit insurers like Aetna, a stock company. The Blue Cross and Blue Shield network of plans consists of non-profit organizations licensed under special state laws. HMOS are integrated insurers and providers that operate under federal and state supervision. The structure of insurance coverage provided by these health insurers can take many forms. Thirty years ago fee-for-service plans covered almost the entire market. Emerging home maintenance organizations were providing coverage for a small market segment, and preferred provider organizations and point-of-service plans were largely unheard of. In an attempt to hold down the rising cost of medical care, alternative strategies for health care reimbursement have been implemented.

Managed care A health management program that attempts to provide adequate care while containing costs.

Managed care is the current term applied to a health insurance plan that puts together a coherent network of providers. Your primary care physician usually serves as the gatekeeper to this network. It is the gatekeeper's job to guide you through the network to ensure that you receive appropriate medical care most efficiently and inexpensively.

Many companies have introduced the managed care concept to hold down the heavy cost of medical care and the rising level of health insurance premiums. The three basic cost-containment features employed by managed care plans are preadmission certification for hospital stays, utilization review for the appropriateness of care, and second opinions for nonemergency surgical procedures. Each of these features limits you or your doctor's choice of medical care. The hope is that eliminating unnecessary or excessively costly choices will provide you with better health care for each dollar spent.

Fee-for-Service (FFS)

Fee-for-service health insurance Reimburses medical providers selected by the insured.

Fee-for-service health insurance providers offer the greatest choice of health care services. You choose your doctor and the hospital. The insurer reimburses service providers at your community's UCR (usual, customary, and reasonable) rates. The UCR is based on fees charged in your local area and is typically set at a level that would provide complete reimbursement for bills submitted by most physicians. Your physician may require a supplemental fee arrangement under which you will pay any excess charges not paid by your insurer.

Fee-for-service providers typically require deductibles and coinsurance payments. However, total out-of-pocket expenses may be limited under the major medical provisions. Typically, it's the most expensive plan.

HMOs

Health maintenance organization (HMO) An insurer and provider of health care offering comprehensive health care services on a prepaid basis.

A **health maintenance organization (HMO)** differs from the other insurers because it is not only the provider of insurance but also the provider of the health care. The HMO premium represents a prepayment for future medical services, which are then provided as needed at little or no out-of-pocket cost.

Group-staff HMO Health services delivered by physicians working on a salaried or contractual basis.

Individual practice arrangement (IPA) HMO Independent physicians are reimbursed by the HMO for services performed.

There are two basic types of HMOs: the group-staff arrangement and the individual practice arrangement. The **group-staff HMO** provides services at one or more locations with salaried physicians. The **individual practice arrangement (IPA) HMO** contracts with private physicians who maintain their own offices and then pays them on a fee-for-service schedule. Individuals then choose from among the participating physicians for their needed medical services. IPAs generally offer a greater choice of physicians and more conveniently located medical services. They are slightly more costly than group-staff HMOs.

An HMO is likely to cover more basic health care benefits than a fee-for-service plan. Some advocates of HMOs have suggested that they are better than traditional insurers because they concentrate on preventive rather than curative medicine. Because the physician has a financial interest in seeing you remain healthy, you supposedly receive better preventive care and, therefore, remain healthier. Critics argue that the physician also has a financial incentive to hold back medical care. There is evidence that hospital stays are shorter for patients of HMOs, but the reasons are unclear. As of now, it is not possible to make any generalizations about the quality of care provided by any particular category of health care plans.

Point of Service (POS)

Recently, some HMOs have begun to offer a **point-of-service plan (POS)**. Under an open-ended plan, you may select non-HMO providers if you are willing to incur additional costs in the form of higher deductibles and coinsurances. This provides a health care alternative for those who find that they are dissatisfied with the HMO's choice of providers.

PPOs

Virtually nonexistent in the mid-1980s, **preferred provider organizations (PPOs)** currently enroll about 40 percent of the participants in employer-sponsored plans. A PPO is only a provider, not an insurer. It works either directly with an employer or through the employer's insurer to provide medical services at less than customary rates to the company's employees. Those who choose a PPO option may still be able to utilize non-PPO services at increased cost. This is not true for persons who belong to an *EPO (exclusive provider organization)*. They must receive care from an affiliated provider or pay the entire cost themselves.

> **TOPIC LINKS**
>
> Check accreditation status of health care organizations.

Point-of-service plan (POS) An HMO plan in which members may use providers outside the HMO for less than full reimbursement.

Preferred provider organizations (PPOs) Selectively offered health care services providing care at reduced out-of-pocket cost.

Employment-Related Health Care Insurance

As shown in Figure 14.5, about 71 percent of workers have employer-sponsored health insurance. Many who don't are probably covered by employer-sponsored insurance covering a spouse or a parent. The cost of these plans from about $4,000 for single coverage to over $10,000 is significant. For this reason, most employers require that employees partially offset some of these costs through individual contributions from participating employees. Employees contribute about 31 percent of the premiums for single coverage and about 50 percent of the premiums for family insurance.

Figure 14.5 also lists the percent of workers who have access to various types of employer-sponsored health care benefits. For many people, health insurance selection is tied to employment selection. As a result, a few individuals in ill health may be deterred from looking for a job. They fear that employers, concerned about rising medical costs, may be reluctant to hire them. The Americans with Disabilities Act of 1990 provides some help to these prospective workers by setting down hiring restrictions on businesses. Basically, an employer cannot deny a person a job because of potential insurance claims or higher insurance premiums. Preexisting conditions, however, can be excluded from coverage as long as these same exclusions are applied to all other workers.

Even a uniformly applied preexisting condition clause can deter workers from changing jobs. In response to that concern, the Health Insurance Portability and Accountability

Figure 14.5
Facts on Employer Provided Health Care Benefits

Source: National Compensation Survey: Employee Benefits in Private Industry in the United States, March 2006, U.S. Bureau of Labor Statistics.

Percent of all workers with access to health care plans

Medical care	71%
Dental care	46%
Vision care	29%
Prescription drug coverage	67%
Short-term disability	39%
Long-term disability	30%

Health insurance contributions

Single coverage

Percent without required contribution	25%
Average flat monthly employer premium	$327
Percent with required contribution	7%
Average flat monthly employer premium	$247
Average flat monthly employee contribution	$76

Family coverage

Percent without required contribution	13%
Average flat monthly employer premium	$789
Percent with required contribution	87%
Average flat monthly employer premium	$592
Average flat monthly employee contribution	$297

Act (HIPAA) limits the period that insurers could deny or limit coverage because of a pre-existing condition to 12 months. Moreover, employees who have not experienced a significant lapse in coverage cannot be forced to wait through more than one 12-month period during their entire work life.

Interim Coverage

Previously, workers who lost their jobs were also likely to lose their health insurance protection. To remedy this doubly disastrous situation, Congress now requires employers with 20 or more workers to provide terminating employees with continued health care coverage under a law called COBRA. This must be made available to those ex-workers who cannot obtain either alternative group insurance or Medicare coverage. The employer may charge you for the insurance, but in most instances the cost to you cannot be more than 102 percent of group insurance rates.

Mandated continuation periods are listed in Figure 14.6. When the continuation period ends, the group coverage must be convertible to an individual policy. Although the individual policy can have a higher price and provide fewer benefits, it still may be wise for you to exercise your conversion rights. An entirely new policy would exclude preexisting conditions and require a waiting period before full coverage began. The continuation and conversion of previous health insurance coverage can be used to eliminate any gaps in coverage due to a change in employment or marital status.

Family members also have a right to request a continuation of benefits for three years with the right of conversion thereafter. The circumstances under which benefits would be continued include death of the covered worker, separation or divorce from the covered spouse, or loss of dependent status by a child of an insured parent.

Figure 14.6
*Continuation Period for
Group Health Insurance*

Qualifying Events	Beneficiary	Term of Coverage
Termination	Employee	18 months
Reduced hours	Spouse	(For individuals who qualify
	Dependent child	for Social Security disability
		benefits, special rules extend
		coverage an additional 11 months)
Employee entitled to Medicare	Spouse	36 months
Divorce or legal separation	Dependent child	
Death of covered employee		
Loss of "dependent child" status	Dependent child	36 months

Workers' Compensation

All states have **workers' compensation** programs that help pay for medical expenses and lost income resulting from work-related illnesses or injuries. However, not all workers are covered nor is coverage required in all states. You should ask your employer whether you are covered. If you are, the type and amount of benefits you may receive are set down in state laws. Your personnel office or the state compensation office can provide you with a schedule of potential benefits.

Workers' compensation provides no-fault insurance for workplace injuries. You are covered regardless of fault. In return for the no-fault coverage, the employer's liability is limited by a prescribed schedule of benefits. Employees, however, are not restricted from filing lawsuits against third parties, such as a product manufacturer, that may have contributed to the injury or in special situations from suing an employer that was grossly or intentionally negligent.

Workers' compensation State programs providing health and disability income coverage for work-related illnesses and injuries.

Health Care Spending Accounts

New government regulations on tax-advantaged employee benefits have allowed employers to experiment with new types of plans that might save costs. An employer may set up a **defined contribution health plan**, where the employee receives a set amount of money to purchase health care benefits. These contributions may be in addition to other primary health insurance benefits. Typically, they are used to fund a tax advantaged spending account consisting of either a health savings account, a flexible spending account, a medical spending account, or a health reimbursement arrangement. Contributions are made out of pretax dollars and you do not owe taxes on distributions used for qualified medical expenses.

Defined contribution health plans Employer provides a fixed amount of dollars for employee-purchased health insurance.

Health Savings Account (HSA)

You don't need an employer to set up a **health savings account (HSA)**. The accounts are set up through a trustee, such as a bank, an insurance company, or anyone else the IRS approves as a trustee for individual retirement accounts. Contributions made by you or your employer are excluded from your gross income and earnings on the account are tax-free. The contributions remain in your account from year to year until you use them. Distributions must be used for qualified medical expenses. Qualified medical expenses are

Health savings account (HSA) A tax-advantaged account for qualified medical expenses that requires a high deductible health plan.

those that meet IRS guidelines and cover most professionally prescribed medical services. These are medical and dental expenses that would generally qualify as an itemized deduction on your federal income taxes. However, you don't have to itemize deductions to gain a tax benefit.

To qualify for an HSA you must be covered by a high deductible health plan (HDHP). In 2008, your insurance plan must have a deductible of at least $1,100 for individual coverage and $2,200 for family coverage. Additional requirements can be found in IRS Pub. 969 "Health Savings Accounts and Other Tax-Favored Health Plans." An HDHP is a medical plan with a high deductible and a maximum limit on deductibles. The annual amount you can contribute to the HSA is basically determined by your deductible. The government hopes that the high deductible will provide an incentive for health care cost containment by making you a more selective consumer of medical services.

Flexible Spending Account (FSA)

Flexible spending account (FSA) Employee-funded accounts for paying health care expenditures with pretax dollars.

If you don't have an HSA, your employer might provide a **flexible spending account (FSA)**. An FSA is funded through a voluntary salary reduction agreement with your employer. You must designate how much you plan to contribute at the beginning of the year. Your planned contribution is then periodically deducted from your salary. Contributions by you and your employer are excluded from your gross income.

Like the HSA, withdrawals must be used for qualified medical expenses. Unlike the HSA, any amount left in the account at the end of the year does not rollover to the next

FINANCIAL PLANNING *for*
young adults 14.2

Insurance Options for Young Adults

Young adults between ages 18 to 24 are more likely to be without health insurance than any other group. Luckily, they are less likely to need medical care than their elders. However, they are more likely to find themselves with catastrophic injuries that can leave them with a lifetime of medical bills and any illness that requires a hospital stay can result in thousands of dollars in bills. The lack of insurance among young adults is the direct result of their labor market experience. They have a higher unemployment rate and job turnover rate than the rest of the labor force.

As long as you are a student and below a certain age (generally age 25) you are likely to be covered under your parent's health insurance. This coverage lapses when you are no longer a full-time student. Young adults who are in the workforce, therefore, are likely to find themselves without coverage during periods of unemployment and job search.

This gap in coverage could be filled by either extending previous employment-related coverage or by purchasing an interim health insurance policy. As discussed in this chapter, workers have a right to retain their health coverage for some time after they leave employment. This right also extends to dependents who were covered under their parent's policy, but are no longer eligible because they are no longer in school. If you are a young worker who is unemployed or without coverage in your new job, continuing coverage under your parent's plan is a good idea. To extend this coverage, you must pay the full cost to the employer plus a 2 percent administrative fee. Unfortunately, a comprehensive health care plan may be too costly for someone who is unemployed.

University health plans that cover about one-quarter of college students typically end a few months after graduation. However, some schools allow students to extend coverage for an additional limited period.

Another option is to purchase interim coverage for only major medical. This does not cover preexisting conditions and should only be used for limited periods of job search and unemployment. eHealthInsurance found that the average monthly cost for single major medical coverage was $125 in 2004. But if you need temporary coverage only, you can purchase a nonrenewable short-term policy for as little as $50 a month or less. The *Wall Street Journal* reports that Humana has policies for young adults with a high deductible of several thousand dollars that start for as little as $24 a month.

year. It is forfeited to your employer. Therefore, the amount you plan to contribute to an FSA requires careful financial planning.

Health Reimbursement Arrangement (HRA)

A **health reimbursement arrangement (HRA)** must be solely funded by your employer. Reimbursements from the account for qualified medical expenses are tax-free. Unused amounts in the account may be rolled over to the next year. Any unused amount that is payable to you at the end of year, must be included in your gross income. An employer may provide an HRA in place of health insurance or as a supplement to cover non-insured medical expenses.

Health reimbursement arrangement (HRA) A tax-advantaged fund for qualified medical expenses that is solely funded by an employer.

Medical Savings Accounts (MSA)

A **medical savings account (MSA)** is designed for self-employed individuals and small businesses. Like the HSA, this is a trustee plan and requires a high deductible health plan that determines the maximum contribution. However, unlike the HSA, the minimum deductible is larger under the MSA and the annual maximum out-of-pocket limit is lower. Also unlike the HSA, an MSA may not contain contributions from both you and your employer in any single year.

Medical savings account (MSA) A tax-advantaged account for self-employed individuals who require a high deductible health plan.

Public Health Services

Medicare and Medicaid are federal programs designed to improve the health of the indigent and the elderly. **Medicaid** is neither an insurer nor a provider of health care. It is a joint federal–state effort to cover the medical expenses of the indigent. Unless you find yourself in this group, you will not have contact with Medicaid services. The coverage and quality of the services offered differ from state to state. Information can be obtained at your state's welfare office.

Medicaid A joint federal–state-sponsored program covering medical expenses for the indigent.

In one way or another, **Medicare** concerns us all. Either we have a relative who is affected by the program, or eventually we will consider enrolling ourselves. A federal health insurance program for those 65 or older or those with chronic kidney failure or certain other disabilities, Medicare consists of three parts: Part A is hospital insurance, Part B is medical insurance, and Part C is an alternative to Parts A and B. Under Part C you can contract with private insurance for substitute coverage under an HMO or PPO plan. Current coverage limits can be found at the Medicare Web site. The hospital insurance is financed through the Social Security taxes you pay while you work. The medical insurance is voluntary and is partly paid by premiums from those who choose to participate. Beginning in 2007, monthly premiums are based on income. These programs are administered through the Social Security Administration. You should contact a local office for information and apply for benefits three months before reaching age 65.

Medicare A federal health insurance program for those age 65 or older, or those with certain sicknesses or disabilities.

TOPIC LINKS

Medicare.

Both Medicare hospital and medical insurance are a good buy at the time you become eligible. Medicare will, however, leave some serious gaps in your health care coverage. You can consider closing these gaps with a private supplemental health insurance policy. Medicare includes substantial deductibles and coinsurance payments. In the event of catastrophic illness, these payments could deplete the investment portfolio generating your retirement income.

Medigap Insurance

Medigap insurance is designed to fill the gap between expenses that are covered by Medicare and those that are not. It's sold by private insurers. A medigap policy that places a realistic limit on deductibles and coinsurance payments is an excellent choice.

Medigap insurance Private insurance meant to cover (partially or totally) those health care expenses that are not reimbursed by Medicare.

Furthermore, if you purchase a medigap policy within six months of turning age 65 and enrolling in Medicare Part B, federal law states that you cannot be turned down or charged extra because of your health status or medical condition. And once you have coverage, a medigap policy may not be canceled or a renewal refused because of your ill health.

Under directions from the U.S. Congress, the National Association of Insurance Commissioners (NIAC) has developed 10 standardized policies. Medigap insurers can promote only those policies as supplemental Medicare insurance; all must sell at least a basic policy that addresses the major gaps in Medicare benefits.

Medicare Prescription Drug Coverage

Medicare beneficiaries may choose to enroll in Part D of the program. Through Part D enrollees can now obtain prescription drug coverage through either a stand-alone prescription drug plan or a Medicare Advantage plan offered by private insurers. The premiums for these plans are subsidized by the government. The plans contain a deductible and coinsurance on payments above the deductible.

Medicare Advantage

Medicare Advantage
Privately run medical plans that replace a traditional Medicare plan.

Medicare Advantage plans are privately run medical plans meant to replace the benefits provided under a traditional Medicare plan. They include all types of plans from fee-for-service to HMOs. They offer at least the same benefits as traditional Medicare. Many are meant to replace both Medicare and a supplemental Medigap policy by closing many of the gaps in Medicare coverage. Plan types include both managed care plans and traditional fee-for-service plans. At the Medicare Web site, you can review and compare the costs and coverage of plans in your area.

Individually Selected Health Care Insurance

Group coverage is generally less expensive than individual insurance. If you are one of the few who cannot take part in a group plan at work, look into group policies offered through fraternal and professional organizations. But be careful. Some insurers advertise their policies as part of a group plan but provide none of the expected cost savings. When the identifiable group is not likely to be in any better health than the population as a whole, there is little reason to believe the policy is a good buy.

The market for individually purchased health insurance has been expanding as corporations cut back on health care benefits that they provide to retirees. Several health insurance companies have been designing policies for older retirees who do not yet qualify for Medicare.

Cost of Coverage

Most group insurance plans offer expensive comprehensive health coverage that includes basic health and major medical benefits. Similar individual policies cost 30 to 40 percent more, with a comprehensive family policy costing over $10,000 a year. A survey of individual policies at the beginning of 2007 by American Health Insurance Plans indicated that the average annual cost of single coverage was $2,613 and the average cost of family coverage was $5,799. This ranged from $1,163 for persons under age 18 for single coverage to $9,201 for family coverage with a head of household aged 60 through 64.

You can hold down premiums by purchasing only major medical coverage with large deductibles and making out-of-pocket payments for your basic health needs. Increasing the deductible from $100 to $1,000 can cut your premiums by 40 to 50 percent. If you set aside an emergency fund, you can use those resources to self-insure against unexpected

saving money 14.3

A Flexible Spending Account for Medical Expenditures

Employer-provided flexible spending accounts generally permit you to allocate a portion of your salary for this purpose. Sometimes employers match employee contributions or contribute a fixed amount. If tax-qualified, the salary dollars paid into this account are tax exempt. These dollars may then be used to pay for expenses that would be deductible from personal income taxes under IRS guidelines.

One popular use of flexible spending accounts is to pay for the deductibles and coinsurance on health insurance plans. The money placed in the flexible spending account can be used to pay the difference between the employee's medical expenses and the amount paid for by the company's health plan. Normally, you would have to earn $138.89 in taxable income to pay for a $100 deductible if you were in the 28 percent marginal

tax bracket and your total medical expenses for the year did not exceed 7.5 percent of your family's gross income. Using tax-exempt dollars through a flexible spending account would result in savings of $38.89, regardless of your proportional medical expenses.

As employers increase deductibles and coinsurance payments in order to hold down the increasing cost of medical insurance, the tax savings provided by flexible spending accounts become greater. There is, however, one significant drawback. At the end of the year, any unused funds you have allocated to this account are forfeited. You either use it or lose it.

For persons engaging in personal financial planning, this should not be a serious problem. If you review previous budgets and your upcoming medical needs in the pro forma budget, you should be in a good position to estimate your flexible account needs conservatively and obtain the maximum tax advantage.

basic health costs. Meanwhile, the major medical insurance provides you with the backup protection you need in case of catastrophic illness or injury. Review the checklist in Figure 14.7 before shopping for private health insurance.

Even healthy persons may find it difficult to purchase comprehensive individual coverage including maternity and mental health benefits. If you have a specific health problem, you will encounter additional difficulties. You are likely to be denied coverage, charged an additional risk premium, or offered a policy that specifically excludes coverage for your preexisting condition. Different insurers apply differing restrictions on coverage for those in less than perfect health; therefore, it pays to shop around. Remember, purchasing health insurance after your illness or accident is like trying to purchase homeowner's insurance after a fire.

Figure 14.7
Checklist: Shopping for Private Health Insurance

✓ **Comparison Shop**
Coverage and costs differ widely.

✓ **Check for Preexisting Condition Exclusions and Beware of Giving Up an Existing Policy**
Statements such as "no medical examination required" do not relieve you of a preexisting condition clause.

✓ **Be Aware of Maximum Benefits and Major Medical Coverage**
You need insurance to avoid major financial losses.

✓ **Check Your Right to Renew**
Avoid policies that permit the company to cancel policies on an individual basis.

✓ **Know with Whom You Are Dealing**
Check out both the agent and the company.

✓ **Don't Put Up with High-Pressure Sales Tactics**
High-pressure sales tactics typically indicate high commissions, high cost, and low quality.

The Insurance Company

Be sure to investigate the financial soundness of the medical insurer. A bankrupt insurer could leave you financially ruined. In many states commercial insurers are covered by a state guarantee fund that protects policyholders if an insurer gets into financial trouble. Technically, however, Blue Cross/Blue Shield companies are not viewed as insurance companies and, thus, are not covered by the guarantee funds in most states.

In the event they become insolvent, HMOs that are federally qualified by the Health Care Financing Administration must carry insurance to cover the unpaid bills of patients. They are also required to include clauses in all contracts with doctors and patients prohibiting the providers of medical services from collecting directly from patients.

Disability Income Protection

Only those workers with dependents need life insurance, but every worker needs disability income protection. Young workers often purchase life insurance while ignoring the much greater risk of disability. A survey by American Health Insurance Plans found that about one-third of adults believe there is about a 5 percent chance they will suffer a disability that would force them to miss three or more months of work and that over half of adults believe the probability is around 10 percent. These misperceptions are troubling, because your chances of suffering a serious disability are surprisingly high. The Social Security Administration estimates that a 20-year-old has more than a 25 percent probability of experiencing an insured disability before reaching age 65 (see Table 14.1). Since the requirements for an insured disability are rather strict, it's likely that many more individuals will experience a significant earnings loss at some point in their work life. In fact, over one-fifth of 55- to 64-year-olds state that they have a work-related disability that limits the kind or amount of work they do.

Long-term disability insurance that bridges at least part of the gap between when short-term benefits end and retirement begins is an employer-sponsored benefit for approximately 30 percent of the workforce. In smaller establishments only about one-fifth of employees are similarly covered. Those without long-term disability protection must rely entirely on Social Security benefits or a declining bank account. Furthermore, few will be able to collect the Social Security benefits they may be depending on. The rules are quite strict. You must be able to prove that the disability is total and will last for at least one year or terminate in death. Nothing is paid out for partial disability unless it is preceded by a period of total disability. And if you do qualify, benefit checks do not begin until at least six months after you become disabled.

Table 14.1
Probability of Death and/or Disability Before Normal Retirement Age (NRA)

	Male	Female
Probability of Death Before NRA	8.6%	5.6%
Probability of Disability Before NRA	29.3%	25.2%
Probability of Survival and Never Disabled to NRA	62.1%	69.2%

Note: Probabilities are for an age 20 individual in 2005

Source: Actuarial Note Social Security Administration Number 2005.6 (February 2006) A Death and Disability Life Table for Insured Workers Born In 1985 by Robert Baldwin and Sharon Chu.

Sources of Disability Income

If you become disabled, you will probably have to rely on a variety of sources for support. The following are some common means of support used by the disabled during periods of reduced market income.

Disability Income Insurance

As with health care insurance, the cheapest **disability income insurance** is obtained through group coverage sponsored by employers. Group benefits are typically integrated with Social Security payments and workers' compensation to provide a level of benefits dependent upon current wages. This usually does not exceed 60 percent of salary.

Disability income insurance Partially replaces lost income during a period of defined disability.

Individual disability income policies generally provide a set dollar amount of coverage. Premiums may be stated in terms of each $100 of monthly disability benefits purchased. Various endorsements and riders are available to tailor the policy to individual needs. For example, the amount of benefits may be dependent upon whether you qualify for Social Security disability benefits.

Both short-term and long-term disability income plans are available. *Short-term coverage* usually begins immediately after an accident but has a short waiting period for disabilities resulting from sickness. Benefit payments may then continue for six months, or at most, two years. *Long-term disability* income insurance has a longer waiting period, but benefits will continue for either a stated number of years or until normal retirement age (65 to 67).

The conditions for receiving disability payments are generally more stringent under long-term disability insurance and may even change with the duration of the disability. For example, you may be considered disabled over the first two to five years if you cannot perform the duties of your current occupation. Payments after this period, however, may continue only if you are unable to engage in any occupation for which you are reasonably qualified by education, training, or experience.

Private disability benefits may or may not be taxable. Specifically excluded are payouts related to military service and terrorist attack. Also, if you pay for premiums on an individual policy with after-tax dollars, the benefits are not taxable. Alternatively, payouts from group employment policies funded with pretax dollars are taxable. Payments received from private sources, including both company plans or individually purchased disability insurance, do not reduce your Social Security disability benefits. However, public benefits from programs such as workers' compensation may lower your Social Security benefits. These are reduced if the combined payments from all public programs exceed 80 percent of your average current earnings.

Social Security

To be considered disabled under the Social Security law, you must have a physical condition that prevents you from doing any substantial gainful work and that is expected to last 12 months or result in death. In 2008, if you could earn over $940 a month in gross wages (higher if you are blind) after deductions for medical services and equipment required because of your impairment, you were considered capable of substantial gainful employment. The disability must be expected to last at least one year or result in death. You may not receive benefits for a partial disability or short-term disability. Moreover, benefits do not begin until six months after the onset of the disability.

Obviously, these requirements rule out Social Security payments for all but the severely and, apparently, permanently disabled. Because you and your family could suffer a severe reduction in income and still be ineligible for disability income from Social

Security, you will likely have a need for private disability income insurance. Plans that integrate private benefits and Social Security benefits provide additional income security by increasing the monthly payout if you do not qualify for governmental benefits.

To be eligible for Social Security disability benefits, you must have accumulated 20 quarters of coverage within the last 10 years. However, younger workers can be eligible with fewer credits. You earn a quarter of coverage for each $1,050 (in 2008) of wages you receive, with a four-quarter maximum for one calendar year. You are also automatically enrolled in Medicare, the government's health insurance program, after two years of disability benefits.

The Disability Planner at the government's Social Security Web site should help you determine potential government-funded disability benefits. You, your dependent children, and a caretaking spouse may all be eligible for benefits. The basic disability benefit is received by the disabled worker. Mothers caring for dependent children under age 16 and earning no more than an annually determined maximum would additionally receive 50 percent of the basic monthly disability benefit. Children under 18 years of age would also get 50 percent of the basic benefit. However, there is a cap on the total benefits a household can receive. Sample benefits are listed in Table 14.2.

Upon reentering the workforce, your Social Security benefits need not end immediately. You may be eligible for a certain trial period in which you will continue to receive unreduced disability benefits. The cost of rehabilitation and the fear of losing Medicare coverage have deterred some beneficiaries from rejoining the workforce. Under the Ticket to Work Program, workers receive a ticket that may be used to obtain vocational rehabilitation, job training, and other support services. They also retain their Medicare coverage for a substantial time period after they return to work.

Workers' Compensation

If the disabling injury or illness is work related, you may also be entitled to disability benefits under your state's workers' compensation statutes. These laws hold employers strictly liable for injuries in the workplace. This means that the employer is responsible, regardless of who is at fault. In return for assuming strict liability, compensation paid by employers is limited to mandated amounts. The benefits vary from state to state and are generally set equal to a given percentage of the average weekly wage within the state.

Specific types of injuries, such as loss of an arm, may come under the state's definition of permanent partial disabilities. For such injuries, the worker may receive a lump-sum payment or weekly payments for a limited time.

Many states also provide maintenance and benefits for workers undergoing rehabilitation. Workers' compensation or related programs may handle this coverage. Again, specifics can be provided at your state's workers' compensation office.

Table 14.2
Estimates of Monthly Disability Benefits from the SSA Quick Benefits Planner

	Current Annual Earnings			
	20,000	40,000	80,000	160,000
	Monthly Disability Benefit			
Worker alone	829	1,265	1,907	2,234
Family maximum	1,265	2,403	3,383	3,934
	Percent of Income Replaced by SSA Benefit			
Worker alone	50%	38%	29%	17%
Family maximum	76%	72%	51%	30%

Source: SSA Quick Planner, based on 35-year-old worker qualifying for disability benefits.

Pension Plans

Instead of purchasing separate group disability insurance, some employers will incorporate a disability option into the existing pension plan. If you are disabled before normal retirement age, you may be able to receive an immediate pension under a disability clause in the pension plan. The method for calculating monthly benefits may or may not differ from that used for normal retirement. However, even at reduced benefit levels, this alternative may be desirable.

Also look for a waiver of contributions clause. Under this option the employer will continue to contribute to your pension plan for as long as you are disabled. Thus, at normal retirement age you could collect the full retirement pension even though you had not worked up until normal retirement age.

Accident Insurance

Also called *dismemberment insurance,* **accident insurance** pays the insured a set dollar amount for the loss of life, limb, or sight. It pays nothing when the physical loss is caused by an illness rather than an accident. Furthermore, the amount paid is unrelated to your actual income loss. Its major selling point is its low price. One company charges $2 a month for $150,000 of accident life, with smaller payments for dismemberment. The price is low because your chances of collecting are small. Avoid this purchase; you need better income disability protection.

Accident insurance Pays a set dollar amount in the event of physical dismemberment.

Waiver of Premium or Payment Clauses

Life and health insurance policies should be examined for clauses that waive future premium payments in the event of disability. If you have mortgage life insurance on your home or credit life insurance on a car loan, examine these policies for a waiver of premium clause.

Savings

If you have not adequately planned for your disability income needs, you may have no choice but to rely on accumulated savings. An emergency fund may provide support in the short run. Over an extended period, you may have to consider disposing of assets that were held for long-term purposes. You may be able to borrow against the cash value on a life insurance policy. For those who are severely disabled or terminally ill, some life policies provide an early payout while you are still alive. Retirement accounts are another potential source of support in times of extreme need. Normally, early withdrawals from tax-advantaged accounts before age $59\frac{1}{2}$ trigger tax penalties. However, the penalties may be waived if you are disabled or if the withdrawals were made to satisfy qualifying medical expenses.

Insurance Clauses Affecting Disability Benefits

The quality of your disability insurance protection will depend on more than just the promised monthly benefits. It will be determined largely by the duration and conditions under which the benefits will be paid.

Definition of Disability

How disabled must you be before you can collect benefits? The answer depends on the exact wording in the insurance contract. A policy that considers you disabled if you cannot perform the main duties of your regular occupation is better than one that considers you disabled if you are unable to engage in any occupation for which you are reasonably suited by education and experience. For example, a surgeon suffering the loss of a hand would be considered disabled under the first definition, but not necessarily under the second, if he or she could practice some other medical specialty. Obviously, both of these are better than a policy that considers you disabled only when you cannot engage in any type of paid work. The definition of disability may depend on the duration of your condition, applying a strict interpretation over longer periods.

Most policies provide for some compensation in case of partial disability. Some definitions of partial disability are related to income loss, while others are defined in terms of the physical handicap. In many policies, however, you must experience a period of total disability before you collect partial benefits. The level of partial benefits may be equal to a set percentage of total disability benefits or geared to the income loss created by the partial disability. For example, if you earned $2,000 a month before the disability and now earn $500 a month, you have suffered a 75 percent reduction in income. If the maximum monthly benefit under the insurance policy is $1,000, you will receive a partial benefit equal to 75 percent of the $1,000 maximum monthly benefit. Thus, partial disability benefits would be $750 per month.

Elimination or Waiting Period

The time between the onset of the disability and the beginning of disability payments is the **disability elimination (or waiting) period**. The longer the elimination period, the less likely you are to collect and, therefore, the lower your premium.

A good method of holding down your insurance costs is to opt for the longest elimination period you feel comfortable with. An emergency fund of highly liquid assets would permit you to continue to meet your financial obligations during this time period. Choosing a longer waiting period is a highly rewarding strategy. Increasing the waiting period from 7 days to 60 days can reduce premiums by more than 50 percent; from 7 days to a year reduces them by more than 65 percent.

Be sure you understand how the policy handles intermittent disabilities. If you are disabled and then return to work after recuperating, must you again go through a waiting period if you have a relapse? Most policies don't require another elimination period if you are disabled by the same cause within six months after returning to work.

Benefit Period

Depending on the policy, benefit payments may last one, five, ten years, or until age 65. Your greatest financial risk is a lifetime disability. The best risk-reduction strategy is to opt for the policy with the longer **benefit period** and to hold down your premiums by choosing a longer elimination period. If this strategy proves too expensive, policies with shorter benefit periods may be used to protect income during a readjustment period or during the financially demanding childrearing years.

Coordination of Benefits Clause

Many policies use a **coordination of benefits clause** to state the maximum disability income you may receive from all insurance sources, both public and private. The maximum is usually stated as a percentage of your current income. This is to ensure you do not earn more by owning multiple policies and not working.

Social Insurance Substitute

The **social insurance substitute** may be included as a rider or as part of the basic policy. In the event you are disabled but still do not satisfy the strict requirements for Social Security benefits or are not covered by workers' compensation, this provision will replace

Disability elimination (or waiting) period The time between the onset of the disability and the beginning of disability benefits.

Benefit period The duration of disability benefits.

Coordination of benefits clause Ensures that disability benefits received from all sources do not exceed a stated percentage of previous earnings.

Social insurance substitute Provision of private disability income benefits in the event that social insurance benefits are not forthcoming.

those benefits with private insurance payments. This is a highly desirable provision because it eliminates an important source of uncertainty regarding your total disability payments, thus permitting you to estimate potential disability income more accurately.

Provision for Rehabilitation

Some policies explicitly provide for the continuation of benefits while you are in a rehabilitation program. This provision ensures that your benefits will not be terminated if you enter a work-related program. Some policies even state that tuition and equipment expenses for such programs will be covered. If you are disabled, and your policy does not contain this provision, you should check with the insurance company anyway. They may be more than willing to cover these expenses. After all, they have an incentive in seeing you return to gainful employment.

Renewability

The disability policy should be renewable without evidence of insurability; however, renewability provisions do vary.

The most unfavorable provision is found in policies that are **class cancelable**. This means the insurance company has the right to cancel an entire class of policies. For example, it can cancel all policies written before a specific date or within a specific state. If you are in poor health, this action can leave you in the position of finding expensive alternative coverage.

Next best are policies that are guaranteed renewable. These cannot be canceled as long as you pay your premiums; however, the premiums can increase. Better yet are policies that are *guaranteed renewable and noncancelable.* Such a provision gives you the right to renew your policy at the same premium.

Class cancelable The insurer can cancel policies for an entire class of insureds.

Inflation Protection

A policy written to cover a certain percentage of your salary will provide inflation protection. As your salary increases, your insurance protection will increase correspondingly. If instead you have a policy that provides fixed-dollar payments, an *option to purchase* rider should be considered. It permits you to purchase additional protection in the future without evidence of insurability.

Ensuring that you have the appropriate level of protection at the beginning of the disability provides only partial protection against inflation. Inflation will erode the value of level dollar benefits. However, Social Security benefit payments are adjusted for increases in the cost of living, so that at least a portion of your disability payments will receive inflation protection. Although, some disability policies provide for a dollar-for-dollar reduction in benefits to offset increases in Social Security payments, thus leaving your total compensation from Social Security and private disability insurance unchanged. A policy that establishes the company's dollar payments at the beginning of the disability period and that does not permit future reductions in these payments is preferred. Better yet is one with a cost-of-living rider that automatically adjusts dollar payments during the disability period for inflation.

Determining Disability Income Insurance Requirements

Your disability income requirements will depend on the duration and severity of the disability. For disabilities lasting six months or less, you may have to rely on sick leave, short-term group disability benefits provided by an employer or workers' compensation if the disability is work related. Lacking those, an emergency fund equal to six months' wages can provide the needed support through this interim period. For disabilities lasting longer than six months, you will have to consider your income needs until, typically, age 65 to 67, when retirement benefits begin. A good rule of thumb is that you should plan to replace about 60 to 70 percent of your lost gross income. This figure is based on the assumptions that some of your disability benefits will be nontaxable and that you will no longer incur work-related expenses. (Employer-provided benefits will be largely taxed, but privately purchased disability benefits will be tax free.) In any case, you may find it difficult to replace a larger percentage of your income through private insurance, since most insurers do not want to provide an incentive for not working.

Starting with your monthly income replacement requirements on line 1 of Figure 14.8, you can then reduce this amount by potential sources of disability income. If you are married, you might include spousal support. The personnel office at your place of work should provide you with an estimate of employer-provided benefits. Individually funded benefits would include investment income and benefits from individually purchased disability income protection.

The Social Security Administration will provide you with a "Personal Earnings and Benefit Statement" that lists potential disability benefits. You can also use the Benefits Planners at its Web site for an estimate of your disability benefits on line 5. Sample results for the Benefits Planner are listed in Table 14.2. You should notice that benefits replace a smaller percentage of lost income as market earnings increase.

Your total integrated benefits are listed on line 6. This is not necessarily equal to the sum of lines 2 to 5. You must examine each of your policies for coordination of benefits clauses and social insurance substitute riders. Participation limits set down in these sections of the disability policies may limit your total integrated benefits to less than the summed total of lines 2 to 5.

If you subtract your total integrated benefits from your total income replacement requirements on line 1, you will have determined your need for additional income insurance protection on line 7. You may be able to satisfy this need through additional individual or group disability insurance. If you do purchase additional insurance, make sure its benefits will not be offset by a reduction in prospective payments under your present policies.

Periodically review your disability income needs and your health care plan. You should also review your plans at all of life's major changes. A marriage, the birth of a child, or a divorce may require different strategies. You may not be able to avoid the pain and suffering accompanying an accident or ill health, but with proper planning you should be able to reduce the accompanying financial risks.

TOPIC LINKS

Use the Social Security Disability Planner.

TOPIC LINKS

Review advance directives.

Figure 14.8
Estimating Your Monthly
Disability Insurance Needs

1. Income replacement requirements
   (60%–70% of gross income lost)   _____
2. Spouse's income   _____
3. Employer-provided disability benefits   _____
4. Individually funded benefits   _____
5. Social Security benefits   _____
6. Total integrated benefits   (_____)
7. Additional disability insurance needed   _____

SIMPLIFYING financial planning 14.4

Have a Living Will

Breakthroughs in medical science now make it possible to extend life far beyond what we had thought likely only a few decades ago. But advances in the extension of life do not always go hand in hand with improvements in the quality of life. For those who worry about being kept alive in a vegetative state with little or no chance of recovery, the "living will" can be the answer.

A living will is really not a will at all. It is a medical directive indicating the type of life support you are willing or unwilling to receive in the event you are unconscious or in a coma and unable to speak for yourself. In most states it is a legal document and, therefore, the state you live in may specify the precise form it must take. In order for a living will to be effective, it must state your wishes precisely, so that your intent is clear.

The Patient Self–Determination Act of 1991 requires that all institutions receiving Medicare or Medicaid funds inform patients upon admission of their right to sign an "advance directive." This includes a living will in which you have the right to refuse life–sustaining treatment and a health care power of attorney in which you appoint someone to make health care decisions for you if you are unable to. You don't have to sign an advance directive, but if you do, a record of it should be kept in your medical file.

The time to make these decisions, however, is not upon entry into a health care facility. By that point you may be incapacitated and your family may be in crisis. It's better to plan for such emergencies well in advance, when both your health care and financial concerns can be combined into a fully integrated plan. In addition to a living will and a health care power of attorney, this plan should include a last will and testament and a durable power of attorney. Similar to the health care power of attorney, the durable power of attorney enables a designated guardian to manage your financial and legal matters if you are unable to.

Review these documents periodically to ensure that they still conform to your wishes. As you get older or your family situation changes, the kind of medical care you desire may also change.

key terms

accident insurance (p. 392)
basic health care insurance (p. 377)
benefit period (p. 394)
class cancelable (p. 394)
coinsurance (p. 378)
comprehensive health insurance (p. 377)
coordination of benefits clause (p. 394)
copayment (p. 378)
defined contribution health plan (p. 385)
dental insurance (p. 379)
disability elimination period (p. 393)
disability income insurance (p. 390)
fee-for-service health insurance (p. 382)
flexible spending account (FSA) (p. 385)
group-staff HMO (p. 382)
guaranteed renewability (p. 380)
health maintenance organization (HMO) (p. 382)
health reimbursement arrangement (HRA) (p. 386)
health savings account (HSA) (p. 385)
hospital expense insurance (p. 377)
hospital insurance (p. 377)
indemnity insurance (p. 377)

individual practice arrangement (IPA) HMO (p. 382)
long-term care policies (p. 378)
major medical insurance (p. 378)
managed care (p. 380)
Medicaid (p. 387)
medical savings account (MSA) (p. 386)
Medicare (p. 387)
Medicare Advantage (p. 387)
medigap insurance (p. 387)
physicians' expense insurance (p. 377)
point-of-service plan (POS) (p. 382)
preexisting conditions clause (p. 380)
preferred provider organizations (PPOs) (p. 382)
prescription drug coverage (p.378)
service benefit coverage (p. 377)
social insurance substitute (p. 394)
surgical expense insurance (p. 377)
usual, customary, and reasonable (UCR) (p. 377)
waiting period (disability) (p. 393)
waiting period (health care) (p. 380)
workers' compensation (p. 384)

follow-up on the Steele family

Reread the chapter-opening vignette.

1. How might the Steeles hold down their out-of-pocket health care expenses?
2. Should the Steeles consider supplementing their employer coverage with privately purchased health or disability insurance? Why or why not?
3. Suppose Arnold lost his job. What options would the Steeles have for continuing or replacing their present coverage?

problems and review questions

1. What kinds of insurance provide protection against the financial consequences of illness and injury?
2. What is the difference between hospital indemnity insurance and hospital expense insurance? Which is the preferred coverage? Explain why.
3. What is the difference between medical insurance and major medical insurance? Which is more important? Explain why?
4. Suppose you have $5,000 of health care expenses that are not covered by your basic health insurance. You have a major medical policy with $500 deductible and 20 percent coinsurance. What are your out-of-pocket expenses?
5. For certain procedures, a fee-for-service plan agrees to pay the physician a UCR fee. What does UCR stand for and how is this fee determined?
6. How does an HMO differ from traditional fee-for-service insurance? How would you go about comparing the relative benefits of fee-for-service insurance and an HMO?
7. How does an HMO differ from a PPO?
8. Which health insurance plans allow you to choose your primary care physician?
9. Name the two government programs that provide health care benefits. Which one is run entirely by the federal government?
10. Where do most individuals obtain group insurance coverage?
11. Which age group is most likely to be without health insurance?
12. How does Social Security define "substantial gainful employment"? Explain how definitions of disability contained in private insurance policies can determine the quality of the insurance protection.
13. It's impossible to purchase disability insurance covering 100 percent of lost income. Why?
14. What part does the elimination period play when planning for adequate disability income protection?
15. Discuss some disability income protection strategies that can help you cope with the erosion of benefits due to inflation.
16. What type of nursing home care is traditionally not reimbursed under health insurance plans?
17. What is the purpose of a living will?
18. What should comprehensive health insurance cover?

19. How can an employer-sponsored flexible spending plan help save you tax dollars? How can you lose dollars with a flexible spending plan?

20. What is meant by managed care?

case 14.1

The Hurleys Compare Disability Insurance

The Hurleys have narrowed their choice of disability insurance for Mr. Hurley down to two policies. They cost the same and are identical except for those differences outlined in the following table. They are guaranteed renewable and have an elimination period of 30 days.

	Policy 1	Policy 2
Maximum monthly benefit	$4,000	$3,000
Benefit period	10 years	To age 65
Maximum replacement from all sources	Lesser of $4,000 a month, or 60% of income	60% of income

Mr. Hurley is currently 35 years of age with two children. Over the next 10 years his child-rearing responsibilities should end. His current job pays $60,000 a year and is covered by Social Security. He calculates potential family disability benefits from Social Security at about $2,500 a month while the children are still at home. He is currently in line for an upper-level management position. Should he get it, his salary will increase substantially.

Questions
1. From the Hurleys' point of view, discuss the relative merits of each policy. Which would you recommend?
2. Which policy provides the better inflation protection? Why?
3. Do these policies provide adequate income replacement for the Hurleys?
4. Suppose the Hurleys must limit the amount spent on disability insurance to the cost of these policies. Are there any changes in coverage that might lower their risk without increasing their premiums? Explain.

case 14.2

Evaluate Walter Simon's Health Care Coverage

As long as Walter Simon was a full-time student he was covered under his parents' health insurance policy. He recently dropped out of school, which effectively eliminated him from his parents' plan. Since then he has worked in a number of temporary jobs, none of which included employer-provided health care coverage. However, he is covered by workers' compensation when on the job. He recently enrolled in a hospital expense insurance plan that will pay him $200 a day for each day he remains in the hospital after an initial three day stay. For a minimal fee he has also purchased accident insurance that pays him set dollar amounts for a long list of possible injuries.

Walter is pretty pleased with himself. By buying low-cost insurance policies he believes he has been able to obtain comprehensive health care coverage at minimal cost.

Questions
1. Does Walter have good reasons to be pleased with his current health care coverage?
2. What health insurance alternatives should Walter consider?

working out
on the Web

Exercises to Strengthen Your Use of the Internet
(Internet links for the following exercises can be found at **www.prenhall.com/frasca.**)

Exercise 14.1 Comparison Shopping for Health Care Plans

There are many Internet sites that offer comparative quotes on health insurance. EHealthInsurance (**www.ehealthinsurance.com**) provides comparative quotes without registration.

Q. Select different types of plans. What are the comparative costs and benefits?

Exercise 14.2 Obtaining Comparative Data on Hospitals

American Hospital Directory (**www.ahd.com**) offers a comprehensive database of information on hospitals. The raw data were collected by the government. There is a free service and a subscription service for using this database. The free service provides only summary data. However, this is probably sufficient information for most consumers. You can also search a database at the Joint Commission on Accreditation of Healthcare Organizations (**www.jointcommission.org**) to review your hospital's accreditation status.

Q. Check on a hospital in your area. What is the average length of stay in this hospital? Is it accredited by some reviewing agency?

Exercise 14.3 Consider a Living Will

The U.S. Living Will Registry (**www.uslivingwillregistry.com**) electronically stores advanced directives for a small fee and makes them available to health care providers. A link to state specific "Advance Directive Forms" can be found under the home page link for "Individuals."

Q. Review a form for your state. What would you put in an advanced directive that reflects your own wishes?

Exercise 14.4 Get a Report Card on Your Local Managed Care Plans

The National Committee on Quality Assurance (**www.ncqa.org**) has derived a system called HEDIS for rating managed care providers. It accredits those health care plans that meet its standards. Find out about the accreditation standards and determine whether the managed care plans in your area are accredited at this Web site by clicking "Report Cards."

Q. Select a managed care plan in your area. Is this an accredited plan?

Exercise 14.5 Obtaining an Estimate of Social Security Disability Benefits

If If you did not already receive a Social Security statement in the mail you can now obtain an estimate of your Personal Earnings and Benefit Estimate Statement from Social Security Online (**www.ssa.gov**). You will receive a reply to your electronic request by snail mail. Alternatively, you can also obtain an estimate of your potential disability benefits by using their "Benefits Calculator." There should be a "Calculate your benefits" line on the home page.

Q. What are your estimated monthly disability benefits?

Life Insurance and Estate Planning

protecting your dependents

15

Objectives

1. To calculate your life insurance protection needs
2. To understand the important provisions in a life insurance policy
3. To describe the major kinds of life insurance
4. To be able to choose the type and amount of protection that is best for you
5. To understand the purpose of a will and what happens if you die without a will
6. To be able to plan for the orderly transition of a death estate

Steele family

Each year Arnold receives a personal benefits statement from his employer that lists the dollar value of all his fringe benefits. They consist of legally required benefits, such as Social Security and unemployment insurance, and elective employer–paid benefits, such as pension plan, medical insurance, and group term life insurance. Arnold is always amazed to find that these benefits represent a significant portion of his total compensation.

Currently, one benefit that concerns the Steeles is the employer–provided term life insurance of about $120,000. Arnold's employer provides employees with term insurance protection equal to one and a half times their annual salary. The only other life insurance the Steeles have is a $50,000 cash value policy on Arnold that he purchased from a fellow classmate shortly after graduation. The policy's cash value is $4,000 against which he has

taken a low–interest $2,000 loan. Lately, he has been wondering whether he has sufficient death protection. He tried a number of life insurance calculators while surfing the Internet. They all seem to indicate that he needs more protection. He is not sure he should trust these calculations. After all, most of these Web sites have a financial interest in selling him additional protection.

Arnold and Sharon have not totally ignored their own mortality. Before the children were born, they had separate wills drawn up naming each other as primary beneficiary. If something happens to either one of them, the entire estate will go to the surviving spouse. Given that they are both professionals, they have not given life insurance much thought. If need be, they expect that either of them could generate enough income to support their children.

TOPIC LINKS

Follow the **Topic Links** in each chapter for your interactive Personal Finance exercise on the Web. Go to: **www.prenhall.com/frasca**.

Most people would rather not discuss l life insurance. Anything that concerns our mortality is almost always distasteful. In addition, we confront a special language we don't understand and costs that are difficult to compare. Moreover, we are sometimes subjected to high-pressure sales tactics from aggressive life insurance agents. It would be very nice if the whole problem of life insurance would just go away. Unfortunately, avoidance is often not the best policy.

A more positive attitude can produce substantial rewards. Life insurance is an integral part of a well-thought-out financial plan. It can provide your dependents with security against possible financial hardship resulting from your premature death. Without life insurance, these contingencies must be covered by your present savings. If you first had to accumulate substantial savings before providing this security, you might be overly cautious in your career decisions and your financial investments.

The life insurance decision requires a considerable amount of effort. First, you must examine the reasons why you need life insurance. If you think you need additional insurance, you must decide on the appropriate kind and amount of insurance protection. This means gathering information on the life insurance market. Life insurance policies differ widely in both cost and coverage, and you can easily misunderstand what is offered you. Finally, you must engage in comparison shopping with insurance agents who may be overly aggressive. Most people do not devote this much effort to the life insurance decision. This is the reason for the industry adage, "Life insurance is sold, not bought."

Similar attitudes affect estate planning. In addition, there is the erroneous belief that only the rich have to worry about estate planning. Tax exemptions are generous on death transfers. But estate planning is more than just limiting tax liability. Its main purpose is the orderly transition of your assets. Without specific instructions, heirs can find themselves in legal entanglements that waste needed resources.

Estimating Your Life Insurance Needs

The two most important reasons for buying life insurance are that it can serve as a convenient means of saving and it can provide financial security for dependents. You must judge its performance as a form of savings against all alternative methods. However, there is no substitute for the death protection it provides. You may *want* to use life insurance as a savings vehicle, but you *need* it for the insurance protection.

Young adults often buy life insurance when they graduate from college. Many times these policies are purchased from other recently hired and inexperienced people. Later, the insured tend not to review the adequacy of their coverage. The paradoxical result is that those who don't need protection have too much, and those who really need protection have too little. To avoid this situation, evaluate your life insurance needs at least once every three years. Also, recalculate whenever your family undergoes a significant change, such as the birth of a child or the purchase of a home.

Be sure to estimate the insurance needs for each adult in the family unit. In most families both spouses are in the job market. Consequently, the absence of either parent can mean a significant decline in family income. Even when the absent spouse is a full-time homemaker, the financial consequences should be considered. Replacing the services of a homemaker can be expensive.

The needs of survivors may be many and varied. All estimates of need, however, must focus on three basic considerations: a transition fund, a maintenance fund, and a specialized needs fund. The dollars to cover all of these expenses must come either from the liquidation of your family's present net assets or from your life insurance proceeds. After you decide what assets might be used to support your survivors, any needs in excess of this amount must either be covered by life insurance or remain unsatisfied. The accompanying worksheets and text will help you judge your life insurance protection needs and the adequacy of your present coverage.

The Transition Fund

It's important that you prepare for expenses that will be incurred at the time of death. These can be budgeted for in a **transition fund**. Include all likely expenses that must be paid at the time of death and any liabilities that would be convenient or preferable to liquidate at this time. The typical items included in a transition fund are listed on the sample worksheet shown in Figure 15.1.

Transition fund Funds immediate death–related expenses.

Funeral and Burial Costs

The price of a funeral and burial can vary widely, depending on your style of departure. The National Funeral Directors Association estimates that the average cost of a funeral is now above $6,500, not including cemetery costs for a plot and a headstone. Many funerals cost more than $10,000, but you can choose cremation for about $1,000.

TOPIC LINKS

FTC Consumer's Guide for Funerals

Estate Taxes

Both the state and the federal government may collect taxes on the death estate. These are discussed in Chapter 4 on taxes.

Under federal estate tax laws, an unlimited amount may be transferred to your spouse tax free. If you have a substantial estate and a nonspousal estate transfer, you will have to estimate your tax liability at this point. This is particularly important if you own a business. Covering the tax liabilities will allow your beneficiaries to avoid a forced sale in a possibly depressed market.

TOPIC LINKS

Estate tax calculators

Probate Costs

The lawyer who wrote your will can probably estimate the probate costs associated with the validation of your will and the distribution of your estate. As a second-best estimate, you may calculate probate costs at 4 percent of the value of the assets distributed through the probate process. For example, you would incur about $6,000 on an estate with $150,000 in assets. These assets should not include life insurance proceeds, since life insurance payouts to beneficiaries other than the estate avoid probate, as do other contractual transfers such as joint bank accounts and joint home ownership.

Uninsured Medical Costs

Your estimate of uninsured medical costs will depend on the quality of your health insurance coverage (see Chapter 14). You can generally count on the cost of your medical care

Figure 15.1
Transition Fund Worksheet

	Sample Entries
1. Funeral and burial costs	$10,000
2. Estate taxes	—
3. Probate costs	6,000
4. Uninsured medical expenses	1,300
5. Outstanding loans due	16,000
Total transition fund	$33,300

at death exceeding deductibles on your medical insurance policy. Therefore, enter any deductibles as an uninsured medical cost. In addition, you might enter another $500 to $1,000 for expenses that are medically related but not covered by medical insurance. Consequently, if you had a $300 deductible on your medical insurance, you might conservatively enter $1,300 for uninsured medical costs.

Outstanding Loans Due

The amount you enter under *outstanding loans due* will be equal to the value of the loans you would like to see repaid at the time of your death. Generally, it's a good idea to include any consumer type loans you may have. These are probably at high rates of interest and will represent an unnecessary burden on your dependents. If you had $1,000 payable on your credit cards and a $15,000 auto loan, you might enter $16,000 for outstanding loans due.

The outstanding balance on a home mortgage may or may not be included in the transition fund. The payments on any loan that is not included in the transition fund must be covered under the family maintenance fund.

The Family Maintenance Fund

Family maintenance fund
Funds the ongoing support of dependent family members.

The most important of your insurance protection needs is the **family maintenance fund**. It will insure the viability of the dependent family unit. The size of the fund will reflect the level of living you would like to see maintained. You want to budget an amount at least large enough to eliminate the need for major financial adjustments. On the other hand, you don't want to budget an amount that makes you worth more to your family dead than alive.

Using a computer spreadsheet, you should be able to arrive at a good estimate of the needed support for survivors. The following steps and the worksheet shown in Figure 15.2 will lead you through the computations.

Step 1: Calculate the monthly expenses for the dependent family unit. If you keep a family budget, you can estimate the monthly living expenses for the surviving family members on the basis of these data. Be sure to include all items that are jointly consumed and exclude only those items that are independently consumed by the insured. For example, the home must still be heated and maintained, but the family may no longer need a second car.

If you have not kept track of your monthly expenses, or you find it difficult to identify marginal expenses for the insured, use data based on average family budgets. Various studies tend to support the percentage of income consumed by the head of household presented in Figure 15.3. To estimate the amount spent for the exclusive support of the insured, multiply total family take-home pay by the appropriate percentage. If you subtract the result-

Figure 15.2
Family Maintenance Fund:
Needs Approach

		Sample Entries
Step 1. Monthly survivors' expenses		$ 4,000
Step 2. Monthly survivors' take–home pay	$ 670	
Step 3. Monthly survivors' benefits	1,980	
Total contribution by survivors		− 2,650
Step 4. Monthly maintenance requirement		$ 1,350
Step 5. Calculate size of maintenance fund		× 12
(a) Annual requirement		$ 16,200
(b) Multiply by annuity factor		× 9.1622
Family maintenance fund		$148,428

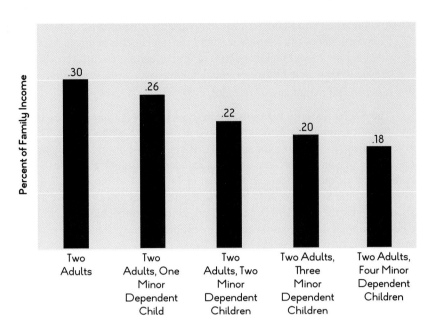

Figure 15.3
Family Head's Consumption Expenditure as Percentage of Family Income

ing amount from the family's take-home pay, you are left with the approximate expenditures necessary to provide for the continued support of the surviving members in a typical household.

The entries in Figure 15.2 assume combined take-home pay of $5,000 per month and a family with three dependent children. Consumption by one of the adult family members in a three-child family would be equal to 0.20 × $5,000, or $1,000 per month. Therefore, the dependent family would require $4,000 per month in maintenance expenditure.

You may want to add any additional expenditures the family might incur with the death of the insured. This may include additional homemaking expenses and lost fringe benefits. For example, many workers receive family medical insurance as a fringe benefit, but this coverage may lapse at their death. In this situation, the monthly cost of medical insurance should be added to living expenses in order to assure the family's continued protection.

Step 2: Calculate total monthly survivors' take-home pay. You will have to estimate the amount the surviving family members can contribute to their own support. After the death of the insured, survivors may find new sources of income. On the other hand, the additional homemaking responsibilities placed on the surviving spouse may reduce that person's ability to participate in the labor market. The example shown in Figure 15.2 assumes that the surviving spouse will bring home part-time earnings of $670 per month. This represents expected earnings after taxes and other payroll deductions.

Step 3: Calculate total monthly survivors' benefits. It's likely that your survivors may be eligible for monthly Social Security death benefits. To be eligible, you must either have recent employment or a history of past employment. Given a fully insured status, a wide range of close relatives might qualify for benefits. These may include the following:

- A widow, widower, or divorced spouse at normal retirement age or reduced benefits as early as age 60. A disabled widow, widower, or divorced spouse can get benefits at age 50 to 60.

- A widow, widower, or divorced spouse at any age if she or he takes care of your child who is under age 16 or disabled.

- An unmarried child under 18 (or up to age 19 if he or she is attending elementary or secondary school full time). Your child can get benefits at any age if he or she was disabled before 22 and remains disabled. Under certain circumstances, benefits can also be paid to your stepchildren or grandchildren.
- A dependent parent age 62 or older.

The Social Security Administration (SSA) mails out annually a "Personal Earnings and Benefit Estimate Statement" to most workers age 25 and older. This statement lists potential benefits available for survivors. If you do not have a statement, you can request one online or you can use the online calculator for a quick estimate. Some sample estimates from the quick calculator are listed in Table 15.1. A more detailed calculator is also available at the Social Security Web site if you want a more precise estimate. Each child should receive the indicated benefit so long as total family payments are less than the indicated maximum. In that case, benefits are proportionately reduced to each survivor so that total benefits do not exceed this limit.

TOPIC LINKS

Use the SSA death benefits calculator.

Benefits paid to a surviving spouse with children are significantly reduced if he or she has significant annual market earnings ($13,560 before age 65 and $36,120 thereafter in 2008). In addition, benefits paid to a dependent child end at age 18 and benefits paid to the caretaking spouse end when the child reaches age 16. The surviving parent then enters a "blackout" period during which benefits are discontinued. Later, when he or she reaches age 60, benefits may again be paid under a widow(er)'s pension.

If you have a private insurance plan that provides monthly survivors' benefits, you will want to add this to any Social Security benefits to arrive at total survivors' benefits. For example, if Social Security provides $1,880 per month and a private pension plan provides $100 per month, then total monthly benefits will be $1,980.

Employer-sponsored retirement plans will often provide some type of benefit for the surviving spouse. In fact, when retirement annuities are offered to employees, both preretirement and postretirement spousal survivorship benefits are in most instances required under the Retirement Equity Act of 1984. These benefits are mandatory and can be withdrawn only with the consent of the nonemployee spouse.

Step 4: Calculate the monthly maintenance requirement. The monthly maintenance requirement is equal to the difference between the expenditure needs of the dependent

Table 15.1
Estimates of Monthly Death Benefits from SSA Quick Calculator

	Current Annual Earnings			
	$20,000	$40,000	$80,000	$160,000
	Monthly Benefit			
Child	632	969	1,449	1,689
Spouse caring for child	632	969	1,449	1,689
Spouse at full retirement age	843	1,292	1,932	2,253
Family maximum	1,265	2,403	3,383	3,944
Percent of Income Replaced by SSA Benefit				
Child	38%	29%	22%	13%
Spouse caring for child	38%	29%	22%	13%
Spouse at full retirement age	51%	39%	29%	17%
Family maximum	76%	72%	51%	30%

Source: SSA Quick Calculator, based on 35-year-old worker qualifying for death benefits.

family unit and the support provided by potential income and benefits. To calculate this amount, add survivors' take-home pay in step 2 and survivors' total benefits in step 3, and subtract the sum from total monthly expenses in step 1. For the sample data, the monthly maintenance requirement is $1,350.

The requirement may change over time. However, some of the changes may offset each other; for example, Social Security benefits are reduced as children become self-supporting. Thus, your estimate of a monthly maintenance requirement for the present age structure of your family may hold up reasonably well until the youngest child reaches age 16. If the surviving spouse does not expect to become self-supporting after the youngest child reaches age 16, you may want to calculate a separate monthly maintenance requirement for the surviving spouse over the years that Social Security benefits are blacked out or include early retirement benefits in a specialized fund.

Step 5: Calculate the size of the maintenance fund.   The monthly maintenance requirements must be paid out of the maintenance fund. In estimating the appropriate size of the maintenance fund, you should consider two important facts: one, with inflation, monthly expenses will rise over time; and two, the maintenance fund will be invested and will earn an interest return. You have to estimate a real rate of return. The real return on your funds is approximately equal to the market rate of interest less the rate of inflation. For example, if these funds can be invested at an annual rate of 5 percent and the rate of inflation is 3 percent, then the real return on your assets is about 2 percent (5 − 3). The larger the expected real return on the maintenance fund, the smaller is the amount of needed funding. To find the size of the needed maintenance fund you can use a financial calculator, our online worksheet, or the annuity tables at the end of the text.

FINANCIAL PLANNING *for*
young adults 15.1

Do Children and Young Adults Need Life Insurance?

The quick answer is a definite "no" for children and a "maybe" for young adults. Life insurance can replace lost market earnings and provide financial security for survivors. The death of a child is a tremendous emotional loss, but typically it's not a financial loss. The government estimates that it costs the typical household more than $190,000 to raise a child to age 18. This doesn't include lost parental earnings or the cost of a college education.

Life insurance agents often target young adults who have just graduated from college. This is the time to start building for the future and life insurance is presented as an important part of the needed foundation. Do you really need the death protection at this point in your life? A single individual with no family or parents to support may receive sufficient protection through employer-provided group term insurance. After all, the only financial cost to your survivors would be funeral and burial expenses.

If you don't need the death protection, what about buying cash value insurance as an investment? To answer this question, you must compare it with other investments. In particular, you should compare it with other tax-advantaged investments such as tax-qualified retirement accounts. It may seem strange to start thinking about retirement when you have just entered the workforce. However, the dollars you put aside today are going to buy a lot more retirement benefits than those you purchase tomorrow.

Young adults with families or parental obligations will need life insurance. Moreover, they probably need a lot more than they might realize. The death of either spouse in a young family with children is a huge financial loss. The affordable answer for most young families is low-cost term protection on both spouses.

The deciding factor on the right strategy is the financial need of your survivors. If you are single without financial obligations, think about retirement planning first. If you have family obligations, be sure you have an adequate amount of life insurance.

For the current example, assume that the real return on the fund will be 2 percent and the fund will need to last 10 years, when the youngest child reaches the age of majority. As shown in Table A.4 at the end of the text, the present value of a $1 annuity that earns 2 percent a year and pays out for 10 years is $8.9826. This is the present value of an inflation adjusted $1 annuity that will pay out at the end of each of the next 10 years.

Unfortunately, this is not quite what you need. You really need a payout at time of death and then a payout at the beginning of each of the subsequent nine years. An *annuity due* is an annuity that pays out at the beginning of each year. To find the value of a 10-year annuity due of $1, you find the value for a nine-year annuity of $1 and then add one for the immediate payment. In the current example, a nine-year annuity of $1 that earns a 2 percent real return has a present value of $8.1622. Therefore, the present value of this $1 annuity due would be $9.1622 ($1 + $8.1622). This is the annuity factor you enter in Figure 15.2.

9-year annuity of $1 at 2%	=	$8.1622
Payment at beginning of first year	=	1.0000
10-year annuity due of $1 at 2%	=	$9.1622

Try not to be too optimistic when assuming an after-tax return on your death estate. Although you may be an experienced investor, it's your survivors who will be making the investment decisions. Furthermore, you should not employ an interest assumption that requires speculative investments. Your life insurance objective is to reduce risk, not to increase it.

Specialized Funds

You might consider setting up various specialized funds to meet temporary needs that are not covered by the maintenance fund. Special funds for emergencies, education, and retirement are definitely worth thinking about and are listed on the specialized fund worksheet shown in Figure 15.4. When these funds, such as the educational fund are needed, will determine how much should be funded at your death. To make things simple, we are simply going to add the needed amounts in current dollars without discounting. You could adjust these values using the present value methods discussed in Chapter 2.

Figure 15.4
Specialized Fund Worksheet

	Sample Entries
	Sample Entries
1. Emergency fund	$ 12,000
2. Educational fund	
Cost per child	$64,000
Number of children	× 3
	$192,000
3. Retirement fund	
Annual requirement	$ 5,000
Retirement years	× 20
	$ 100,000
4. Other funds	—
Total specialized fund	$304,000

An Emergency Fund

You may want to be fairly generous in estimating the size of your emergency fund, since emergencies might be more difficult to handle in a single-parent household. A good rule of thumb is three to six months of the survivors' expenses included in Figure 15.2. If most of these expenses are guaranteed by survivors' benefits, a multiple of 3 might be sufficient.

An Educational Fund

College students over 18 years of age are not entitled to survivors' benefits under Social Security. Therefore, if you plan to provide a college education for your children, you should consider the need for an educational fund. The College Board estimates that tuition and fees, room and board, books and supplies, transportation, and personal expenses for a resident student are now over $16,000 per year at public institutions and $33,000 at private institutions. Thus, you should budget at least $64,000 for four years for a resident student at a public institution.

TOPIC LINKS

College Board on educational costs

A Retirement Fund

If you think that pension benefits from private plans and Social Security might not provide enough support for the surviving spouse, you might want to set an additional amount aside in a retirement fund to eliminate this deficiency. If you multiply the annual deficiency in support times 20 years, you will have a decent estimate of the amount needed in the retirement fund, assuming retirement at age 65. If you want payments to begin during the "blackout" period on Social Security benefits, you will need a larger multiple. More accurate techniques for estimating a retirement fund are contained in Chapter 16 on retirement and pension planning.

TOPIC LINKS

Download insurance planning worksheets.

The Insurance Protection Gap

Once you have estimated the total needs of the dependent family—consisting of the transition fund, the maintenance fund, and specialized funds—the next task is to determine how these needs will be met. Figure 15.5 contains a worksheet for calculating the insurance protection gap.

Figure 15.5
Worksheet: The Life Insurance Gap

	Sample Entries	
Funding Needs		
1. Clean-up fund	$ 33,300	
2. Maintenance fund	148,428	
3. Specialized funds	304,000	
Total needs		$485,728
Funding Sources		
1. Financial investments	$ 56,000	
2. Tangible goods	10,000	
3. Life insurance		
(a) Group insurance	$ 50,000	
(b) Individual insurance	—	
(c) Social Security	255	
Total sources		($116,255)
Unfunded Needs		$369,473
Unfunded Estate Liquidity		—
The Life Insurance Protection Gap		$369,473

Funding sources will consist of the following:

1. Financial investments. These should be counted at present market value after taxes. Include your personal portfolio, plus any lump-sum distributions from retirement plans that pay out upon death. Remember, if you are using pension payouts to fund maintenance expenditure, you may want to offset this by including a specialized fund for the dependent survivor's retirement.

2. Tangible goods. You may have some items the family will no longer require. These should be valued at their market price after taxes and selling costs. Do not include lifestyle assets that will be utilized by the survivors.

3. Life insurance. The face amount of your present policies, minus outstanding loans on those policies, is available for future support. Include any group coverage you have at work, plus the $255 death benefit under Social Security.

Funding needs less funding sources represents your survivors' unfunded needs. You obviously will have to provide sufficient insurance protection for your survivors' unfunded needs. However, covering only unfunded needs may not protect your survivors adequately from immediate financial hardship. Your survivors may be hard-pressed to convert the funding sources into cash in order to meet immediate death-related expenses such as estate taxes. For this reason, you should check your funding needs and sources in Figure 15.5 to ensure that your liquid resources—those readily convertible into cash—are sufficient to cover the transition fund, which should include all immediate death-related expenses. The deficiency in liquid resources must be entered under unfunded estate liquidity.

Your survivors' unfunded needs plus their unfunded estate liquidity equals your **life insurance protection gap**. If a gap exists on your worksheet, it's time to consider additional life insurance coverage.

Life insurance protection gap Unfunded needs plus unfunded estate liquidity.

The Special Language of Life Insurance Policies

A life insurance policy is a contract between you and the insurance company. As with all contracts, you should read it carefully and understand it fully before you sign. This may require some tenacity on your part, since many companies provide sample policies only with great reluctance. Furthermore, to understand the agreement you must first master the special language of the life insurance industry. However, the efforts are worth the trouble. Purchasing the wrong kind of insurance or the wrong type of policy can prove costly.

The Basic Policy

In return for amounts paid to the insurance company while you are living, the life insurance agreement obligates the company to pay out a stated amount at the time of your death. Although policies differ widely in language and coverage, the basic agreement should contain some common terminology.

Face Amount

Face amount The dollar amount of life insurance protection stated on the face of the policy.

The dollar amount stated on the face of the policy is the **face amount**. In the absence of special provisions or additions, the face amount minus any outstanding loans on the policy is the amount paid out at death. Special provisions, such as an accidental death clause, which increases the payout when death is due to accidental circumstances, may affect the actual payout at death.

$$\text{Face Amount of Policy} + \text{Accidental Death Benefit} - \text{Outstanding Loans} = \text{Death Benefit}$$

$$\text{Cash Value} - \text{Outstanding Loans} - \text{Surrender Charges} = \text{Surrender Value}$$

Cash and Surrender Value

The **cash value** of a life insurance policy is equal to the savings accumulated during the existence of the policy contract. Not all insurance policies have a cash value; only those that allocate a part of each year's premium to savings do. In many insurance policies, the insured may borrow against the policy's cash value at an interest rate either specified in the policy or set periodically by the insurance company. Closely related to the policy's cash value is its **surrender value**. This is the amount returned to the policyholder when coverage is terminated. Typically, the surrender value of the policy is equal to the cash value plus surrender dividends, minus outstanding loans and surrender charges.

Cash value The savings accumulated during the existence of the policy contract.

Surrender value The amount paid the policyholder when coverage is terminated.

Lives Covered

Most policies are taken out on the life of one person and are called **single life policies**. However, there are policies with more complicated coverage. A **joint life policy** covers more than one person. On a joint life policy, the face amount is paid out at the first death. This may be important to a family that desires to replace the income lost at the death of either spouse. In this case, a $100,000 joint life policy can be considerably less expensive than a single life policy of $100,000 on the husband and a single life policy of $100,000 on the wife.

A **survivorship joint life** policy operates in the reverse manner. It pays out on the death of the last individual in the group. This policy is particularly useful in estate planning, when taxes must be paid at the death of the surviving spouse.

Many insurance companies issue what is commonly called a **family policy** or family rider. It provides coverage for several family members in one policy. The coverage provided generally consists of whole life insurance on the primary breadwinner and small amounts of term protection on the children, including those born after the policy is issued. Coverage on the children is usually convertible into whole life insurance when the term protection ends at some stated age.

Single life policy Covers a single life and is payable at the end of that life.

Joint life policy Covers more than one life and pays out at the death of the first.

Survivorship joint life Covers more than one life and pays out on the death of the last.

Family policy Covers several family members in one contract.

Premium

The periodic payment made to the insurance company is called the **premium**. Depending on the particular policy, this payment may be made annually, semiannually, monthly, or even weekly. A service charge is usually added for premiums that are paid other than annually.

Premium The periodic payment made to the insurance company.

Nonparticipating insurance The earnings and mortality experience of the insurer do not influence premiums.

Dividend

Insurance may be purchased from either mutual insurance companies or stock insurance companies. Typically, mutual insurance companies issue participating policies, and stock insurance companies issue **nonparticipating insurance**. However, a few stock companies do write policies with limited participation.

Participating insurance gets its name from the fact that policyholders participate in the earnings and mortality experience of the insurer. If the mutual insurance company pays out less in claims than it expected, the policyholders participate in this good fortune by receiving back the surplus funds in the form of what is called a **dividend**. This dividend is considered a partial return of your initial premium and is therefore nontaxable.

Participating insurance Policyholders participate in the earnings and mortality experience of the insurer through dividend adjustments.

Dividend A partial return of premium dependent upon the earnings of the insurer.

If the company had only unexpected gains, participating insurance would be a great buy. However, policyholders may participate in both unexpected gains and losses. Mutual insurance companies tend to charge higher premiums than stock insurance companies in order to create a fund to cover any unexpected costs. Should these costs occur, dividends need not be paid out. A dividend payment is not guaranteed, and payments will fluctuate with the earnings experience of the mutual insurance company.

Beneficiary

Beneficiary The individual who receives the proceeds from the life insurance policy.

Contingent beneficiary The one who receives the proceeds if the primary beneficiary dies first.

The person or instrument (e.g., a trust fund) that receives the proceeds of the policy when you die is the **beneficiary**. If two or more individuals are to share the proceeds, then they are known as *cobeneficiaries.* You may also specify a primary beneficiary and a contingent beneficiary. The **contingent beneficiary**, also termed the *secondary beneficiary,* receives the proceeds if the primary beneficiary dies before you do. You may name more than one person as either a primary or a contingent beneficiary. For example, suppose Arnold Steele takes out a policy naming his wife, Sharon, as primary beneficiary and their two children, Nancy and John, as contingent beneficiaries. If Sharon dies before Arnold, the children, or more likely a trust fund for the children, will receive the insurance proceeds. The unexpected could happen in a fatal car crash.

Special Provisions

Rider A specialized provision meant to modify or extend coverage in an insurance contract.

The worth of a life insurance policy will depend on more than just the policy's face amount or cash value. It will also be influenced by the various specialized provisions contained in the policy and the addition of any options, also called **riders**, to the insurance contract. The features you are most likely to encounter are described in Figure 15.6. Some of these provisions are determined by state law, and others can be added by the insured.

 finance news 15.2

Living Benefits Insurance and Life Settlements

The availability of living benefits provisions, also called accelerated death benefits, has expanded rapidly over the last few years. More than 18 million Americans now have these provisions in their policies. Playing on the fear of the high cost of long-term health care, living benefits insurance is meant to allay that concern by either providing for your survivors in case of sudden death or providing for you in case of a protracted illness.

In most cases, the payment of living benefits reduces potential death benefits, but not necessarily on a dollar-for-dollar basis. A partial prepayment of benefits while living may entail the elimination of potentially larger future death benefits. On one such policy, patients given 18 to 24 months to live can get from 50 to 75 percent of the policy's face value. However, acceptance of this partial sum wipes out all death benefits, in effect placing a very high opportunity cost on the prepayment of death benefits.

There are also viatical companies that purchase the insurance policies directly from the policyholders. (The word *viatical* comes from the Latin word *viaticum,* meaning provisions for a journey.) They typically pay the dying only about $0.50 to $0.80 on the dollar. Such high discounts on future payments might be avoided by arranging private loans from relatives in return for naming them as beneficiaries on the policy.

You don't have to be terminally ill to sell your insurance policy. The industry is increasingly engaging in what are termed "life settlements." You sell your policy to an investor who pays the premiums on the policy and collects the payout. This can be an ideal solution for those who no longer need the insurance protection or who do not want to continue paying premiums. For older insured, the market value of the life settlement can exceed the surrender value on the policy. Even term policies that have no cash value may be of interest to an investor in life settlements. Consequently, it may be a preferred alternative to either surrendering the policy or letting your coverage lapse.

Provision	Description
Accelerated death benefits	Also known as living benefits. Predeath benefits that may be triggered by catastrophic illness or terminal illness.
Accidental death benefit	This option provides that, if the death of the insured is accidental, the death benefit will be some multiple of the face amount of the policy. If it doubles the face amount, it is sometimes known as a *double indemnity* provision.
Convertibility	You can exchange one kind of insurance for another without a medical examination. For example, your term insurance policy might be convertible to a specified amount of whole life at each age.
Cost-of-living adjustment	Automatically increases both the face amount of the policy and the premium. You have the right to reject this inflation-adjusted coverage, but if you do so, you may forfeit your right to all future cost-of-living adjustments in the face value of the policy.
Disability waiver of premium	If you become disabled, this rider requires the insurance company to take over premium payments on the policy. It usually takes effect six months after the beginning of the disability period.
Grace period	If you stop making payments and the cash value of your policy is depleted, coverage must cease but not until the specified grace period ends. This period is usually 31 days.
Guaranteed insurability	Allows you to increase the face amount of the policy by stated amounts and at specified dates without a medical examination. A worthwhile option for those who expect a future increase in insurance protection needs.
Incontestability	Prohibits the insurance company, after some period of time, from challenging your unintentional mistakes and omissions on the insurance application.
Nonforfeiture clause	This clause ensures that you will not lose the cash value of your policy if you cease making payments. The cash value may be disposed of in one of three ways: You may receive it in cash; you may use it to extend premium payments of the life insurance coverage; or you may use it to purchase a reduced amount of paid-up life insurance.
Renewability	Allows you to renew your coverage without a medical examination. However, your premiums for subsequent periods may be higher.
Settlement option	This provision determines how the face amount of the policy will be paid out. The choice of settlement option can also be left to the beneficiary.

Figure 15.6
Checklist: Special Provisions of Life Insurance Policies

Life Insurance Formats

Life insurance can be grouped into two basic categories: term and cash value. Most policies can be easily classified under one of these headings. A few, however, such as universal life, discussed later in this chapter, have the characteristics of both term insurance and cash value insurance.

Term Insurance

Term insurance Has no cash value buildup; provides only death protection.

Term insurance provides only death protection. A term policy does not build up a cash value. If the insured discontinues premium payments, the coverage simply lapses after a specified grace period. Life insurance agents sometimes attempt to discourage people from purchasing term insurance by suggesting that if they survive the period of coverage, they have, in effect, paid for nothing, since the policy has no residual value. This is not true. They have paid for and received a reduction in the financial risks associated with the possibility of dying. Such risk reduction is not costless, nor is it valueless.

As we will see, there are many kinds of term insurance. Some are sold under the name *term insurance* and others are not. In addition, some policies that are sold under the *term* label are not true term policies. The distinguishing feature of a term policy is that it does not have a savings component. Under a true term policy, the entire premium pays for death protection. Therefore, term provides the greatest amount of death protection for each premium dollar.

Because of tax advantages extended to employer-provided term life insurance, this is the type of group life insurance that is typically provided by employers. The face amount of the employer-supplied insurance is on average equal to about one-and-a-half times the employee's annual salary. This coverage is particularly attractive to older workers. Current law prohibits employers from providing such workers with less insurance protection than younger workers, even though the cost of a given face amount of term protection may be much greater for this group. The cost of the first $50,000 of group term protection purchased by your employer is not included in your taxable income. Employer-paid premiums for additional coverage is a taxable fringe benefit; consequently, employees are often given the option of refusing the additional coverage.

Increasing-Premium Term

Renewable term Term insurance that may be periodically renewed over some defined term without a medical examination.

Each year as you age, you experience a greater risk of mortality. Therefore, a pure term policy that provides a level death benefit must have increasing premiums in order to offset age-related risks. Yearly **renewable term** is the most common type of increasing-premium term. Figure 15.7 illustrates the premium structure for a representative policy. Renewability indicates that a policy may be extended without proof of insurability such as a medical exam. The renewability provision may last for some specified number of years or until you reach some specified age, typically age 65. Since the premium covers only death protection, it is lowest in the early years. Consequently, it is ideal for families with young children who need large amounts of insurance protection at minimal cost. After age 65, term protection may be nonexistent or prohibitively expensive.

Level-Premium Term

There are also *level-premium term* policies for 5-, 10-, and 15-year periods that may be renewable for subsequent periods. The level-term policies hold the premium constant over the specified period by requiring a higher premium than yearly term in the early years and a lower premium than yearly term in the later years. The lower premiums at the end of the policy's term are paid for by the overcharges in the earlier years.

Policies that hold the premium level over a large number of years may actually build up a cash value in the early years. *Life-expectancy term* provides level premiums over the insured's life expectancy. The leveling of the premium over this extended period creates a cash value that increases and then declines to zero at the termination of the policy. The same holds for *term-to-age-65* (or 70), which provides a shorter period of protection than life-expectancy term.

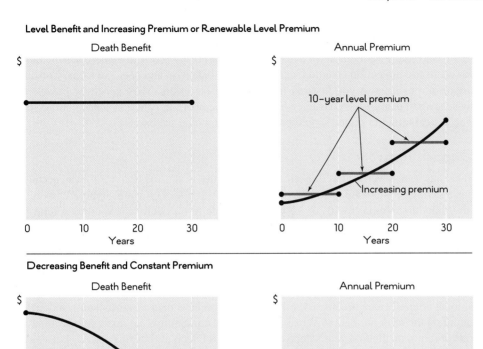

Figure 15.7
Structure of Term Policy Coverage and Premiums

Decreasing Term

Decreasing term is usually packaged as a one-year renewable policy. Its premium remains constant over time. The increased risk of mortality is reflected in a declining amount of death protection, so your insurance coverage automatically decreases as you age. It is useful for those who can anticipate a declining need for insurance protection.

Decreasing term A term policy with level premiums but decreasing death protection.

Group Mortgage Life and Credit Life

A form of decreasing term insurance, **group mortgage life** is designed to pay off the remaining balance on a mortgage. The death benefit declines as the remaining balance on the mortgage falls. As with traditional decreasing term insurance, the premium remains level over the term of the mortgage. The face amount at any time may not exactly equal the remaining balance, so, if you die, the beneficiary will receive an amount only approximately equal to the remaining balance.

Group mortgage life Pays off the remaining balance on the mortgage at death.

Group mortgage life is usually sold through the bank that holds your mortgage. The bank collects a commission from the insurance company for functioning as a sales agent. The bank also benefits in another way: It's the beneficiary on the insurance policy. This arrangement ensures that the mortgage is paid off at your death. Your family will have no say in how the proceeds are spent. If you have a low-interest mortgage, paying it off may not be the wisest use of insurance proceeds.

Credit life insurance Prepays a remaining loan balance at death.

Group mortgage life is only one form of **credit life insurance** that pays off your loan balance at death. Too many consumers purchase credit life because they wrongly believe that it is a required condition for a loan. You have probably received numerous solicitations for credit life protection on auto loans, credit card balances, and personal loans. Consumer organizations suggest you just say no to all of these offers. They generally believe that these are bad deals, with consumers only receiving $0.42 in benefits on each dollar spent. The typical term life policy should provide a much better payback.

Deposit Term

Deposit term insurance Returns a lump-sum amount at the end of the term protection; not true term insurance.

What has been advertised as **deposit term insurance** is not true term insurance, because it has a savings component. With a typical deposit term policy, you are supposedly purchasing something similar to 10- or 15-year renewable term. Each year you pay a term premium on the policy. However, during the first year of coverage you pay an extra premium, which is the deposit. At the end of the coverage period you may get back an amount equal to double the extra premium paid during the first year. This represents the saving component. In reality, the deposit you made in the first year may be going to pay the sales commission received by the agent. The insurance company is able to pay you back a lump-sum amount after 10 years because over the 10 years you have paid a higher-than-standard premium on the term protection. When these excessive premiums are taken into account, the rate of return on the first year's deposit is much less than it at first appears. Also, if you terminate the policy before a specified number of years, you may lose the deposit. Most insurance analysts have been highly critical of deposit term and suggest you avoid purchasing this type of policy.

Cash Value Insurance

Cash value insurance Provides both death protection and cash value buildup.

Cash value insurance functions both as death protection and as a savings vehicle. There are many reasons why people purchase cash value insurance: The periodic premium payments provide a convenient method for accumulating savings; the cash value may be a comparatively attractive investment; and, for most insurance products, the cash buildup is relatively safe. In some states the cash values and death benefits may even be protected from creditors.

If a cash value policy is terminated, you receive the cash value buildup less any surrender charges and outstanding loans. Such payouts may trigger tax liabilities; however, these may be conveniently handled by transferring the funds into retirement annuities. Also significant for your later years is the fact that cash value insurance can continue to provide death protection after term insurance has expired. Consequently, cash value insurance is an important tool in estate planning, supplying needed funds to pay estate taxes and an efficient method for transferring wealth to your heirs. Furthermore, under recently introduced policy options, some insureds may receive benefits before death in order to offset the unexpected cost of catastrophic illness.

One characteristic that often attracts people to cash value policies is that the insured may borrow from the insurance company an amount equal to the cash value at an attractive rate of interest. If the insured should die while owing money on the policy, the amount paid to beneficiaries will be reduced by the amount of the loan.

Figure 15.8 illustrates the death benefit and the death protection for a hypothetical cash value life policy with a face amount of $100,000. It's assumed that there are no special provisions, such as an accidental death benefit, that provide for an additional payout under special circumstances. The death benefit is equal to the face amount less any outstanding policy loans at the time of death. The actual death protection, the insurance com-

	Death Benefit*	Death Protection	Cash Surrender Value
Face amount	$100,000	$100,000	
Cash value		–30,000	$30,000
Outstanding loans	–10,000		–10,000
Surrender charges			–500
	$90,000	$70,000	$19,500

Figure 15.8
Death Benefit and Death Protection for a Hypothetical Policy

*Does not include additional amounts that may be paid out under an accidental death provision.

ponent, is equal to the face amount less the policy's cash value. It's also equal to the death benefit less the net cash value (cash value less outstanding policy loans). An increase in the policy's cash value reduces the risk to the insurance company.

Whole Life

With **whole life**, also called **straight** or **ordinary life**, premium payments are level over the lifetime of the insured. On a cash value policy the amount of death protection is equal to the difference between the policy's face value and its cash value. Figure 15.9 indicates how the cash value and the death protection vary over the term of the policy. In the early years, much of the premium must go toward purchasing the death protection component. As the cash value builds up, and the required death protection declines, more of the premium can be added to the cash value. Thus, the buildup in cash value will be more rapid in the later years. At age 100, the cash value of the policy equals the face amount, and the insured receives the face amount if he or she is still living. The rise in the cash value is predetermined, and the insured is often presented with a schedule indicating what the cash value of the policy will be at each year of age.

Whole life or straight or ordinary life Cash value insurance with level lifetime payments.

Limited Payment Life

Under a **limited payment life** policy, premium payments remain level up to a certain age, usually 65, and then cease. However, the insurance protection remains effective over the entire life span. This protection is accomplished by charging higher premiums than on a comparable straight life policy over fewer payment years in order to provide a more rapid buildup in cash value. The insurance company then uses part of the interest earned on the

Limited payment life Cash value insurance with level premiums over a limited number of years and lifetime protection.

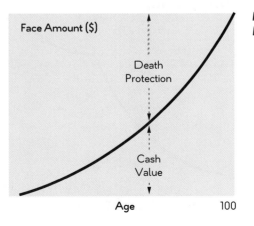

Figure 15.9
Level-Premium Whole Life

cash value to provide continued protection after premium payments terminate. The allocation of death protection and cash value is illustrated in Figure 15.10.

Endowment Life

Endowment life Rapid buildup of cash value, with payoff of face value after a set number of years.

An **endowment life** policy pays off its face value after a set number of years, thus providing rapid cash value buildup with death protection. With past changes in the tax law, the cash value buildup on most traditional endowment policies no longer qualifies for tax deferral. Consequently, such policies are rarely sold anymore.

Modified Whole Life

Modified whole life Level premiums with varying death protection tied to life-cycle needs.

Most families require less insurance protection in later years. **Modified whole life** attempts to fit the needs of the family throughout the life cycle by automatically reducing the death benefit as the insured ages. As in a whole life policy, the premium payments remain level for life. However, premium payments on a modified life plan will be lower than those on a whole life policy providing identical protection in the early years.

Adjustable Life

Adjustable life The face amount may be adjusted by specified amounts at defined time intervals.

Under an **adjustable life** plan, both the premium payments and the face amount of the policy are adjustable. You are allowed to change coverage as need varies and to change premium payments as income varies. The basic idea seems to be a good one, but this plan has some characteristics you should be wary of.

The face amount of the policy may be increased only by specified amounts at specified time intervals. Unless the policy contains a guaranteed insurability rider, you may have to take another medical exam when you desire to increase the face amount. In addition, a sales charge may be built in to pay the insurance agent a second commission when you increase the insurance coverage. With the added sales charge and the medical exam, increasing the face amount of an adjustable life policy may cost about as much as taking out a new whole life policy.

The premiums are adjusted by allowing the insured to move between term protection and cash value protection. When the insured's income increases, higher premiums can be paid in order to build up cash value. During periods of financial distress, premiums can be cut by opting for lower-cost term protection. The implicit assumption is that when you can afford it, you purchase the more expensive cash value insurance.

Figure 15.10
Limited Payment Life

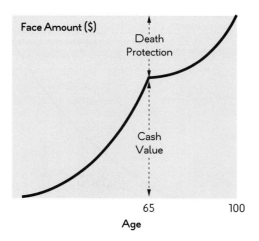

Universal Life

Unlike traditional whole life, **universal life** permits flexible premium payments, affecting the size of the cash buildup. The premium payment on universal life is often called a *contribution* and, within certain limits, is voluntary. Out of this contribution the insurance company deducts a charge for term insurance protection and the cost of management. The remainder is deposited in an interest-bearing account. The interest earned either is determined periodically by the insurance company or is tied to an agreed-upon index.

Universal life Permits flexible premium payments, affecting the size of the cash buildup.

You receive periodic reports on a universal life policy indicating the cost of the term protection, the management expenses, and the earned return on cash value. This provides a significant advantage over traditional whole life, where you may have no idea how much you are really paying for death protection or how much you are really earning on the policy's cash value. Given the more detailed information on a universal life policy, you are in a better position to judge the relative merits of purchasing term insurance separately and investing the difference.

Those who have compared universal life with traditional whole life have concluded that universal life does generally provide a better return on the invested cash value. Indeed, the primary reason for consumer interest in universal life has been the high advertised rate on the investment account. However, there are additional attractions. Within limits set by the company and the government, the insured may borrow against the accumulated cash value. Furthermore, most universal life policies allow the insured to increase the death protection, although another medical examination may be required.

On all policies that have an interest-sensitive cash buildup, you should critically evaluate seller illustrations of future benefits. These may be based on assumed rates of return that never materialize.

SIMPLIFYING
financial planning 15.3

Borrowing Your Cash Value

The cash value on your life insurance can represent a convenient source of liquidity. In most cases, you can promptly tap the cash value with a policy loan. Since the loan is 100 percent collateralized by the policy's cash value, there is no need for a credit check or other financial inquiries that can delay a typical bank loan.

To your advantage, policy loans need never be repaid, and policy loan rates are often substantially below those on other consumer financing. On the negative side, loans will reduce the death benefits, which is probably the primary reason you purchased life insurance in the first place.

When deciding on a policy loan, you should be sure to look at the true opportunity cost of borrowing, which may exceed the policy loan rate. The cash value on your life insurance will earn interest and grow over time. However, if you borrow against the policy, the cash value is used as collateral for the loan. Because the loan may be made at an interest rate that is below what the insurance company can earn on its invested assets, this may

reduce the rate earned on the policy's cash value. This practice is called "direct recognition."

For example, suppose you have a universal life policy currently earning 8 percent on cash value, on which you may obtain a policy loan for 5 percent. If you decide to borrow against the policy, the insurance company may reduce the rate earned on the collateralized portion of the cash value to only 3 percent, thus forcing you to give up an additional 5 percent return on the cash value. The true opportunity cost of borrowing is, therefore, equal to 10 percent, the policy loan rate of 5 percent plus the reduced interest rate on the cash value of 5 percent.

When deciding whether to borrow in order to invest your funds elsewhere, the true opportunity cost, and not the policy loan rate, is the starting point for comparison purposes. Tax considerations, of course, can make comparative valuations much more complicated. Interest earned on the cash value is tax deferred until the policy is surrendered. If the policy is never surrendered, income taxes need never be paid on the death benefits.

Variable Life

Variable life Selective investment of premiums in a market portfolio that determines the cash value in the policy.

In many ways, **variable life** is similar to universal life. Like universal life, it has a term insurance component and an investment component. A minimum death benefit is guaranteed by the term insurance, while the cash value buildup and additional death benefit protection depend on the performance of selected market portfolios of stocks, bonds, or money market funds. You may be permitted to decide how the cash value will be allocated among the available portfolios and when funds should be switched between portfolios.

If your market portfolio does poorly, the cash value buildup will be less than with either whole or universal life. The speculative risk associated with variable life reduces its ability to secure the financial future of your survivors. Variable life should be compared with other tax-advantageous investments and only secondarily looked upon as death benefit protection. The government recognizes its speculative characteristics by requiring that only registered security dealers be permitted to sell this policy. As on universal life policies, management fees and early withdrawal penalties should be examined closely.

Variable life provides less flexibility than universal life. Annual premiums are fixed by the insurer. Regardless of how the market may look, you must contribute to at least one of the policy's portfolios to keep the policy in force. In contrast, universal life permits you to vary the amount you contribute each year and even to skip payments when there is sufficient cash value to cover the cost of insurance protection.

Variable-Universal Life

Variable-universal life Combines the flexible premiums of universal life with the investment selection of variable life.

Variable-universal life is also sold under various other names, such as universal life II. It combines the flexible premiums permitted under universal life with the investment selection permitted by variable life. Depending on your outlook, you can say it blends the best or the worst of each. By allowing both contributions and investments to vary, it becomes a more flexible speculative investment. However, like a traditional variable life policy, if your cash value falls far enough, you may be required to contribute additional funds or lose your family's insurance protection. Furthermore, a forced payout of cash value will require the immediate payment of all deferred tax. This may present a severe hardship for those who have borrowed against the policy's cash value. After repaying those loans, they may have nothing left with which to pay the tax bill.

Selecting the Right Policy

Policy selection may be looked upon as the following three-step process:

1. Determine your life insurance needs.
2. Select the type of policy that best fits those needs.
3. Compare specific policies and companies.

By now you should have an understanding as to how much insurance you require and information on the various types of policies that may satisfy your needs. You are in a good position to select the appropriate insurance vehicle and comparison shop the best price. Selecting the right policy will save you money and protect your family.

Insurance Needs

Once you have determined your death protection needs, it may be easy to decide on the type of insurance protection you need. Young families with small children are going to need large amounts of death protection. Unfortunately, it is these same families who are on tight budgets and can ill afford to pay high premiums for life insurance. They need to get the greatest amount of insurance protection per dollar spent, and that means purchasing term insurance. It's a mistake to settle for less than needed protection today, in the expectation of some investment return in the future. The American Council of Life Insurers reports that 40 percent of individual life policies sold in 2005 were term life policies. The other 60 percent consisted of whole life and endowment policies. Although the number of whole life policies sold was greater, the term life policies provided more than twice as much face amount protection.

Term or Cash Value Insurance?

Commissions are significantly higher on cash value insurance than on term insurance. Consequently, insurance agents have stronger incentives for selling cash value insurance. This may lead them to exaggerate the benefits of cash value policies and understate the benefits of term insurance. The unique benefit of cash value insurance is the savings feature. It's often promoted as a method of forced savings for retirement and as a "can't-lose" proposition. If you die, you have the insurance protection; if you live, you have the savings. Unfortunately, the savings have often accumulated at unattractive rates of interest.

Cash value insurance should be looked upon as an alternative to term insurance for those who can comfortably afford it. If you can, then you may want to consider purchasing cash value insurance as a supplement to your investment portfolio or as part of your estate plan. As part of your investment portfolio, it should be evaluated like any other investment.

Term Plus a Saving Plan

For many years Consumers Union has suggested that individuals would be better off purchasing lower-cost term and investing the difference. One such plan is illustrated in Table 15.2. You would have $25,000 worth of death protection if the face amount of the term policy plus the amount in the savings account averaged $25,000 over each year. This is the way payments are allocated in Table 15.2. Assuming the side savings fund earned a 5 percent annual return after taxes, the amount in the side savings fund would equal $5,677.44 after 10 years.

Year	Term Rate Per $1,000	Term Expenditures	Annual Deposit	Term Protection*	End-of-Year Side Savings
1	$2.57	$63.12	$482.38	$24,517.62	$ 506.50
2	2.75	65.93	479.57	24,013.93	1,035.37
3	3.00	70.62	439.63	23,525.00	1,548.75
4	3.15	72.60	432.40	23,018.85	2,080.21
5	3.31	74.37	425.38	22,494.41	2,630.87
6	3.51	77.16	417.34	21,951.79	3,200.62
7	3.79	81.08	408.17	21,391.22	3,789.22
8	4.05	84.22	399.78	20,811.00	4,398.45
9	4.35	88.13	390.62	20,210.93	5,028.53
10	4.75	92.69	378.56	19,592.92	5,677.44

Table 15.2
Buying Term and Investing the Difference at 5 Percent After Taxes

*The term protection plus the amount in the side savings fund will equal about $25,000 each year.

If the amount in the side savings fund after the specified time period is greater than the after-tax surrender value on the cash value policy, then purchasing term and investing the difference should be the preferred option.

Unbundled Whole Life

Consumers have been increasingly purchasing term rather than cash value insurance. The industry has responded by introducing universal life, variable life, and, finally, variable-universal life. As previously discussed, each of these products unbundles the insurance premium into a payment for death protection and a contribution to savings; thus, they do exactly what the critics of whole life have suggested. They combine term and a side savings account into one convenient package. The important benefit is that you know how much you are paying for term protection and how much of a return you are earning on your investment. This is a significant benefit over traditional whole life, where it may be difficult to understand what you are paying for and what you are getting in return.

On all policies, such as universal, variable, and variable-universal, that have an interest-sensitive cash buildup, it's important to examine the historical returns of the companies' market portfolios. These returns should be compared with returns on other investments, such as mutual funds, that have similar levels of risk. But remember, past returns are no guarantee of similar future returns. Illustrations of future premiums and cash buildup based upon historically high returns may be overly optimistic.

The quality of the coverage will depend upon both the cost of the underlying term insurance and the return on the cash value. If you are paying for expensive term coverage, a high return on the cash value may be no bargain. The insurance company will subtract from each premium the cost of insurance protection and a sales commission; what is left goes to build cash value. If you consider the sales commission on the savings component, your actual return may be much less than the advertised rates. Commissions on universal life policies vary from 5 percent to 90 percent of the first year's premium. Moreover, there may be significant charges if you surrender your policy in the early years.

Weighing the Tax Advantage of Cash Value Insurance

A major selling point for cash value insurance has been the tax advantage for individuals in high tax brackets. The interest earned on the policy's cash value avoids taxes at the time it's credited to the savings component. A 9 percent tax-sheltered yield on the cash value is equivalent to a 12.5 percent taxable yield for someone in the 28 percent marginal tax bracket. However, if you decide to surrender the policy, you will have to pay tax on the interest earnings at that time. One alternative is to borrow against the cash value instead of surrendering the policy. But, again, you may run into problems. Both the company and the government can limit the amount you may be permitted to borrow.

The basic tax rule is that if you surrender a policy, you must pay taxes on the difference between the value of savings and the cost of the policy. The cost of the policy is equal to the sum of premiums paid less the sum of dividends received. However, the immediate tax impact may be avoided if you engage in an IRC Section 1035 exchange. To qualify for a nontaxable exchange, you must roll over the cash value into another life insurance policy or an annuity contract. The exchange of life insurance for a retirement annuity can provide supplementary income if you no longer need insurance protection in your later years.

All life insurance, whether it is whole life or term, provides certain tax benefits at death. Beneficiaries can receive a tax-free payout. In addition, if the insurance contract is properly structured so that the insured gives up all rights of ownership, the proceeds can reduce estate taxes.

Comparison Shopping

Traditional whole life policies have been particularly difficult to compare, because insurance companies have not supplied information on the rate of return for the savings component. Also, life insurance agents have been known to misrepresent the actual cost of the policy. The agent would add up the premiums paid over the 20-year period and subtract from this amount the dividends received and the cash value at the end of the 20 years. The result would often be negative, erroneously indicating to the buyer that the insurance did not "cost" anything. Of course, this calculation ignores the time value of money. Had the consumer been depositing the net premiums into an account paying a competitive market rate of interest over the same period, the total amount in the account at the end of 20 years would have been much greater than the cash value of the policy at that time. The difference between the value in this imaginary account and the cash value of the policy at the end of the 20-year period represents the real cost of the life insurance policy.

Comparison Indexes

From the previous discussion, it should be apparent that when policies differ in premiums, cash buildup, and expected dividends, comparing their relative value is no easy task. Comparison indexes provide a single statistic for ranking the worth of different insurance illustrations. The National Association of Insurance Commissioners (NAIC) has promoted the use of the 10-year and 20-year **interest-adjusted net cost index**, also called the **surrender cost index**. About three-quarters of states now require that the insurance company provide this information. The index takes into account annual premiums, annual dividends, and the cash accumulation at the end of a 10- and a 20-year period. Assuming you can earn a 5 percent return on alternative investments, the index calculates the annual cost for a given dollar amount of insurance protection. The formula for the index is quite complex. However, all you really need to know is that the higher the index, the greater the cost of the insurance protection.

Interest-adjusted net cost index or surrender cost index A useful industry-provided index for comparing the relative costs of similar life insurance policies.

You must be careful not to use the index for comparing the relative cost of dissimilar policies. Most important, don't use the index to compare the cost of term insurance with the cost of cash value insurance. The cash value insurance will always appear cheaper if you do. The reason for this is simple. The interest-adjusted net cost index measures the cost of a given face amount of life insurance and not a given amount of death protection. If you purchase a term policy with a $10,000 face amount, you are receiving a full $10,000 of death protection over the period of coverage. On the other hand, when you purchase a $10,000 cash value policy, the amount of death protection is equal to the face amount of the policy less the policy's cash value.

The interest-adjusted net cost index also has another shortcoming. It's based on an assumed rate of return on savings of 5 percent. When market rates are above this amount, the net cost index will not perfectly reflect the relative value of two dissimilar policies. It will tend to understate the relative cost of policies that have higher current premiums but lower future premiums and higher future dividends.

In California, the Department of Insurance has replaced the interest-adjusted net cost index with the **net payment cost index and yield comparison index (YCI)**. These indexes take into account the interest credited, the estimated value of the death protection, and the expenses charged. The net payment cost index allows the consumer to rank policies in terms of cost per $1,000 of coverage. It assumes that you continue to pay premiums and do not withdraw the cash value. The YCI, which is a measure of cash value growth over the index period, is expressed as a percentage. A higher YCI indicates a better buy; however, it should not be confused with the rate of return on cash value.

Net payment cost index and yield comparison index (YCI) Indexes for ranking life insurance policies in terms of cost effectiveness.

The problem with these indexes is that they are dependent on policy illustrations. In most cases, illustrations are based on assumptions about interest rates, mortality rates, and policy lapses that are not guaranteed. Therefore, even though one policy might have a better index value than another, it may actually turn out to be more costly. Even with a comparison index, you must still examine the underlying assumptions.

The Insurance Company

Check the financial rating of the insurance company before you buy a policy. If you have cash value insurance, you should continue to monitor the financial health of the company for as long as you hold the policy. Firms that rate the financial soundness of an insurance company provide the consumer with help on this matter. The five major rating services are A.M. Best Company, Fitch Ratings, Moody's Investors Service, Standard & Poor's Insurance Rating Services, and the Weiss Group. Publications issued by some of these services can be found at most university and public libraries. The top solvency rating given by each of these firms is shown in Figure 15.11. There has been much bickering among company representatives as to which firm does the best job of rating the insurance companies. Because ratings often differ by rating agency, it's a good idea to monitor several services.

TOPIC LINKS

Review ratings for insurance companies.

Switching Policies

The general feeling among industry analysts is that the industry is basically sound, and that policyholders should be wary of insurance agents who exaggerate the difficulties faced by some insurers. This may be merely an unjustified attempt at "churning," replacing an existing policy with a new one simply to generate commissions. However, if your insurance company is down-rated, consider the associated benefits and costs of changing insurers. This is not an easy decision. If you surrender your policy, you may incur substantial surrender penalties and tax liabilities. The tax liabilities can be eliminated or deferred if you decide to switch your investment earnings into another policy and fill out a "1035 exchange form" with the new company. But there may be no way of avoiding additional high first-year commissions and another medical exam to prove insurability on a new pol-

Figure 15.11
Top Insurance Industry
Ratings

Provision	Highest Rating	Criteria
A.M. Best Company www.ambest.com	A++	Superior ability to meet policyholder and other contractual obligations.
Fitch Ratings www.fitchrating.com	AAA	Strong capacity to meet contract obligations and commitments to policyholders.
Moody's Investors Service www.moodys.com	Aaa	Best quality and smallest degree of credit risk. The financial strength of these companies is likely to change, but changes are unlikely to impair their fundamentally strong position.
Standard & Poor's Insurance Rating Services www.standardpoors.com	AAA	Superior financial security on both an absolute and relative basis; they possess the highest safety and have an overwhelming capacity to meet policyholder obligations.
Weiss Group www.weissratings.com	A+	Excellent financial security; strong ability to deal with economic adversity.

icy. One intermediate step between doing nothing and switching insurers is to take out a policy loan. By borrowing against the policy instead of surrendering it, you at least enhance your own liquidity while avoiding surrender charges and protecting death benefits. If the company fails, you have a portion of your money; and if it recovers, you can always repay the loan.

Participating Versus Nonparticipating Insurance

Historically, policyholders with participating insurance do better when interest rates rise, because mutual insurance companies pass on part of the higher return on their investment portfolios as dividends to policyholders. On the other hand, those with nonparticipating insurance may have cash values accumulating at a historically low rate set at the time coverage was initiated. In an effort to compete, stock insurance companies have been offering policies with a type of participation. Universal life and variable life are two such policies, because the policyholder participates in current market returns.

Some policy illustrations for participating life policies show *vanishing premiums* at a point in the future. The premium vanishes when the interest or dividend earnings become large enough to cover the premium. If dividends fall below those anticipated in the illustration, then the premium may not vanish. This fact was learned the hard way by many policyholders who purchased insurance in the 1980s when interest rates were higher. For a significant number, their expectations of vanishing premiums did not materialize, and some whose premiums had vanished found them reinstated as interest rates dropped.

Other Factors

You should recognize that life insurance will differ in cost because of policy riders. The riders attached to a contract play an important role in determining the worth of the policy and should be weighed carefully when making comparisons. The first step is to make sure you are not comparing apples and oranges. The second step is to take a close look at the apples. The same company may sell a high-commission and low-commission version of the same policy with identical riders. At times, unethical insurance agents have pointed to an independent survey indicating that their company's product was rated favorably, while forgetting to tell the prospective buyer that the rated policy was different from the higher-cost policy being offered.

If you deal through an independent life insurance agent, choose one who is a Chartered Life Underwriter. It will indicate that this individual has a minimum of three years' experience, has met basic educational requirements, and agrees to abide by a code of ethics. Ask the agent how much of each year's premium goes toward commissions. You may then inquire as to whether you might receive part of that commission as a rebate. This is a hot issue in the industry. Some insurance agents feel that commission rebates are unethical or illegal; others think that rebates simply signal a competitive market.

Make sure you understand all of the assumptions underlying the illustrated benefits. The agent should explain how sensitive the illustration is to the underlying assumptions. In particular, you should request alternative illustrations of future dividends, premiums, and cash value based on guaranteed rates of return.

Ask for a specimen policy before you buy. When you receive the actual policy, read it carefully and be sure you understand every term. Also, find out the legally required cooling-off period during which you may change your mind and have your premiums returned without penalty. Finally, after you have decided to keep the policy, make copies for your beneficiaries. It is important that they understand the benefits they are entitled to and how the proceeds will be paid. Most policies offer settlement options consisting of either a lump-sum payment at death or an annuity for survivors. You may choose the settlement option or leave the choice to your beneficiaries.

Estate Planning

Death estate Property and wealth transferred at death.

Upon death, the property you leave is termed your **death estate**. It should be large enough to provide for the care and support of the surviving spouse and children. However, all your planning and all your saving may accomplish little if your estate is squandered on legal costs or is transferred to the wrong individual. To make sure this does not happen, you will need some expert advice. Estate planning is not a do-it-yourself project. For small estates the help of an attorney may prove sufficient, but for large estates, especially those over $1 million, the aid of either an accountant or a financial planner specializing in estate transfer should also be enlisted.

The transfer of death estates can trigger tax consequences as discussed in Chapter 4 on taxes. These tax liabilities are scheduled to change erratically over the next few years, challenging the best of financial plans. In this section, we will limit the discussion to the methods of transfer and refer you to Chapter 4 for a discussion of potential tax liabilities.

Estate planning has two basic objectives: to transfer your assets at death in a manner consistent with your wishes, and to transfer those assets as intact as possible. The first objective can be achieved through a well-thought-out will. Depending on the amount and nature of your wealth, the second objective can be either very simple or very difficult.

Intestate To die without a valid will.

An overwhelming number of Americans die each year without a valid will. In these situations the deceased is said to have died **intestate**. When this occurs, the state supplies a ready-made will dividing the estate according to that state's laws of intestacy. The division is uniquely determined by each state, but the laws generally follow the format outlined in Figure 15.12.

The chance is very small that the state-mandated distribution of your assets will reflect your own desires. In fact, for many families with minor children, the distribution directed by the state is likely to run counter to the best interest of the family. Typically, under the laws of intestacy a surviving spouse with children receives only one-half to one-third of the estate. The rest is distributed to the children of the deceased. For those who have not yet reached the age of majority, court-appointed trustees will have to manage these funds in the children's interest. The surviving spouse may then be required to gain the agreement of the trustees on how and when these funds may be spent. For most families, this arrangement is undesirable and inconvenient. In addition, the associated administrative and legal costs may use up resources needed to support the surviving spouse and children.

Figure 15.12
Possible Division of Estate Under Typical Intestate Provisions

Survivors	Division of Property
Spouse and one child	Spouse and child each receive one-half
Spouse and two or more children	Spouse receives one-third. The other two-thirds is divided equally among the children
Spouse and parents surviving, no children	Spouse receives 50–75% of estate, surviving parents receive the rest
Spouse surviving, no children, and parents deceased	Spouse receives 50–100% of estate, surviving brothers and sisters receive remaining balance
Parents surviving, no spouse or children	Parents receive all
Brother(s) and/or sister(s) surviving, no spouse or children, parents deceased	Brother(s) and/or sisters(s) receive equal shares

The Last Will and Testament

A **will** is a legal declaration of how you wish your property to be disposed of at your death. It should be drawn up under the supervision of an attorney knowledgeable in estate planning. The presence of an attorney is essential because there are myriad reasons for challenging a will and contesting the distribution of an estate. For example, unless the will is properly witnessed, according to state-mandated guidelines, you may not have a valid will. Should the will be declared invalid for any reason, the estate will be distributed under the laws of intestacy. Furthermore, an improperly written will that does not foreclose future court proceedings may be more costly to your intended beneficiaries than dying with no will at all.

Your estate planning objectives will not be achieved if you simply write a will and then forget it. Review the document periodically to ensure that it reflects your current familial status and needs. Be sure to review your will whenever you change your state of residency or your family structure. Don't assume that just because you previously wrote a will with the help of a knowledgeable attorney that it is necessarily still valid. The laws differ among states, and a valid will in one state may be invalid in another.

A person who leaves a valid will is said to die **testate** and is referred to as either the **testator** or the **testatrix**. The correct suffix depends on whether the person is a male, requiring a *tor* ending, or a female, requiring a *trix* ending. You as the testator or testatrix can accomplish several objectives through the use of a will. You can name the executor for your estate. You can choose the guardian for your children. You can specify how your estate should be divided among beneficiaries. And finally, you can create investment trusts to provide for the future support and welfare of the beneficiaries.

Naming an Executor

The person named in the will who manages your estate from the time of death until all the assets are distributed is called the **executor or executrix**. Because he or she is given extensive powers to handle your affairs and distribute your property according to your wishes, pick someone who is exceedingly trustworthy. Furthermore, discuss your choice with your potential executor, explaining what is required and who might provide additional information on the handling of your estate. This information should also be contained in the "letter of last instructions" discussed later. If you die without a will, or the named executor refuses

Will A legal declaration of how property will be transferred at death.

TOPIC LINKS

Review sample estate planning forms.

Testate To die with a valid will.

Testator The male author of a valid will.

Testatrix The female author of a valid will.

Executor or executrix The person who manages the distribution of the death estate according to the wishes expressed in the will.

 ## saving money 15.4

Staying Healthy

Life insurance companies have been lowering premiums over the last decade to reflect the increasing longevity of the U.S. population. Part of this increase has been due to improvements in medical science, but part is a result of a healthier lifestyle.

If you have a healthy lifestyle, you will benefit from a preferred lower premium. Life insurance companies differ in their risk ratings; therefore, comparison shop for health-related discounts. The three factors you have some control over are cholesterol, body weight, and smoking. Not smoking can save you a significant amount in premiums. Moreover, on a term life policy the savings from remaining tobacco-free will increase with age and time.

Leading a healthy lifestyle can mean more than just avoiding disease-related risks. A high-risk occupation or hobby, such as scuba diving, as well as a poor driving record, can increase your premiums.

Don't try to avoid higher premiums by lying. The insurer has access to your medical record. If you are caught, you will be denied coverage. If you get coverage, it can be canceled and you could be charged with fraud. Should an investigation after your death discover fraud, the premiums may be returned and the payout may be denied.

Administrator or administratrix The court–appointed manager of the death estate and will.

to serve, the court chooses someone termed the **administrator or administratrix** to handle your estate. This choice may not coincide with your own desires.

An executor will normally be paid a fee for services performed, but the person you select may agree to serve free. More important, unless the will specifically states otherwise, the executor will be required to post a bond to cover any potential mismanagement of the estate. This is expensive and will eventually be charged to the estate. Assuming you have picked a trustworthy individual, you may waive the need for posting bond in the will.

Specifying Guardianship

For those who have children, the will is used to name a guardian in the event both parents die before the children reach the age of majority. As in the case of executor, make sure the proposed guardian will accept the assigned role. It is also worthwhile appointing successor guardians who care for the children, if for some reason the primary guardians are not available. If you leave surviving children without a named guardian, or a named guardian refuses to serve, the court chooses one. In some cases this assignment provides the incentive for a lengthy and emotional custody battle among relatives. A potentially undesirable outcome is that guardianship of the children may be split. Consequently, brothers and sisters may grow up emotionally and physically separated from each other.

Dividing the Estate

Bequest or legacy Property given by a wish expressed in a will.

In the will, you also indicate how your property should be disposed of. You may divide your estate into percentage shares or provide for absolute dollar payments for each beneficiary. You may also make a specific **bequest**, also termed a **legacy**, leaving a specific item of property to a particular individual.

Most property is distributed under either a *per capita* or a *per stirpes* division. Suppose Arnold and Sharon Steele have two grandchildren by their son, John, as illustrated in Figure 15.13. Furthermore, assume John dies before his parents. At Arnold's and Sharon's subsequent death, how will their property be divided among the grandchildren and the surviving daughter, Nancy? The answer will depend on whether the Steeles specified a per capita or a per stirpes distribution in their will. In a **per capita (per cap'-i-ta) division**, all of the survivors would share equally. One-third would go to Nancy, and one-third would go to each of the grandchildren. In a **per stirpes (per stir'-pez) division**, each *branch* of the family would share equally. Nancy would receive one-half of the property, and each of John's children would receive one-quarter.

Per capita division Inheritance is divided equally among surviving family members.

Per stirpes division Inheritance is divided equally among branches of the family.

The way in which the estate is divided may affect estate taxes, inheritance taxes, and the income taxes of beneficiaries. In addition, there are some potential legal problems that should be considered. First, property cannot be left directly to minor children. If you have minor children, you will have to provide for their continued support through a trust arrangement. An attorney can help you formulate one that reflects your intentions. Second, who is included and who is not included in your will may determine who might challenge the validity of the will. Under state law you may have no choice but to leave part of your estate to your spouse. Your failure to do so in your will may later provide the basis for contesting your intended distribution of your death estate.

Changing or Revoking the Will

Codicil An amendment to an existing will, modifying or explaining specific items.

If you wish to change only a few specific items in the will, you can do so through a **codicil**, which is usually a one-page document indicating the desired changes in the existing will. Like the initial will, the codicil should also be drawn up and witnessed in a manner satisfying state law. Thus, an attorney should also be used when amending an existing will with a codicil.

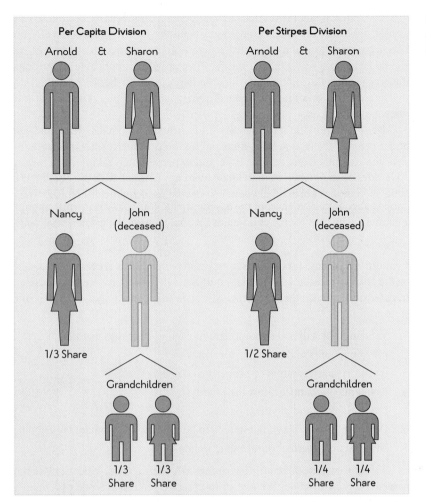

Figure 15.13
Alternative Estate Distributions

For matters that require more than a few simple changes, the old will should be revoked and a new will written. The old will can be revoked by expressly stating so in the new will. Most people do not realize that a previously valid will may be automatically revoked by a change in family status. Marriage, divorce, or the birth of a child can all automatically revoke an existing will. The exact result of this change will, again, depend on state law. Naturally, you should consult an attorney whenever family arrangements change.

The Letter of Last Instructions

If you desire, you can leave your relatives with a few well-chosen words, but not in the will. Everything in it is subject to legal interpretation and challenge. Therefore, to minimize the possibility of misinterpretation and conflict, do not include unnecessary statements. Your last words of wisdom or insult should be contained in the **letter of last instructions**. In it you might explain why you structured your bequests as you did, what you hoped to accomplish in the specified distribution of your assets, and what you hope your beneficiaries might accomplish in the future.

Letter of last instructions A document providing advice on the management of your death estate and the distribution of your assets.

The letter of last instructions should also have a more practical objective. It can serve as a roadmap for your survivors, pointing the way to information on your estate. Since a roadmap is most useful at the beginning of a trip, inform your beneficiaries where it might be found and keep copies at several locations.

The letter of last instructions should contain an inventory of your assets and the location of important documents, beginning with the location of your will. You may want to keep a copy of the will along with the letter of last instructions. However, the original will should be kept on file at the attorney's office or, where applicable, at the county office with the register of wills and not in your safe-deposit box or home. It may take a while before the safe-deposit box may be opened after your death, and wills left at home have been known to disappear.

Be sure to provide information on life insurance policies, death and survivor benefits under pension plans, and your financial holdings. Such readily available information can save the executor considerable time and expense when taking inventory of your estate. Also provide the names of individuals who are familiar with the operation of your estate, such as your stockbroker, accountant, lawyer, and financial planner. The executor may have to rely on their help in the management and distribution of your assets.

Probate

Probate A court process for transferring assets according to a will or the laws of intestacy.

Probate is the name for the court process in which assets are transferred subject to the will or the laws of intestacy. A special court, known as the probate court, exists to handle the transfer of death estates. The proceedings in this court may be divided into seven major steps as follows:

1. Validation of will and appointment of executor or administrator
2. Informing heirs and claimants of death
3. Inventory and valuation of property and debts
4. Payments of claims against the estate
5. Determination and payment of taxes due
6. Determination of how the estate is to be divided and who are the legal heirs
7. Division and distribution of estate to heirs

In the first step the court determines whether a valid will exists. If there is one, the named executor oversees the rest of the process. In the absence of a valid will, the court will appoint an administrator to help manage the probate process.

Not all property is distributed through the will and the probate process. Property may be passed outside of the will. Since probate costs are usually equal to a percentage of the assets transferred, even a partial transfer of assets outside the will can result in cost savings. However, this need not result in any tax savings. Estate taxes are based on the value of the gross estate, which will include property transferred both within and outside of the will.

Transferring Your Estate Outside the Will

One way of transferring property and avoiding probate is to give your assets away while you are still living. Most of us would like to retain control over our property in case of future need, however, so this method isn't always desirable. There are several ways in which property may transfer at death, thus leaving us with control while living and yet still avoiding probate. Joint tenancy, trusts, and contracts are the three most important ways in which this is accomplished. Each has advantages and drawbacks, and none should be entered into just to avoid probate. The indiscriminate use of these estate planning instruments could result in increased tax liabilities, increased estate management costs, and an undesirable distribution of your estate. Accordingly, each should be used with care and forethought, and never as a substitute for a will. Rather, they should be looked upon as individual instruments in your estate planning tool kit.

Joint Tenancy with Right of Survivorship

When property is held under the form of ownership called *joint tenancy with right of survivorship,* it automatically passes at death to the surviving co-owner. It is not distributed through the will and, therefore, avoids probate. In a **joint tenancy**, each owner has an undivided interest in the property, meaning that each has an equal right to make use of and enjoy the entire property.

Most estate planners tend to look upon joint tenancy unfavorably, because too many people use it as a substitute for a will. It is not. Even when most of your assets are held in joint tenancy, you still need a will to specify how the property is to be distributed at the death of the surviving owner. Joint tenants who are husband and wife might die simultaneously in an accident; only a will can specify how the jointly held property would then be disposed of.

Joint tenancy should not be confused with other forms of multiple ownership such as *tenancy in common* or *community property*. **Tenancy in common** is similar to joint tenancy in that each owner shares an undivided interest, even when each owns an unequal share. However, an important difference for estate planning is that the property does not necessarily pass to the co-owner(s) at death. Each owner can transfer his or her share in the tenancy in common as desired in both life and death. Thus, ownership will pass through the will the same as individually owned property.

Some states employ the concept of **community property**. This is property acquired during the marriage from the joint efforts of husband and wife. Each is assumed to share equally in the ownership of such assets. Upon the death of either spouse, community property is treated much the same as in tenancy in common. The surviving spouse receives one-half of the property. The other half is disposed of through the will of the deceased spouse or through the laws of intestacy.

Trusts

A **trust** is an arrangement whereby the right to property is held by one party, the **trustee**, for the benefit of another, the **beneficiary**. The trustee is said to have a **fiduciary responsibility** to the beneficiary. This means that the trustee has a legal obligation to manage the trust in the best interests of the beneficiary. If the trustee does not honor this obligation, he or she may be held liable for any damages suffered by the beneficiary.

The person who establishes and funds the trust is known as the **grantor**. The grantor may arrange for the trust to become operational either at his or her death or while the grantor is still alive. Each arrangement can play an important role in estate planning.

Testamentary and living trusts. A trust specified in the will and taking effect at death is called a **testamentary trust**. The most common reason for including a testamentary trust in a will is to provide for the support and care of dependent children. A minor cannot receive the proceeds from an estate directly. When property is left to a minor and the funds are not placed in a testamentary trust, the court will create a trust fund to manage the bequest in the minor's interest. By preempting the court, you can specify who will manage the fund, for what purpose the funds may be used, and when the funds may be paid out.

Since funding for a testamentary trust must be specified in the will, the trust funds are generally liable for both probate costs and estate taxes. An **inter vivos trust** is one established during the grantor's lifetime and is also termed a **living trust**. Funds in a living trust pass outside the will and the probate process, saving probate costs. This occurs because probate includes only those items held in the name of the deceased. The property in a living trust is held in the name of the trust.

Joint tenancy Each co-owner has an undivided interest in the property and the property passes to the co-owner at death.

Tenancy in common Each co-owner has an undivided interest in the property, but the property can be individually transferred.

Community property Property acquired during the marriage by the joint efforts of husband and wife.

Trust A legal arrangement in which property is held by one party for the benefit of another.

Trustee The one who controls the property in a trust.

Beneficiary The one who benefits from the trust.

Fiduciary responsibility Legal responsibility for managing the trust in the best interests of the beneficiary.

Grantor The one who establishes and funds the trust.

Testamentary trust A trust that takes effect at death.

Inter vivos or living trust A trust that takes effect during the grantor's lifetime.

Revocable trust A trust that can be changed or revoked by the grantor.

Irrevocable trust A trust that cannot be changed by the grantor once it is established.

Revocable and irrevocable trusts. Although funds in a living trust escape probate, they still may be taxable as part of the decedent's estate. The deciding factor for estate tax liability is whether the trust fund is *revocable* or *irrevocable*. A **revocable trust** can be changed or revoked by the grantor at any time. In reality the property still remains under the control of the person who established the trust and is, therefore, part of the deceased's taxable estate. The same is not true for an **irrevocable trust**. The terms of an irrevocable trust cannot be changed after it is established. Thus, the grantor loses all effective future control of the property placed in the trust, which eliminates future estate tax liabilities but creates immediate gift tax liabilities. Naturally, irrevocable trusts should be set up only after considerable thought.

In a living trust, the grantor, the trustee, and the beneficiary may all be the same person. Setting up a revocable living trust can provide for your own welfare while you are still alive and then for the welfare of your survivors after your death. If you are considering setting up a revocable living trust, you would probably be better off if you first discussed the matter with an attorney specializing in estate planning. You will learn that this arrangement has both advantages and disadvantages. Property placed in the trust is not so easily exchanged as property outside the trust. Moreover, you may still need a will. Such things as naming a guardian for your children can be accomplished only through a will.

Contractual Transfers

Life insurance proceeds are directly assigned to beneficiaries in the life insurance contract, thus passing outside the will and probate. This represents a contractual transfer. Other investments such as retirement accounts and bank accounts may also be directly transferred to beneficiaries at death.

In states that have adopted the Uniform Probate Code, a bank account with the designation "Arnold Steele, payable on death to Sharon Steele," would pass directly to Sharon at Arnold's death. In other states the same type of transfer may be accomplished through a **trustee bank account**, also called a savings account trust or Totten trust. The designation for this type of account would be "Arnold Steele, as trustee for Sharon Steele."

Trustee bank account An account that provides for contractual transfer at death.

Because no trust is actually created, the terminology used in setting up a trustee bank account is confusing. In the present example, Arnold would not owe Sharon any fiduciary responsibility. Moreover, Sharon would have absolutely no right to the bank account while Arnold is alive. However, at his death, the funds in the account would pass directly to Sharon, thus circumventing probate.

Life insurance and estate planning are to a large extent selfless acts. The time and effort you devote to proper planning show how much you appreciate those who have supported you. Be sure to revisit both of these topics every few years or when you experience a significant change. This will ensure the financial well-being of those who depend on your care and support.

key terms

adjustable life (p. 418)	contingent beneficiary (p. 412)
administrator(trix) (p. 428)	credit life insurance (p. 416)
beneficiary (life insurance) (p. 431)	death estate (p. 426)
beneficiary (trust) (p. 412)	decreasing term (p. 415)
bequest (p. 428)	deposit term insurance (p. 416)
cash value (p. 411)	dividend (p. 411)
cash value insurance (p. 416)	endowment life (p. 418)
codicil (p. 428)	executor(trix) (p. 427)
community property (p. 431)	face amount (p. 410)

family maintenance fund (p. 404)

family policy (p. 411)

fiduciary responsibility (p. 431)

grantor (p. 431)

group mortgage life (p. 415)

irrevocable trust (p. 432)

interest-adjusted net cost index (p. 423)

inter vivos trust (p. 431)

intestate (p. 426)

joint life policy (p. 411)

joint tenancy (p. 431)

legacy (p. 428)

letter of last instructions (p. 429)

life insurance protection gap (p. 410)

limited payment life (p. 417)

living trust (p. 431)

modified whole life (p. 418)

net payment cost index (p. 423)

nonparticipating insurance (p. 411)

ordinary life (p. 417)

participating insurance (p. 411)

per capita division (p. 428)

per stirpes division (p. 428)

premium (p. 411)

probate (p. 430)

renewable term (p. 414)

revocable trust (p. 432)

rider (p. 412)

single life policy (p. 411)

straight life (p. 417)

surrender cost index (p. 423)

surrender value (p. 411)

survivorship joint life (p. 411)

tenancy in common (p. 431)

term insurance (p. 414)

testamentary trust (p. 431)

testate (p. 427)

testator(trix) (p. 427)

transition fund (p. 403)

trust (p. 431)

trustee (p. 431)

trustee bank account (p. 432)

universal life (p. 419)

variable life (p. 420)

variable-universal life (p. 420)

whole life (p. 417)

will (p. 427)

yield comparison index (p. 423)

---

follow-up on the
Steele family

Reread the chapter-opening vignette.

1. Are the Steeles likely to have too much or too little life insurance? About how much life insurance protection should a family like the Steeles have?

2. Should the Steeles consider purchasing life insurance on other family members besides Arnold? If so, who else in the family might need insurance protection?

3. If the Steeles were to purchase additional life insurance, what types of policies would best fit their current and future needs?

4. Arnold and Sharon both have wills. Given the relatively small size of their estate, is it necessary for them to engage in estate planning?

---

problems
and review
questions

1. Explain the primary reason for having life insurance. For what other reasons might people hold life insurance?

2. What three funding categories are used to estimate life insurance needs? Explain the purpose of each.

3. Why might a family consider life insurance coverage for both spouses?

4. What types of family assets might be used to satisfy death protection funding requirements?

5. What is the difference between joint life and survivorship joint life?

6. One life insurance expert suggests that people should never buy participating life insurance, because the purpose of life insurance is to reduce risk, not to increase it. Discuss.

7. Renewability and guaranteed insurability are not the same. Explain the difference.

8. If a young family expects that its life insurance needs will increase in the near future, what policy options might they find desirable?

9. What is the distinguishing characteristic of term insurance? Why isn't deposit term true term insurance?

10. What kinds of insurance might offer the best protection against unexpected inflation? Explain why.

11. Suppose you wanted to leave your dependents with enough funds to pay off the home mortgage. Under what conditions would you prefer decreasing term insurance over group mortgage life, and vice versa?

12. If you perceive a need for insurance protection in your retirement years, might you prefer whole life over term life today? Why? Can you think of situations in which you might need insurance protection in your later years?

13. Suppose you took out a universal life insurance policy that charges a 20 percent sales commission on each dollar paid into the policy and pays a 10 percent annual return on the policy's cash value. What is the actual percentage return at the end of one year on each premium dollar placed in the savings component?

14. How does universal life differ from variable life? Which one entails greater risk?

15. What are the pros and cons of life insurance comparison indexes?

16. What are the basic objectives of estate planning?

17. What does it mean to die intestate? How might your estate be divided if you died intestate?

18. What can be accomplished only with a will? How would these matters be handled in the absence of a will? When certain changes occur, it's important that you review your will. What are these changes, and why is it important to review your will when they occur?

19. For estate planning purposes, what is the difference between *joint tenancy* and *tenancy in common?*

20. What is a trust? What obligation does the trustee have?

---

case 15.1

The Wright Family Maintenance Fund

Sue and Tom Wright are assistant professors at the local university. They each take home about $40,000 per year after taxes. Sue is 37 years old and Tom is 35. Their two children, Mike and Karen, are 13 and 11.

Were either one to die, they estimate that the remaining family members would need about 75 percent of the present combined take-home pay to retain their current standard of living while the children are still dependent. This does not include an extra $50 per month in child-care expenses that would be required in a single-parent household. They estimate that survivors' benefits would total about $1,000 per month in child support.

Both Sue and Tom are knowledgeable investors. In the past, average after-tax returns on their investment portfolio have exceeded the rate of inflation by about 3 percent.

Questions

1. If Sue died today, how much would the Wrights need in the family maintenance fund? Explain the reasons behind your calculations.

2. Suppose the Wrights found that Sue and Tom each had a life insurance protection gap of $50,000. How might they go about searching for protection to close that gap?

David Lombard is considering the purchase of a $100,000 face amount, nonparticipating, whole life policy. The life insurance agent tells David that the $100,000 insurance protection really won't cost him anything. The annual premiums on the policy are $5,000, and at the end of 10 years the surrender value after taxes will be $50,000. Therefore, David can get back all of his premium payments at the end of the 10 years.

David decides to make some calculations on his own. He figures that if he deposited $5,000 annually in a savings account that had a 5 percent annual return after taxes, he would have $66,034 after 10 years. He wonders if the insurance policy is really the great deal the agent says it is.

Questions

1. How much is the death protection provided by the whole life policy really costing David?
2. How might David figure out whether term protection would be cheaper?
3. What other factors might David take into consideration when deciding between term and whole life?

Exercises to Strengthen Your Use of the Internet
(Internet links for the following exercises can be found at **www.prenhall.com/frasca**.)

Exercise 15.1 Calculating Your Financial Worth to Your Dependents

The Life and Health Insurance Foundation for Education (**lifehappens.org**) provides two different calculators for estimating insurance needs. Under "Life Insurance" and "How Much Do I Need" you will find the "Human Life Value Calculator" and the "Insurance Needs Calculator." The "Human Life Calculator" estimates the financial loss to your survivors from your death. It calculates the amount needed in the family maintenance fund to replace the support you will provide your family. The present value of the investment fund is based on an assumed interest rate, inflation rate, and tax rate.

Enter the following information: Assume a young married couple with a child and choose what you feel are appropriate values for the inputs.

Q. Given these assumptions, what is the net present value of the lost support from the death of either spouse according to the Human Value Calculator?

Exercise 15.2 Calculating Your Insurance Needs

The Life and Health Insurance Foundation for Education (**lifehappens.org**) also provides an "Insurance Needs Calculator." The "Insurance Needs Calculator" takes into account additional financial expenses that may be related to your death. You begin by entering the cash needs at death, the mortgage payoff, and anticipated college funding. To this amount it adds the present value of maintenance for the surviving spouse less current investments and existing life insurance.

Enter the amounts you think are appropriate for a married couple with two children and a 30-year-old head of household.

Q. If this family does not have any life insurance, what is the life insurance protection gap?

Exercise 15.3 Get a Quick Estimate of Future Social Security Benefits

Want to know how much your survivors will receive in Social Security benefits? Review your Personal Earnings and Benefit Estimate Statement. If you do not have one, you can order a copy at Social Security Online (**www.ssa.gov**) . You can obtain an instantaneous estimate by using the Quick Calculator. You will find it under "Retirement" and "Calculate Your Benefits."

Q. Assume a worker age 30 with a child and earning $40,000 a year. At the death of the worker, how much would the child receive in monthly payments?

Exercise 15.4 What Is Your Probability of Survival?

Life tables, like those included in the Social Security Statistical Tables published by the Social Security Administration, can provide estimates on your probability of survival. For a given age group they predict how many individuals are likely to survive to subsequent ages. On the Social Security (**www.ssa.gov**) home page go to Actuarial Resources/Actuarial Publications/Statistical Tables/Life Table.

Q. Look at the life table. For an individual of your age and gender, what is your probability of survival over the next year? What is your probability of survival over the next 10 years? Hint: Given 100,000 males born alive, if 97,578 are alive at age 25 and 96,025 are alive at age 35, then the probability of surviving from age 25 to age 35 is .984 = (96,025 / 97,578).

Exercise 15.5 Playing the Longevity Game

How long can you expect to live? Northwestern Mutual Life's (**www.nmfn.com**) online life expectancy calculator factors in genetic and lifestyle characteristics to estimate your life expectancy. The "Longevity Game" can be found under the "Learning Center" menu. The probabilities of survival are based on data gathered by private life insurance companies and public agencies. Remember, you are calculating an average. This means that half the population with similar characteristics is expected to exceed this life expectancy and half is not.

Q. Enter you own characteristics. What is your life expectancy? Change one of the lifestyle characteristics you have control over. How does this change your life expectancy?

Exercise 15.6 Pricing Term Insurance

Numerous sites on the Web will provide a price quote on term insurance. Most, however, require that you be willing to provide the insurance company with some personal information. LifeInsure.Com (**www.lifeinsure.com**) seems to provide anonymous quotes. Price a $100,000 five-year term policy for yourself at age 25 and at age 45.

Q. How does your annual premium at age 45 differ from that at age 25?

Exercise 15.7 Checking the Ratings on Insurance Companies

Insure.com provides Standard & Poor's financial ratings on an extensive list of life and health insurance companies. "Insurance Company Ratings" are located under "Insurance Shopping Tools."

Q. How does First MetLife Investors Insurance Co. rank?

Retirement Planning

planning for your long-term needs

Objectives

1. To evaluate the features of a company pension plan
2. To analyze alternative company retirement plans
3. To list individual tax-deferred methods of saving
4. To estimate your retirement needs
5. To learn how to establish a personal saving plan for retirement

Steele family

Arnold's parents visited over the holidays. They spent a few days with the Steeles before continuing on to Florida for their traditional winter vacation. Both Arnold and Sharon were impressed with how well Arnold's parents seemed to have planned their retirement. They have enough saved so that they can afford to take several trips each year. Arnold's parents spend a couple of weeks in a southern resort in the winter and take an extended camping trip out West in the summer.

Sharon's parents are self-sufficient, but they do not seem to have the funds to enjoy many extras. It's been a long time since they have seen their grandchildren. They do not travel much and rarely go out for entertainment. Her mom told Sharon that she enjoys staying home and really does not care to visit what she calls tourist traps. Sharon wonders if this is just a convenient excuse. The real reason may be that her mom and dad have to watch their pennies a lot more closely than Arnold's parents do.

Arnold and Sharon have discussed how they would like to remain active like Arnold's parents have. They know they need to start planning now if this is to become a reality. The only investments that have been specifically tagged for retirement are those in Arnold's defined contribution plan at his place of work. The contributions can be invested in a choice of bond funds and stock funds. Arnold has allocated 100 percent of his previous contributions to a government bond fund. On his last annual statement, the total value of this fund was $41,000. His employer matches the first 5 percent on a dollar-for-dollar basis. Over the past few years he has contributed just enough to receive the employer's matching contribution. He worries that his retirement savings may not be on track to a comfortable retirement.

Sharon does not receive any employer-provided retirement benefits from her part-time employment. However, she expects to qualify for employer-provided retirement benefits when she returns to work full-time. As of now, the Steeles have put off planning for retirement until the future appears a little more certain.

TOPIC LINKS

Follow the **Topic Links** in each chapter for your interactive Personal Finance exercise on the Web. Go to: **www.prenhall.com/frasca**.

Most financial planners will advise you to begin planning for retirement as soon as you enter the workforce. If you put off retirement planning until your forties and fifties, altering projected retirement benefits during your remaining working years will be much more difficult. In addition, you will have missed most of the tax advantages that come from funding tax-deferred retirement plans.

You probably realize this is good advice, but if you are in your early twenties and retirement is far off, you may find it very difficult to follow. Unless you have a crystal ball, forecasting more than a few years ahead is usually fruitless. Changes in tax rates, interest rates, inflation rates, and Social Security benefits may all upset well-intended retirement plans. For this reason, a retirement plan should not be viewed as something set in concrete. It should change as circumstances change. And remember: The sooner you get started, the easier it will be to accommodate that plan to your changing financial environment.

Retirement planning is long-term planning that takes into account your family's needs and resources. Figure 16.1 illustrates a typical family's earnings and expenditures with respect to the age of the primary market worker. During the worker's twenties, thirties, and forties, both income and expenditures will likely increase. Savings accumulated during these early years will have more time to grow and accumulate tax-deferred returns until they are needed in retirement. Unfortunately, this is also the time when families like the Steeles experience the significant financial demands of childrearing, which culminates with the high cost of a college education. In the worker's fifties, most of the children will have left the household, and savings will dramatically rise as expenditures drop. Saving will be easier at this time, but the money set aside will have fewer years in which to accumulate returns.

Earnings for the average market worker begin to decline in his or her early sixties as work time decreases and leisure time increases. Many individuals who retire from a full-time position find alternative employment as part-time workers. Self-employed individuals may experience no clear division between preretirement and postretirement years as they reduce their market efforts. Financially, retirement may be said to occur when expenses begin to exceed earnings. Retirement years are ones of dissaving, when the wealth accumulated over the preretirement years is slowly depleted. This dissaving is illustrated by the change in age-related net worth (assets – liabilities) of households in Figure 16.2. The standard of living in retirement will depend largely on the family's accumulated savings and, therefore, on plans begun and actions taken many years before.

When and how much to save are personal decisions. There is not one "right" retirement plan for everyone. In saving for retirement, you are trading-off present consumption

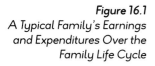

Figure 16.1
A Typical Family's Earnings and Expenditures Over the Family Life Cycle

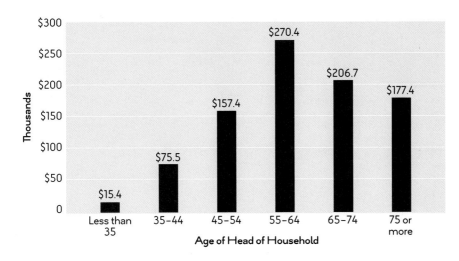

Figure 16.2
*Median Net Worth by Age
of Head of Household*

*Source: Survey of Consumer
Finances: 2004*, The Federal
Reserve Board. Values updated to
mid–2007 with the Consumer
Price Index

for future consumption. How much you plan to save will depend on how much weight you place on each of these needs. Your retirement plan may be to consume everything today and leave nothing for tomorrow. As long as you realize that this decision means someday you will have to survive on minimal benefits provided under an uncertain system of Social Security, we have no quarrel with your choice.

In this chapter, first we will examine the traditional ways of saving for retirement. Once you understand how you can save, we will address the question of how much you need to save to achieve your goals.

Saving and Investing for Retirement

Is saving for retirement different from other types of saving? Like most questions in personal finance, this one can be answered with both a "yes" and a "no." Retirement saving is different because in many cases the government permits it to be treated differently. Qualified retirement savings receive special tax treatment. In most instances the tax isn't forgiven; it's just deferred until the funds are needed in your later years.

Retirement saving is also different because the funding need is not immediate. This means the savings can be channeled into less liquid investments that possibly penalize short-term withdrawals but pay a high return on long-term holdings.

Other than these two characteristics, saving and investing for retirement are the same as for any other purpose. Accordingly, investments for retirement should satisfy all of the guidelines for investments discussed in previous chapters. Most important, there should be a proper diversification of holdings, and the acceptable risk-return trade-off should depend on the size of your nest egg. Only after you have provided for a needed safety margin in your later years should you consider speculative deals with potentially more rewarding and more damaging outcomes.

Company Pension Plans

Company-sponsored retirement plans have become an increasingly important source of income for retired workers. Recent estimates by the Bureau of Labor Statistics reveal that 70 percent of all full-time employees have access to a retirement plan (see Table 16.1).

Table 16.1
Percent of private workers with access and participating in retirement plans

	All Plans		Defined Benefit Plans		Defined Contribution Plans	
	Access	Participation	Access	Participation	Access	Participation
All workers	61	51	21	20	55	43
Full time	70	60	24	23	64	50
Part time	31	23	10	9	27	18
Union	84	81	69	67	49	41
Nonunion	58	47	15	15	56	43
Average wage less than $15 per hour	47	36	11	10	44	30
Average wage $15 per hour or higher	76	69	33	32	69	57

Source: National Compensation Survey: Employee Benefits in Private Industry in the United States, March 2007, U.S. Dept. of Labor.

Employee Retirement Income Security Act (ERISA) Federal act regulating tax–qualified, employer–sponsored pension plans.

Qualified retirement plan One that qualifies for special tax advantages.

The passage of the **Employee Retirement Income Security Act (ERISA)** in 1974 eliminated much of the uncertainty surrounding the payment of company benefits. ERISA sets down certain standards for funding of company-sponsored retirement plans, including guidelines for employee coverage and contributions. When a plan meets all of the government-mandated requirements, it becomes a **qualified retirement plan**. This means that taxes are deferred on employer contributions to the retirement fund and on interest earned by the retirement fund. Taxes do not become due until the benefits of the retirement fund are received by the employee.

A pension is nothing more than a promissory note. If you have a pension, what you have is a promise that you will receive certain payments at retirement. Before the passage of ERISA it was not uncommon to hear of workers nearing retirement losing all of the promised pension benefits they had been depending on. Some firms purposely terminated workers right before retirement so that they would not have to pay pension benefits. Other, better-intentioned firms found they simply could not afford to pay the promised benefits.

ERISA requires that all qualified pension plans be adequately funded. It established the Pension Benefit Guaranty Corporation (PBGC) to insure promised benefits against unexpected loss. However, an employee may still end his or her career without a pension. Employers are not required to provide employees pensions. Furthermore, ERISA does not set standards for minimum benefits. At retirement you may find that your benefits are not as generous as you thought. For these reasons, and because the pension plan is often a valuable component of the salary package, it deserves close examination.

TOPIC LINKS

Check out pension guaranties at the PBGC.

A careful study of the plan documents listed in Figure 16.3 will provide essential information on the operation of your pension plan. If you have trouble reading these documents, the personnel officer or plan administrator may explain the contents. Be sure you know the answers to the checklist questions in Figure 16.4.

The Advantage of Tax Deferral

Because qualified plans offer significant tax advantages, almost all company plans satisfy the ERISA requirements. To understand the advantages of tax deferral, look at the example

Participants in qualified plans are entitled to receive certain documents providing important information on the operation of the plan and their particular interest in the plan. In most cases, these documents will be routinely made available. If they are not, you should demand copies of the following:

Summary Plan Description This general overview of how the retirement plan operates should be written in a clear and understandable form. It contains essential information on the structure of the plan, explaining how benefits are calculated, when they may be received, and most important, how you might lose them.

Summary Annual Report It provides updated information on the plan and its financial status. If the pension fund depends upon an underlying portfolio of investments, it should indicate how well those investments performed over the previous year.

Personal Benefits Statement This may be included within the Summary Annual Report. It will indicate the total amount of your pension benefits that are currently accrued and vested. Each participant is entitled to receive an updated statement once a year. If you have not received one in the last 12 months the plan administrator (listed in the Summary Plan Description) must provide it within 30 days upon written request.

Statement of Deferred Vested Benefits for Terminating Employees If you leave your current employer, and you have a vested right to benefits, you should receive a statement describing those rights and benefits. Copies of this statement are kept on file by the Secretary of Health and Human Resources. If you lose your copy, or for some reason the firm will not provide you one, a duplicate is obtainable through the Social Security Administration upon written request.

Figure 16.3
Qualified Plan Documents

✓ What type of pension plan do I have (defined benefit or defined contribution)?

✓ Is it a qualified retirement plan covered by ERISA and insured by the PBGC?

✓ In order to participate, must I contribute to the pension plan? If so, how much?

✓ Can I make voluntary contributions to my employer's pension plan? What are the tax consequences of these contributions?

✓ Are my benefits fully vested? If not, how long must I remain employed before they are?

✓ How many years of credited service have I accumulated? How many hours do I have to work to earn a year of credited service?

✓ How is a break in service defined? What happens to my benefits if I have a break in service?

✓ What are my likely benefits at normal retirement age? How much would I receive at normal retirement age if I terminated employment today?

✓ How are my benefits at normal retirement age calculated? What is the benefit formula?

✓ Is there an early retirement age? If so, how are my benefits reduced for early retirement?

✓ If I become disabled before retirement, may I receive disability benefits through the pension plan?

✓ If I die, will my spouse or dependents receive any payout from my pension plan?

✓ What are the payout options at retirement? Can I receive a lump-sum distribution at termination or retirement?

✓ At retirement will I receive a single life annuity or a joint life annuity? If I am to receive a joint life annuity, how will benefits be reduced at the first death?

Figure 16.4
Checklist of Questions for Your Pension Plan Review

shown in Table 16.2. The comparison is based on an assumed flat tax rate of 28 percent. In Case One, the monies placed into the fund and the interest on the fund are taxed; in Case Two the tax is applied when the fund matures at the end of the 20-year period. In the first example, $2,000 in compensation is set aside each year for investment, but only $1,440 can be invested after taxes. Given an assumed pretax interest rate of 10 percent, the effective after-tax interest rate is reduced to 7.2 percent. After 20 years, this nontax-deferred investment fund will accumulate to $64,683.27.

Table 16.2
The Power of Tax Deferral Under a Flat 28 Percent Tax Rate

	Case One: No Deferral of Taxes		
Year	Contribution After Taxes	Interest Income After Taxes (After–Tax Rate 7.2%)	Ending Balance
1	$1,440	$ 103.68	$ 1,543.68
2	1,440	214.82	3,198.50
3	1,440	333.97	4,972.48
.	.	.	.
.	.	.	.
.	.	.	.
18	1,440	$ 3,593.48	53,502.97
19	1,440	3,955.89	58,898.87
20	1,440	4,344.40	64,683.27
		Taxes due at maturity	—
		Ending year's balance after taxes	$ 64,683.27

	Case Two: Deferral of Taxes (Deductible IRA)		
Year	Tax–Deferred Contribution	Tax–Deferred Interest Income (Tax–Deferred Rate 10%)	Ending Balance
1	$2,000	$ 200.00	$ 2,200.00
2	2,000	420.00	4,620.00
3	2,000	662.00	7,282.00
.	.	.	.
.	.	.	.
.	.	.	.
18	2,000	9,119.83	100,318.00
19	2,000	10,231.80	112,550.00
20	2,000	11,455.00	126,005.00
		Taxes due at maturity	(−35,281.40)
		Ending year's balance after taxes	$ 90,723.60

	Case Three: Tax–Free Returns (Roth IRA)		
Year	Contribution After Taxes	Interest Income (Tax–Free Rate 10%)	Ending Balance
1	$1,440	$ 144.00	$ 1,584.00
2	1,440	302.40	3,326.40
3	1,440	476.64	5,243.04
.	.	.	.
.	.	.	.
.	.	.	.
18	1,440	6,566.28	72,229.09
19	1,440	7,366.91	81,036.00
20	1,440	8,247.60	90,723.60
		Taxes due at maturity	—
		Ending year's balance after taxes	$ 90,723.60

In Case Two, the full $2,000 of compensation can be invested at a pretax interest rate of 10 percent. Taxes on both the contribution and the investment returns are postponed until the funds are withdrawn. When the fund matures at the end of 20 years, taxes become due. This is the tax advantage provided by a typical tax-deferred company-sponsored retirement account or a traditional individual retirement account (IRA). Applying the same

28 percent tax rate to the distributions, we find that you are still over $26,000 ahead on the tax-deferred investment. This is the power of tax deferral.

Case Three illustrates how funds would accumulate in a retirement plan with nondeductible contributions and nontaxable withdrawals. This is how taxes would accrue on a Roth IRA. Contributions to the fund must be made out of after-tax income. However, returns on the fund and withdrawals from the fund are tax free. In this example, the available funds at the end of 20 years are the same as in Case Two. This is because we are assuming that the marginal tax rate remains the same over the entire 20-year period. Consequently, taking taxes out of the initial contribution provides exactly the same result as taking taxes out of the final distribution.

If your real income declines after retirement, then the marginal tax rate will likely be lower when the funds are finally withdrawn. This would increase the return in Case Two relative to Case Three. On the other hand, for the lucky few that might find themselves in a higher marginal tax bracket after retirement, Case Three would be the preferred choice. It's clear, however, that tax-advantaged funds are almost always preferred to no tax advantage as in Case One.

There is one significant exception that results from the different tax rates on capital gains and ordinary income. Capital gains on the appreciation of such assets as stocks are taxed at a much lower rate than ordinary income. Because all disbursements from tax-deferred retirement accounts are taxed at ordinary income rates, investments that generate significant capital gains and very little income may do better in a nontax-deferred account.

Defined Benefit and Defined Contribution Plans

All pension plans can be classified as defined benefit plans, defined contribution plans, or some combination of the two. As seen in Table 16.1, most union workers have access to defined benefit plans, whereas white-collar workers are largely offered defined contribution plans. With the decline in union membership over the last few decades, a much larger share of the workforce has increasingly relied on defined contribution plans to fund their retirement years.

A **defined benefit plan** specifies the monthly benefit you will receive when you reach retirement age. Each year the employer contributes to a retirement fund an amount necessary to pay for those promised future benefits. The present contribution is actuarially determined; that is, it is based on assumed investment returns and probabilities of survival. Defined benefit plans are insured by a government agency, the Pension Benefit Guaranty Corporation (PBGC). Up to a given monthly limit, the PBGC insures the future payout of defined benefits. The PBGC does not insure benefits in defined contribution plans.

Under a **defined contribution plan** you are not guaranteed a specific benefit at retirement. Instead, your benefits will depend on the investment performance of the retirement fund. Employer contributions go into a separate retirement account for each worker, where they accumulate until retirement. The current value of this account should be indicated on the personal benefits statement (see Figure 16.3).

In most defined contribution plans, the funds accumulated in the retirement account may be converted at retirement to an annuity that generates lifetime income. The cost of the annuity and the income generated by the annuity will depend on financial factors at the retirement date. Sometimes personal benefits statements for defined contribution plans will contain an example of the monthly benefits that might be purchased with your retirement account. This example is only an illustration and should not be mistaken for a guaranteed monthly benefit.

Defined benefit and defined contribution plans have offsetting advantages and disadvantages as listed in Figure 16.5. With a defined benefit plan, you know how much you will receive, but you don't know how much those dollars will be worth. Inflation can

Defined benefit plan A pension plan that specifies the monthly benefit paid at retirement age.

TOPIC LINKS

Consumer information on retirement plans from the Department of Labor

Defined contribution plan A pension plan that defines the current pension plan contribution. Future retirement benefits are dependent portfolio performance.

Figure 16.5
Pension Unknowns

Accumulation Phase	Growth Phase	Disbursement Phase
Defined benefit plans		
How much is the employer contributing today?	When will the benefits vest? Will the pension fund be there when I retire?	How much will those defined dollar benefits be worth in the future?
Defined contribution plans		
How much do I need to contribute today?	When will the benefits vest? Will my funds earn an adequate return?	How many dollars will I have in the future?

severely erode the purchasing power of benefits that currently appear quite respectable. With a defined contribution plan, you know how much your retirement fund is currently worth, but you don't know how many dollars you will have at retirement. Remember, this will depend on future contributions and yet-to-be-determined investment returns.

Both defined benefit and defined contribution plans can be integrated with the Social Security system. When they are, your company's benefits and contributions may be less than expected. Defined benefit plans can be written so that benefit payments from the plan are reduced as Social Security benefits increase. Defined contribution plans sometimes include part of the Social Security tax in calculating the company's contribution.

Contributions

A few plans require mandatory contributions from employees who wish to participate in the company retirement plan. Those who elect not to participate should find out under what conditions, if any, they may later join. Most do not require employee contributions. However, many defined contribution plans permit the employee to make a tax-advantaged voluntary contribution into a 401(k) account, discussed later.

Vesting

Accrued benefit Accumulated pension benefit based on previous credited service.

Vested benefits Nonforfeitable pension benefits.

When you participate in a pension plan, you accrue pension benefits. The **accrued benefit** is the benefit that a pension plan participant has accumulated to a particular point in time. Some or all of your accrued benefits may be lost if you leave your present employer. Your rights to your currently promised benefits will depend on whether they are *vested*. **Vested benefits** are not forfeitable for any reason other than death. You may be fired, or you may quit, but in either case you still retain the right to receive all vested retirement benefits.

All qualified pension plans must satisfy the minimum vesting schedules in Figure 16.6 as established by the Pension Protection Act of 2006. ERISA requires that all employee contributions to a retirement plan must immediately vest. However, there may be a specified waiting period before employer contributions are partially or fully vested. Employer contributions are subject to either cliff vesting or graded vesting. Under cliff vesting none of the employer contributions are vested until minimum years of service are accumulated, after which contributions are 100 percent vested. Graded vesting gradually vests contributions over several years.

Credited Service

For several reasons, you may have fewer years of credited service than calendar years of employment. Under all plans, you are credited with a year of service only if you have worked a sufficient number of hours within a 12-month period. The required number of hours, typically 1,000, can be found in the Summary Plan Description.

Vesting Schedule	Employer Contributions			Employee Contributions
	Defined Contribution Plans	"Applicable Defined Benefit Plan" (Cash Balance Type Plans)	Defined Benefit (Traditional Plans)	All Plans
Cliff Vesting	Full vesting after 3 years of service, with no vesting before then	Full vesting after 3 years of service, with no vesting before then	Full vesting after 5 years of service, with no vesting before then	100% Immediate Vesting
Graded Vesting		Not applicable		
20% vested after	2 years		3 years	
40% vested after	3 years		4 years	
60% vested after	4 years		5 years	
80% vested after	5 years		6 years	
100% vested after	6 years		7 years	

Figure 16.6
Minimum Vesting Schedules

In the Summary Plan Description you will also find a definition for a break in service. Plans generally require that you work at least 500 hours per 12-month period to avoid a break in service. A break in service may delay the vesting of benefits and cause a forfeiture of nonvested benefits. Under federal law, qualified retirement plans cannot terminate non-vested benefits unless the break in service is greater than five years. Furthermore, firms cannot interrupt vesting for maternity or paternity leaves of one year or less.

Retirement Age

Most plans specify age 65 as **normal retirement age**. At this age, you are eligible to receive the full pension benefits. Many plans also specify an **early retirement age** at which you can retire with reduced benefits. A common requirement for early retirement benefits is the attainment of age 55 and the completion of 10 years of service. The reduction in benefits will depend upon the time interval between the early retirement age and the normal retirement age. You may be given a schedule of reduced payments or a formula for calculating the reduction factor.

Normal retirement age Age at which you are entitled to full retirement benefits.

Early retirement age Earliest age at which you can retire with reduced benefits.

For almost all occupations, the law forbids an employer from requiring you to retire at any age. If the normal retirement age is 65, you have a right to postpone receiving benefits until age 70. Furthermore, the company must provide you with additional retirement benefits for years of service beyond normal retirement age.

Calculation of Benefits

If you have a defined contribution plan, the calculation of benefits at retirement age is simple. The value in the account determines either a lump-sum payout or the value of the retirement annuity. The funds available at retirement will depend on annual contributions to the account and investment returns on the account. Your employer may provide several investment funds into which your annual contribution may be deposited. These may range from short-term bond funds to high-growth equity funds. A benefit formula, typically expressed as a percentage of your salary, will determine how much is contributed by your employer each year. Most plans permit employees to make voluntary tax-advantaged contributions to the plan. In addition, a majority of employers match employee contributions with additional employer contributions.

Flat benefit formula Pension benefits are equal to a specified percentage of compensation or a specific dollar benefit.

Unit benefit formula Pension benefits depend directly upon units of credited service.

With a defined benefit plan, you must apply a specific formula contained in the plan documents to calculate your monthly benefits at retirement. Most defined benefit plans compute benefits using a flat benefit, a unit benefit, or a cash balance formula. With a **flat benefit formula**, monthly benefits are equal to either a specific percentage of compensation or a specific dollar payment. Most plans use a **unit benefit formula**, where length of service is entered directly into the calculation of benefits. For example, the formula might state that your monthly normal retirement benefit will be $20 times your years of service. Alternatively, it might employ a percentage formula, such as 2 percent of salary times your years of service.

Regardless of whether the flat or unit method is employed, you will receive better inflation protection when benefits are stated not in specific dollars but rather as a percentage of your salary. This is so because your salary at retirement should reflect the higher cost of living at that time. Percentage formulas use either the career average approach or the final average approach. With the *career average approach,* percentage benefits are based on your average compensation over all years of service. It's more common for plans to use the *final average approach.* This bases benefits on a percentage of your average compensation over the last three or five years. Since the final average approach responds more rapidly to an inflationary rise in wages, it is usually preferred.

As you near retirement age you might decide to reduce the number of hours you work. This can affect pension benefits based on final earnings. Be sure to discuss the potential impact of these reduced earnings on your pension benefits with your firm's personnel officer.

Cash balance plan Pension plan with defined cash value benefits.

Lately, many employers have adopted a specific form of a defined benefit plan called a **cash balance plan** that looks like a defined contribution plan. The cash balance plan defines promised benefits in terms of an account balance for each employee. Each year the account is credited by a dollar amount that depends on years of service and an interest rate that is either fixed or linked to some interest rate index. The market returns on the plan's underlying investments do not affect the stated accumulations of the employee, since a defined benefit plan must have a promised benefit. When the employee retires, the account balance is converted into an annuity, or if the company plan permits, it's received in a lump-sum payment. Cash balance plans often permit employees who leave employment before retirement to receive the lump-sum value of the account balance.

There has been some dissatisfaction among older workers in companies that have converted an existing traditional defined benefit plan to a cash balance plan. Traditional defined benefit plans that base benefits on years of service tend to favor older employees. When a company switches from a traditional defined benefit plan to a cash balance plan, employees who expected to accumulate significant benefits at the end of their career may see that prospect eroded. In some firms, employees have sued employers for reducing what they perceived as promised benefits. To reduce dissatisfaction among experienced workers, some employers have permitted older employees the choice of accumulating future retirement benefits under the previous defined benefit plan or the new cash balance plan.

Medical Benefits

You do not qualify for enrollment in the Medicare program until you are age 65. If you presently have health insurance through your employer and you plan to retire before age 65, be sure you have adequate alternative coverage between when you retire and when you and your spouse turn 65. The Kaiser Family Foundation reports that about 60 percent of retirees age 55 to 64 receive some assistance from their previous employer in obtaining and paying for health insurance. Even so, after young adults, early retirees make this the second age group most likely to be without health insurance. Moreover, older adults spend over five times as much on out-of-pocket health care expenses as those under age 65.

finance news 16.1

Employers Expand the Number of Cash Balance Plans

Over the last decade, employers have been steadily replacing traditional defined benefit plans with cash balance plans. A plan conversion can have a dramatic impact on benefits for older workers. In general, a defined benefit plan credits a worker with future benefits for each year of service. Suppose a younger worker and an older worker are both promised additional monthly benefits at retirement based on their previous year of service. Assume this entitles each to an additional $10 a month in pension benefits beginning at age 65. Since the older worker is closer to retirement, that $10 a month annuity is a lot more attractive to the older worker than it is to the younger worker. It is also more costly for the employer. The present value of a $10 annuity that begins payouts 10 years from today is a lot more expensive than the present value of a $10 annuity that begins payments 30 years from now. Actuarially, traditional defined benefit plans tend to be backloaded, with most of the benefits earned in the last years before retirement.

Many workers in traditional defined benefit plans probably never realize that the value of the benefits each has earned over the previous year are significantly different. With a cash balance plan, the present value of the benefit is obvious. The worker's "hypothetical" account is credited with the present value of a future benefit. In addition, if the plan provides a cash-out option upon termination, the employee has a good dollar estimate of the lump-sum payment. This is especially beneficial for mobile younger workers who are changing jobs.

So, why do so many workers complain when an employer converts a traditional defined benefit plan to a cash balance plan? The problem is that the conversion is usually accompanied by a change in the distribution of future benefit accumulations. If the new plan promises identical cash additions to both the younger and older workers' "hypothetical" accounts, this likely represents a reduction in benefits for the older worker.

In response to these plan conversions, workers have sued employers, arguing that the company breached a promise of future pension accruals. Typically, however, the law only protects previously earned benefits; it does not require the employer to provide future benefits. A few companies have responded by canceling a planned conversion; some have provided larger cash balance credits for older workers; and others have allowed older workers to choose between remaining in the old plan or going with the new cash balance plan. This is a difficult decision; however, your likelihood of making the right decision is better when you understand how the time value of money affects your pension benefits.

Regardless of whether your employer subsidizes medical benefits for retired workers, you still may have the right to continued coverage under a group health plan sponsored by an employer with 20 or more workers. Your rights are set down in the Consolidated Omnibus Reconciliation Act of 1985 (COBRA). For 60 days after retiring, you may elect to continue group health coverage. If you make this election, you can extend the group health coverage for another 18 months, after which the group policy may be converted to an individual policy. The employer does not have to pay for your insurance after you leave employment. However, by continuing coverage under the employer-sponsored plan, you avoid having to satisfy preexisting conditions clauses that might exclude reimbursements under a new insurance plan.

When you do turn age 65, you most likely will qualify for enrollment in the Medicare program. Moreover, for six months after you turn 65, you cannot be denied private "medigap" insurance because of any preexisting illness. See Chapter 14 for details on both of these programs.

Disability Benefits

Most company retirement plans also include some type of disability income protection. Contributions by the company to the retirement plan may continue during periods of disability. In other situations, the plan may begin paying out monthly benefits at the onset of the disability, regardless of the employee's age. Furthermore, the monthly benefits may be computed under a more generous disability benefit formula. A review of the sections in Chapter 14 on disability insurance will help you determine the quality of this coverage.

Survivors' Benefits

Joint and last survivor annuity Periodic benefits continue as long as you or your spouse is alive.

ERISA requires that if you die before your retirement benefits begin, the vested portion of your benefits must be used to provide death benefits for your spouse. It also mandates that married workers automatically be provided a **joint and last survivor annuity** at retirement, unless both spouses elect otherwise. This means that payments will continue as long as either you or your spouse is still alive, although the amount may be reduced after the first death. Federal law requires that monthly payments from the survivor's annuity be more than 50 percent, but less than 100 percent, of the amount paid when both the spouse and the participant were alive. The law also specifies that the benefits cannot be reduced if the surviving spouse remarries. The alternative is a **single life annuity**, for which all payments cease at the pensioner's death. The value of the single life annuity and the joint and last survivor annuity must be actuarially equivalent. That means that the total expected payouts under the two annuity options should be the same. Accordingly, since the potential benefit period under a single life annuity is less than a joint and last survivor annuity, the single life option will provide larger monthly benefits.

Single life annuity All periodic payments cease at the death of the annuitant.

The choice is a difficult one. Do you select larger monthly payments over your life or lower monthly payments over both your life and your spouse's? Given life expectancies and interest returns, the two annuities are worth the same. Accordingly, if both you and your spouse need the cash flow generated by the joint and survivor annuity and you are both in average health, don't gamble on the single life annuity. You may do better under the single life annuity, but the odds are just as good that you will do worse, in which case the surviving spouse may suffer financial hardships.

Distributions

Distributions from a retirement account may occur for reasons other than just retirement. If you die, become disabled, leave your current employment, or suffer financial hardship, you may be entitled to receive the funds in your retirement plan. The distribution may consist of a single payment, termed a lump-sum distribution, or an annuity, a series of periodic payments. When you receive the distributions, you must pay ordinary income taxes on the proceeds from all tax-deferred accumulations. However, the tax consequences may be postponed further if you roll over the distribution into another tax-deferred retirement account. Generally, spreading out the distributions over your and your spouse's lifetime can reduce the tax due.

TOPIC LINKS

See IRS Pub. 575 "Pension and Annuity Income."

An early or late withdrawal of funds from a retirement account may trigger tax penalties in addition to income taxes. There is a uniform set of penalties on early and late withdrawals from almost all types of group and individual retirement accounts, including those discussed later in this chapter. An early withdrawal is defined as any withdrawal before age 59½. With a few exceptions, such as death, disability, excessive medical expenses, or a lifetime annuity, a 10 percent tax penalty is levied on all early withdrawals.

The penalty on late withdrawals is much worse. Payouts from most retirement funds must begin by April 1 of the next calendar year after you reach 70½. In addition, these payouts must be large enough to distribute the fund over your own or your spouse's life expectancy. If you fail to meet the minimum required distribution, there is an onerous 50 percent tax penalty on the difference between the actual distribution and the minimum required distribution.

Other Company Retirement Plans

Companies may offer savings vehicles that differ from the pension format discussed above in one of two ways: One, they may not provide the same type of scheduled contributions or benefits expected of a long-term pension plan; or, two, they may be used to save for needs other than retirement. Such plans are often offered as a supplement to, rather than an alternative to, a typical pension plan. By not tying the employer or the employee into a scheduled set of contributions, they allow each to supplement the basic benefits afforded by the pension plan whenever possible.

ERISA specifies limits on the total amount contributed to company-sponsored retirement plans by both the employer and employee. The guidelines, recently expanded under the Tax Relief Act of 2001, are complicated but generous. Most middle-income taxpayers are not likely to be affected. Moreover, workers age 50 and older may be able to contribute more than the normal limits under what have been termed *catch-up* provisions.

401(k), 403(b), and 457 Plans

The name for each account is derived from the applicable section of the Internal Revenue Code. These plans are provided by private, (401(k)) nonprofit (403(b)), and public institutions (457), respectively. Under each of these plans, you may defer a portion of your compensation for retirement through a salary reduction agreement. Although you may currently owe Social Security taxes on the earnings, federal income taxes are deferred until you receive the money. Alternatively, you may elect to have all or part of your contribution to these plans taxed like a Roth IRA. Under this option, the contributions would be out of after-tax income and all distributions from the account would be tax free.

Usually the employer provides a choice of investment vehicles into which the funds may be placed while earning tax-deferred returns. Furthermore, many employers offer matching contributions. These contributions, plus the current reduction in income taxes, typically make salary-reduction plans an excellent long-term investment.

Profit-Sharing Plans

A **profit-sharing plan** is a type of defined contribution plan whereby the employer makes contributions into an individual employee's account according to a predetermined formula. Qualified profit-sharing plans must satisfy many of the same rules governing qualified pension plans. Unlike a pension plan, however, the employee may not have to wait until retirement to receive distributions. The plan can be set to pay out after a fixed number of years. One disadvantage for planning purposes is that the firm must contribute only when it earns a profit.

Profit-sharing plan A defined contribution plan with contributions contingent upon the profitability of the firm.

Employee Stock Ownership Plans (ESOPs)

An **employee stock ownership plan (ESOP)** can function in many different ways, but most operate like profit-sharing plans. The difference is that contributions are invested primarily in the employer's stock, and contributions are not necessarily dependent on profits. In addition, all distributions must be made in the form of stock.

An employee stock ownership program is an inappropriate instrument for retirement savings. Because most of the funds are concentrated in the stock of one company, it does not provide any safety through diversification. The value of the fund is likely to swing widely as the company's fortunes change. You could lose both your job and your savings at the same time. Fortunately, federal regulations allow certain employees nearing retirement to place part of their ESOP account in diversified investments.

Employee stock ownership plan (ESOP) A savings plan that provides employees benefits in company stock.

Simplified Employee Pension Plans (SEPs)

A **simplified employee pension plan (SEP)** has advantages for both the employer and employee. For the employer, the paperwork and administrative costs are much less than

Simplified employee pension plan (SEP) An employer-sponsored retirement plan utilizing individual retirement accounts.

under a qualified pension plan. For the employee, all amounts deposited in the SEP are immediately vested. As an alternative to a qualified pension plan, the SEP plan permits the employer to set up a tax-deferred individual retirement account for each employee.

Savings Incentive Match Plans for Employees (SIMPLE)

The SIMPLE may be set up as part of a 401(k) plan or as an IRA. This is a new tax-advantaged retirement plan for small employers. Employees enter into a written agreement with their employer to defer some of their current income into a tax-advantaged retirement account. Over specified limits, the employer must also make matching contributions into this account.

Individual Retirement Plans

If you do not have a company retirement plan or you would like to supplement a company plan through additional private savings, the benefits of tax deferral can also be achieved through noncorporate-sponsored investments. The rules governing early and late withdrawals from individual retirement plans are generally the same as for company-sponsored plans. Distributions before age 59½ incur a 10 percent penalty tax. However, there are significant exceptions for withdrawals satisfying criteria related to hardship, medical expenses, disability, and death. Insufficient withdrawals after age 70½ suffer a 50 percent tax penalty on tax-deferred IRAs.

Individual Retirement Accounts (IRAs)

Individual retirement account (IRA) An individual retirement account that qualifies for special tax treatment under IRS regulations.

The **individual retirement account (IRA)** is a trust or custodial account approved by the Internal Revenue Service. In a trust or custodial relationship, the funds are temporarily held by someone other than the investor. However, you as the investor may still retain control over how the funds are managed. The IRS approval indicates that the form of the IRA satisfies the requirements for special tax treatment. It does not suggest anything about the

saving money 16.2

Consolidating Pension Accounts through Rollovers

If you opened several IRAs over the last several years, or you have pension accounts from previous employers, you probably have trouble keeping track of your retirement savings. Many small accounts can also be costly, since each is likely to charge a management fee. By consolidating these accounts, you can simplify your bookkeeping and achieve economies of scale in your investments.

On tax-deferred retirement accounts, taxes become due when the funds are withdrawn. Taxes, however, can be deferred further if the funds are redeposited in another tax-deferred retirement account within 60 days. This tax-free transfer of assets from one retirement plan to another is termed a rollover. In order to ensure that you don't violate the 60-day limit, it's best to arrange a direct transfer from one account to another, so that you never have receipt of the funds.

A rollover is also useful for deferring taxes on a lump-sum distribution from a qualified retirement plan. A distribution of previously nontaxable contributions to retirement savings might occur upon termination of employment. In most cases, this can have severe tax consequences. If your age is less than 59½ years, you will have to pay both ordinary income taxes and a 10 percent penalty on funds you withdraw. Using a tax-free rollover, however, you can avoid the penalty by postponing receipt until after age 59½ and allow your savings to continue earning tax-deferred income.

If you decide to take the distribution and not roll it over, there are still some ways to hold your taxes down. Under certain circumstances, the 10 percent penalty might be avoided. These include disability, receipt of an annuity, exorbitant medical expenses, and payment under a divorce or separation agreement.

merits of investing in this particular account. Poorly managed IRAs can offer low returns and high risks while still maintaining IRS approval of their tax status.

For the majority of Americans, an IRA is probably the most convenient, and most tax advantageous, means to save individually for retirement. Taxes on income earned by funds in a traditional account are deferred until the earnings are withdrawn. For many workers the annual contributions are either partially or fully deductible against current income. This effectively defers taxes on the contribution until it is withdrawn from the account in later years.

For certain special circumstances an IRA may also be a convenient means of saving for shorter-term goals. As stated previously, there are several exceptions to the early withdrawal penalty. Three notable items are exceptions for qualified higher education expenses, excessive medical expenditures, and first-time home buyers.

Eligibility

Every individual receiving earned income, or alimony, can contribute to an IRA. You may even open an IRA for a spouse with no earned income. You can contribute up to the lesser of your income or $5,000 to an IRA account for you and your spouse, and an additional $1,000 for each individual over age 50. After 2008, contribution limits are set to rise with the rate of inflation.

Part or all of the IRA may be taken as an adjustment to gross income on your individual tax return. The full amount is deductible for those who are not covered by a retirement plan at work. For those who are, the size of the deduction will depend on adjusted gross income before the IRA deduction. Tax deductible contributions are phased out according to an inflation adjusted income limit. For 2008, the deduction is phased out in the following income ranges:

- More than $85,000 but less than $105,000 for a married couple filing a joint return or a qualifying widow(er)
- More than $53,000 but less than $63,000 for a single individual or head of household
- Less than $10,000 for a married individual filing a separate return

Taxes on deductible IRA contributions are delayed, not forgiven. When contributions are withdrawn, taxes will become due on the portion of the withdrawal resulting from previously untaxed contributions and investment earnings. A deductible IRA contribution can be an excellent tax-advantageous investment for young adults with moderate incomes. They are able to capture both the immediate benefit of the tax reduction and the long-term benefit of tax deferral over the many years until retirement. As was demonstrated in Table 16.2, the benefits of tax deferral can be substantial.

There is a tax credit for contributions to individual retirement accounts for low-income households. The credits may also be applied to 401(k) plans and other types of employer-sponsored pension plans. The maximum credit is $1,000 ($2,000 if filing jointly); the credit rate varies depending on your income. Unfortunately, you cannot receive the tax credit if you are a full-time student or you are listed as a dependent on someone else's tax return. However, those just entering the job market are likely to qualify. This provides an incentive for early retirement planning by young workers. To qualify, you must earn less than an annually inflation adjusted maximum. For 2008, you may be able to claim a retirement savings contribution credit if your adjusted gross income is not more than:

- $53,000 if your filing status is married filing jointly
- $39,750 if your filing status is head of household
- $26,500 if your filing status is single, married filing separately, or qualifying widow(er)

TOPIC LINKS

See IRS Pub. 590 "Individual Retirement Arrangements."

Investments. You cannot invest your IRA funds in life insurance or in collectibles other than gold or silver U.S. coins. Nor can you borrow from the account, use it as collateral for a loan, or engage in investments that put you at risk for more than the value of the IRA. Other than these few rules, how you invest your IRA is a matter of considerable choice. You can place it in CDs, annuities, mutual funds, or real estate, or you can open a self-directed IRA through a brokerage house and organize your own portfolio of stocks and bonds.

The IRA is only one component of your investment portfolio. Where you should invest your IRA will depend on the risk-return trade-off that is acceptable to you and the diversity and risk in your non-IRA investments. In general, however, you probably want to consider investments that generate high ordinary income as candidates for inclusion in an IRA. Taxes are deferred on both deductible contributions and investment returns. It makes no sense to use the IRA for investments that generate uncertain tax-postponed capital gains, since taxes are already deferred.

Roth IRA

You cannot contribute to a traditional IRA if you reach 70½ before the end of the year. However, there is no age limit on contributing to a Roth IRA. With a Roth IRA, contributions are not tax deductible. However, the returns on the account and qualified distributions from the account are tax free. Typically, a qualified distribution is any withdrawal from the account after it has existed for five years and you have attained age 59½. Unlike a traditional IRA, the fund does not have to be distributed over the owner's lifetime.

Contribution limits are the same as for a traditional IRA, although these limits must be reduced by any amounts you have contributed to a traditional IRA. There is also a phase-out on allowable contributions for high-income individuals that is annually adjusted. For individuals with incomes in 2008 between $101,000 and $116,000 ($159,000 to $169,000 for married couples filing jointly) the allowable contribution is proportionately phased out.

For individuals who do not qualify for a tax-deductible contribution to a traditional IRA, the Roth IRA is a good alternative. In fact, for individuals who expect to be in a higher marginal tax bracket in their retirement years, a Roth IRA will provide greater benefits than a traditional tax-deductible IRA. The preferred retirement account will depend on the marginal tax rate during the accumulation phase and the marginal tax rate during the withdrawal phase. Assuming the same stream of contributions as in Table 16.2, the relative tax advantage of a traditional tax-deductible IRA to the Roth alternative for differing marginal tax rates is indicated in Figure 16.7. As also shown in Table 16.2, both accounts produce identical returns when the marginal tax rate remains unchanged. A Roth IRA may be an excellent choice for young part-time workers who owe minimal taxes.

Figure 16.7
The Relative Advantage of Traditional Tax–Deductible IRA*

| | Tax Rate Accumulation Period | | | |
Tax Rate in Payout Period	10%	15%	25%	35%
10%	—	$ 6,300	$ 18,901	$ 31,501
15%	$ (6,300)	—	$ 12,600	$ 25,201
25%	$ (18,901)	$ (12,600)	—	$ 12,600
35%	$ (31,501)	$ (25,201)	$ (12,600)	—

*Assuming an annual $2,000 contribution for 20 years and a lump-sum distribution in the twentieth year. The contribution to the Roth IRA is out of after-tax funds.

Keogh (HR-10) Plans

If you derive any of your earnings from self-employment, you can set up a **Keogh (HR-10) plan**. Suppose you work by day for a corporation with a qualified corporate pension plan, but by night you run your own business. Part of the earned income from your self-employment may be tax-sheltered for retirement in a Keogh, even though you are already participating in the corporate retirement plan as an employee. Moreover, the limits on contributions to a Keogh are more generous than those governing IRAs.

Keogh (HR-10) plan A tax-deferred pension account for self-employed individuals.

TOPIC LINKS

See IRS Pub. 560 "Retirement Plans for Small Business."

Retirement Annuities

In the early years of the family life cycle, when you have many responsibilities, it's important that you provide an estate for the protection of your survivors. In the later years, when you have fewer family responsibilities, it is more important to protect yourself against the possibility that your estate may run out before your death. Annuities can provide such assurance. These are often purchased as part of a tax-advantaged individual retirement plan.

Annuity contracts sold by life insurance companies are a convenient means of saving for retirement and of providing security in retirement. Coinciding with these two objectives, annuities have two distinct periods: the accumulation period and the liquidation period.

Annuity contract A contract that provides for periodic payments.

During the **accumulation period** the principal builds through investments and returns on investments, while benefits are deferred. The annuity contract may allow the buyer to make a single investment (a single premium annuity) or a series of investments during the accumulation period.

Accumulation period The term over which the principal in the contract is building.

You can purchase either fixed or variable annuities. The distinction has to do with the preservation of principal during the accumulation period. The value of a **fixed annuity** can only increase, whereas the value of a variable annuity can move both up and down. Typically, the interest rate on fixed annuities is guaranteed for a short period of time, such as a year. After this initial period, the interest rate can be changed at the discretion of the insurance company, so long as it doesn't fall below some guaranteed minimal interest rate, such as 3 percent.

Fixed annuity An annuity in which the principal is guaranteed.

The principal in a **variable annuity** is invested in a portfolio of securities. Therefore, the value of a variable annuity will increase or decrease with the changing value of the underlying securities. The future worth of the annuity will depend on the portfolio's financial performance. If it does poorly, you could lose some or all of your principal.

Variable annuity The value of the annuity is dependent upon the market performance of a specified investment fund.

Equity-indexed annuities are a hybrid product. The return on the cash value is linked to some market index, such as the Standard & Poor's 500 Index. You are guaranteed repayment of principal and a moderate annual return. In return for the reduced risk, you must share an increase in the equity with the insurance company. The policy may also place a cap on the maximum annual appreciation in your fund.

When the accumulation period ends, you can typically receive the accumulated cash value in a lump-sum payment or in the form of an annuity. In the **liquidation period** the owner receives the annuity benefit in monthly or annual installments. When you elect the type of payments to be received, you are said to annuitize the contract. The **annuity starting date** is the point in time when the liquidation period begins.

Liquidation period The term over which the annuity pays out periodic benefits.

Annuity starting date The date when the annuity begins periodic payments.

An **immediate annuity** begins payments one period from the date it is purchased. How much income an annuity might purchase is indicated in Figure 16.8. Annuities that defer benefits until some later period are called **deferred annuities**. During the accumulation period, when benefits are deferred, taxes on the investment buildup of principal are also postponed. This makes deferred annuities a tax-advantageous savings vehicle. As with other retirement accounts, income taxes become due when the tax-deferred accumulations are withdrawn. Likewise, there is a 10 percent tax penalty on early distributions before age

Immediate annuity Payments begin one period from the current date.

Deferred annuity Payments are deferred until some later period.

Figure 16.8
How Much Will
$100,000 Buy?

Suppose you purchase a single life annuity with a single payment of $100,000. The monthly payments begin immediately and end at your death. How much would you receive each month? The answers below indicate that the older you are and the higher the rate of interest, the better your monthly benefits will be.

	Males		
	Starting Age		
Interest Rate	60	65	70
9%	$929	$1,026	$1,165
8%	866	964	1,103
7%	803	902	1,041
6%	741	840	979

	Females		
	Starting Age		
Interest Rate	60	65	70
9%	$847	$910	$1,005
8%	783	847	943
7%	719	784	882
6%	656	723	821

Note: Calculations are based on the 1983 Group Annuity Mortality Table published by the Society of Actuaries.

59½. The early withdrawal penalty does not apply in cases of death or disability or when payments are received as an annuity over the life of the annuitant or his or her spouse.

In addition to the penalties levied by the government on early withdrawal, the insurance company may impose a surrender charge in the early years. Some policies contain a bailout provision that permits you to surrender the policy without charges if the rate paid on the annuity falls below some initially guaranteed rate. Together, tax penalties and surrender charges restrict the use of annuities to long-term savings objectives, such as retirement. Retirement annuities receive the same tax treatment as nondeductible IRA contributions, but there is no limit on the amount you may invest. Taxes on investment earnings are deferred until they are withdrawn during the liquidation period.

There are many ways you may collect the proceeds from the annuity. You can elect to receive a single life or a joint and last survivor annuity, already discussed in the section on survivors' benefits in qualified retirement plans. Under these options you are assured of receiving benefits no matter how long you (single life annuity) or you and your spouse (joint and last survivor annuity) may live.

Of course, if benefits are based entirely on survival, the possibility of an early death means you, the annuitant, may never receive the cost of the annuity in expected benefits. For this reason, many annuitants desire a *refund feature.* This guarantees that payments will continue until they have at least refunded the cost of the annuity. Should you die during the guaranteed period, payments would continue to your named beneficiary for the remainder of the guaranteed refund period.

The period of guaranteed payments need not coincide with the refund period. Annuities can be written to guarantee any number of payments. Of course, the longer the guarantee period, the smaller will be the annuity payment. A single life annuity with all payments ceasing at death will provide the greatest periodic benefit per dollar of cost.

Purchasing an annuity with guaranteed payments does not guarantee that the life insurance company selling the annuity will be around to make those payments. Given the recent volatility in financial markets and the long-term nature of the relationship, it is essential that you check out the financial stability of the company issuing the policy in *Best's Insurance Reports.*

Home Ownership

For many people, home ownership is an integral part of their retirement plan. They look forward to having the mortgage paid off and seeing an end to the monthly mortgage payments. Thus, equity in a home, equal to market value less the mortgage balance, represents an important source of savings for the elderly. The home ownership rate among those in the early retirement ages of 55 to 64 is close to 80 percent.

Obviously, owning a home is considered by many an important means of saving for retirement. Interest payments on the mortgage are tax deductible, and in most situations there is no tax on the capital gain. Consequently, home ownership can be an important source of savings for the future. There are, however, some potential disadvantages you should be aware of. Markets may rise and fall, and in efficient financial markets the past may be an inaccurate guide to the future. At the turn of this century no one was forecasting the current problems in the subprime mortgage market. What impact this may have on housing prices is presently uncertain. In this potential market, those who rely on the equity in a home for financial support in retirement may be very disappointed.

The main point is that you should always attempt to reduce your risks through diversification. Don't rely on home ownership, or any other single investment, as the only source of retirement income. As one component in a comprehensive and diversified savings plan, it is likely to be a sound tax-advantageous investment.

Reverse Mortgages

Having a good chunk of your retirement savings locked up in your home can also be a problem if you need those savings for maintenance expenditures. A reverse mortgage could let you have your savings and your home at the same time. With a **reverse mortgage**, also called an *equity conversion* loan, the equity in your home serves as collateral for the loan. What makes this loan unique is that repayment of principal and interest is deferred until the house is sold, regardless of when that may be. The loan may provide a line of credit, a lump-sum payment, or, as is the most common option, monthly disbursements. The monthly payout may extend over a fixed number of years or for as long as you remain in the home.

When the home is sold, the lender is repaid debt plus interest. Your obligation to the lender is limited by the value of the home at the time it is sold. The Federal Housing Administration (FHA) insures reverse mortgages up to specified limits, thus guaranteeing lenders that the equity would be sufficient to cover the amount owed at sale. The FHA also protects you by ensuring that your loan payments will continue if the lender defaults.

Reverse mortgage Retirees remain in their home while accessing the home equity for supplemental income.

TOPIC LINKS

AARP reverse mortgage calculator

Establishing a Personal Retirement Plan

We have already examined the various forms your retirement savings might take, but we have not yet answered the question of how much to save. The easy response is that you should save enough to meet your goals. All planning involves a statement of goals and a method for achieving those goals. In retirement planning the goal is a specific standard of living in your later years. Your standard is a personal decision.

Your present income, your ability and willingness to save, and your expected Social Security benefits will affect your goals. You might begin by setting a goal and then calculating how much you would have to save to achieve it. If the required savings appear out of line with your present abilities, then revise the goal and repeat your calculations. You should eventually arrive at a goal and a level of current savings that balance your immediate and future needs.

Financial planners often state that retirement planning should be thought of as a three-legged stool, with Social Security, company pensions, and private savings providing each of the essential supporting legs. The relative size of each leg is illustrated in Figure 16.9. As expected, the relative importance of Social Security benefits declines as retirement income increases. Those retirees with the highest income must generate a larger portion of their support from private pensions and personal savings.

Social Security Benefits

You should have a Social Security card with your current name. If you change your name because of marriage or divorce, notify the Social Security Office and order a new card (Form SS-5). Your employer reports your earnings using the name you supply. For the Social Security Administration to correctly track your earnings, it is important that they have them listed under the correct name and Social Security number.

A record of your historic earnings will be contained in your personal Social Security Statement. These are automatically mailed to all persons age 25 and over who are not currently receiving benefits. If you have not received one, you can request a copy at the Social Security Administration Web site or by contacting the office nearest you. Review your record of historical earnings that are listed on this statement. It is estimated that one person in 13 has not had covered earnings credited correctly. This is unfortunate because future benefits depend on historic earnings.

The Social Security taxes you pay each year do not go into an investment fund where they accumulate for your retirement years. The Social Security tax is simply a transfer tax. It transfers income from working Americans to those receiving Social Security benefits.

Figure 16.9
Persons Age 65 or Older: Shares of Aggregate Income for the Lowest and Highest Income Quintiles, by Source, 2004

Source: Income of the Aged Chartbook, 2004, Social Security Administration www.ssa.gov/policy/docs/chartbooks/income_aged/2004/. The income limit on the lowest quintile was $10,399 and the income floor on the highest quintile was $44,129.

Lowest Quintile
Public assistance 8.4%
Earnings 1.2%
Asset income 2.3%
Pensions 3.5%
Other 2%
Social Security 82.6%

Highest Quintile
Other 1.9%
Public assistance 0.1%
Social Security 18.9%
Earnings 40.1%
Pensions 21.2%
Asset income 17.8%

Congress is currently discussing options that would allow you to invest part of your Social Security contribution in an individual retirement account, but the prospects for any change in the near future do not seem good.

Because there is no investment fund, and because the government retains the power to tax, the system technically cannot go bankrupt. However, the average age of the population is expected to increase into the twenty-first century. There are currently five working persons for each elderly person; by the year 2030 there will be only two and one-half working persons for each elderly person. As this trend continues, the government will confront a difficult choice. It must either increase taxes on the working population or reduce benefits. In anticipation of future problems, some changes are already set to go into effect.

TOPIC LINKS

Use the Social Security Quick Calculator.

Retirement Age

For many years, the normal retirement age for full Social Security benefits has been age 65. You will probably have to wait a little longer. Normal retirement age increases in installments until it reaches age 67 in 2027 when it impacts all individuals born after 1960.

Additional incentives for delayed retirement should also hold down the cost of benefits. For each year you delay receiving benefits beyond age 65 up to age 71, benefits are increased. For those born after 1942, the yearly increase for delayed retirement is 8 percent.

There are no plans to change the early retirement age of 62. However, benefits at early retirement will eventually fall from 80 to 70 percent of monthly benefits at normal retirement age.

Retirement Benefits

To qualify for Social Security retirement benefits you must be "fully insured" at retirement. This requires 40 quarters of covered earnings (10 years). A quarter of earnings is defined as a minimum dollar amount, $1,050 in 2008, that is adjusted upward each year to reflect rising national wages. If you qualify for retirement benefits, other members of your family may also be entitled to monthly benefits. These may include the following:

- Your spouse age 62 or older
- Your spouse under age 62, if she or he is taking care of your child who is under age 16 or disabled
- Your former spouse age 62 or older and children up to age 18
- Children ages 18 and 19, if they are full-time students through grade 12
- Children over age 18, if they are disabled

Two-earner couples can each qualify separately for a pension, or one may qualify as a dependent on the other's earning record. A dependent spouse at normal retirement age will receive benefits equal to 50 percent of the benefits received by the retired wage earner. Whether you should qualify on your own record or your spouse's will depend on who generates more in retirement benefits.

In a complicated manner, Social Security benefits are based on the amount you paid into the system and your age at retirement. Your estimate of future benefits in today's dollars will be contained in the personal benefits statement prepared by the Social Security Administration (SSA). You can use the online Social Security Quick Calculator to get a rough idea of your future benefits in today's dollars. A few sample estimates from the Quick Calculator are listed in Table 16.3. Notice that benefits do not increase proportionately with covered earnings. Social Security benefits replace a declining percentage of market earnings as income increases.

| Retirement age | Current Earnings | | | |
| | $20,000 | $40,000 | $80,000 | $160,000 |
	Monthly Benefit and Percentage Replacement			
62 in 2007	$560	$822	$1,315	$1,598
	34%	25%	20%	12%
66 in 2011	$775	$1,155	$1,805	$2,178
	47%	35%	27%	16%
70 in 2015	$1,062	$1,604	$2,456	$2,936
	64%	48%	37%	22%

Source: SSA Quick Calculator, http://www.ssa.gov/OACT/quickcalc/

Retirement Test

Before 2001, if you were under age 70 and earned too much income, you could see your Social Security benefits reduced. The retirement test no longer applies to individuals who have reached normal retirement age. The year after you reach normal retirement age, you can now earn wage income without fear of losing any of your benefits.

The retirement test, however, still holds for those who receive early retirement benefits. It deters individuals with earned income from applying for early benefits. In 2008, benefits were reduced by $1 for every $2 you earn above $13,560. The earned income limits are increased each year for changes in the average national wage.

Taxation of Social Security Benefits

Income from other sources will affect your Social Security Tax. Up to 85 percent of your Social Security benefits may be included in taxable income. The calculations for determining the taxable portion are complicated. A simplified rule is that if the total of nonbenefit income plus one-half of Social Security benefits exceeds $25,000 to $34,000 for single individuals and $32,000 to $44,000 for married couples, then 50 to 85 percent of the earnings could be taxed.

Cost-of-Living Adjustments

One particularly attractive characteristic of Social Security retirement pensions is that they are periodically increased to offset the rise in average national wages. Most private pensions provide for fixed dollar benefits during retirement. Over time these constant dollar benefits will purchase fewer goods and services. Having Social Security as part of your retirement income ensures you will receive at least partial inflation protection.

Divorced and Surviving Spouse Benefits

Dependent spouses can receive 100 percent of the deceased spouse's benefits. If the dependent spouse was previously receiving spousal benefits at 50 percent of the basic monthly benefit, then total household income will decline by one-third after the death of the partner. Be sure to budget for these contingencies in your retirement plan.

Remarried spouses may qualify for widow's benefits, but they cannot receive both spousal benefits and widow's benefits. Divorced spouses may also qualify for benefits based on the ex-spouse's work record. They may even receive benefits before the ex-spouse applies for benefits and after the ex-spouse is deceased.

When Should You Begin Benefits?

Your need for financial support may determine when you begin your benefits. However, for many this will be a difficult financial decision. By delaying your retirement, you increase your monthly benefits but reduce the number of years that you receive benefits. The Quick Calculator at **www.ssa.gov** can be used to estimate when you break even by delaying retirement and thus increasing your monthly benefit. For example, if you retire at normal retirement age instead of early retirement age, you are likely to more than recover the benefits you lost in the early years with larger monthly benefits if you live beyond age 76. If you delay retirement between normal retirement age and age 70, you only come out ahead if you live beyond age 81.

The optimal decision, however, will depend on more than just your survival probabilities. As discussed previously, early retirement benefits are reduced by the retirement test. Moreover, alternative income may increase the marginal tax rate on Social Security benefits at any age. Therefore, your earning capacity and the timing of alternative income streams will also influence your decision on when you should begin receiving your Social Security monthly benefit.

Estimating Your Retirement Needs

You can begin you retirement planning by first estimating your retirement needs and then calculating the annual savings necessary to meet your targeted retirement lifestyle. Each year, as new information becomes available, it can be incorporated into your retirement planning, and a new savings requirement can be calculated. Although the target may move each year, if you take the indicated steps you should arrive at your retirement goals. The calculations in this section use the financial tools discussed in Chapter 2.

Future Income Needs

If your planned retirement age is far off, your future may appear highly uncertain. Do not let this prevent you from beginning you retirement planning. It's far better to gloss over uncertainties with simplifying assumptions, while building in a safety margin to cover potential misfortunes. Reaching your goals will become increasing more difficult if you delay.

Figure 16.10 contains a worksheet that may be used for retirement planning by either a single individual or a household with a single market worker. In households where both spouses have separate retirement plans, and they expect to retire at different ages or dates, separate worksheets may be prepared by each market worker. In the current example we are assuming a married couple dependent upon the wages of a single market worker. The market worker plans to retire at age 67, at which time the spouse will be age 65.

Begin your analysis by entering your current salary on line 1. On line 2, estimate the percentage of that salary you would have to replace to retain an adequate standard of living during your retirement years. This figure should be based on the assumption that you will not have any work-related expenses or dependent children to support. The historic rule of thumb is that you will need about 60 percent of your final salary to retain your current living standard during retirement. If you are planning on your home being fully paid for by then, this percentage may be reduced accordingly. Alternatively, if you intend to pursue an active lifestyle, as many retirees do today, you may want to input a higher replacement ratio of about 80 percent. With improved health care and specialized retirement communities, seniors are much more active today than they were even a few decades ago.

Figure 16.10
Retirement Planning
Worksheet

	Sample Data
1. Current salary	$ 60,000
2. Replacement percentage	× 0.60
3. Retirement income target	$ 36,000
4. Minus vested defined benefits	(0)
5. Minus Social Security benefits	$ 17,503
6. Required supplemental income from investment fund	$ 18,497
7. Income adjustment	
Number of periods until retirement 30	
Inflation rate to retirement 3%	
Future value of $1 (see Appendix Table A.1)	× 2.4273
Future value of supplemental retirement income	$ 44,897
8. Required funding at retirement	
Number of periods of retirement income (See life expectancy Table 16.5) 26	
Net discount rate (after–tax interest rate minus the inflation rate) 4%	
Present value of a $1 annuity due (see Appendix Table A.4)	× 16.6221
Lump sum needed at retirement to provide annual supplemental income	$ 746,283
9. Future value of retirement resources	
After–tax return on investments 7%	
Present retirement resources $50,000	
Future value of a $1 investment (see Appendix Table A.1) × 7.6123	
Future value of current resource	–380,613
10. Additional savings needed at retirement	$ 365,670
Future value of $1 annuity to retirement (see Appendix Table A.2)	÷ 94.4608
11. Current annual savings needed to achieve target	$ 3,871

The retirement income target on line 3 will have to be covered by pension benefits or investment accumulations. To estimate the needed investment fund, first subtract annual pension benefits. Line 4 contains defined benefit payments from corporate pension plans or independently purchased annuities. Enter only benefits that are vested and accrued—that is, future benefits you would receive at the expected retirement date were you to terminate employment and further contributions today. These should be estimated in terms of today's dollars. The purchasing power of future dollar benefits may be significantly eroded by future inflation.

FINANCIAL PLANNING *for* young adults 16.3

Participate in Your Company's Pension Plan

Young workers often make a serious financial mistake by not participating in their company's pension plan. An employer-sponsored defined contribution plan may require a voluntary contribution before any matching contributions contributed by the employer are deposited in the account. This is often a good deal for at least two reasons. First, the funds you deposit reduce your taxable income today and generate tax-free compounding. Taxes are delayed until the funds are withdrawn. Second, if the employer matches your contributions, you receive a significant return on your initial investment.

On a dollar-for-dollar match, you generate an instantaneous return of 100 percent on your investment. You can't find an investment better than that. Consider a short-term loan if you are temporarily short of the funds needed for a matched voluntary contribution. As long as the matched rate is greater than the interest rate on borrowed funds, you should come out ahead after vesting.

If you leave your current employment, any contributions you made are vested. At this time you can most likely receive these funds in a lump-sum distribution at any age. An early distribution before age 59½ can trigger income taxes and a 10 percent tax penalty. However, even after the 10 percent penalty you may come out ahead if you received a dollar-for-dollar match on your previous contributions. Of course, that assumes the employer's contributions have vested. Check your vesting schedule. Especially with cliff vesting, it may be worth delaying your search for a new job.

You may also have penalty-free access to these funds at any age if you use them for a qualified purpose such as a down payment on a home or a medical emergency. A discussion of these exemptions can be found in IRS Publication 575, "Pension and Annuity Income."

In spite of all these benefits, a significant percentage of young adults don't participate in their company's defined contribution plan. Recognizing that fact, the Pension Protection Act of 2006 now provides for an automatic plan contribution. Employers can set default contributions if they provide a matching contribution and vest all benefits within two years. There is an initial period during which employees can opt out of the plan. The hope is that by forcing employees to opt out of rather than opt into the pension plan more workers will participate.

Enter an estimate of your Social Security benefits on line 5. The Social Security Administration will provide an estimate of these benefits at normal retirement age and any other retirement age for which you may be planning. The estimates are in today's dollars, unadjusted for future inflation. Consequently, they may be entered directly into Figure 16.10 on line 5. If you do not have a personalized estimate prepared by the Social Security Administration, you can use the Quick Calculator at its Web site.

After subtracting annual payments under government and nongovernment pension programs, you have the annual income you must generate from investments in defined contribution plans and individual investment accounts. This is in today's dollars. To find your income needs in future dollars, future rates of inflation must be taken into account. (Present value and future value computations can be complicated. In order that you might understand the methodology, we will calculate these values using the tables in the Appendix at the end of the text and the tools presented in Chapter 2. If you prefer an easier approach, the online worksheet will automatically enter the needed values.)

Appendix Table A.1 provides the future value of $1 compounded over various periods at several different rates of growth. If there are 30 years to retirement and you assume a 3 percent annual rate of inflation, what costs $1.00 today will cost $2.4273 at 30 years from now. When you multiply 2.4273 (the future value of $1) by $18,497 on line 6, you will find that you will actually need a supplemental dollar income of $44,897 in the year you retire.

Your Retirement Years

You must next estimate your retirement years. Table 16.4 contains unisex single and joint life expectancies published by the IRS. The single life expectancy represents the number of years an individual is expected to survive. Of course, 50 percent will live fewer years, and 50 percent will live more years. The joint life expectancy is based on two lives; the expected number of years until both are deceased is the joint life expectancy. Given a married couple age 67 and age 65 at retirement, their joint life expectancy at that date is 25.4 years, which is rounded up to 26 years. If you want to build in a safety margin, you can add a few years to your life expectancy.

Required Funding at Retirement

Appendix Table A.4 provides the present value of a $1 annuity payable over various periods. If you multiply the present value of a $1 annuity payable over your retirement years by $44,897, you can find how much you would need to fund this annuity at retirement. Of course, if you want your standard of living to remain constant, what you really desire is an annuity that begins at $44,897 and then is adjusted upward each year for any increase in the cost of living. The present value of an inflation-adjusted annuity can be found by using a net discount rate, which is approximately equal to the rate of inflation minus the rate of interest. For example, if you assume an after-tax return on your investments of 7 percent and a rate of inflation of 3 percent, then the net discount rate is 4 percent.

According to Appendix Table A.4, the present value of a $1 annuity payable for 26 years at a net discount rate of 4 percent is $15.9828. However, this is the present value of an annuity that pays out at the end of each year. What you really need in this example is a payment at the beginning of the year in which you retire, and then 25 future payments, each at the beginning of a subsequent year. An annuity that pays out at the beginning of each period is termed an *annuity due*. The present value of an *n*-period $1 annuity due can be found by taking the present value of an (*n* − 1)-period $1 annuity and adding 1 to it. Accordingly, the present value of a 25-period annuity due at a net discount rate of 4 percent is $16.221. This is equal to $15.6221 (the present value of a 25-period annuity discounted at 4 percent) plus $1. Multiplying the present value of a $1 annuity due by the required supplemental income indicates that the lump sum needed at retirement is $746,283.

Future Value of Current Resources

Retirement needs may be funded by both previously accumulated resources and future savings. Current resources may consist of savings in defined contribution plans and personal retirement accounts. Those resources you have already accumulated will continue to earn investment income until they are needed. If you assume that the annual after-tax return on your current resources is 7 percent, then Appendix Table A.1 indicates that $1 of present funding will grow to $7.6123 in 30 years. Therefore, the future value of present resources at retirement will be $380,613 ($50,000 × 7.6123). Thus, the additional savings needed at retirement will be equal to the difference between future needs and the future value of present resources, or $365,670 ($746,283 − 380,613).

Annual Retirement Savings

You now have to determine a savings plan for closing the shortfall in future resources. The future value of a $1 annuity is given in Appendix Table A.2. This indicates how much you would have in an investment fund after the given number of years if you deposited $1 in the account each year and the amount deposited earned interest at the indicated rate. For example, the future value of a $1 annual payment made over each of the next 30 years,

Table 16.4
Single and Joint Life Expectancies in Years

Source: Internal Revenue Service, Publication 939, Unisex Tables V and VI, January 2003.

Single Life Annuity Life Expectancy (Earnings Multiple)

Age	50	51	52	53	54	55	56	57	58	59	60	61	62	63	64	65	66	67	68	69	70
	34.2	33.3	32.3	31.4	30.5	29.6	28.7	27.9	27.0	26.1	25.2	24.4	23.5	22.7	21.8	21.0	20.2	19.4	18.6	17.8	17.0

Joint Life Annuity Joint Life Expectancy (Earnings Multiple)

Age	50	51	52	53	54	55	56	57	58	59	60	61	62	63	64	65	66	67	68	69	70
50	40.4	40.0	39.5	39.1	38.7	38.3	38.0	37.6	37.3	37.1	36.8	36.6	36.3	36.1	35.9	35.8	35.6	35.5	35.3	35.2	35.1
51		39.5	39.0	38.5	38.1	37.7	37.4	37.0	36.7	36.4	36.1	35.8	35.6	35.4	35.2	35.0	34.8	34.7	34.5	34.4	34.3
52			38.5	38.0	37.6	37.2	36.8	36.4	36.0	35.7	35.4	35.1	34.9	34.6	34.4	34.2	34.0	33.9	33.7	33.6	33.4
53				37.5	37.1	36.6	36.2	35.8	35.4	35.1	34.8	34.5	34.2	33.9	33.7	33.5	33.3	33.1	32.9	32.8	32.6
54					36.6	36.1	35.7	35.2	34.8	34.5	34.1	33.8	33.5	33.2	33.0	32.7	32.5	32.3	32.1	32.0	31.8
55						35.6	35.1	34.7	34.3	33.9	33.5	33.2	32.9	32.6	32.3	32.0	31.8	31.6	31.4	31.2	31.1
56							34.7	34.2	33.7	33.3	32.9	32.6	32.2	31.9	31.6	31.4	31.1	30.9	30.7	30.5	30.3
57								33.7	33.2	32.8	32.4	32.0	31.6	31.3	31.0	30.7	30.4	30.2	29.9	29.7	29.5
58									32.8	32.3	31.9	31.4	31.1	30.7	30.4	30.0	29.8	29.5	29.2	29.0	28.8
59										31.8	31.3	30.9	30.5	30.1	29.8	29.4	29.1	28.8	28.6	28.3	28.1
60											30.9	30.4	30.0	29.6	29.2	28.8	28.5	28.2	27.9	27.6	27.4
61												29.9	29.5	29.0	28.6	28.3	27.9	27.6	27.3	27.0	26.7
62													29.0	28.5	28.1	27.7	27.3	27.0	26.7	26.4	26.1
63														28.1	27.6	27.2	26.8	26.4	26.1	25.7	25.4
64															27.1	26.7	26.3	25.9	25.5	25.2	24.8
65																26.2	25.8	25.4	25.0	24.6	24.3
66																	25.3	24.9	24.5	24.1	23.7
67																		24.4	24.0	23.6	23.2
68																			23.5	23.1	22.7
69																				22.6	22.2
70																					21.8

SIMPLIFYING
financial planning 16.4

Target Retirement with a Retirement Allocation Fund

You take your chances when you're young. As you approach retirement you want the quiet life. Well, not exactly the quiet life. You want to travel and try new things. Financially, however, the quiet life would suit you just fine. To prepare for financial independence, you will need to continuously restructure your portfolio as your expected date of retirement approaches. You can do this each year by gradually moving toward safer investments as you age or you can depend on a target retirement fund to do the work for you.

You can select a target fund that corresponds to the year you plan to retire. There are numerous mutual funds that target different retirement dates. Vanguard has funds that target retirement in five year intervals between 2005 and 2050. The funds assume an estimated retirement age of approximately 65. The

mix between stocks, bonds, and cash is gradually changed as the targeted retirement date approaches. Over time the portfolio is progressively shifted out of stocks into more conservative investments such as bonds and money market funds.

Each of the major categories (stock, bond and, cash) is invested in several underlying funds that also change as the fund matures. You should examine the types of underlying funds the target funds are invested in. There are many target retirement funds and they don't all target the same allocation of investments. Some start out with a more aggressive or conservative portfolio and then vary the mix differently. If you choose a target fund, be sure to choose one that matches your own risk preference. You don't have to choose a fund that exactly matches your date of retirement. You could choose a fund target at an earlier or later date, if you feel that portfolio better matches your lifestyle needs.

Changing Portfolio Allocation by Target Retirement Year

where these payments earn an annual after-tax return of 7 percent, is $94.4608. Dividing $365,670 (the additional savings needed at retirement) by 94.4608, you will find that equal annual contributions of $3,871 will cover the shortfall in future funding needs. Unfortunately, equal annual contributions do not take into consideration the declining value of the dollar. Consequently, a $3,871 payment in the early years will be more burdensome than the same dollar payment in the later years when your earnings are likely to be greater because of productivity increases and inflation.

Suppose instead of level annual contributions, you wanted to assume increasing annual contributions. Your initial contribution could be less than $3,871, if you were to contribute a larger amount in the later years. Given a planned increase in your annual contributions, the online worksheet for Figure 16.10 will calculate a stream of increasing funding that will allow you to meet your savings target. For example, if you planned to increase your annual contribution by 3 percent each year, your initial contribution would begin at $2,389. After 30 years, the annual contribution would have risen to $6,213 and you would have created an identical fund of $365,670. Assuming a 3 percent rate of inflation, the real dollar value of your $6,213 contribution in the thirtieth year would be the same as your initial contribution of $2,389.

You may use either graduated contributions or level contributions to attain your retirement goals. The most important choice you can make is to plan and to plan early. Change some of the assumptions in the worksheet and notice how dramatically savings requirements can change. We tend to think that the market conditions that exist today will inevitably hold into the future. A brief review of historic market conditions should convince you that market returns and rate of inflation could change unexpectedly and dramatically. Periodic updates will ensure that you hit your targeted goals. The closer you are to retirement, the harder it is to overcome poor planning in your early years. Be sure to review your goals and savings each year to guarantee that you are on the right path. Retirement is not as far away as you might think.

key terms

accrued benefit (p. 444)
accumulation period (p. 453)
annuity contract (p. 453)
annuity starting date (p. 453)
cash balance plan (p. 446)
deferred annuity (p. 453)
defined benefit plan (p. 443)
defined contribution plan (p. 443)
early retirement age (p. 445)
Employee Retirement Income Security Act (ERISA) (p. 440)
employee stock ownership plan (ESOP) (p. 449)
fixed annuity (p. 453)
flat benefit formula (p. 446)
immediate annuity (p. 453)

individual retirement account (IRA) (p. 450)
joint and last survivor annuity (p. 448)
Keogh (HR-10) plan (p. 453)
liquidation period (p. 453)
normal retirement age (p. 445)
profit-sharing plan (p. 449)
qualified retirement plan (p. 440)
reverse mortgage (p. 455)
simplified employee pension plan (SEP) (p. 449)
single life annuity (p. 448)
unit benefit formula (p. 446)
variable annuity (p. 453)
vested benefits (p. 444)

follow-up on the Steele family

Reread the chapter-opening vignette. Arnold is age 37 and Sharon is age 35. The children, Nancy and John, are ages 9 and 7.

1. Arnold has allocated all of his contributions in his retirement plan to a government bond fund. Is this choice consistent with long-term retirement planning?

2. The Steeles would like to plan for early retirement when Arnold reaches age 62 in 25 years. About how much would

they have to save each year in order to afford a comfortable retirement?

3. Suppose the Steeles delayed retirement until Arnold is age 67 when he qualifies for Social Security benefits. How would this affect their savings decision?

4. If the Steeles decided to increase saving for retirement, what tax-advantaged investments might they consider?

problems and review questions

1. "Retirement planning should be put off until you can accurately assess your later needs." Do you agree or disagree with this statement? Explain.

2. What does the term *qualified* indicate when describing a pension plan? Why is it important that a pension plan be qualified?

3. What is the difference between a defined benefit plan and a defined contribution plan? What are the advantages and disadvantages of each?

4. Why is it important that benefits be vested?

5. How does cliff vesting differ from graded vesting?

6. Up to what age must the company provide you with additions to your retirement benefits? You cannot be forced into retirement before what age?

7. Which approach for calculating defined benefits responds more rapidly to the effects of inflation: the career average approach or the final average approach? Why?

8. How does a pension plan differ from a profit-sharing plan?

9. Which tax-deferred retirement plans could a self-employed individual take advantage of?

10. How do fixed annuities differ from variable annuities?

11. Why is it unwise to place the majority of your retirement savings into your home?

12. What is normal retirement age for Social Security benefits? How is this expected to change?

13. How are Social Security benefits reduced for part-time employment?

14. Are Social Security benefits tax free? Explain.

15. Why might you prefer a Roth IRA to a traditional IRA?

16. You want to change the mutual fund you have your IRA invested in. How might you change funds without triggering a tax on your withdrawal?

17. When might deferral of taxes on a retirement account be an unwise choice?

18. How does health care planning before age 65 differ from health care planning after age 65?

19. Does the nonemployee spouse have any rights to a pension plan participant's defined benefits?

20. Why do the ages 59½ and 70½ have special significance for qualified retirement plans?

21. Change the income replacement target in the Retirement Planning Worksheet (Figure 16.10) from 60 percent to 80 percent. How does this affect required annual savings?

case 16.1

Steve Deutsch Plans for Retirement

Steve Deutsch's company pension and his expected Social Security benefits are his only sources of retirement income. He would like to retire in 10 years at age 62, but he is worried that these programs will not provide enough in early retirement benefits for him to live in his normal style. He figures he would need to generate an additional income of $10,000 from a supplemental investment fund for him to live comfortably in early retirement. He expects that the after-tax returns on his investments will average 9 percent, and future inflation will average 5 percent.

Questions

1. What is the target amount he would need in this investment fund?

2. What is his current savings target, given the target investment fund?

3. Where might Steve consider placing these additional funds for retirement?

case 16.2

Janet Myrnic
Considers Changing
Jobs

Janet Myrnic has been offered an executive position at a competing firm. The salary is substantially above what her present employer is paying. Therefore, it is very likely she will accept the offer.

However, before leaving her old job, she would like to review her participation in that company's pension plan and understand her rights. She has participated in the company's defined contribution plan for the last five years, during which the employer matched each dollar she contributed to the retirement fund. Combined contributions currently total $11,320.

Questions

1. Under minimum graded vesting, what percentage of these benefits must be vested?
2. Suppose the entire amount in Janet's retirement account was fully vested; how much is she definitely entitled to receive in a lump-sum payment at termination of employment?
3. Assuming she leaves some funds in the retirement plan, what document should she receive at termination?
4. What are her investment options if she decides to receive a lump-sum payment?

Exercises to Strengthen Your Use of the Internet

(Internet links for the following exercises can be found at **www.prenhall.com/frasca**.)

working out
on the Web

Exercise 16.1 The Cost of Waiting

New York Life (**www.newyorklife.com**) has a calculator that demonstrates the power of tax deferral. Under "Planning Tools" you will find the "Lump Sum Tax Deferral" calculator. Enter your monthly savings and your tax bracket, and it calculates how much more you would save at retirement by putting your funds in a tax-deferred account.

Q. Suppose you are in the 25 percent marginal tax bracket and you set aside $100 a month. How much will you have accumulated by the end of 25 years in a taxable account and a nontaxable account?

Exercise 16.2 Roth IRA or Traditional IRA?

BankSite (**www.banksite.com**) has a calculator that lets you compare accumulations from a Roth IRA and a traditional IRA. Depending on your current income and relative marginal tax bracket in your retirement years, one of these IRAs may provide a more favorable outcome. The "Roth v. traditional IRA" calculator can be found on the "Calculators" page.

Q. By assuming different marginal tax rates in the contribution and retirement years, provide an example in which the Roth IRA is the preferred investment vehicle. Now repeat your analysis and provide an example in which the traditional IRA is the preferred investment vehicle. How do you explain your results?

Exercise 16.3 How Long Do You Need to Plan For?

MetLife (**www.metlife.com**) has a "Life Expectancy Calculator." It provides the age at which you have a 50 percent chance of survival and a 25 percent chance of survival. Go to Individuals/Retirement/Retirement Toolbox/Life Expectancy Calculator.

Q. What are the ages at which you have a 50 and 25 percent chance of survival?

Exercise 16.4 How Much Do You Need to Save for Retirement?

Choose-to-Save (**www.choosetosave.org**) is a public program designed to promote personal financial security. Using the simplified methodology at this site you can generate a

"Ballpark Estimate" estimate of how much you need to save for retirement.

Q. What's your ballpark estimate?

Exercise 16.5 How Much Income Will $100,000 Buy?

ImmediateAnnuities.com (**www.immediateannuities.com**) lets you estimate the present cost of a future retirement annuity. The cost will depend on many factors. The major ones will be your present age and future retirement age, interest returns on the annuity accumulation, and the method of payout.

Q. Enter your gender and present age into the calculator. Find the cost of an immediate single life annuity that would pay out $1,000 a month beginning at age 40. Now find the cost of the same annuity at age 65.

Time-Value-of-Money Concepts

Chapter 1 introduced the basic concepts regarding the time value of money. This appendix provides greater detail about these concepts, and it includes present value and future value of $1 tables.

Future Value of a Single Payment

Finding the future value, *FV*, of a sum of money invested today answers the question: "How much will my money grow if I invest it today and leave it in the investment for a specified number of time periods, assuming it earns a specified rate of return each period?" For example, $100 invested for three years and earning 10 percent each year grows to $133.10 as follows:

FV end of year 1 = $100 + 0.10($100) = $110.00

FV end of year 2 = $110 + 0.10($110) = $121.00

FV end of year 3 = $121 + 0.10($121) = $133.10

The year-by-year solution is long and unnecessary, because there are two much quicker solutions. If you have a calculator, simply use the *FV* of a single payment formula, which is

$$FV = PV(1.0 + i)^n \qquad (A1)$$

where

FV = the future value

PV = the present value (the amount invested today)

i = the interest rate per period

n = the number of periods the PV is invested

In the preceding example, we have

$$FV = \$100(1.0 + 0.10)^3 = \$100(1.10)^3 = \$100(1.331) = \$133.10$$

The other approach for finding an *FV* is to refer to a future value (also called compound value) table. These are widely available, and they show the future value of $1 for various investment periods and rates. Table A.1 illustrates a future value table, and if you go down the left-hand column to period 3 (indicating three holding periods) and across to the 10 percent column, you find the number 1.3310. (Of course, this is the same number we have already calculated.) Since this shows the future value of $1, the final step is to multiply the *FV* of $1 by the amount of dollars invested, as we have already done.

Table A.1
Future Value (FV) of $1 at the End of n Periods: $FV_5 (1.01i)^n$

Number of Periods	1%	2%	3%	4%	5%	6%	7%	8%	9%	10%	12%	14%	15%	16%	18%	20%	24%	28%	32%	36%
1	1.0100	1.0200	1.0300	1.0400	1.0500	1.0600	1.0700	1.0800	1.0900	1.1000	1.1200	1.1400	1.1500	1.1600	1.1800	1.2000	1.2400	1.2800	1.3200	1.3600
2	1.0201	1.0404	1.0609	1.0816	1.1025	1.1236	1.1449	1.1664	1.1881	1.2100	1.2544	1.2996	1.3225	1.3456	1.3924	1.4400	1.5376	1.6384	1.7424	1.8496
3	1.0303	1.0612	1.0927	1.1249	1.1576	1.1910	1.2250	1.2597	1.2950	1.3310	1.4049	1.4815	1.5209	1.5609	1.6430	1.7280	1.9066	2.0972	2.3000	2.5155
4	1.0406	1.0824	1.1255	1.1699	1.2155	1.2625	1.3108	1.3605	1.4116	1.4641	1.5735	1.6890	1.7490	1.8106	1.9388	2.0736	2.3642	2.6844	3.0360	3.4210
5	1.0510	1.1041	1.1593	1.2167	1.2763	1.3382	1.4026	1.4693	1.5386	1.6105	1.7623	1.9254	2.0114	2.1003	2.2878	2.4883	2.9316	3.4360	4.0075	4.6526
6	1.0615	1.1262	1.1941	1.2653	1.3401	1.4185	1.5007	1.5869	1.6771	1.7716	1.9738	2.1950	2.3131	2.4364	2.6996	2.9860	3.6352	4.3980	5.2899	6.3275
7	1.0721	1.1487	1.2299	1.3159	1.4071	1.5036	1.6058	1.7138	1.8280	1.9487	2.2107	2.5023	2.6600	2.8262	3.1855	3.5832	4.5077	5.6295	6.9826	8.6054
8	1.0829	1.1717	1.2668	1.3686	1.4775	1.5938	1.7182	1.8509	1.9926	2.1436	2.4760	2.8526	3.0590	3.2784	3.7589	4.2998	5.5895	7.2058	9.2170	11.703
9	1.0937	1.1951	1.3048	1.4233	1.5513	1.6895	1.8385	1.9990	2.1719	2.3579	2.7731	3.2519	3.5179	3.8030	4.4355	5.1598	6.9310	9.2234	12.166	15.916
10	1.1046	1.2190	1.3439	1.4802	1.6289	1.7908	1.9672	2.1589	2.3674	2.5937	3.1058	3.7072	4.0456	4.4114	5.2338	6.1917	8.5944	11.805	16.059	21.646
11	1.1157	1.2434	1.3842	1.5395	1.7103	1.8983	2.1049	2.3316	2.5804	2.8531	3.4785	4.2262	4.6524	5.1173	6.1759	7.4301	10.657	15.111	21.198	29.439
12	1.1268	1.2682	1.4258	1.6010	1.7959	2.0122	2.2522	2.5182	2.8127	3.1384	3.8960	4.8179	5.3502	5.9360	7.2876	8.9161	13.214	19.342	27.982	40.037
13	1.1381	1.2936	1.4685	1.6651	1.8856	2.1329	2.4098	2.7196	3.0658	3.4523	4.3635	5.4924	6.1528	6.8858	8.5994	10.699	16.386	24.758	36.937	54.451
14	1.1495	1.3195	1.5126	1.7317	1.9799	2.2609	2.5785	2.9372	3.3417	3.7975	4.8871	6.2613	7.0757	7.9875	10.147	12.839	20.319	31.691	48.756	74.053
15	1.1610	1.3459	1.5580	1.8009	2.0789	2.3966	2.7590	3.1722	3.6425	4.1772	5.4736	7.1379	8.1371	9.2655	11.973	15.407	25.195	40.564	64.358	100.71
16	1.1726	1.3728	1.6047	1.8730	2.1829	2.5404	2.9522	3.4259	3.9703	4.5950	6.1304	8.1372	9.3576	10.748	14.129	18.488	31.242	51.923	84.953	136.96
17	1.1843	1.4002	1.6528	1.9479	2.2920	2.6928	3.1588	3.7000	4.3276	5.0545	6.8660	9.2765	10.761	12.467	16.672	22.186	38.740	66.461	112.13	186.27
18	1.1961	1.4282	1.7024	2.0258	2.4066	2.8543	3.3799	3.9960	4.7171	5.5599	7.6900	10.575	12.375	14.462	19.673	26.623	48.038	85.070	148.02	253.33
19	1.2081	1.4568	1.7535	2.1068	2.5270	3.0256	3.6165	4.3157	5.1417	6.1159	8.6128	12.055	14.231	16.776	23.214	31.948	59.567	108.89	195.39	344.53
20	1.2202	1.4859	1.8061	2.1911	2.6533	3.2071	3.8697	4.6610	5.6044	6.7275	9.6463	13.743	16.366	19.460	27.393	38.337	73.864	139.37	257.91	468.57
21	1.2324	1.5157	1.8603	2.2788	2.7860	3.3996	4.1406	5.0338	6.1088	7.4002	10.803	15.667	18.821	22.574	32.323	46.005	91.591	178.40	340.44	637.26
22	1.2447	1.5460	1.9161	2.3699	2.9253	3.6035	4.4304	5.4365	6.6586	8.1403	12.100	17.861	21.644	26.186	38.142	55.206	113.57	228.35	449.39	866.67
23	1.2572	1.5769	1.9736	2.4647	3.0715	3.8197	4.7405	5.8715	7.2579	8.9543	13.552	20.361	24.891	30.376	45.007	66.247	140.83	292.30	593.19	1178.6
24	1.2697	1.6084	2.0328	2.5633	3.2251	4.0489	5.0724	6.3412	7.9111	9.8497	15.178	23.212	28.625	35.236	53.108	79.496	174.63	374.14	783.02	1602.9
25	1.2824	1.6406	2.0938	2.6658	3.3864	4.2919	5.4274	6.8485	8.6231	10.834	17.000	26.461	32.918	40.874	62.668	95.396	216.54	478.90	1033.5	2180.0
26	1.2953	1.6734	2.1566	2.7725	3.5557	4.5494	5.8074	7.3964	9.3992	11.918	19.040	30.166	37.856	47.414	73.948	114.47	268.51	612.99	1364.3	2964.9
27	1.3082	1.7069	2.2213	2.8834	3.7335	4.8223	6.2139	7.9881	10.245	13.110	21.324	34.389	43.535	55.000	87.259	137.37	332.95	784.63	1800.9	4032.2
28	1.3213	1.7410	2.2879	2.9987	3.9201	5.1117	6.6488	8.6271	11.167	14.421	23.883	39.204	50.065	63.800	102.96	164.84	412.86	1004.3	2377.2	5483.8
29	1.3345	1.7758	2.3566	3.1187	4.1161	5.4184	7.1143	9.3173	12.172	15.863	26.749	44.693	57.575	74.008	121.50	197.81	511.95	1285.5	3137.9	7458.0
30	1.3478	1.8114	2.4273	3.2434	4.3219	5.7435	7.6123	10.062	13.267	17.449	29.959	50.950	66.211	85.849	143.37	237.37	634.81	1645.5	4142.0	10143.
40	1.4889	2.2080	3.2620	4.8010	7.0400	10.285	14.974	21.724	31.409	45.259	93.050	188.88	267.86	378.72	750.32	1469.7	5455.9	19426.	66520.	•
50	1.6446	2.6916	4.3839	7.1067	11.467	18.420	29.457	46.901	74.357	117.39	289.00	700.23	1083.6	1670.7	3927.3	9100.4	46890.	•	•	•
60	1.8167	3.2810	5.8916	10.519	18.679	32.987	57.946	101.25	176.03	304.48	897.59	2595.9	4383.9	7370.1	20555.	56347.	•	•	•	•

Note: n = number of periods; i = interest rate per period.

Future Value of a Stream of Equal Payments (An Annuity)

Very often an investment program calls for an equal amount invested each period. For example, suppose your budget allows a $100 investment each year. You are curious about how much you will accumulate at the end of three years, assuming you begin making payments at the end of each of the next three years. This total future value is calculated as follows:

FV of the payment made at the end of year 1 = $100(1.10)^2$ = $100(1.21) = $121.00

FV of the payment made at the end of year 2 = $100(1.10)^1$ = $100(1.10) = $110.00

FV of the payment made at the end of year 3 = $100.00

Total future value = $331.00

Just as in the case of the FV of a single payment, you can use a formula to find the future value of a stream of equal investments—that is, of an annuity. It is

$$FV = \frac{\left[(1.0+i)^n - 1.0\right] \times A}{i} \tag{A2}$$

where, FV, i, and n have the same meaning as before, and A = the amount of the annuity.

Substituting the preceding values, we have

$$FV = \frac{\left[(1.0+0.10)^3 - 1.0\right] \times 100}{0.10} = \frac{\left[(1.10)^3 - 1.0\right] \times 100}{0.10}$$

$$= \frac{(1.331-1.0) \times 100}{0.10} = \frac{0.331 \times 100}{0.10} = \frac{33.10}{0.10} = \$331.10$$

There are also future value of an annuity tables that can be consulted for a quick answer. Table A.2 is an example of such a table. To find the answer to the preceding example, again simply go down to period 3 and across to the 10 percent column to find the answer for the future value of a $1 annuity invested for three periods at a rate of 10 percent each period. It is 3.31. Multiply the amount of the annuity, $100, by this number to arrive at the correct answer: $331.00.

The preceding example assumes that the annuity payments begin at the end of the first period. However, you might encounter situations where the payments begin immediately. Let's assume that to be the case using the preceding example. This change offers no particular problem: Simply assume four holding periods instead of three and then subtract 1.0 from the FV coefficient. In Table A.2 the coefficient for four periods at 10 percent is 4.641. Subtracting 1.0 from this gives 3.641, which is the future value of $1 invested for three periods with payments beginning immediately. So $100 invested in this fashion would grow to $364.10, a somewhat larger amount than in the previous illustration. Of course, this answer makes sense because your money is invested one year longer.

Table A.2
Future Value of $1 Annuity: $FV = \dfrac{(1.0+i)^n - 1.0}{i}$

Number of Periods	1%	2%	3%	4%	5%	6%	7%	8%	9%	10%	12%	14%	15%	16%	18%	20%	24%	28%	32%	36%
1	1.0000	1.0000	1.0000	1.0000	1.0000	1.0000	1.0000	1.0000	1.0000	1.0000	1.0000	1.0000	1.0000	1.0000	1.0000	1.0000	1.0000	1.0000	1.0000	1.0000
2	2.0100	2.0200	2.0300	2.0400	2.0500	2.0600	2.0700	2.0800	2.0900	2.1000	2.1200	2.1400	2.1500	2.1600	2.1800	2.2000	2.2400	2.2800	2.3200	2.3600
3	3.0301	3.0604	3.0909	3.1216	3.1525	3.1836	3.2149	3.2464	3.2781	3.3100	3.3744	3.4396	3.4725	3.5056	3.5724	3.6400	3.7776	3.9184	4.0624	4.2096
4	4.0604	4.1216	4.1836	4.2465	4.3101	4.3746	4.4399	4.5061	4.5731	4.6410	4.7793	4.9211	4.9934	5.0665	5.2154	5.3680	5.6842	6.0156	6.3624	6.7251
5	5.1010	5.2040	5.3091	5.4163	5.5256	5.6371	5.7507	5.8666	5.9847	6.1051	6.3528	6.6101	6.7424	6.8771	7.1542	7.4416	8.0484	8.6999	9.3983	10.146
6	6.1520	6.3081	6.4684	6.6330	6.8019	6.9753	7.1533	7.3359	7.5233	7.7156	8.1152	8.5355	8.7537	8.9775	9.4420	9.9299	10.980	12.135	13.405	14.798
7	7.2135	7.4343	7.6625	7.8983	8.1420	8.3938	8.6540	8.9228	9.2004	9.4872	10.089	10.730	11.066	11.413	12.141	12.915	14.615	16.533	18.695	21.126
8	8.2857	8.5830	8.8923	9.2142	9.5491	9.8975	10.259	10.636	11.028	11.435	12.299	13.232	13.726	14.240	15.327	16.499	19.122	22.163	25.678	29.731
9	9.3685	9.7546	10.159	10.582	11.026	11.491	11.978	12.487	13.021	13.579	14.775	16.085	16.785	17.518	19.085	20.798	24.712	29.369	34.895	41.435
10	10.462	10.949	11.463	12.006	12.577	13.180	13.816	14.486	15.192	15.937	17.548	19.337	20.303	21.321	23.521	25.958	31.643	38.592	47.061	57.351
11	11.566	12.168	12.807	13.486	14.206	14.971	15.783	16.645	17.560	18.531	20.654	23.044	24.349	25.732	28.755	32.150	40.237	50.398	63.121	78.998
12	12.682	13.412	14.192	15.025	15.917	16.869	17.888	18.977	20.140	21.384	24.133	27.270	29.001	30.850	34.931	39.580	50.894	65.510	84.320	108.43
13	13.809	14.680	15.617	16.626	17.713	18.882	20.140	21.495	22.953	24.522	28.029	32.088	34.351	36.786	42.218	48.496	64.109	84.852	112.30	148.47
14	14.947	15.973	17.086	18.291	19.598	21.015	22.550	24.214	26.019	27.975	32.392	37.581	40.504	43.672	50.818	59.195	80.496	109.61	149.23	202.92
15	16.096	17.293	18.598	20.023	21.578	23.276	25.129	27.152	29.360	31.772	37.279	43.842	47.580	51.659	60.965	72.035	100.81	141.30	197.99	276.97
16	17.257	18.639	20.156	21.824	23.657	25.672	27.888	30.324	33.003	35.949	42.753	50.980	55.717	60.925	72.939	87.442	126.01	181.86	262.35	377.69
17	18.430	20.012	21.761	23.697	25.840	28.212	30.840	33.750	36.973	40.544	48.883	59.117	65.075	71.673	87.068	105.93	157.25	233.79	347.30	514.66
18	19.614	21.412	23.414	25.645	28.132	30.905	33.999	37.450	41.301	45.599	55.749	68.394	75.836	84.140	103.74	128.11	195.99	300.25	459.44	700.93
19	20.810	22.840	25.116	27.671	30.539	33.760	37.379	41.446	46.018	51.159	63.439	78.969	88.211	98.603	123.41	154.74	244.03	385.32	607.47	954.27
20	22.019	24.297	26.870	29.778	33.066	36.785	40.995	45.762	51.160	57.275	72.052	91.024	102.44	115.37	146.62	186.68	303.60	494.21	802.86	1298.8
21	23.239	25.783	28.676	31.969	35.719	39.992	44.865	50.422	56.764	64.002	81.698	104.76	118.81	134.84	174.02	225.02	377.46	633.59	1060.7	1767.3
22	24.471	27.299	30.536	34.248	38.505	43.392	49.005	55.456	62.873	71.402	92.502	120.43	137.63	157.41	206.34	271.03	469.05	811.99	1401.2	2404.6
23	25.716	28.845	32.452	36.617	41.430	46.995	53.436	60.893	69.531	79.543	104.60	138.29	159.27	183.60	244.48	326.23	582.62	1040.3	1850.6	3271.3
24	26.973	30.421	34.426	39.082	44.502	50.815	58.176	66.764	76.789	88.497	118.15	158.65	184.16	213.97	289.49	392.48	723.46	1332.6	2443.8	4449.9
25	28.243	32.030	36.459	41.645	47.727	54.864	63.249	73.105	84.700	98.347	133.33	181.87	212.79	249.21	342.60	471.98	898.09	1706.8	3226.8	6052.9
26	29.525	33.670	38.553	44.311	51.113	59.156	68.676	79.954	93.323	109.18	150.33	208.33	245.71	290.08	405.27	567.37	1114.6	2185.7	4260.4	8233.0
27	30.820	35.344	40.709	47.084	54.669	63.705	74.483	87.350	102.72	121.09	169.37	238.49	283.56	337.50	479.22	681.85	1383.1	2798.7	5624.7	11197.9
28	32.129	37.051	42.930	49.967	58.402	68.528	80.697	95.338	112.96	134.20	190.69	272.88	327.10	392.50	566.48	819.22	1716.0	3583.3	7425.6	15230.2
29	33.450	38.792	45.218	52.966	62.322	73.639	87.346	103.96	124.13	148.63	214.58	312.09	377.16	456.30	669.44	984.06	2128.9	4587.6	9802.9	20714.1
30	34.784	40.568	47.575	56.084	66.438	79.058	94.460	113.28	136.30	164.49	241.33	356.78	434.74	530.31	790.94	1181.8	2640.9	5873.2	12940.	28172.2
40	48.886	60.402	75.401	95.025	120.79	154.76	199.63	259.05	337.88	442.59	767.09	1342.0	1779.0	2360.7	4163.2	7343.2	22728.	69377.	•	•
50	64.463	84.579	112.79	152.66	209.34	290.33	406.52	573.76	815.08	1163.9	2400.0	4994.5	7217.7	10435.	21813.	45497.	•	•	•	•
60	81.669	114.05	163.05	237.99	353.58	533.12	813.52	1253.2	1944.7	3034.8	7471.6	18535.	29219.	46057.	•	•	•	•	•	•

Note: n = number of periods; i = interest rate per period.

Present Value of a Single Payment

To find the present value, *PV,* of a single payment, you just reverse the process of finding a future value. Referring to Equation (A1), you simply rearrange terms to get

$$PV = \frac{FV}{\left(1.0+i\right)^{n}} \text{ or } PV = FV \times \frac{1.0}{\left(1.0+i\right)^{n}} \qquad (A3)$$

Thus, the present value of 133.10 received three years from today is $100.

$$PV = \frac{\$133.10}{\left(1.0+0.10\right)} = \frac{\$133.10}{\left(1.10\right)} = \frac{\$133.10}{1.331} = \$100$$

Table A.3 shows a present value of $1 table. It is used in exactly the same manner as a future value table. The number in the period 3 row and 10 percent column is 0.7513, which is 1 divided by $(1.10)^3$. Multiplying 0.7513 by $133.10 gives $100.

Present Value of a Stream of Equal Payments (An Annuity)

The following formula can be used to calculate the present value of a stream of equal payments to be received beginning at the end of the first period and assuming that each payment is discounted at the discount rate applicable each period.

$$PV = \frac{\left[1.0 - 1.0 / \left(1.0+i\right)^{n}\right] \times A}{i} \qquad (A4)$$

If you receive $100 at the end of each of the next three periods, the present value of this stream is

$$PV = \frac{\left[1.0 - 1.0/\left(1.0+0.10\right)^{3}\right] \times \$100}{0.10} = \frac{\left[1.0 - 1.0/\left(1.10\right)^{3}\right] \times \$100}{0.10}$$

$$= \frac{\left[1.0 - \left(1.0/1.331\right)\right] \times \$100}{0.10}$$

$$= \frac{\left(1.0 - 0.7513\right) \times \$100}{0.10} = \frac{0.24869 \times \$100}{0.10} = \frac{\$24.869}{0.10}$$

$$= \$248.69$$

The same answer can be found by referring to a present value of an annuity table, such as the one shown in Table A.4, and finding the value for $n = 3$ and $i = 10$ percent. This is 2.4869, and multiplying it by the $100 annuity gives $248.69. Figure A.1 shows some applications of *FV* and *PV* techniques; exercises to test your understanding of the material follow.

Table A.3
Present Value of $1: $PV = \dfrac{1.0}{(1.0+i)^n}$

Number of Periods	1%	2%	3%	4%	5%	6%	7%	8%	9%	10%	12%	14%	15%	16%	18%	20%	24%	28%	32%	36%
1	.9901	.9804	.9709	.9615	.9524	.9434	.9346	.9259	.9174	.9091	.8929	.8772	.8696	.8621	.8475	.8333	.8065	.7813	.7576	.7353
2	.9803	.9612	.9426	.9246	.9070	.8900	.8734	.8573	.8417	.8264	.7972	.7695	.7561	.7432	.7182	.6944	.6504	.6104	.5739	.5407
3	.9706	.9423	.9151	.8890	.8638	.8396	.8163	.7938	.7722	.7513	.7118	.6750	.6575	.6407	.6086	.5787	.5245	.4768	.4348	.3975
4	.9610	.9238	.8885	.8548	.8227	.7921	.7629	.7350	.7084	.6830	.6355	.5921	.5718	.5523	.5158	.4823	.4230	.3725	.3294	.2923
5	.9515	.9057	.8626	.8219	.7835	.7473	.7130	.6806	.6499	.6209	.5674	.5194	.4972	.4761	.4371	.4019	.3411	.2910	.2495	.2149
6	.9420	.8880	.8375	.7903	.7462	.7050	.6663	.6302	.5963	.5645	.5066	.4556	.4323	.4104	.3704	.3349	.2751	.2274	.1890	.1580
7	.9327	.8706	.8131	.7599	.7107	.6651	.6227	.5835	.5470	.5132	.4523	.3996	.3759	.3538	.3139	.2791	.2218	.1776	.1432	.1162
8	.9235	.8535	.7894	.7307	.6768	.6274	.5820	.5403	.5019	.4665	.4039	.3506	.3269	.3050	.2660	.2326	.1789	.1388	.1085	.0854
9	.9143	.8368	.7664	.7026	.6446	.5919	.5439	.5002	.4604	.4241	.3606	.3075	.2843	.2630	.2255	.1938	.1443	.1084	.0822	.0628
10	.9053	.8203	.7441	.6756	.6139	.5584	.5083	.4632	.4224	.3855	.3220	.2697	.2472	.2267	.1911	.1615	.1164	.0847	.0623	.0462
11	.8963	.8043	.7224	.6496	.5847	.5268	.4751	.4289	.3875	.3505	.2875	.2366	.2149	.1954	.1619	.1346	.0938	.0662	.0472	.0340
12	.8874	.7885	.7014	.6246	.5568	.4970	.4440	.3971	.3555	.3186	.2567	.2076	.1869	.1685	.1372	.1122	.0757	.0517	.0357	.0250
13	.8787	.7730	.6810	.6006	.5303	.4688	.4150	.3677	.3262	.2897	.2292	.1821	.1625	.1452	.1163	.0935	.0610	.0404	.0271	.0184
14	.8700	.7579	.6611	.5775	.5051	.4423	.3878	.3405	.2992	.2633	.2046	.1597	.1413	.1252	.0985	.0779	.0492	.0316	.0205	.0135
15	.8613	.7430	.6419	.5553	.4810	.4173	.3624	.3152	.2745	.2394	.1827	.1401	.1229	.1079	.0835	.0649	.0397	.0247	.0155	.0099
16	.8528	.7284	.6232	.5339	.4581	.3936	.3387	.2919	.2519	.2176	.1631	.1229	.1069	.0930	.0708	.0541	.0320	.0193	.0118	.0073
17	.8444	.7142	.6050	.5134	.4363	.3714	.3166	.2703	.2311	.1978	.1456	.1078	.0929	.0802	.0600	.0451	.0258	.0150	.0089	.0054
18	.8360	.7002	.5874	.4936	.4155	.3503	.2959	.2502	.2120	.1799	.1300	.0946	.0808	.0691	.0508	.0376	.0208	.0118	.0068	.0039
19	.8277	.6864	.5703	.4746	.3957	.3305	.2765	.2317	.1945	.1635	.1161	.0829	.0703	.0596	.0431	.0313	.0168	.0092	.0051	.0029
20	.8195	.6730	.5537	.4564	.3769	.3118	.2584	.2145	.1784	.1486	.1037	.0728	.0611	.0514	.0365	.0261	.0135	.0072	.0039	.0021
21	.8114	.6598	.5375	.4388	.3589	.2942	.2415	.1987	.1637	.1351	.0926	.0638	.0531	.0443	.0309	.0217	.0109	.0056	.0029	.0016
22	.8034	.6468	.5219	.4220	.3418	.2775	.2257	.1839	.1502	.1228	.0826	.0560	.0462	.0382	.0262	.0181	.0088	.0044	.0022	.0012
23	.7954	.6342	.5067	.4057	.3256	.2618	.2109	.1703	.1378	.1117	.0738	.0491	.0402	.0329	.0222	.0151	.0071	.0034	.0017	.0008
24	.7876	.6217	.4919	.3901	.3101	.2470	.1971	.1577	.1264	.1015	.0659	.0431	.0349	.0284	.0188	.0126	.0057	.0027	.0013	.0006
25	.7798	.6095	.4776	.3751	.2953	.2330	.1842	.1460	.1160	.0923	.0588	.0378	.0304	.0245	.0160	.0105	.0046	.0021	.0010	.0005
26	.7720	.5976	.4637	.3607	.2812	.2198	.1722	.1352	.1064	.0839	.0525	.0331	.0264	.0211	.0135	.0087	.0037	.0016	.0007	.0003
27	.7644	.5859	.4502	.3468	.2678	.2074	.1609	.1252	.0976	.0763	.0469	.0291	.0230	.0182	.0115	.0073	.0030	.0013	.0006	.0002
28	.7568	.5744	.4371	.3335	.2551	.1956	.1504	.1159	.0895	.0693	.0419	.0255	.0200	.0157	.0097	.0061	.0024	.0010	.0004	.0002
29	.7493	.5631	.4243	.3207	.2429	.1846	.1406	.1073	.0822	.0630	.0374	.0224	.0174	.0135	.0082	.0051	.0020	.0008	.0003	.0001
30	.7419	.5521	.4120	.3083	.2314	.1741	.1314	.0994	.0754	.0573	.0334	.0196	.0151	.0116	.0070	.0042	.0016	.0006	.0002	.0001
40	.6717	.4529	.3066	.2083	.1420	.0972	.0668	.0460	.0318	.0221	.0107	.0053	.0037	.0026	.0013	.0007	.0002	.0001	•	•
50	.6080	.3715	.2281	.1407	.0872	.0543	.0339	.0213	.0134	.0085	.0035	.0014	.0009	.0006	.0003	.0001	•	•	•	•
60	.5504	.3048	.1697	.0951	.0535	.0303	.0173	.0099	.0057	.0033	.0011	.0004	.0002	.0001	•	•	•	•	•	•

Note: n = number of periods; i = interest rate per period.

Table A.4
Present Value of an Annuity of $1 per Period for n Periods; $PV = \dfrac{1.0 - \dfrac{1.0}{(1.0+i)^n}}{i}$

Number of Periods	1%	2%	3%	4%	5%	6%	7%	8%	9%	10%	12%	14%	15%	16%	18%	20%	24%	28%	32%
1	0.9901	0.9804	0.9709	0.9615	0.9524	0.9434	0.9346	0.9259	0.9174	0.9091	0.8929	0.8772	0.8696	0.8621	0.8475	0.8333	0.8065	0.7813	0.7576
2	1.9704	1.9416	1.9135	1.8861	1.8594	1.8334	1.8080	1.7833	1.7591	1.7355	1.6901	1.6467	1.6257	1.6052	1.5656	1.5278	1.4568	1.3916	1.3315
3	2.9410	2.8839	2.8286	2.7751	2.7232	2.6730	2.6243	2.5771	2.5313	2.4869	2.4018	2.3216	2.2832	2.2459	2.1743	2.1065	1.9813	1.8684	1.7663
4	3.9020	3.8077	3.7171	3.6299	3.5460	3.4651	3.3872	3.3121	3.2397	3.1699	3.0373	2.9137	2.8550	2.7982	2.6901	2.5887	2.4043	2.2410	2.0957
5	4.8534	4.7135	4.5797	4.4518	4.3295	4.2124	4.1002	3.9927	3.8897	3.7908	3.6048	3.4331	3.3522	3.2743	3.1272	2.9906	2.7454	2.5320	2.3452
6	5.7955	5.6014	5.4172	5.2421	5.0757	4.9173	4.7665	4.6229	4.4859	4.3553	4.1114	3.8887	3.7845	3.6847	3.4976	3.3255	3.0205	2.7594	2.5342
7	6.7282	6.4720	6.2303	6.0021	5.7864	5.5824	5.3893	5.2064	5.0330	4.8684	4.5638	4.2883	4.1604	4.0386	3.8115	3.6046	3.2423	2.9370	2.6775
8	7.6517	7.3255	7.0179	6.7327	6.4632	6.2098	5.9713	5.7466	5.5348	5.3349	4.9676	4.6389	4.4873	4.3436	4.0776	3.8372	3.4212	3.0758	2.7860
9	8.5660	8.1622	7.7861	7.4353	7.1078	6.8017	6.5152	6.2469	5.9952	5.7590	5.3282	4.9464	4.7716	4.6065	4.3030	4.0310	3.5655	3.1842	2.8681
10	9.4713	8.9826	8.5302	8.1109	7.7217	7.3601	7.0236	6.7101	6.4177	6.1446	5.6502	5.2161	5.0188	4.8332	4.4941	4.1925	3.6819	3.2689	2.9304
11	10.3676	9.7868	9.2526	8.7605	8.3064	7.8869	7.4987	7.1390	6.8052	6.4951	5.9377	5.4527	5.2337	5.0286	4.6560	4.3271	3.7757	3.3351	2.9776
12	11.2551	10.5753	9.9540	9.3851	8.8633	8.3838	7.9427	7.5361	7.1607	6.8137	6.1944	5.6603	5.4206	5.1971	4.7932	4.4392	3.8514	3.3868	3.0133
13	12.1337	11.3484	10.6350	9.9856	9.3936	8.8527	8.3577	7.9038	7.4869	7.1034	6.4235	5.8424	5.5831	5.3423	4.9095	4.5327	3.9124	3.4272	3.0404
14	13.0037	12.1062	11.2961	10.5631	9.8986	9.2950	8.7455	8.2442	7.7862	7.3667	6.6282	6.0021	5.7245	5.4675	5.0081	4.6106	3.9616	3.4587	3.0609
15	13.8651	12.8493	11.9379	11.1184	10.3797	9.7122	9.1079	8.5595	8.0607	7.6061	6.8109	6.1422	5.8474	5.5755	5.0916	4.6755	4.0013	3.4834	3.0764
16	14.7179	13.5777	12.5611	11.6523	10.8378	10.1059	9.4466	8.8514	8.3126	7.8237	6.9740	6.2651	5.9542	5.6685	5.1624	4.7296	4.0333	3.5026	3.0882
17	15.5623	14.2919	13.1661	12.1657	11.2741	10.4773	9.7632	9.1216	8.5436	8.0216	7.1196	6.3729	6.0472	5.7487	5.2223	4.7746	4.0591	3.5177	3.0971
18	16.3983	14.9920	13.7535	12.6593	11.6896	10.8276	10.0591	9.3719	8.7556	8.2014	7.2497	6.4674	6.1280	5.8178	5.2732	4.8122	4.0799	3.5294	3.1039
19	17.2260	15.6785	14.3238	13.1339	12.0853	11.1581	10.3356	9.6036	8.9501	8.3649	7.3658	6.5504	6.1982	5.8775	5.3162	4.8435	4.0967	3.5386	3.1090
20	18.0456	16.3514	14.8775	13.5903	12.4622	11.4699	10.5940	9.8181	9.1285	8.5136	7.4694	6.6231	6.2593	5.9288	5.3527	4.8696	4.1103	3.5458	3.1129
21	18.8570	17.0112	15.4150	14.0292	12.8212	11.7641	10.8355	10.0168	9.2922	8.6487	7.5620	6.6870	6.3125	5.9731	5.3837	4.8913	4.1212	3.5514	3.1158
22	19.6604	17.6580	15.9369	14.4511	13.1630	12.0416	11.0612	10.2007	9.4424	8.7715	7.6446	6.7429	6.3587	6.0113	5.4099	4.9094	4.1300	3.5558	3.1180
23	20.4558	18.2922	16.4436	14.8568	13.4886	12.3034	11.2722	10.3711	9.5802	8.8832	7.7184	6.7921	6.3988	6.0442	5.4321	4.9245	4.1371	3.5592	3.1197
24	21.2434	18.9139	16.9355	15.2470	13.7986	12.5504	11.4693	10.5288	9.7066	8.9847	7.7843	6.8351	6.4338	6.0726	5.4509	4.9371	4.1428	3.5619	3.1210
25	22.0232	19.5235	17.4131	15.6221	14.0939	12.7834	11.6536	10.6748	9.8226	9.0770	7.8431	6.8729	6.4641	6.0971	5.4669	4.9476	4.1474	3.5640	3.1220
26	22.7952	20.1210	17.8768	15.9828	14.3752	13.0032	11.8258	10.8100	9.9290	9.1609	7.8957	6.9061	6.4906	6.1182	5.4804	4.9563	4.1511	3.5656	3.1227
27	23.5596	20.7069	18.3270	16.3296	14.6430	13.2105	11.9867	10.9352	10.0266	9.2372	7.9426	6.9352	6.5135	6.1364	5.4919	4.9636	4.1542	3.5669	3.1233
28	24.3164	21.2813	18.7641	16.6631	14.8981	13.4062	12.1371	11.0511	10.1161	9.3066	7.9844	6.9607	6.5335	6.1520	5.5016	4.9697	4.1566	3.5679	3.1237
29	25.0658	21.8444	19.1885	16.9837	15.1411	13.5907	12.2777	11.1584	10.1983	9.3696	8.0218	6.9830	6.5509	6.1656	5.5098	4.9747	4.1585	3.5687	3.1240
30	25.8077	22.3965	19.6004	17.2920	15.3725	13.7648	12.4090	11.2578	10.2737	9.4268	8.0552	7.0027	6.5660	6.1772	5.5168	4.9789	4.1601	3.5693	3.1242
40	32.8347	27.3555	23.1148	19.7928	17.1591	15.0463	13.3317	11.9246	10.7574	9.7791	8.2438	7.1050	6.6418	6.2335	5.5482	4.9966	4.1659	3.5712	3.1250
50	39.1961	31.4236	25.7298	21.4822	18.2559	15.7619	13.8007	12.2335	10.9617	9.9148	8.3045	7.1327	6.6605	6.2463	5.5541	4.9995	4.1666	3.5714	3.1250
60	44.9550	34.7609	27.6756	22.6235	18.9293	16.1614	14.0392	12.3766	11.0480	9.9672	8.3240	7.1401	6.6651	6.2492	5.5553	4.9999	4.1667	3.5714	3.1250

Note: n = number of periods; i = interest rate per period.

Figure A.1
Some Applications of FV and PV Techniques

Problem	Solution
1. Alicia invests $350 today and expects to earn 20% on the investment each year for the next 20 years. How much will she have?	Find the future value, *FV*, of $1 for 20% and 20 years; 38.337. Multiply 38.337 times $350 to get the answer; it is $13,417.95.
2. Manuel's uncle plans to give him a graduation present of $500 at graduation or $700 three years later if Manuel agrees to complete a graduate program. Considering the value of the gift only and assuming Manuel could invest at 8% in each of the three years, which is the better alternative?	You can use either future or present value of $1 tables. Using the former, find the *FV* for 8% and three years; it is 1.2597. The future value of $500 is $629.85 ($500 × 1.2597). Since this is less than $700, Manuel is better off waiting three years for his uncle's gift. If you use the present value of $1, you find the present value coefficient for 8% and three years; it is 0.7938. You then find the present value, *PV*, of $700, which is $555.66 (0.7938 × $700). Since the present value is greater than the immediate $500, Manuel should accept the future $700.
3. Gunther's stockbroker is trying to convince Gunther to purchase a security that will be worth $10,000 in 30 years. The cost of the security today is $1,500. Gunther isn't sure whether this is a good or bad investment but believes he could make a better decision if he knew the approximate rate of return on the investment. What is it?	You can find a rate of return by dividing the future value of an investment by its cost to arrive at a future value of $1 coefficient. Relate this coefficient then to the number of periods and the approximate value of *i*. You have a coefficient of 6.667 ($10,000/$1,500). Since the number of periods is 30, go across the 30 row until you come as close as possible to 6.667. As you see, the number corresponds to an *i* value of 6%, which is 5.7435. Since 6.667 is somewhat larger than 5.7435, you conclude the rate of return is greater than 6% but far less than 8% (in which case the coefficient would be 10.0620). As a rough approximation, you conclude it is about 6.5%. (You could use more accurate interpolation techniques, but such accuracy is not necessary in many cases. Moreover, for greater accuracy you should use expanded tables or an appropriate calculating device.)

Exercises

1. You receive $500 in graduation presents and plan to invest it for your retirement in 40 years. Assuming you can earn 8 percent interest each year, how much will you have at retirement? (*Answer*: $10,862.) How much will you have if you could earn 12 percent each year? (*Answer*: $46,526.)

2. Suppose you cannot make an immediate investment for retirement but can afford $100 each year for the next 30 years, with the first payment starting in one year. Assuming a 14 percent investment rate each year, how much will you accumulate at the end of 30 years? (*Answer*: $35,678.) Suppose your target was to accumulate $50,000; how much must you invest each year? (*Answer*: $140.14.) Suppose your target was $50,000, but you had only 20 years and could earn only 10 percent each year. What would be your yearly contribution? (*Answer*: $872.98.)

3. You are thinking of buying a zero coupon bond. It matures in 10 years for $1,000, pays no yearly interest, and currently costs $200. You look at other similar bonds and see that they are yielding 16 percent. Since you feel the zero coupon bond should also yield 16 percent, the most you are willing to pay for it is _____. (*Answer*: $226.70.) Should you or should you not buy the bond? (*Answer*: Should.) Suppose you bought the bond and interest rates fell immediately afterward, such that your bond yielded only 10 percent based on its current market price. How much would its current market price be? (*Answer*: $385.50.)

4. You are thinking of buying an annuity to provide future income to your spouse in the event of your death. The insurance company selling the annuity offers two alternatives: The first calls for an immediate payment of $10,000, and the other requires annual payments of $1,500 for the next 10 years with payments beginning in one year. You are pretty sure you can invest your money at 6 percent interest each year for the next 10 years. If this is true, which alternative should you prefer? (*Answer*: The first, since the present value of the second is $11,040, which is greater than $10,000.) Suppose you could earn 10 percent; now which would be better? (*Answer*: The second; its present value is $9,217.)

Index